The Writings of
Henry D. Thoreau

Excursions

Textual Center

The Writings of Henry D. Thoreau

Northern Illinois University and

The University of California, Santa Barbara

HENRY D. THOREAU

Excursions

EDITED BY JOSEPH J. MOLDENHAUER

PRINCETON, NEW JERSEY

PRINCETON UNIVERSITY PRESS

MMVII

COMMITTEE ON
SCHOLARLY EDITIONS
AN APPROVED EDITION

MODERN LANGUAGE
ASSOCIATION OF AMERICA

®

*The Committee's emblem indicates that this volume is based on an
examination of all available relevant textual sources, that it is edited
according to principles articulated in the volume, that the source texts and
the edited text's deviations from them are fully described, that the editorial
principles and the text and the apparatus have undergone a peer review,
that a rigorous schedule of verification and proofreading was followed to
insure a high degree of accuracy in the presentation of the edition, and
that the text is accompanied by appropriate textual and other historical
contextual information.*

*The editorial preparation of this volume, and costs associated with its
publication, were supported by grants from the National Endowment for
the Humanities, an independent federal agency.*

Library of Congress Cataloging-in-Publication Data

Thoreau, Henry David, 1817-1862.
Excursions / Henry D. Thoreau ; edited by Joseph J. Moldenhauer.
p. cm. — (The writings of Henry D. Thoreau)
Includes index.
ISBN-13: 978-0-691-06450-5 (cl. : alk. paper)
ISBN-10: 0-691-06540-4 (cl. : alk. paper)
*I. Moldenhauer, Joseph J., 1934- II. Title. III. Series: Thoreau, Henry David,
1817-1862. Works. 1971.*
PS3045.A1 206   814'.3—cd22   2006043895

*The paper used in this publication meets the minimum requirements of
ANSI/NISO Z39.48-1992 (R 1997) (Permanence of Paper)*

www.pup.princeton.edu

Printed in the United States of America

10   9   8   7   6   5   4   3   2   1

Contents

Excursions

Natural History of Massachusetts.

*Reports–on the Fishes, Reptiles, and Birds; the Herba-
ceous Plants and Quadrupeds; the Insects Injurious to
Vegetation; and the Invertebrate Animals–of Massachusetts.* Published agreeably to an Order of the
Legislature, by the Commissioners on the Zoological
and Botanical Survey of the State.

Books of natural history make the most cheerful
winter reading. I read in Audubon with a thrill of delight, when the snow covers the ground, of the magno-
lia, and the Florida keys, and their warm sea breezes;
of the fence-rail, and the cotton-tree, and the migrations of the rice-bird; of the breaking up of winter in
Labrador, and the melting of the snow on the forks of
the Missouri; and owe an accession of health to these
reminiscences of luxuriant nature.

> Within the circuit of this plodding life
> There enter moments of an azure hue,
> Untarnished fair as is the violet
> Or anemone, when the spring strews them
> By some meandering rivulet, which make
> The best philosophy untrue that aims
> But to console man for his grievances.
> I have remembered when the winter came,
> High in my chamber in the frosty nights,
> When in the still light of the cheerful moon,
> On every twig and rail and jutting spout,
> The icy spears were adding to their length
> Against the arrows of the coming sun,
> How in the shimmering noon of summer past
> Some unrecorded beam slanted across
> The upland pastures where the Johnswort grew;
> Or heard, amid the verdure of my mind,
> The bee's long smothered hum, on the blue flag
> Loitering amidst the mead; or busy rill,
> Which now through all its course stands still and dumb

Its own memorial,–purling at its play
Along the slopes, and through the meadows next,
Until its youthful sound was hushed at last
In the staid current of the lowland stream;
Or seen the furrows shine but late upturned,
And where the fieldfare followed in the rear,
When all the fields around lay bound and hoar
Beneath a thick integument of snow.
So by God's cheap economy made rich
To go upon my winter's task again.

I am singularly refreshed in winter when I hear of service berries, poke-weed, juniper. Is not heaven made up of these cheap summer glories? There is a singular health in those words Labrador and East Main, which no desponding creed recognises. How much more than federal are these states. If there were no other vicissitudes than the seasons, our interest would never tire. Much more is adoing than Congress wots of. What journal do the persimmon and the buck-eye keep, and the sharp-shinned hawk? What is transpiring from summer to winter in the Carolinas, and the Great Pine Forest, and the Valley of the Mohawk? The merely political aspect of the land is never very cheering; men are degraded when considered as the members of a political organization. On this side all lands present only the symptoms of decay. I see but Bunker Hill and Sing-Sing, the District of Columbia and Sullivan's Island, with a few avenues connecting them. But paltry are they all beside one blast of the east or the south wind which blows over them.

In society you will not find health, but in nature. Unless our feet at least stood in the midst of nature, all our faces would be pale and livid. Society is always diseased, and the best is the most so. There is no scent in it so wholesome as that of the pines, nor any fragrance so penetrating and restorative as the life-everlasting in high pastures. I would keep some book of natural history always by me as a sort of elixir, the reading of which should restore the tone of the system. To the sick, indeed, nature is sick, but to the well, a fountain of health. To him who contemplates a trait of natural beauty no harm nor disappointment can come. The doctrines of despair, of spiritual or political tyranny or servitude, were never taught by such as shared the serenity of nature. Surely good courage will not flag here on the Atlantic border, as long as we are flanked by the Fur Countries. There is enough in that sound to cheer one under any circumstances. The spruce, the hemlock, and the pine will not countenance despair. Methinks some creeds in vestries and churches do forget the hunter wrapped in furs by the Great Slave Lake, and that the Esquimaux sledges are drawn by dogs, and in the twilight of the northern night, the hunter does not give over to follow the seal and walrus on the ice. They are of sick and diseased imaginations who would toll the world's knell so soon. Cannot these sedentary sects do better than prepare the shrouds and write the epitaphs of those other busy living men? The practical faith of all men belies the preacher's consolation. What is any man's discourse to me, if I am not sensible of something in it as steady and cheery as the creak of crickets? In it the woods must be relieved against the sky. Men tire me when I am not constantly greeted and refreshed as by the flux of sparkling streams. Surely joy is the condition of life. Think of the young fry that leap in ponds, the myriads of insects ushered into being on a summer evening, the incessant note of the hyla with which the woods ring in the spring, the nonchalance of the butterfly carrying accident and change painted in a thousand hues upon its wings, or the brook minnow stoutly stemming the current, the lustre of whose scales worn bright by the attrition is reflected upon the bank.

We fancy that this din of religion, literature, and philosophy, which is heard in pulpits, lyceums, and parlors, vibrates through the universe, and is as catholic a sound as the creaking of the earth's axle; but if a man sleep soundly, he will forget it all between sunset and dawn. It is the three-inch swing of a pendulum in a cupboard, which the great pulse of nature vibrates by and through each instant. When we lift our eyelids and open our ears, it disappears with smoke and rattle like the cars on a railroad. When I detect a beauty in any of the recesses of nature, I am reminded, by the serene and retired spirit in which it requires to be contemplated, of the inexpressible privacy of a life,–how silent and unambitious it is. The beauty there is in mosses must be considered from the holiest, quietest nook. What an admirable training is science for the more active warfare of life. Indeed, the unchallenged bravery, which these studies imply, is far more impressive than the trumpeted valor of the warrior. I am pleased to learn that Thales was up and stirring by night not unfrequently, as his astronomical discoveries prove. Linnæus, setting out for Lapland, surveys his "comb" and "spare shirt," "leathern breeches" and "gauze cap to keep off gnats," with as much complacency as Bonaparte a park of artillery for the Russian campaign. The quiet bravery of the man is admirable. His eye is to take in fish, flower, and bird, quadruped and biped. Science is always brave, for to know, is to know good; doubt and danger quail before her eye. What the coward overlooks in his hurry, she calmly scrutinizes, breaking ground like a pioneer for the array of arts that follow in her train. But cowardice is unscientific; for there cannot be a science of ignorance. There may be a science of bravery, for that advances; but a retreat is rarely well conducted;

if it is, then is it an orderly advance in the face of circumstances.

But to draw a little nearer to our promised topics. Entomology extends the limits of being in a new direction, so that I walk in nature with a sense of greater space and freedom. It suggests besides, that the universe is not rough-hewn, but perfect in its details. Nature will bear the closest inspection; she invites us to lay our eye level with the smallest leaf, and take an insect view of its plain. She has no interstices; every part is full of life. I explore, too, with pleasure, the sources of the myriad sounds which crowd the summer noon, and which seem the very grain and stuff of which eternity is made. Who does not remember the shrill roll-call of the harvest fly? There were ears for these sounds in Greece long ago, as Anacreon's ode will show.

> "We pronounce thee happy, Cicada,
> For on the tops of the trees,
> Drinking a little dew,
> Like any king thou singest.
> For thine are they all,
> Whatever thou seest in the fields,
> And whatever the woods bear.
> Thou art the friend of the husbandmen,
> In no respect injuring any one;
> And thou art honored among men,
> Sweet prophet of summer.
> The Muses love thee,
> And Phœbus himself loves thee,
> And has given thee a shrill song;
> Age does not wrack thee,
> Thou skilful, earthborn, song-loving,
> Unsuffering, bloodless one;
> Almost thou art like the gods."

In the autumn days, the creaking of crickets is heard at noon over all the land, and as in summer they are heard chiefly at night-fall, so then by their incessant chirp they usher in the evening of the year. Nor can all the vanities that vex the world alter one whit the measure that night has chosen. Every pulse-beat is in exact time with the cricket's chant and the tickings of the deathwatch in the wall. Alternate with these if you can.

About two hundred and eighty birds either reside permanently in the State, or spend the summer only, or make us a passing visit. Those which spend the winter with us have obtained our warmest sympathy. The nuthatch and chicadee flitting in company through the dells of the wood, the one harshly scolding at the intruder, the other with a faint lisping note enticing him on, the jay screaming in the orchard, the crow cawing in unison with the storm, the partridge, like a russet link extended over from autumn to spring, preserving unbroken the chain of summers, the hawk with warrior-like firmness abiding the blasts of winter, the robin* and lark lurking by warm springs in the woods, the familiar snow-bird culling a few seeds in the garden, or a few crumbs in the yard, and occasionally the shrike, with heedless and unfrozen melody bringing back summer again;–

> His steady sails he never furls
> At any time o' year,
> And perching now on Winter's curls,
> He whistles in his ear.

As the spring advances and the ice is melting in the river, our earliest and straggling visitors make their ap-

---

* A white robin and a white quail have occasionally been seen. It is mentioned in Audubon as remarkable that the nest of a robin should be found on the ground; but this bird seems to be less particular than most in the choice of a building spot. I have seen its nest placed under the thatched roof of a deserted barn, and in one instance, where the adjacent country was nearly destitute of trees, together with two of the phœbe, upon the end of a board in the loft of a sawmill, but a few feet from the saw, which vibrated several inches with the motion of the machinery.

pearance. Again does the old Teian poet sing as well for New England as for Greece, in the

RETURN OF SPRING.

"Behold, how spring appearing,
The Graces send forth roses;
Behold, how the wave of the sea
Is made smooth by the calm;
Behold, how the duck dives;
Behold, how the crane travels;
And Titan shines constantly bright.
The shadows of the clouds are moving;
The works of man shine;
The earth puts forth fruits;
The fruit of the olive puts forth.
The cup of Bacchus is crowned,
Along the leaves, along the branches,
The fruit, bending them down, flourishes."

The ducks alight at this season in the still water, in company with the gulls, which do not fail to improve an east wind to visit our meadows, and swim about by twos and threes, pluming themselves, and diving to peck at the root of the lily, and the cranberries which the frost has not loosened. The first flock of geese is seen beating to north, in long harrows and waving lines, the gingle of the song-sparrow salutes us from the shrubs and fences, the plaintive note of the lark comes clear and sweet from the meadow, and the bluebird, like an azure ray, glances past us in our walk. The fish-hawk, too, is occasionally seen at this season sailing majestically over the water, and he who has once observed it will not soon forget the majesty of its flight. It sails the air like a ship of the line, worthy to struggle with the elements, falling back from time to time like a ship on its beam ends, and holding its talons up as if ready for the arrows, in the attitude of the national bird. It is a great presence, as of the master of river and forest. Its eye would not quail before

the owner of the soil, but make him feel like an intruder on its domains. And then its retreat, sailing so
steadily away, is a kind of advance. I have by me one of
a pair of ospreys, which have for some years fished in
this vicinity, shot by a neighboring pond, measuring
more than two feet in length, and six in the stretch of
its wings. Nuttall mentions that "The ancients, particularly Aristotle, pretended that the ospreys taught
their young to gaze at the sun, and those who were unable to do so were destroyed. Linnæus even believed,
on ancient authority, that one of the feet of this bird
had all the toes divided, while the other was partly
webbed, so that it could swim with one foot, and grasp
a fish with the other." But that educated eye is now
dim, and those talons are nerveless. Its shrill scream
seems yet to linger in its throat, and the roar of the sea
in its wings. There is the tyranny of Jove in its claws,
and his wrath in the erectile feathers of the head and
neck. It reminds me of the Argonautic expedition, and
would inspire the dullest to take flight over Parnassus.

The booming of the bittern, described by Goldsmith
and Nuttall, is frequently heard in our fens, in the
morning and evening, sounding like a pump, or the
chopping of wood in a frosty morning in some distant
farm-yard. The manner in which this sound is produced I have not seen anywhere described. On one occasion, the bird has been seen by one of my neighbors
to thrust its bill into the water, and suck up as much as
it could hold, then raising its head, it pumped it out
again with four or five heaves of the neck, throwing it
two or three feet, and making the sound each time.

At length the summer's eternity is ushered in by the
cackle of the flicker among the oaks on the hill-side,
and a new dynasty begins with calm security.

In May and June the woodland quire is in full tune,
and given the immense spaces of hollow air, and this

curious human ear, one does not see how the void could be better filled.

> Each summer sound
> Is a summer round.

As the season advances, and those birds which make us but a passing visit depart, the woods become silent again, and but few feathers ruffle the drowsy air. But the solitary rambler may still find a response and expression for every mood in the depths of the wood.

> Sometimes I hear the veery's* clarion,
> Or brazen trump of the impatient jay,
> And in secluded woods the chicadee
> Doles out her scanty notes, which sing the praise
> Of heroes, and set forth the loveliness
> Of virtue evermore.

The phœbe still sings in harmony with the sultry weather by the brink of the pond, nor are the desultory hours of noon in the midst of the village without their minstrel.

> Upon the lofty elm tree sprays
> The vireo rings the changes sweet,
> During the trivial summer days,
> Striving to lift our thoughts above the street.

With the autumn begins in some measure a new spring. The plover is heard whistling high in the air over the dry pastures, the finches flit from tree to tree, the bobolinks and flickers fly in flocks, and the goldfinch rides on the earliest blast, like a winged hyla

---

* This bird, which is so well described by Nuttall, but is apparently unknown by the author of the Report, is one of the most common in the woods in this vicinity, and in Cambridge I have heard the college yard ring with its trill. The boys call it *"yorrick,"* from the sound of its querulous and chiding note, as it flits near the traveller through the underwood. The cowbird's egg is occasionally found in its nest, as mentioned by Audubon.

peeping amid the rustle of the leaves. The crows, too, begin now to congregate; you may stand and count them as they fly low and straggling over the landscape, singly or by twos and threes, at intervals of half a mile, until a hundred have passed.

I have seen it suggested somewhere that the crow was brought to this country by the white man; but I shall as soon believe that the white man planted these pines and hemlocks. He is no spaniel to follow our steps; but rather flits about the clearings like the dusky spirit of the Indian, reminding me oftener of Philip and Powhatan, than of Winthrop and Smith. He is a relic of the dark ages. By just so slight, by just so lasting a tenure does superstition hold the world ever; there is the rook in England, and the crow in New England.

> Thou dusky spirit of the wood,
> Bird of an ancient brood,
> Flitting thy lonely way,
> A meteor in the summer's day,
> From wood to wood, from hill to hill,
> Low over forest, field, and rill,
> What wouldst thou say?
> Why shouldst thou haunt the day?
> What makes thy melancholy float?
> What bravery inspires thy throat,
> And bears thee up above the clouds,
> Over desponding human crowds,
> Which far below
> Lay thy haunts low?

The late walker or sailer, in the October evenings, may hear the murmuring of the snipe, circling over the meadows, the most spirit-like sound in nature; and still later in the autumn, when the frosts have tinged the leaves, a solitary loon pays a visit to our retired ponds, where he may lurk undisturbed till the season of moulting is passed, making the woods ring with his wild laughter. This bird, the Great Northern Diver, well deserves its name; for when pursued with a boat, it will dive, and swim like a fish under water, for sixty rods or more, as fast as a boat can be paddled, and its pursuer, if he would discover his game again, must put his ear to the surface to hear where it comes up. When it comes to the surface, it throws the water off with one shake of its wings, and calmly swims about until again disturbed.

These are the sights and sounds which reach our senses oftenest during the year. But sometimes one hears a quite new note, which has for back ground other Carolinas and Mexicos than the books describe, and learns that his ornithology has done him no service.

It appears from the Report that there are about forty quadrupeds belonging to the State, and among these one is glad to hear of a few bears, wolves, lynxes, and wildcats.

When our river overflows its banks in the spring, the wind from the meadows is laden with a strong scent of musk, and by its freshness advertises me of an unexplored wildness. Those backwoods are not far off then. I am affected by the sight of the cabins of the musk-rat, made of mud and grass, and raised three or four feet along the river, as when I read of the barrows of Asia. The musk-rat is the beaver of the settled States. Their number has even increased within a few years in this vicinity. Among the rivers which empty into the Merrimack, the Concord is known to the boatmen as a dead stream. The Indians are said to have called it Musketaquid, or Prairie river. Its current being much more sluggish, and its water more muddy than the rest, it abounds more in fish and game of every kind. According to the History of the town, "The fur trade here was once very important. As early as 1641, a company was formed in the colony, of which Major Willard of Concord was superintendent, and had the exclusive right to trade with the Indians in furs and other articles; and for this right they were obliged to pay into the public treasury one twentieth of all the furs they obtained." There are trappers in our midst still, as well as on the streams of the far west, who night and morning go the round of their traps, without fear of the Indian. One of these takes from one hundred and fifty to two hundred musk-rats in a year, and even thirty-six have been shot by one man in a day. Their fur, which is not nearly as valuable as formerly, is in good condition in the winter and spring only; and upon the breaking up of the ice, when they are driven out of their holes by the water, the greatest number is shot from boats, either swimming or resting on their stools, or slight supports of grass and reeds, by the side of the stream. Though they exhibit considerable cunning at other times, they are easily taken in a trap, which has only to be placed in their holes, or wherever they frequent, without any bait being used, though it is sometimes rubbed with their musk. In the winter the hunter cuts holes in the ice, and shoots them when they come to the surface. Their burrows are usually in the high banks of the river, with the entrance under water, and rising within to above the level of high water. Sometimes their nests, composed of dried meadow grass and flags, may be discovered where the bank is low and spongy, by the yielding of the ground under the feet. They have from three to seven or eight young in the spring.

Frequently, in the morning or evening, a long ripple is seen in the still water, where a musk-rat is crossing the stream, with only its nose above the surface, and sometimes a green bough in its mouth to build its house with. When it finds itself observed, it will dive and swim five or six rods under water, and at length conceal itself in its hole, or the weeds. It will remain under water for ten minutes at a time, and on one occasion has been seen, when undisturbed, to form an

air bubble under the ice, which contracted and expanded as it breathed at leisure. When it suspects
danger on shore, it will stand erect like a squirrel, and
survey its neighborhood for several minutes, without
moving.

In the fall, if a meadow intervene between their burrows and the stream, they erect cabins of mud and
grass, three or four feet high, near its edge. These are
not their breeding places, though young are sometimes found in them in late freshets, but rather their
hunting lodges, to which they resort in the winter with
their food, and for shelter. Their food consists chiefly
of flags and fresh water muscles, the shells of the latter
being left in large quantities around their lodges in the
spring.

The Penobscot Indian wears the entire skin of a
musk-rat, with the legs and tail dangling, and the head
caught under his girdle, for a pouch, into which he
puts his fishing tackle, and essences to scent his traps
with.

The bear, wolf, lynx, wildcat, deer, beaver, and mar-
ten, have disappeared from this vicinity; the otter is
rarely if ever seen here at present; and the mink is less
common than formerly.

Perhaps of all our untamed quadrupeds, the fox has
obtained the widest and most familiar reputation,
from the time of Pilpay and Æsop to the present day.
His recent tracks still give variety to a winter's walk. I
tread in the steps of the fox that has gone before me by
some hours, or which perhaps I have started, with
such a tiptoe of expectation, as if I were on the trail of
the Spirit itself which resides in the wood, and expected soon to catch it in its lair. I am curious to
know what has determined its graceful curvatures,
and how surely they were coincident with the fluctua-
tions of some mind. I know which way a mind wended,
what horizon it faced, by the setting of these tracks,

and whether it moved slowly or rapidly, by their greater or less intervals and distinctness; for the swiftest step leaves yet a lasting trace. Sometimes you will see the trails of many together, and where they have gambolled and gone through a hundred evolutions, which testify to a singular listlessness and leisure in nature.

When I see a fox run across the pond on the snow, with the carelessness of freedom, or at intervals trace his course in the sunshine along the ridge of a hill, I give up to him sun and earth as to their true proprietor. He does not go in the sun, but it seems to follow him, and there is a visible sympathy between him and it. Sometimes, when the snow lies light, and but five or six inches deep, you may give chase and come up with one on foot. In such a case he will show a remarkable presence of mind, choosing only the safest direction, though he may lose ground by it. Notwithstanding his fright, he will take no step which is not beautiful. His pace is a sort of leopard canter, as if he were in no wise impeded by the snow, but were husbanding his strength all the while. When the ground is uneven, the course is a series of graceful curves, conforming to the shape of the surface. He runs as though there were not a bone in his back, occasionally dropping his muzzle to the ground for a rod or two, and then tossing his head aloft, when satisfied of his course. When he comes to a declivity, he will put his fore feet together, and slide swiftly down it, shoving the snow before him. He treads so softly that you would hardly hear it from any nearness, and yet with such expression, that it would not be quite inaudible at any distance.

Of fishes, seventy-five genera and one hundred and seven species are described in the Report. The fisherman will be startled to learn that there are but about a dozen kinds in the ponds and streams of any inland town; and almost nothing is known of their habits. Only their names and residence make one love fishes. I would know even the number of their fin rays, and how many scales compose the lateral line. I am the wiser in respect to all knowledges, and the better qualified for all fortunes, for knowing that there is a minnow in the brook. Methinks I have need even of his sympathy and to be his fellow in a degree.

I have experienced such simple delight in the trivial matters of fishing and sporting, formerly, as might have inspired the muse of Homer or Shakspeare; and now when I turn the pages and ponder the plates of the Angler's Souvenir, I am fain to exclaim,–

> "Can these things be,
> And overcome us like a summer's cloud?"

Next to nature it seems as if man's actions were the most natural, they so gently accord with her. The small seines of flax stretched across the shallow and transparent parts of our river, are no more intrusion than the cobweb in the sun. I stay my boat in mid current, and look down in the sunny water to see the civil meshes of his nets, and wonder how the blustering people of the town could have done this elvish work. The twine looks like a new river weed, and is to the river as a beautiful memento of man's presence in nature, discovered as silently and delicately as a footprint in the sand.

When the ice is covered with snow, I do not suspect the wealth under my feet; that there is as good as a mine under me wherever I go. How many pickerel are poised on easy fin fathoms below the loaded wain. The revolution of the seasons must be a curious phenomenon to them. At length the sun and wind brush aside their curtain, and they see the heavens again.

Early in the spring, after the ice has melted, is the time for spearing fish. Suddenly the wind shifts from north-east and east to west and south, and every icicle, which has tinkled on the meadow grass so long, trickles down its stem, and seeks its level unerringly with a million comrades. The steam curls up from every roof and fence.

> I see the civil sun drying earth's tears,
> Her tears of joy, which only faster flow.

In the brooks is heard the slight grating sound of small cakes of ice, floating with various speed, full of content and promise, and where the water gurgles under a natural bridge, you may hear these hasty rafts hold conversation in an under tone. Every rill is a channel for the juices of the meadow. In the ponds the ice cracks with a merry and inspiriting din, and down the larger streams is whirled grating hoarsely, and crashing its way along, which was so lately a highway for the woodman's team and the fox, sometimes with the tracks of the skaters still fresh upon it, and the holes cut for pickerel. Town committees anxiously inspect the bridges and causeways, as if by mere eye-force to intercede with the ice, and save the treasury.

> The river swelleth more and more,
> Like some sweet influence stealing o'er
> The passive town; and for a while
> Each tussuck makes a tiny isle,
> Where, on some friendly Ararat,
> Resteth the weary water-rat.
>
> No ripple shows Musketaquid,
> Her very current e'en is hid,
> As deepest souls do calmest rest,
> When thoughts are swelling in the breast,
> And she that in the summer's drought
> Doth make a rippling and a rout,
> Sleeps from Nahshawtuck to the Cliff,
> Unruffled by a single skiff.

But by a thousand distant hills
The louder roar a thousand rills,
And many a spring which now is dumb,
And many a stream with smothered hum,
Doth swifter well and faster glide,
Though buried deep beneath the tide.

Our village shows a rural Venice,
Its broad lagoons where yonder fen is;
As lovely as the Bay of Naples
Yon placid cove amid the maples;
And in my neighbor's field of corn
I recognise the Golden Horn.

Here Nature taught from year to year,
When only red men came to hear,
Methinks 't was in this school of art
Venice and Naples learned their part,
But still their mistress, to my mind,
Her young disciples leaves behind.

The fisherman now repairs and launches his boat. The best time for spearing is at this season, before the weeds have begun to grow, and while the fishes lie in the shallow water, for in summer they prefer the cool depths, and in the autumn they are still more or less concealed by the grass. The first requisite is fuel for your crate; and for this purpose the roots of the pitch pine are commonly used, found under decayed stumps, where the trees have been felled eight or ten years.

With a crate, or jack, made of iron hoops, to contain your fire, and attached to the bow of your boat about three feet from the water, a fish-spear with seven tines, and fourteen feet long, a large basket, or barrow, to carry your fuel and bring back your fish, and a thick outer garment, you are equipped for a cruise. It should be a warm and still evening; and then with a fire crackling merrily at the prow, you may launch forth like a cucullo into the night. The dullest soul cannot go upon such an expedition without some of the spirit of adventure; as if he had stolen the boat of Charon and gone down the Styx on a midnight expedition into the realms of Pluto. And much speculation does this wandering star afford to the musing night-walker, leading him on and on, jack-o'lantern-like, over the meadows; or if he is wiser, he amuses himself with imagining what of human life, far in the silent night, is flitting moth-like round its candle. The silent navigator shoves his craft gently over the water, with a smothered pride and sense of benefaction, as if he were the phosphor, or light-bringer, to these dusky realms, or some sister moon, blessing the spaces with her light. The waters, for a rod or two on either hand and several feet in depth, are lit up with more than noon-day distinctness, and he enjoys the opportunity which so many have desired, for the roofs of a city are indeed raised, and he surveys the midnight economy of the fishes. There they lie in every variety of posture, some on their backs, with their white bellies uppermost, some suspended in mid water, some sculling gently along with a dreamy motion of the fins, and others quite active and wide awake,–a scene not unlike what the human city would present. Occasionally he will encounter a turtle selecting the choicest morsels, or a musk-rat resting on a tussuck. He may exercise his dexterity, if he sees fit, on the more distant and active fish, or fork the nearer into his boat, as potatoes out of a pot, or even take the sound sleepers with his hands. But these last accomplishments he will soon learn to dispense with, distinguishing the real object of his pursuit, and find compensation in the beauty and never ending novelty of his position. The pines growing down to the water's edge will show newly as in the glare of a conflagration, and as he floats under the willows with his light, the song-sparrow will often wake on her perch, and sing that strain at midnight, which she had meditated for the morning. And when he has done, he may have to steer his way home through the dark by the north star, and he will feel himself some degrees nearer to it for having lost his way on the earth.

The fishes commonly taken in this way are pickerel, suckers, perch, eels, pouts, breams, and shiners,–from thirty to sixty weight in a night. Some are hard to be recognised in the unnatural light, especially the perch, which, his dark bands being exaggerated, acquires a ferocious aspect. The number of these transverse bands, which the Report states to be seven, is, however, very variable, for in some of our ponds they have nine and ten even.

It appears that we have eight kinds of tortoises, twelve snakes,–but one of which is venomous,–nine frogs and toads, nine salamanders, and one lizard, for our neighbors.

I am particularly attracted by the motions of the serpent tribe. They make our hands and feet, the wings of the bird, and the fins of the fish seem very superfluous, as if nature had only indulged her fancy in making them. The black snake will dart into a bush when pursued, and circle round and round with an easy and graceful motion, amid the thin and bare twigs, five or six feet from the ground, as a bird flits from bough to bough, or hang in festoons between the forks. Elasticity and flexibleness in the simpler forms of animal life are equivalent to a complex system of limbs in the higher; and we have only to be as wise and wily as the serpent, to perform as difficult feats without the vulgar assistance of hands and feet.

In May, the snapping turtle, *Emysaurus serpentina*, is frequently taken on the meadows and in the river. The fisherman, taking sight over the calm surface, discovers its snout projecting above the water, at the distance of many rods, and easily secures his prey through its unwillingness to disturb the water by swimming hastily away, for, gradually drawing its head under, it remains resting on some limb or clump of grass. Its eggs, which are buried at a distance from the water, in some soft place, as a pigeon bed, are frequently devoured by the skunk. It will catch fish by daylight, as a toad catches flies, and is said to emit a transparent fluid from its mouth to attract them.

Nature has taken more care than the fondest parent for the education and refinement of her children. Consider the silent influence which flowers exert, no less upon the ditcher in the meadow than the lady in the bower. When I walk in the woods, I am reminded that a wise purveyor has been there before me; my most delicate experience is typified there. I am struck with the pleasing friendships and unanimities of nature, as when the lichens on the trees take the form of their leaves. In the most stupendous scenes you will see delicate and fragile features, as slight wreaths of vapor, dew-lines, feathery sprays, which suggest a high refinement, a noble blood and breeding, as it were. It is not hard to account for elves and fairies; they represent this light grace, this ethereal gentility. Bring a spray from the wood, or a crystal from the brook, and place it on your mantel, and your household ornaments will seem plebeian beside its nobler fashion and bearing. It will wave superior there, as if used to a more refined and polished circle. It has a salute and a response to all your enthusiasm and heroism.

In the winter, I stop short in the path to admire how the trees grow up without forethought, regardless of the time and circumstances. They do not wait as man does, but now is the golden age of the sapling. Earth, air, sun, and rain, are occasion enough; they were no better in primeval centuries. The "winter of *their* discontent" never comes. Witness the buds of the native poplar standing gaily out to the frost on the sides of its bare switches. They express a naked confidence. With cheerful heart one could be a sojourner in the wilderness, if he were sure to find there the catkins of the willow or the alder. When I read of them in the accounts of northern adventurers, by Baffin's Bay or Mackenzie's river, I see how even there too I could dwell. They are our little vegetable redeemers. Methinks our virtue will hold out till they come again. They are worthy to have had a greater than Minerva or Ceres for their inventor. Who was the benignant goddess that bestowed them on mankind?

Nature is mythical and mystical always, and works with the license and extravagance of genius. She has her luxurious and florid style as well as art. Having a pilgrim's cup to make, she gives to the whole, stem, bowl, handle, and nose, some fantastic shape, as if it were to be the car of some fabulous marine deity, a Nereus or Triton.

In the winter, the botanist needs not confine himself to his books and herbarium, and give over his outdoor pursuits, but may study a new department of vegetable physiology, what may be called crystalline botany, then. The winter of 1837 was unusually favorable for this. In December of that year the Genius of vegetation seemed to hover by night over its summer haunts with unusual persistency. Such a hoar-frost, as is very uncommon here or anywhere, and whose full effects can never be witnessed after sunrise, occurred several times. As I went forth early on a still and frosty morning, the trees looked like airy creatures of darkness caught napping, on this side huddled together with their grey hairs streaming in a secluded valley, which the sun had not penetrated, on that hurrying off in Indian file along some water-course, while the shrubs and grasses, like elves and fairies of the night, sought to hide their diminished heads in the snow. The river, viewed from the high bank, appeared of a yellowish green color, though all the landscape was white. Every tree, shrub, and spire of grass, that could raise its head above the snow, was covered with a dense ice-foliage, answering, as it were, leaf for leaf to its summer dress. Even the fences had put forth leaves in the night. The centre, diverging, and more minute fibres were perfectly distinct, and the edges regularly indented. These leaves were on the side of the twig or stubble opposite to the sun, meeting it for the most part at right angles, and there were others standing out at all possible angles upon these and upon one another, with no twig or stubble supporting them. When the first rays of the sun slanted over the scene, the grasses seemed hung with innumerable jewels, which jingled merrily as they were brushed by the foot of the traveller, and reflected all the hues of the rainbow as he moved from side to side. It struck me that these ghost leaves and the green ones whose forms they assume, were the creatures of but one law; that in obedience to the same law the vegetable juices swell gradually into the perfect leaf, on the one hand, and the crystalline particles troop to their standard in the same order, on the other. As if the material were indifferent, but the law one and invariable, and every plant in the spring but pushed up into and filled a permanent and eternal mould, which, summer and winter forever, is waiting to be filled.

This foliate structure is common to the coral and the plumage of birds, and to how large a part of animate and inanimate nature. The same independence of law on matter is observable in many other instances, as in the natural rhymes, when some animal form, color, or odor, has its counterpart in some vegetable. As, indeed, all rhymes imply an eternal melody, independent of any particular sense.

As confirmation of the fact, that vegetation is but a kind of crystallization, every one may observe how, upon the edge of the melting frost on the window, the needle-shaped particles are bundled together so as to resemble fields waving with grain, or shocks rising here and there from the stubble; on one side the vegetation of the torrid zone, high towering palms and wide-spread bannians, such as are seen in pictures of oriental scenery; on the other, arctic pines stiff frozen, with downcast branches.

Vegetation has been made the type of all growth; but as in crystals the law is more obvious, their material being more simple, and for the most part more transient and fleeting, would it not be as philosophical as convenient, to consider all growth, all filling up within the limits of nature, but a crystallization more or less rapid?

On this occasion, in the side of the high bank of the river, wherever the water or other cause had formed a cavity, its throat and outer edge, like the entrance to a citadel, bristled with a glistening ice-armor. In one place you might see minute ostrich feathers, which seemed the waving plumes of the warriors filing into the fortress; in another, the glancing, fan-shaped banners of the Lilliputian host; and in another, the needle-shaped particles collected into bundles, resembling the plumes of the pine, might pass for a phalanx of spears. From the under side of the ice in the brooks, where there was a thicker ice below, depended a mass of crystallization, four or five inches deep, in the form of prisms, with their lower ends open, which, when the ice was laid on its smooth side, resembled the roofs and steeples of a Gothic city, or the vessels of a crowded haven under a press of canvass. The very mud in the road, where the ice had melted, was crystallized with deep rectilinear fissures, and the crystalline masses in the sides of the ruts resembled exactly asbestos in the disposition of their needles. Around the roots of the stubble and flower-stalks, the frost was gathered into the form of irregular conical shells, or fairy rings. In some places the ice-crystals were lying upon granite rocks, directly over crystals of quartz, the frost-work of a longer night, crystals of a longer period, but to some eye unprejudiced by the short term of human life, melting as fast as the former.

In the Report on the Invertebrate Animals, this singular fact is recorded, which teaches us to put a new value on time and space. "The distribution of the marine shells is well worthy of notice as a geological fact. Cape Cod, the right arm of the Commonwealth, reaches out into the ocean, some fifty or sixty miles. It is nowhere many miles wide; but this narrow point of land has hitherto proved a barrier to the migrations of many species of Mollusca. Several genera and numerous species, which are separated by the intervention of only a few miles of land, are effectually prevented from mingling by the Cape, and do not pass from one side to the other. * * * * Of the one hundred and ninety-seven marine species, eighty-three do not pass to the south shore, and fifty are not found on the north shore of the Cape."

That common muscle, the *Unio complanatus*, or more properly *fluviatilis*, left in the spring by the musk-rat upon rocks and stumps, appears to have been an important article of food with the Indians. In one place, where they are said to have feasted, they are found in large quantities, at an elevation of thirty feet above the river, filling the soil to the depth of a foot, and mingled with ashes and Indian remains.

The works we have placed at the head of our chapter, with as much license as the preacher selects his text, are such as imply more labor than enthusiasm. The State wanted complete catalogues of its natural riches, with such additional facts merely as would be directly useful.

The Reports on Fishes, Reptiles, Insects, and Invertebrate Animals, however, indicate labor and research, and have a value independent of the object of the legislature.

Those on Herbaceous Plants and Birds cannot be of much value, as long as Bigelow and Nuttall are accessible. They serve but to indicate, with more or less exactness, what species are found in the State. We detect several errors ourselves, and a more practised eye would no doubt expand the list.

The Quadrupeds deserved a more final and instructive report than they have obtained.

These volumes deal much in measurements and minute descriptions, not interesting to the general reader, with only here and there a colored sentence to allure him, like those plants growing in dark forests, which bear only leaves without blossoms. But the ground was comparatively unbroken, and we will not complain of the pioneer, if he raises no flowers with his first crop. Let us not underrate the value of a fact; it will one day flower in a truth. It is astonishing how few facts of importance are added in a century to the natural history of any animal. The natural history of man himself is still being gradually written. Men are knowing enough after their fashion. Every countryman and dairymaid knows that the coats of the fourth stomach of the calf will curdle milk, and what particular mushroom is a safe and nutritious diet. You cannot go into any field or wood, but it will seem as if every stone had been turned, and the bark on every tree ripped up. But after all, it is much easier to discover than to see when the cover is off. It has been well said that "the attitude of inspection is prone." Wisdom does not inspect, but behold. We must look a long time before we can see. Slow are the beginnings of philosophy. He has something demoniacal in him, who can discern a law, or couple two facts. We can imagine a time when,– "Water runs down hill,"–may have been taught in the schools. The true man of science will know nature better by his finer organization; he will smell, taste, see, hear, feel, better than other men. His will be a deeper and finer experience. We do not learn by inference and deduction, and the application of mathematics to philosophy, but by direct intercourse and sympathy. It is with science as with ethics, we cannot know truth by contrivance and method; the Baconian is as false as any other, and with all the helps of machinery and the arts, the most scientific will still be the healthiest and friendliest man, and possess a more perfect Indian wisdom.

A Walk to Wachusett.

The needles of the pine,
All to the west incline.

CONCORD, JULY 19, 1842.

SUMMER and winter our eyes had rested on the dim outline of the mountains in our horizon, to which distance and indistinctness lent a grandeur not their own, so that they served equally to interpret all the allusions of poets and travellers; whether with Homer, on a spring morning, we sat down on the many-peaked Olympus, or, with Virgil, and his compeers, roamed the Etrurian and Thessalian hills, or with Humboldt measured the more modern Andes and Teneriffe. Thus we spoke our mind to them, standing on the Concord cliffs.–

With frontier strength ye stand your ground,
With grand content ye circle round,
Tumultuous silence for all sound,
Ye distant nursery of rills,
Monadnock, and the Peterboro' hills;
Like some vast fleet,
Sailing through rain and sleet,
Through winter's cold and summer's heat;
Still holding on, upon your high emprise,
Until ye find a shore amid the skies;
Not skulking close to land,
With cargo contraband,
For they who sent a venture out by ye
Have set the sun to see
Their honesty.
Ships of the line, each one,
Ye to the westward run,
Always before the gale,
Under a press of sail,
With weight of metal all untold.

I seem to feel ye, in my firm seat here,
Immeasurable depth of hold,
And breadth of beam, and length of running gear.

Methinks ye take luxurious pleasure
In your novel western leisure;
So cool your brows, and freshly blue,
As Time had nought for ye to do;
For ye lie at your length,
An unappropriated strength,
Unhewn primeval timber,
For knees so stiff, for masts so limber;
The stock of which new earths are made,
One day to be our western trade,
Fit for the stanchions of a world
Which through the seas of space is hurled.

While we enjoy a lingering ray,
Ye still o'ertop the western day,
Reposing yonder, on God's croft,
Like solid stacks of hay.
Edged with silver, and with gold,
The clouds hang o'er in damask fold,
And with such depth of amber light
The west is dight,
Where still a few rays slant,
That even heaven seems extravagant.
On the earth's edge mountains and trees
Stand as they were on air graven,
Or as the vessels in a haven
Await the morning breeze.
I fancy even
Through your defiles windeth the way to heaven;
And yonder still, in spite of history's page,
Linger the golden and the silver age;
Upon the laboring gale
The news of future centuries is brought,
And of new dynasties of thought,
From your remotest vale.

But special I remember thee,
Wachusett, who like me
Standest alone without society.

Thy far blue eye,
A remnant of the sky,
Seen through the clearing or the gorge,
Or from the windows of the forge,
Doth leaven all it passes by.
Nothing is true,
But stands 'tween me and you,
Thou western pioneer,
Who know'st not shame nor fear,
By venturous spirit driven,
Under the eaves of heaven,
And canst expand thee there,
And breathe enough of air?
Upholding heaven, holding down earth,
Thy pastime from thy birth,
Not steadied by the one, nor leaning on the other;
May I approve myself thy worthy brother!

At length, like Rasselas, and other inhabitants of happy valleys, we resolved to scale the blue wall which bound the western horizon, though not without misgivings, that thereafter no visible fairy land would exist for us. But we will not leap at once to our journey's end, though near, but imitate Homer, who conducts his reader over the plain, and along the resounding sea, though it be but to the tent of Achilles. In the spaces of thought are the reaches of land and water, where men go and come. The landscape lies far and fair within, and the deepest thinker is the farthest travelled.

At a cool and early hour on a pleasant morning in July, my companion and I passed rapidly through Acton and Stow, stopping to rest and refresh us on the bank of a small stream, a tributary of the Assabet, in the latter town. As we traversed the cool woods of Acton, with stout staves in our hands, we were cheered by the song of the red-eye, the thrushes, the phœbe, and the cuckoo; and as we passed through the open country, we inhaled the fresh scent of every field, and all nature lay passive, to be viewed and travelled. Every rail, every farm-house, seen dimly in the twilight, every tinkling sound told of peace and purity, and we moved happily along the dank roads, enjoying not such privacy as the day leaves when it withdraws, but such as it has not profaned. It was solitude with light, which is better than darkness. But anon, the sound of the mower's rifle was heard in the fields, and this, too, mingled with the lowing of kine.

This part of our route lay through the country of hops, which plant perhaps supplies the want of the vine in American scenery, and may remind the traveller of Italy, and the South of France, whether he traverses the country when the hop-fields, as then, present solid and regular masses of verdure, hanging in graceful festoons from pole to pole, the cool coverts where lurk the gales which refresh the way-farer, or in September, when the women and children, and the neighbors from far and near, are gathered to pick the hops into long troughs, or later still, when the poles stand piled in vast pyramids in the yards, or lie in heaps by the roadside.

The culture of the hop, with the processes of picking, drying in the kiln, and packing for the market, as well as the uses to which it is applied, so analogous to the culture and uses of the grape, may afford a theme for future poets.

The mower in the adjacent meadow could not tell us the name of the brook on whose banks we had rested, or whether it had any, but his younger companion, perhaps his brother, knew that it was Great Brook. Though they stood very near together in the field, the things they knew were very far apart; nor did they suspect each other's reserved knowledge, till the stranger came by. In Bolton, while we rested on the rails of a cottage fence, the strains of music which issued from

within, probably in compliment to us sojourners, reminded us that thus far men were fed by the accustomed pleasures. So soon did we, wayfarers, begin to
learn that man's life is rounded with the same few
facts, the same simple relations everywhere, and it is
vain to travel to find it new. The flowers grow more
various ways than he. But coming soon to higher
land, which afforded a prospect of the mountains, we
thought we had not travelled in vain, if it were only
to hear a truer and wilder pronunciation of their
names, from the lips of the inhabitants; not *Way*-tatic,
Way-chusett, but *Wor*-tatic, *Wor*-chusett. It made us
ashamed of our tame and civil pronunciation, and we
looked upon them as born and bred farther west than
we. Their tongues had a more generous accent than
ours, as if breath was cheaper where they wagged. A
countryman, who speaks but seldom, talks copiously,
as it were, as his wife sets cream and cheese before
you without stint. Before noon we had reached the
highlands overlooking the valley of Lancaster, (afford-
ing the first fair and open prospect into the west,) and
there, on the top of a hill, in the shade of some oaks,
near to where a spring bubbled out from a leaden
pipe, we rested during the heat of the day, reading Virgil, and enjoying the scenery. It was such a place as
one feels to be on the outside of the earth, for from it
we could, in some measure, see the form and structure
of the globe. There lay Wachusett, the object of our
journey, lowering upon us with unchanged proportions, though with a less ethereal aspect than had
greeted our morning gaze, while further north, in successive order, slumbered its sister mountains along
the horizon.

We could get no further into the Æneid than

-atque altæ mœnia Romæ,
-and the wall of high Rome,

before we were constrained to reflect by what myriad tests a work of genius has to be tried; that Virgil, away in Rome, two thousand years off, should have to unfold his meaning, the inspiration of Italian vales, to the pilgrim on New England hills. This life so raw and modern, that so civil and ancient, and yet we read Virgil, mainly to be reminded of the identity of human nature in all ages, and by the poet's own account, we are both the children of a late age, and live equally under the reign of Jupiter.

> "He shook honey from the leaves, and removed fire,
> And stayed the wine, everywhere flowing in rivers,
> That experience, by meditating, might invent various arts
> By degrees, and seek the blade of corn in furrows,
> And strike out hidden fire from the veins of the flint."

The old world stands serenely behind the new, as one mountain yonder towers behind another, more dim and distant. Rome imposes her story still upon this late generation. The very children in the school we had that morning passed, had gone through her wars, and recited her alarms, ere they had heard of the wars of neighboring Lancaster. The roving eye still rests inevitably on her hills, and she still holds up the skirts of the sky on that side, and makes the past remote.

The lay of the land hereabouts is well worthy the attention of the traveller. The hill on which we were resting made part of an extensive range, running from south-west to north-east, across the country, and separating the waters of the Nashua from those of the Concord, whose banks we had left in the morning, and by bearing in mind this fact, we could easily determine whither each brook was bound that crossed our path. Parallel to this, and fifteen miles further west, beyond the deep and broad valley in which lie Groton, Shirley, Lancaster, and Boylston, runs the Wachusett range, in the same general direction. The descent into the valley on the Nashua side is, by far, the most sudden; and a couple of miles brought us to the southern branch of the Nashua, a shallow but rapid stream, flowing between high and gravelly banks. But we soon learned that these were no *gelidæ valles* into which we had descended, and missing the coolness of the morning air, feared it had become the sun's turn to try his power upon us.

> "The sultry sun had gained the middle sky,
> And not a tree, and not an herb was nigh,"

and with melancholy pleasure we echoed the melodious plaint of our fellow-traveller Hassan, in the desert,

> "Sad was the hour, and luckless was the day,
> When first from Schiraz' walls I bent my way."

The air lay lifeless between the hills, as in a seething caldron, with no leaf stirring, and instead of the fresh odor of grass and clover, with which we had before been regaled, the dry scent of every herb seemed merely medicinal. Yielding, therefore, to the heat, we strolled into the woods, and along the course of a rivulet, on whose banks we loitered, observing at our leisure the products of these new fields. He who traverses the woodland paths, at this season, will have occasion to remember the small drooping bell-like flowers and slender red stem of the dogs-bane, and the coarser stem and berry of the poke, which are both common in remoter and wilder scenes; and if "the sun casts such a reflecting heat from the sweet fern," as makes him faint, when he is climbing the bare hills, as they complained who first penetrated into these parts, the cool fragrance of the swamp pink restores him again, when traversing the valleys between.

As we went on our way late in the afternoon, we refreshed ourselves by bathing our feet in every rill that crossed the road, and anon, as we were able to walk in

the shadows of the hills, recovered our morning elasticity. Passing through Sterling, we reached the banks
of the Stillwater, in the western part of the town, at
evening, where is a small village collected. We fancied
that there was already a certain western look about
this place, a smell of pines and roar of water, recently
confined by dams, belying its name, which were exceedingly grateful. When the first inroad has been
made, a few acres levelled, and a few houses erected,
the forest looks wilder than ever. Left to herself, nature
is always more or less civilized, and delights in a certain refinement; but where the axe has encroached
upon the edge of the forest, the dead and unsightly
limbs of the pine, which she had concealed with green
banks of verdure, are exposed to sight. This village
had, as yet, no post-office, nor any settled name. In the
small villages which we entered, the villagers gazed
after us, with a complacent, almost compassionate
look, as if we were just making our debut in the world,
at a late hour. "Nevertheless," did they seem to say,
"come and study us, and learn men and manners." So
is each one's world but a clearing in the forest, so
much open and inclosed ground. The landlord had
not yet returned from the field with his men, and the
cows had yet to be milked. But we remembered the
inscription on the wall of the Swedish inn, "You will
find at Trolhate excellent bread, meat, and wine, provided you bring them with you," and were contented.
But I must confess it did somewhat disturb our pleasure, in this withdrawn spot, to have our own village
newspaper handed us by our host, as if the greatest
charm the country offered to the traveller was the fa-
cility of communication with the town. Let it recline
on its own everlasting hills, and not be looking out
from their summits for some petty Boston or New York
in the horizon.

At intervals we heard the murmuring of water, and the slumberous breathing of crickets throughout the night, and left the inn the next morning in the grey twilight, after it had been hallowed by the night air, and when only the innocent cows were stirring, with a kind of regret. It was only four miles to the base of the mountain, and the scenery was already more picturesque. Our road lay along the course of the Stillwater, which was brawling at the bottom of a deep ravine, filled with pines and rocks, tumbling fresh from the mountains, so soon, alas! to commence its career of usefulness. At first a cloud hung between us and the summit, but it was soon blown away. As we gathered the raspberries, which grew abundantly by the roadside, we fancied that that action was consistent with a lofty prudence, as if the traveller who ascends into a mountainous region should fortify himself by eating of such light ambrosial fruits as grow there, and drinking of the springs which gush out from the mountain sides, as he gradually inhales the subtler and purer atmosphere of those elevated places, thus propitiating the mountain gods, by a sacrifice of their own fruits. The gross products of the plains and valleys are for such as dwell therein; but it seemed to us that the juices of this berry had relation to the thin air of the mountain tops.

In due time we began to ascend the mountain, passing, first, through a grand sugar maple wood, which bore the marks of the auger, then a denser forest, which gradually became dwarfed, till there were no trees whatever. We at length pitched our tent on the summit. It is but nineteen hundred feet above the village of Princeton, and three thousand above the level of the sea; but by this slight elevation, it is infinitely removed from the plain, and when we reached it, we felt a sense of remoteness, as if we had travelled into distant regions, to Arabia Petrea, or the farthest east. A robin upon a staff, was the highest object in sight. Swallows were flying about us, and the chewink and cuckoo were heard near at hand. The summit consists of a few acres, destitute of trees, covered with bare rocks, interspersed with blueberry bushes, raspberries, gooseberries, strawberries, moss, and a fine wiry grass. The common yellow lily, and dwarf cornel, grow abundantly in the crevices of the rocks. This clear space, which is gently rounded, is bounded a few feet lower by a thick shrubbery of oaks, with maples, aspens, beeches, cherries, and occasionally a mountain-ash intermingled, among which we found the bright blue berries of the Solomon's Seal, and the fruit of the pyrola. From the foundation of a wooden observatory, which was formerly erected on the highest point, forming a rude hollow structure of stone, a dozen feet in diameter, and five or six in height, we could see Monadnock, in simple grandeur, in the north-west, rising nearly a thousand feet higher, still the "far blue mountain," though with an altered profile. The first day the weather was so hazy that it was in vain we endeavored to unravel the obscurity. It was like looking into the sky again, and the patches of forest here and there seemed to flit like clouds over a lower heaven. As to voyagers of an aerial Polynesia, the earth seemed like a larger island in the ether; on every side, even as low as we, the sky shutting down, like an unfathomable deep, around it. A blue Pacific island, where who knows what islanders inhabit? and as we sail near its shores we see the waving of trees, and hear the lowing of kine.

We read Virgil and Wordsworth in our tent, with new pleasure there, while waiting for a clearer atmosphere, nor did the weather prevent our appreciating the simple truth and beauty of Peter Bell:

"And he had lain beside his asses,
On lofty Cheviot hills."

"And he had trudged through Yorkshire dales,
Among the rocks and winding *scars*,
Where deep and low the hamlets lie
Beneath their little patch of sky,
And little lot of stars."

Who knows but this hill may one day be a Helvellyn, or even a Parnassus, and the Muses haunt here, and other Homers frequent the neighboring plains,

Not unconcerned Wachusett rears his head
Above the field, so late from nature won,
With patient brow reserved, as one who read
New annals in the history of man.

The blueberries which the mountain afforded, added to the milk we had brought, made our frugal supper, while for entertainment, the even-song of the wood-thrush rung along the ridge. Our eyes rested on no painted ceiling, nor carpeted hall, but on skies of nature's painting, and hills and forests of her embroidery. Before sunset, we rambled along the ridge to the north, while a hawk soared still above us. It was a place where gods might wander, so solemn and solitary, and removed from all contagion with the plain. As the evening came on, the haze was condensed in vapor, and the landscape became more distinctly visible, and numerous sheets of water were brought to light,

Et jam summa procul villarum culmina fumant,
Majoresque cadunt altis de montibus umbræ.

And now the tops of the villas smoke afar off,
And the shadows fall longer from the high mountains.

As we stood on the stone tower while the sun was setting, we saw the shades of night creep gradually over the valleys of the east, and the inhabitants went into their houses, and shut their doors, while the moon silently rose up, and took possession of that part. And then the same scene was repeated on the west side, as far as the Connecticut and the Green Mountains, and the sun's rays fell on us two alone, of all New England men.

It was the night but one before the full of the moon, so bright that we could see to read distinctly by moonlight, and in the evening strolled over the summit without danger. There was, by chance, a fire blazing on Monadnock that night, which lighted up the whole western horizon, and by making us aware of a community of mountains, made our position seem less solitary. But at length the wind drove us to the shelter of our tent, and we closed its door for the night, and fell asleep.

It was thrilling to hear the wind roar over the rocks, at intervals, when we waked, for it had grown quite cold and windy. The night was, in its elements, simple even to majesty in that bleak place–a bright moonlight and a piercing wind. It was at no time darker than twilight within the tent, and we could easily see the moon through its transparent roof as we lay; for there was the moon still above us, with Jupiter and Saturn on either hand, looking down on Wachusett, and it was a satisfaction to know that they were our fellow-travellers still, as high and out of our reach as our own destiny. Truly the stars were given for a consolation to man. We should not know but our life were fated to be always grovelling, but it is permitted to behold them, and surely they are deserving of a fair destiny. We see laws which never fail, of whose failure we never conceived; and their lamps burn all the night, too, as well as all day, so rich and lavish is that nature, which can afford this superfluity of light.

The morning twilight began as soon as the moon had set, and we arose and kindled our fire, whose blaze might have been seen for thirty miles around. As the day-light increased, it was remarkable how rapidly the wind went down. There was no dew on the summit, but coldness supplied its place. When the dawn had reached its prime, we enjoyed the view of a distinct horizon line, and could fancy ourselves at sea, and the distant hills the waves in the horizon, as seen from the deck of a vessel. The cherry-birds flitted around us, the nuthatch and flicker were heard among the bushes, the titmouse perched within a few feet, and the song of the woodthrush again rung along the ridge. At length we saw the sun rise up out of the sea, and shine on Massachusetts, and from this moment the atmosphere grew more and more transparent till the time of our departure, and we began to realize the extent of the view, and how the earth, in some degree, answered to the heavens in breadth, the white villages to the constellations in the sky. There was little of the sublimity and grandeur which belong to mountain scenery, but an immense landscape to ponder on a summer's day. We could see how ample and roomy is nature. As far as the eye could reach, there was little life in the landscape; the few birds that flitted past did not crowd. The travellers on the remote highways, which intersect the country on every side, had no fellow-travellers for miles, before or behind. On every side, the eye ranged over successive circles of towns, rising one above another, like the terraces of a vineyard, till they were lost in the horizon. Wachusett is, in fact, the observatory of the state. There lay Massachusetts, spread out before us in its length and breadth, like a map. There was the level horizon, which told of the sea on the east and south, the well-known hills of

New Hampshire on the north, and the misty summits of the Hoosac and Green Mountains, first made visible to us the evening before, blue and unsubstantial, like some bank of clouds which the morning wind would dissipate, on the north-west and west. These last distant ranges, on which the eye rests unwearied, commence with an abrupt boulder in the north, beyond the Connecticut, and travel southward, with three or four peaks dimly seen. But Monadnock, rearing its masculine front in the north-west, is the grandest feature. As we beheld it we knew that it was the height of land between the two rivers, on this side the valley of the Merrimack, on that of the Connecticut, fluctuating with their blue seas of air,–these rival vales, already teeming with Yankee men along their respective streams, born to what destiny who shall tell? Watatic, and the neighboring hills in this state and in New Hampshire, are a continuation of the same elevated range on which we were standing. But that New Hampshire bluff–that promontory of a state–lowering day and night on this our state of Massachusetts, will longest haunt our dreams.

We could, at length, realize the place mountains occupy on the land, and how they come into the general scheme of the universe. When first we climb their summits, and observe their lesser irregularities, we do not give credit to the comprehensive intelligence which shaped them; but when afterward we behold their outlines in the horizon, we confess that the hand which moulded their opposite slopes, making one to balance the other, worked round a deep centre, and was privy to the plan of the universe. So is the least part of nature in its bearings referred to all space. These lesser mountain ranges, as well as the Alleghanies, run from north-east to south-west, and parallel with these mountain streams are the more fluent rivers, answering to the general direction of the coast, the bank of the great ocean stream itself. Even the clouds, with their thin bars, fall into the same direction by preference, and such even is the course of the prevailing winds, and the migration of men and birds. A mountain chain determines many things for the statesman and philosopher. The improvements of civilization rather creep along its sides than cross its summit. How often is it a barrier to prejudice and fanaticism? In passing over these heights of land, through their thin atmosphere, the follies of the plain are refined and purified; and as many species of plants do not scale their summits, so many species of folly no doubt do not cross the Alleghanies; it is only the hardy mountain plant that creeps quite over the ridge, and descends into the valley beyond.

We get a dim notion of the flight of birds, especially of such as fly high in the air, by having ascended a mountain. We can now see what landmarks mountains are to their migrations; how the Catskills and Highlands have hardly sunk to them, when Wachusett and Monadnock open a passage to the north-east– how they are guided, too, in their course by the rivers and valleys, and who knows but by the stars, as well as the mountain ranges, and not by the petty landmarks which we use. The bird whose eye takes in the Green Mountains on the one side, and the ocean on the other, need not be at a loss to find its way.

At noon we descended the mountain, and having returned to the abodes of men, turned our faces to the east again; measuring our progress, from time to time, by the more ethereal hues, which the mountain assumed. Passing swiftly through Stillwater and Sterling, as with a downward impetus, we found ourselves almost at home again in the green meadows of Lancaster, so like our own Concord, for both are watered by two streams which unite near their centres, and have many other features in common. There is an unexpected refinement about this scenery; level prairies of great extent, interspersed with elms, and hop-fields, and groves of trees, give it almost a classic appearance. This, it will be remembered, was the scene of Mrs. Rowlandson's capture, and of other events in the Indian wars, but from this July afternoon, and under that mild exterior, those times seemed as remote as the irruption of the Goths. They were the dark age of New England. On beholding a picture of a New England village as it then appeared, with a fair open prospect, and a light on trees and river, as if it were broad noon, we find we had not thought the sun shone in those days, or that men lived in broad daylight then. We do not imagine the sun shining on hill and valley during Philip's war, nor on the war-path of Paugus, or Standish, or Church, or Lovell, with serene summer weather, but a dim twilight or night did those events transpire in. They must have fought in the shade of their own dusky deeds.

At length, as we plodded along the dusty roads, our thoughts became as dusty as they; all thought indeed stopped, thinking broke down, or proceeded only passively in a sort of rhythmical cadence of the confused material of thought, and we found ourselves mechanically repeating some familiar measure which timed with our tread; some verse of the Robin Hood ballads, for instance, which one can recommend to travel by.

> "Sweavens are swift, sayd lyttle John,
>   As the wind blows over the hill;
> For if it be never so loud this night,
>   To-morrow it may be still."

And so it went up hill and down till a stone interrupted the line, when a new verse was chosen.

"His shoote it was but loosely shot,
Yet flewe not the arrowe in vaine,
For it met one of the sheriffe's men,
And William-a-Trent was slaine."

There is, however, this consolation to the most way-
worn traveller, upon the dustiest road, that the path
his feet describe is so perfectly symbolical of human
life–now climbing the hills, now descending into the
vales. From the summits he beholds the heavens and
the horizon, from the vales he looks up to the heights
again. He is treading his old lessons still, and though
he may be very weary and travel-worn, it is yet sincere
experience.

Leaving the Nashua, we changed our route a little,
and arrived at Stillriver village, in the western part of
Harvard, just as the sun was setting. From this place,
which lies to the northward, upon the western slope of
the same range of hills, on which we had spent the
noon before, in the adjacent town, the prospect is
beautiful, and the grandeur of the mountain outlines
unsurpassed. There was such a repose and quiet here
at this hour, as if the very hill-sides were enjoying the
scene, and as we passed slowly along, looking back
over the country we had traversed, and listening to the
evening song of the robin, we could not help contrasting the equanimity of nature with the bustle and impa-
tience of man. His words and actions presume always
a crisis near at hand, but she is forever silent and unpretending.

And now that we have returned to the desultory life
of the plain, let us endeavor to import a little of that
mountain grandeur into it. We will remember within
what walls we lie, and understand that this level life
too has its summit, and why from the mountain top
the deepest valleys have a tinge of blue; that there is
elevation in every hour, as no part of the earth is so low

that the heavens may not be seen from it, and we have only to stand on the summit of our hour to command an uninterrupted horizon.

We rested that night at Harvard, and the next morning, while one bent his steps to the nearer village of Groton, the other took his separate and solitary way to the peaceful meadows of Concord; but let him not forget to record the brave hospitality of a farmer and his wife, who generously entertained him at their board, though the poor wayfarer could only congratulate the one on the continuance of hayweather, and silently accept the kindness of the other. Refreshed by this instance of generosity, no less than by the substantial viands set before him, he pushed forward with new vigor, and reached the banks of the Concord before the sun had climbed many degrees into the heavens.

The Landlord.

UNDER the one word, house, are included the school house, the alms house, the jail, the tavern, the dwelling house; and the meanest shed or cave in which men live, contains the elements of all these. But no where on the earth stands the entire and perfect house. The Parthenon, St. Peter's, the Gothic minster, the palace, the hovel, are but imperfect executions of an imperfect idea. Who would dwell in them? Perhaps to the eye of the gods, the cottage is more holy than the Parthenon, for they look down with no especial favor upon the shrines formally dedicated to them, and that should be the most sacred roof which shelters most of humanity. Surely, then, the gods who are most interested in the human race preside over the Tavern, where especially men congregate. Methinks I see the thousand shrines erected to Hospitality shining afar in all countries, as well Mahometan and Jewish, as Christian, khans, and caravansaries, and inns, whither all pilgrims without distinction resort.

Likewise we look in vain east or west over the earth to find the perfect man; but each represents only some particular excellence. The Landlord is a man of more open and general sympathies, who possesses a spirit of hospitality which is its own reward, and feeds and shelters men from pure love of the creatures. To be sure, this profession is as often filled by imperfect characters, and such as have sought it from unworthy motives, as any other, but so much the more should we prize the true and honest Landlord when we meet with him.

Who has not imagined to himself a country inn, where the traveller shall really feel *in*, and at home, and at his public house, who was before at his private house; whose host is indeed a *host*, and a *lord* of the *land*, a self-appointed brother of his race; called to his place, beside, by all the winds of heaven and his good genius, as truly as the preacher is called to preach; a man of such universal sympathies, and so broad and genial a human nature, that he would fain sacrifice the tender but narrow ties of private friendship, to a broad, sunshiny, fair-weather-and-foul friendship for his race; who loves men, not as a philosopher, with philanthropy, nor as an overseer of the poor, with charity, but by a necessity of his nature, as he loves dogs and horses; and standing at his open door from morning till night, would fain see more and more of them come along the highway, and is never satiated. To him the sun and moon are but travellers, the one by day and the other by night; and they too patronise his house. To his imagination all things travel save his sign-post and himself; and though you may be his neighbor for years, he will show you only the civilities of the road. But on the other hand, while nations and individuals are alike selfish and exclusive, he loves all men equally; and if he treats his nearest neighbor as a stranger, since he has invited all nations to share his hospitality, the farthest travelled is in some measure kindred to him who takes him into the bosom of his family.

He keeps a house of entertainment at the sign of the Black Horse or the Spread Eagle, and is known far and wide, and his fame travels with increasing radius every year. All the neighborhood is in his interest, and if the traveller ask how far to a tavern, he receives some such answer as this: "Well, sir, there's a house about three miles from here, where they haven't taken down their sign yet; but it's only ten miles to Slocum's, and that's a capital house, both for man and beast." At three miles he passes a cheerless barrack, standing desolate behind its sign-post, neither public nor private, and has glimpses of a discontented couple who have mistaken their calling. At ten miles see where the Tavern stands,–really an *entertaining* prospect,–so public and inviting that only the rain and snow do not enter. It is no gay pavilion, made of bright stuffs, and furnished with nuts and gingerbread, but as plain and sincere as a caravansary; located in no Tarrytown, where you receive only the civilities of commerce, but far in the fields it exercises a primitive hospitality, amid the fresh scent of new hay and raspberries, if it be summer time, and the tinkling of cow-bells from invisible pastures; for it is a land flowing with milk and honey, and the newest milk courses in a broad deep stream across the premises.

In these retired places the tavern is first of all a house–elsewhere, last of all, or never–and warms and shelters its inhabitants. It is as simple and sincere in its essentials as the caves in which the first men dwelt, but it is also as open and public. The traveller steps across the threshold, and lo! he too is master, for he only can be called proprietor of the house here who behaves with most propriety in it. The Landlord stands clear back in nature, to my imagination, with his axe and spade felling trees and raising potatoes with the vigor of a pioneer; with Promethean energy making nature yield her increase to supply the wants of so many; and he is not so exhausted, nor of so short a stride, but that he comes forward even to the highway to this wide hospitality and publicity. Surely, he has solved some of the problems of life. He comes in at his back door, holding a log fresh cut for the hearth upon his shoulder with one hand, while he greets the newly arrived traveller with the other.

Here at length we have free range, as not in palaces, nor cottages, nor temples, and intrude no where. All the secrets of housekeeping are exhibited to the eyes of men, above and below, before and behind. This is the necessary way to live, men have confessed, in these days, and shall he skulk and hide? And why should we have any serious disgust at kitchens? Perhaps they are the holiest recess of the house. There is the hearth, after all,–and the settle, and the faggots, and the kettle, and the crickets. We have pleasant reminiscences of these. They are the heart, the left ventricle, the very vital part of the house. Here the real and sincere life which we meet in the streets was actually fed and sheltered. Here burns the taper that cheers the lonely traveller by night, and from this hearth ascend the smokes that populate the valley to his eyes by day. On the whole, a man may not be so little ashamed of any other part of his house, for here is his sincerity and earnest, at least. It may not be here that the besoms are plied most–it is not here that they need to be, for dust will not settle on the kitchen floor more than in nature.

Hence it will not do for the Landlord to possess too fine a nature. He must have health above the common accidents of life, subject to no modern fashionable diseases; but no taste, rather a vast relish or appetite. His sentiments on all subjects will be delivered as freely as the wind blows; there is nothing private or individual in them, though still original, but they are public, and of the hue of the heavens over his house,–a certain out-of-door obviousness and transparency not to be disputed. What he does, his manners are not to be complained of, though abstractly offensive, for it is what man does, and in him the race is exhibited. When he eats, he is liver and bowels, and the whole digestive apparatus to the company, and so all admit the thing is done. He must have no idiosyncrasies, no particular bents or tendencies to this or that, but a general, uniform, and healthy development, such as his portly person indicates, offering himself equally on all sides to men. He is not one of your peaked and inhospitable men of genius, with particular tastes, but, as we said before, has one uniform relish, and taste which never aspires higher than a tavern sign, or the cut of a weather-cock. The man of genius, like a dog with a bone, or the slave who has swallowed a diamond, or a patient with the gravel, sits afar and retired, off the road, hangs out no sign of refreshment for man and beast, but says, by all possible hints and signs, I wish to be alone–good-bye–farewell. But the landlord can afford to live without privacy. He entertains no private thought, he cherishes no solitary hour, no sabbath day, but thinks–enough to assert the dignity of reason–and talks, and reads the newspaper. What he does not tell to one traveller, he tells to another. He never wants to be alone, but sleeps, wakes, eats, drinks, sociably, still remembering his race. He walks abroad through the thoughts of men, and the Iliad and Shakspeare are tame to him, who hears the rude but homely incidents of the road from every traveller. The mail might drive through his brain in the midst of his most lonely solilo-quy, without disturbing his equanimity, provided it brought plenty of news and passengers. There can be no *pro*-fanity where there is no fane behind, and the whole world may see quite round him. Perchance his lines have fallen to him in dustier places, and he has heroically sat down where two roads meet, or at the Four Corners, or the Five Points, and his life is sub-limely trivial for the good of men. The dust of travel blows ever in his eyes, and they preserve their clear, complacent look. The hourlies and half-hourlies, the dailies and weeklies, whirl on well worn tracks, round and round his house, as if it were the goal in the sta-dium, and still he sits within in unruffled serenity, with no show of retreat. His neighbor dwells timidly behind a screen of poplars and willows, and a fence with sheaves of spears at regular intervals, or defended against the tender palms of visitors by sharp spikes,–

but the traveller's wheels rattle over the door-step of the tavern, and he cracks his whip in the entry. He is truly glad to see you, and sincere as the bull's-eye over his door. The traveller seeks to find, wherever he goes, some one who will stand in this broad and catholic relation to him, who will be an inhabitant of the land to him a stranger, and represent its human nature, as the rock stands for its inanimate nature; and this is he. As his crib furnishes provender for the traveller's horse, and his larder provisions for his appetite, so his conversation furnishes the necessary aliment to his spirits. He knows very well what a man wants, for he is a man himself, and as it were the farthest travelled, though he has never stirred from his door. He understands his needs and destiny. He would be well fed and lodged, there can be no doubt, and have the transient sympathy of a cheerful companion, and of a heart which always prophesies fair weather. And after all the greatest men, even, want much more the sympathy which every one can give, than that which the great only can impart. If he is not the most upright, let us allow him this praise, that he is the most downright of men. He has a hand to shake and to be shaken, and takes a sturdy and unquestionable interest in you, as if he had assumed the care of you, but if you will break your neck, he will even give you the best advice as to the method.

The great poets have not been ungrateful to their landlords. Mine host of the Tabard inn, in the Prologue to the Canterbury Tales, was an honor to his profession:

"A semely man our Hoste was, with alle,
For to han been an marshal in an halle.
A large man he was, with eyen stepe;
A fairer burgeis is ther non in Chepe:

> Bold of his speche, and wise, and well ytaught,
> And of manhood him lacked righte naught.
> Eke thereto, was he right a mery man,
> And after souper plaien he began,
> And spake of mirthe amonges other thinges,
> Whan that we hadden made our reckoninges."

He is the true house-band, and centre of the company–of greater fellowship and practical social talent
than any. He it is, that proposes that each shall tell a
tale to while away the time to Canterbury, and leads
them himself, and concludes with his own tale:

> "Now, by my fader's soule that is ded,
> But ye be mery, smiteth of my hed:
> Hold up your hondes withouten more speche."

If we do not look up to the Landlord, we look round
for him on all emergencies, for he is a man of infinite
experience, who unites hands with wit. He is a more
public character than a statesman–a publican, and not
consequently a sinner; and surely, he, if any, should
be exempted from taxation and military duty.

Talking with our host is next best and instructive to
talking with one's self. It is a more conscious solilo-
quy; as it were, to speak generally, and try what we
would say provided we had an audience. He has indul-
gent and open ears, and does not require petty and
particular statements. "Heigho!" exclaims the traveller. Them's my sentiments, thinks mine host, and
stands ready for what may come next, expressing the
purest sympathy by his demeanor. "Hot as blazes!"
says the other,–"Hard weather, sir,–not much stirring
now-a-days," says he. He is wiser than to contradict
his guest in any case; he lets him go on, he lets him
travel.

The latest sitter leaves him standing far in the night,
prepared to live right on, while suns rise and set, and

his "good-night" has as brisk a sound as his "good-morning," and the earliest riser finds him tasting his liquors in the bar ere flies begin to buzz, with a countenance fresh as the morning star over the sanded floor,–and not as one who had watched all night for travellers. And yet, if beds be the subject of conversation, it will appear that no man has been a sounder sleeper in his time.

Finally, as for his moral character, we do not hesitate to say, that he has no grain of vice or meanness in him, but represents just that degree of virtue which all men relish without being obliged to respect. He is a good man, as his bitters are good–an unquestionable goodness. Not what is called a good man,–good to be considered, as a work of art in galleries and museums,–but a good fellow, that is, good to be associated with. Who ever thought of the religion of an innkeeper–whether he was joined to the Church, partook of the sacrament, said his prayers, feared God, or the like? No doubt he has had his experiences, has felt a change, and is a firm believer in the perseverance of the saints. In this last, we suspect, does the peculiarity of his religion consist. But he keeps an inn, and not a conscience. How many fragrant charities, and sincere social virtues are implied in this daily offering of himself to the public. He cherishes good will to all, and gives the wayfarer as good and honest advice to direct him on his road, as the priest.

To conclude, the tavern will compare favorably with the church. The church is the place where prayers and sermons are delivered, but the tavern is where they are to take effect, and if the former are good, the latter cannot be bad.

A Winter Walk.

THE WIND has gently murmured through the blinds, or puffed with feathery softness against the windows, and occasionally sighed like a summer zephyr lifting the leaves along, the livelong night. The meadow mouse has slept in his snug gallery in the sod, the owl has sat in a hollow tree in the depth of the swamp, the rabbit, the squirrel, and the fox have all been housed. The watch-dog has lain quiet on the hearth, and the cattle have stood silent in their stalls. The earth itself has slept, as it were its first, not its last sleep, save when some street-sign or wood-house door has faintly creaked upon its hinge, cheering forlorn nature at her midnight work–the only sound awake twixt Venus and Mars,–advertising us of a remote inward warmth, a divine cheer and fellowship, where gods are met together, but where it is very bleak for men to stand. But while the earth has slumbered, all the air has been alive with feathery flakes descending, as if some northern Ceres reigned, showering her silvery grain over all the fields.

At length we awake to the still reality of a winter morning. The snow lies warm as cotton or down upon the window-sill; the broadened sash and frosted panes admit a dim and private light, which enhances the snug cheer within. The stillness of the morning is impressive. The floor creaks under our feet as we move toward the window to look abroad through some clear space over the fields. We see the roofs stand under their snow burden. From the eaves and fences hang stalactites of snow, and in the yard stand stalagmites covering some concealed core. The trees and shrubs rear white arms to the sky on every side, and where were walls and fences, we see fantastic forms stretching in frolic gambols across the dusky landscape, as if nature had strewn her fresh designs over the fields by night as models for man's art.

Silently we unlatch the door, letting the drift fall in, and step abroad to face the cutting air. Already the stars have lost some of their sparkle, and a dull leaden mist skirts the horizon. A lurid brazen light in the east proclaims the approach of day, while the western landscape is dim and spectral still, and clothed in a sombre Tartarean light, like the shadowy realms. They are Infernal sounds only that you hear,–the crowing of cocks, the barking of dogs, the chopping of wood, the lowing of kine, all seem to come from Pluto's barn-yard and beyond the Styx;–not for any melancholy they suggest, but their twilight bustle is too solemn and mysterious for earth. The recent tracks of the fox or otter, in the yard, remind us that each hour of the night is crowded with events, and the primeval nature is still working and making tracks in the snow. Open-ing the gate, we tread briskly along the lone country road, crunching the dry and crisped snow under our feet, or aroused by the sharp clear creak of the wood-sled, just starting for the distant market, from the early farmer's door, where it has lain the summer long, dreaming amid the chips and stubble; while far through the drifts and powdered windows we see the farmer's early candle, like a paled star, emitting a lonely beam, as if some severe virtue were at its matins there. And one by one the smokes begin to ascend from the chimneys amidst the trees and snows.

> The sluggish smoke curls up from some deep dell,
> The stiffened air exploring in the dawn,
> And making slow acquaintance with the day;
> Delaying now upon its heavenward course,
> In wreathed loiterings dallying with itself,
> With as uncertain purpose and slow deed,
> As its half-wakened master by the hearth,

Whose mind still slumbering and sluggish thoughts
Have not yet swept into the onward current
Of the new day;–and now it streams afar,
The while the chopper goes with step direct,
And mind intent to swing the early axe.
     First in the dusky dawn he sends abroad
His early scout, his emissary, Smoke,
The earliest latest pilgrim from the roof,
To feel the frosty air, inform the day,
And while he crouches still beside the hearth,
Nor musters courage to unbar the door,
'T has been far down the glen with the new wind,
And o'er the plain unfurled its venturous wreath,
Draped the tree tops, loitered upon the hill,
And warmed the pinions of the early bird;
And now, perchance, high in the crispy air,
Has caught sight of the day o'er the earth's edge,
And greets its master's eye at his low door,
As some refulgent cloud in the upper sky.

We hear the sound of wood-chopping at the farmers' doors, far over the frozen earth, the baying of the house dog, and the distant clarion of the cock. Though the thin and frosty air conveys only the finer particles of sound to our ears, with short and sweet vibrations, as the waves subside soonest on the purest and lightest liquids, in which gross substances sink to the bottom, they come clear and bell-like and from a greater distance in the horizon, as if there were fewer impediments than in summer to make them faint and ragged. The ground is sonorous, like seasoned wood, and even the ordinary rural sounds are melodious, and the jingling of the ice on the trees is sweet and liquid. There is the least possible moisture in the atmosphere, all being dried up or congealed, and it is of such extreme tenuity and elasticity that it becomes as much a source of delight as anything. The withdrawn and tense sky seems groined like the aisles of a cathedral, and the polished air sparkles as if there were crystals of ice floating in it, as they who have resided in Greenland tell us, that when it freezes, "the sea smokes like burning turf land, and a fog or mist arises, called frost smoke," which "cutting smoke frequently raises blisters on the face and hands, and is very pernicious to the health." But this pure stinging cold is an elixir to the lungs, and not so much a frozen mist, as a crystallized mid-summer haze, refined and purified by cold.

The sun at length rises through the distant woods, as if with the faint clashing swinging sound of cymbals, melting the air with his beams, and with such rapid steps the morning travels, that already his rays are gilding the distant western mountains. Meanwhile we step hastily along through the powdery snow, warmed by an inward heat, a protestant warmth, enjoying an Indian summer still in the increased glow of thought and feeling. Probably if our lives were more conformed to nature, we should not need to defend ourselves against her heats and colds, but find her our constant nurse and friend as do plants and quadrupeds. If our bodies were fed with pure and simple elements, and not with a stimulating and heating diet, they would afford no more pasture for cold than a leafless twig, but thrive like the trees, which find even winter genial to their expansion.

The wonderful purity of nature at this season is a most pleasing fact. Every decayed stump and moss-grown stone and rail, and the dead leaves of autumn, are concealed by a clean napkin of snow. In the bare fields and tinkling woods, see what virtue survives. In the coldest and bleakest places the warmest charities still maintain a foothold. A cold and searching wind drives away all contagion, and nothing can withstand it but what has a virtue in it; and, accordingly, whatever we meet with in cold and bleak places, as the tops of mountains, we respect for a sort of sturdy innocence, a Puritan toughness. All things beside seem to be called in for shelter, and what stays out must be part of the original frame of the universe, and of such valor as God himself. It is invigorating to breathe the cleansed air. Its greater fineness and purity are visible to the eye, and we would fain stay out long and late, that the gales may sigh through us too, as through the leafless trees, and fit us for the winter:–as if we hoped so to borrow some pure and steadfast virtue, which will stead us in all seasons.

There is a slumbering subterranean fire in nature which never goes out, and which no cold can chill. It finally melts the great snow, and in January or July is only buried under a thicker or thinner covering. In the coldest day it flows somewhere, and the snow melts around every tree. This field of winter rye, which sprouted late in the fall, and now speedily dissolves the snow, is where the fire is very thinly covered. We feel warmed by it. In the winter, warmth stands for all virtue, and we resort in thought to a trickling rill, with its bare stones shining in the sun, and to warm springs in the woods, with as much eagerness as rabbits and robins. The steam which rises from swamps and pools, is as dear and domestic as that of our own ket-tle. What fire could ever equal the sunshine of a winter's-day, when the meadow mice come out by the wallsides, and the chicadee lisps in the defiles of the wood? The warmth comes directly from the sun, and is not radiated from the earth, as in summer; and when we feel his beams on our backs as we are treading some snowy dell, we are grateful as for a special kind-ness, and bless the sun which has followed us into that by-place.

This subterranean fire has its altar in each man's breast, for in the coldest day, and on the bleakest hill, the traveller cherishes a warmer fire within the folds of his cloak than is kindled on any hearth. A healthy man, indeed, is the complement of the seasons, and in winter, summer is in his heart. There is the south. Thither have all birds and insects migrated, and around the warm springs in his breast are gathered the robin and the lark.

At length having reached the edge of the woods, and shut out the gadding town, we enter within their covert as we go under the roof of a cottage, and cross its threshold, all ceiled and banked up with snow. Our voices ring hollowly through them as through a chamber and the twigs crackle under feet with private and household echoes. They are glad and warm still, and as genial and cheery in winter as in summer. As we stand in the midst of the pines, in the flickering and checkered light which straggles but little way into their maze, we wonder if the towns have ever heard their simple story. It seems to us that no traveller has ever explored them, and notwithstanding the wonders which science is elsewhere revealing every day, who would not like to hear their annals? Our humble villages in the plain, are their contribution. We borrow from the forest the boards which shelter, and the sticks which warm us. How important is their evergreen to the winter, that portion of the summer which does not fade, the permanent year, the unwithered grass. Thus simply, and with little expense of altitude, is the surface of the earth diversified. What would human life be without forests, those natural cities? From the tops of mountains they appear like smooth shaven lawns, yet whither shall we walk but in this taller grass? Nothing is so beautiful as the tree tops. A pine or two with a dash of vapor in the sky–and our elysium is made.– Each tree takes my own attitude sometime. Yonder pine stands like Caesar. I see Cromwell, and Jesus, and George Fox in the wood, with many savages beside. A fallen pine, with its green branches still freshly drooping, lies like Tecumseh with his blanket about him.

In this glade covered with bushes of a year's growth, see how the silvery dust lies on every seared leaf and twig, deposited in such infinite and luxurious forms as by their very variety atone for the absence of color. Observe the tiny tracks of mice around every stem, and the triangular tracks of the rabbit. A pure elastic heaven hangs over all, as if the impurities of the summer sky, refined and shrunk by the chaste winter's cold, had been winnowed from the heavens upon the earth.

Nature confounds her summer distinctions at this season. The heavens seem to be nearer the earth. The elements are less reserved and distinct. Water turns to ice, rain to snow. The day is but a Scandinavian night. The winter is an arctic summer.

How much more living is the life that is in nature, the furred life which still survives the stinging nights, and, from amidst fields and woods covered with frost and snow, sees the sun rise.

> "The foodless wilds
> Pour forth their brown inhabitants."

The grey-squirrel and rabbit are brisk and playful in the remote glens, even on the morning of the cold Friday. Here is our Lapland and Labrador, and for our Esquimaux and Knistenaux, Dog-ribbed Indians, Novazemblaites, and Spitzbergeners, are there not the ice-cutter and wood-chopper, the fox, muskrat, and mink?

Still, in the midst of the arctic day, we may trace the summer to its retreats, and sympathize with some contemporary life. Stretched over the brooks, in the midst of the frost-bound meadows, we may observe the submarine cottages of the caddis worms, the larvae of the Plicipennes. Their small cylindrical cases built around themselves, composed of flags, sticks, grass and withered leaves, shells and pebbles, in form and color like the wrecks which strew the bottom–now drifting along over the pebbly bottom, now whirling in tiny eddies and dashing down steep falls, or sweeping rapidly along with the current, or else swaying to and fro at the end of some grass blade or root. Anon they will leave their sunken habitations, and crawling up the stems of plants, or floating to the surface like gnats, as perfect insects henceforth flutter over the surface of the water, or sacrifice their short lives in the flame of our candles at evening.

We have come down into some little wintry glen this bright morning, where too the pure snow has fallen, as into an arena for more than Greek or Roman virtue. The shrubs are drooping under their burden, and the red alder berries contrast with the white ground. Here are the marks of a myriad feet which have already been abroad. The sun rises as proudly over such a glen, as over the valley of the Seine or the Tiber, and it seems the residence of a pure and self-subsistent valor such as they never witnessed; which never knew defeat nor fear. Here reign the simplicity and purity of a primitive age, and a health and hope far remote from towns and cities. Standing quite alone, far in the forest, while the wind is shaking down snow from the trees, and leaving the only human tracks behind us, we find our reflections of richer variety than the life of cities. The chicadee and nuthatch are more inspiring society than statesmen and philosophers, and we shall return to them at length, as to more vulgar companions. In this lonely glen, with its brook draining the slopes, its creased ice and crystals of all hues, which shame the galleries of Florence and Rome, where the pines and hemlocks stand up on either side, and the rush and sere wild oats in the rivulet itself, our lives are more serene and worthy to contemplate.

As the day advances the heat of the sun is reflected by the hillsides, and we hear a faint but sweet music, where flows the rill released from its fetters, and the icicles are melting on the trees, and the nut-hatch and partridge are heard and seen. The south wind melts the snow at noon, and the bare ground appears with its withered grass and leaves, and we are invigorated by the perfume which exhales from it, as by the scent of strong meats.

> The apples thaw
> The ravens caw
> The squirrels gnaw
> The frozen fruit;
>
> To their retreat
> We track the feet
> Of mice that eat
> The apple's root.
>
> The snow dust falls
> The otter crawls
> The partridge calls
> Far in the wood.
>
> The traveller dreams
> The tree-ice gleams
> The blue jay screams
> In angry mood.
>
> The Rabbit leaps
> The mouse outcreeps
> The flag out-peeps
> Beside the brook.
>
> The ferret weeps
> The marmot sleeps
> The owlet keeps
> In his snug nook.

The willows droop
The alders stoop
The pheasants group
  Beneath the snow.

The catkins green
Cast o'er the scene
A summer sheen
  A genial glow.

Let us go into this deserted woodman's hut, and see how he has passed the long winter nights and the short and stormy days. For here man has lived under this south hill-side, and it seems a civilized and public spot. We have such associations as when the traveller stands by the ruins of Palmyra or Hecatompolis. Singing birds and flowers perchance have begun to appear here, for flowers as well as weeds follow in the footsteps of man. These hemlocks whispered over his head, these hickory logs were his fuel, and these pitch-pine roots kindled his fire; yonder fuming rill in the hollow, whose thin and airy vapor still ascends as busily as ever, though he is far off now, was his well. These hemlock boughs, and the straw upon this raised platform, were his bed, and this broken dish held his drink. But he has not been here this season, for the phœbes built their nest upon this shelf last summer. I find some embers left, as if he had but just gone out, where he baked his pot of beans, and while at evening he smoked his pipe, whose stemless bowl lies in the ashes, chatted with his only companion, if perchance he had any, about the depth of the snow on the morrow, already falling fast and thick without, or disputed whether the last sound was the screech of an owl, or the creak of a bough, or imagination only; and through this broad chimney throat, in the late winter evening, ere he stretched himself upon the straw, he looked up to learn the progress of the storm, and seeing the bright stars of Cassiopeia's chair shining brightly down upon him, fell contentedly asleep.

See how many traces from which we may learn the chopper's history. From this stump we may guess the sharpness of his axe, and from the slope of the stroke, on which side he stood, and whether he cut down the tree without going round it or changing hands; and from the flexure of the splinters we may know which way it fell. This one chip contains inscribed on it the whole history of the wood-chopper and of the world. On this scrap of paper which held his sugar or salt, perchance, or was the wadding of his gun, sitting on a log in the forest, with what interest we read the tattle of cities, of those larger huts, empty and to let like this, in High-streets, and Broad-ways. The eaves are dripping on the south side of this simple roof, while the titmouse lisps in the pine, and the genial warmth of the sun around the door is somewhat kind and human. What means this vision of scattered logs and chips gilt by his rays? Our thoughts are like loose-strife in the noon of a summer day, and we could easily evaporate, and ascend into the sun.

After two seasons this rude dwelling does not deform the scene. Already the birds resort to it to build their nests, and you may track to its door the feet of many quadrupeds. Thus for a long time nature overlooks the incroachment and profanity of man. The wood still cheerfully and unsuspiciously echoes the strokes of the axe that fells it, and while they are few and seldom, they enhance its wildness, and all the elements strive to naturalize the sound.

Now our path begins to ascend gradually to the top of this high hill, from whose precipitous south side we can look over the broad country, of forest, and field, and river, to the distant snowy mountains. See yonder thin column of smoke curling up through the woods from some invisible farm-house;–the standard raised over some human and domestic life. There must be a warmer and more genial spot there below, as where we detect the vapor from a spring forming a cloud above the trees. What fine relations are established between the traveller who discovers this airy column from some eminence in the forest, and him who sits below. Up goes the smoke as silently and naturally as the vapor exhales from the leaves, and as busy disposing itself in wreaths as the housewife on the hearth below. It is a hieroglyphic of man's life, and suggests more intimate and important things than the boiling of a pot. Where its fine column rises above the forest, like an ensign, some human life has planted itself,–and such is the beginning of Rome, the establishment of the arts, and the foundation of empires, whether on the prairies of America, or the steppes of Asia.

And now we descend again to the brink of this woodland lake, which lies in a hollow of the hills, as if it were their expressed juice, and that of the leaves which are annually steeped in it. Without outlet or inlet to the eye, it has still its history, in the lapse of its waves, in the rounded pebbles on its shore, and in the pines which grow down to its brink. It has not been idle, though sedentary, but, like Abu Musa, teaches that "Sitting still at home is the heavenly way. The going out is the way of the world." Yet in its evaporation it travels as far as any. In summer it is the earth's liquid eye; a mirror in the breast of nature. The sins of the wood are washed out in it. See how the woods form an amphitheatre about it, and it is an arena for all the genialness of nature. All trees direct the traveller to its brink, all paths seek it out, birds fly to it, quadrupeds flee to it, and the very ground inclines toward it. It is nature's saloon, where she has sat down to her toilet.

Consider her silent economy and tidiness; how the sun comes with his evaporation to sweep the dust from its surface each morning, and a fresh surface is constantly welling up; and annually, after whatever impurities have accumulated herein, its liquid transparency appears again in the spring. In summer a hushed music seems to sweep across its surface. But now a plain sheet of snow conceals it from our eyes, except where the wind has swept the ice bare, and the sere leaves are gliding from side to side, tacking and veering on their tiny voyages. Here is one just keeled up against a pebble on shore, a dry beech leaf, rocking still, as if it would soon start again. A skilful engineer, methinks, might project its course since it fell from the parent stem. Here are all the elements for such a calculation. Its present position, the direction of the wind, the level of the pond, and how much more is given. In its scarred edges and veins is its log rolled up.

We fancy ourselves in the midst of some domestic scene. The surface of the pond is our deal table or sanded floor, and the woods rise abruptly from its edge, like the walls of a cottage. The lines set to catch pickerel through the ice look like a larger culinary preparation, and the men stand about on the white ground like pieces of forest furniture. The actions of these men, at the distance of half a mile over the ice and snow, impress us as when we read the exploits of Alexander in history. They seem not unworthy of the scenery and as momentous as the conquest of kingdoms.

Again we have wandered through the arches of the wood, until from its skirts we hear the distant booming of ice from yonder bay of the river, as if it were moved by some other and subtler tide than oceans know. It is a strange domestic sound and thrilling as the voice of one's distant and noble kindred. A mild summer sun shines over forest and lake, and though there is but one green leaf for many rods, yet nature enjoys a serene health. God is not more well. Every sound is fraught with the same mysterious assurance of health, as well now the creaking of the boughs in January, as the soft sough of the wind in July.

When Winter fringes every bough
    With his fantastic wreath,
And puts the seal of silence now
    Upon the leaves beneath;

When every stream in its pent-house
    Goes gurgling on its way,
And in his gallery the mouse
    Nibbleth the meadow hay;

Methinks the Summer still is nigh,
    And lurketh underneath,
As that same meadow mouse doth lie
    Snug in the last year's heath.

And if perchance the chicadee
    Lisp a faint note anon,
The snow is Summer's canopy,
    Which she herself put on.

Fair blossoms deck the cheerful trees,
    And dazzling fruits depend,
The north wind sighs a summer breeze,
    The nipping frosts to fend,

Bringing glad tidings unto me,
    The while I stand all ear,
Of a serene eternity,
    Which need not winter fear.

Out on the silent pond straightway
    The restless ice doth crack,
And pond sprites merry gambols play
    Amid the deaf'ning rack.

Eager I hasten to the vale,
   As if I heard brave news,
How nature held high festival,
   Which it were hard to lose.

I crack me with my neighbor ice
   And sympathizing quake,
As each new crack darts in a trice
   Across the gladsome lake.

One with the cricket in the ground,
   And faggot on the hearth,
Resounds the rare domestic sound
   Along the forest path.

Before night we will take a journey on skates along the course of this meandering river, as full of novelty to one who sits by the cottage fire all the winter's day, as if it were over the polar ice, with captain Parry or Franklin; following the winding of the stream, now flowing amid hills, now spreading out into fair meadows, and forming a myriad coves and bays where the pine and hemlock overarch. The river flows in the rear of the towns, and we see all things from a new and wilder side. The fields and gardens come down to it with a sort of unpretension and frankness, as they do not front upon the highway. It is the outside and edge of the earth. Our eyes are not offended by violent contrasts. The last rail of the farmer's fence is some swaying willow bough, which still preserves its freshness, and here at length all fences stop, and we no longer cross any road. We may go far up within the country now by the most retired and level road, never climbing a hill, but by broad levels ascending to the upland meadows. It is a beautiful illustration of the law of obedience, the flow of a river; the path for a sick man, a highway down which an acorn cup may float secure with its freight. Its slight occasional falls, whose precipices would not diversify the landscape, are celebrated by mist and spray, and attract the traveller from far and near. From the remote interior its current conducts him by broad and easy steps or by one gentle inclined plane, to the sea. Thus by an early and constant yielding to the inequalities of the ground, it secures itself the easiest passage.

No domain of nature is quite closed to man at all times, and now we draw near to the empire of the fishes. Our feet glide swiftly over unfathomed depths where in summer our line tempted the pout and perch, and where the stately pickerel lurked in the long corridors, formed by the bulrushes. The deep impenetrable marsh, where the heron waded, and bittern squatted, is made pervious to our swift shoes, as if a thousand railroads had been made into it. With one impulse we are carried to the cabin of the muskrat, that earliest settler, and see him dart away under the transparent ice, like a furred fish, to his hole in the bank; and we glide rapidly over meadows where lately "the mower whet his scythe," through beds of frozen cranberries mixed with meadow grass. We skate near to where the blackbird, the pewee, and the kingbird, hung their nests over the water, and the hornets builded from the maple in the swamp. How many gay warblers now following the sun, have radiated from this nest of silver birch and thistle down. On the swamp's outer edge was hung the supermarine village, where no foot penetrated. In this hollow tree the wood-duck reared her brood, and slid away each day to forage in yonder fen.

In winter nature is a cabinet of curiosities, full of dried specimens, in their natural order and position. The meadows and forests are a *hortus siccus*. The leaves and grasses stand perfectly pressed by the air without screw or gum, and the birds' nests are not hung on an artificial twig, but where they builded them. We go about dry-shod to inspect the summer's work in the rank swamp, and see what a growth have got the alders, the willows, and the maples; testifying to how many warm suns, and fertilizing dews and showers. See what strides their boughs took in the luxuriant summer,–and anon these dormant buds will carry them onward and upward another span into the heavens.

Occasionally we wade through fields of snow, under whose depths the river is lost for many rods, to appear again to the right or left, where we least expected; still holding on its way underneath with a faint stertorous rumbling sound, as if, like the bear and marmot, it too had hibernated, and we had followed its faint summer trail to where it earthed itself in snow and ice. At first we should have thought that rivers would be empty and dry in mid winter, or else frozen solid till the spring thawed them; but their volume is not diminished even, for only a superficial cold bridges their surface. The thousand springs which feed the lakes and streams are flowing still. The issues of a few surface springs only are closed, and they go to swell the deep reservoirs. Nature's wells are below the frost. The summer brooks are not filled with snow water, nor does the mower quench his thirst with that alone. The streams are swollen when the snow melts in the spring, because nature's work has been delayed, the water being turned into ice and snow, whose particles are less smooth and round, and do not find their level so soon.

Far over the ice, between the hemlock woods and snow-clad hills, stands the pickerel fisher, his lines set in some retired cove, like a Finlander, with his arms thrust into the pouches of his dreadnought; with dull, snowy, fishy thoughts, himself a finless fish, separated a few inches from his race. Dumb, erect, and made to be enveloped in clouds and snows, like the pines on shore. In these wild scenes men stand about in the scenery, or move deliberately and heavily, having sacrificed the sprightliness and vivacity of towns to the dumb sobriety of nature. He does not make the scenery less wild, more than the jays and muskrats, but stands there as a part of it, as the natives are represented in the voyages of early navigators, at Nootka Sound, and on the North-West coast, with their furs about them, before they were tempted to loquacity by a scrap of iron. He belongs to the natural family of man, and is planted deeper in nature and has more root than the inhabitants of towns. Go to him, ask what luck, and you will learn that he too is a worshipper of the unseen. Hear with what sincere deference and waving gesture in his tone, he speaks of the lake pickerel, which he has never seen, his primitive and ideal race of pickerel. He is connected with the shore still, as by a fish-line, and yet remembers the season when he took fish through the ice on the pond, while the peas were up in his garden at home.

But now, while we have loitered, the clouds have gathered, and a few straggling snow-flakes are beginning to descend. Faster and faster they fall, shutting out the distant objects from sight. The nearest drive straight to the ground, weaving their thick woof in the air, while the more distant seem to float like a quivering bank of feathers. The snow falls on every wood and field, and no crevice is forgotten; by the river and the pond, on the hill and in the valley. Quadrupeds are confined to their coverts, and the birds sit upon their perches this peaceful hour. There is not so much sound as in fair weather, but silently and gradually every slope, and the grey walls and fences, and the polished ice, and the sere leaves, which were not buried before, are concealed, and the tracks of men and beasts are lost. With so little effort does nature reassert her rule, and blot out the traces of men. Hear how Homer has described the same. "The snow-flakes fall thick and fast on a winter's day. The winds are lulled, and the snow falls incessant, covering the tops of the mountains, and the hills, and the plains where the lotus tree grows, and the cultivated fields. And they are falling by the inlets and shores of the foaming sea, but are silently dissolved by the waves". The snow levels all things and infolds them deeper in the bosom of nature, as in the slow summer vegetation creeps up to the entablature of the temple, and the turrets of the castle, and helps her to prevail over art.

The surly night wind rustles through the wood, and warns us to retrace our steps, while the sun goes down behind the thickening storm, and birds seek their roosts, and cattle their stalls.

> "Drooping the lab'rer ox
> Stands covered o'er with snow, and *now* demands
> The fruit of all his toil."

Douglas' "Description of Wynter wyth his grete Stormis and Tempestis", is true enough for this occasion.

> "The wynd maid waif the rede wede on the dyk,
> Bedowin[1] in donkis[2] depe was every sike;[3]
> Ouer craggis and the frontis of rochys sere
> Hang grete yse schokkilis lang as ony spere:
> The grund stade barrane, widderit, dosk and gray,
> Herbis, flouris and gerssis wallowit away:
> Woddis, forestis with naket bewis blout
> Stude stripit of thare wede in every hout;
> Sa bustouslic Boreas his bugill blew,
> The dere full derne[4] doun in the dailis drew:

[1] sprinkled. [2] pools. [3] rill.
[4] secretly.

Small birdis flokand throw ilk ronnys[5] thrang,
In chirmynge, and with cheping changit thare sang,
Sekand hidlis[6] and hirnys[7] thame to hyde
Fra ferefull thuddis of the tempestuus tyde:
The wattir linnys rowtis, and every lynd
Quhislit and brayit of the souchand wynd:
Pure lauboraris and byssy husband men
Went weet and wery draglit in the fen.
The cilly schepe and thare litill hird-gromes
Lurkis under lye of bankis, woddis and bromes:
And utheris dantit[8] greter beistial,
Within thare stabill sesit in thare stall,
Sic as mulis, hors, oxin or ky,
Fed tuskit baris, and fat swyne in sty,
Sustenit war be mannis governance
On hervist and on someris purviance:
Widequhare with fors so Eolus schoutis schill,
In this congelit sesoun scharp and chill,
The callour are penetrative and pure
Dasing the blude in every creature,
Made seik warme stovis and bene fyris hote,
In doubill garmont cled, and welecote,
With mychty drink, and metis confortive,
Aganis the sterne wynter for to strive."–

Though Winter is represented in the almanack as an old man, facing the wind and sleet, and drawing his cloak about him, we rather think of him as a merry wood-chopper, and warm-blooded youth, as blithe as Summer. The unexplored grandeur of the storm keeps up the spirits of the traveller. It does not trifle with us but has a sweet earnestness. In winter we lead a more inward life. Our hearts are warm and cheery, like cottages under drifts, whose windows and doors are half concealed, but from whose chimneys the smoke cheerfully ascends. The imprisoning drifts increase the sense of comfort which the house affords, and in the coldest days we are content to sit over the hearth,

[5]briars.   [6-7]hiding places.   [8]tamed

and see the sky through the chimney top, enjoying the quiet and serene life that may be had in a warm corner by the chimney side, or feeling our pulse by listening to the low of cattle in the street, or the sound of the flail in distant barns, all the long afternoon. No doubt a skilful physician could determine our health by observing how these simple and natural sounds affected us. We enjoy now, not an oriental, but a boreal leisure, around warm stoves and fire-places, and watch the shadow of motes in the sunbeams.

Sometimes our fates grow too homely and familiarly serious ever to be cruel. Consider how for three months the human destiny is wrapped in furs. The good Hebrew revelation takes no cognizance of all this cheerful snow. Is there no religion for the temperate and frigid zones? We know of no scripture which records the pure benignity of the gods on a New England winter night. Their praises have never been sung, only their wrath deprecated. But even God cannot frighten a good man. The best scripture after all records but a meagre faith. Its saints live reserved and austere. Let a brave devout man spend the year in the woods of Maine or Labrador, and see if the Hebrew scripture speaks adequately to his condition and experience, from the setting in of winter to the breaking up of the ice.

Now commences the long winter evening around the farmer's hearth, when the thoughts of the indwellers travel far abroad, and men are by nature and necessity charitable and liberal to all creatures. Now is the happy resistance to cold, when the farmer reaps his reward, and thinks of his preparedness for winter, and through the glistering panes, sees with equanimity "the mansion of the northern bear", for now the storm is over,

"The full ethereal round,
Infinite worlds disclosing to the view,
Shines out intensely keen; and all one cope
Of starry glitter glows from pole to pole."

   Pray to what earth does this sweet cold belong,
Which asks no duties and no conscience?
The moon goes up by leaps her cheerful path
In some far summer stratum of the sky,
While stars with their cold shine bedot her way.
The fields gleam mildly back upon the sky,
And far and near upon the leafless shrubs
The snow dust still emits a silvery light.
Under the hedge, where drift banks are their screen,
The titmice now pursue their downy dreams,
As often in the sweltering summer nights,
The bee doth drop asleep in the flower cup,
Where evening overtakes him with his load.
By the brooksides, in the still genial night,
The more adventurous wanderer may hear
The crystals shoot and form, and winter slow
Increase his rule by gentlest summer means.

But to return to Douglas.

"Repatirrit[1] wele, and by the chymnay bekit,[2]
At evin be tyme doun in ane bed me strekit,
Warpit my hede, kest on claithis thrynfald
For to expell the perellous persand cald:"–

From our comfortable pillows, we lend our warm sympathy to the Siberian traveller, on whose morning route the sun is rising, and in imagination frequent the encampment of the lonely fur-trader on lake Winnipeg, and climb the Ural and the Jura, or range the Andes and Rocky mountains and traverse the shaggy solitudes of the glaciers in our dreams, hugging the furs about us. Or perhaps we have visions of Greece and Italy, the AEgean sea, and the Sicilian coast, or an-

[1]fed.   [2]bent

ticipate the coming in of spring like a pomp through the gate of a city.

> "I crosit me syne bownit[3] for to slepe:
> Quhare lemand throw the glas I did take kepe
> Latonia the lang irksum nycht
> Hir subtell blenkis sched and watry lycht,
> Full hie up quhirlit in hir region,
> Till Phebus richt in opposicioun,
> Into the Crab hir propir mansioun draw,
> Haldand the hicht althocht the son went law;
> The hornyt byrd quhilk we clepe the nicht owle,
> Within hir caverne hard I schout and youle,
> Laithely of forme, with crukit camscho beik,
> Ugsum to here was hir wyld elrische skreik.
> The wyld geis eik claking by nychtis tyde
> Attour the ciete fleand hard I glyde,
> On slummer I slade full sone, and slepyt sound,
> Quhill the horisont upwart can rebound:"–

[3] went.

A Yankee in Canada.

*"New England is by some affirmed to be an island,
bounded on the north with the river Canada so called
from Monsieur Cane."*

Josselyn's Rarities.

And still older, in Thomas Morton's "New English
Canaan," published in 1637, it is said, on page 97,
"From this Lake [Erocoise] Northwards is derived the
famous River of Canada, so named, of Monsier de
Cane, a French Lord, who first planted a Colony of
French in America."

I. Concord to Montreal.

I FEAR that I have not got much to say about
Canada, not having seen much; what I got by going to
Canada was a cold. I left Concord, Massachusetts,
Wednesday morning Sep. 25th 1850, for Quebec. Fare
seven dollars there and back; distance from Boston
five hundred and ten miles; being obliged to leave
Montreal on the return as soon as Friday Oct. 4th, or
within ten days. I will not stop to tell the reader the
names of my fellow travellers; there were said to be
fifteen hundred of them. I wished only to be set down
in Canada, and take one honest walk there, as I might
in Concord woods for an afternoon.

The country was new to me beyond Fitchburg. In
Ashburnham and afterward, as we were whirled rapidly along, I noticed the woodbine, (*ampelopsis quin-
quefolia*), its leaves now changed, for the most part on
dead trees, draping them like a red scarf. It was not a
little exciting, suggesting bloodshed, or at least a military life, like an epaulet or sash, as if it were dyed with

the blood of the trees whose wounds it was inadequate to staunch. For now the bloody autumn was come, and an Indian warfare was waged through the forest. These military trees appeared very numerous, for our rapid progress connected those that were even some miles apart. Does the woodbine prefer the elm? The first view of Monadnoc was obtained five or six miles this side of Fitzwilliam, but nearest and best at Troy and beyond. Then there were the Troy cuts and embankments. Keene street strikes the traveller favorably, it is so wide, level, straight, and long. I have heard one of my relatives who was born and bred there say that you could see a chicken run across it a mile off. I have also been told that when this town was settled they laid out a street four rods wide, but at a subsequent meeting of the proprietors one rose and remarked, "We have plenty of land, why not make the street eight rods wide?" and so they voted that it should be eight rods wide, and the town is known far and near for its handsome street. It was a cheap way of securing comfort, as well as fame, and I wish that all new towns would take pattern from this. It is best to lay our plans widely in youth, for then land is cheap, and it is but too easy to contract our views afterward. Youths so laid out, with broad avenues and parks, that they may make handsome and liberal old men! Show me a youth whose mind is like some Washington city of magnificent distances, prepared for the most remotely successful and glorious life after all, when those spaces shall be built over, and the idea of the founder be realized. I trust that every New England boy will begin by laying out a Keene street through his head, eight rods wide. I know one such Washington-city of a man, whose lots are as yet only surveyed and staked out, and, except a cluster of shanties here and there, only the Capitol stands there for all structures, and any day you may see from afar his princely idea borne coach-wise along the spacious but yet empty avenues. Keene is built on a remarkably large and level interval, like the bed of a lake, and the surrounding hills, which are remote from its street, must afford some good walks. The scenery of mountain towns is commonly too much crowded. A town which is built on a plain of some extent, with an open horizon, and surrounded by hills at a distance, affords the best walks and views.

As we travel north-west up the country, sugar-maples, beeches, birches, hemlocks, spruce, butter-nuts and ash-trees prevail more and more. To the rapid traveller the number of elms in a town is the measure of its civility. One man in the cars has a bottle full of some liquor. The whole company smile when-ever it is exhibited. I find no difficulty in containing myself. The Westmoreland country looked attractive. I heard a passenger giving the very obvious derivation of this name, West-more-land, as if it were purely American, and he had made a discovery; but I thought of "my cousin Westmoreland" in England. Every one will remember the approach to Bellows' Falls, under a high cliff which rises from the Connecticut. I was dis-appointed in the size of the river here; it appeared shrunk to a mere mountain stream. The water was evi-dently very low. The rivers which we had crossed this forenoon possessed more of the character of moun-tain streams than those in the vicinity of Concord, and I was surprised to see everywhere traces of recent freshets which had carried away bridges and injured the rail-road, though I had heard nothing of it. In Lud-low, Mt Holly, and beyond, there is interesting moun-tain scenery, not rugged and stupendous, but such as you could easily ramble over, long narrow mountain vales through which to see the horizon. You are in the midst of the Green Mountains. A few more elevated blue peaks are seen from the neighborhood of Mt Holly, perhaps Killington Peak is one. Sometimes, as on the Western rail-road, you are whirled over mountainous embankments, from which the scared horses in the valleys appear diminished to hounds. All the hills blush. I think that autumn must be the best season to journey over even the *Green* Mountains. You frequently exclaim to yourself, What *red* maples! The sugar-maple is not so red. You see some of the latter with rosy spots or cheeks only, blushing on one side like fruit, while all the rest of the tree is green, proving either some partiality in the light or frosts, or some prematurity in particular branches. Tall and slender ash trees whose foliage is turned to a dark mulberry color, are frequent. The butter-nut which is a remarkably spreading tree, is turned completely yellow, thus proving its relation to the hickories. I was also struck by the bright yellow tints of the yellow-birch. The sugar-maple is remarkable for its clean ankle. The groves of these trees looked like vast forest sheds, their branches stopping short at a uniform height, four or five feet from the ground, like eaves, as if they had been trimmed by art, so that you could look under and through the whole grove with its leafy canopy, as under a tent whose curtain is raised.

As you approach Lake Champlain you begin to see the New York mountains. The first view of the lake at Vergennes is impressive, but rather from association than from any peculiarity in the scenery. It lies there so small (not appearing in that proportion to the width of the state that it does on the map,) but beautifully quiet, like a picture of the Lake of Lucerne on a music box, where you trace the name Lucerne among the foliage; far more ideal than ever it looked on the map. It

does not say, "Here I am, Lake Champlain", as the
conductor might for it, but having studied the geography thirty years, you crossed over a hill one afternoon and beheld it. But it is only a glimpse that you get
here. At Burlington you rush to a wharf and go on
board a steamboat two-hundred-and thirty-two miles
from Boston. We left Concord at twenty minutes before eight in the morning, and were in Burlington
about six at night, but too late to see the lake. We got
our first fair view of the lake at dawn, just before reaching Plattsburg, and saw blue ranges of mountains on
either hand, in New York and in Vermont, the former
especially grand. A few white schooners like gulls were
seen in the distance, for it is not waste and solitary like
a lake in Tartary, but it was such a view as leaves not
much to be said; indeed I have postponed Lake Champlain to another day.

The oldest reference to these waters that I have met
with is in the account of Cartier's discovery and exploration of the St. Lawrence in 1535. Samuel Champlain
actually discovered and paddled up the lake in July
1609, eleven years before the settlement of Plymouth,
accompanying a war party of the Canadian Indians
against the Iroquois. He describes the islands in it as
not inhabited although they are pleasant, on account
of the continual wars of the Indians, in consequence
of which they withdraw from the rivers and lakes into
the depths of the land, that they may not be surprised.
"Continuing our course", says he "in this lake, on the
western side, viewing the country, I saw on the eastern
side very high mountains, where there was snow on
the summit. I inquired of the savages if those places
were inhabited. They replied that they were, and that
they were Hiroquois, and that in those places there
were beautiful valleys and plains fertile in corn, such

as I have eaten in this country, with an infinity of other fruits". This is the earliest account of what is now Vermont.

The number of French Canadian gentlemen and ladies among the passengers, and the sound of the French language, advertised us by this time, that we were being whirled toward some foreign vortex. And now we have left Rouse's Point, and entered the Sorel River, and passed the invisible barrier between the States and Canada. The shores of the Sorel, Richelieu, or St John's River, were flat and reedy, where I had expected something more rough and mountainous for a natural boundary between two nations. Yet I saw a difference at once, in the few huts, in the pirogues on the shore, and as it were, in the shore itself. This was an interesting scenery to me, and the very reeds or rushes in the shallow water, and the tree tops in the swamps, have left a pleasing impression. We had still a distant view behind us of two or three blue mountains in Vermont and New York. About nine o'clock in the forenoon we reached St Johns, an old frontier post three hundred and six miles from Boston and twenty-four from Montreal. We now discovered that we were in a foreign country, in a station-house of another nation. This building was a barn-like structure looking as if it were the work of the villagers combined, like a log-house in a new settlement. My attention was caught by the double advertisements in French and English fastened to its posts, by the formality of the English, and the covert or open reference to their queen and the British lion. No gentlemanly conductor appeared, none whom you would know to be the conductor by his dress and demeanor; but ere long we began to see here and there a solid, red-faced, burly-looking Englishman, a little pursy perhaps, who made us ashamed of ourselves and our thin and nervous countrymen. A grandfatherly personage at home in his great coat, who looked as if he might be a stage proprietor, certainly a rail-road director, and knew, or had a right to know when the cars did start. Then there were two or three pale-faced, black-eyed, loquacious Canadian French gentlemen there, shrugging their shoulders; pitted, as if they had all had the small pox. In the meanwhile some soldiers, red-coats, belonging to the barracks nearby, were turned out to be drilled. At every important point in our route the soldiers showed themselves ready for us. Though they were evidently rather raw recruits here, they manoeuvred far better than our soldiers; yet, as usual, I heard some Yankees talk as if they were no great shakes, and they had seen the Acton Blues manoeuvre as well. The officers spoke sharply to them and appeared to be doing their part thoroughly. I heard one, suddenly coming to the rear, exclaim–"Michael Donolly, take his name!" though I could not see what the latter did or omitted to do. It was whispered that Michael Donolly would have to suffer for that. I heard some of our party discussing the possibility of their driving these troops off the field with their umbrellas. I thought that the Yankee, though undisciplined, had this advantage at least, that he especially is a man who, everywhere and under all circumstances, is fully resolved to better his condition essentially, and therefore he could afford to be beaten at first; while the virtue of the Irishman, and to a great extent the Englishman, consists in merely maintaining his ground, or condition. The Canadians here, a rather poor looking race clad in grey homespun, which gave them the appearance of being covered with dust, were riding about in caleches and small one-horse carts called charettes. The Yankees assumed that all the riders were racing, or at least exhibiting the paces of their horses, and saluted them accordingly. We saw but little of the village here, for nobody could tell us when the cars would start; that was kept a profound secret, perhaps for political reasons; and therefore we were tied to our seats. The inhabitants of St Johns and vicinity are described by an English traveller as "singularly unprepossessing," and before completing his period he adds, "besides, they are generally very much disaffected to the British Crown". I suspect that that "besides" should have been a because.

At length about noon the cars began to roll toward La Prairie. The whole distance of fifteen miles was over a remarkably level country, resembling a western prairie, with the mountains about Chambly visible in the north-east. This novel, but monotonous, scenery was exciting. At La Prairie we first took notice of the tinned roofs, but, above all, of the St. Lawrence, which looked like a lake, in fact it is considerably expanded here; it was nine miles across diagonally to Montreal. Mount Royal in the rear of the city and the island of St. Helens opposite to it, were now conspicuous. We could also see the Sault St. Louis about five miles up the river, and the Sault Norman still further eastward. The former are described as the most considerable rapids in the St. Lawrence; but we could see merely a gleam of light there as from a cobweb in the sun. Soon the city of Montreal was discovered with its tin roofs shining afar. Their reflections fell on the eye like a clash of cymbals on the ear. Above all the church of Notre Dame was conspicuous, and anon the Bonsecours Market-House occupying a commanding position on the quay, in the rear of the shipping. This city makes the most favorable impression from being approached by water, and also being built of stone, a gray limestone found on the island. Here, after travelling directly inland the whole breadth of New England, we had struck upon a city's harbor,–it made on me the impression of a sea-port,–to which ships of six hundred tons can ascend, and where vessels drawing fifteen feet lie close to the wharf,–five hundred and forty miles from the Gulf; the St Lawrence being here two miles wide. There was a great crowd assembled on the ferry-boat wharf, and on the quay, to receive the Yankees, and flags of all colors were streaming from the vessels to celebrate their arrival. When the gun was fired, the gentry hurrahed again and again, and then the Canadian caleche drivers, who were the most interested in the matter, and who, I perceived, were separated from the former by a fence, hurrahed their welcome; first the broad-cloth, then the home-spun.

It was early in the afternoon when we stepped ashore. With a single companion I soon found my way to the church of Notre Dame. I saw that it was of great size and signified something. It is said to be the largest ecclesiastical structure in North America, and can seat ten thousand. It is two hundred fifty-five and a half feet long, and the groined ceiling is eighty feet above your head. The Catholic are the only churches which I have seen worth remembering, which are not almost wholly prophane. I do not speak only of the rich and splendid like this, but of the humblest of them as well. Coming from the hurrahing mob and the rattling carriages, we pushed aside the listed door of this church and found ourselves instantly in an atmosphere which might be sacred to thought and religion if one had any. There sat one or two women who had stolen a moment from the concerns of the day as they were passing; but if there had been fifty people there, it would still have been the most solitary place imaginable. They did not look up at us, nor did one regard another. We walked softly down the broad-aisle with our hats in our hands.

Presently came in a troop of Canadians, in their home-spun, who had come to the city in the boat with us, and one and all kneeled in the aisle before the high altar to their devotions, somewhat awkwardly, as cattle prepare to lie down, and there we left them. As if you were to catch some farmers' sons from Marl-boro', come to Cattleshow, silently kneeling in Con-cord meetinghouse some Wednesday! Would there not soon be a mob peeping in at the windows? It is true, these Roman Catholics, priests and all, impress me as a people who have fallen far behind the sig-nificance of their symbols. It is as if an ox had strayed into a church and were trying to bethink himself. Nev-ertheless, they are capable of reverence; but we Yan-kees are a people in whom this sentiment has nearly died out, and in this respect we cannot bethink our-selves even as oxen. I did not mind the pictures nor the candles, whether tallow or tin. Those of the former which I looked at appeared tawdry. It matters little to me whether the pictures are by a neophyte of the Al-gonquin or the Italian tribe. But I was impressed by the quiet religious atmosphere of the place. It was a great cave in the midst of a city,–and what were the altars and the tinsel but the sparkling stalactites,–into which you entered in a moment, and where the still atmosphere and the sombre light disposed to serious and profitable thought. Such a cave at hand, which you can enter any day, is worth a thousand of our churches which are open only on Sundays,–hardly long enough for an airing,–and then filled with a bus-tling congregation. A church where the priest is the least part, where you do your own preaching, where the universe preaches to you and can be heard. I am not sure but this Catholic religion would be an admi-rable one if the priest were quite omitted. I think that I might go to church myself sometimes, some Monday, if I lived in a city where there was such a one to go to. In Concord, to be sure, we do not need such. Our forests are such a church, far grander and more sacred. We dare not leave *our* meetinghouses open for fear they would be prophaned. Such a cave, such a shrine, in one of our groves, for instance, how long would it be respected–for what purposes would it be entered, by such baboons as we are? I think of its value not only to religion, but to philosophy and poetry; beside a Reading Room to have a Thinking Room in every city! Perchance the time will come when every house even will have not only its sleeping rooms, and dining room, and talking room or parlor, but its Thinking Room also, and the architects will put it into their plans. Let it be furnished and ornamented with whatever conduces to serious and creative thought. I should not object to the holy water, or any other simple symbols if it were consecrated by the imagination of the worshippers.

I heard that some Yankees bet that the candles here were not wax but tin. A European assured them that they were wax; but inquiring of the sexton he was surprised to learn that they were tin filled with oil. The church was too poor to afford wax. As for the protestant churches, here, as elsewhere, they did not interest me, for it is only as caves that churches interest me at all, and in that respect they were inferior.

Montreal makes the impression of a larger city than you had expected to find, though you may have heard that it contains nearly sixty thousand inhabitants. In the newer parts it appeared to be growing fast like a small New York, and to be considerably Americanized. The names of the squares reminded you of Paris–the Champ de Mars, the Place d'Armes, and others, and you felt as if a French revolution might break out any moment. Glimpses of Mount Royal rising behind the town, and the names of some streets in that direction made one think of Edinburgh. That hill sets off this city wonderfully. I inquired at a principal bookstore for books published in Montreal. They said that there were none but school books, and the like, they got their books from the States. From time to time we met a priest in the streets, for they are distinguished by their dress, like the *civil* police. Like clergymen generally, with or without the gown, they made on us the impression of effeminacy. We also met some Sisters of Charity, dressed in black, with Shaker-shaped black bonnets and crosses, and cadaverous faces, who looked as if they had almost cried their eyes out,–their complexions parboiled with scalding tears; insulting the daylight by their presence, having taken an oath not to smile. By cadaverous, I mean that their faces were like the faces of those who have been dead and buried for a year, and then untombed, with the life's grief upon them, and yet, for some unaccountable reason, the process of decay arrested.

> "Truth never fails her servant, Sir, nor leaves him
> With the day's shame upon him."

They waited demurely on the side-walk while a truck laden with raisins was driven in at the seminary of St Sulpice, never once lifting their eyes from the ground.

The soldier here, as everywhere in Canada, appeared to be put forward, and by his best foot. They were in the proportion of the soldiers to the laborers in an African ant-hill. The inhabitants evidently rely on them in a great measure, for music and entertainment. You would meet with them pacing back and forth before some guard-house or passage way, guarding, regarding, and disregarding all kinds of law by turns, apparently for the sake of the discipline to themselves,

and not because it was important to exclude anybody
from entering that way. They reminded me of the men
who are paid for piling up bricks and then throwing
them down again. On every prominent ledge you
could see England's hands holding the Canadas, and I
judged by the redness of her knuckles that she would
soon have to let go. In the rear of such a guard-house,
in a large gravelled square or parade ground, called
the Champ de Mars, we saw a large body of soldiers
being drilled, we being as yet the only spectators. But
they did not appear to notice us any more than the
devotees in the church, but were seemingly as indifferent to fewness of spectators as the phenomena of
nature are, whatever they might have been thinking
under their helmets of the Yankees that were to come.
Each man wore white kid gloves. It was one of the most
interesting sights which I saw in Canada. The problem
appeared to be, how to smooth down all individual
protuberances or idiosyncrasies, and make a thousand men move as one man, animated by one central
will, and there was some approach to success. They
obeyed the signals of a commander who stood at a
great distance, wand in hand, and the precision, and
promptness, and harmony of their movements, could
not easily have been matched. The harmony was far
more remarkable than that of any quire or band, and
obtained, no doubt, at a greater cost. They made on
me the impression, not of many individuals, but of one
vast centipede of a man, good for all sorts of pulling
down;–and why not then for some kinds of building
up? If men could combine thus earnestly, and pa-
tiently, and harmoniously, to some really worthy end,
what might they not accomplish! They now put their
hands, and partially perchance their heads, together
and the result is that they are the imperfect tools of
an imperfect and tyrannical government. But if they

could put their hands and heads and hearts and all together, such a cooperation and harmony would be the
very end and success for which government now exists in vain–a government, as it were, not only with
tools, but stock to trade with.

I was obliged to frame some sentences that sounded
like French in order to deal with the market women,
who, for the most part, cannot speak English. According to the guide-book the relative population of this
city stands nearly thus. Two fifths are French Canadian; nearly 1/5 British Canadian; one and one half
fifth English, Irish, and Scotch; somewhat less than
one half fifth Germans, United States people, and
others. I saw nothing like pie for sale, and no good
cake to put in my bundle, such as you can easily find in
our towns, but plenty of fair-looking apples, for which
Montreal Island is celebrated, and also pears, cheaper
and I thought better than ours, and peaches, which,
though they were probably brought from the south,
were as cheap as they commonly are with us. So imperative is the law of demand and supply that, as I
have been told, the market of Montreal is sometimes
supplied with green apples from the state of New York
some weeks even before they are ripe in the latter
place. I saw here the spruce wax which the Canadians
chew, done up in little silvered papers, a penny a roll;
also a small and shrivelled fruit which they called
cerises mixed with many little stems somewhat like
raisins, but I soon returned what I had bought, finding
them rather insipid, only putting a sample in my
pocket. Since my return, I find on comparison that it is
the fruit of the sweet viburnum (viburnum lentago)
which with us rarely holds on till it is ripe.

I stood on the deck of the steamer John Munn, late
in the afternoon, when the second and third ferry-
boats arrived from La Prairie bringing the remainder

of the Yankees. I never saw so many caleches, cabs, charettes, and similar vehicles, collected before, and doubt if New York could easily furnish more. The handsome and substantial stone quay which stretches a mile along the river side and protects the street from the ice, was thronged with the citizens who had turned out on foot and in carriages to welcome or to behold the Yankees. It was interesting to see the caleche drivers dash up and down the slopes of the quay with their active little horses. They drive much faster than in our cities. I am told that some of them come nine miles into the city every morning and return every night, without changing their horses during the day. In the midst of the crowd of carts, I observed one deep one loaded with sheep with their legs tied together, and their bodies piled one upon another. As if the driver had forgotten that they were sheep and not yet mutton. A sight, I trust, peculiar to Canada, though I fear that it is not.

II. Quebec and Montmorenci.

ABOUT six o'clock we started for Quebec, one hundred and eighty miles distant by the river; gliding past Longueil and Boucherville on the right, and *Pointe aux Trembles*, "so called from having been originally covered with aspens," and *Bout de l'Isle*, or End of the Island, on the left. I repeat these names not merely for want of more substantial facts to record, but because they sounded singularly poetic to my ears. There certainly was no lie in them. They suggested that some simple and perchance heroic human life might have transpired there. There is all the poetry in the world in a name. It is a poem which the mass of men hear and read. What is poetry in the common sense but a string of such jingling names. I want nothing better than a good word. The name of a thing may easily be more than the thing itself to me. Inexpressibly beautiful appears the recognition by man of the least natural fact, and the allying his life to it; all the world reiterating this slender truth, that aspens once grew there; and the swift inference is, that men were there to see them. And so it would be with the names of our native and neighboring villages, if we had not profaned them.

The daylight now failed us and we went below, but I endeavored to console myself for being obliged to make this voyage by night by thinking that I did not lose a great deal, the shores being low and rather unattractive, and that the river itself was much the most interesting object. I heard something in the night about the boat being at William Henry, Three Rivers, and in the Richelieu Rapids, but I was still where I had been when I lost sight of *Pointe aux Trembles*. To hear a man who has been waked up at midnight in the cabin of a steamboat, inquiring,–"Waiter, where are we now?"–is as if at any moment of the earth's revolution round the sun, or of the system round its centre, one were to raise himself up and inquire of one of the deck hands,–Where are we now?

I went on deck at daybreak, when we were thirty or forty miles above Quebec. The banks were now higher and more interesting. There was an "uninterrupted succession of white-washed cottages" on each side of the river. This is what every traveller tells. But it is not to be taken as an evidence of the populousness of the country in general, hardly even of the river banks. They have presented a similar appearance for a hundred years. The Swedish traveller and naturalist Kalm, who descended this river in 1749, says "It could really be called a village, beginning at Montreal and ending at Quebec, which is a distance of more than one hundred and eighty miles; for the farm-houses are never above five arpens, and sometimes but three asunder, a few places excepted." Even in 1684 Hontan said that the houses were not more than a gunshot apart at most. Ere long we passed Cap Rouge, eight miles above Quebec, the mouth of the Chaudiere on the opposite or south side, New Liverpool Cove with its lumber rafts and some shipping; then Sillery and Wolfe's Cove and the Heights of Abraham on the north, with now a view of Cape Diamond and the citadel in front. The approach to Quebec was very imposing. It was about six o'clock in the morning when we arrived. There is but a single street under the cliff on the south side of the cape, which was made by blasting the rock and filling up the river. Three story houses did not rise more than one fifth or one sixth the way up the nearly perpendicular rock, whose summit is three hundred and forty-five feet above the water. We saw, as we glided past, the sign on the side of the precipice, part way up, pointing to the spot where Montgomery was killed in 1775. Formerly it was the custom for those who went to Quebec for the first time, to be ducked, or else pay a fine. Not even the Governor General escaped. But we were too many to be ducked, even if the custom had not been abolished.*

Here we were, in the harbor of Quebec, still three hundred and sixty miles from the mouth of the St. Lawrence, in a basin two miles across, where the

---

* Hierosme Lalemant says in 1648, in his relation, he being Superior: "All those who come to New France know well enough the mountain of Notre Dame, because the pilots and sailors, being arrived at that part of the Great River which is opposite to those high mountains, baptize ordinarily for sport the new passengers, if they do not turn aside by some present the inundation of this baptism which one makes flow plentifully upon their heads."

greatest depth is twenty-eight fathoms, and though the water is fresh, the tide rises seventeen to twenty-four feet, a harbor "large and deep enough," says a British traveller, "to hold the English navy." I may as well state that in 1844 the county of Quebec contained about 45000 inhabitants, (the city and suburbs having about 43000.)
about 28000 being Canadians of French origin.
    "   8000   "   "   " British   "
over   7000   " natives of Ireland;
        1500   "   "   " England;
the rest Scotch and others. 36000 belong to the Church of Rome.

Separating ourselves from the crowd we walked up a narrow street, thence ascended by some wooden steps, called the Break-neck Stairs, into another steep narrow and zigzag street, blasted through the rock, which last led through a low massive stone portal, called Prescott Gate, the principal thoroughfare, into the Upper Town. This passage was defended by cannon, with a guard-house over it, a sentinel at his post, and other soldiers at hand ready to relieve him. I rubbed my eyes to be sure that I was in the nineteenth century, and was not entering one of those portals which sometimes adorn the frontispieces of new editions of old black-letter volumes. I thought it would be a good place to read Froissart's Chronicles. It was such a reminiscence of the middle ages as Scott's novels. Men apparently dwelt there for security. Peace be unto them! As if the inhabitants of New York were to go over to Castle William to live! What a place it must be to bring up children. Being safe through the gate we naturally took the street which was steepest, and after a few turns found ourselves on the Durham Terrace, a wooden platform on the site of the old Castle of St. Louis, still one hundred and fifteen feet below the summit of the citadel, overlooking the Lower Town, the wharf where we had landed, the harbor, the Isle of Orleans, and the river and surrounding country to a great distance. It was literally a *splendid* view. We could see six or seven miles distant in the north-east an indentation in the lofty shore of the northern channel, apparently on one side of the harbor, which marked the mouth of the Montmorenci, whose celebrated fall was only a few rods in the rear.

At a shoe-shop, whither we were directed for this purpose we got some of our American money changed into English. I found that American hard money would have answered as well, excepting cents, which fell very fast before their pennies, it taking two of the former to make one of the latter, and often the penny which had cost us two cents did us the service of one cent only. Moreover, our robust cents were compelled to meet on even terms a crew of vile half-penny tokens and bung-town coppers, which had more brass in their composition, and so perchance made their way in the world. Wishing to get into the citadel, we were directed to the Jesuits' Barracks,–a good part of the public buildings here are barracks,–to get a pass of the Town Major. We did not heed the sentries at the gate, nor did they us, and what under the sun they were placed there for, unless to hinder a free circulation of the air, was not apparent. There we saw soldiers eating their breakfasts in their mess room, from bare wooden tables in camp fashion. We were continually meeting with soldiers in the streets, carrying funny little tin pails of all shapes, even semicircular, as if made to pack conveniently. I supposed that they contained their dinners, so many slices of bread and butter to each, perchance. Sometimes they were carrying some kind of military chest on a sort of bier or hand barrow, with a springy, undulating, military step, all passengers giving way to them, even the charette drivers stopping for them to pass,–as if the battle were being lost from an inadequate supply of powder. There was a regiment of Highlanders, and, as I understood, of Royal Irish, in the city; and by this time there was a regiment of Yankees also. I had already observed, looking up even from the water, the head and shoulders of some General Poniatowski, with an enormous cocked hat and gun peering over the roof of a house, away up where the chimney caps commonly are with us, as it were a caricature of war and military awfulness; but I had not gone far up St Louis street before my riddle was solved, by the apparition of a real live Highlander under a cocked hat, and with his knees out, standing and marching sentinel on the ramparts between St Louis and St John's Gates. (It must be a holy war that is waged there.) We stood close by without fear and looked at him. His legs were somewhat tanned, and the hair had begun to grow on them as some of our wise men predict that it will in such cases, but I did not think they were remarkable in any respect. Notwithstanding all his warlike gear, when I inquired of him the way to the Plains of Abraham, he could not answer me without betraying some bashfulness through his broad Scotch. Soon after, we passed another of these creatures standing sentry at the St Louis Gate, who let us go by without shooting us or even demanding the countersign. We then began to go through the gate, which was so thick and tunnel-like as to remind me of those lines in Claudian's Old Man of Verona, about the getting out of the gate being the greater part of a journey;–as you might imagine yourself crawling through an architectural vignette *at the end* of a black-letter volume. We were then reminded that we had been in a fortress, from which we emerged by numerous zigzags in a ditch-like road, going a considerable distance to advance a few rods, where they could have shot us two or three times over, if their minds had been disposed as their guns were. The greatest, or rather the most prominent, part of this city was constructed with the design to offer the deadest resistance to leaden and iron missiles that might be cast against it. But it is a remarkable meteorological and psychological fact, that it is rarely known to rain lead with much violence, except on places so constructed. Keeping on about a mile we came to the Plains of Abraham; for having got through with the Saints, we come next to the Patriarchs. Here the Highland regiment was being reviewed, while the band stood on one side and played–methinks it was "La Claire Fontaine," the national air of the Canadian French. This is the site where a real battle once took place, to commemorate which they have had a sham fight here almost every day since. The Highlanders manoeuvred very well, and if the precision of their movement was less remarkable, they did not appear so stiffly erect as the English or Royal Irish, but had a more elastic and graceful gait, like a herd of their own red deer, or as if accustomed to stepping down the sides of mountains. But they made a sad impression on the whole, for it was obvious that all true manhood was in the process of being drilled out of them. I have no doubt that soldiers well drilled are as a class peculiarly destitute of originality and independence. The officers appeared like men dressed above their condition. It is impossible to give the soldier a good education without making him a deserter. His natural foe is the government that drills him. What would any philanthropist who felt an interest in these men's welfare naturally do, but first of all teach them so to respect themselves that they could not be hired for this work, whatever might be the consequences to this government or that;–not drill a few, but educate

all. I observed one older man among them, grey as a
wharf-rat and supple as the devil, marching lock-step
with the rest, who would have to pay for that elastic
gait.

We returned to the citadel along the heights, pluck-
ing such flowers as grew there. There was an abundance of succory still in blossom, broadleaved golden-
rod, butter-cups, thorn-bushes, Canada thistles, and
ivy, on the very summit of Cape Diamond. I also found
the bladder-campion in the neighborhood. We there
enjoyed an extensive view which I will describe in another place. Our pass, which stated that all the rules
were "to be strictly enforced," as if they were determined to keep up the semblance of reality to the last
gasp, opened to us the Dalhousie Gate, and we were
conducted over the citadel by a bare-legged Highlander in cocked hat and full regimentals. He told us
that he had been here about three years, and had formerly been stationed at Gibraltar. As if his regiment,
having perchance been nestled amid the rocks of
Edinburgh Castle, must flit from rock to rock thenceforth over the earth's surface, like a bald eagle, or other
bird of prey, from eyrie to eyrie. As we were going
out we met the Yankees coming in in a body, headed
by a red-coated officer called the commandant, and
escorted by many citizens both English and French
Canadian; I therefore immediately fell into the proces-
sion, and went round the citadel again with more in-
telligent guides, carrying, as before, all my effects with
me. Seeing that nobody walked with the red-coated
commandant, I attached myself to him, and though I
was not what is called well-dressed, he did not know
whether to repel me or not, for I talked like one who
was not aware of any deficiency in that respect. Probably there was not one among all the Yankees who went
to Canada this time, who was not more splendidly

dressed than I was. It would have been a poor story if I had not enjoyed some distinction. I had on my "bad weather clothes", like Olaf Tryggvesson the Northman when he went to the Thing in England, where, by the way, he won his bride. As we stood by the thirty-two pounder on the summit of Cape Diamond, which is fired three times a day, the commandant told me that it would carry to the Isle of Orleans, four miles distant, and that no hostile vessel could come round the island. I now saw the subterranean or rather "casemated barracks" of the soldiers, which I had not noticed before, though I might have walked over them. They had very narrow windows, serving as loopholes for musketry, and small iron chimneys rising above the ground. There we saw the soldiers at home and in an undress, splitting wood,–I looked to see whether with swords or axes–and in various ways endeavoring to realize that their nation was now at peace with this part of the world. A part of each regiment, chiefly officers, are allowed to marry. A grandfatherly would-be-witty Englishman could give a Yankee whom he was patronizing no reason for the bare knees of the Highlanders, other than oddity. The rock within the citadel is a little convex, so that shells falling on it would roll toward the circumference, where the barracks of the soldiers and officers are; it has been proposed therefore to make it slightly concave, so that they may roll into the centre, where they would be comparatively harmless, and it is estimated that to do this would cost twenty thousand pounds sterling. It may be well to remember this when I build my next house, and have the roof "all correct" for bomb-shells.

At mid-afternoon we made haste down Sault au Matelot street towards the Falls of Montmorenci, about eight miles down the St. Lawrence on the north side, leaving the further examination of Quebec till our return. On our way we saw men in the streets sawing logs pit-fashion, and afterward with a common wood-saw and horse cutting the planks into squares for paving the streets. This looked very shiftless, especially in a country abounding in water-power, and reminded me that I was no longer in Yankee land. I found on inquiry that the excuse for this was, that labor was so cheap, and I thought with some pain,–how cheap men are here! I have since learned that the English traveller Warburton, remarked soon after landing at Quebec, that everything was cheap there but men. That must be the difference between going thither from New and from Old England. I had already observed the dogs harnessed to their little milk-carts, which contain a single large can, lying asleep in the gutters, regardless of the horses, while they rested from their labors, at different stages of the ascent in the Upper Town. I was surprised at the regular and extensive use made of these animals for drawing, not only milk, but groceries, wood, &c. It reminded me that the dog commonly is not put to any use. Cats catch mice; but dogs only worry the cats. Kalm, a hundred years ago, saw sledges here for ladies to ride in drawn by a pair of dogs. He says, "A middle-sized dog is sufficient to draw a single person when the roads are good," and he was told by old people that horses were very scarce in their youth, and almost all the land carriage was then effected by dogs. They made me think of the Esquimaux, who, in fact, are the next people on the north. Charlevoix says that the first horses were introduced in 1665.

We crossed Dorchester Bridge over the St Charles,–the little river in which Cartier, the discoverer of the St Lawrence, put his ships, and spent the winter of 1535,–and found ourselves on an excellent macadamized road, called Le Chemin de Beauport. We had left

Concord Wednesday morning, and we endeavored to realise that now, Friday morning, we were taking a walk in Canada, in the Seigniory of Beauport, a foreign country, which a few days before had seemed almost as far off as England and France. Instead of rambling to Flint's Pond or the Sudbury Meadows, we found ourselves, after being a little detained in cars and steamboats,–after spending half a night at Burlington, and half a day at Montreal,–taking a walk down the bank of the St. Lawrence to the Falls of Montmorenci and elsewhere. Well, I thought to myself, here I am in a foreign country, let me have my eyes about me and take it all in. It already looked and felt a good deal colder than it had in New England, as we might have expected it would. I realized fully that I was four degrees nearer the pole, and shuddered at the thought; and I wondered if it were possible that the peaches might not all be gone when I returned. It was an atmosphere that made me think of the fur-trade, which is so interesting a department in Canada, for I had for all head covering a thin palm-leaf hat without lining, that cost twenty-five cents, and over my coat one of those unspeakably cheap, as well as thin, brown linen sacks of the Oak Hall pattern, which every summer appear all over New England, thick as the leaves upon the trees. It was a thoroughly Yankee costume, which some of my fellow travellers wore in the cars to save their coats a dusting. I wore mine at first because it looked better than the coat it covered, and last because two coats were warmer than one, though one was thin and dirty. I never wear my best coat on a journey; though perchance I could show a certificate to prove that I have a more costly one, at least, at home, if that were all that a gentleman required. It is not wise for a traveller to go dressed. I should no more think of it than of putting on a clean dicky and blacking my

shoes to go a fishing. As if you were going out to dine,
when in fact the genuine traveller is going out to work
hard and fare harder, to eat a crust by the way-side
whenever he can get it. Honest travelling is about as
dirty work as you can do. Why, a man needs a pair of
overalls for it. As for blacking my shoes in such a case,
I should as soon think of blacking my face. I carry a
piece of tallow to preserve the leather, and keep out
the water, that's all; and many an officious shoe-black,
who carried off my shoes when I was slumbering, mis-
taking me for a gentleman, has had occasion to repent
it before he produced a gloss on them. My pack, in
fact, was soon made, for I keep a short list of those
articles, which, from frequent experience I have found
indispensable to the foot traveller, and when I am
about to start, I have only to consult that to be sure
that nothing is omitted, and, what is more important,
nothing superfluous inserted. Most of my fellow travellers carried carpet-bags or valises. Sometimes one
had two or three ponderous yellow valises in his clutch
at each hitch of the cars, as if we were going to have
another rush for seats; and when there was a rush in
earnest, and there were not a few, I would see my man
in the crowd, with two or three affectionate lusty fellows along each side of his arm, between his shoulder
and his valises, which last held them tight to his back,
like the nut on the end of a screw. I could not help
asking in my mind,–what so great cause for showing
Canada to those valises, when perchance your very
nieces had to stay at home for want of an escort. I
should have liked to be present when the custom-
house officer came aboard of him, and asked him to
declare upon his honor if he had anything but wearing
apparel in them. Even the elephant carries but a small
trunk on his journeys. The perfection of travelling is to
travel without baggage. After considerable reflection

and experience, I have concluded that the best bag for the foot traveller is made with a handkerchief, or if he studies appearances, a piece of stiff brown paper, well tied up, with a fresh piece within to put outside when the first is torn. That is good for both town and country, and none will know but you are carrying home the silk for a new gown for your wife, when it may be a dirty shirt. A bundle which you can carry literally under your arm, and which will shrink and swell, with its contents. I never found the carpet-bag of equal capacity which was not a bundle of itself. We styled ourselves the knights of the umbrella and the bundle, for wherever we went, whether to Notre Dame, or Mount Royal, or the Champ de Mars, to the Town Major's, or the Bishop's Palace, to the Citadel with a barelegged Highlander for our escort, or to the Plains of Abraham, to dinner or to bed, the umbrella and the bundle went with us, for we wished to be ready to digress at any moment. We made it our home nowhere in particular, but everywhere where our umbrella and bundle were. It would have been an amusing circumstance if the mayor of one of those cities had politely asked us where we were staying; we could only have answered that we were staying with his honor for the time being. I was amused when, after our return, some green ones inquired if we found it easy to get accommodated, as if we went abroad to get accommodated, when we can get that at home. There was no crowd where we put up. The best houses, in my opinion, are never crowded. But to proceed with my story.

We met with many charettes bringing wood and stone to the city. The most ordinary looking horses travelled faster than ours, or perhaps they were ordinary looking because, as I am told, the Canadians do not use the curry-comb. Moreover, it is said that on the approach of winter their horses acquire an increased quantity of hair to protect them from the cold. If this is true, some of our horses would make you think winter was approaching even in mid summer. We soon began to see women and girls at work in the fields, digging potatoes alone, or bundling up the grain which the men cut. They appeared in rude health with a great deal of color in their cheeks, and if their occupation had made them coarse, it impressed me as better in its effects than making shirts at four-pence apiece, or doing nothing at all, unless it be chewing slate-pencils, with still smaller results. They were much more agreeable objects with their great broad-brimmed hats and flowing dresses, than the men and boys. We afterward saw them doing various other kinds of work; indeed I thought that we saw more women at work out of doors than men. On our return we observed in this town a girl with Indian boots nearly two feet high taking the harness off a dog. The purity and transparency of the atmosphere were wonderful. When we had been walking an hour we were surprised on turning round to see how near the city with its glittering tin roofs still looked. A village ten miles off did not appear to be more than three or four. I was convinced that you could see objects distinctly there much farther than here. It is true, the villages are of a dazzling white, but the dazzle is to be referred perhaps to the transparency of the atmosphere as much as to the whitewash.

We were now fairly in the village of Beauport, though there was still but one road. The houses stood close upon this without any front-yards, and at any angle with it, as if they had dropped down, being set with more reference to the road which the sun travels. It being about sundown and the falls not far off, we began to look round for a lodging, for we preferred to put up at a private house, that we might see more of the inhabitants. We inquired first at the most promising looking houses, if indeed any were promising. When we knocked they shouted some French word for Come in, perhaps *Entrez*, and we asked for a lodging in English; but we found, unexpectedly, that they spoke French only. Then we went along and tried another house, being generally saluted by a rush of two or three little curs which readily distinguished a foreigner, and which we were prepared now to hear bark in French. Our first question would be, *Parlez vous Anglais?* but the invariable answer was, *non Monsieur*; and we soon found that the inhabitants were exclusively French Canadian, and nobody spoke English at all any more than in France; that in fact we were in a foreign country, where the inhabitants uttered not one familiar sound to us. Then we tried by turns to talk French with them, in which we succeeded sometimes pretty well, but for the most part pretty ill. *Pouvez vous nous donner un lit ce nuit?* we would ask, and then they would answer with French volubility, so that we could catch only a word here and there. We could understand the women and children generally better than the men, and they us; and thus after a while we would learn that they had no more beds than they used. So we were compelled to inquire *Y a-t-il une maison publique ici?*–(*auberge* we should have said perhaps, for they seemed never to have heard of the other,) and they answered at length that there was no tavern, unless we could get lodging at the mill, *le moulin*, which we had passed; or they would direct us to a grocery, and almost every house had a small grocery at one end of it. We called on the public notary or village lawyer, but he had no more beds nor English than the rest. At one house there was so good a misunderstanding at once established, through the politeness of all parties, that we were encouraged to walk in and sit down and ask for a glass of water; and having drunk their water, we thought it was as good as to have tasted their salt. When our host and his wife spoke of their poor accommodations, meaning for themselves, we assured them that they were good enough, for we thought that they were only apologizing for the poorness of the accommodations they were about to offer us, and we did not discover our mistake till they took us up a ladder into a loft and showed to our eyes what they had been laboring in vain to communicate to our brains through our ears, that they had but that one apartment with its few beds for the whole family. We made our *a-dieus* forthwith, and with gravity, perceiving the literal significance of that word. We were finally taken in at a sort of public-house, whose master worked for Patterson, the proprietor of the extensive saw-mills driven by a portion of the Montmorenci stolen from the fall, whose roar we now heard. We here talked or murdered French all the evening with the master of the house and his family, and probably had a more amusing time than if we had completely understood one another. At length they showed us to a bed in their best chamber, very high to get into, with a low wooden rail to it. It had no cotton sheets, but coarse home-made dark-colored linen ones. Afterward we had to do with sheets still coarser than these, and nearly the color of our blankets. There was a large open buffet crowded with crockery in one corner of the room, as if to display their wealth to travellers, and pictures of Scripture scenes, French, Italian, and Spanish, hung around. Our hostess came back directly to inquire if we would have brandy for breakfast. The next morning when I asked their names she took down the temperance pledges of herself and husband and children, which were hanging against the wall.

They were Jean Baptiste Binet and his wife Genevieve Binet. Jean Baptiste is the sobriquet of the French Canadians.

After breakfast we proceeded to the fall, which was within half a mile, and at this distance its rustling sound, like the wind among the leaves, filled all the air. We were disappointed to find that we were in some measure shut out from the west side of the fall by the private grounds and fences of Patterson, who appropriates not only a part of the water for his mill, but a still larger part of the prospect, so that we were obliged to trespass. This gentleman's mansion-house and grounds were formerly occupied by the Duke of Kent, father to Queen Victoria. It appeared to me in bad taste for an individual, though he were the father of Queen Victoria, to obtrude himself with his land titles, or at least his fences, on so remarkable a natural phenomenon, which should in every sense belong to mankind. Some falls should even be kept sacred from the intrusion of mills and factories, as water-privileges in another than the mill-wright's sense. This small river falls perpendicularly nearly two hundred and fifty feet at one pitch. The St. Lawrence falls only 164 feet at Niagara. It is a very simple and noble fall, and leaves nothing to be desired; but the most that I could say of it would only have the force of one other testimony to assure the reader that it is there. We looked directly down on it from the point of a projecting rock, and saw far below us, on a low promontory, the grass kept fresh and green by the perpetual drizzle, looking like moss. The rock is a kind of slate, in the crevices of which grew ferns and golden-rods. The prevailing trees on the shores were spruce and arbor-vitae, the latter very large and now full of fruit; also aspens, alders, and the mountain ash with its berries. Every immigrant who arrives in this country by way of the St Lawrence, as he

opens a point on the Isle of Orleans sees the Montmorenci tumbling into the Great River thus magnifi-
cently in a vast white sheet, making its contribution
with emphasis. Roberval's Pilot, Jean Alphonse, saw
this fall thus and described it in 1542. It is a splendid
introduction to the scenery of Quebec. Instead of an
artificial fountain in its squares, Quebec has this magnificent natural waterfall to adorn one side of its harbor. Within the mouth of the chasm below, which can
be entered only at ebb tide, we had a grand view at
once of Quebec and of the fall. Kalm says that the
noise of the fall is sometimes heard at Quebec about
eight miles distant, and is a sign of a north-east wind.
The side of this chasm, of soft and crumbling slate too
steep to climb, was among the memorable features of
the scene. In the winter of 1829 the frozen spray of the
fall descending on the ice of the St Lawrence made a
hill one hundred and twenty-six feet high. It is an annual phenomenon which some think may help explain
the formation of glaciers.

In the vicinity of the fall we began to notice what
looked like our red-fruited thorn bushes grown to the
size of ordinary apple trees, very common and full of
large red or yellow fruit which the inhabitants called
pommettes, but I did not learn that they were put to
any use.

III. St. Anne.

By the middle of the forenoon, though it was a
rainy day, we were once more on our way down the
north bank of the St. Lawrence, in a north-easterly direction, toward the Falls of St. Anne, which are about
thirty miles from Quebec. The settled, more level,

and fertile portion of Canada East, may be described rudely as a triangle, with its apex slanting toward the north-east, about one hundred miles wide at its base, and from two to three, or even four hundred miles long, if you reckon its narrow north-eastern extremity; it being the immediate valley of the St. Lawrence and its tributaries, rising by a single or by successive terraces toward the mountains on either hand. Though the words Canada East on the map, stretch over many rivers and lakes and unexplored wildernesses, the actual Canada, which might be the colored portion of the map, is but a little clearing on the banks of the river, which one of those syllables would more than cover. The banks of the St. Lawrence are rather low from Montreal to the Richelieu Rapids, about forty miles above Quebec. Thence they rise gradually to Cape Diamond, or Quebec. Where we now were, eight miles north-east of Quebec, the mountains which form the northern side of this triangle were only five or six miles distant from the river, gradually departing further and further from it, on the west, till they reach the Ottawa, and making haste to meet it on the east, at Cape Tourmente, now in plain sight about twenty miles distant. So that we were travelling in a very narrow and sharp triangle between the mountains and the river, tilted up toward the mountains on the north, never losing sight of our great fellow-traveller on our right. According to Bouchette's Topographical Description of the Canadas, we were in the Seigniory of the Côte de Beaupré, in the County of Montmorenci, and the District of Quebec; in that part of Canada which was the first to be settled, and where the face of the country and the population have undergone the least change from the beginning, where the influence of the States and of Europe is least felt, and the inhabitants see little or nothing of the world over the walls of Quebec. This

Seigniory was granted in 1636, and is now the property of the Seminary of Quebec. It is the most mountainous one in the province. There are some half-a-dozen parishes in it, each containing a church, parsonage-house, grist-mill, and several saw-mills. We were now in the most westerly parish called Ange Gardien, or the Guardian Angel, which is bounded on the west by the Montmorenci. The north bank of the St. Lawrence here is formed on a grand scale. It slopes gently, either directly from the shore, or from the edge of an interval, till at the distance of about a mile, it attains the height of four or five hundred feet. The single road runs along the side of the slope two or three hundred feet above the river at first, and from a quarter of a mile to a mile distant from it, and affords fine views of the north channel, which is about a mile wide, and of the beautiful Isle of Orleans, about twenty miles long by five wide, where grow the best apples and plums in the Quebec District.

Though there was but this single road, it was a continuous village for as far as we walked this day and the next, or about thirty miles down the river, the houses being as near together all the way as in the middle of one of our smallest straggling country villages, and we could never tell by their number when we were on the skirts of a parish, for the road never ran through the fields or woods. We were told that it was just six miles from one parish church to another. I thought that we saw every house in Ange Gardien. Therefore, as it was a muddy day, we never got out of the mud, nor out of the village, unless we got over the fence; then indeed, if it was on the north side, we were out of the civilized world. There were sometimes a few more houses near the church, it is true, but we had only to go a quarter of a mile from the road to the top of the bank to find ourselves on the verge of the uninhabited, and, for the most part, unexplored wilderness stretching toward Hudson's Bay. The farms accordingly were extremely long and narrow, each having a frontage on the river. Bouchette accounts for this peculiar manner of laying out a village by referring to "the social character of the Canadian peasant, who is singularly fond of neighborhood," also to the advantage arising from a concentration of strength in Indian times. Each farm, called *terre*, he says, is, in nine cases out of ten, three arpents wide by thirty deep, that is, very nearly thirty-five by three hundred and forty-nine of our rods; sometimes one-half arpent by thirty, or one to sixty; sometimes in fact a few yards by half a mile. Of course it costs more for fences. A remarkable difference between the Canadian and the New England character appears from the fact that in 1745, the French government were obliged to pass a law forbidding the farmers or *censitaires* building on land less than one and a half arpents front by thirty or forty deep, under a certain penalty, in order to compel emigration, and bring the seigneurs' estates all under cultivation; and it is thought that they have now less reluctance to leave the paternal roof than formerly, "removing beyond the sight of the parish spire, or the sound of the parish bell." But I find that in the previous or 17th century, the complaint, often renewed, was of a totally opposite character, namely, that the inhabitants dispersed and exposed themselves to the Iroquois. Accordingly, about 1664, the king was obliged to order that "they should make no more clearings except one next to another, and that they should reduce their parishes to the form of the parishes in France as much as possible." The Canadians of those days at least, possessed a roving spirit of adventure which carried them further, in exposure to hardship and danger, than ever the New England colonist went, and led them, though not to clear and colonize the wilderness, yet to range over it as *cou-reurs de bois*, or runners of the woods, or as Hontan prefers to call them, *coureurs de risques*, runners of risks; to say nothing of their enterprising priesthood; and Charlevoix thinks that if the authorities had taken the right steps to prevent the youth from ranging the woods (*de courir les bois*) they would have had an excellent militia to fight the Indians and English.

The road, in this clayey looking soil, was exceedingly muddy in consequence of the night's rain. We met an old woman directing her dog, which was harnessed to a little cart, to the least muddy part of the road. It was a beggarly sight. But harnessed to the cart as he was, we heard him barking after we had passed, though we looked any where but to the cart to see where the dog was that barked. The houses commonly fronted the south, whatever angle they might make with the road; and frequently they had no door nor cheerful window on the roadside. Half the time, they stood fifteen to forty rods from the road, and there was no very obvious passage to them, so that you would suppose that there must be another road running by them; they were of stone, rather coarsely mortared, but neatly whitewashed, almost invariably one story high, and long in proportion to their height, with a shingled roof, the shingles being pointed, for ornament, at the eaves, like the pickets of a fence, and also, one row half way up the roof. The gables sometimes projected a foot or two at the ridge-pole only. Yet they were very humble and unpretending dwellings. They commonly had the date of their erection on them. The windows opened in the middle, like blinds, and were frequently provided with solid shutters. Sometimes, when we walked along the back side of a house, which stood near the road, we observed stout stakes leaning against it, by which the shutters, now pushed half open, were fastened at night; within, the houses were neatly ceiled with wood not painted. The oven was commonly out of doors, built of stone and mortar, frequently on a raised platform of planks. The cellar was often on the opposite side of the road, in front of or behind the houses, looking like an ice-house with us, with a lattice door for summer. The very few mechanics whom we met had an old-Bettyish look, in their aprons and *bonnets rouges*, like fools' caps. The men wore commonly the same *bonnet rouge*, or red woollen, or worsted cap, or sometimes blue or gray, looking to us as if they had got up with their night-caps on, and in fact, I afterwards found that they had. Their clothes were of the cloth of the country, *étoffe du pays*, gray or some other plain color. The women looked stout, with gowns that stood out stiffly, also, for the most part, apparently of some home-made stuff. We also saw some specimens of the more characteristic winter dress of the Canadian, and I have since frequently detected him in New England by his coarse gray home-spun capote and picturesque red sash, and his well furred cap, made to protect his ears against the severity of his climate.

It drizzled all day, so that the roads did not improve. We began now to meet with wooden crosses frequently, by the road-side, about a dozen feet high, often old and toppling down, sometimes standing on a square wooden platform, sometimes in a pile of stones, with a little niche containing a picture of the virgin and child, or of Christ alone, sometimes with a string of beads, and covered with a piece of glass to keep out the rain, with the words, *pour la vierge*, or *Inri*, on them. Frequently, on the cross-bar, there would be quite a collection of symbolical knick-knacks, looking like an Italian's board; the representation in wood of a hand, a hammer, spikes, pincers, a

flask of vinegar, a ladder, &c., the whole perchance
surmounted by a weathercock; but I could not look
at an honest weathercock in this walk, without mis-
trusting that there was some covert reference in it to
St. Peter. From time to time we passed a little one story
chapel-like building, with a tin-roofed spire, a shrine,
perhaps it would be called, close to the path-side, with
a lattice door, through which we could see an altar,
and pictures about the walls; equally open, through
rain and shine, though there was no getting into it. At
these places the inhabitants kneeled and perhaps
breathed a short prayer. We saw one school-house in
our walk, and listened to the sounds which issued
from it; but it appeared like a place where the process,
not of enlightening, but of obfuscating the mind was
going on, and the pupils received only so much light as
could penetrate the shadow of the Catholic church.
The churches were very picturesque, and their interior
much more showy than the dwelling houses promised. They were of stone, for it was ordered in 1699,
that that should be their material. They had tinned
spires, and quaint ornaments. That of l'Ange Gardien
had a dial on it, with the middle age Roman numerals
on its face, and some images in niches on the outside.
Probably its counterpart has existed in Normandy for
a thousand years. At the church of Chateau Richer,
which is the next parish to l'Ange Gardien, we read,
looking over the wall, the inscriptions in the adjacent
church-yard, which began with, "*Ici git*" or "*repose*,"
and one over a boy contained, "*Priez pour lui.*" This
answered as well as Père la Chaise. We knocked at the
door of the curé's house here, when a sleek friar-like
personage, in his sacerdotal robe appeared. To our
Parlez-vous Anglais? even he answered, "*Non, Monsieur;*" but at last we made him understand what we
wanted. It was to find the ruins of the old chateau. "*Ah!*

oui! oui!" he exclaimed, and donning his coat, hastened forth, and conducted us to a small heap of rubbish which we had already examined. He said that fifteen years before, it was *plus considérable.* Seeing at that moment three little red birds fly out of a crevice in the ruins, up into an arbor-vitæ tree, which grew out of them, I asked him their names, in such French as I could muster, but he neither understood me, nor ornithology; he only inquired where we had *appris à parler Français;* we told him, *dans les Etats-Unis;* and so we bowed him into his house again. I was surprised to find a man wearing a black coat, and with apparently no work to do, even in that part of the world.

The universal salutation from the inhabitants whom we met was *bon jour,* at the same time touching the hat; with *bon jour,* and touching your hat, you may go smoothly through all Canada East. A little boy, meeting us would remark, "*Bon jour, Monsieur; le chemin est mauvais:*" Good morning, sir; it is bad walking. Sir Francis Head says that the immigrant is forward to "appreciate the happiness of living in a land in which the old country's servile custom of touching the hat does not exist," but he was thinking of Canada West, of course. It would, indeed, be a serious bore to be obliged to touch your hat several times a day. A Yankee has not leisure for it.

We saw peas, and even beans, collected into heaps in the fields. The former are an important crop here, and, I suppose, are not so much infested by the weevil as with us. There were plenty of apples, very fair and sound, by the road-side, but they were so small as to suggest the origin of the apple in the crab. There was also a small red fruit which they called *snells,* and another, also red and very acid, whose name a little boy wrote for me "pinbéna." It is probably the same with, or similar to the *pembina* of the voyageurs, a species of viburnum, which, according to Richardson, has given its name to many of the rivers of Rupert's Land. The forest trees were spruce, arbor-vitæ, firs, birches, beeches, two or three kinds of maple, bass-wood, wild-cherry, aspens, &c., but no pitch pines (pinus rigida). I saw very few, if any, trees which had been set out for shade or ornament. The water was commonly running streams or springs in the bank by the road-side, and was excellent. The parishes are commonly separated by a stream, and frequently the farms. I noticed that the fields were furrowed or thrown into beds seven or eight feet wide to dry the soil.

At the *Rivière du Sault à la Puce*, which, I suppose, means the River of the Fall of the Flea, was advertised in English, as the sportsmen are English, "the best snipe-shooting grounds," over the door of a small public-house. These words being English affected me as if I had been absent now ten years from my country, and for so long had not heard the sound of my native language, and every one of them was as interesting to me as if I had been a snipe-shooter, and they had been snipes. The prunella or self-heal, in the grass here, was an old acquaintance. We frequently saw the inhabitants washing, or cooking for their pigs, and in one place hackling flax by the road-side. It was pleasant to see these usually domestic operations carried on out of doors, even in that cold country.

At twilight we reached a bridge over a little river, the boundary between Chateau Richer and St. Anne, *le premier pont de Ste. Anne*, and at dark the church of *La Bonne Ste. Anne*. Formerly vessels from France, when they came in sight of this church, gave "a general discharge of their artillery," as a sign of joy that they had escaped all the dangers of the river. Though all the while we had grand views of the adjacent country far up and down the river, and, for the most part, when we turned about, of Quebec in the horizon behind us, and we never beheld it without new surprise and admiration; yet, throughout our walk, the Great River of Canada on our right hand was the main feature in the landscape, and this expands so rapidly below the Isle of Orleans, and creates such a breadth of level horizon above its waters in that direction, that, looking down the river as we approached the extremity of that island, the St. Lawrence seemed to be opening into the ocean, though we were still about three hundred and twenty-five miles from what can be called its mouth.*

When we inquired here for a *maison publique* we were directed apparently to that private house where we were most likely to find entertainment. There were no guide-boards where we walked, because there was but one road; there were no shops nor signs, because there were no artisans to speak of, and the people raised their own provisions; and there were no taverns because there were no travellers. We here bespoke lodging and breakfast. They had, as usual, a large old-fashioned, two-storied box stove in the middle of the room, out of which, in due time, there was sure to be forthcoming a supper, breakfast, or dinner. The lower half held the fire, the upper the hot air, and as it was a cool Canadian evening, this was a comforting sight to us. Being four or five feet high it warmed the whole person as you stood by it. The stove was plainly a very important article of furniture in Canada, and was not set aside during the summer. Its size, and the respect which was paid to it, told of the severe winters which it

* From McCulloch's Geographical Dictionary we learn that "immediately beyond the Island of Orleans it is eleven miles broad; where the Saguenay joins it, eighteen miles; at Point Pelee, upwards of thirty; at the Bay of Seven Islands, seventy miles; and at the Island of Anticosti (about three hundred and fifty miles from Quebec) it rolls a flood into the ocean nearly one hundred miles across."

had seen and prevailed over. The master of the house, in his long-pointed, red woollen cap, had a thoroughly antique physiognomy of the old Norman stamp. He might have come over with Jacques Cartier. His was the hardest French to understand of any we had heard yet, for there was a great difference between one speaker and another, and this man talked with a pipe in his mouth beside, a kind of tobacco French. I asked him what he called his dog. He shouted *Brock!* (the name of the breed). We like to hear the cat called *min–min! min! min!* I inquired if we could cross the river here to the Isle of Orleans, thinking to return that way when we had been to the Falls. He answered, "*S'il ne fait pas un trop grand vent,*" if there is not too much wind. They use small boats or pirogues, and the waves are often too high for them. He wore, as usual, something between a moccasin and a boot, which he called *bottes Indiennes*, Indian boots, and had made himself. The tops were of calf or sheep-skin, and the soles of cow-hide turned up like a moccasin. They were yellow or reddish, the leather never having been tanned nor colored. The women wore the same. He told us that he had travelled ten leagues due north into the bush. He had been to the Falls of St. Anne, and said that they were more beautiful, but not greater, than Montmorenci, *plus beau mais non plus grand que Montmorenci.* As soon as we had retired the family commenced their devotions. A little boy officiated, and for a long time we heard him muttering over his prayers.

In the morning, after a breakfast of tea, maple sugar, bread and butter, and what I suppose is called a *potage* (potatoes and meat boiled with flour), the universal dish as we found, perhaps the national one, I ran over to the Church of La Bonne Ste. Anne, whose matin bell we had heard, it being Sunday morning. Our book said that this church had "long been an object of interest, from the miraculous cures said to have been wrought on visitors to the shrine." There was a profusion of gilding, and I counted more than twenty-five crutches suspended on the walls, some for grown persons, some for children, which it was to be inferred so many sick had been able to dispense with; but they looked as if they had been made to order by the carpenter who made the church. There were one or two villagers at their devotions at that early hour, who did not look up, but when they had sat a long time with their little book before the picture of one saint, went to another. Our whole walk was through a thoroughly Catholic country, and there was no trace of any other religion. I doubt if there are any more simple and unsophisticated Catholics any where. In early times the court gave very precise orders to prevent protestants entering New France–or the exercise of any other than the Catholic religion there. Emery de Caen, Champlain's contemporary, told the Huguenot sailors that "Monseigneur, the Duke de Ventadour (Viceroy), did not wish that they should sing psalms in the Great River."

On our way to the falls, we met the habitans coming to the Church of La Bonne Ste. Anne, walking or riding in charettes by families. I remarked that they were universally of small stature. The toll-man at the bridge, over the St. Anne, was the first man we had chanced to meet since we left Quebec, who could speak a word of English. How good French the inhabitants of this part of Canada speak, I am not competent to say; I only know that it is not made impure by being mixed with English. I do not know why it should not be as good as is spoken in Normandy. Charlevoix, who was here a hundred years ago, observed, "the French language is nowhere spoken with greater purity, there being no accent perceptible;" and Potherie said "they had no dialect, which, indeed, is generally lost in a colony."

The falls, which we were in search of, are three miles up the St. Anne. We followed for a short distance a foot-path up the east bank of this river, through handsome sugar-maple and arbor-vitæ groves. Having lost the path which led to a house where we were to get further directions, we dashed at once into the woods, steering by guess and by compass, climbing directly through woods, a steep hill, or mountain, five or six hundred feet high, which was, in fact, only the bank of the St. Lawrence. Beyond this we by good luck fell into another path, and following this or a branch of it, at our discretion, through a forest consisting of large white pines,–the first we had seen in our walk,–we at length heard the roar of falling water, and came out at the head of the Falls of St. Anne. We had descended into a ravine or cleft in the mountain, whose walls rose still a hundred feet above us, though we were near its top, and we now stood on a very rocky shore, where the water had lately flowed a dozen feet higher, as appeared by the stones and drift-wood, and large birches twisted and splintered as a farmer twists a withe. Here the river, one or two hundred feet wide, came flowing rapidly over a rocky bed out of that interesting wilderness which stretches toward Hudson's Bay and Davis's Straits. Ha-ha Bay, on the Saguenay, was about one hundred miles north of where we stood. Looking on the map, I find that the first country on the north which bears a name, is that part of Rupert's Land called East Main. This river, called after the holy Anne, flowing from such a direction, here tumbled over a precipice, at present by three channels, how far down I do not know, but far enough for all our purposes, and to as good a distance as if twice as far. It matters little whether you call it one, or two, or three hundred feet; at any rate, it was a sufficient water-privilege for us. I crossed the principal channel directly over the verge of the fall, where it was contracted to about fifteen feet in width, by a dead tree which had been dropped across and secured in a cleft of the opposite rock, and a smaller one a few feet higher, which served for a hand-rail. This bridge was rotten as well as small and slippery, being stripped of bark, and I was obliged to seize a moment to pass when the falling water did not surge over it, and mid-way, though at the expense of wet feet, I looked down probably more than a hundred feet, into the mist and foam below. This gave me the freedom of an island of precipitous rock, by which I descended as by giant steps, the rock being composed of large cubical masses, clothed with delicate, close-hugging lichens of various colors, kept fresh and bright by the moisture, till I viewed the first fall from the front, and looked down still deeper to where the second and third channels fell into a remarkably large circular basin worn in the stone. The falling water seemed to jar the very rocks, and the noise to be ever increasing. The vista down stream was through a narrow and deep cleft in the mountain, all white suds at the bottom; but a sudden angle in this gorge prevented my seeing through to the bottom of the fall. Returning to the shore, I made my way down stream through the forest to see how far the fall extended, and how the river came out of that adventure. It was to clamber along the side of a precipitous mountain of loose mossy rocks, covered with a damp primitive forest, and terminating at the bottom in an abrupt precipice over the stream. This was the east side of the fall. At length, after a quarter of a mile, I got down to still water, and on looking up through the winding gorge, I could just see to the foot of the fall which I had before examined; while from the opposite side of the stream, here much contracted, rose a perpendicular wall, I will not venture to say how many hundred feet, but only that it was the highest perpendicular wall of bare rock that I ever saw. In front of me tumbled in from the summit of the cliff a tributary stream, making a beautiful cascade, which was a remarkable fall in itself, and there was a cleft in this precipice, apparently four or five feet wide, perfectly straight up and down from top to bottom, which from its cavernous depth and darkness, appeared merely as *a black streak*. This precipice is not sloped, nor is the material soft and crumbling slate as at Montmorenci, but it rises perfectly perpendicular, like the side of a mountain fortress, and is cracked into vast cubical masses of gray and black rock shining with moisture, as if it were the ruin of an ancient wall built by Titans. Birches, spruces, mountain-ashes with their bright red berries, arbor-vitæs, white pines, alders, &c., overhung this chasm on the very verge of the cliff and in the crevices, and here and there were buttresses of rock supporting trees part way down, yet so as to enhance, not injure, the effect of the bare rock. Take it altogether, it was a most wild and rugged and stupendous chasm, so deep and narrow where a river had worn itself a passage through a mountain of rock, and all around was the comparatively untrodden wilderness.

This was the limit of our walk down the St. Lawrence. Early in the afternoon we began to retrace our steps, not being able to cross the north channel and return by the Isle of Orleans, on account of the *trop grand vent*, or too great wind. Though the waves did run pretty high, it was evident that the inhabitants of Montmorenci County were no sailors, and made but little use of the river. When we reached the bridge, between St. Anne and Chateau Richer, I ran back a little way to ask a man in a field the name of the river which we were crossing, but for a long time I could not make out what he said, for he was one of the more unintelli-

gible Jacques Cartier men. At last it flashed upon me
that it was *La Rivière au Chien*, or the Dog River, which
my eyes beheld, which brought to my mind the life of
the Canadian *voyageur* and *coureur de bois*, a more
western and wilder Arcadia, methinks, than the world
has ever seen; for the Greeks, with all their wood and
river gods, were not so qualified to name the natural
features of a country, as the ancestors of these French
Canadians; and if any people had a right to substi-
tute their own for the Indian names, it was they. They
have preceded the pioneer on our own frontiers, and
named the *prairie* for us. *La Rivière au Chien* cannot,
by any licence of language, be translated into Dog
River, for that is not such a giving it to the dogs, and
recognizing their place in creation as the French implies. One of the tributaries of the St. Anne is named,
La Rivière de la Rose; and further east are, *La Rivière de
la Blondelle*, and *La Rivière de la Friponne*. Their very
rivière meanders more than our *river*.

Yet the impression which this country made on me,
was commonly different from this. To a traveller from
the Old World, Canada East may appear like a new
country, and its inhabitants like colonists, but to me,
coming from New England, and being a very green
traveller withal–notwithstanding what I have said
about Hudson's Bay,–it appeared as old as Normandy
itself, and realized much that I had heard of Europe
and the Middle Ages. Even the names of humble Canadian villages, affected me as if they had been those of
the renowned cities of antiquity. To be told by a habitan, when I asked the name of a village in sight, that it
is *St. Fereole* or *St. Anne*, the *Guardian Angel* or the
Holy Joseph's, or of a mountain, that it was *Belange*, or
St. Hyacinthe! As soon as you leave the States, these
saintly names begin. *St. Johns* is the first town you stop
at (fortunately we did not see it), and thenceforward,

the names of the mountains and streams, and villages,
reel, if I may so speak, with the intoxication of poetry;–
Chambly, Longueil, Pointe aux Trembles, Bartholomy,
&c., &c.; as if it needed only a little foreign accent, a
few more liquids and vowels perchance in the language, to make us locate our ideals at once. I began to
dream of Provence and the Troubadours, and of
places and things which have no existence on the
earth. They veiled the Indian and the primitive forest,
and the woods toward Hudson's Bay were only as the
forests of France and Germany. I could not at once
bring myself to believe that the inhabitants who pronounced daily those beautiful, and to me, significant
names, lead as prosaic lives as we of New England.
In short, the Canada which I saw, was not merely a
place for railroads to terminate in, and for criminals
to run to.

When I asked the man to whom I have referred, if
there were any falls on the Rivière au Chien, for I saw
that it came over the same high bank with the
Montmorenci and St. Anne; he answered that there
were. How far? I inquired; *Trois quatres lieue.* How
high? *Je pense, quatre-vingt-dix pieds*; that is, ninety
feet. We turned aside to look at the falls of the *Rivière
du Sault à la Puce*, half a mile from the road, which
before we had passed in our haste and ignorance, and
we pronounced them as beautiful as any that we saw;
yet they seemed to make no account of them there,
and when first we inquired the way to the Falls, directed us to Montmorenci, seven miles distant. It was
evident that this was the country for waterfalls; that
every stream that empties into the St. Lawrence, for
some hundreds of miles, must have a great fall or cascade on it, and in its passage through the mountains,
was, for a short distance, a small Saguenay, with its
upright walls. This fall of La Puce, the least remarkable

of the four which we visited in this vicinity, we had never heard of till we came to Canada, and yet, so far as I know, there is nothing of the kind in New England to be compared with it. Most travellers in Canada would not hear of it, though they might go so near as to hear it. Since my return I find that in the topographical description of the country mention is made of "two or three romantic falls" on this stream, though we saw and heard of but this one. Ask the inhabitants respecting any stream, if there is a fall on it, and they will perchance tell you of something as interesting as Bashpish or the Catskill, which no traveller has ever seen, or if they have not found it, you may possibly trace up the stream and discover it yourself. Falls there are a drug; and we became quite dissipated in respect to them. We had drunk too much of them. Beside these which I have referred to, there are a thousand other falls on the St. Lawrence and its tributaries which I have not seen nor heard of; and above all there is one which I have heard of, called Niagara, so that I think that this river must be the most remarkable for its falls of any in the world.

At a house near the western boundary of Chateau Richer, whose master was said to speak a very little English, having recently lived at Quebec, we got lodging for the night. As usual, we had to go down a lane to get round to the south side of the house where the door was, away from the road. For these Canadian houses have no front door, properly speaking. Every part is for the use of the occupant exclusively, and no part has reference to the traveller or to travel. Every New England house, on the contrary, has a front and principal door opening to the great world, though it may be on the cold side, for it stands on the highway of nations, and the road which runs by it, comes from the Old World and goes to the Far West; but the Canadian's door opens into his back yard and farm alone, and the road which runs behind his house leads only from the church of one saint to that of another. We found a large family, hired men, wife, and children, just eating their supper. They prepared some for us afterwards. The hired men were a merry crew of short black-eyed fellows, and the wife a thin-faced, sharp-featured French Canadian woman. Our host's English staggered us rather more than any French we had heard yet; indeed, we found that even we spoke better French than he did English, and we concluded that a less crime would be committed on the whole, if we spoke French with him, and in no respect aided or abetted his attempts to speak English. We had a long and merry chat with the family this Sunday evening in their spacious kitchen. While my companion smoked a pipe and parlez-vous'd with one party, I parleyed and gesticulated to another. The whole family was enlisted, and I kept a little girl writing what was otherwise unintelligible. The geography getting obscure, we called for chalk, and the greasy oiled table-cloth having been wiped,–for it needed no French, but only a sentence from the universal language of looks on my part, to indicate that it needed it,–we drew the St. Lawrence with its parishes thereon, and thenceforward went on swimmingly, by turns handling the chalk and committing to the table-cloth what would otherwise have been left in a limbo of unintelligibility. This was greatly to the entertainment of all parties. I was amused to hear how much use they made of the word *oui* in conversation with one another. After repeated single insertions of it one would suddenly throw back his head at the same time with his chair, and exclaim rapidly, *oui! oui! oui! oui!* like a Yankee driving pigs. Our host told us that the farms thereabouts were generally two acres, or three hundred and sixty French feet wide, by one and a half leagues (?) or a little more than four and a half of our miles deep. This use of the word acre as long measure, arises from the fact that the French acre or arpent, the arpent of Paris, makes a square of ten perches of eighteen feet each on a side, a Paris foot being equal to 1.06575 English feet. He said that the wood was cut off about one mile from the river. The rest was "bush," and beyond that the "Queen's bush." Old as the country is, each land-holder bounds on the primitive forest, and fuel bears no price. As I had forgotten the French for sickle, they went out in the evening to the barn and got one, and so clenched the certainty of our understanding one another. Then, wishing to learn if they used the cradle, and not knowing any French word for this instrument, I set up the knives and forks on the blade of the sickle to represent one; at which they all exclaimed that they knew and had used it. When *snells* were mentioned they went out in the dark and plucked some. They were pretty good. They said that they had three kinds of plums growing wild, blue, white, and red, the two former much alike, and the best. Also they asked me if I would have *des pommes*, some apples, and got me some. They were exceedingly fair and glossy, and it was evident that there was no worm in them, but they were as hard almost as a stone, as if the season was too short to mellow them. We had seen no soft and yellow apples by the road-side. I declined eating one, much as I admired it, observing that it would be good *dans le printemps*, in the spring. In the morning when the mistress had set the eggs a frying, she nodded to a thick-set jolly-looking fellow, who rolled up his sleeves, seized the long-handled griddle, and commenced a series of revolutions and evolutions with it, ever and anon tossing its contents into the air, where they turned completely topsy-turvey and came down t'other side up; and this he repeated till they were done. That appeared to be his duty when eggs were concerned. I did not chance to witness this performance, but my companion did, and he pronounced it a master-piece in its way. This man's farm, with the buildings, cost seven hundred pounds; some smaller ones, two hundred.

In 1827, Montmorenci County, to which the Isle of Orleans has since been added, was nearly as large as Massachusetts, being the eighth county out of forty (in Lower Canada) in extent; but by far the greater part still must continue to be waste land, lying, as it were, under the walls of Quebec.

I quote these old statistics, not merely because of the difficulty of obtaining more recent ones, but also because I saw there so little evidence of any recent growth. There were in this county, at the same date, five Roman Catholic churches, and no others, five curés and five presbyteries, two schools, two corn-mills, four saw-mills, one carding-mill,–no medical man, or notary or lawyer,–five shopkeepers, four taverns (we saw no *sign* of any, though, after a little hesitation, we were sometimes directed to some undistinguished hut as such), thirty artisans, and five river craft, whose tonnage amounted to sixty-nine tons! This, notwithstanding that it has a frontage of more than thirty miles on the river, and the population is almost wholly confined to its bank. This describes nearly enough what we saw. But double some of these figures, which, however, its growth will not warrant, and you have described a poverty which not even its severity of climate and ruggedness of soil will suffice to account for. The principal productions were wheat, potatoes, oats, hay, peas, flax, maple-sugar, &c., &c.; linen, cloth, or *étoffe du pays*, flannel, and homespun, or *petite étoffe*.

In Lower Canada, according to Bouchette, there are two tenures,–the feudal and the soccage. Tenanciers, censitaires, or holders of land *en roture*, pay a small annual rent to the seigneurs, to which "is added some article of provision, such as a couple of fowls, or a goose, or a bushel of wheat." "They are also bound to grind their corn at the *moulin banal*, or the lord's mill, where one fourteenth part of it is taken for his use" as toll. He says that the toll is one twelfth in the United States, where competition exists. It is not permitted to exceed one sixteenth in Massachusetts. But worse than this monopolizing of mill rents is what are called *lods et ventes*, or mutation fines. According to which the seigneur has "a right to a twelfth part of the purchase-money of every estate within his seigniory that changes its owner by sale." This is over and above the sum paid to the seller. In such cases, moreover, "the lord possesses the *droit de retrait*, which is the privilege of pre-emption at the highest bidden price within forty days after the sale has taken place,"–a right which, however, is said to be seldom exercised. "Lands held by Roman Catholics are further subject to the payment to their curates of one twenty-sixth part of all the grain produced upon them, and to occasional assessments for building and repairing churches," &c.,– a tax to which they are not subject if the proprietors change their faith; but they are not the less attached to their church in consequence. There are, however, various modifications of the feudal tenure. Under the soccage tenure, which is that of the townships or more recent settlements, English, Irish, Scotch, and others, and generally of Canada West, the landholder is wholly unshackled by such conditions as I have quoted, and "is bound to no other obligations than those of allegiance to the king and obedience to the laws." Throughout Canada "a freehold of forty shillings yearly value, or the payment of ten pounds rent annually, is the qualification for voters." In 1846 more than one sixth of the whole population of Canada East were qualified to vote for members of Parliament,–a greater proportion than enjoy a similar privilege in the United States.

The population which we had seen the last two days,–I mean the habitans of Montmorenci County,– appeared very inferior, intellectually and even physically, to that of New England. In some respects they were incredibly filthy. It was evident that they had not advanced since the settlement of the country, that they were quite behind the age, and fairly represented their ancestors in Normandy a thousand years ago. Even in respect to the common arts of life, they are not so far advanced as a frontier town in the West three years old. They have no money invested in railroad stock, and probably never will have. If they have got a French phrase for a railroad, it is as much as you can expect of them. They are very far from a revolution; have no quarrel with Church or State, but their vice and their virtue is content. As for annexation, they have never dreamed of it; indeed, they have not a clear idea what or where the States are. The English government has been remarkably liberal to its Catholic subjects in Canada, permitting them to wear their own fetters, both political and religious, as far as was possible for subjects. Their government is even too good for them. Parliament passed "an act [in 1825] to provide for the extinction of feudal and seigniorial rights and burdens on lands in Lower Canada, and for the gradual conversion of those tenures into the tenure of free and common soccage," &c. But as late as 1831, at least, the design of the act was likely to be frustrated, owing to the reluctance of the seigniors and peasants. It has been observed by another that the French Canadians do not extend nor perpetuate their influence. The British, Irish, and other immigrants, who have settled the townships, are found to have imitated the American settlers, and not the French. They reminded me in this of the Indians, whom they were slow to displace and to whose habits of life they themselves more readily conformed than the Indians to theirs. The Governor-General Denonville remarked, in 1685, that some had long thought that it was necessary to bring the Indians near them in order to Frenchify (*franciser*) them, but that they had every reason to think themselves in an error; for those who had come near them and were even collected in villages in the midst of the colony had not become French, but the French, who had haunted them, had become savages. Kalm said: "Though many nations imitate the French customs, yet I observed, on the contrary, that the French in Canada, in many respects, follow the customs of the Indians, with whom they converse every day. They make use of the tobacco-pipes, shoes, garters, and girdles of the Indians. They follow the Indian way of making war with exactness; they mix the same things with tobacco (he might have said that both French and English learned the use itself of this weed of the Indian); they make use of the Indian bark-boats, and row them in the Indian way; they wrap square pieces of cloth round their feet instead of stockings; and have adopted many other Indian fashions." Thus, while the descendants of the Pilgrims are teaching the English to make pegged boots, the descendants of the French in Canada are wearing the Indian moccasin still. The French, to their credit be it said, to a certain extent respected the Indians as a separate and independent people, and spoke of them and contrasted themselves with them as the English have never done. They not only went to war with them as allies, but they lived at home with them as neighbors. In 1627 the French king declared "that the descendants of the French, settled in" New France, "and the savages who should be brought to the knowledge of the faith, and should make profession of it, should be counted and reputed French born (*Naturels François*); and as such could emigrate to France, when it seemed good to them, and there acquire, will, inherit, &c., &c., without obtaining letters of naturalization." When the English had possession of Quebec, in 1630, the Indians, attempting to practise the same familiarity with them that they had with the French, were driven out of their houses with blows; which accident taught them a difference between the two races, and attached them yet more to the French. The impression made on me was, that the French Canadians were even sharing the fate of the Indians, or at least gradually disappearing in what is called the Saxon current.

The English did not come to America from a mere love of adventure, nor to truck with or convert the savages, nor to hold offices under the crown, as the French to a great extent did, but to live in earnest and with freedom. The latter overran a great extent of country, selling strong water, and collecting its furs, and converting its inhabitants,–or at least baptizing its dying infants (*enfans moribonds*),–without *improving* it. First, went the *coureur de bois* with the *eau de vie;* then followed, if he did not precede, the heroic missionary with the *eau d'immortalité.* It was freedom to hunt, and fish, and convert, not to work, that they sought. Hontan says that the *coureurs de bois* lived like sailors ashore. In no part of the seventeenth century could the French be said to have had a foothold in Canada; they held only by the fur of the wild animals which they were exterminating. To enable the poor seigneurs to get their living, it was permitted by a decree passed in the reign of Louis the Fourteenth, in 1685, "to all nobles and gentlemen settled in Canada, to engage in commerce, without being called to account or reputed to have done anything derogatory." The reader can infer to what extent they had engaged in agriculture, and how their farms must have shone by this time. The New England youth, on the other hand, were never *coureurs de bois* nor *voyageurs*, but backwoodsmen and sailors rather. Of all nations the English undoubtedly have proved hitherto that they had the most business here.

Yet I am not sure but I have most sympathy with that spirit of adventure which distinguished the French and Spaniards of those days, and made them especially the explorers of the American Continent,–which so early carried the former to the Great Lakes and the Mississippi on the north, and the latter to the same river on the south. It was long before our frontiers reached their settlements in the West. So far as inland discovery was concerned, the adventurous spirit of the English was that of sailors who land but for a day, and their enterprise the enterprise of traders.

There was apparently a greater equality of condition among the habitans of Montmorenci County than in New England. They are an almost exclusively agricultural, and so far independent, population, each family producing nearly all the necessaries of life for itself. If the Canadian wants energy, perchance he possesses those virtues, social and others, which the Yankee lacks, in which case he cannot be regarded as a poor man.

IV. The Walls of Quebec.

AFTER spending the night at a farm-house in Chateau-Richer, about a dozen miles northeast of Quebec, we set out on our return to the city. We stopped at the next house, a picturesque old stone mill, over the *Chi-pré*,–for so the name sounded,–such as you will nowhere see in the States, and asked the millers the age of the mill. They went up stairs to call the master; but the crabbed old miser asked why we wanted to know, and would tell us only for some compensation. I wanted French to give him a piece of my mind. I had got enough to talk on a pinch, but not to quarrel; so I had to come away, looking all I would have said. This was the utmost incivility we met with in Canada. In Beauport, within a few miles of Quebec, we turned aside to look at a church which was just being completed,–a very large and handsome edifice of stone, with a green bough stuck in its gable, of some significance to Catholics. The comparative wealth of the Church in this country was apparent; for in this village we did not see one good house besides. They were all humble cottages; and yet this appeared to me a more imposing structure than any church in Boston. But I am no judge of these things.

Re-entering Quebec through St. John's Gate, we took a caleche in Market Square for the Falls of the Chaudière, about nine miles southwest of the city, for which we were to pay so much, beside forty sous for tolls. The driver, as usual, spoke French only. The number of these vehicles is very great for so small a town. They are like one of our chaises that has lost its top, only stouter and longer in the body, with a seat for the driver where the dasher is with us, and broad leather ears on each side to protect the riders from the wheel and keep children from falling out. They had an easy jaunting look, which, as our hours were numbered, persuaded us to be riders. We met with them on every road near Quebec these days, each with its complement of two inquisitive-looking foreigners and a Canadian driver, the former evidently enjoying their novel experience, for commonly it is only the horse whose language you do not understand; but they were one remove further from him by the intervention of an equally unintelligible driver. We crossed the St. Lawrence to Point Levi in a French-Canadian ferry-boat, which was inconvenient and dirty, and managed with great noise and bustle. The current was very strong and tumultuous, and the boat tossed enough to make some sick, though it was only a mile across; yet the wind was not to be compared with that of the day before, and we saw that the Canadians had a good excuse for not taking us over to the Isle of Orleans in a pirogue, however shiftless they may be for not having provided any other conveyance. The route which we took to the Chaudière did not afford us those views of Quebec which we had expected, and the country and inhabitants appeared less interesting to a traveller than those we had seen. The Falls of the Chaudière are three miles from its mouth on the south side of the St. Lawrence. Though they were the largest which I saw in Canada, I was not proportionately interested by them, probably from satiety. I did not see any *peculiar* propriety in the name *Chaudière*, or caldron. I saw here the most brilliant rainbow that I ever imagined. It was just across the stream below the precipice, formed on the mist which this tremendous fall produced; and I stood on a level with the key-stone of its arch. It was not a few faint prismatic colors merely, but a full semicircle, only four or five rods in diameter, though as wide as usual, so intensely bright as to pain the eye, and apparently as substantial as an arch of stone. It changed its position and colors as we moved, and was the brighter because the sun shone so clearly and the mist was so thick. Evidently a picture painted on mist for the men and animals that came to the falls to look at; but for what special purpose beyond this, I know not. At the farthest point in this ride, and when most inland, unexpectedly at a turn in the road we descried the frowning citadel of Quebec in the horizon, like the beak of a bird of prey. We returned by the river-road under the bank, which is very high, abrupt, and rocky. When we were opposite to Quebec, I was surprised to see that in the Lower Town, under the shadow of the rock, the lamps were lit, twinkling not unlike crystals in a cavern, while the citadel high above, and we, too, on the south shore, were in broad daylight. As we were too late for the ferry-boat that night, we put up at a *maison de pension* at Point Levi. The usual two-story stove was here placed against an opening in the partition shaped like a fireplace, and so warmed several rooms. We could not understand their French here very well, but the *potage* was just like what we had had before. There were many small chambers with doorways but no doors. The walls of our chamber, all around and overhead, were neatly ceiled, and the timbers cased with wood unpainted. The pillows were checkered and tasselled, and the usual long-pointed red woollen or worsted night-cap was placed on each. I pulled mine out to see how it was made. It was in the form of a double cone, one end tucked into the other; just such, it appeared, as I saw men wearing all day in the streets. Probably I should have put it on if the cold had been then, as it is sometimes there, thirty or forty degrees below zero.

When we landed at Quebec the next morning, a man lay on his back on the wharf, apparently dying, in the midst of a crowd and directly in the path of the horses, groaning, "*O ma conscience!*" I thought that he pronounced his French more distinctly than any I heard, as if the dying had already acquired the accents of a universal language. Having secured the only unengaged berths in the Lord Sydenham steamer, which was to leave Quebec before sundown, and being resolved, now that I had seen somewhat of the country, to get an idea of the city, I proceeded to walk round the Upper Town, or fortified portion, which is two miles and three quarters in circuit, alone, as near as I could get to the cliff and the walls, like a rat looking for a hole; going round by the southwest, where there is but a single street between the cliff and the water, and up the long, wooden stairs, through the suburbs northward to the King's Woodyard, which I thought must have been a long way from his fireplace, and under the cliffs of the St. Charles, where the drains issue under the walls, and the walls are loopholed for musketry; so returning by Mountain Street and Prescott Gate to the Upper Town. Having found my way by an obscure passage near the St. Louis Gate to the glacis on the north of the citadel proper,–I believe that I was the only visitor then in the city who got in there,– I enjoyed a prospect nearly as good as from within the citadel itself, which I had explored some days before. As I walked on the glacis I heard the sound of a bagpipe from the soldiers' dwellings in the rock, and was further soothed and affected by the sight of a soldier's cat walking up a cleated plank into a high loophole, designed for *mus-catry*, as serene as Wisdom herself, and with a gracefully waving motion of her tail, as if her ways were ways of pleasantness and all her paths were peace. Scaling a slat fence, where a small force might have checked me, I got out of the esplanade into the Governor's Garden, and read the well-known inscription on Wolfe and Montcalm's monument, which for saying much in little, and that to the purpose, undoubtedly deserved the prize medal which it received:

MORTEM . VIRTUS . COMMUNEM .

FAMAM . HISTORIA .

MONUMENTUM . POSTERITAS .

DEDIT.

Valor gave them one death, history one fame, posterity one monument. The Government Garden has for nose-gays, amid kitchen vegetables, beside the common garden flowers, the usual complement of cannon directed toward some future and possible enemy. I then returned up St. Louis Street to the esplanade and ramparts there, and went round the Upper Town once more, though I was very tired, this time on the *inside* of the wall; for I knew that the wall was the main thing in Quebec, and had cost a great deal of money, and therefore I must make the most of it. In fact, these are the only remarkable walls we have in North America, though we have a good deal of Virginia fence, it is true. Moreover, I cannot say but I yielded in some measure to the soldier instinct, and, having but a short time to spare, thought it best to examine the wall thoroughly, that I might be the better prepared if I should ever be called that way again in the service of my country. I committed all the gates to memory in their order, which did not cost me so much trouble as it would have done at the hundred-gated city, there being only five; nor were they so hard to remember as those seven of Bœotian Thebes; and, moreover, I thought that, if seven champions were enough against the latter, one would be enough against Quebec, though he bore for all armor and device only an umbrella and a bundle. I took the nunneries as I went, for I had learned to distinguish them by the blinds; and I observed also the foundling hospitals and the convents, and whatever was attached to, or in the vicinity of the walls. All the rest I omitted, as naturally as one would the inside of an inedible shell-fish. These were the only pearls, and the wall the only mother-of-pearl for me. Quebec is chiefly famous for the thickness of its parietal bones. The technical terms of its conchology may stagger a beginner a little at first, such as *banlieue, esplanade, glacis, ravelin, cavalier,* &c., &c., but with the aid of a comprehensive dictionary you soon learn the nature of your ground. I was surprised at the extent of the artillery barracks, built so long ago,–*Casernes Nouvelles,* they used to be called,–nearly six hundred feet in length by forty in depth, where the sentries, like peripatetic philosophers, were so absorbed in thought, as not to notice me when I passed in and out at the gates. Within, are "small arms of every description, sufficient for the equipment of twenty thousand men," so arranged as to give a startling *coup d'œil* to strangers. I did not enter, not wishing to get a black eye; for they are said to be "in a state of complete repair and readiness for immediate use." Here, for a short time, I lost sight of the wall, but I recovered it again on emerging from the barrack yard. There I met with a Scotchman who appeared to have business with the wall, like myself; and, being thus mutually drawn together by a similarity of tastes, we had a little conversation *sub mœnibus,* that is, by an angle of the wall which sheltered us. He lived about thirty miles northwest of Quebec; had been nineteen years in the country; said he was disappointed that he was not brought to America after all, but found himself still under British rule and where his own language was not spoken; that many Scotch, Irish, and English were disappointed in like manner, and either went to the States, or pushed up the river to Canada West, nearer to the States, and where their language was spoken. He talked of visiting the States some time; and, as he seemed ignorant of geography, I warned him that it was one thing to visit the State of Massachusetts, and another to visit the State of California. He said it was colder there than usual at that season, and he was lucky to have brought his thick togue, or frock-coat, with him; thought it would snow, and then be pleasant and warm. That is the way we are always thinking. However, his words were music to me in my thin hat and sack.

At the ramparts on the cliff near the old Parliament House I counted twenty-four thirty-two-pounders in a row, pointed over the harbor, with their balls piled pyramid-wise between them,–there are said to be in all about one hundred and eighty guns mounted at Quebec,–all which were faithfully kept dusted by officials, in accordance with the motto, "In time of peace prepare for war"; but I saw no preparations for peace: she was plainly an uninvited guest.

Having thus completed the circuit of this fortress, both within and without, I went no further by the wall for fear that I should become wall-eyed. However, I think that I deserve to be made a member of the Royal Sappers and Miners.

In short, I observed everywhere the most perfect arrangements for keeping a wall in order, not even permitting the lichens to grow on it, which some think an ornament; but then I saw no cultivation nor pasturing within it to pay for the outlay, and cattle were strictly forbidden to feed on the glacis under the severest penalties. Where the dogs get their milk I don't know, and I fear it is bloody at best.

The citadel of Quebec says, "I *will* live here, and you sha'n't prevent me." To which you return, that you have not the slightest objection; live and let live. The Martello towers looked, for all the world, exactly like abandoned wind-mills which had not had a grist to grind these hundred years. Indeed, the whole castle here was a "folly,"–England's folly,–and, in more senses than one, a castle in the air. The inhabitants and the government are gradually waking up to a sense of this truth; for I heard something said about their abandoning the wall around the Upper Town, and confining the fortifications to the citadel of forty

acres. Of course they will finally reduce their intrench-
ments to the circumference of their own brave hearts.

The most modern fortifications have an air of antiquity about them; they have the aspect of ruins in better
or worse repair from the day they are built, because
they are not really the work of this age. The very place
where the soldier resides has a peculiar tendency to
become old and dilapidated, as the word *barrack* implies. I couple all fortifications in my mind with the
dismantled Spanish forts to be found in so many parts
of the world; and if in any place they are not actually
dismantled, it is because that there the intellect of the
inhabitants is dismantled. The commanding officer of
an old fort near Valdivia in South America, when a
traveller remarked to him that, with one discharge, his
gun-carriages would certainly fall to pieces, gravely
replied, "No, I am sure, sir, they would stand two."
Perhaps the guns of Quebec would stand three. Such
structures carry us back to the Middle Ages, the siege
of Jerusalem, and St. Jean d'Acre, and the days of the
Bucaniers. In the armory of the citadel they showed
me a clumsy implement, long since useless, which
they called a Lombard gun. I thought that their whole
citadel was such a Lombard gun, fit object for the
museums of the curious. Such works do not consist
with the development of the intellect. Huge stone
structures of all kinds, both in their erection and by
their influence when erected, rather oppress than
liberate the mind. They are tombs for the souls of men,
as frequently for their bodies also. The sentinel with
his musket beside a man with his umbrella is spectral. There is not sufficient reason for his existence.
Does my friend there, with a bullet resting on half an
ounce of powder, think that he needs that argument in
conversing with me? The fort was the first institution
that was founded here, and it is amusing to read in

Champlain how assiduously they worked at it almost from the first day of the settlement. The founders of the colony thought this an excellent site for a wall,– and no doubt it was a better site, in some respects, for a wall than for a city,–but it chanced that a city got behind it. It chanced, too, that a Lower Town got before it, and clung like an oyster to the outside of the crags, as you may see at low tide. It is as if you were to come to a country village surrounded by palisades in the old Indian fashion,–interesting only as a relic of antiquity and barbarism. A fortified town is like a man cased in the heavy armor of antiquity, with a horse-load of broadswords and small arms slung to him, endeavoring to go about his business. Or is this an indispensable machinery for the good government of the country? The inhabitants of California succeed pretty well, and are doing better and better every day, without any such institution. What use has this fortress served, to look at it even from the soldiers' point of view? At first the French took care of it; yet Wolfe sailed by it with impunity, and took the town of Quebec without experiencing any hinderance at last from its fortifications. They were only the bone for which the parties fought. Then the English began to take care of it. So of any fort in the world,–that in Boston harbor, for instance. We shall at length hear that an enemy sailed by it in the night, for it cannot sail itself, and both it and its inhabitants are always benighted. How often we read that the enemy occupied a position which commanded the old, and so the fort was evacuated. Have not the school-house and the printing-press occupied a position which commands such a fort as this?

However, this is a ruin kept in remarkably good repair. There are some eight hundred or thousand men there to exhibit it. One regiment goes bare-legged to increase the attraction. If you wish to study the muscles of the leg about the knee, repair to Quebec. This universal exhibition in Canada of the tools and sinews of war reminded me of the keeper of a menagerie showing his animals' claws. It was the English leopard showing his claws. Always the *royal* something or other; as, at the menagerie, the Royal Bengal Tiger. Silliman states that "the cold is so intense in the winter nights, particularly on Cape Diamond, that the sentinels cannot stand it more than one hour, and are relieved at the expiration of that time"; "and even, as it is said, at much shorter intervals, in case of the most extreme cold." What a natural or unnatural fool must that soldier be,–to say nothing of his government,–who, when quicksilver is freezing and blood is ceasing to be quick, will stand to have his face frozen, watching the walls of Quebec, though, so far as they are concerned, both honest and dishonest men all the world over have been in their beds nearly half a century,–or at least for that space travellers have visited Quebec only as they would read history. I shall never again wake up in a colder night than usual, but I shall think how rapidly the sentinels are relieving one another on the walls of Quebec, their quicksilver being all frozen, as if apprehensive that some hostile Wolfe may even then be scaling the Heights of Abraham, or some persevering Arnold about to issue from the wilderness; some Malay or Japanese, perchance, coming round by the northwest coast, have chosen that moment to assault the citadel! Why I should as soon expect to find the sentinels still relieving one another on the walls of Nineveh, which have so long been buried to the world! What a troublesome thing a wall is! I thought it was to defend me, and not I it. Of course, if they had no wall they would not need to have any sentinels.

You might venture to advertise this farm as well fenced with substantial stone walls (saying nothing about the eight hundred Highlanders and Royal Irish who are required to keep them from toppling down); stock and tools to go with the land if desired. But it would not be wise for the seller to exhibit his farm-book.

Why should Canada, wild and unsettled as it is, impress us as an older country than the States, unless because her institutions are old? All things appeared to contend there, as I have implied, with a certain rust of antiquity,–such as forms on old armor and iron guns,–the rust of conventions and formalities. It is said that the metallic roofs of Montreal and Quebec keep sound and bright for forty years in some cases. But if the rust was not on the tinned roofs and spires, it was on the inhabitants and their institutions. Yet the work of burnishing goes briskly forward. I imagined that the government vessels at the wharves were laden with rotten-stone and oxalic acid,–that is what the first ship from England in the spring comes freighted with,–and the hands of the colonial legislature are cased in wash-leather. The principal exports must be *gun*ny bags, verdigrease, and iron rust. Those who first built this fort, coming from Old France with the memory and tradition of feudal days and customs weighing on them, were unquestionably behind their age; and those who now inhabit and repair it are behind their ancestors or predecessors. Those old chevaliers thought that they could transplant the feudal system to America. It has been set out, but it has not thriven. Notwithstanding that Canada was settled first, and, unlike New England, for a long series of years enjoyed the fostering care of the mother country,–notwithstanding that, as Charlevoix tells us, it had more of the ancient *noblesse* among its early settlers than any other of the French colonies, and perhaps than all the others together,–there are in both the Canadas but

600,000 of French descent to-day,–about half so many as the population of Massachusetts. The whole population of both Canadas is but about 1,700,000 Canadians, English, Irish, Scotch, Indians, and all, put together! Samuel Laing, in his essay on the Northmen, to whom especially, rather than the Saxons, he refers the energy and indeed the excellence of the English character, observes that, when they occupied Scandinavia, "each man possessed his lot of land without reference to, or acknowledgment of, any other man,– without any local chief to whom his military service or other quit-rent for his land was due,–without tenure from, or duty or obligation to, any superior, real or fictitious, except the general sovereign. The individual settler held his land, as his descendants in Norway still express it, by the same right as the king held his crown,–by udal right, or adel,–that is, noble right." The French have occupied Canada, not *udally*, or by noble right, but *feudally*, or by ignoble right. They are a nation of peasants.

It was evident that, both on account of the feudal system and the aristocratic government, a private man was not worth so much in Canada as in the United States; and, if your wealth in any measure consists in manliness, in originality, and independence, you had better stay here. How could a peaceable, free-thinking man live neighbor to the Forty-ninth Regiment? A New-Englander would naturally be a bad citizen, probably a rebel, there,–certainly if he were already a rebel at home. I suspect that a poor man who is not servile is a much rarer phenomenon there and in England than in the Northern United States. An Englishman, methinks,–not to speak of other European nations,–habitually regards himself merely as a constituent part of the English nation; he is a member of the royal regiment of Englishmen, and is proud of his company, as he has reason to be proud of it. But an American,–one who has made a tolerable use of his opportunities,–cares, comparatively, little about such things, and is advantageously nearer to the primitive and the ultimate condition of man in these respects. It is a government, that English one,–like most other European ones,–that cannot afford to be forgotten, as you would naturally forget it; under which one cannot be wholesomely neglected, and grow up a man and not an Englishman merely,–cannot be a poet even without danger of being made poet-laureate! Give me a country where it is the most natural thing in the world for a government that does not understand you to let you alone. One would say that a true Englishman could speculate only within bounds. (It is true the Americans have proved that they, in more than one sense, can *speculate* without bounds.) He has to pay his respects to so many things, that, before he knows it, he *may* have paid away all he is worth. What makes the United States government, on the whole, more tolerable,–I mean for us lucky *white* men,–is the fact that there is so much less of government with us. Here it is only once in a month or a year that a man *needs* remember that institution; and those who go to Congress can play the game of the Kilkenny cats there without fatal consequences to those who stay at home,–their term is so short: but in Canada you are reminded of the government every day. It parades itself before you. It is not content to be the servant, but will be the master; and every day it goes out to the Plains of Abraham or to the Champ de Mars and exhibits itself and its tools. Everywhere there appeared an attempt to make and to preserve trivial and otherwise transient distinctions. In the streets of Montreal and Quebec you met not only with soldiers in red, and shuffling priests in unmistakable black and white, with Sisters of Charity gone into mourning for their deceased relative,–not to mention the nuns of various orders depending on the fashion of a tear, of whom you heard,–but youths belonging to some seminary or other, wearing coats edged with white, who looked as if their expanding hearts were already repressed with a piece of tape. In short, the inhabitants of Canada appeared to be suffering between two fires,–the soldiery and the priesthood.

V. The Scenery of Quebec; and the River St. Lawrence.

ABOUT twelve o'clock this day, being in the Lower Town, I looked up at the signal-gun by the flagstaff on Cape Diamond, and saw a soldier up in the heavens there making preparations to fire it,–both he and the gun in bold relief against the sky. Soon after, being warned by the boom of the gun to look up again, there was only the cannon in the sky, the smoke just blowing away from it, as if the soldier, having touched it off, had concealed himself for effect, leaving the sound to echo grandly from shore to shore, and far up and down the river. This answered the purpose of a dinner-horn.

There are no such restaurants in Quebec or Montreal as there are in Boston. I hunted an hour or two in vain in this town to find one, till I lost my appetite. In one house, called a restaurateur, where lunches were advertised, I found only tables covered with bottles and glasses innumerable, containing apparently a sample of every liquid that has been known since the earth dried up after the flood, but no scent of solid food did I perceive gross enough to excite a hungry mouse. In short, I saw nothing to tempt me there, but a large map of Canada against the wall. In another place I once more got as far as the bottles, and then asked for a bill of fare; was told to walk up stairs; had no bill of fare, nothing but fare. "Have you any pies or puddings?" I inquired, for I am obliged to keep my savageness in check by a low diet. "No, sir; we've nice mutton-chop, roast beef, beef-steak, cutlets," and so on. A burly Englishman, who was in the midst of the siege of a piece of roast beef, and of whom I have never had a front view to this day, turned half round, with his mouth half full, and remarked, "You'll find no pies nor puddings in Quebec, sir; they don't make any here." I found that it was even so, and therefore bought some musty cake and some fruit in the open market-place. This market-place by the water-side, where the old women sat by their tables in the open air, amid a dense crowd jabbering all languages, was the best place in Quebec to observe the people; and the ferry-boats, continually coming and going with their motley crews and cargoes, added much to the entertainment. I also saw them getting water from the river, for Quebec is supplied with water by cart and barrel. This city impressed me as wholly foreign and French, for I scarcely heard the sound of the English language in the streets. More than three fifths of the inhabitants are of French origin; and if the traveller did not visit the fortifications particularly, he might not be reminded that the English have any foothold here; and, in any case, if he looked no further than Quebec, they would appear to have planted themselves in Canada only as they have in Spain at Gibraltar; and he who plants upon a rock cannot expect much increase. The novel sights and sounds by the water-side made me think of such ports as Boulogne, Dieppe, Rouen, and Havre de Grace, which I have never seen; but I have no doubt that they present similar scenes. I was much amused from first to last with the sounds made by the charette and caleche drivers. It was that part of their foreign language that you heard the most of,–the French they talked to their horses,–and which they talked the loudest. It was a more novel sound to me than the French of conversation. The streets resounded with the cries, "*Qui donc!*" "*March tôt!*" I suspect that many of our horses which came from Canada would prick up their ears at these sounds. Of the shops, I was most attracted by those where furs and Indian works were sold, as containing articles of genuine Canadian manufacture. I have been told that two townsmen of mine, who were interested in horticulture, travelling once in Canada, and being in Quebec, thought it would be a good opportunity to obtain seeds of the real Canada crook-neck squash. So they went into a shop where such things were advertised, and inquired for the same. The shopkeeper had the very thing they wanted. "But are you sure," they asked, "that these are the genuine Canada crook-neck?" "O yes, gentlemen," answered he, "they are a lot which I have received directly from Boston." I resolved that my Canada crook-neck seeds should be such as had grown in Canada.

Too much has not been said about the scenery of Quebec. The fortifications of Cape Diamond are omnipresent. They preside, they frown over the river and surrounding country. You travel ten, twenty, thirty miles up or down the river's banks, you ramble fifteen miles amid the hills on either side, and then, when you have long since forgotten them, perchance slept on them by the way, at a turn of the road or of your body, there they are still, with their geometry against the sky. The child that is born and brought up thirty miles distant, and has never travelled to the city, reads his country's history, sees the level lines of the citadel amid the cloud-built citadels in the western horizon, and is told that that is Quebec. No wonder if Jacques Cartier's pilot exclaimed in Norman French, *Que bec!*– "What a beak!–" when he saw this cape, as some suppose. Every modern traveller involuntarily uses a similar expression. Particularly it is said that its sudden apparition on turning Point Levi makes a memorable impression on him who arrives by water. The view from Cape Diamond has been compared by European travellers with the most remarkable views of a similar kind in Europe, such as from Edinburgh Castle, Gibraltar, Cintra, and others, and preferred by many. A main peculiarity in this, compared with other views which I have beheld, is that it is from the ramparts of a fortified city, and not from a solitary and majestic river cape alone that this view is obtained. I associate the beauty of Quebec with the steel-like and flashing air, which may be peculiar to that season of the year, in which the blue flowers of the succory and some late golden-rods and buttercups on the summit of Cape Diamond were almost my only companions,–the former bluer than the heavens they faced. Yet even I yielded in some degree to the influence of historical associations, and found it hard to attend to the geology of Cape Diamond or the botany of the Plains of Abraham. I still remember the harbor far beneath me, sparkling like silver in the sun,–the answering highlands of Point Levi on the southeast,–the frowning Cap Tourmente abruptly bounding the sea-ward view far in the northeast,–the villages of Lorette and Charlesbourg on the north,–and further west the distant Val Cartier, sparkling with white cottages, hardly removed by distance through the clear air,–not to mention a few blue mountains along the horizon in that direction. You look out from the ramparts of the citadel beyond the frontiers of civilization. Yonder small group of hills, according to the guide-book, forms "the portal of the wilds which are trodden only by the feet of the Indian hunters as far as Hudson's Bay." It is but a few years since Bouchette declared that the country ten leagues north of the British capital of North America was as little known as the middle of Africa. Thus the citadel under my feet, and all historical associations, were swept away again by an influence from the wilds and from nature, as if the beholder had read her history,–an influence which, like the Great River itself, flowed from the Arctic fastnesses and Western forests with irresistible tide over all.

The most interesting object in Canada to me was the River St. Lawrence, known far and wide, and for centuries, as the Great River. Cartier, its discoverer, sailed up it as far as Montreal in 1535,–nearly a century before the coming of the Pilgrims; and I have seen a pretty accurate map of it so far, containing the city of "Hochelaga" and the river "Saguenay," in Ortelius's *Theatrum Orbis Terrarum*, printed at Antwerp in 1575,–the first edition having appeared in 1570,–in which the famous cities of "Norumbega" and "Orsinora" stand on the rough-blocked continent where New England is to-day, and the fabulous but unfortunate Isle of Demons, and Frislant, and others, lie off and on in the unfrequented sea, some of them prowling near what is now the course of the Cunard steamers. In this ponderous folio of the "Ptolemy of his age," said to be the first general atlas published after the revival of the sciences in Europe, only one page of which is devoted to the topography of the *Novus Orbis*, the St. Lawrence is the only large river, whether drawn from fancy or from observation, on the east side of North America. It was famous in Europe before the other rivers of North America were heard of, notwithstanding that the mouth of the Mississippi is said to have been discovered first, and its stream was reached by Soto not long after; but the St. Lawrence had attracted settlers to its cold shores long before the Mississippi, or even the Hudson, was known to the world. (Schoolcraft was misled by Gallatin into saying that Narvaez discovered the Mississippi. De Vaca does *not* say so.) The first explorers declared that the summer in that country was as warm as France, and they named one of the bays in the Gulf of St. Lawrence the Bay of Chaleur, or of warmth; but they said nothing about the winter being as cold as Greenland. In the manuscript account of Cartier's second voyage, attributed by some to that navigator himself, it is called "the greatest river, without comparison, that is known to have ever been seen." The savages told him that it was the "*chemin du Canada*,"–the highway to Canada,– "which goes so far that no man had ever been to the end that they had heard." The Saguenay, one of its tributaries, which the panorama has made known to New England within three years, is described by Cartier, in 1535, and still more particularly by Jean Alphonse, in 1542, who adds, "I think that this river comes from the sea of Cathay, for in this place there issues a strong current, and there runs there a terrible tide." The early explorers saw many whales and other sea-monsters far up the St. Lawrence. Champlain, in his map, represents a whale spouting in the harbor of Quebec, three hundred and sixty miles from what is called the mouth of the river; and Charlevoix takes his reader to the summit of Cape Diamond to see the "porpoises, white as snow," sporting on the surface of the harbor of Quebec. And Boucher says in 1664, "from there (Tadoussac) to Montreal is found a great quantity of *Marsouins blancs*." Several whales have been taken pretty high up the river since I was there. P. H. Gosse, in his "Canadian Naturalist," p. 171 (London,

1840), speaks of "the white dolphin of the St. Lawrence (*Delphinus Canadensis*)," as considered different from those of the sea. "The Natural History Society of Montreal offered a prize, a few years ago, for an essay on the *Cetacea* of the St. Lawrence, which was, I believe, handed in." In Champlain's day it was commonly called "the Great River of Canada." More than one nation has claimed it. In Ogilby's "America" of 1670, in the map *Novi Belgii*, it is called "De Groote Rivier van Niew Nederlandt." It bears different names in different parts of its course, as it flows through what were formerly the territories of different nations. From the Gulf to Lake Ontario it is called at present the St. Lawrence; from Montreal to the same place it is frequently called the Cataraqui; and higher up it is known successively as the Niagara, Detroit, St. Clair, St. Mary's, and St. Louis rivers. Humboldt, speaking of the Orinoco, says that this name is unknown in the interior of the country; so likewise the tribes that dwell about the sources of the St. Lawrence have never heard the name which it bears in the lower part of its course. It rises near another father of waters,–the Mississippi,– issuing from a remarkable spring far up in the woods, called Lake Superior, fifteen hundred miles in circumference; and several other springs there are thereabouts which feed it. It makes such a noise in its tumbling down at one place as is heard all round the world. Bouchette, the Surveyor-General of the Canadas, calls it "the most splendid river on the globe"; says that it is two thousand statute miles long (more recent geographers make it four or five hundred miles longer); that at the Rivière du Sud it is eleven miles wide; at the Traverse, thirteen; at the Paps of Matane, twenty-five; at the Seven Islands, seventy-three; and at its mouth, from Cape Rosier to the Mingan Settlements in Labrador, near one hundred and five (?)

miles wide. According to Captain Bayfield's recent chart it is about *ninety-six* geographical miles wide at the latter place, measuring at right angles with the stream. It has much the largest estuary, regarding both length and breadth, of any river on the globe. Humboldt says that the river Plate, which has the broadest estuary of the South American rivers, is ninety-two geographical miles wide at its mouth; also he found the Orinoco to be more than three miles wide at five hundred and sixty miles from its mouth; but he does not tell us that ships of six hundred tons can sail up it so far, as they can up the St. Lawrence to Montreal,–an equal distance. If he had described a fleet of such ships at anchor in a city's port so far inland, we should have got a very different idea of the Orinoco. Perhaps Charlevoix describes the St. Lawrence truly as the most *navigable* river in the world. Between Montreal and Quebec it averages about two miles wide. The tide is felt as far up as Three Rivers, four hundred and thirty-two miles, which is as far as from Boston to Washington. As far up as Cap aux Oyes, sixty or seventy miles below Quebec, Kalm found a great part of the plants near the shore to be marine, as glass-wort (*Salicornia*), seaside pease (*Pisum maritimum*), sea-milkwort (*Glaux*), beach-grass (*Psamma arenaria*), seaside plantain (*Plantago maritima*), the sea-rocket (*Bunias cakile*), &c.

The geographer Guyot observes that the Maranon is three thousand miles long, and gathers its waters from a surface of a million and a half square miles; that the Mississippi is also three thousand miles long, but its basin covers only from eight to nine hundred thousand square miles; that the St. Lawrence is eighteen hundred miles long, and its basin covers more than a million square miles (Darby says five hundred thousand); and speaking of the lakes, he adds, "These vast fresh-water seas, together with the St. Lawrence, cover a surface of nearly one hundred thousand square miles, and it has been calculated that they contain almost one half of all the fresh water on the surface of our planet." But all these calculations are necessarily very rude and inaccurate. Its tributaries, the Ottawa, St. Maurice, and Saguenay, are great rivers themselves. The latter is said to be more than one thousand (?) feet deep at its mouth, while its cliffs rise perpendicularly an equal distance above its surface. Pilots say there are no soundings till one hundred and fifty miles up the St. Lawrence. The greatest sounding in the river, given on Bayfield's chart of the gulf and river, is two hundred and twenty-eight fathoms. Mac-Taggart, an engineer, observes that "the Ottawa is larger than all the rivers in Great Britain, were they running in one." The traveller Gray writes: "A dozen Danubes, Rhines, Taguses, and Thameses would be nothing to twenty miles of fresh water in breadth (as where he happened to be), from ten to forty fathoms in depth." And again: "There is not perhaps in the whole extent of this immense continent so fine an approach to it as by the river St. Lawrence. In the Southern States you have, in general, a level country for many miles inland; here you are introduced at once into a majestic scenery, where everything is on a grand scale,–mountains, woods, lakes, rivers, precipices, waterfalls."

We have not yet the data for a minute comparison of the St. Lawrence with the South American rivers; but it is obvious that, taking it in connection with its lakes, its estuary, and its falls, it easily bears off the palm from all the rivers on the globe; for though, as Bouchette observes, it may not carry to the ocean a greater volume of water than the Amazon and Mississippi, its surface and cubic mass are far greater than theirs. But, unfortunately, this noble river is closed by ice from the beginning of December to the middle of April. The arrival of the first vessel from England when the ice breaks up is, therefore, a great event, as when the salmon, shad, and alewives come up a river in the spring to relieve the famishing inhabitants on its banks. Who can say what would have been the history of this continent if, as has been suggested, this river had emptied into the sea where New York stands!

After visiting the Museum and taking one more look at the wall, I made haste to the Lord Sydenham steamer, which at five o'clock was to leave for Montreal. I had already taken a seat on deck, but finding that I had still an hour and a half to spare, and remembering that large map of Canada which I had seen in the parlor of the restaurant in my search after pudding, and realizing that I might never see the like out of the country, I returned thither, asked liberty to look at the map, rolled up the mahogany table, put my handkerchief on it, stood on it, and copied all I wanted before the maid came in and said to me standing on the table, "Some gentlemen want the room, sir"; and I retreated without having broken the neck of a single bottle, or my own, very thankful and willing to pay for all the solid food I had got. We were soon abreast of Cap Rouge, eight miles above Quebec, after we got underway. It was in this place, then called "*Fort du France Roy*," that the Sieur de Roberval with his company, having sent home two of his three ships, spent the winter of 1542-43. It appears that they fared in the following manner (I translate from the original): "Each mess had only two loaves, weighing each a pound, and half a pound of beef. They ate pork for dinner, with half a pound of butter, and beef for supper, with about two handfuls of beans, without butter. Wednesdays, Fridays, and Saturdays they ate salted cod, and sometimes green, for dinner, with butter; and porpoise and beans for supper. Monsieur Roberval administered good justice, and punished each according to his offence. One, named Michel Gaillon, was hung for theft; John of Nantes was put in irons and imprisoned for his fault; and others were likewise put in irons; and many were whipped, both men and women; by which means they lived in peace and tranquillity." In an account of a voyage up this river, printed in the Jesuit Relations in the year 1664, it is said: "It was an interesting navigation for us in ascending the river from Cap Tourment to Quebec, to see on this side and on that, for the space of eight leagues, the farms and the houses of the company, built by our French, all along these shores. On the right, the seigniories of Beauport, of Notre Dame des Anges; and on the left, this beautiful Isle of Orleans." The same traveller names among the fruits of the country observed at the Isles of Richelieu, at the head of Lake St. Peter, "kinds (*des espèces*) of little apples or haws (*senelles*), and of pears, which only ripen with the frost."

Night came on before we had passed the high banks. We had come from Montreal to Quebec in one night. The return voyage, against the stream, takes but an hour longer. Jacques Cartier, the first white man who is known to have ascended this river, thus speaks of his voyage from what is now Quebec to the foot of Lake St. Peter, or about half-way to Montreal: "From the said day, the 19th, even to the 28th of the said month, [September, 1535] we had been navigating up the said river without losing hour or day, during which time we had seen and found as much country and lands as level as we could desire, full of the most beautiful trees in the world," which he goes on to describe. But we merely slept and woke again to find that we had passed through all that country which he was eight days in sailing through. He must have had a troubled sleep. We were not long enough on the river to realize that it had length; we got only the impression of its breadth, as if we had passed over a lake a mile or two in breadth and several miles long, though we might thus have slept through a European kingdom. Being at the head of Lake St. Peter, on the above-mentioned 28th of September, dealing with the natives, Cartier says: "We inquired of them by signs if this was the route to Hochelaga [Montreal]; and they answered that it was, and that there were yet three days' journeys to go there." He finally arrived at Hochelaga on the 2d of October.

When I went on deck at dawn we had already passed through Lake St. Peter, and saw islands ahead of us. Our boat advancing with a strong and steady pulse over the calm surface, we felt as if we were permitted to be awake in the scenery of a dream. Many vivacious Lombardy poplars along the distant shores gave them a novel and lively, though artificial, look, and contrasted strangely with the slender and graceful elms on both shores and islands. The church of Varennes, fifteen miles from Montreal, was conspicuous at a great distance before us, appearing to belong to, and rise out of, the river; and now, and before, Mount Royal indicated where the city was. We arrived about seven o'clock, and set forth immediately to ascend the mountain, two miles distant, going across lots in spite of numerous signs threatening the severest penalties to trespassers, past an old building known as the McTavish property,–Simon McTavish, I suppose, whom Silliman refers to as "in a sense the founder of the Northwestern Company." His tomb was behind in the woods, with a remarkably high wall and higher monument. The family returned to Europe. He could not have imagined how dead he would be in a few years, and all the more dead and forgotten for being buried under such a mass of gloomy stone, where not even memory could get at him without a crowbar. Ah! poor man, with that last end of his! However, he may have been the worthiest of mortals for aught that I know. From the mountain-top we got a view of the whole city; the flat, fertile, extensive island; the noble sea of the St. Lawrence swelling into lakes; the mountains about St. Hyacinth, and in Vermont and New York; and the mouth of the Ottawa in the west, overlooking that St. Ann's where the voyageur sings his "parting hymn," and bids adieu to civilization,–a name, thanks to Moore's verses, the most suggestive of poetic associations of any in Canada. We, too, climbed the hill which Cartier, first of white men, ascended, and named Mont-real, (the 3d of October, O. S., 1535,) and, like him, "we saw the said river as far as we could see, *grand, large, et spacieux*, going to the southwest," toward that land whither Donnacona had told the discoverer that he had been a month's journey from Canada, where there grew "*force Canelle et Girofle*," much cinnamon and cloves, and where also, as the natives told him, were three great lakes and afterward *une mer douce*,–a sweet sea,–*de laquelle n'est mention avoir vu le bout*, of which there is no mention to have seen the end. But instead of an Indian town far in the interior of a new world, with guides to show us where the river came from, we found a splendid and bustling stone-built city of white men, and only a few squalid Indians offered to sell us baskets at the Lachine Railroad Depot, and Hochelaga is, perchance, but the fancy name of an engine company or an eating-house.

We left Montreal Wednesday, the 2d of October, late in the afternoon. In the La Prairie cars the Yankees made themselves merry, imitating the cries of the charette-drivers to perfection, greatly to the amusement of some French-Canadian travellers, and they kept it up all the way to Boston. I saw one person on board the boat at St. John's, and one or two more elsewhere in Canada, wearing homespun gray great-coats, or capotes, with conical and comical hoods, which fell back between their shoulders like small bags, ready to be turned up over the head when occasion required, though a hat usurped that place now. They looked as if they would be convenient and proper enough as long as the coats were new and tidy, but would soon come to have a beggarly and unsightly look, akin to rags and dust-holes. We reached Burlington early in the morning, where the Yankees tried to pass off their Canada coppers, but the news-boys knew better. Returning through the Green Mountains, I was reminded that I had not seen in Canada such brilliant autumnal tints as I had previously seen in Vermont. Perhaps there was not yet so great and sudden a contrast with the summer heats in the former country as in these mountain valleys. As we were passing through Ashburnham, by a new white house which stood at some distance in a field, one passenger exclaimed, so that all in the car could hear him, "There, there's not so good a house as that in all Canada!" I did not much wonder at his remark, for there is a neatness, as well as evident prosperity, a certain elastic easiness of circumstances, so to speak, when not rich, about a New England house, as if the proprietor could at least afford to make repairs in the spring, which the Canadian houses do not suggest. Though of stone, they are no better constructed than a stone barn would be with us; the only building, except the chateau, on which money and taste are expended, being the church. In Canada an ordinary New England house would be mistaken for the chateau, and while every village here contains at least several gentlemen or "squires," *there* there is but one to a seigniory.

I got home this Thursday evening, having spent just one week in Canada and travelled eleven hundred miles. The whole expense of this journey, including two guidebooks and a map, which cost one dollar twelve and a half cents, was twelve dollars seventy-five cents. I do not suppose that I have seen all British America; that could not be done by a cheap excursion, unless it were a cheap excursion to the Icy Sea, as seen by Hearne or Mackenzie, and then, no doubt, some interesting features would be omitted. I wished to go a little way behind that word *Canadense*, of which naturalists make such frequent use; and I should like still right well to make a longer excursion on foot through the wilder parts of Canada, which perhaps might be called *Iter Canadense.*

An Address on the Succession of Forest Trees.

Ladies and Gentlemen:

EVERY MAN is entitled to come to Cattle-show, even a transcendentalist; and for my part I am more interested in the men than in the cattle. I wish to see once more those old familiar faces, whose names I do not know, which for me represent the Middlesex country, and come as near being indigenous to the soil as a white man can; the men who are not above their business, whose coats are not too black, whose shoes do not shine very much, who never wear gloves to conceal their hands. It is true, there are some queer specimens of humanity attracted to our festival, but all are welcome. I am pretty sure to meet once more that weak-minded and whimsical fellow, generally weak-bodied too, who prefers a crooked stick for a cane; perfectly useless, you would say, only bizarre, fit for a cabinet, like a petrified snake. A ram's horn would be as convenient, and is yet more curiously twisted. He brings that much indulged bit of the country with him, from some town's end or other, and introduces it to Concord groves, as if he had promised it so much sometime. So some, it seems to me, elect their rulers for their crookedness. But I think that a straight stick makes the best cane, and an upright man the best ruler. Or why choose a man to do plain work who is distinguished for his oddity? However, I do not know but you will think that they have committed this mistake who invited me to speak to you to-day.

In my capacity of surveyor, I have often talked with some of you, my employers, at your dinner-tables, after having gone round and round and behind your farming, and ascertained exactly what its limits were. Moreover, taking a surveyor's and a naturalist's liberty, I have been in the habit of going across your lots much oftener than is usual, as many of you, perhaps to your sorrow, are aware. Yet many of you, to my relief, have seemed not to be aware of it; and when I came across you in some out-of-the-way nook of your farms, have inquired, with an air of surprise, if I were not lost, since you had never seen me in that part of the town or county before; when, if the truth were known, and it had not been for betraying my secret, I might with more propriety have inquired if *you* were not lost, since I had never seen *you* there before. I have several times shown the proprietor the shortest way out of his woodlot.

Therefore, it would seem that I have some title to speak to you to-day; and considering what that title is, and the occasion that has called us together, I need offer no apology if I invite your attention, for the few moments that are allotted me, to a purely scientific subject.

At those dinner-tables referred to, I have often been asked, as many of you have been, if I could tell how it happened, that when a pine wood was cut down an oak one commonly sprang up, and *vice versa*. To which I have answered, and now answer, that I can tell—that it is no mystery to me. As I am not aware that this has been clearly shown by any one, I shall lay the more stress on this point. Let me lead you back into your woodlots again.

When, hereabouts, a single forest tree or a forest springs up naturally where none of its kind grew before, I do not hesitate to say, though in some quarters still it may sound paradoxical, that it came from a seed. Of the various ways by which trees are *known* to be propagated—by transplanting, cuttings, and the

like–this is the only supposable one under these circumstances. No such tree has ever been known to
spring from any thing else. If any one asserts that it
sprang from something else, or from nothing, the burden of proof lies with him.

It remains then only to show how the seed is trans-
ported from where it grows to where it is planted. This
is done chiefly by the agency of the wind, water and
animals. The lighter seeds, as those of pines and
maples, are transported chiefly by wind and water;
the heavier, as acorns and nuts, by animals.

In all the pines, a very thin membrane, in appearance much like an insect's wing, grows over and
around the seed, and independent of it, while the latter is being developed within its base. Indeed this is
often perfectly developed, though the seed is abortive,
nature being, you would say, more sure to provide the
means of transporting the seed, than to provide the
seed to be transported. In other words, a beautiful thin
sack is woven around the seed, with a handle to it such
as the wind can take hold of, and it is then committed
to the wind, expressly that it may transport the seed
and extend the range of the species; and this it does as
effectually as when seeds are sent by mail in a different
kind of sack from the patent office. There is a patent
office at the seat of government of the universe, whose
managers are as much interested in the dispersion of
seeds as any body at Washington can be, and their operations are infinitely more extensive and regular.

There is then no necessity for supposing that the
pines have sprung up from nothing, and I am aware
that I am not at all peculiar in asserting that they come
from seeds, though the mode of their propagation *by
nature* has been but little attended to. They are very
extensively raised from the seed in Europe, and are beginning to be here.

When you cut down an oak wood, a pine wood will not *at once* spring up there unless there are, or have been, quite recently, seed-bearing pines near enough for the seeds to be blown from them. But, adjacent to a forest of pines, if you prevent other crops from growing there, you will surely have an extension of your pine forest, provided the soil is suitable.

As for the heavy seeds and nuts which are not furnished with wings, the notion is still a very common one that, when the trees which bear these spring up where none of their kind were noticed before, they have come from seeds or other principles spontaneously generated there in an unusual manner, or which have lain dormant in the soil for centuries, or perhaps been called into activity by the heat of a burning. I do not believe these assertions, and I will state some of the ways in which, according to my observation, such forests are planted and raised.

Every one of these seeds, too, will be found to be winged or legged in another fashion. Surely it is not wonderful that cherry-trees of all kinds are widely dispersed, since their fruit is well known to be the favorite food of various birds. Many kinds are called bird-cherries, and they appropriate many more kinds, which are not so called. Eating cherries is a bird-like employment, and unless we disperse the seeds occasionally, as they do, I shall think that the birds have the best right to them. See how artfully the seed of a cherry is placed in order that a bird may be compelled to transport it–in the very midst of a tempting pericarp, so that the creature that would devour this must commonly take the stone also into its mouth or bill. If you ever ate a cherry, and did not make two bites of it, you must have perceived it–right in the centre of the luscious morsel, a large earthy residuum left on the tongue. We thus take into our mouths cherry stones as big as peas, a dozen at once, for Nature can persuade us to do almost anything when she would compass her ends. Some wild men and children instinctively swallow these, as the birds do when in a hurry, it being the shortest way to get rid of them. Thus, though these seeds are not provided with vegetable wings, Nature has impelled the thrush tribe to take them into their bills and fly away with them, and they are winged in another sense, and more effectually than the seeds of pines, for these are carried even against the wind. The consequence is, that cherry trees grow not only here but there. The same is true of a great many other seeds.

But to come to the observation which suggested these remarks. As I have said, I suspect that I can throw some light on the fact, that when hereabouts a dense pine wood is cut down, oaks and other hard woods may at once take its place. I have got only to show that the acorns and nuts, provided they are grown in the neighborhood, are regularly planted in such woods; for I assert that if an oak tree has not grown within ten miles, and man has not carried acorns thither, then an oak wood will not spring up *at once* when a pine wood is cut down.

Apparently, there were only pines there before. They are cut off, and after a year or two you see oaks and other hard woods springing up there, with scarcely a pine amid them, and the wonder commonly is how the seed could have lain in the ground so long without decaying. But the truth is, that it has not lain in the ground so long, but is regularly planted each year by various quadrupeds and birds.

In this neighborhood, where oaks and pines are about equally dispersed, if you look through the thickest pine wood, even the seemingly unmixed pitch-pine ones, you will commonly detect many little oaks, birches, and other hard woods, sprung from seeds carried into the thicket by squirrels and other animals, and also blown thither, but which are overshadowed and choked by the pines. The denser the evergreen wood, the more likely it is to be well planted with these seeds, because the planters incline to resort with their forage to the closest covert. They also carry it into birch and other woods. This planting is carried on annually, and the oldest seedlings annually die; but when the pines are cleared off, the oaks, having got just the start they want, and now secured favorable conditions, immediately spring up to trees.

The shade of a dense pine wood is more unfavorable to the springing up of pines of the same species than of oaks within it, though the former may come up abundantly when the pines are cut, if there chance to be sound seed in the ground.

But when you cut off a lot of hard wood, very often the little pines mixed with it have a similar start, for the squirrels have carried off the nuts to the pines, and not to the more open wood, and they commonly make pretty clean work of it; and moreover, if the wood was old, the sprouts will be feeble or entirely fail; to say nothing about the soil being, in a measure, exhausted for this kind of crop.

If a pine wood is surrounded by a white oak one chiefly, white oaks may be expected to succeed when the pines are cut. If it is surrounded instead by an edging of shruboaks, then you will probably have a dense shruboak thicket.

I have no time to go into details, but will say, in a word, that while the wind is conveying the seeds of pines into hard woods and open lands, the squirrels and other animals are conveying the seeds of oaks and walnuts into the pine woods, and thus a rotation of crops is kept up.

I affirmed this confidently many years ago, and an occasional examination of dense pine woods confirmed me in my opinion. It has long been known to observers that squirrels bury nuts in the ground, but I am not aware that any one has thus accounted for the regular succession of forests.

On the 24th of September, in '57, as I was paddling down the Assabet, in this town, I saw a red squirrel run along the bank under some herbage, with something large in its mouth. It stopped near the foot of a hemlock, within a couple of rods of me, and, hastily pawing a hole with its fore feet, dropped its booty into it, covered it up, and retreated part way up the trunk of the tree. As I approached the shore to examine the deposit, the squirrel, descending part way, betrayed no little anxiety about its treasure, and made two or three motions to recover it before it finally retreated. Digging there, I found two green pig nuts joined together, with the thick husks on, buried about an inch and a half under the reddish soil of decayed hemlock leaves– just the right depth to plant it. In short, this squirrel was then engaged in accomplishing two objects, to wit, laying up a store of winter food for itself, and planting a hickory wood for all creation. If the squirrel was killed, or neglected its deposit, a hickory would spring up. The nearest hickory tree was twenty rods distant. These nuts were there still just fourteen days later, but were gone when I looked again, Nov. 21, or six weeks later still.

I have since examined more carefully several dense woods, which are said to be, and are apparently exclusively pine, and always with the same result. For instance, I walked the same day to a small, but very dense and handsome white-pine grove, about fifteen rods square, in the east part of this town. The trees are large for Concord, being from ten to twenty inches in diameter, and as exclusively pine as any wood that I know. Indeed, I selected this wood because I thought it the least likely to contain anything else. It stands on an open plain or pasture, except that it adjoins another small pine wood, which has a few little oaks in it, on the south-east side. On every other side, it was at least thirty rods from the nearest woods. Standing on the edge of this grove and looking through it, for it is quite level and free from underwood, for the most part bare, red-carpeted ground, you would have said that there was not a hard wood tree in it, young or old. But on looking carefully along over its floor I discovered, though it was not till my eye had got used to the search, that, alternating with thin ferns, and small blueberry bushes, there was, not merely here and there, but as often as every five feet, and with a degree of regularity, a little oak, from three to twelve inches high, and in one place I found a green acorn dropped by the base of a pine.

I confess I was surprised to find my theory so perfectly proved in this case. One of the principal agents in this planting, the red squirrels, were all the while curiously inspecting me, while I was inspecting their plantation. Some of the little oaks had been browsed by cows, which resorted to this wood for shade.

After seven or eight years, the hard woods evidently find such a locality unfavorable to their growth, the pines being allowed to stand. As an evidence of this, I observed a diseased red maple twenty-five feet long, which had been recently prostrated, though it was still covered with green leaves, the only maple in any position in the wood.

But although these oaks almost invariably die if the pines are not cut down, it is probable that they do better for a few years under their shelter than they would anywhere else.

The very extensive and thorough experiments of the English have at length led them to adopt a method of raising oaks almost precisely like this, which somewhat earlier had been adopted by nature and her squirrels here; they have simply re-discovered the value of pines as nurses for oaks. The English experimenters seem early and generally to have found out the importance of using trees of some kind as nurse plants for the young oaks. I quote from Loudon what he describes as "the ultimatum on the subject of planting and sheltering oaks"–an "abstract of the practice adopted by the Government officers in the national forests" of England, prepared by Alexander Milne.

At first some oaks had been planted by themselves, and others mixed with Scotch pines; "but in all cases," says Mr. Milne, "where oaks were planted actually among the pines, and surrounded by them, [though the soil might be inferior,] the oaks were found to be much the best." "For several years past, the plan pursued has been to plant the inclosures with Scotch pines only, [a tree very similar to our pitch pine,] and when the pines have got to the height of five or six feet, then to put in good strong oak plants of about four or five years' growth among the pines–not cutting away any pines at first, unless they happen to be so strong and thick as to overshadow the oaks. In about two years, it becomes necessary to shred the branches of the pines, to give light and air to the oaks, and in about two or three more years to begin gradually to remove the pines altogether, taking out a certain number each year, so that, at the end of twenty or twenty-five years, not a single Scotch pine shall be left; although, for the first ten or twelve years, the plantation may have appeared to contain nothing else but pine. The advantage of this mode of planting has been found to be that the pines dry and ameliorate the soil, destroying the coarse grass and brambles which frequently choke and injure oaks; and that no mending over is necessary, as scarcely an oak so planted is found to fail."

Thus much the English planters have discovered by patient experiment, and, for aught I know, they have taken out a patent for it; but they appear not to have discovered that it was discovered before, and that they are merely adopting the method of Nature, which she long ago made patent to all. She is all the while planting the oaks amid the pines without our knowledge, and at last, instead of Government officers, we send a party of wood-choppers to cut down the pines, and so rescue an oak forest, at which we wonder as if it had dropped from the skies.

As I walk amid hickories, even in August, I hear the sound of green pig-nuts falling from time to time, cut off by the chickaree over my head. In the fall, I notice on the ground, either within or in the neighborhood of oak woods, on all sides of the town, stout oak twigs three or four inches long, bearing half-a-dozen empty acorn-cups, which twigs have been gnawed off by squirrels, on both sides of the nuts, in order to make them more portable. The jays scream and the red squirrels scold while you are clubbing and shaking the chestnut trees, for they are there on the same errand, and two of a trade never agree. I frequently see a red or gray squirrel cast down a green chestnut bur, as I am going through the woods, and I used to think, sometimes, that they were cast at me. In fact, they are so busy about it, in the midst of the chestnut season, that you cannot stand long in the woods without hearing one fall. A sportsman told me that he had, the day before–that was in the middle of October–seen a green chestnut bur dropt on our great river meadow, fifty

rods from the nearest wood, and much further from
the nearest chestnut tree, and he could not tell how it
came there. Occasionally, when chestnutting in mid-
winter, I find thirty or forty nuts in a pile, left in its
gallery, just under the leaves, by the common wood-
mouse (*mus leucopus.*)

But especially in the winter the extent to which this
transportation and planting of nuts is carried on is
made apparent by the snow. In almost every wood,
you will see where the red or gray squirrels have
pawed down through the snow in a hundred places,
sometimes two feet deep, and almost always directly
to a nut or a pine-cone, as directly as if they had
started from it and bored upward–which you and I
could not have done. It would be difficult for us to find
one before the snow falls. Commonly, no doubt, they
had deposited them there in the fall. You wonder if
they remember the localities, or discover them by the
scent. The red squirrel commonly has its winter abode
in the earth under a thicket of evergreens, frequently
under a small clump of evergreens in the midst of a
deciduous wood. If there are any nut-trees, which still
retain their nuts, standing at a distance without the
wood, their paths often lead directly to and from them.
We, therefore, need not suppose an oak standing here
and there *in* the wood in order to seed it, but if a few
stand within twenty or thirty rods of it, it is sufficient.

I think that I may venture to say that every white-
pine cone that falls to the earth naturally in this town,
before opening and losing its seeds, and almost every
pitch-pine one that falls at all, is cut off by a squirrel,
and they begin to pluck them long before they are ripe,
so that when the crop of white-pine cones is a small
one, as it commonly is, they cut off thus almost every
one of these before it fairly ripens. I think, moreover,

that their design, if I may so speak, in cutting them off green, is, partly, to prevent their opening and losing their seeds, for these are the ones for which they dig through the snow, and the only white-pine cones which contain anything then. I have counted in one heap, within a diameter of four feet, the cores of 239 pitch-pine cones which had been cut off and stripped by the red squirrel the previous winter.

The nuts thus left on the surface, or buried just beneath it, are placed in the most favorable circumstances for germinating. I have sometimes wondered how those which merely fell on the surface of the earth got planted; but, by the end of December, I find the chestnuts of the same year partially mixed with the mold, as it were, under the decaying and moldy leaves, where there is all the moisture and manure they want, for the nuts fall first. In a plentiful year, a large proportion of the nuts are thus covered loosely an inch deep, and are, of course, somewhat concealed from squirrels. One winter, when the crop had been abundant, I got, with the aid of a rake, many quarts of these nuts as late as the 10th of January, and though some bought at the store the same day were more than half of them moldy, I did not find a single moldy one among these which I picked from under the wet and moldy leaves, where they had been snowed on once or twice. Nature knows how to pack them best. They were still plump and tender. Apparently, they do not heat there, though wet. In the spring they were all sprouting.

Loudon says that "when the nut [of the common walnut of Europe] is to be preserved through the winter for the purpose of planting in the following spring, it should be laid in a rot heap, as soon as gathered, with the husk on; and the heap should be turned over frequently in the course of the winter."

Here, again, he is stealing Nature's "thunder." How can a poor mortal do otherwise? for it is she that finds fingers to steal with, and the treasure to be stolen. In the planting of the seeds of most trees, the best gardeners do no more than follow Nature, though they may not know it. Generally, both large and small ones are most sure to germinate, and succeed best, when only beaten into the earth with the back of a spade, and then covered with leaves or straw. These results to which planters have arrived, remind us of the experience of Kane and his companions at the North, who, when learning to live in that climate, were surprised to find themselves steadily adopting the customs of the natives, simply becoming Esquimaux. So, when we experiment in planting forests, we find ourselves at last doing as Nature does. Would it not be well to consult with Nature in the outset? for she is the most extensive and experienced planter of us all, not excepting the Dukes of Athol.

In short, they who have not attended particularly to this subject are but little aware to what an extent quadrupeds and birds are employed, especially in the fall, in collecting, and so disseminating and planting the seeds of trees. It is the almost constant employment of the squirrels at that season and you rarely meet with one that has not a nut in its mouth, or is not just going to get one. One squirrel-hunter of this town told me that he knew of a walnut tree which bore particularly good nuts, but that on going to gather them one fall, he found that he had been anticipated by a family of a dozen red squirrels. He took out of the tree, which was hollow, one bushel and three pecks by measurement, without the husks, and they supplied him and his family for the winter. It would be easy to multiply instances of this kind. How commonly in the fall you see

the cheek-pouches of the striped squirrel distended
by a quantity of nuts! This species gets its scientific
name *Tamias*, or the steward, from its habit of storing
up nuts and other seeds. Look under a nut-tree a
month after the nuts have fallen, and see what proportion of sound nuts to the abortive ones and shells you
will find ordinarily. They have been already eaten, or
dispersed far and wide. The ground looks like a platform before a grocery, where the gossips of the village
sit to crack nuts and less savory jokes. You have come,
you would say, after the feast was over, and are presented with the shells only.

Occasionally, when threading the woods in the fall,
you will hear a sound as if some one had broken a twig,
and, looking up, see a jay pecking at an acorn, or you
will see a flock of them at once about it, in the top of an
oak, and hear them break them off. They then fly to a
suitable limb, and, placing the acorn under one foot,
hammer away at it busily, making a sound like a wood
pecker's tapping, looking round from time to time to
see if any foe is approaching, and soon reach the meat,
and nibble at it, holding up their heads to swallow,
while they hold the remainder very firmly with their
claws. Nevertheless, it often drops to the ground before the bird has done with it. I can confirm what Wm.
Bartram wrote to Wilson, the Ornithologist, that "The
jay is one of the most useful agents in the economy of
nature, for disseminating forest trees and other nuciferous and hard-seeded vegetables on which they feed.
Their chief employment during the autumnal season
is foraging to supply their winter stores. In performing
this necessary duty they drop abundance of seed in
their flight over fields, hedges, and by fences where
they alight to deposit them in the post-holes, &c. It is
remarkable what numbers of young trees rise up in

fields and pastures after a wet winter and spring. These birds alone are capable, in a few years time, to replant all the cleared lands."

I have noticed that squirrels also frequently drop their nuts in open land, which will still further account for the oaks and walnuts which spring up in pastures, for, depend on it, every new tree comes from a seed. When I examine the little oaks, one or two years old, in such places, I invariably find the empty acorn from which they sprung.

So far from the seed having lain dormant in the soil since oaks grew there before, as many believe, it is well known that it is difficult to preserve the vitality of acorns long enough to transport them to Europe; and it is recommended in Loudon's Arboretum, as the safest course, to sprout them in pots on the voyage. The same authority states that "very few acorns of any species will germinate after having been kept a year," that beech mast "only retains its vital properties one year," and the black walnut, "seldom more than six months after it has ripened." I have frequently found that in November almost every acorn left on the ground had sprouted or decayed. What with frost, drouth, moisture, and worms, the greater part are soon destroyed. Yet it is stated by one botanical writer that "acorns that have lain for centuries, on being plowed up, have soon vegetated."

Mr. George B. Emerson, in his valuable Report on the Trees and Shrubs of this State, says of the pines: "The tenacity of life of the seeds is remarkable. They will remain for many years unchanged in the ground, protected by the coolness and deep shade of the forest above them. But when the forest is removed, and the warmth of the sun admitted, they immediately vegetate." Since he does not tell us on what observation his remark is founded, I must doubt its truth. Besides, the experience of nurserymen makes it the more questionable.

The stories of wheat raised from seed buried with an ancient Egyptian, and of raspberries raised from seed found in the stomach of a man in England, who is supposed to have died sixteen or seventeen hundred years ago, are generally discredited, simply because the evidence is not conclusive.

Several men of science, Dr. Carpenter among them, have used the statement that beach-plums sprang up in sand which was dug up forty miles inland in Maine, to prove that the seed had lain there a very long time, and some have inferred that the coast has receded so far. But it seems to me necessary to their argument to show, first, that beach-plums grow only on a beach. They are not uncommon here, which is about half that distance from the shore, and I remember a dense patch a few miles north of us, twenty-five miles inland, from which the fruit was annually carried to market. How much further inland they grow, I know not. Dr. Chas. T. Jackson speaks of finding "beach-plums" (perhaps they were this kind) more than one hundred miles inland in Maine.

It chances that similar objections lie against all the more notorious instances of the kind on record.

Yet I am prepared to believe that some seeds, especially small ones, may retain their vitality for centuries under favorable circumstances. In the spring of 1859, the old Hunt House, so called, in this town, whose chimney bore the date 1703, was taken down. This stood on land which belonged to John Winthrop, the first Governor of Massachusetts, and a part of the house was evidently much older than the above date, and belonged to the Winthrop family. For many years, I have ransacked this neighborhood for plants, and I consider myself familiar with its productions. Thinking of the seeds which are said to be sometimes dug up at an unusual depth in the earth, and thus to reproduce long extinct plants, it occurred to me last fall that some new or rare plants might have sprung up in the cellar of this house, which had been covered from the light so long. Searching there on the 22d of September, I found, among other rank weeds, a species of nettle (Urtica urens) which I had not found before; dill, which I had not seen growing spontaneously; the Jerusalem oak, (Chenopodium botrys) which I had seen wild in but one place; black nightshade (Solanum nigrum,) which is quite rare hereabouts, and common tobacco, which, though it was often cultivated here in the last century, has for fifty years been an unknown plant in this town, and a few months before this not even I had heard that one man in the north part of the town was cultivating a few plants for his own use. I have no doubt that some or all of these plants sprang from seeds which had long been buried under or about that house, and that that tobacco is an additional evidence that the plant was formerly cultivated here. The cellar has been filled up this year, and four of those plants, including the tobacco, are now again extinct in that locality.

It is true, I have shown that the animals consume a great part of the seeds of trees, and so, at least, effectually prevent their becoming trees; but in all these cases, as I have said, the consumer is compelled to be at the same time the disperser and planter, and this is the tax which he pays to nature. I think it is Linnæus who says that while the swine is rooting for acorns he is planting acorns.

Though I do not believe that a plant will spring up where no seed has been, I have great faith in a seed–a, to me, equally mysterious origin for it. Convince me that you have a seed there, and I am prepared to expect wonders. I shall even believe that the millennium is at hand, and that the reign of justice is about to commence, when the Patent Office, or Government, begins to distribute, and the people to plant the seeds of these things.

In the spring of '57, I planted six seeds sent to me from the Patent Office, and labeled, I think, "*Poitrine jaune grosse*," large yellow squash. Two came up, and one bore a squash which weighed 123 1-2 pounds, the other bore four, weighing together 186 1-4 pounds. Who would have believed that there were 310 pounds of *poitrine jaune grosse* in that corner of my garden? These seeds were the bait I used to catch it, my ferrets which I sent into its burrow, my brace of terriers which unearthed it. A little mysterious hoeing and manuring was all the *abra cadabra presto-change*, that I used, and lo! true to the label, they found for me 310 pounds of *poitrine jaune grosse* there, where it never was known to be, nor was before. These talismans had perchance sprung from America at first, and returned to it with unabated force. The big squash took a premium at your fair that fall, and I understood that the man who bought it intended to sell the seeds for ten cents a piece. (Were they not cheap at that?) But I have more hounds of the same breed. I learn that one which I dispatched to a distant town, true to its instinct, points the large yellow squash there too, where no hound ever found it before, as its ancestors did here and in France.

Other seeds I have which will find other things in that corner of my garden, in like fashion, almost any fruit you wish, every year for ages, until the crop more than fills the whole garden. You have but little more to do than throw up your cap for entertainment these American days. Perfect alchemists I keep, who can transmute substances without end; and thus the corner of my garden is an inexhaustible treasure chest. Here you can dig, not gold, but the value which gold merely represents; and there is no Signor Blitz about it. Yet farmers' sons will stare by the hour to see a juggler draw ribbons from his throat, though he tells them it is all deception. Surely, men love darkness rather than light.

Walking

I WISH to speak a word for Nature, for absolute Freedom and Wildness, as contrasted with a Freedom and Culture merely civil,–to regard man as an inhabitant, or a part and parcel of Nature, rather than a member of society. I wish to make an extreme statement, if so I may make an emphatic one, for there are enough champions of civilization; the minister, and the school-committee, and every one of you will take care of that.

I have met with but one or two persons in the course of my life who understood the art of Walking, that is, of taking walks, who had a genius, so to speak, for *sauntering*; which word is beautifully derived "from idle people who roved about the country, in the middle ages, and asked charity, under pretence of going *à la sainte terre*"–to the holy land, till the children exclaimed, "There goes a *sainte-terrer*", a saunterer–a holy-lander. They who never go to the holy land in their walks, as they pretend, are indeed mere idlers and vagabonds, but they who do go there are saunterers in the good sense, such as I mean. Some, however, would derive the word from *sans terre*, without land or a home, which, therefore, in the good sense, will mean, having no particular home, but equally at home everywhere. For this is the secret of successful sauntering. He who sits still in a house all the time may be the greatest vagrant of all, but the Saunterer, in the good sense, is no more vagrant than the meandering river, which is all the while sedulously seeking the shortest course to the sea. But I prefer the first, which indeed is the most probable derivation. For every walk is a sort of crusade, preached by some Peter the Hermit in us, to go forth and reconquer this holy land from the hands of the Infidels.

It is true, we are but faint hearted crusaders, even the walkers, now-a-days, who undertake no persevering never ending enterprises. Our expeditions are but tours and come round again at evening to the old hearth side from which we set out. Half the walk is but retracing our steps. We should go forth on the shortest walk, perchance, in the spirit of undying adventure, never to return; prepared to send back our embalmed hearts only, as relics to our desolate kingdoms. If you are prepared to leave father and mother, and brother and sister, and wife and child and friends, and never see them again; if you have paid your debts, and made your will, and settled all your affairs, and are a free man; then you are ready for a walk.

To come down to my own experience, my companion and I, for I sometimes have a companion, take pleasure in fancying ourselves knights of a new, or rather an old, order–not Equestrians or Chevaliers, not Ritters or Riders, but Walkers, a still more ancient and honorable class I trust. The chivalric and heroic spirit which once belonged to the rider seems now to reside in–or perchance to have subsided into the Walker–not the Knight but Walker Errant. He is a sort of 4th estate– outside to Church and State and People.

We have felt that we almost alone hereabouts practised this noble art; though, to tell the truth, at least, if their own assertions are to be received, most of my townsmen would fain walk sometimes, as I do, but they cannot. No wealth can buy the requisite leisure, freedom, and independence, which are the capital in this profession. It comes only by the grace of God. It requires a direct dispensation from heaven to become a walker. You must be born into the family of the Walkers. *Ambulator nascitur, non fit.* Some of my townsmen, it is true, can remember, and have described to me some walk which they took ten years ago, in which they were so blessed as to lose themselves for half an hour in the woods, but I know very well that they have confined themselves to the highway ever since, whatever pretensions they may make to belong to this select class. No doubt, they were elevated for a moment as by the reminiscence of a previous state of existence, when even they were foresters and outlaws.

> "When he came to grene wode,
>   In a mery mornynge,
> There he herde the notes small,
>   Of byrdes mery syngynge.
>
> "It is ferre gone, sayd Robyn,
>   That I was last here,
> Me lyste a lytell for to shote,
>   At the donne dere."

I think that I cannot preserve my health and spirits unless I spend four hours a day at least–and it is commonly more than that–sauntering through the woods and over the hills and fields absolutely free from all worldly engagements. You may safely say a penny for your thoughts, or a thousand pounds. When sometimes I am reminded that the mechanics and shopkeepers stay in their shops not only all the forenoon, but all the afternoon too, sitting with crossed legs, so many of them–as if the legs were made to sit upon, and not to stand or walk upon–I think that they deserve some credit for not having all committed suicide long ago.

I who cannot stay in my chamber for a single day without acquiring some rust, and when sometimes I have stolen forth for a walk at the eleventh hour of four o'clock in the afternoon, too late to redeem the day, when the shades of night were already beginning to be mingled with the day-light–have felt as if I had committed some sin to be atoned for, I confess that I am astonished at the power of endurance–to say nothing of the moral insensibility of my neighbors who confine themselves to shops and offices the whole day for weeks and months, aye and years almost together. I know not what manner of stuff they are of–sitting there now at 3 o'clock in the afternoon, as if it were 3 o'clock in the morning. Buonaparte may talk of the 3 o'clock in the morning courage, but it is nothing to the courage which can sit down cheerfully at this hour in the afternoon over against one's self whom you have known all the morning,–to starve out a garrison to whom you are bound by such strong ties of sympathy. I wonder that about these times, or say between four and five o'clock in the afternoon, too late for the morning papers and too early for the evening ones, there is not a general explosion heard up and down the street, scattering a legion of antiquated and house-bred notions and whims to the four winds for an airing–and so the evil cure itself.

How womankind, who are confined to the house still more than men, stand it I do not know; but I have ground to suspect that most of them do not *stand* it at all. When, early in a summer afternoon, we have been shaking the dust of the village from the skirts of our garments–making haste past those houses with purely Doric or Gothic fronts, which have such an air of repose about them, my companion whispers that probably about these times their occupants are all gone to bed.– Then it is that I appreciate the beauty and the glory of architecture, which itself never turns in, but forever stands out and erect, keeping watch over the slumberers.

No doubt temperament, and above all age, have a good deal to do with it. As a man grows older his ability to sit still and follow in-door occupations increases.

He grows vespertinal in his habits, as the evening of life approaches, till at last he comes forth only just before sundown, and gets all the walk that he requires in half an hour.

But the walking of which I speak has nothing in it akin to taking exercise as it is called, as the sick take medicine at stated hours–as the swinging of dumb-bells or chairs; but is itself the enterprise and adventure of the day. If you would get exercise go in search of the springs of life. Think of a man's swinging dumb-bells for his health, when those springs are bubbling up in far off pastures unsought by him.

Moreover, you must walk like a camel which is said to be the only beast which ruminates when walking. When a traveller asked Wordsworth's servant to show him her master's study, she answered "Here is his library, but his study is out of doors."

Living much out of doors, in the sun and wind, will no doubt produce a certain roughness of character–will cause a thicker cuticle to grow over some of the finer qualities of our nature, as on the face and hands, or as severe manual labor robs the hands of some of their delicacy of touch. So staying in the house on the other hand may produce a softness and smoothness, not to say thinness of skin, accompanied by an increased sensibility to certain impressions. Perhaps we should be more susceptible to some influences important to our intellectual and moral growth, if the sun had shone and the wind blown on us a little less; and no doubt it is a nice matter to proportion rightly the thick and thin skin. But methinks that is a scurf that will fall off fast enough–that the natural remedy is to be found in the proportion which the night bears to the day, the winter to the summer, thought to experience. There will be so much the more air and sunshine in our thoughts. The callous palms of the laborer are

conversant with finer tissues of selfrespect and heroism whose touch thrills the heart, than the languid fingers of idleness. That is mere sentimentality that lies
abed by day and thinks itself white, far from the tan
and callus of experience.

When we walk we naturally go to the fields and
woods; what would become of us if we walked only in
a garden or a mall? Even some sects of philosophers
have felt the necessity of importing the woods to
themselves since they did not go to the woods, "They
planted groves and walks of Platans" where they took
subdiales ambulationes in porticoes open to the air. Of
course, it is of no use to direct our steps to the woods,
if they do not carry us thither. I am alarmed when it
happens that I have walked a mile into the woods
bodily, without getting there in spirit. In my afternoon
walk I would fain forget all my morning occupations,
and my obligations to society. But it sometimes happens that I cannot easily shake off the village. The
thought of some work will run in my head, and I am
not where my body is; I am out of my senses. In my
walks I would fain return to my senses. What business have I in the woods, if I am thinking of something
out of the woods? I suspect myself, and cannot help
a shudder, when I find myself so implicated even in
what are called good works–for this may sometimes
happen.–

My vicinity affords many good walks, and though I
have walked almost every day for so many years, and
sometimes for several days together, I have not yet exhausted them. An absolutely new prospect is a great
happiness, and I can still get this any afternoon. Two
or three hours' walking will carry me to as strange a
country as I expect ever to see. A single farm-house
which I had not seen before is sometimes as good as
the dominions of the king of Dahomey. There is in fact

a sort of harmony discoverable between the capabili-
ties of the landscape within a circle of ten miles radius,
or the limits of an afternoon walk, and the three-score-
years and ten of human life. It will never become quite
familiar to you.

Now a days, almost all man's improvements, so
called, as the building of houses, and the cutting down
of the forest, and of all large trees, simply deform the
landscape, and make it more and more tame and
cheap.

A people who would begin by burning the fences
and let the forest stand! I saw the fences half consumed, their ends lost in the middle of the prairie, and
some worldly miser with a surveyor looking after his
bounds, while heaven had taken place around him,
and he did not see the angels going to and fro, but was
looking for an old post-hole in the midst of paradise. I
looked again and saw him standing in the middle of a
boggy stygian fen surrounded by devils, and he had
found his bounds without a doubt, three little stones
where a stake had been driven, and looking nearer I
saw that the Prince of Darkness was his surveyor.

I can easily walk ten, fifteen, twenty, any number of
miles, commencing at my own door, without going by
any house, without crossing a road except where the
fox and the mink do. First along by the river, and then
the brook, and then the meadow and the wood-side.
There are square miles in my vicinity which have no
inhabitant. From many a hill I can see civilization and
the abodes of man afar. The farmers and their works
are scarcely more obvious than woodchucks and their
burrows. Man and his affairs, church and state–and
school, trade and commerce, and manufactures and
agriculture,–even politics, the most alarming of them
all,–I am pleased to see how little space they occupy in
the landscape. Politics is but a narrow field, and that

still narrower highway yonder leads to it. I sometimes direct the traveller thither. If you would go to the political world, follow the great road,–follow that market man, keep his dust in your eyes, and it will lead you straight to it–for it too has its place merely, and does not occupy all space. I pass from it as from a bean field into the forest, and it is forgotten. In one half hour I can walk off to some portion of the earth's surface where a man does not stand from one year's end to another and there consequently politics are not, for they are but as the cigar smoke of a man.

The village is the place to which the roads tend, a sort of expansion of the highway as a lake of a river. It is the body of which roads are the arms and legs; a trivial or quadrivial place, the thoroughfare and ordinary of travellers. The word is from the Latin *villa*, which together with *via*, a way, or more anciently *ved* and *vella*, Varro derives from *veho* to carry, because the villa is the place to and from which things are carried. They who got their living by teaming were said *vellaturam facere*. Hence too apparently the Latin word *vilis* and our *vile; also *villain*. This suggests what kind of degeneracy villagers are liable to. They are way-worn by the travel that goes by and over them, without travelling themselves.

Some do not walk at all, others walk in the highways; a few walk across lots. Roads are made for horses and men of business. I do not travel in them much comparatively, because I am not in a hurry to get to any tavern, or grocery, or livery stable, or depot to which they lead. I am a good horse to travel but not from choice a roadster. The landscape painter uses the figures of men to mark a road. He would not make that use of my figure. I walk out into a nature such as the old prophets and poets Menu, Moses, Homer, Chaucer, walked in. You may name it America, but it is not America. Neither Americus Vespucius, nor Columbus, nor the rest were the discoverers of it. There is a truer account of it in Mythology than in any history of America so called that I have seen.

However, there are a few old roads that may be trodden with profit, as if they led some where now that they are nearly discontinued. There is the Old Marlboro Road, which does not go to Marlboro now methinks, unless that is Marlboro where it carries me. I am the bolder to speak of it here, because I presume that there are one or two such roads in every town.

THE OLD MARLBORO ROAD.

Where they once dug for money
But never found any;
Where sometimes Martial Miles
Singly files,
And Elijah Wood,
I fear for no good.
No other man
Save Elisha Dugan—
O man of wild habits,
Partridges and rabbits,
Who hast no cares
Only to set snares,
Who liv'st all alone,
Close to the bone;
And where life is sweetest
Constantly eatest.
When the spring stirs my blood
With the instinct to travel,
I can get enough gravel
On the Old Marlboro Road.
Nobody repairs it,
For nobody wears it;
It is a living way,
As the Christians say,
Not many there be
Who enter therein,
Only the guests of the
Irishman Quin.

What is it, what is it
But a direction out there,
And the bare possibility
Of going somewhere?
Great guide boards of stone
But travellers none.
Cenotaphs of the towns
Named on their crowns.
It is worth going to see
Where you *might* be.
What king
Did the thing,
I am still wondering–
Set up how or when,
By what select men,
Gourgas or Lee,
Clark or Darby?
They're a great endeavor
To be something forever.
Blank tablets of stone,
Where a traveller might groan,
And in one sentence
Grave all that is known
Which another might read
In his extreme need.
I know one or two
Lines that would do,
Literature that might stand
All over the land,
Which a man could remember
Till next December,
And read again in the spring,
After the thawing.
If with fancy unfurled
   You leave your abode,
You may go round the world
   By the Old Marlboro Road.

At present, in this vicinity, the best part of the land is
not private property; the landscape is not owned, and
the walker enjoys comparative freedom. But possibly
the day will come when it will be partitioned off into

so-called pleasure grounds, in which a few will take a narrow and exclusive pleasure only,–when fences shall be multiplied, and man traps and other engines invented to confine men to the *public* road; and walking over the surface of God's earth, shall be construed to mean trespassing on some gentleman's grounds. To enjoy a thing exclusively is commonly to exclude yourself from the true enjoyment of it. Let us improve our opportunities then before the evil days come.

What is it that makes it so hard sometimes to determine whither we will walk? I believe that there is a subtile magnetism in Nature, which, if we unconsciously yield to it, will direct us aright. It is not indifferent to us which way we walk. There is a right way; but we are very liable from heedlessness and stupidity to take the wrong one. We would fain take that walk, never yet taken by us through this actual world, which is perfectly symbolical of the path which we love to travel in the interior and ideal world; and sometimes, no doubt, we find it difficult to choose our direction, because it does not yet exist distinctly in our idea.

When I go out of the house for a walk, uncertain as yet whither I will bend my steps, and submit myself to my instinct to decide for me, I find, strange and whimsical as it may seem, that I finally and inevitably settle south-west, toward some particular wood or meadow or deserted pasture or hill in that direction. My needle is slow to settle–varies a few degrees, and does not always point due south-west, it is true, and it has good authority for this variation, but it always settles between west and south-south-west. The future lies that way to me, and the earth seems more unexhausted and richer on that side. The outline which would bound my walks, would be, not a circle, but a parabola, or rather like one of those cometary orbits, which have been thought to be non-returning curves, in this case opening westward, in which my house occupies the place of the sun. I turn round and round irresolute sometimes for a quarter of an hour, until I decide for the thousandth time, that I will walk into the south-west or west. Eastward I go only by force; but westward I go free. Thither no business leads me. It is hard for me to believe that I shall find fair landscapes, or sufficient Wildness and Freedom behind the eastern horizon. I am not excited by the prospect of a walk thither; but I believe that the forest which I see in the western horizon stretches uninterruptedly towards the setting sun, and that there are no towns nor cities in it of enough consequence to disturb me. Let me live where I will, on this side is the city, on that the wilderness, and ever I am leaving the city more and more, and withdrawing into the wilderness. I should not lay so much stress on this fact, if I did not believe that something like this is the prevailing tendency of my countrymen. I must walk toward Oregon, and not toward Europe. And that way the nation is moving, and I may say that mankind progress from east to west. Within a few years we have witnessed the phenomenon of a south-eastward migration, in the settlement of Australia; but this affects us as a retrograde movement, and, judging from the moral and physical character of the first generation of Australians, has not yet proved a successful experiment. The eastern Tartars think that there is nothing west beyond Thibet. "The World ends there," say they, "beyond there is nothing but a shoreless sea." It is unmitigated East where they live.

We go eastward to realize history, and study the works of art and literature, retracing the steps of the race,–we go westward as into the future, with a spirit of enterprise and adventure. The Atlantic is a Lethean stream, in our passage over which we have had an opportunity to forget the old world and its institutions. If we do not succeed this time, there is perhaps one more chance for the race left before it arrives on the banks of the Styx; and that is in the Lethe of the Pacific, which is three times as wide.

I know not how significant it is, or how far it is an evidence of singularity, that an individual should thus consent in his pettiest walk, with the general movement of the race; but I know that something akin to the migratory instinct in birds and quadrupeds,–which, in some instances, is known to have affected the squirrel tribe, impelling them to a general and mysterious movement, in which they were seen, say some, crossing the broadest rivers, each on its particular chip, with its tail raised for a sail, and bridging narrower streams with their dead,–that something like the *furor* which affects the domestic cattle in the spring, and which is referred to a worm in their tails,–affects both nations and individuals, either perennially or from time to time. Not a flock of wild geese cackles over our town but it to some extent unsettles the value of real estate here, and if I were a broker I should probably take that disturbance into account.–

> "Than longen folk to gon on pilgrimages,
> And palmeres for to seken strange strondes."

Every sunset which I witness inspires me with the desire to go to a west as distant and as fair as that into which the Sun goes down. He appears to migrate westward daily and tempt us to follow him. He is the Great Western Pioneer whom the nations follow. We dream all night of those mountain ridges in the horizon, though they may be of vapor only, which were last gilded by his rays. The island of Atlantis, and the islands and gardens of the Hesperides, a sort of terrestrial paradise, appear to have been the Great West of

the ancients, enveloped in mystery and poetry. Who
has not seen in imagination, when looking into the
sunset sky, the gardens of the Hesperides, and the
foundation of all those fables?

Columbus felt the westward tendency more strongly
than any before. He obeyed it, and found a New World
for Castile and Leon. The herd of men in those days
scented fresh pastures from afar.–

> "And now the sun had stretched out all the hills,
> And now was dropt into the western bay;
> At last *he* rose, and twitch'd his mantle blue;
> To-morrow to fresh woods and pastures new."

Where on the Globe can there be found an area of
equal extent with that occupied by the bulk of our
states, so fertile and so rich and varied in its productions, and at the same time so habitable by the European, as this is? Michaux who knew but part of them,
says that "the species of large trees are much more
numerous in North America than in Europe: in the
United States there are more than 140 species that exceed thirty feet in height; in France there are but thirty
that attain this size." Later botanists more than confirm his observations. Humboldt came to America to
realize his youthful dreams of a tropical vegetation,
and he beheld it in its greatest perfection in the primitive forests of the Amazon, the most gigantic wilderness on the earth, which he has so eloquently described. The geographer Guyot, himself a European,
goes further–further than I am ready to follow him, yet
not when he says "As the plant is made for the animal,
as the vegetable world is made for the animal world,
America is made for the man of the Old World."

"The man of the Old World sets out upon his way.
Leaving the highlands of Asia, he descends from station to station, towards Europe. Each of his steps is
marked by a new civilization superior to the preced-

ing, by a greater power of development. Arrived at the Atlantic, he pauses on the shore of this unknown Ocean, the bounds of which he knows not, and turns upon his foot prints for an instant." When he has exhausted the rich soil of Europe and reinvigorated himself–"Then recommences his adventurous career westward as in the earliest ages."–So far Guyot.

From this western impulse coming in contact with the barrier of the Atlantic sprang the commerce and enterprise of modern times. The younger Michaux, in his Travels West of the Alleghanies in 1802, says that the common inquiry in the newly settled West was– "From what part of the world have you come? As if these vast and fertile regions would naturally be the place of meeting and common country of all the inhabitants of the globe."

To use an obsolete Latin word, I might say *Ex oriente lux; ex occidente* FRUX. From the East light; from the West fruit.

Sir Francis Head,–an English traveller, and a Governor General of Canada,–tells us that "in both the northern and southern hemispheres of the new world, Nature has not only outlined her works on a larger scale, but has painted the whole picture with brighter and more costly colors than she used in delineating and in beautifying the old world." "The heavens of America appear infinitely higher–the sky is bluer–the air is fresher–the cold is intenser–the moon looks larger–the stars are brighter–the thunder is louder–the lightning is vivider–the wind is stronger–the rain is heavier–the mountains are higher–the rivers larger– the forests bigger–the plains broader.–" This statement will do at least to set against Buffon's account of this part of the world and its productions.

Linnaeus said long ago Nescio quae facies *laeta, glabra* plantis Americanis. I know not what there is of joyous and smooth in the aspect of American plants; and

I think that in this country there are no, or at most, very few, *Africanae bestiae*, African beasts, as the Romans called them, and that in this respect also it is peculiarly fitted for the habitation of man. We are told that within three miles of the center of the East Indian city of Singapore some of the inhabitants are annually carried off by tigers;–but the traveller can lie down in the woods at night almost anywhere in North America without fear of wild beasts.

These are encouraging testimonies. If the moon looks larger here than in Europe, probably the sun looks larger also. If the heavens of America appear infinitely higher, the stars brighter, I trust that these facts are symbolical of the height to which the philosophy and poetry and religion of her inhabitants may one day soar. At length perchance the immaterial heaven will appear as much higher to the American mind, and the intimations that star it as much brighter. For I believe that climate does thus react on man–as there is something in the mountain air that feeds the spirit and inspires. Will not man grow to greater perfection intellectually as well as physically under these influences? Or is it unimportant how many foggy days there are in his life? I trust that we shall be more imaginative; that our thoughts will be clearer, fresher and more ethereal, as our sky–our understanding more comprehensive and broader, like our plains–our intellect generally on a grander scale, like our thunder and lightning, our rivers and mountains and forests,–and our hearts shall even correspond in breadth and depth and grandeur to our inland seas. Perchance there will appear to the traveller something, he knows not what, of *laeta* and *glabra*– of joyous and serene, in our very faces. Else, to what end does the world go on, and why was America discovered?

To Americans I hardly need to say–

"Westward the star of empire takes its way."

As a true patriot I should be ashamed to think that Adam in paradise was more favorably situated on the whole than the backwoodsman in this country.

Our sympathies in Massachusetts are not confined to New England, though we may be estranged from the south, we sympathize with the west. There is the home of the younger sons, as among the Scandinavians they took to the sea for their inheritance. It is too late to be studying Hebrew; it is more important to understand even the slang of today.

Some months ago I went to see a panorama of the Rhine. It was like a dream of the Middle Ages. I floated down its historic stream in something more than imagination, under bridges built by the Romans, and repaired by later heroes, past cities and castles whose very names were music to my ears, and each of which was the subject of a legend. There were Ehren-breitstein and Rolandseck and Coblentz, which I knew only in history. They were ruins that interested me chiefly. There seemed to come up from its waters and its vine-clad hills and valleys a hushed music as of cru-saders departing for the Holy Land. I floated along under the spell of enchantment, as if I had been trans-ported to a heroic age, and breathed an atmosphere of chivalry.

Soon after I went to see a panorama of the Missis-sippi, and as I worked my way up the stream in the light of to-day,–and saw the steamboats wooding up–counted the rising cities, gazed on the fresh ruins of Nauvoo–beheld the Indians moving west across the stream, and, as before I had looked up the Moselle, now looked up the Ohio and the Missouri, and heard the legends of Dubuque and of Wenona's Cliff–still

thinking more of the future than of the past or present–I saw that this was a Rhine stream of a different
kind; that the foundations of castles were yet to be
laid, and the famous bridges were yet to be thrown
over the stream; and I felt that *this was the Heroic Age
itself*, though we know it not, for the hero is commonly
the simplest and obscurest of men.

The West of which I speak is but another name for
the Wild; and what I have been preparing to say is, that
in Wildness is the preservation of the world. Every tree
sends its fibres forth in search of the Wild. The cities
import it at any price. Men plow and sail for it. From
the forest and wilderness come the tonics and barks
which brace mankind. Our ancestors were savages.
The story of Romulus and Remus being suckled by a
wolf is not a meaningless fable. The founders of every
state which has risen to eminence, have drawn their
nourishment and vigor from a similar wild source. It is
because the children of the empire were not suckled
by the wolf that they were conquered and displaced by
the children of the northern forests who were.

I believe in the forest, and in the meadow, and in the
night in which the corn grows. We require an infusion
of hemlock spruce or Arbor vitae in our tea. There is a
difference between eating and drinking for strength
and from mere gluttony. The Hottentots eagerly devour the marrow of the Koodoo and other antelopes
raw, as a matter of course. Some of our northern Indians eat raw the marrow of the Arctic reindeer, as well
as various other parts, including the summits of the
antlers as long as they are soft. And herein perchance
they have stolen a march on the cooks of Paris. They
get what usually goes to feed the fire. This is probably
better than stall-fed beef and slaughter-house pork to
make a man of. Give me a Wildness whose glance no
civilization can endure,–as if we lived on the marrow
of koodoos devoured raw.

There are some intervals which border the strain of the wood-thrush, to which I would migrate–wild lands where no settler has squatted; to which, methinks, I am already acclimated.

The African hunter Cumming tells us that the skin of the Eland, as well as that of most other antelopes just killed, emits the most delicious perfume of trees and grass. I would have every man so much a wild antelope, so much a part and parcel of Nature, that his very person should thus sweetly advertise our senses of his presence, and remind us of those parts of nature which he most haunts. I feel no disposition to be satirical when the trapper's coat emits the odor of musquash even; it is a sweeter scent to me than that which commonly exhales from the merchant's or the scholar's garments. When I go into their wardrobes and handle their vestments, I am reminded of no grassy plains and flowery meads which they have frequented, but of dusty merchants' exchanges and libraries rather.

A tanned skin is something more than respectable, and perhaps olive is a fitter color than white for a man–a denizen of the woods. "The pale white man!" I do not wonder that the African pitied him. Darwin the naturalist says "A white man bathing by the side of a Tahitian was like a plant bleached by the gardener's art compared with a fine, dark green one growing vigorously in the open fields."

Ben Jonson exclaims,–

> "How near to good is what is fair!"

So I would say–

> How near to good is what is *wild*!

Life consists with Wildness. The most alive is the wildest. Not yet subdued to man, its presence refreshes him. One who pressed forward incessantly and never rested from his labors, who grew fast and made infinite demands on life, would always find himself in a new country or wilderness, and surrounded by the raw material of life. He would be climbing over the prostrate stems of primitive forest trees.

Hope and the future for me are not in lawns and cultivated fields, not in towns and cities, but in the impervious and quaking swamps. When, formerly, I have analysed my partiality for some farm which I had contemplated purchasing, I have frequently found that I was attracted solely by a few square rods of impermeable and unfathomable bog–a natural sink in one corner of it. That was the jewel which dazzled me. I derive more of my subsistence from the swamps which surround my native town than from the cultivated gardens in the village. There are no richer parterres to my eyes than the dense beds of dwarf andromeda (*Cassandra calyculata*) which cover these tender places on the earth's surface. Botany cannot go further than tell me the names of the shrubs which grow there–the high-blueberry, panicled andromeda,–lamb-kill, azalea–and rhodora–all standing in the quaking sphagnum. I often think that I would like to have my house front on this mass of dull red bushes, omitting other flower plots and borders, transplanted spruce and trim box, even gravelled walks–to have this fertile spot under my windows, not a few imported barrow-fuls of soil only, to cover the sand which was thrown out in digging the cellar. Why not put my house–my parlor–behind this plot instead of behind that meagre assemblage of curiosities–that poor apology for a Nature and art, which I call my front yard? It is an effort to clear up and make a decent appearance when the carpenter and mason have departed, though done as much for the passer by as the dweller within. The most tasteful front-yard fence was never an agreeable object of study to me; the most elaborate ornaments, acorn tops, or what not, soon wearied and disgusted me. Bring your sills up to the very edge of the swamp then, (though it may not be the best place for a dry cellar,) so that there be no access on that side to citizens. Front-yards are not made to walk in, but, at most, through, and you could go in the back way.

Yes; though you may think me perverse, if it were proposed to me to dwell in the neighborhood of the most beautiful garden that ever human art contrived, or else of a dismal swamp, I should certainly decide for the swamp.– How vain then have been all your labors, citizens, for me!

My spirits infallibly rise in proportion to the out-ward dreariness. Give me the Ocean, the desert, or the wilderness. In the desert a pure air and solitude compensate for want of moisture and fertility. The traveller Burton says of it "Your *morale* improves; you become frank and cordial, hospitable and single-minded. . . . . . In the desert spirituous liquors excite only disgust. There is a keen enjoyment in a mere ani-mal existence." They who have been travelling long on the steppes of Tartary, say "On reentering cultivated lands, the agitation, perplexity and turmoil of civiliza-tion oppressed and suffocated us; the air seemed to fail us, and we felt every moment as if about to die of asphyxia." When I would recreate myself, I seek the darkest wood, the thickest and most interminable, and, to the citizen, most dismal swamp. I enter a swamp as a sacred place–a *sanctum sanctorum*. There is the strength–the marrow of Nature. The wild wood covers the virgin mould,–and the same soil is good for men and for trees. A man's health requires as many acres of meadow to his prospect as his farm does loads of muck. There are the strong meats on which he feeds. A town is saved, not more by the righteous men

in it, than by the woods and swamps that surround it.
A township where one primitive forest waves above,
while another primitive forest rots below–such a town
is fitted to raise not only corn and potatoes, but poets
and philosophers for the coming ages. In such a soil
grew Homer and Confucius and the rest, and out of
such a wilderness comes the reformer eating locusts
and wild honey.

To preserve wild animals, implies generally the creation of a forest for them to dwell in or resort to. So is
it with man. A hundred years ago they sold bark in our
streets peeled from our own woods. In the very aspect
of those primitive and rugged trees, there was methinks a tanning principle which hardened and con-
solidated the fibres of men's thoughts. Ah! already I
shudder for these comparatively degenerate days of
my native village, when you cannot collect a load of
bark of good thickness–and we no longer produce tar
and turpentine.

The civilized nations–Greece, Rome, England, are
sustained by the primitive forests which anciently rot-
ted where they stand. They survive as long as the soil is
not exhausted. Alas for human culture! little is to be
expected of a nation when the vegetable mould is exhausted, and it is compelled to make manure of the
bones of its fathers. There the poet sustains himself
merely by his own superfluous fat, and the philosopher comes down on to his marrow bones.

It is said to be the task of the American, "to work the
virgin soil," and that "Agriculture here already assumes proportions unknown everywhere else." I think
that the farmer displaces the Indian even because he
redeems the meadow, and so makes himself stronger
and in some respects more natural. I was surveying for
a man the other day a single straight line 132 rods long
through a swamp, at whose entrance might have been

written the words which Dante read over the entrance to the Infernal regions–Leave all hope ye that enter–that is of ever getting out again; where at one time I saw my employer actually up to his neck and swimming for his life in his property, though it was still winter. He had another similar swamp which I could not survey at all because it was completely under water, and nevertheless, with regard to a third swamp which I did *survey* from a distance, he remarked to me, true to his instincts, that he would not part with it for any consideration, on account of the mud which it contained. And that man intends to put a girdling ditch round the whole in the course of 40 months, and so redeem it by the magic of his spade. I refer to him only as the type of a class.

The weapons with which we have gained our most important victories, which should be handed down as heirlooms from father to son, are not the sword and the lance, but the bush-whack–the turf-cutter, the spade, and the bog-hoe, rusted with the blood of many a meadow, and begrimed with the dust of many a hard-fought field. The very winds blew the Indian's corn-field into the meadow, and pointed out the way which he had not the skill to follow. He had no better implement with which to intrench himself in the land than a clam-shell. But the farmer is armed with plow and spade.

In Literature, it is only the wild that attracts us. Dulness is but another name for tameness. It is the uncivilized free and wild thinking in Hamlet and the Iliad, in all the scriptures and mythologies, not learned in the Schools, that delights us. As the wild duck is more swift and beautiful than the tame, so is the wild–the mallard–thought, which, 'mid falling dews wings its way above the fens. A truly good book is something as natural, and as unexpectedly and unaccountably fair and perfect, as a wild flower discovered on the prairies of the west, or in the jungles of the east. Genius is a light which makes the darkness visible, like the lightning's flash, which perchance shatters the temple of knowledge itself–and not a taper lighted at the hearthstone of the race which pales before the light of common day.

English literature from the days of the minstrels to the Lake Poets–Chaucer and Spenser and Milton, and even Shakspeare included, breathes no quite fresh and in this sense wild strain. It is an essentially tame and civilized literature reflecting Greece and Rome. Her wilderness is a green-wood–her wild man a Robinhood. There is plenty of genial love of nature, but not so much of Nature herself. Her chronicles inform us when her wild animals, but not when the wild man in her, became extinct.

The science of Humboldt is one thing, poetry is another thing. The poet today, notwithstanding all the discoveries of science, and the accumulated learning of mankind, enjoys no advantage over Homer.

Where is the literature which gives expression to Nature? He would be a poet who could impress the winds and streams into his service, to speak for him; who nailed words to their primitive senses, as farmers drive down stakes in the spring which the frost has heaved; who derived his words as often as he used them–transplanted them to his page with earth adhering to their roots;–whose words were so true, and fresh, and natural that they would appear to expand like the buds at the approach of spring, though they lay half smothered between two musty leaves in a library,–aye, to bloom and bear fruit there after their kind annually for the faithful reader, in sympathy with surrounding Nature.

I do not know of any poetry to quote which adequately expresses this yearning for the Wild. Approached from this side the best poetry is tame. I do not know where to find in any literature, ancient or modern, any account which contents me, of that Nature with which even I am acquainted. You will perceive that I demand something which no Augustan nor Elizabethan age–which no *culture* in short can give. Mythology comes nearer to it than anything. How much more fertile a nature at least has Grecian mythology its root in than English Literature! Mythology is the crop which the old world bore before its soil was exhausted, before the fancy and imagination were affected with blight;–and which it still bears wherever its pristine vigor is unabated. All other literatures endure only as the elms which overshadow our houses, but this is like the great Dragon tree of the Western isles, as old as mankind, and whether that does or not, will endure as long; for the decay of other literatures makes the soil in which it thrives.

The West is preparing to add its fables to those of the east. The valleys of the Ganges, the Nile, and the Rhine, having yielded their crop, it remains to be seen what the valleys of the Amazon, the Plate, the Orinoco–the St Lawrence and the Mississippi will produce. Perchance, when in the course of ages, American Liberty has become a fiction of the past,–as it is to some extent a fiction of the present,–the poets of the world will be inspired by American Mythology.

The wildest dreams of wild men, even, are not the less true, though they may not recommend themselves to the sense which is most common among Englishmen and Americans to-day. It is not every truth that recommends itself to the common sense. Nature has a place for the wild clematis as well as for the

cabbage. Some expressions of truth are reminiscent,–
others merely *sensible*, as the phrase is–others pro-
phetic. Some forms of disease even may prophesy
forms of health. The geologist has discovered that the
figures of serpents, griffins, flying dragons, and other
fanciful embellishments of heraldry, have their proto-
types in the forms of fossil species which were extinct
before man was created, and hence "indicate a faint
and shadowy knowledge of a previous state of organic
existence." The Hindoos dreamed that the earth
rested on an elephant, and the elephant on a tortoise,
and the tortoise on a serpent; and though it may be an
unimportant coincidence, it will not be out of place
here to state, that a fossil tortoise has lately been discovered in Asia large enough to support an elephant. I
confess that I am partial to these wild fancies, which
transcend the order of time and development. They
are the sublimest recreation of the intellect. The partridge loves peas, but not those that go with her into
the pot.

In short, all good things are wild and free. There is
something in a strain of music, whether produced by
an instrument or by the human voice–take the sound
of a bugle in a summer night, for instance,–which by
its wildness, to speak without satire, reminds me of the
cries emitted by wild beasts in their native forests. It is
so much of their wildness as I can understand. Give
me for my friends and neighbors wild men, not tame
ones. The wildness of the savage is but a faint symbol
of the awful ferity with which good men and lovers
meet.

I love even to see the domestic animals reassert
their native rights–any evidence that they have not
wholly lost their original wild habits and vigor; as
when my neighbor's cow breaks out of her pasture
early in the Spring and boldly swims the river, a cold

grey tide, twenty-five or thirty rods wide, swollen by the melted snow. It is the Buffalo crossing the Mississippi. This exploit confers some dignity on the herd in my eyes–already dignified. The seeds of instinct are preserved under the thick hides of cattle and horses, like seeds in the bowels of the earth, an indefinite period.

Any sportiveness in cattle is unexpected. I saw one day a herd of a dozen bullocks and cows running about and frisking in unwieldly sport, like huge rats, even like kittens. They shook their heads, raised their tails, and rushed up and down a hill, and I perceived by their horns, as well as by their activity, their relation to the deer tribe. But, alas! a sudden loud *who!* would have damped their ardor at once, reduced them from venison to beef, and stiffened their sides and sinews like the locomotive. Who but the Evil One has cried Who! to mankind?– Indeed, the life of cattle, like that of many men, is but a sort of locomotiveness, they move a side at a time, and Man by his machinery is meeting the horse and ox half way. Whatever part the whip has touched is thenceforth palsied. Who would ever think of a *side* of any of the supple cat tribe, as we speak of a *side* of beef.

I rejoice that horses and steers have to be broken before they can be made the slaves of men, and that men themselves have some wild oats still left to sow before they become submissive members of society. Undoubtedly, all men are not equally fit subjects for civilization, and because the majority, like dogs and sheep are tame by inherited disposition, is no reason why the others should have their natures broken that they may be reduced to the same level. Men are in the main alike, but they were made several in order that they might be various. If a low use is to be served, one man will do nearly or quite as well as another; if a high one, individual excellence is to be regarded. Any man can stop a hole to keep the wind away, but no other man could serve so rare a use as the author of this illustration did. Confucius says "The skins of the tiger and the leopard when they are tanned, are as the skins of the dog and the sheep tanned." But it is not the part of a true culture to tame tigers, any more than it is to make sheep ferocious, and tanning their skins for shoes is not the best use to which they can be put.

When looking over a list of men's names in a foreign language, as of military officers or of authors who have written on a particular subject, I am reminded once more that there is nothing in a name. The name Menschikoff, for instance, has nothing in it to my ears more human than a whisker, and it may belong to a rat. As the names of the Poles and Russians are to us, so are ours to them. It is as if they had been named by the child's rigmarole–*Iery-wiery ichery van, tittle-tol-tan*. I see in my mind a herd of wild creatures swarming over the earth, and to each the herdsman has affixed some barbarous sound in his own dialect. The names of men are of course as cheap and meaningless as *Bose* and *Tray*, the names of dogs.

Methinks it would be some advantage to philosophy if men were named merely in the gross as they are known. It would be necessary only to know the genus, and perhaps the race or variety, to know the individual. We are not prepared to believe that every private soldier in a Roman army had a name of his own– because we have not supposed that he had a character of his own. At present our only true names are nicknames. I knew a boy who from his peculiar energy was called "Buster" by his playmates, and this rightly supplanted his Christian name. Some travellers tell us that an Indian had no name given him at first, but earned it, and his name was his fame; and among some tribes he acquired a new name with every new exploit. It is pitiful when a man bears a name for convenience merely, who has earned neither name nor fame.

I will not allow mere names to make distinctions for me, but still see men in herds for all them. A familiar name cannot make a man less strange to me. It may be given to a savage who retains in secret his own wild title earned in the woods. We have a wild savage in us, and a savage name is perchance somewhere recorded as ours. I see that my neighbor, who bears the familiar epithet William, or Edwin, takes it off with his jacket. It does not adhere to him when asleep or in anger, or aroused by any passion or inspiration. I seem to hear pronounced by some of his kin at such a time, his original wild name in some jaw-breaking or else melodious tongue.

Here is this vast, savage, howling Mother of ours, Nature lying all around, with such beauty, and such affection for her children, as the leopard,–and yet we are so early weaned from her breast to society–to that culture which is exclusively an interaction of man on man,–a sort of breeding in and in, which produces at most a merely English nobility, a civilization destined to have a speedy limit.

In society, in the best institutions of men it is easy to detect a certain precocity. When we should still be growing children, we are already little men. Give me a culture which imports much muck from the meadows, and deepens the soil, not that which trusts to heating manures, and improved implements and modes of culture only.

Many a poor sore-eyed student that I have heard of, would grow faster both intellectually and physically, if, instead of sitting up so very late, he honestly slumbered a fool's allowance.

There may be an excess even of informing light. Niepce, a Frenchman, discovered "actinism," that power in the sun's rays which produces a chemical effect; that granite rocks, and stone structures, and statues of metal "are all alike destructively acted upon during the hours of sunshine, and but for provisions of nature no less wonderful, would soon perish under the delicate touch of the most subtile of the agencies of the universe". But he observed "that those bodies which underwent this change during the day-light possessed the power of restoring themselves to their original conditions during the hours of night, when this excitement was no longer influencing them." Hence it has been inferred that "The hours of darkness are as necessary to the inorganic creation, as we know night and sleep are to the organic kingdom." Not even does the moon shine every night, but gives place to darkness.

I would not have every man nor every part of a man cultivated, any more than I would have every acre of earth cultivated; part will be tillage, but the greater part will be meadow and forest, not only serving an immediate use, but preparing a mould against a distant future, by the annual decay of the vegetation which it supports.

There are other letters for the child to learn than those which Cadmus invented. The Spaniards have a good term to express this wild and dusky knowledge– *Gramatica parda*–tawny grammar–a kind of mother wit derived from that same leopard to which I have referred.

We have heard of a Society for the Diffusion of Useful Knowledge. It is said that Knowledge is power; and the like. Methinks there is equal need of a Society for the Diffusion of Useful Ignorance, what we will call Beautiful Knowledge, a knowledge useful in a higher sense; for what is most of our boasted so-called knowledge but a conceit that we know something which robs us of the advantage of our actual ignorance? What we

call knowledge is often our positive ignorance; ignorance our negative knowledge. By long years of patient
industry and reading of the newspapers,–for what are
the libraries of science but files of newspapers?–a man
accumulates a myriad facts, lays them up in his memory, and then when in some spring of his life he saun-
ters abroad into the Great Fields of thought, he as it
were goes to grass like a horse, and leaves all his harness behind in the stable. I would say to the Society for
the Diffusion of Useful Knowledge, sometimes–Go to
grass. You have eaten hay long enough. The Spring has
come with its green crop. The very cows are driven to
their country pastures before the end of May; though
I have heard of one unnatural farmer who kept his
cow in the barn and fed her on hay all the year round.
So, frequently the Society for the Diffusion of Useful
Knowledge treats its cattle.

A man's ignorance sometimes is not only useful, but
beautiful, while his knowledge, so called, is oftentimes
worse than useless beside being ugly. Which is the
best man to deal with, he who knows nothing about
a subject, and what is extremely rare, knows that he
knows nothing,–or he who really knows something
about it, but thinks that he knows all?

My desire for knowledge is intermittent; but my desire to bathe my head in atmospheres unknown to my
feet is perennial and constant. The highest that we
can attain to is not Knowledge, but Sympathy with Intelligence. I do not know that this higher knowledge
amounts to anything more definite than a novel and
grand surprise on a sudden revelation of the insuffi-
ciency of all that we called Knowledge before–a discovery that there are more things in heaven and earth
than are dreamed of in our philosophy. It is the lighting up of the mist by the sun. Man cannot *know* in any
higher sense than this, any more than he can look

serenely and with impunity in the face of the sun; ʿως τὶ νοῶν, ὀυ κεινον νοήςεις–"You will not perceive that as perceiving a particular thing," say the Chaldean Oracles.

There is something servile in the habit of seeking after a law which we may obey. We may study the laws of matter at and for our convenience, but a successful life knows no law. It is an unfortunate discovery certainly, that of a law which binds us where we did not know before that we were bound. Live free, Child of the Mist–and with respect to knowledge we are all children of the mist.– The man who takes the liberty to live is superior to all the laws both of heaven and earth, by virtue of his relation to the Law-maker. "That is active duty", says the Vishnu Purana, "which is not for our bondage; that is knowledge which is for our liberation; all other duty is good only unto weariness; all other knowledge, is only the cleverness of an artist."

It is remarkable how few events or crises there are in our histories; how little exercised we have been in our minds; how few experiences we have had. I would fain be assured that I am growing apace and rankly, though my very growth disturb this dull equanimity,–though it be with struggle through long dark muggy nights or seasons of gloom. It would be well if all our lives were a divine tragedy even, instead of this trivial comedy or farce. Christ, Dante, Bunyan, and others, appear to have been exercised in their minds more than we;– they were subjected to a kind of culture such as our district schools and colleges do not contemplate. Even Mahomet, though Christians may scream at his name, had a good deal more to live for, aye and to die for than they have commonly.

When, at rare intervals, some thought visits one, as perchance he is walking on a railroad, then indeed the cars go by without his hearing them. But soon, by some inexorable law our life goes by and the cars return.–

> "Gentle breeze that wanderest unseen,
> And bendest the thistles round Loira of storms
> Traveller of the windy glens,
> Why hast thou left my ear so soon?"

While almost all men feel an attraction drawing them to Society, few are attracted strongly to Nature. In their relation to Nature men appear to me for the most part, not-withstanding their arts, lower than the animals. It is not often a beautiful relation, as in the case of the animals. How little appreciation of the beauty of the landscape there is among us! We have to be told that the Greeks called the world Κοσμος Beauty–or Order, but we do not see clearly why they did so, and we esteem it at best only a curious philo-logical fact.

For my part, I feel, that with regard to Nature, I live a sort of border life, on the confines of a world, into which I make occasional and transient forays only, and my patriotism and allegiance to the state into whose territories I seem to retreat are those of a moss-trooper. Unto a life which I call natural I would gladly follow even a will o' the wisp through bogs and sloughs unimaginable, but no moon nor fire-fly has shown me the cause-way to it. Nature is a personality so vast and universal that we have never seen one of her features. The walker in the familiar fields which stretch around my native town, sometimes finds himself in another land than is described in their owners' deeds, as it were in some far away field on the confines of the ac-tual Concord, where her jurisdiction ceases, and the idea which the word Concord suggests ceases to be suggested. These farms which I have myself surveyed, these bounds which I have set up appear dimly still as through a mist; but they have no chemistry to fix them; they fade from the surface of the glass; and the picture which the painter painted stands out dimly from beneath. The world with which we are commonly acquainted leaves no trace, and it will have no anniversary.

I took a walk on Spaulding's Farm the other afternoon. I saw the setting sun lighting up the opposite side of a stately pine-wood. Its golden rays straggled into the aisles of the wood as into some noble hall. I was impressed as if some ancient and altogether admirable and shining family had seated there in that part of the land called Concord, unknown to me; to whom the Sun was servant; who had not gone into society in the village; who had not been called on. I saw their park, their pleasure ground, beyond through the wood, in Spaulding's cranberry meadow. The pines furnished them with gables as they grew. Their house was not obvious to vision; the trees grew through it. I do not know whether I heard the sounds of a suppressed hilarity or not. They seemed to recline on the sunbeams. They have sons and daughters. They are quite well. The farmer's cart path which leads directly through their hall does not in the least put them out,–as the muddy bottom of a pool is sometimes seen through the reflected skies. They never heard of Spaulding, and do not know that he is their neighbor,– notwithstanding that I heard him whistle as he drove his team through the house. Nothing can equal the serenity of their lives. Their coat of arms is simply a lichen. I saw it painted on the pines and oaks. Their attics were in the tops of the trees. They are of no politics. There was no noise of labor. I did not perceive that they were weaving or spinning. Yet I did detect, when the wind lulled and hearing was done away, the finest imaginable sweet musical hum,–as of a distant hive in May, which perchance was the sound of their thinking. They had no idle thoughts, and no one without could see their work, for their industry was not as in knots and excrescences embayed.

But I find it difficult to remember them. They fade irrevocably out of my mind even now that I speak and endeavor to recall them, and recollect myself. It is only after a long and serious effort to recollect my best thoughts that I become again aware of their cohabitancy. If it were not for such families as this I think I should move out of Concord.

We are accustomed to say in New England that few and fewer pigeons visit us every year. Our forests furnish no mast for them. So, it would seem, few and fewer thoughts visit each growing man from year to year, for the grove in our minds is laid waste,–sold to feed unnecessary fires of ambition, or sent to mill, and there is scarcely a twig left for them to perch on. They no longer build nor breed with us. In some more genial season, perchance, a faint shadow flits across the landscape of the mind, cast by the *wings* of some thought in its vernal or autumnal migration, but looking up, we are unable to detect the substance of the thought itself. Our winged thoughts are turned to poultry. They no longer soar, and they attain only to a Shanghai and Cochin China grandeur. Those *gra-a-ate thoughts*–those *gra-a-ate men*–you hear of.

We hug the earth–how rarely we mount! Methinks we might elevate ourselves a little more. We might climb a tree at least. I found my account in climbing a tree once. It was a tall white pine on the top of a hill, and though I got well pitched I was well payed for it, for I discovered new mountains in the horizon which I had never seen before,–so much more of the earth and the heavens. I might have walked about the foot of the tree for three score years and ten, and yet I certainly should never have seen them. But, above all, I discovered around me,–it was near the end of June, on the ends of the topmost branches only, a few minute and delicate red cone-like blossoms, the fertile flower of the white pine looking heavenward. I carried straightway to the village the topmost spire, and showed it to stranger jurymen who walked the streets,–for it was court week–and to farmers and lumber dealers, and wood-choppers and hunters, and not one had ever seen the like before, but they wondered as at a star dropped down! Tell of ancient architects finishing their works on the tops of columns as perfectly as on the lower and more visible parts! Nature has from the first expanded the minute blossoms of the forest only toward the heavens, above men's heads and unobserved by them. We see only the flowers that are under our feet in the meadows. The pines have developed their delicate blossoms on the highest twigs of the wood every summer for ages, as well over the heads of Nature's red children, as of her white ones.– Yet scarcely a farmer or hunter in the land has ever seen them.

Above all, we cannot afford not to live in the present. He is blessed over all mortals who loses no moment of the passing life in remembering the past. Unless our philosophy hears the cock crow in every barn-yard within our horizon, it is belated. That sound commonly reminds us that we are growing rusty and antique in our employments and habits of thought. His philosophy comes down to a more recent time than ours. There is something suggested by it not in Plato nor the New Testament. It is a newer testament–the Gospel according to this moment. He has not fallen astern; he has got up early, and kept up early, and to be where he is, is to be in season, in the foremost rank of time. It is an expression of the health and soundness of

Nature, a brag for all the world–healthiness as of a spring burst forth–a new fountain of the Muses, to celebrate this last instant of time. Where he lives no fugitive slave laws are passed. Who has not betrayed his master many times since last he heard that note?

The merit of this bird's strain is in its freedom from all plaintiveness. The singer can easily move us to tears or to laughter, but where is he who can excite in us a pure morning joy? When, in doleful dumps, breaking the awful stillness of our wooden side-walk on a Sunday–or perchance a watcher in the house of mourning–I hear a cockerel crow far or near, I think to myself there is one of us well at any rate, and with a sudden gush return to my senses.

We had a remarkable sunset one day last November. I was walking in a meadow the source of a small brook, when the sun at last, just before setting, after a cold grey day, reached a clear stratum in the horizon, and the softest brightest morning sun-light fell on the dry grass and on the stems of the trees in the opposite horizon, and on the leaves of the shrub-oaks on the hillside, while our shadows stretched long over the meadow eastward, as if we were the only motes in its beams. It was such a light as we could not have imagined a moment before, and the air also was so warm and serene that nothing was wanting to make a paradise of that meadow. When we reflected that this was not a solitary phenomenon, never to happen again, but that it would happen forever and ever an infinite number of evenings, and cheer and reassure the latest child that walked there, it was more glorious still.

The sun sets on some retired meadow, where no house is visible, with all the glory and splendor that it lavishes on cities, and perchance, as it has never set before,–where there is but a solitary marsh hawk to have his wings gilded by it, or only a musquash looks out from his cabin, and there is some little black-veined brook in the midst of the marsh, just beginning to meander, winding slowly round a decaying stump.– We walked in so pure and bright a light, gilding the withered grass and leaves, so softly and serenely bright–I thought I had never bathed in such a golden flood, without a ripple or a murmur to it. The west side of every wood and rising ground gleamed like the boundary of elysium, and the sun on our backs seemed like a gentle herdsman, driving us home at evening.

So we saunter toward the Holy Land; till one day the sun shall shine more brightly than ever he has done, shall perchance shine into our minds and hearts, and light up our whole lives with a great awakening light, so warm and serene and golden as on a bank-side in Autumn.

Autumnal Tints.

EUROPEANS coming to America are surprised by the brilliancy of our autumnal foliage. There is no account of such a phenomenon in English poetry, because the trees acquire but few bright colors there. The most that Thomson says on this subject in his "Autumn" is contained in the lines–

> "But see the fading many-colored woods,
> Shade deepening over shade, the country round
> Imbrown; a crowded umbrage, dusk and dun,
> Of every hue, from wan-declining green
> To sooty dark."–

And the line in which he speaks of

> "Autumn beaming o'er the yellow woods."

The autumnal change of our woods has not made a deep impression on our own literature yet. October has hardly tinged our poetry.

A great many, who have spent their lives in cities, and have never chanced to come into the country at this season, have never seen this the flower, or rather ripe fruit, of the year. I remember riding with one such citizen, who, though a fortnight too late for the most brilliant tints, was taken by surprise, and would not believe that there had been any brighter. He had never heard of this phenomenon before. Not only many in our towns have never witnessed it, but it is scarcely remembered by the majority from year to year.

Most appear to confound changed leaves with withered ones, as if they were to confound ripe apples with rotten ones. I think that the change to some higher color in a leaf is an evidence that it has arrived at a late and perfect maturity, answering to the maturity of fruits. It is generally the lowest and oldest leaves which change first. But as the perfect winged and usually bright-colored insect is short-lived, so the leaves ripen but to fall.

Generally, every fruit, on ripening, and just before it falls, when it commences a more independent and individual existence, requiring less nourishment from any source, and that not so much from the earth through its stem as from the sun and air, acquires a bright tint. So do leaves. The physiologist says it is "due to an increased absorption of oxygen." That is the scientific account of the matter,—only a reassertion of the fact. But I am more interested in the rosy cheek than I am to know what particular diet the maiden fed on. The very forest and herbage, the pellicle of the earth, must acquire a bright color, an evidence of its ripeness,—as if the globe itself were a fruit on its stem, with ever a cheek toward the sun.

Flowers are but colored leaves, fruits but ripe ones. The edible part of most fruits is, as the physiologist says, "the parenchyma or fleshy tissue of the leaf" of which they are formed.

Our appetites have commonly confined our views of ripeness and its phenomena, color, mellowness, and perfectness, to the fruits which we eat, and we are wont to forget that an immense harvest which we do not eat, hardly use at all, is annually ripened by Nature. At our annual Cattle Shows and Horticultural Exhibitions, we make, as we think, a great show of fair fruits, destined, however, to a rather ignoble end, fruits not valued for their beauty chiefly. But round about and within our towns there is annually another show of fruits, on an infinitely grander scale, fruits which address our taste for beauty alone.

October is the month of painted leaves. Their rich glow now flashes round the world. As fruits and leaves and the day itself acquire a bright tint, just before they fall, so the year near its setting. October is its sunset sky; November the later twilight.

I formerly thought that it would be worth the while to get a specimen leaf from each changing tree, shrub and herbaceous plant, when it had acquired its brightest characteristic color, in its transition from the green to the brown state, outline it and copy its color exactly with paint in a book, which should be entitled October, or Autumnal Tints. Beginning with the earliest reddening–woodbine and the lake of radical leaves, and coming down through the maples, hickories and sumacs, and many beautifully freckled leaves less generally known, to the latest oaks and aspens. What a memento such a book would be! You would need only to turn over its leaves to take a ramble through the Autumn woods whenever you pleased. Or if I could preserve the leaves themselves unfaded, it would be better still. I have made but little progress toward such a book, but I have endeavored instead to describe all these bright tints in the order in which they present themselves. The following are some extracts from my notes.

The Purple Grasses.

By the twentieth of August, everywhere in woods and swamps, we are reminded of the fall, both by the richly spotted Sarsaparilla-leaves and Brakes, and the withering and blackened Skunk-Cabbage and Hellebore, and, by the river-side, the already blackening Pontederia.

The Purple Grass (*Eragrostis pectinacea*) is now in the height of its beauty. I remember still when I first noticed this grass particularly. Standing on a hill-side near our river, I saw, thirty or forty rods off, a stripe of purple half a dozen rods long, under the edge of a wood, where the ground sloped toward a meadow. It was as high-colored and interesting, though not quite so bright, as the patches of Rhexia, being a darker purple, like a berry's stain laid on close and thick. On going to and examining it, I found it to be a kind of grass in bloom, hardly a foot high, with but few green blades, and a fine spreading panicle of purple flowers, a shallow, purplish mist trembling around me. Close at hand it appeared but a dull purple, and made little impression on the eye. It was even difficult to detect, and if you plucked a single plant you were surprised to find how thin it was, and how little color it had. But viewed at a distance in a favorable light, it was of a fine lively purple, flower-like, enriching the earth. Such puny causes combine to produce these decided effects. I was the more surprised and charmed because grass is commonly of a sober and humble color.

With its beautiful purple blush it reminds me and supplies the place of the rhexia which is now leaving off, and it is one of the most interesting phenomena of August. The finest patches of it grow on waste strips or selvedges of land at the base of dry hills, just above the edge of the meadows, where the greedy mower does not deign to swing his scythe; for this is a thin and poor grass, beneath his notice. Or, it may be, because it is so beautiful he does not know that it exists; for the same eye does not see this and timothy. He carefully gets the meadow hay and the more nutritious grasses which grow next to that, but he leaves this fine purple mist for the walker's harvest–fodder for his fancy stock. Higher up the hill perchance grow also blackberries, johnswort and neglected, withered and wiry June-grass. How fortunate that it grows in such places and not in the midst of the rank grasses which are annually cut! Nature thus keeps use and beauty distinct.

I know many such localities where it does not fail to present itself annually and paint the earth with its blush. It grows either in a continuous patch, or in scattered and rounded tufts a foot in diameter on the gentle slopes, and it lasts till it is killed by the first smart frosts.

In most plants the corolla or calyx is the part which attains the highest color, and is the most attractive; in many it is the seed-vessel or fruit; in others, as the Red Maple, the leaves; and in others still it is the very culm itself which is the principal flower or blooming part.

The last is especially the case with the Poke or Garget (*Phytolacca decandra*). Some which stand under our cliffs quite dazzle me with their purple stems now and early in September. They are as interesting to me as most flowers, and one of the most important fruits of our autumn. Every part is flower, (or fruit,) such is its superfluity of color,–stem, branch, peduncle, pedicel, petiole, and even the at length yellowish purple-veined leaves. Its cylindrical racemes of berries of various hues, from green to dark purple, six or seven inches long, are gracefully drooping on all sides, offering repasts to the birds; and even the sepals from which the birds have picked the berries are a brilliant lake-red, with crimson flame-like reflections, equal to anything of the kind,–all on fire with ripeness. Hence the *lacca*, from *lac*, lake. There are at the same time flower-buds, flowers, green berries, dark purple or ripe ones, and these flower-like sepals, all on the same plant.

We love to see any redness in the vegetation of the temperate zone. It is the color of colors. This plant speaks to our blood. It asks a bright sun on it to make it show to best advantage, and it must be seen at this season of the year. On warm hill-sides its stems are ripe by the twenty-third of August. At that date I walked through a beautiful grove of them, six or seven feet high, on the side of one of our cliffs, where they ripen early. Quite to the ground they were a deep brilliant purple with a bloom, contrasting with the still clear green leaves. It appears a rare triumph of Nature to have produced and perfected such a plant, as if this were enough for a summer. What a perfect maturity it arrives at! It is the emblem of a successful life, concluded by a death not premature, which is an ornament to nature. What if we were to mature as perfectly, root and branch, glowing in the midst of our decay, like the Poke! I confess, that it excites me to behold them. I cut one for a cane, for I would fain handle and lean on it. I love to press the berries between my fingers, and see their juice staining my hand. To walk amid these upright branching casks of purple wine, which retain and diffuse a sunset glow, tasting each one with your eye, instead of counting the pipes on a London dock, what a privilege! For Nature's vintage is not confined to the vine. Our poets have sung of wine, the product of a foreign plant which commonly they never saw, as if our own plants had no juice in them more than the singers. Indeed, this has been called by some the American Grape, and, though a native of America, its juices are used in some foreign countries to improve the color of the wine; so that the poetaster may be celebrating the virtues of the Poke without knowing it. Here are berries enough to paint afresh the western sky, and play the bacchanal with, if you will. And what flutes its ensanguined stems would make, to be used in such a dance! It is truly a royal plant. I could spend the evening of the year musing amid the Poke-stems. And perchance amid these groves might arise at last a new school of philosophy or poetry. It lasts all through September.

At the same time with this, or near the end of August, a to me very interesting genus of grasses, Andropogons, or Beard-Grasses, is in its prime. *Andropogon furcatus*, Forked Beard-Grass, or call it Purple-Fingered Grass; *Andropogon scoparius*, Purple Wood-Grass; and *Andropogon* (now called *Sorghum*) *nutans*, Indian-Grass. The first is a very tall and slender-culmed grass, three to seven feet high, with four or five purple finger-like spikes raying upward from the top. The second is also quite slender, growing in tufts two feet high by one wide, with culms often somewhat curving, which, as the spikes go out of bloom, have a whitish fuzzy look. These two are prevailing grasses at this season on dry and sandy fields and hill-sides. The culms of both, not to mention their pretty flowers, reflect a purple tinge, and help to declare the ripeness of the year. Perhaps I have the more sympathy with them because they are despised by the farmer, and occupy sterile and neglected soil. They are high-colored, like ripe grapes, and express a maturity which the spring did not suggest. Only the August sun could have thus burnished these culms and leaves. The farmer has long since done his upland haying, and he will not condescend to bring his scythe to where these slender wild grasses have at length flowered thinly; you often see spaces of bare sand amid them. But I walk encouraged between the tufts of Purple Wood-Grass, over the sandy fields, and along the edge of the Shrub-Oaks, glad to recognize these simple contemporaries. With thoughts cutting a broad swathe I "get" them, with horse-raking thoughts I gather them into windrows. The fine-eared poet may hear the whetting of my scythe. These two were almost the first grasses that I learned to distinguish, for I had not known by how many friends I was surrounded,–I had seen them simply as grasses standing. The purple of their culms also excites me like that of the Poke-Weed stems.

Think what refuge there is for one, before August is over, from college commencements and society that isolates! I can skulk amid the tufts of Purple Wood-Grass on the borders of the "Great Fields." Wherever I walk these afternoons, the Purple-Fingered Grass also stands like a guide-board, and points my thoughts to more poetic paths than they have lately travelled.

A man shall perhaps rush by and trample down plants as high as his head, and cannot be said to know that they exist, though he may have cut many tons of them, littered his stables with them, and fed them to his cattle for years. Yet, if he ever favorably attends to them, he may be overcome by their beauty. Each humblest plant, or weed, as we call it, stands there to express some thought or mood of ours; and yet how long it stands in vain! I had walked over those Great Fields so many Augusts, and never yet distinctly recognized these purple companions that I had there. I had brushed against them and trodden on them, forsooth; and now, at last, they, as it were, rose up and blessed me. Beauty and true wealth are always thus cheap and despised. Heaven might be defined as the place which men avoid. Who can doubt that these grasses, which the farmer says are of no account to him, find some compensation in your appreciation of them? I may say that I never saw them before,–though, when I came to look them face to face, there did come down to me a purple gleam from previous years; and now, wherever I go, I see hardly anything else. It is the reign and presidency of the Andropogons.

Almost the very sands confess the ripening influence of the August sun, and methinks, together with the slender grasses waving over them, reflect a purple tinge. The impurpled sands! Such is the consequence of all this sunshine absorbed into the pores of plants and of the earth. All sap or blood is now wine-colored. At last we have not only the purple sea, but the purple land.

The Chestnut Beard-Grass, Indian-Grass, or Wood-Grass, growing here and there in waste places, but more rare than the former, (from two to four or five feet high,) is still handsomer and of more vivid colors than its congeners, and might well have caught the Indian's eye. It has a long, narrow, one-sided, and slightly nodding panicle of bright purple and yellow flowers, like a banner raised above its reedy leaves. These bright standards are now advanced on the distant hill-sides, not in large armies, but in scattered troops or single file, like the red men. They stand thus fair and bright, representative of the race which they are named after, but for the most part unobserved as they. The expression of this grass haunted me for a week, after I first passed and noticed it, like the glance of an eye. It stands like an Indian chief taking a last look at his favorite hunting-grounds.

The Red Maple

By the 25th of September, the Red Maples generally are *beginning* to be ripe. Some large ones have been conspicuously changing for a week, and some single trees are now very brilliant. I notice a small one, half a mile off across a meadow, against the green wood-side there, a far brighter red than the blossoms of any tree in summer, and more conspicuous. I have observed this tree for several autumns invariably changing earlier than its fellows, just as one tree ripens its fruit earlier than another. It might serve to mark the season perhaps. I should be sorry if it were cut down.

I know of 2 or 3 such trees in different parts of my town, which might perhaps be propagated from as early ripeners or September trees, and their seed be advertised in the market, as well as that of radishes, if we cared as much about them.

At present, these burning bushes stand chiefly along the edge of the meadows, or I distinguish them afar on the hill-sides here and there. Sometimes you will see many small ones in a swamp turned quite crimson when all other trees around are still perfectly green, and the former appear so much the brighter for it. They take you by surprise as you are going by on one side, across the fields, thus early in the season, as if it were some gay encampment of the redmen, or other foresters, of whose arrival you had not heard.

Some single trees, wholly bright scarlet, seen against others of their kind still freshly green, or against evergreens, are more memorable than whole groves will be by and by. How beautiful when a whole tree is like one great scarlet fruit, full of ripe juices, every leaf, from lowest limb to topmost spire, all a-glow, especially if you look toward the sun. What more remarkable object can there be in the landscape? Visible for miles, too fair to be believed. If such a phenomenon occurred but once, it would be handed down by tradition to posterity, and get into the mythology at last.

The whole tree thus ripening in advance of its fellows attains a singular preëminence, and sometimes maintains it for a week or two. I am thrilled at the sight of it, bearing aloft its scarlet standard for the regiment of green-clad foresters around, and I go half a mile out of my way to examine it. A single tree becomes thus the crowning beauty of some meadowy vale, and the expression of the whole surrounding forest is at once more spirited for it.

A small Red Maple has grown, perchance, far away at the head of some retired valley, a mile from any road, unobserved. It has faithfully discharged the duties of a Maple there, all winter and summer, neglected none of its economies, but added to its stature in the virtue which belongs to a Maple, by a steady growth for so many months, never having gone gadding abroad, and is nearer heaven than it was in the spring. It has faithfully husbanded its sap, and afforded a shelter to the wandering bird, has long since ripened its seeds and committed them to the winds, and has the satisfaction of knowing, perhaps, that a thousand little well-behaved Maples are already settled in life somewhere. It deserves well of Mapledom. Its leaves have been asking it from time to time, in a whisper, "When shall we redden?" And now, in this month of September, this month of travelling, when men are hastening to the sea-side, or the mountains, or the lakes, this modest Maple, still without budging an inch, travels in its reputation,–runs up its scarlet flag on that hill-side, which shows that it has finished its summer's work before all other trees, and withdraws from the contest. At the eleventh hour of the year, the tree which no scrutiny could have detected here when it was most industrious is thus, by the tint of its maturity, by its very blushes, revealed at last to the careless and distant traveller, and leads his thoughts away from the dusty road into those brave solitudes which it inhabits. It flashes out conspicuous with all the virtue and beauty of a Maple,–*Acer rubrum*. We may now read its title, or *rubric*, clear. Its *virtues*, not its sins, are as scarlet.

Notwithstanding that the Red Maple is the most intense scarlet of any of our trees, the Sugar Maple has been the most celebrated, and Michaux, in his Sylva does not speak of the autumnal color of the former. About the 2nd of October these trees, both large and small, are most brilliant, though many are still green. In sprout-lands they seem to vie with one another, and ever some particular one in the midst of the crowd will be of a peculiarly pure scarlet, and by its more intense color attract our eye even at a distance, and carry off the palm. A large Red Maple swamp, when at the height of its change, is the most obviously brilliant of all tangible things, where I dwell, so abundant is this tree with us. It varies much both in form and color. A great many are merely yellow, more Scarlet, others scarlet deepening into crimson, more red than common. Look at yonder swamp of Maples mixed with Pines, at the base of a pine-clad hill, a quarter of a mile off, so that you get the full effect of the bright colors, without detecting the imperfections of the leaves and see their yellow, scarlet and crimson fires, of all tints, mingled and contrasted with the green.

Some Maples are yet green, only yellow or crimson-tipt on the edges of their flakes, as the edges of a hazel-nut burr, some are wholly brilliant scarlet, raying out regularly and finely every way, bilaterally, like the veins of a leaf; others, of more irregular form, when I turn my head slightly, emptying out some of its earthiness and concealing the trunk of the tree, seem to rest heavily flake on flake like yellow and scarlet clouds, wreath upon wreath, or like snow drifts driving through the air, stratified by the wind. It adds greatly to the beauty of such a swamp at this season, that, even though there may be no other trees interspersed, it is not seen as a simple mass of color, but different trees being of different colors and hues the outline of each crescent tree top is distinct, and where one laps onto another. Yet a painter would hardly venture to make them thus distinct a quarter of a mile off.

As I go across a meadow directly towards a low rising ground this bright afternoon, I see, some fifty rods off toward the sun the top of a Maple swamp just appearing over the sheeny russet edge of the hill, a stripe apparently twenty rods long by ten feet deep, of the most intensely brilliant scarlet, orange and yellow equal to any flowers or fruits, or any tints ever painted. As I advance, lowering the edge of the hill which makes the firm foreground or lower frame of the picture, the depth of the brilliant grove revealed steadily increases, suggesting that the whole of the enclosed valley is filled with such color. One wonders that the tithing men and fathers of the town are not out to see what the trees mean by their high colors and exuberance of spirits, fearing that some mischief is brewing. I do not see what the Puritans did at this season when the maples blaze out in scarlet. They certainly could not have worshipped in groves then. Perhaps that is what they built meeting houses and fenced them round with horse-sheds for.

THE ELM.

Now, too, the first of October, or later, the Elms are at the height of their autumnal beauty, great brownish-yellow masses, warm from their September oven, hanging over the highway. Their leaves are perfectly ripe. I wonder if there is any answering ripeness in the lives of the men who live beneath them. As I look down our street, which is lined with them, they remind me both by their form and color of yellowing sheaves of grain, as if the harvest had indeed come to the village itself, and we might expect to find some maturity and *flavor* in the thoughts of the villagers at last. Under those bright rustling yellow piles just ready to fall on the heads of the walkers, how can any crudity or greenness of thought or act prevail? When I stand where half a dozen large Elms droop over a house, it is as if I stood within a ripe pumpkin-rind, and I feel as mellow as if I were the pulp, though I may be somewhat stringy and seedy withal. What is the late greenness of the English Elm, like a cucumber out of season, which does not know when to have done, compared with the early and golden maturity of the American tree? The street is the scene of a great harvest-home. It would be worth the while to set out these trees, if only for their autumnal value. Think of these great yellow canopies or parasols held over our heads and houses by the mile together, making the village all one and compact,–an *ulmarium*, which is at the same time a nursery of men! And then how gently and unobserved they drop their burden and let in the sun when it is wanted, their leaves not heard when they fall on our roofs and in our streets; and thus the village parasol is shut up and put away! I see the market-man driving into the village, and disappearing under its canopy of Elm-tops, with *his* crop, as into a great granary or barn-yard. I am tempted to go thither as to a husking of thoughts, now dry and ripe and ready to be separated from their integuments; but alas! I foresee that it will be chiefly husks and little thought, blasted pig-corn, fit only for cob-meal–for as you sow so shall you reap.

Fallen Leaves.

By the sixth of October the leaves generally begin to fall, in successive showers, after frost or rain; but the principal leaf-harvest, the acme of the *Fall*, is commonly about the sixteenth. Some morning at that date there is perhaps a harder frost than we have seen, and ice formed under the pump, and now, when the morning wind rises, the leaves come down in denser showers than ever. They suddenly form thick beds or carpets on the ground, in this gentle air, or even without wind, just the size and form of the tree above. Some trees, as small Hickories, appear to have dropped their leaves instantaneously, as a soldier grounds arms at a signal; and those of the Hickory, being bright yellow still, though withered, reflect a blaze of light from the ground where they lie. Down they have come on all sides, at the first earnest touch of autumn's wand, making a sound like rain.

Or else it is after moist and rainy weather that we notice how great a fall of leaves there has been in the night, though it may not yet be the touch that loosens the Rock-Maple leaf. The streets are thickly strewn with the trophies, and fallen Elm-leaves make a dark brown pavement under our feet. After some remarkably warm Indian-summer day or days, I perceive that it is the unusual heat which, more than anything, causes the leaves to fall, there having been, perhaps, no frost nor rain for some time. The intense heat suddenly ripens and wilts them, just as it softens and ripens peaches and other fruits, and causes them to drop.

The leaves of late Red Maples, still bright, strew the earth, often crimson-spotted on a yellow ground, like some wild apples,–though they preserve these bright colors on the ground but a day or two, especially if it rains. On causeways I go by trees here and there all bare and smoke-like, having lost their brilliant clothing; but there it lies, nearly as bright as ever, on the ground on one side, and making nearly as regular a figure as lately on the tree. I would rather say that I first observe the trees thus flat on the ground like a permanent colored shadow, and they suggest to look for the boughs that bore them. A queen might be proud to walk where these gallant trees have spread their bright cloaks in the mud. I see wagons roll over them as a shadow or a reflection, and the drivers heed them just as little as they did their shadows before.

Birds'-nests, in the Huckleberry and other shrubs, and in trees, are already being filled with the withered leaves. So many have fallen in the woods, that a squirrel cannot run after a falling nut without being heard. Boys are raking them in the streets, if only for the pleasure of dealing with such clean crisp substances. Some sweep the paths scrupulously neat, and then stand to see the next breath strew them with new trophies. The swamp-floor is thickly covered, and the *Lycopodium lucidulum* looks suddenly greener amid them. In dense woods they half-cover pools that are three or four rods long. The other day I could hardly find a well-known spring, and even suspected that it had dried up, for it was completely concealed by freshly fallen leaves; and when I swept them aside and revealed it, it was like striking the earth, with Aaron's rod, for a new spring. Wet grounds about the edges of swamps look dry with them. At one swamp, where I was surveying, thinking to step on a leafy shore from a rail, I got into the water more than a foot deep.

When I go to the river the day after the principal fall of leaves, the sixteenth I find my boat all covered, bottom and seats, with the leaves of the Golden Willow, under which it is moored, and I set sail with a cargo of them rustling under my feet. If I empty it it will be full again tomorrow. I do not regard them as litter to be swept out, but accept them as suitable straw or matting for the bottom of my carriage. When I turn up into the mouth of the Assabet, which is wooded, large fleets of leaves are floating on its surface, as it were getting out to sea, with room to tack, but next the shore, a little

further up, they are thicker than foam, quite concealing the water for a rod in width, under and amid the
Alders, Button-bushes and Maples, still perfectly light
and dry with fiber unrelaxed; and at a rocky bend,
where they are met and stopped by the morning wind,
they sometimes form a broad and dense crescent,
quite across the river. When I turn my prow that way
and the wave which it makes strikes them, list what a
pleasant rustling from these dry substances, grating
on one another. Often it is their undulation only which
reveals the water beneath them. Also every motion of
the wood turtle on the shore is betrayed by their rustling there. Or even in mid channel, when the wind
rises, I hear them blown with a rustling sound. Higher
up they are slowly moving round and round in some
great eddy which the river makes, as that at the "Leaning Hemlocks", where the water is deep, and the current is wearing into the bank.

Perchance, in the afternoon of such a day, when the
water is perfectly calm and full of reflections, I paddle
gently down the main stream, and turning up the Assabet reach a quiet cove where I unexpectedly find
myself surrounded by myriads of leaves like fellow
voyagers which seem to have the same purpose or
want of purpose, with myself. See this great fleet of
scattered leaf-boats which we paddle amid, in this
smooth river bay, each one curled up on every side by
the sun's skill; each nerve a stiff Spruce knee; like
boats of hide and of all patterns, Charon's boat probably among the rest, and some with lofty prows and
poops like the stately vessels of the ancients, scarcely
moving in the sluggish current,–like the great fleets,
the dense Chinese cities, of boats, with which you
mingle on entering some great mart, some New York
or Canton, which we are all steadily approaching
together.

How gently each has been deposited on the water. No violence has been used towards them yet, though perchance palpitating hearts were present at the launching. And painted ducks too, the splendid Wood-duck, among the rest, often come to sail and float amid the painted leaves–barks of a nobler model still!

What wholesome herb drinks are to be had in the swamps now! What strong medicinal but rich scents from the decaying leaves! The rain falling on the freshly dried herbs and leaves, and filling the pools and ditches into which they have dropped thus clean and rigid, will soon convert them into tea–green, black, brown and yellow teas, of all degrees of strength, enough to set all Nature a-gossiping. Whether we drink them or not, as yet, before their strength is drawn, these leaves, dried on Great Nature's coppers, are of such various pure and delicate tints as might make the fame of oriental teas.

How they are mixed up, of all species, Oak, and Maple, and Chestnut, and Birch. But Nature is not cluttered with them. She is a perfect husbandman; she stores them all. Consider what a vast crop is thus annually shed on the earth! This more than any mere grain or seed is the great harvest of the year. The trees are now repaying the earth with interest–what they have taken from it. They are discounting. They are about to add a leaf's thickness to the depth of the soil. This is the beautiful way in which Nature gets her muck, while I chaffer with this man and that, who talks to me about sulphur and the cost of carting. We are all the richer for their decay. I am more interested in this crop than in the English grass alone or in the corn. It prepares the virgin mould for future cornfields and forests, on which the earth fattens. It keeps our homestead in good heart.

For beautiful variety no crop can be compared with this. Here is not merely the plain yellow of the grains, but nearly all the colors that we know, the brightest blue not excepted. The early blushing Maple, the poison Sumac blazing its sins as scarlet, the mulberry Ash, the rich chrome yellow of the Poplars, the brilliant red Huckleberry, with which the hills' backs are painted, like those of sheep. The frost touches them, and with the slightest breath of returning day or jarring of earth's axle, see in what showers they come floating down. The ground is all particolored with them. But they still live in the soil whose fertility and bulk they increase, and in the forests that spring from it. They stoop to rise, to mount higher in coming years, by subtle chemistry, climbing by the sap in the trees, and the sapling's first fruits thus shed, transmuted at last, may adorn its crown, when in after years, it has become the monarch of the forest.

It is pleasant to walk over the beds of these fresh, crisp, and rustling leaves. How beautifully they go to their graves! how gently lay themselves down and turn to mould!–painted of a thousand hues, and fit to make the beds of us living. So they troop to their last resting-place, light and frisky. They put on no weeds, but merrily they go scampering over the earth, selecting the spot, choosing a lot, ordering no iron fence, whispering all through the woods about it,–some choosing the spot where the bodies of men are mouldering beneath, and meeting them half-way. How many flutterings before they rest quietly in their graves! They that soared so loftily, how contentedly they return to dust again, and are laid low, resigned to lie and decay at the foot of the tree, and afford nourishment to new generations of their kind, as well as to flutter on high! They teach us how to die. One wonders if the time will ever

come when men, with their boasted faith in immortal-
ity, will lie down as gracefully and as ripe,–with such
an Indian-summer serenity will shed their bodies, as
they do their hair and nails.

When the leaves fall, the whole earth is a cemetery
pleasant to walk in. I love to wander and muse over
them in their graves. Here are no lying nor vain epitaphs. What though you own no lot at Mount Auburn?
Your lot is surely cast somewhere in this vast cemetery, which has been consecrated from of old. You
need attend no auction to secure a place. There is
room enough here. The Loose-strife shall bloom and
the Huckleberry-bird sing over your bones. The woodman and hunter shall be your sextons, and the children shall tread upon the borders as much as they will.
Let us walk in the cemetery of the leaves,–this is your
true Greenwood Cemetery.

The Sugar Maple

But think not that the splendor of the year is over, for
if one leaf does not make a summer neither does
one fallen leaf make an Autumn. The smallest Sugar
Maples in our streets make a great show as early as the
fifth of October, more than any trees there. As I look up
the Main Street they appear like painted screens
standing before the houses, yet many are green. But
now, or generally by the 17th of October, when almost
all Red Maples, and some White Maples are bare, the
large Sugar Maples also are in their glory, glowing with
yellow and red and show unexpectedly bright and delicate tints. They are remarkable for the contrast they
often afford of deep blushing red on one half, and
green on the other. They become at length dense
masses of rich yellow with a deep scarlet blush, or
more than blush, on the exposed surfaces. They are
the brightest trees now in the street.

The large ones on our common are particularly beautiful. A delicate, but warmer than golden yellow is now the prevailing color, with scarlet cheeks. Yet standing on the east side of the Common just before sundown, when the western light is transmitted through them, I see that their yellow even, compared with the pale lemon yellow of an Elm close by, amounts to a scarlet, without noticing the bright scarlet portions. Generally, they are great regular oval masses of yellow and scarlet. All the sunny warmth of the season, the Indian summer, seems to be absorbed in their leaves. The lowest and inmost leaves next the bole are, as usual, of the most delicate yellow and green, like the complexion of young men brought up in the house. There is an auction on the Common to-day, but its red flag is hard to be discerned amid this blaze of color.

Little did the fathers of the town anticipate this brilliant success, when they caused to be imported from further in the country some straight poles with their tops cut off, which they called Sugar-Maples; and, as I remember, after they were set out, a neighboring merchant's clerk, by way of jest, planted beans about them. Those which were then jestingly called bean-poles are to-day far the most beautiful objects noticeable in our streets. They are worth all and more than they have cost,–though one of the selectmen, while setting them out, took the cold which occasioned his death,–if only because they have filled the open eyes of children with their rich color unstintedly so many Octobers. We will not ask them to yield us sugar in the spring, while they afford us so fair a prospect in the autumn. Wealth in-doors may be the inheritance of few, but it is equally distributed on the Common. All children alike can revel in this golden harvest.

Surely trees should be set in our streets with a view to their October splendor; though I doubt whether this is ever considered by the "Tree Society." Do you not think it will make some odds to these children that they were brought up under the Maples? Hundreds of eyes are steadily drinking in this color, and by these teachers even the truants are caught and educated the moment they step abroad. Indeed, neither the truant nor the studious are at present taught colors in the schools. These are instead of the bright colors in apothecaries' shops and city windows. It is a pity that we have no more *Red* Maples, and some Hickories, in our streets as well. Our paint-box is very imperfectly filled. Instead of, or beside, supplying such paint-boxes as we do, we might supply these natural colors to the young. Where else will they study color under greater advantages? What School of Design can vie with this? Think how much the eyes of painters of all kinds, and of manufacturers of cloth and paper, and paper-stainers, and countless others, are to be educated by these autumnal colors. The stationer's envelopes may be of very various tints, yet not so various as those of the leaves of a single tree. If you want a different shade or tint of a particular color, you have only to look further within or without the tree or the wood. These leaves are not many dipped in one dye, as at the dye-house, but they are dyed in light of infinitely various degrees of strength, and left to set and dry there.

Shall the names of so many of our colors continue to be derived from those of obscure foreign localities, as Naples yellow, Prussian blue, raw Sienna, burnt Umber, Gamboge?–(surely the Tyrian purple must have faded by this time)–or from comparatively trivial articles of commerce,–chocolate, lemon, coffee, cinnamon, claret?–(shall we compare our Hickory to a

lemon, or a lemon to a Hickory?)–or from ores and ox-
ides which few ever see? Shall we so often, when describing to our neighbors the color of something we
have seen, refer them, not to some natural object in
our neighborhood, but perchance to a bit of earth
fetched from the other side of the planet, which possibly they may find at the apothecary's, but which probably neither they nor we ever saw? Have we not an
earth under our feet,–ay, and a sky over our heads? Or
is the last *all* ultramarine? What do we know of sap-
phire, amethyst, emerald, ruby, amber, and the like,–
most of us who take these names in vain? Leave these
precious words to cabinet keepers, virtuosos and
maids of honor, to the Nabobs, Begums and Chobdars
of Hindostan,–or wherever else. I do not see why,
since America and her autumn woods have been discovered, our leaves should not compete with the precious stones in giving names to colors, and, indeed, I
believe that in course of time, the names of some of
our trees and shrubs as well as flowers will get into our
popular chromatic nomenclature.

But of much more importance than a knowledge of
the names and distinctions of color, is the joy and ex-
hilaration which these colored leaves excite. Already
these brilliant trees throughout the street, without any
more variety, are at least equal to an annual festival
and holiday, or a week of such. These are cheap and
innocent galadays, celebrated by one and all without
the aid of committees or marshals, such a show as may
safely be licensed, not attracting gamblers nor rum-
sellers, nor requiring any special police to keep the
peace; and poor indeed must be that New England village's October which has not the Maple in its streets.
This October festival costs no powder, nor ringing of
bells, but every tree is a living liberty pole on which a
thousand bright flags are waving.

No wonder that we must have our annual cattle-show, and Fall Training, and perhaps Cornwallis–our September Courts, and the like–Nature herself holds her annual Fair in October, not only in the streets, but in every hollow and on every hill side. When lately we looked into that Red Maple swamp all a-blaze, where the trees were clothed in their vestures of most dazzling tints, did it not suggest a thousand Gypsies beneath–a race capable of wild delight–or even the fabled fawns, satyrs and wood-nymphs come back to earth? Or was it only a congregation of wearied wood choppers, or of proprietors come to inspect their lots, that we thought of? Or, earlier still, when we paddled on the river through that fine-grained September air, did there not appear to be something new going on under the sparkling surface of the stream, a shaking of props, at least, so that we made haste in order to be up in time? Did not the rows of yellowing willows and button-bushes on each side seem like rows of booths under which perhaps some fluviatile egg-pop equally yellow was effervescing? –Did not all these suggest that man's spirits should rise as high as Nature's–should hang out their flag, and the routine of his life be interrupted by an analogous expression of joy and hilarity?

No annual training or muster of soldiery, no celebration with its scarfs and banners, could import into the town a hundredth part of the annual splendor of our October. We have only to set the trees, or let them stand, and Nature will find the colored drapery,–flags of all her nations, some of whose private signals hardly the botanist can read,–while we walk under the triumphal arches of the Elms. Leave it to Nature to appoint the days, whether the same as in neighboring States or not, and let the clergy read her proclamations, if they can understand them. Behold what a brilliant drapery is her Woodbine flag! What public-spirited merchant, think you, has contributed this part of the show? There is no handsomer shingling and paint than this vine, at present covering a whole side of some houses. I do not believe that the Ivy *never sear* is comparable to it. No wonder it has been extensively introduced into London. Let us have a good many Maples and Hickories and Scarlet Oaks, then, I say. Blaze away! Shall that dirty roll of bunting in the gun-house be all the colors a village can display? A village is not complete, unless it have these trees to mark the season in it. They are important, like the town-clock. A village that has them not will not be found to work well. It has a screw loose, an essential part is wanting. Let us have Willows for spring, Elms for summer, Maples and Walnuts and Tupeloes for autumn, Evergreens for winter, and Oaks for all seasons. What is a gallery in a house to a gallery in the streets, which every market-man rides through, whether he will or not? Of course, there is not a picture-gallery in the country which would be worth so much to us as is the western view at sunset under the Elms of our main street. They are the frame to a picture which almost daily is painted behind them. An avenue of elms as large as our largest and 3 miles long would seem to lead to some admirable place though only C———. were at the end of it.

A village needs these innocent stimulants of bright and cheering prospects to keep off melancholy and superstition. Show me two villages, one embowered in trees and blazing with all the glories of October, the other a merely trivial and treeless waste, or with only a single tree or 2 for suicides, and I shall be sure that in the latter will be found the most starved and bigoted religionists, and the most desperate drinkers.

Every wash-tub, and milk-can, and grave-stone will be exposed. The inhabitants will disappear abruptly behind their barns and houses, like desert Arabs amid their rocks, and I shall look to see spears in their hands. They will be ready to accept the most barren and forlorn doctrine–as that the world is speedily coming to an end, or has already got to it, or that they themselves are turned wrong side outward. They will perchance crack their dry joints at one another and call it a spiritual communication.

But to confine ourselves to the Maples. What if we were to take half as much pains in protecting them as we do in setting them out! not stupidly tie our horses to our dahlia stems!

What meant the Fathers by establishing this *perfectly living* institution before the church? this institution which needs no repairing nor re-painting, which is continually "enlarged and repaired" by its growth?

Surely–they

> "Wrought in a sad sincerity;
> Themselves from God they could not free;
> They *planted* better than they knew;–
> The conscious *trees* to beauty grew."

Verily these maples are cheap preachers, permanently settled, which preach their half-century, and century, aye and century and a half sermons, with constantly increasing unction and influence, ministering to many generations of men, and the least we can do is to supply them with suitable colleagues as they grow infirm.

The Scarlet Oak

Belonging to a genus which is remarkable for the beautiful form of its leaves, I suspect that some Scarlet Oak leaves surpass those of all other Oaks in the rich and wild beauty of their outlines. I judge from an acquaintance with 12 species and from drawings which I have seen, of many others.

Stand under this tree and see how finely its leaves are cut against the sky, as it were, only a few sharp points extending from a midrib. They look like double, treble or quadruple crosses. They are far more ethereal than the less deeply scolloped oak leaves. They have so little leafy terra-firma that they appear melting away in the light, and scarcely obstruct our view. The leaves of very young plants, are, like those of full grown oaks of other species, more entire, simple and lumpish in their outlines, but these, raised high on old trees, have solved the leafy problem. Lifted higher and higher and sublimated more and more, putting off some earthiness and cultivating more intimacy with the light each year, they have at length the least possible amount of earthy matter, and the greatest spread and grasp of skyey influences. There they dance, arm in arm with the light, tripping it on fantastic points, fit partners in those aerial halls. So intimately mingled are they with it, that what with their slenderness and their glossy surfaces, you can hardly tell at last what in the dance is leaf and what is light. And when no zephyr stirs, they are at most but a rich tracery to the forest windows.

I am again struck with their beauty, when, a month later they thickly strew the ground in the woods, piled one upon another under my feet. They are then brown above but purple beneath. With their narrow lobes and their bold deep scollops reaching almost to the middle, they suggest that the material must be cheap, or else there has been a lavish expense in their creation, as if so much had been cut out. Or else they seem to us, the remnants of the stuff out of which leaves have been cut with a die. Indeed when they lie

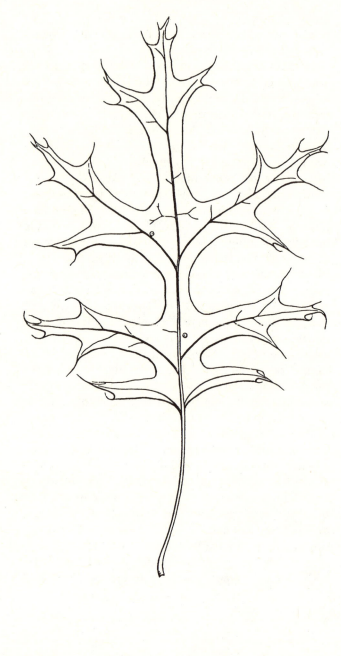

thus one upon another, they remind me of a pile of scrap tin.*

Or bring one home and study it closely at your leisure, by the fireside. It is a type not from any Oxford font, not in the Basque nor the arrow headed character–not found on the Rosetta Stone, but destined to be copied in sculpture one day, if they ever get to whittling stone here. What a wild and pleasing outline, a combination of graceful curves and angles! The eye rests with equal delight on what is not leaf and on what is leaf,–on the broad, free, open sinuses, and on the long, sharp, bristle-pointed lobes. A simple oval outline would include it all, if you connected the points of the leaf; but how much richer is it than that, with its half-dozen deep scollops, in which the eye and thought of the beholder are embayed! If I were a drawing-master, I would set my pupils to copying these leaves, that they might learn to draw firmly and gracefully.

Regarded as water, it is like a pond with half a dozen broad rounded promontories extending nearly to its middle, half from each side, while its watery bays extend far inland, like sharp friths, at each of whose heads several fine streams empty in,–almost a leafy archipelago.

But it oftener suggests land, and, as Dionysius and Pliny compared the form of the Morea to that of the leaf of the Oriental Plane-tree, so this leaf reminds me of some fair wild island in the ocean, whose extensive coast, alternate rounded bays with smooth strands, and sharp-pointed rocky capes, mark it as fitted for the habitation of man, and destined to become a centre of civilization at last. To the sailor's eye, it is a

---

* The original of the leaf on the opposite page was picked from such a pile.

much-indented shore. Is it not, in fact, a shore to the aërial ocean, on which the windy surf beats? At sight of this leaf we are all mariners,–if not vikings, bucca-neers, and filibusters. Both our love of repose and our spirit of adventure are addressed. In our most casual glance, perchance, we think, that, if we succeed in doubling those sharp capes, we shall find deep, smooth, and secure havens in the ample bays. How different from the White-Oak leaf, with its rounded headlands, on which no light-house need be placed! That is an England, with its long civil history, that may be read. This is some still unsettled New-found Island or Celebes. Shall we go and be rajahs there?

By the 26th of October the large Scarlet Oaks are in their prime, when other oaks are usually withered. They have been kindling their fires for a week past, and now generally burst into a blaze. This alone of *our* in-digenous deciduous trees (excepting the Dogwood, of which I do not know half a dozen, and they are but large bushes), is now in its glory. The two Aspens and the Sugar Maple come nearest to it in date, but they have lost the greater part of their leaves. Of evergreens, only the pitch pine is still commonly bright.

But it requires a particular alertness, if not devotion to these phenomena, to appreciate the wide spread, but late and unexpected glory of the Scarlet Oaks. I do not speak here of the small trees and shrubs, which are commonly observed, and which are now withered, but of the large trees. Most go in and shut their doors, thinking that bleak and colorless November has al-ready come, when some of the most brilliant and memorable colors are not yet lit.

This very perfect and vigorous one, about forty feet high, standing in an open pasture, which was quite glossy green on the 12th, is now, the 26th, completely changed to bright dark scarlet, every leaf, between you and the sun as if it had been dipped into a scarlet dye. The whole tree is much like a heart in form, as well as color. Was not this worth waiting for? Little did you think ten days ago, that that cold green tree would assume such color as this. Its leaves are still firmly attached, while those of other trees, are falling around it. It seems to say–I am the last to blush, but I blush deeper than any of ye. I bring up the rear in my red coat. We Scarlet ones, alone of oaks, have not given up the fight.

The sap is now, and even far into November, frequently flowing fast in these trees, as in Maples in the spring; and apparently their bright tints, now that most other Oaks are withered, are connected with this phenomenon. They are full of life. It has a pleasantly astringent, acorn-like taste, this strong Oak-wine, as I find on tapping them with my knife.

Looking across this woodland valley, a quarter of a mile wide, how rich those Scarlet Oaks, embosomed in Pines, their bright red branches intimately intermingled with them! They have their full effect there. The Pine-boughs are the green calyx to their red petals. Or, as we go along a road in the woods, the sun striking endwise through it, and lighting up the red tents of the Oaks, which on each side are mingled with the liquid green of the Pines, makes a very gorgeous scene. Indeed, without the evergreens for contrast, the autumnal tints would lose much of their effect.

The Scarlet Oak asks a clear sky and the brightness of late October days. These bring out its colors. If the sun goes into a cloud, they become comparatively indistinct. As I sit on a cliff in the southwest part of our town, the sun is now getting low, and the woods in Lincoln, south and east of me, are lit up by its more level rays; and in the Scarlet Oaks, scattered so equally over the forest, there is brought out a more brilliant redness than I had believed was in them. Every tree of this species which is visible in those directions, even to the horizon, now stands out distinctly red. Some great ones lift their red backs high above the woods, in the next town, like huge roses with a myriad of fine petals; and some more slender ones, in a small grove of White Pines on Pine Hill in the east, on the very verge of the horizon, alternating with the Pines on the edge of the grove, and shouldering them with their red coats, look like soldiers in red amid hunters in green. This time it is Lincoln green, too. Till the sun got low, I did not believe that there were so many redcoats in the forest army. Theirs is an intense burning red, which would lose some of its strength, methinks, with every step you might take toward them; for the shade that lurks amid their foliage does not report itself at this distance, and they are unanimously red. The focus of their reflected color is in the atmosphere far on this side. Every such tree becomes a nucleus of red, as it were, where, with the declining sun, that color grows and glows. It is partly borrowed fire, gathering strength from the sun on its way to your eye. It has only some comparatively dull red leaves for a rallying-point, or kindling-stuff, to start it, and it becomes an intense scarlet or red mist, or fire, which finds fuel for itself in the very atmosphere. So vivacious is redness. The very rails reflect a rosy light at this hour and season. You see a redder tree than exists.

If you wish to count the Scarlet Oaks, do it now. In a clear day stand thus on a hill-top in the woods, when the sun is an hour high, and every one within range of your vision, excepting in the west, will be revealed. You might live to the age of Methuselah and never find a tithe of them, otherwise. Yet sometimes even in a dark day I have thought them as bright as I ever saw them. Looking westward, their colors are lost in a blaze of light; but in other directions the whole forest is a flower-garden, in which these late roses burn, alternating with green, while the so-called "gardeners," walking here and there, perchance, beneath, with spade and water-pot, see only a few little asters amid withered leaves.

These are *my* China-asters, *my* late garden-flowers. It costs me nothing for a gardener. The falling leaves, all over the forest, are protecting the roots of my plants. Only look at what is to be seen, and you will have garden enough, without deepening the soil in your yard. We have only to elevate our view a little, to see the whole forest as a garden. The blossoming of the Scarlet Oak,–the forest-flower, surpassing all in splendor (at least since the Maple)! I do not know but they interest me more than the Maples, they are so widely and equally dispersed throughout the forest; they are so hardy, a nobler tree on the whole;–our chief November flower, abiding the approach of winter with us, imparting warmth to early November prospects. It is remarkable that the latest bright color that is general should be this deep, dark scarlet and red, the intensest of colors. The ripest fruit of the year; like the cheek of a hard, glossy, red apple from the cold Isle of Orleans, which will not be mellow for eating till next spring! When I rise to a hill-top, a thousand of these great Oak roses, distributed on every side, as far as the horizon! I admire them four or five miles off! This my unfailing prospect for a fortnight past! This late forest-flower surpasses all that spring or summer could do. Their colors were but rare and dainty specks comparatively, (created for the near-sighted, who walk amid the humblest herbs and underwoods,) and made no impression on a distant eye. Now it is an extended forest or a mountain-side, through or along which we journey from day to day, that bursts into bloom. Comparatively, our gardening is on a petty scale,–the gardener still nursing a few asters amid dead weeds, ignorant of the gigantic asters and roses, which, as it were, overshadow him, and ask for none of his care. It is like a little red paint ground on a saucer, and held up against the sunset sky. Why not take more elevated and broader views, walk in the great garden, not skulk in a little "debauched" nook of it? consider the beauty of the forest, and not merely of a few impounded herbs?

Let your walks now be a little more adventurous; ascend the hills. If, about the last of October, you ascend any hill in the outskirts of our town, and probably of yours, and look over the forest, you may see—well, what I have endeavored to describe. All this you surely *will* see, and much more, if you are prepared to see it,–if you *look* for it. Otherwise, regular and universal as this phenomenon is, whether you stand on the hilltop or in the hollow, you will think for threescore years and ten that all the wood is, at this season, sear and brown. Objects are concealed from our view, not so much because they are out of the course of our visual ray as because we do not bring our minds and eyes to bear on them; for there is no power to see in the eye itself, any more than in any other jelly. We do not realize how far and widely, or how near and narrowly, we are to look. The greater part of the phenomena of Nature are for this reason concealed from us all our lives. The gardener sees only the gardener's garden. Here, too, as in political economy, the supply answers to the demand. Nature does not cast pearls before swine. There is just as much beauty visible to us in the landscape as we are prepared to appreciate,–not a grain more. The actual objects which one man will see from a particular hill-top are just as different from those which another will see as the beholders are different.

The Scarlet Oak must, in a sense, be in your eye when you go forth. We cannot see anything until we are possessed with the idea of it, take it into our heads,–and then we can hardly see anything else. In my botanical rambles, I find that, first, the idea, or image, of a plant occupies my thoughts, though it may seem very foreign to this locality–no nearer than Hudson's Bay–and for some weeks or months I go thinking of it, and expecting it, unconsciously, and at length I surely see it. This, is the history of my finding a score or more of rare plants, which I could name.

A man sees only what concerns him. A botanist absorbed in the study of grasses, does not distinguish the grandest pasture oaks. He, as it were, tramples down oaks unwittingly in his walk, or at most sees only their shadows. I have found that it required a different intention of the eye, in the same locality, to see different plants, even when they were closely allied,–as *Juncaceae* and *Gramineae;*–when I was looking for the former, I did not see the latter, in their midst. How much more then it requires different intentions of the eye and of the mind, to attend to different departments of knowledge! How differently the poet and the naturalist look at objects!

Take a New England Select Man, and set him on the highest of our hills, and tell him to look–sharpening his sight to the utmost, and putting on the glasses that suit him best, (aye, using a spy-glass, if he likes),–and make a full report. What, probably, will he *spy*?–what will he *select* to look at? Of course, he will see a Brocken spectre of himself. He will see several meeting-houses, at least, and perhaps that somebody ought to be assessed higher than he is, since he has so handsome a woodlot. Now take Julius Caesar–or Emanuel Swedenborg–or a Fejee Islander, and set him up there! Or suppose all together and let them compare notes afterward. Will it appear that they have enjoyed the same prospect? What they will see will be as different as Rome was from Heaven or Hell, or the last from the Fejee Islands.– For aught we know, as strange a man as any of these, is always at our elbow.

Why, it takes a sharp shooter to bring down even such trivial game, as snipes and woodcocks, he must take very particular aim, and know what he is aiming at. He would stand a very small chance, if he fired at random into the sky, being told that snipes were flying there. And so is it with him that shoots at beauty; though he wait till the sky falls, he will not bag any, if he does not already know its seasons and haunts, and the color of its wing,–if he has not dreamed of it, so that he can *anticipate* it; then, indeed, he flushes it at every step, shoots double and on the wing, with both barrels, even in cornfields. The sportsman trains himself, dresses and watches unweariedly, and loads and primes for his particular game. He prays for it, and offers sacrifices, and so he gets it. After due and long preparation, schooling his eye and hand, dreaming awake and asleep, with gun and paddle and boat he goes out after meadow-hens, which most of his townsmen never saw nor dreamed of, and paddles for miles against a head-wind, and wades in water up to his knees, being out all day without his dinner, and *therefore* he gets them. He had them half-way into his bag when he started, and has only to shove them down. The true sportsman can shoot you almost any of his game from his windows: what else has he windows or eyes for? It comes and perches at last on the barrel of his gun; but the rest of the world never see it *with the feathers on*. The geese fly exactly under his zenith, and honk when they get there, and he will keep himself supplied by firing up his chimney; twenty musquash have the refusal of each one of his traps before it is empty. If he lives, and his game-spirit increases, heaven and earth shall fail him sooner than game; and when he dies, he will go to more extensive, and, perchance, happier hunting-grounds. The fisherman, too, dreams of fish, sees a bobbing cork in his dreams, till he can almost catch them in his sink-spout. I knew a girl who, being sent to pick huckleberries, picked wild gooseberries by the quart, where no one else knew that there were any, because she was accustomed to pick them up country where she came from. The astronomer knows where to go star-gathering, and sees one clearly in his mind before any have seen it with a glass. The hen scratches and finds her food right under where she stands, but such is not the way with the hawk.

These bright leaves which I have mentioned are not the exception but the rule, for I believe that all leaves, even grasses and mosses, acquire brighter colors just before their fall. When you come to observe faithfully the changes of each humblest plant, you find that each has sooner or later its peculiar autumnal tint, and if you undertake to make a complete list of the bright tints it will be nearly as long as a catalogue of the plants in your vicinity.

Wild Apples.

It is remarkable how closely the history of the Apple-tree is connected with that of man. The geologist tells us that the order of the *Rosaceæ*, which includes the Apple, also the true Grasses, and the *Labiatæ*, or Mints, were introduced only a short time previous to the appearance of man on the globe.

It appears that apples made a part of the food of that unknown primitive people whose traces have lately been found at the bottom of the Swiss lakes, supposed to be older than the foundation of Rome, so old that they had no metallic implements. An entire black and shrivelled Crab-Apple has been recovered from their stores.

Tacitus says of the ancient Germans, that they satisfied their hunger with wild apples (*agrestia poma*) among other things.

Niebuhr observes that "the words for a house, a field, a plough, ploughing, wine, oil, milk, sheep, apples, and others relating to agriculture and the gentler ways of life, agree in Latin and Greek, while the Latin words for all objects pertaining to war or the chase are utterly alien from the Greek." Thus the apple-tree may be considered a symbol of peace no less than the olive.

The apple was early so important, and generally distributed, that its name traced to its root in many languages signifies fruit in general. Μῆλον, in Greek, means an apple, also the fruit of other trees, also a sheep and any cattle, and finally riches in general.

The apple-tree has been celebrated by the Hebrews, Greeks, Romans, and Scandinavians. Some have thought that the first human pair were tempted by its fruit. Goddesses are fabled to have contended for it, dragons were set to watch it, and heroes were employed to pluck it.

The tree is mentioned in at least three places in the Old Testament, and its fruit in two or three more. Solomon sings,–"As the apple-tree among the trees of the wood, so is my beloved among the sons." And again,– "Stay me with flagons, comfort me with apples." The noblest part of man's noblest feature is named from this fruit, "the apple of the eye."

The apple-tree is also mentioned by Homer and Herodotus. Ulysses saw in the glorious garden of Alcinoüs "pears and pomegranates, and apple-trees bearing beautiful fruit" (καὶ μηλέαι ἀγλαόκαρποι). And according to Homer, apples were among the fruits which Tantalus could not pluck, the wind ever blowing their boughs away from him. Theophrastus knew and described the apple-tree as a botanist.

According to the Prose Edda, "Iduna keeps in a box the apples which the gods, when they feel old age approaching, have only to taste of to become young again. It is in this manner that they will be kept in renovated youth until Ragnarök" (or the destruction of the gods).

I learn from Loudon that "the ancient Welsh bards were rewarded for excelling in song by the token of the apple-spray"; and "in the Highlands of Scotland the apple-tree is the badge of the clan Lamont."

The apple-tree (*Pyrus malus*) belongs chiefly to the northern temperate zone. Loudon says, that "it grows spontaneously in every part of Europe except the frigid zone, and throughout Western Asia, China, and Japan." We have also two or three varieties of the apple indigenous in North America. The cultivated apple-tree was first introduced into this country by the earliest settlers, and it is thought to do as well or better here than anywhere else. Probably some of the varieties which are now cultivated were first introduced into Britain by the Romans.

Pliny, adopting the distinction of Theophrastus, says,–"Of trees there are some which are altogether wild (*sylvestres*), some more civilized (*urbaniores*)." Theophrastus includes the apple among the last; and, indeed, it is in this sense the most civilized of all trees. It is as harmless as a dove, as beautiful as a rose, and as valuable as flocks and herds. It has been longer cultivated than any other, and so is more humanized; and who knows but, like the dog, it will at length be no longer traceable to its wild original? It migrates with man, like the dog and horse and cow: first, perchance, from Greece to Italy, thence to England, thence to America; and our Western emigrant is still marching steadily toward the setting sun with the seeds of the apple in his pocket, or perhaps a few young trees strapped to his load. At least a million apple-trees are thus set further westward this year than any cultivated ones grew last year. Consider how the Blossom-Week, like the Sabbath, is thus annually spreading over the prairies; for when man migrates, he carries with him not only his birds, quadrupeds, insects, vegetables, and his very sward, but his orchard also.

The leaves and tender twigs are an agreeable food to many domestic animals, as the cow, horse, sheep, and goat; and the fruit is sought after by the first, as well as by the hog. Thus there appears to have existed a natural alliance between these animals and this tree from the first. "The fruit of the Crab in the forests of France" is said to be "a great resource for the wild-boar."

Not only the Indian, but many indigenous insects, birds, and quadrupeds, welcomed the apple-tree to these shores. The tent-caterpillar saddled her eggs on the very first twig that was formed, and it has since shared her affections with the wild cherry; and the canker-worm also in a measure abandoned the elm to feed on it. As it grew apace, the blue-bird, robin, cherry-bird, king-bird, and many more, came with haste and built their nests and warbled in its boughs, and so became orchard-birds, and multiplied more than ever. It was an era in the history of their race. The downy woodpecker found such a savory morsel under its bark, that he perforated it in a ring quite round the tree, before he left it,–a thing which he had never done before, to my knowledge. It did not take the partridge long to find out how sweet its buds were, and every winter eve she flew, and still flies, from the wood, to pluck them, much to the farmer's sorrow. The rabbit, too, was not slow to learn the taste of its twigs and bark; and when the fruit was ripe, the squirrel half-rolled, half-carried it to his hole; and even the mus-quash crept up the bank from the brook at evening, and greedily devoured it, until he had worn a path in the grass there; and when it was frozen and thawed, the crow and the jay were glad to taste it occasionally. The owl crept into the first apple-tree that became hollow, and fairly hooted with delight, finding it just the place for him; so, settling down into it, he has remained there ever since.

My theme being the Wild Apple, I will merely glance at some of the seasons in the annual growth of the cultivated apple, and pass on to my special province.

The flowers of the apple are perhaps the most beautiful of any tree's, so copious and so delicious to both sight and scent. The walker is frequently tempted to turn and linger near some more than usually handsome one, whose blossoms are two-thirds expanded. How superior it is in these respects to the pear, whose blossoms are neither colored nor fragrant!

By the middle of July, green apples are so large as to remind us of coddling, and of the autumn. The sward is commonly strewed with little ones which fall still-born, as it were,–Nature thus thinning them for us. The Roman writer Palladius said,–"If apples are inclined to fall before their time, a stone placed in a split root will retain them." Some such notion, still surviving, may account for some of the stones which we see placed to be overgrown in the forks of trees. They have a saying in Suffolk, England,–

> "At Michaelmas time, or a little before,
> Half an apple goes to the core."

Early apples begin to be ripe about the first of August; but I think that none of them are so good to eat as some to smell. One is worth more to scent your handkerchief with than any perfume which they sell in the shops. The fragrance of some fruits is not to be forgotten, along with that of flowers. Some gnarly apple which I pick up in the road reminds me by its fragrance of all the wealth of Pomona,–carrying me forward to those days when they will be collected in golden and ruddy heaps in the orchards and about the cider-mills.

A week or two later, as you are going by orchards or gardens, especially in the evenings, you pass through a little region possessed by the fragrance of ripe apples, and thus enjoy them without price, and without robbing anybody.

There is thus about all natural products a certain volatile and ethereal quality which represents their highest value, and which cannot be vulgarized, or bought and sold. No mortal has ever enjoyed the perfect flavor of any fruit, and only the godlike among men begin to taste its ambrosial qualities. For nectar and ambrosia are only those fine flavors of every

earthly fruit which our coarse palates fail to perceive,–
just as we occupy the heaven of the gods without
knowing it. When I see a particularly mean man carrying a load of fair and fragrant early apples to market, I
seem to see a contest going on between him and his
horse, on the one side, and the apples on the other,
and, to my mind, the apples always gain it. Pliny says
that apples are the heaviest of all things, and that the
oxen begin to sweat at the mere sight of a load of them.
Our driver begins to lose his load the moment he tries
to transport them to where they do not belong, that is,
to any but the most beautiful. Though he gets out from
time to time, and feels of them, and thinks they are all
there, I see the stream of their evanescent and celestial
qualities going to heaven from his cart, while the pulp
and skin and core only are going to market. They are
not apples, but pomace. Are not these still Iduna's apples, the taste of which keeps the gods forever young?
and think you that they will let Loki or Thjassi carry
them off to Jötunheim, while they grow wrinkled and
gray? No, for Ragnarök, or the destruction of the gods,
is not yet.

There is another thinning of the fruit, commonly
near the end of August or in September, when the
ground is strewn with windfalls; and this happens especially when high winds occur after rain. In some orchards you may see fully three-quarters of the whole
crop on the ground, lying in a circular form beneath
the trees, yet hard and green,–or, if it is a hill-side,
rolled far down the hill. However, it is an ill wind that
blows nobody any good. All the country over, people
are busy picking up the windfalls, and this will make
them cheap for early apple-pies.

In October, the leaves falling, the apples are more
distinct on the trees. I saw one year in a neighboring

town some trees fuller of fruit than I remembered to have ever seen before, small yellow apples hanging over the road. The branches were gracefully drooping with their weight, like a barberry-bush, so that the whole tree acquired a new character. Even the topmost branches, instead of standing erect, spread and drooped in all directions; and there were so many poles supporting the lower ones, that they looked like pictures of banian-trees. As an old English manuscript says, "The mo appelen the tree bereth, the more sche boweth to the folk."

Surely the apple is the noblest of fruits. Let the most beautiful or the swiftest have it. That should be the "going" price of apples.

Between the fifth and twentieth of October I see the barrels lie under the trees. And perhaps I talk with one who is selecting some choice barrels to fulfil an order. He turns a specked one over many times before he leaves it out. If I were to tell what is passing in my mind, I should say that every one was specked which he had handled; for he rubs off all the bloom, and those fugacious ethereal qualities leave it. Cool evenings prompt the farmers to make haste, and at length I see only the ladders here and there left leaning against the trees.

It would be well, if we accepted these gifts with more joy and gratitude, and did not think it enough simply to put a fresh load of compost about the tree. Some old English customs are suggestive at least. I find them described chiefly in Brand's "Popular Antiquities." It appears that "on Christmas eve the farmers and their men in Devonshire take a large bowl of cider, with a toast in it, and carrying it in state to the orchard, they salute the apple-trees with much ceremony, in order to make them bear well the next season." This salutation consists in "throwing some of the cider about the roots of the tree, placing bits of the toast on the branches," and then, "encircling one of the best bearing trees in the orchard, they drink the following toast three several times:–

> 'Here's to thee, old apple-tree,
> Whence thou mayst bud, and whence thou
>   mayst blow,
> And whence thou mayst bear apples enow!
>   Hats-full! caps-full!
>   Bushel, bushel, sacks-full!
>   And my pockets full, too! Hurra!' "

Also what was called "apple-howling" used to be practised in various counties of England on New-Year's eve. A troop of boys visited the different orchards, and, encircling the apple-trees, repeated the following words:–

> "Stand fast, root! bear well, top!
> Pray God send us a good howling crop:
>   Every twig, apples big;
>   Every bough, apples enow!"

"They then shout in chorus, one of the boys accompanying them on a cow's horn. During this ceremony they rap the trees with their sticks." This is called "wassailing" the trees, and is thought by some to be "a relic of the heathen sacrifice to Pomona."

Herrick sings,–

> "Wassaile the trees that they may beare
> You many a plum and many a peare;
> For more or less fruits they will bring
> As you do give them wassailing."

Our poets have as yet a better right to sing of cider than of wine; but it behooves them to sing better than English Phillips did, else they will do no credit to their Muse.

The Wild Apple.

So much for the more civilized apple-trees (*urban-iores*, as Pliny calls them). I love better to go through the old orchards of ungrafted apple-trees, at whatever season of the year,–so irregularly planted: sometimes two trees standing close together; and the rows so devious that you would think that they not only had grown while the owner was sleeping, but had been set out by him in a somnambulic state. The rows of grafted fruit will never tempt me to wander amid them like these. But I now, alas, speak rather from memory than from any recent experience, such ravages have been made!

Some soils, like a rocky tract called the Easterbrooks Country in my neighborhood, are so suited to the apple, that it will grow faster in them without any care, or if only the ground is broken up once a year, than it will in many places with any amount of care. The owners of this tract allow that the soil is excellent for fruit, but they say that it is so rocky that they have not patience to plough it, and that, together with the distance, is the reason why it is not cultivated. There are, or were recently, extensive orchards there standing without order. Nay, they spring up wild and bear well there in the midst of pines, birches, maples, and oaks. I am often surprised to see rising amid these trees the rounded tops of apple-trees glowing with red or yellow fruit, in harmony with the autumnal tints of the forest.

Going up the side of a cliff about the first of November, I saw a vigorous young apple-tree, which, planted by birds or cows, had shot up amid the rocks and open woods there, and had now much fruit on it, uninjured by the frosts, when all cultivated apples were gathered. It was a rank wild growth, with many green leaves on it still, and made an impression of thorniness. The fruit was hard and green, but looked as if it would be palatable in the winter. Some was dangling on the twigs, but more half-buried in the wet leaves under the tree, or rolled far down the hill amid the rocks. The owner knows nothing of it. The day was not observed when it first blossomed, nor when it first bore fruit, unless by the chickadee. There was no dancing on the green beneath it in its honor, and now there is no hand to pluck its fruit,–which is only gnawed by squirrels, as I perceive. It has done double duty,–not only borne this crop, but each twig has grown a foot into the air. And this is *such* fruit! bigger than many berries, we must admit, and carried home will be sound and palatable next spring. What care I for Iduna's apples so long as I can get these?

When I go by this shrub thus late and hardy, and see its dangling fruit, I respect the tree, and I am grateful for Nature's bounty, even though I cannot eat it. Here on this rugged and woody hill-side has grown an apple-tree, not planted by man, no relic of a former orchard, but a natural growth, like the pines and oaks. Most fruits which we prize and use depend entirely on our care. Corn and grain, potatoes, peaches, melons, etc., depend altogether on our planting; but the apple emulates man's independence and enterprise. It is not simply carried, as I have said, but, like him, to some extent, it has migrated to this New World, and is even, here and there, making its way amid the aboriginal trees; just as the ox and dog and horse sometimes run wild and maintain themselves.

Even the sourest and crabbedest apple, growing in the most unfavorable position, suggests such thoughts as these, it is so noble a fruit.

The Crab.

Nevertheless, *our* wild apple is wild only like myself, perchance, who belong not to the aboriginal race here, but have strayed into the woods from the cultivated stock. Wilder still, as I have said, there grows else-where in this country a native and aboriginal Crab-Apple, *Malus coronaria*, "whose nature has not yet been modified by cultivation." It is found from West-ern New-York to Minnesota, and southward. Michaux says that its ordinary height "is fifteen or eighteen feet, but it is sometimes found twenty-five or thirty feet high," and that the large ones "exactly resemble the common apple-tree." "The flowers are white mingled with rose-color, and are collected in corymbs." They are remarkable for their delicious odor. The fruit, ac-cording to him, is about an inch and a half in diameter, and is intensely acid. Yet they make fine sweet-meats, and also cider of them. He concludes, that, "if, on being cultivated, it does not yield new and palatable varieties, it will at least be celebrated for the beauty of its flowers, and for the sweetness of its perfume."

I never saw the Crab-Apple till May, 1861. I had heard of it through Michaux, but more modern bota-nists, so far as I know, have not treated it as of any peculiar importance. Thus it was a half-fabulous tree to me. I contemplated a pilgrimage to the "Glades," a portion of Pennsylvania where it was said to grow to perfection. I thought of sending to a nursery for it, but doubted if they had it, or would distinguish it from Eu-ropean varieties. At last I had occasion to go to Minne-sota, and on entering Michigan I began to notice from the cars a tree with handsome rose-colored flowers. At first I thought it some variety of thorn; but it was not long before the truth flashed on me, that this was my long-sought Crab-Apple. It was the prevailing flower-ing shrub or tree to be seen from the cars at that sea-son of the year,—about the middle of May. But the cars never stopped before one, and so I was launched on the bosom of the Mississippi without having touched one, experiencing the fate of Tantalus. On arriving at

St. Anthony's Falls, I was sorry to be told that I was too
far north for the Crab-Apple. Nevertheless I succeeded
in finding it about eight miles west of the Falls;
touched it and smelled it, and secured a lingering cor-
ymb of flowers for my herbarium. This must have been
near its northern limit.

How the Wild Apple Grows.

But though these are indigenous, like the Indians, I
doubt whether they are any hardier than those backwoodsmen among the apple-trees, which, though descended from cultivated stocks, plant themselves in
distant fields and forests, where the soil is favorable to
them. I know of no trees which have more difficulties
to contend with, and which more sturdily resist their
foes. These are the ones whose story we have to tell. It
oftentimes reads thus:–

Near the beginning of May, we notice little thickets
of apple-trees just springing up in the pastures where
cattle have been,–as the rocky ones of our Easterbrooks Country, or the top of Nobscot Hill, in Sudbury. One or two of these perhaps survive the drought
and other accidents,–their very birthplace defending
them against the encroaching grass and some other
dangers, at first.

> In two years' time 't had thus
>   Reached the level of the rocks,
> Admired the stretching world,
>   Nor feared the wandering flocks.
>
> But at this tender age
>   Its sufferings began:
> There came a browsing ox
>   And cut it down a span.

This time, perhaps, the ox does not notice it amid the
grass; but the next year, when it has grown more stout,

he recognizes it for a fellow-emigrant from the old country, the flavor of whose leaves and twigs he well knows; and though at first he pauses to welcome it, and express his surprise, and gets for answer, "The same cause that brought you here brought me," he nevertheless browses it again, reflecting, it may be, that he has some title to it.

Thus cut down annually, it does not despair; but, putting forth two short twigs for every one cut off, it spreads out low along the ground in the hollows or between the rocks, growing more stout and scrubby, until it forms, not a tree as yet, but a little pyramidal, stiff, twiggy mass, almost as solid and impenetrable as a rock. Some of the densest and most impenetrable clumps of bushes that I have ever seen, as well on account of the closeness and stubbornness of their branches as of their thorns, have been these wild-apple scrubs. They are more like the scrubby fir and black spruce on which you stand, and sometimes walk, on the tops of mountains, where cold is the demon they contend with, than anything else. No wonder they are prompted to grow thorns at last, to defend themselves against such foes. In their thorniness, however, there is no malice, only some malic acid.

The rocky pastures of the tract I have referred to–for they maintain their ground best in a rocky field–are thickly sprinkled with these little tufts, reminding you often of some rigid gray mosses or lichens, and you see thousands of little trees just springing up between them, with the seed still attached to them.

Being regularly clipped all around each year by the cows, as a hedge with shears, they are often of a perfect conical or pyramidal form, from one to four feet high, and more or less sharp, as if trimmed by the gardener's art. In the pastures on Nobscot Hill and its spurs, they make fine dark shadows when the sun is low. They are also an excellent covert from hawks for many small birds that roost and build in them. Whole flocks perch in them at night, and I have seen three robins' nests in one which was six feet in diameter.

No doubt many of these are already old trees, if you reckon from the day they were planted, but infants still when you consider their development and the long life before them. I counted the annual rings of some which were just one foot high, and as wide as high, and found that they were about twelve years old, but quite sound and thrifty! They were so low that they were unnoticed by the walker, while many of their contemporaries from the nurseries were already bearing considerable crops. But what you gain in time is perhaps in this case, too, lost in power,–that is, in the vigor of the tree. This is their pyramidal state.

The cows continue to browse them thus for twenty years or more, keeping them down and compelling them to spread, until at last they are so broad that they become their own fence, when some interior shoot, which their foes cannot reach, darts upward with joy: for it has not forgotten its high calling, and bears its own peculiar fruit in triumph.

Such are the tactics by which it finally defeats its bovine foes. Now, if you have watched the progress of a particular shrub, you will see that it is no longer a simple pyramid or cone, but that out of its apex there rises a sprig or two, growing more lustily perchance than an orchard-tree, since the plant now devotes the whole of its repressed energy to these upright parts. In a short time these become a small tree, an inverted pyramid resting on the apex of the other, so that the whole has now the form of a vast hour-glass. The spreading bottom, having served its purpose, finally disappears, and the generous tree permits the now harmless cows to come in and stand in its shade, and rub against and redden its trunk, which has grown in spite of them, and even to taste of part of its fruit, and so disperse the seed.

Thus the cows create their own shade and food; and the tree, its hour-glass being inverted, lives a second life, as it were.

It is an important question with some nowadays, whether you should trim young apple-trees as high as your nose or as high as your eyes. The ox trims them up as high as he can reach, and that is about the right height, I think.

In spite of wandering kine, and other adverse circumstances, that despised shrub, valued only by small birds as a covert and shelter from hawks, has its blossom-week at last, and in course of time its harvest, sincere, though small.

By the end of some October, when its leaves have fallen, I frequently see such a central sprig, whose progress I have watched, when I thought it had forgotten its destiny, as I had, bearing its first crop of small green or yellow or rosy fruit, which the cows cannot get at over the bushy and thorny hedge which surrounds it, and I make haste to taste the new and undescribed variety. We have all heard of the numerous varieties of fruit invented by Van Mons and Knight. This is the system of Van Cow, and she has invented far more and more memorable varieties than both of them.

Through what hardships it may attain to bear a sweet fruit! Though somewhat small, it may prove equal, if not superior, in flavor to that which has grown in a garden,–will perchance be all the sweeter and more palatable for the very difficulties it has had to contend with. Who knows but this chance wild fruit, planted by a cow or a bird on some remote and rocky hill-side, where it is as yet unobserved by man, may be the choicest of all its kind, and foreign potentates shall hear of it, and royal societies seek to propagate it, though the virtues of the perhaps truly crabbed owner of the soil may never be heard of,–at least, beyond the limits of his village? It was thus the Porter and the Baldwin grew.

Every wild-apple shrub excites our expectation thus, somewhat as every wild child. It is, perhaps, a prince in disguise. What a lesson to man! So are human beings, referred to the highest standard, the celestial fruit which they suggest and aspire to bear, browsed on by fate; and only the most persistent and strongest genius defends itself and prevails, sends a tender scion upward at last, and drops its perfect fruit on the ungrateful earth. Poets and philosophers and statesmen thus spring up in the country pastures, and outlast the hosts of unoriginal men.

Such is always the pursuit of knowledge. The celestial fruits, the golden apples of the Hesperides, are ever guarded by a hundred-headed dragon which never sleeps, so that it is an Herculean labor to pluck them.

This is one, and the most remarkable way, in which the wild apple is propagated; but commonly it springs up at wide intervals in woods and swamps, and by the sides of roads, as the soil may suit it, and grows with comparative rapidity. Those which grow in dense woods are very tall and slender. I frequently pluck from these trees a perfectly mild and tamed fruit. As Columella says, "*Et injussu consternitur ubere mali*": And the ground is strewn with the fruit of an unbidden apple-tree.

It is an old notion, that, if these wild trees do not bear a valuable fruit of their own, they are the best stocks by which to transmit to posterity the most highly prized qualities of others. However, I am not in search of stocks, but the wild fruit itself, whose fierce gust has suffered no "inteneration." It is not my

> "highest plot
> To plant the Bergamot."

The Fruit, and Its Flavor.

The time for wild apples is the last of October and the first of November. They then get to be palatable, for they ripen late, and they are still perhaps as beautiful as ever. I make a great account of these fruits, which the farmers do not think it worth the while to gather,–wild flavors of the Muse, vivacious and inspiriting. The farmer thinks that he has better in his barrels, but he is mistaken, unless he has a walker's appetite and imagination, neither of which can he have.

Such as grow quite wild, and are left out till the first of November, I presume that the owner does not mean to gather. They belong to children as wild as themselves,–to certain active boys that I know,–to the wild-eyed woman of the fields, to whom nothing comes amiss, who gleans after all the world,–and, moreover, to us walkers. We have met with them, and they are ours. These rights, long enough insisted upon, have come to be an institution in some old countries, where they have learned how to live. I hear that "the custom of grippling, which may be called apple-gleaning, is, or was formerly, practised in Herefordshire. It consists in leaving a few apples, which are called the gripples, on every tree, after the general gathering, for the boys, who go with climbing-poles and bags to collect them."

As for those I speak of, I pluck them as a wild fruit, native to this quarter of the earth,–fruit of old trees that have been dying ever since I was a boy and are not yet dead, frequented only by the woodpecker and the squirrel, deserted now by the owner, who has not faith enough to look under their boughs. From the appearance of the tree-top, at a little distance, you would expect nothing but lichens to drop from it, but your faith is rewarded by finding the ground strewn with spirited fruit,–some of it, perhaps, collected at squirrel-holes, with the marks of their teeth by which they carried them,–some containing a cricket or two silently feeding within, and some, especially in damp days, a shelless snail. The very sticks and stones lodged in the tree-top might have convinced you of the savoriness of the fruit which has been so eagerly sought after in past years.

I have seen no account of these among the "Fruits and Fruit-Trees of America," though they are more memorable to my taste than the grafted kinds; more racy and wild American flavors do they possess, when October and November, when December and January, and perhaps February and March even, have assuaged them somewhat. An old farmer in my neighborhood, who always selects the right word, says that "they have a kind of bow-arrow tang."

Apples for grafting appear to have been selected commonly, not so much for their spirited flavor, as for their mildness, their size, and bearing qualities,–not so much for their beauty, as for their fairness and soundness. Indeed, I have no faith in the selected lists of pomological gentlemen. Their "Favorites" and "None-suches" and "Seek-no-furthers," when I have fruited them, commonly turn out very tame and forgetable. They are eaten with comparatively little zest, and have no real *tang* nor *smack* to them.

What if some of these wildings are acrid and puckery, genuine *verjuice*, do they not still belong to the *Pomaceæ*, which are uniformly innocent and kind to our race? I still begrudge them to the cider-mill. Perhaps they are not fairly ripe yet.

No wonder that these small and high-colored apples are thought to make the best cider. Loudon quotes from the "Herefordshire Report," that "apples of a small size are always, if equal in quality, to be preferred to those of a larger size, in order that the rind and kernel may bear the greatest proportion to the pulp, which affords the weakest and most watery juice." And he says, that, "to prove this, Dr. Symonds, of Hereford, about the year 1800, made one hogshead of cider entirely from the rinds and cores of apples, and another from the pulp only, when the first was found of extraordinary strength and flavor, while the latter was sweet and insipid."

Evelyn says that the "Red-strake" was the favorite cider-apple in his day; and he quotes one Newburgh as saying, "In Jersey 't is a general observation, as I hear, that the more of red any apple has in its rind, the more proper it is for this use. Pale-faced apples they exclude as much as may be from their cider-vat." This opinion still prevails.

All apples are good in November. Those which the farmer leaves out as unsalable, and unpalatable to those who frequent the markets, are choicest fruit to the walker. But it is remarkable that the wild apple, which I praise as so spirited and racy when eaten in the fields or woods, being brought into the house, has frequently a harsh and crabbed taste. The Saunterer's Apple not even the saunterer can eat in the house. The palate rejects it there, as it does haws and acorns, and demands a tamed one; for there you miss the November air, which is the sauce it is to be eaten with. Accordingly, when Tityrus, seeing the lengthening shadows, invites Melibœus to go home and pass the night with him, he promises him *mild* apples and soft chestnuts,–*mitia poma, castaneæ molles*. I frequently pluck wild apples of so rich and spicy a flavor that I wonder all orchardists do not get a scion from that tree, and I fail not to bring home my pockets full. But perchance, when I take one out of my desk and taste it in my chamber, I find it unexpectedly crude,–sour enough to set a squirrel's teeth on edge and make a jay scream.

These apples have hung in the wind and frost and rain till they have absorbed the qualities of the weather or season, and thus are highly *seasoned*, and they *pierce* and *sting* and *permeate* us with their spirit. They must be eaten in *season*, accordingly,–that is, out-of-doors.

To appreciate the wild and sharp flavors of these October fruits, it is necessary that you be breathing the sharp October or November air. The out-door air and exercise which the walker gets give a different tone to his palate, and he craves a fruit which the sedentary would call harsh and crabbed. They must be eaten in the fields, when your system is all aglow with exercise, when the frosty weather nips your fingers, the wind rattles the bare boughs or rustles the few remaining leaves, and the jay is heard screaming around. What is sour in the house a bracing walk makes sweet. Some of these apples might be labelled, "To be eaten in the wind."

Of course no flavors are thrown away; they are intended for the taste that is up to them. Some apples have two distinct flavors, and perhaps one-half of them must be eaten in the house, the other out-doors. One Peter Whitney wrote from Northborough in 1782, for the Proceedings of the Boston Academy, describing an apple-tree in that town "producing fruit of opposite qualities, part of the same apple being frequently sour and the other sweet"; also some all sour, and others all sweet, and this diversity on all parts of the tree.

There is a wild apple on Nawshawtuct Hill in my town which has to me a peculiarly pleasant bitter tang, not perceived till it is three-quarters tasted. It remains on the tongue. As you eat it, it smells exactly like a squash-bug. It is a sort of triumph to eat and relish it.

I hear that the fruit of a kind of plum-tree in Provence is "called *Prunes sibarelles*, because it is impossible to whistle after having eaten them, from their sourness." But perhaps they were only eaten in the house and in summer, and if tried out-of-doors in a stinging atmosphere, who knows but you could whistle an octave higher and clearer?

In the fields only are the sours and bitters of Nature appreciated; just as the wood-chopper eats his meal in a sunny glade, in the middle of a winter day, with content, basks in a sunny ray there and dreams of summer in a degree of cold which, experienced in a chamber, would make a student miserable. They who are at work abroad are not cold, but rather it is they who sit shivering in houses. As with temperatures, so with flavors; as with cold and heat, so with sour and sweet. This natural raciness, the sours and bitters which the diseased palate refuses, are the true condiments.

Let your condiments be in the condition of your senses. To appreciate the flavor of these wild apples requires vigorous and healthy senses, *papillæ* firm and erect on the tongue and palate, not easily flattened and tamed.

From my experience with wild apples, I can understand that there may be reason for a savage's preferring many kinds of food which the civilized man rejects. The former has the palate of an out-door man. It takes a savage or wild taste to appreciate a wild fruit.

What a healthy out-of-door appetite it takes to relish the apple of life, the apple of the world, then!

> "Nor is it every apple I desire,
>   Nor that which pleases every palate best;
> 'T not the lasting Deuxan I require,
>   Nor yet the red-cheeked Queening I request,
>   Nor that which first beshrewed the name of wife,
>   Nor that whose beauty caused the golden strife:
>   No, no! bring me an apple from the tree of life!"

So there is one *thought* for the field, another for the house. I would have my thoughts, like wild apples, to be food for walkers, and will not warrant them to be palatable, if tasted in the house.

THEIR BEAUTY.

Almost all wild apples are handsome. They cannot be too gnarly and crabbed and rusty to look at. The gnarliest will have some redeeming traits even to the eye. You will discover some evening redness dashed or sprinkled on some protuberance or in some cavity. It is rare that the summer lets an apple go without streaking or spotting it on some part of its sphere. It will have some red stains, commemorating the mornings and evenings it has witnessed; some dark and rusty blotches, in memory of the clouds and foggy, mildewy days that have passed over it; and a spacious field of green reflecting the general face of Nature,–green even as the fields; or a yellow ground, which implies a milder flavor,–yellow as the harvest, or russet as the hills.

Apples, these I mean, unspeakably fair,–apples not of Discord, but of Concord! Yet not so rare but that the homeliest may have a share. Painted by the frosts, some a uniform clear bright yellow, or red, or crimson, as if their spheres had regularly revolved, and enjoyed the influence of the sun on all sides alike,–some with the faintest pink blush imaginable,–some brindled with deep red streaks like a cow, or with hundreds of fine blood-red rays running regularly from the stem-dimple to the blossom-end, like meridional lines, on a straw-colored ground,–some touched with a greenish rust, like a fine lichen, here and there, with crimson blotches or eyes more or less confluent and fiery when wet,–and others gnarly, and freckled or peppered all over on the stem side with fine crimson spots on a white ground, as if accidentally sprinkled from the brush of Him who paints the autumn leaves. Others, again, are sometimes red inside, perfused with a beautiful blush, fairy food, too beautiful to eat,–apple of the Hesperides, apple of the evening sky! But like shells and pebbles on the sea-shore, they must be seen as they sparkle amid the withering leaves in some dell in the woods, in the autumnal air, or as they lie in the wet grass, and not when they have wilted and faded in the house.

THE NAMING OF THEM.

It would be a pleasant pastime to find suitable names for the hundred varieties which go to a single heap at the cider-mill. Would it not tax a man's invention,–no one to be named after a man, and all in the *lingua vernacula*? Who shall stand godfather at the christening of the wild apples? It would exhaust the Latin and Greek languages, if they were used, and make the *lingua vernacula* flag. We should have to call in the sunrise and the sunset, the rain-bow and the autumn woods and the wild flowers, and the woodpecker and the purple finch and the squirrel and the jay and the butterfly, the November traveller and the truant boy, to our aid.

In 1836 there were in the garden of the London Horticultural Society more than fourteen hundred distinct sorts. But here are species which they have not in their catalogue, not to mention the varieties which our Crab might yield to cultivation.

Let us enumerate a few of these. I find myself compelled, after all, to give the Latin names of some for the benefit of those who live where English is not spoken,– for they are likely to have a world-wide reputation.

There is, first of all, the Wood-Apple (*Malus sylvatica*); the Blue-Jay Apple; the Apple which grows in Dells in the Woods, (*sylvestrivallis,*) also in Hollows in Pastures (*campestrivallis*); the Apple that grows in an old Cellar-Hole (*Malus cellaris*); the Meadow-Apple; the Partridge-Apple; the Truant's Apple, (*Cessatoris,*) which no boy will ever go by without knocking off some, however *late* it may be; the Saunterer's Apple,– you must lose yourself before you can find the way to that; the Beauty of the Air (*Decus Aëris*); December-Eating; the Frozen-Thawed, (*gelato-soluta,*) good only in that state; the Concord Apple, possibly the same with the *Musketaquidensis;* the Assabet Apple; the Brindled Apple; Wine of New England; the Chickaree Apple; the Green Apple (*Malus viridis*);–this has many synonymes; in an imperfect state, it is the *Cholera morbifera aut dysenterifera, puerulis dilectissima;*–the Apple which Atalanta stopped to pick up; the Hedge-Apple (*Malus Sepium*); the Slug-Apple (*limacea*); the Railroad-Apple, which perhaps came from a core thrown out of the cars; the Apple whose Fruit we tasted in our Youth; our Particular Apple, not to be found in any catalogue,–*Pedestrium Solatium;* also the Apple where hangs the Forgotten Scythe; Iduna's Apples, and the Apples which Loki found in the Wood; and a great many more I have on my list, too numerous to mention,–all of them good. As Bodæus exclaims, referring to the cultivated kinds, and adapting Virgil to his case, so I, adapting Bodæus,–

"Not if I had a hundred tongues, a hundred mouths,
An iron voice, could I describe all the forms
And reckon up all the names of these *wild apples.*"

THE LAST GLEANING.

By the middle of November the wild apples have lost
some of their brilliancy, and have chiefly fallen. A great
part are decayed on the ground, and the sound ones
are more palatable than before. The note of the chickadee sounds now more distinct, as you wander amid
the old trees, and the autumnal dandelion is half-
closed and tearful. But still, if you are a skilful gleaner,
you may get many a pocket-full even of grafted fruit,
long after apples are supposed to be gone out-of-
doors. I know a Blue-Pearmain tree, growing within
the edge of a swamp, almost as good as wild. You
would not suppose that there was any fruit left there,
on the first survey, but you must look according to system. Those which lie exposed are quite brown and rotten now, or perchance a few still show one blooming
cheek here and there amid the wet leaves. Nevertheless, with experienced eyes, I explore amid the bare
alders and the huckleberry-bushes and the withered
sedge, and in the crevices of the rocks, which are full of
leaves, and pry under the fallen and decaying ferns,
which, with apple and alder leaves, thickly strew the
ground. For I know that they lie concealed, fallen into
hollows long since and covered up by the leaves of the
tree itself,–a proper kind of packing. From these lurk-
ing-places, anywhere within the circumference of the
tree, I draw forth the fruit, all wet and glossy, maybe
nibbled by rabbits and hollowed out by crickets and
perhaps with a leaf or two cemented to it, (as Curzon
an old manuscript from a monastery's mouldy cellar,)
but still with a rich bloom on it, and at least as ripe and
well kept, if not better than those in barrels, more crisp

and lively than they. If these resources fail to yield anything, I have learned to look between the bases of the
suckers which spring thickly from some horizontal
limb, for now and then one lodges there, or in the very
midst of an alder-clump, where they are covered by
leaves, safe from cows which may have smelled them
out. If I am sharp-set, for I do not refuse the Blue-
Pearmain, I fill my pockets on each side; and as I retrace my steps in the frosty eve, being perhaps four or
five miles from home, I eat one first from this side, and
then from that, to keep my balance.

I learn from Topsell's Gesner, whose authority appears to be Albertus, that the following is the way in
which the hedge-hog collects and carries home his apples. He says,–"His meat is apples, worms, or grapes:
when he findeth apples or grapes on the earth, he roll-
eth himself upon them, until he have filled all his
prickles, and then carrieth them home to his den,
never bearing above one in his mouth; and if it fortune
that one of them fall off by the way, he likewise shaketh
off all the residue, and walloweth upon them afresh,
until they be all settled upon his back again. So, forth
he goeth, making a noise like a cart-wheel; and if he
have any young ones in his nest, they pull off his load
wherewithal he is loaded, eating thereof what they
please, and laying up the residue for the time to
come."

The "Frozen-Thawed" Apple.

Toward the end of November, though some of the
sound ones are yet more mellow and perhaps more
edible, they have generally, like the leaves, lost their
beauty, and are beginning to freeze. It is finger-cold,
and prudent farmers get in their barrelled apples, and
bring you the apples and cider which they have engaged; for it is time to put them into the cellar. Perhaps

a few on the ground show their red cheeks above the early snow, and occasionally some even preserve their color and soundness under the snow throughout the winter. But generally at the beginning of the winter they freeze hard, and soon, though undecayed, acquire the color of a baked apple.

Before the end of December, generally, they experience their first thawing. Those which a month ago were sour, crabbed, and quite unpalatable to the civilized taste, such at least as were frozen while sound, let a warmer sun come to thaw them, for they are extremely sensitive to its rays, are found to be filled with a rich sweet cider, better than any bottled cider that I know of, and with which I am better acquainted than with wine. All apples are good in this state, and your jaws are the cider-press. Others, which have more substance, are a sweet and luscious food,–in my opinion of more worth than the pine-apples which are imported from the West Indies. Those which lately even I tasted only to repent of it,–for I am semi-civilized,– which the farmer willingly left on the tree, I am now glad to find have the property of hanging on like the leaves of the young oaks. It is a way to keep cider sweet without boiling. Let the frost come to freeze them first, solid as stones, and then the rain or a warm winter day to thaw them, and they will seem to have borrowed a flavor from heaven through the medium of the air in which they hang. Or perchance you find, when you get home, that those which rattled in your pocket have thawed, and the ice is turned to cider. But after the third or fourth freezing and thawing they will not be found so good.

What are the imported half-ripe fruits of the torrid South, to this fruit matured by the cold of the frigid North? These are those crabbed apples with which I cheated my companion, and kept a smooth face that I might tempt him to eat. Now we both greedily fill our pockets with them,–bending to drink the cup and save our lappets from the overflowing juice,–and grow more social with their wine. Was there one that hung so high and sheltered by the tangled branches that our sticks could not dislodge it?

It is a fruit never carried to market, that I am aware of,–quite distinct from the apple of the markets, as from dried apple and cider,–and it is not every winter that produces it in perfection.

The era of the Wild Apple will soon be past. It is a fruit which will probably become extinct in New England. You may still wander through old orchards of native fruit of great extent, which for the most part went to the cider-mill, now all gone to decay. I have heard of an orchard in a distant town, on the side of a hill, where the apples rolled down and lay four feet deep against a wall on the lower side, and this the owner cut down for fear they should be made into cider. Since the temperance reform and the general introduction of grafted fruit, no native apple-trees, such as I see everywhere in deserted pastures, and where the woods have grown up around them, are set out. I fear that he who walks over these fields a century hence will not know the pleasure of knocking off wild apples. Ah, poor man, there are many pleasures which he will not know! Notwithstanding the prevalence of the Baldwin and the Porter, I doubt if so extensive orchards are set out to-day in my town as there were a century ago, when those vast straggling cider-orchards were planted, when men both ate and drank apples, when the pomace-heap was the only nursery, and trees cost nothing but the trouble of setting them out. Men could afford then to stick a tree by every wall-side and let it take its chance. I see nobody planting trees to-day in such out-of-the-way places, along the lonely roads and lanes, and at the bottom of dells in the wood. Now that they have grafted trees, and pay a price for them, they collect them into a plat by their houses, and fence them in,—and the end of it all will be that we shall be compelled to look for our apples in a barrel.

This is "The word of the Lord that came to Joel the son of Pethuel.

"Hear this, ye old men, and give ear, all ye inhabitants of the land! Hath this been in your days, or even in the days of your fathers? . . . .

"That which the palmer-worm hath left hath the locust eaten; and that which the locust hath left hath the canker-worm eaten; and that which the canker-worm hath left hath the caterpillar eaten.

"Awake, ye drunkards, and weep! and howl, all ye drinkers of wine, because of the new wine! for it is cut off from your mouth.

"For a nation is come up upon my land, strong, and without number, whose teeth are the teeth of a lion, and he hath the cheek-teeth of a great lion.

"He hath laid my vine waste, and barked my fig-tree; he hath made it clean bare, and cast it away; the branches thereof are made white. . . . .

"Be ye ashamed, O ye husbandmen! howl, O ye vine-dressers! . . . .

"The vine is dried up, and the fig-tree languisheth; the pomegranate-tree, the palm-tree also, and the apple-tree, even all the trees of the field, are withered: because joy is withered away from the sons of men."

EDITORIAL APPENDIX

Index

THE modern standard form of a proper noun often differs from that used by Thoreau or by a source that Thoreau follows in the text. The current standard spelling and, in parentheses, any alternative standard, as listed in *Webster's Biographical Dictionary* or in *Webster's New Geographical Dictionary*, are given first. Thoreau's spelling in the text follows in square brackets if the two forms vary only slightly, as with "Eskimo(s) [Esquimaux]." A cross-reference is provided where the variation is substantial.

The names of towns and cities in the United States are followed by postal abbreviations of the applicable states. The locations of cities and towns elsewhere, in Canada, England, or France, for example, are identified in square brackets. For topographical and institutional features, such as rivers, mountains, bays, streets, churches, or public gardens, the political location is also reported in square brackets. Conjectural identifications are noted by question marks.

Biographical names are followed by parenthetical birth and death dates. Some other editorially supplied biographical information is given in square brackets, such as the identities of Thoreau's unnamed companions in "A Walk to Wachusett" and "A Yankee in Canada."

A special feature of this index is the identification by author and title of published sources that Thoreau quotes, paraphrases, or alludes to in the text, as determined by the present editor. Authors' names are followed by birth and death dates; titles–often abbreviated for economy–are those of the publications Thoreau himself consulted; page numbers locate the individual places in the *Excursions* text where he employs a source. Poetic quotations from published sources are indexed by author and title. Poems and poetic fragments by Thoreau are indexed by title or, if untitled in the text, by first line.

Notes on Illustrations

"A Winter Walk": page from Thoreau's *Dial*
      manuscript   following p. 342

Like the other surviving leaves of the "Winter Walk" manuscript, this one, page "17", shows both compositional revisions by Thoreau and editorial revision and notations by Emerson. Thoreau sent the manuscript to Emerson from Staten Island on June 8, 1843, for publication in the *Dial*. Extensively modified by Emerson without Thoreau's approval, the essay was printed in the October issue. The text of this manuscript page, which is in Special Collections, University of Delaware Library, Newark, Delaware, corresponds to 62.1-23.

First page of Thoreau's "Walking" manuscript

The entire manuscript of ninety-nine pages, now in William Munroe Special Collections in the Concord Free Public Library, was sent to James T. Fields, editor of the *Atlantic Monthly*, on March 11, 1862, eight weeks before Thoreau died. This page illustrates Thoreau's own revisions in pencil and ink; in the upper left hand corner, Fields' attestation of Thoreau's handwriting can be seen. The cancelled phrase, "this evening" in the opening sentence shows that Thoreau used this leaf as reading text during one of his presentations of "Walking" as a platform lecture. The essay was published in the June 1862 *Atlantic*. The text of this manuscript page corresponds to 185.1-14.

Thoreau's traveling outfit

Thoreau's New Bedford friend Daniel Ricketson drew this sketch after his first encounter with Thoreau in December 1854. The outfit, ideal for the hard work of traveling, conforms essentially to what Thoreau wore and carried on his trip to Canada; see pp. 100-101 and 103-105. Ricketson pasted this sketch into his copy of *A Week on the Concord and Merrimack Rivers* (Boston: James Munroe and Company, 1849), which is in the Albert E. Lownes Collection at the John Hay Library, Brown University.

Detail from "Plan of the City of Quebec"

This fold-out plan by A. Larue was bound into Alfred Hawkins, *The Quebec Guide* (Quebec: W. Cowan and Sons, 1844). The enlarged detail shows many structures, roads, gates, and parts of the city that Thoreau describes in "A Yankee in Canada," including the wharfs, the Lower Town, the fortified Upper Town, the several gardens, and the Citadel. Thoreau was familiar with Hawkins' guidebook and may have used it while touring Quebec City with Ellery Channing in 1850. This copy of the map is at the Harry Ransom Humanities Research Center, The University of Texas at Austin.

Acknowledgments

LONG in preparation, *Excursions* benefitted from the work of many hands: those of editors in *The Writings of Henry D. Thoreau*, those of professional staff in the project's Textual Center, and those of student research assistants at Princeton University, the University of California at Santa Barbara, The University of Texas at Austin, and Northern Illinois University. Preliminary research for the volume dates back almost to the inception of the Thoreau Edition; Mr. Moldenhauer's involvement began in the late 1970s, when in his role of Textual Editor for the series he evaluated work already performed by others and developed detailed plans for editing the most problematic of the component texts, "A Winter Walk" and "A Yankee in Canada." Moldenhauer resumed work on *Excursions* in 1991, when he established the text and wrote the apparatus for "A Yankee in Canada." Supporting work continued at the Edition's Textual Center, and in 1999 Moldenhauer began to edit the remaining eight essays, submitting finished text and apparatus to the Textual Center in 2003.

The remainder of this statement will for the most part be organized categorically by type of task, from the most basic to the relatively advanced, rather than essay by essay or strict chronology. The reader should bear in mind that in modern critical editing of literary documents, repetition of mechanical tasks such as collation of different versions of the text and proofreading of transcripts against their originals is a redundancy necessary to assure the accuracy and completeness of the work. Technical terms whose usage is not self-evident in this statement will be explained in the Textual Introduction.

Textual Center staff, including Minka Misangyi Barton, Sarah Louisa Dennis, Elizabeth Marshall Dubrulle, Tiffany Hayes, Carolyn Kappes, Jette Matzke, Dianne Piper-Rybak, Mary Shelden, Lihong Xie, and Deborah Zak; project editors, including Thomas Blanding, John C. Broderick, William Drake, Robert Hudspeth, Leonard Neufeldt, J. Lyndon Shanley, and Paul O. Williams; and graduate students at The University of Texas at Austin, helped to carry out the tasks described below.

> "Sight" or "hand" collation of various printed forms of the texts of all nine pieces, from the earliest magazine printings through the last major collected editions in the Ticknor and Fields–Houghton Mifflin line.
>
> Optical collation of the texts on the Hinman Collator and the Lindstrand Comparator, for the purpose of ascertaining alterations and text-affecting type deterioration between ostensibly identical impressions of relevant printed forms.
>
> Transcription in type facsimile, letter by letter and line by line, of setting-copy manuscripts that Thoreau sent to his publishers, lecture and essay drafts, and related manuscripts such as commonplace books.
>
> Proofreading against the original manuscripts of transcripts of Thoreau's setting-copy manuscripts (which necessarily serve as copy-text wherever they survived). These readings assured the accuracy of the transcripts, which served as "copy-text," or the basis for this edition's corresponding sections of the texts.

Thoreau's many published sources for quotations and paraphrases in eight of the nine essays were identified by Kevin P. Van Anglen. These identifications were refined and supplemented *in extenso* by staff members at the Textual Center and by Moldenhauer, who together also developed source identifications for the remaining essay, "Succession of Forest Trees."

Background research for the Historical Introduction was undertaken by Blanding. Indeed, Blanding produced in the 1970s an early draft Introduction, which was later useful to Moldenhauer in writing the nine Headnotes and the present Historical Introduction. Elizabeth Hall Witherell and Robert Sattelmeyer wrote early draft Headnotes for "The Landlord" and "A Walk to Wachusett." Elizabeth Marshall Dubrulle gathered background information on "Succession of Forest Trees" and did archival research for the Historical Introduction in the James T. Fields Collection of the Henry E. Huntington Library, archival study which was retraced and refined by Moldenhauer.

WordPerfect files of the texts were prepared at the Textual Center and transmitted to Moldenhauer, for perfection against the copy-texts preliminary to emendation decisions.

Surviving lecture and other working draft leaves were transcribed exactly by various contributing editors and staff, and were systematically correlated by Moldenhauer with setting copy manuscript and first printings.

Copy-texts for the nine component parts of *Excursions* were chosen by Moldenhauer, sometimes in consultation with other editors, and are Moldenhauer's responsibility. He is also responsible for decisions to emend or not emend. He prepared the final versions of text and apparatus for the nine essays, the apparatus consisting of Headnote essays, Textual Notes, lists of Emendations, Rejected Substantives, End-of-Line Hyphenation, and (where applicable) Alterations in manuscript copy-texts and in Thoreau's personal copies of first printings. For all the authorial contents except "A Yankee in Canada" and "Autumnal Tints" and all the apparatus except Headnotes, he was assisted in the preparation of these materials by Eric Lupfer, in Austin. Moldenhauer also wrote the Historical and Textual Introductions and this statement of Acknowledgments.

Moldenhauer planned the text index, which was realized from his marked page-proof at the Textual Center by Andrew Sidle and Dianne Piper-Rybak using CINDEX software.

Prior to the creation of *Excursions* text page proof at the Princeton University Press, photocopies of the copy-texts were read at the Textual Center against the edited text and apparatus by staff members under the supervision of Xie and Witherell. The WordPerfect files for the volume were coded for typesetting at the Textual Center.

Page proof of the *Excursions* text was read aloud against printouts of the nine electronic text files by Moldenhauer and Charles Bradford in Austin and by staff members at the Textual Center.

Printout of the Center's files of Textual Notes and all the tabular apparatus was proofread and perfected against the files originally submitted by Moldenhauer. This proofreading was performed aloud by Moldenhauer and W. Rodney Herring. Page proof of all the back matter (index and editorial commentary) was proofread against the perfected printouts by Moldenhauer and Joanne McConnell Moldenhauer. These procedures were replicated under the direction of Witherell at the Textual Center.

Illustrations were selected by Moldenhauer in consultation with Witherell; Moldenhauer wrote the Notes on Illustrations.

The following repositories have graciously granted permission to refer to and publish manuscript material: Albert A. and Henry W. Berg Collection, The New York Public Library, Astor, Lenox and Tilden Foundations, New York, NY; American Antiquarian Society, Worcester, MA; Archives and Special Collections, Robert H. Goddard Library, Clark University, Worcester, MA; Bierce Library, University of Akron, Akron, OH; Brown University Library, Providence, RI; Bruce Peel Special Collections Library, University of Alberta, Edmonton, Alberta, Canada; City College Archives, The City College of The City University of New York, New York, NY; Clifton Waller Barrett Library of American Literature, Special Collections, University of Virginia Library, Charlottesville, VA; Grasselli Library, John Carroll University, University Heights, OH; Houghton Library, Harvard University, Cambridge, MA; The Huntington Library, San Marino, CA; Julian W. Abernethy Collection of American Literature, Special Collections, Middlebury College Library, Middlebury, VT; Manuscripts and Archives Division, The New York Public Library, Astor, Lenox and Tilden Foundations, New York, NY; The Morgan Library & Museum, New York, NY; Myrin Library, Ursinus College, Collegeville, PA; Princeton University Library, Princeton, NJ; Providence Public Library, Providence, RI; Schlesinger Library, Radcliffe Institute, Harvard University, Cambridge, MA; Special Collections, Davidson Library, University of California, Santa Barbara, Santa Barbara, CA; Special Collections, RIT Libraries, Rochester Institute of Technology, Rochester, NY; Special Collections, University of Delaware Library, Newark, DE; Special Collections and Archives, University of Idaho Library, Moscow, ID; Special Collections Research Center, Morris Library, Southern Illinois University, Carbondale, IL; Thoreau Society Archives, Thoreau Institute at Walden Woods Library, Lincoln, MA; William Munroe Special Collections, Concord Free Public Library, Concord, MA; The

William R. Oliver Special Collections Room, Carnegie Library of Pittsburgh, Pittsburgh, PA. Copies of manuscript and other material used in research for *Excursions* were generously provided by the institutions listed above, as well as by Amherst College Library, Amherst, MA; Andersen Library, University of Minnesota, Twin Cities, Minneapolis, MN; Beinecke Rare Book and Manuscript Library, Yale University, New Haven, CT; Boston Athenaeum, Boston, MA; Brandywine Conservancy, Inc., Chadds Ford, PA; Burritt Library, Central Connecticut State University, New Britain, CT; Cowles Memorial Library, Whitworth College, Spokane, WA; Cullom-Davis Library, Bradley University, Peoria, IL; Du Bois Library, University of Massachusetts, Amherst, MA; Fondren Library, Rice University, Houston, TX; Fruitlands Museum, Harvard, MA; Harry Ransom Humanities Research Center, University of Texas at Austin, Austin, TX; Harvard University, Cambridge, MA; Hillman Library, University of Pittsburgh, Pittsburgh, PA; Horgan Library, New Mexico Military Institute, Roswell, NM; James S. Copley Library, La Jolla, CA; Kuhn Library, University of Maryland, Baltimore County, Baltimore, MD; Library of Congress, Washington, DC; Main Library, University of Iowa, Iowa City, IA; Martin Bodmer Foundation, Geneva, Switzerland; Massachusetts Historical Society, Boston, MA; Massachusetts Horticultural Society, Boston, MA; Milne Library, State University of New York at Geneseo, Geneseo, NY; New York State Library, Albany, NY; Perry-Castañeda Library, University of Texas at Austin, Austin, TX; Richter Library, University of Miami, Coral Gables, FL; Roosevelt University Library, Chicago, IL; Rush Rhees Library, University of Rochester, Rochester, NY; San Diego State University Library, San Diego, CA; Shain Library, Connecticut College, New London, CT; UCSD Libraries, University of California, San Diego, La Jolla, CA; University Library, University of California, Santa Cruz, Santa Cruz, CA; University Library, University of Michigan, Ann Arbor, MI; and USAF Academy Libraries, United States Air Force Academy, Colorado Springs, CO.

The editor is grateful to the following individuals for permission to publish or refer to manuscript material: David Fuller, Theodore Hassan, Dr. George A. Snook, William A. Strutz, and Amy Wallace and David Wallechinsky. He also thanks the following, who provided copies of manuscripts: Mr. and Mrs. Morton H. Baker, Paul R. Bernier, Raymond R. Borst, Paul Brown, James Dawson, J. M. Dorsey, Doris Harris, R. W. Knight, Suzanne Y. H. Kurtz, Mrs. John J. McDevitt III, Richard F. Mullen, Edward Scibilia, Daniel Siegel, and Anne Wanzer. In some cases, manuscripts have changed hands since the Textual Center received copies. An effort has been made to locate current owners; in the list above, the most recent owner known to the Textual Center is acknowledged.

Contributions of time, expertise, and good will were made by Randall Conrad, Bernard Crystal, Bradley P. Dean, Sue Hodson, Austin Meredith, Dick O'Connor, Sandra Harbert Petrulionis, Gayle M. Richardson, Leslie Perrin Wilson, Michael Winship, and Richard E. Winslow III.

Material assistance was generously provided by the National Endowment for the Humanities, The University of Texas at Austin, Princeton University, Georgia State University, the University of California, Santa Barbara, Northern Illinois University, the Universities Research Association, and the Barkley Foundation through the National Trust for the Humanities.

Short Titles

son, and William Rossi (Princeton: Princeton University Press, 1990)

Journal 4 — Henry D. Thoreau, *Journal 4: 1851-1852*, ed. Leonard N. Neufeldt and Nancy Craig Simmons (Princeton: Princeton University Press, 1992)

Journal 5 — Henry D. Thoreau, *Journal 5: 1852-1853*, ed. Patrick F. O'Connell (Princeton: Princeton University Press, 1997)

Journal 6 — Henry D. Thoreau, *Journal 6: 1853*, ed. William Rossi and Heather Kirk Thomas (Princeton: Princeton University Press, 2000)

Journal 7 — Henry D. Thoreau, *Journal 7: 1853-1854*, ed. Nancy Craig Simmons and Ron Thomas (Princeton: Princeton University Press, in proofs, forthcoming 2007)

Journal 8 — Henry D. Thoreau, *Journal 8: 1854*, ed. Sandra Harbert Petrulionis (Princeton: Princeton University Press, 2002)

LMHDT — William L. Howarth, *The Literary Manuscripts of Henry David Thoreau* (Columbus: The Ohio State University Press, 1974)

Maine Woods — Henry D. Thoreau, *The Maine Woods*, ed. Joseph J. Moldenhauer (Princeton: Princeton University Press, 1972)

OED — *The Oxford English Dictionary*, ed. James A. H. Murray, Henry Bradley, W. A. Craigie, and C. T. Onions, 13 vols. (Oxford: At the Clarendon Press, 1970, 1933)

Reform Papers — Henry D. Thoreau, *Reform Papers*, ed. Wendell Glick (Princeton: Princeton University Press, 1973)

Translations — Henry D. Thoreau, *Translations*, ed. K. P. Van Anglen (Princeton: Princeton University Press, 1986)

Walden — Henry D. Thoreau, *Walden*, ed. J. Lyndon Shanley (Princeton: Princeton University Press, 1971)

Walker — John Walker, *A Critical Pronouncing Dictionary . . . of the English Language* (New York: Collins and Hannay, 1823)

Webster   Noah Webster, *An American Dictionary of the English Language*, 15th ed. (New York: N. and J. White, 1836)

A Week   Henry D. Thoreau, *A Week on the Concord and Merrimack Rivers*, ed. Carl F. Hovde et al. (Princeton: Princeton University Press, 1980)

Library Symbols

California

CLjC	James S. Copley Library, La Jolla
CSdS	San Diego State University Library, San Diego
CSmH	The Huntington Library, San Marino
CU-S	UCSD Libraries, University of California, San Diego, La Jolla
CU-SB	Davidson Library, University of California, Santa Barbara, Santa Barbara
CU-SC	University Library, University of California, Santa Cruz, Santa Cruz

Colorado

CoCA	USAF Academy Libraries, United States Air Force Academy, Colorado Springs

Connecticut

CtNbT	Burritt Library, Central Connecticut State University, New Britain
CtNlC	Shain Library, Connecticut College, New London
CtY-BR	Beinecke Rare Book and Manuscript Library, Yale University, New Haven

Delaware

DeU	University of Delaware Library, Newark

District of Columbia

DLC	Library of Congress, Washington

Florida

FMU	Richter Library, University of Miami, Coral Gables

Idaho

IdU	University of Idaho Library, Moscow

Illinois

ICarbS	Morris Library, Southern Illinois University, Carbondale
ICRC	Roosevelt University Library, Chicago
IPB	Cullom-Davis Library, Bradley University, Peoria

Iowa

IaU	Main Library, University of Iowa, Iowa City

Maryland

MdU-BC   Kuhn Library, University of Maryland, Baltimore
            County, Baltimore

Massachusetts

MA   Amherst College Library, Amherst
MaLiTIW   Thoreau Society Archives, Thoreau Institute at
            Walden Woods Library, Lincoln
MBAt   Boston Athenaeum, Boston
MBH   Massachusetts Horticultural Society, Boston
MCo-SC   William Munroe Special Collections, Concord
            Free Public Library, Concord
MCR-S   Schlesinger Library, Radcliffe Institute, Harvard
            University, Cambridge
MH   Harvard University, Cambridge
MH-H   Houghton Library, Harvard University, Cam-
            bridge
MHi   Massachusetts Historical Society, Boston
MHvFM   Fruitlands Museum, Harvard
MU   Du Bois Library, University of Massachusetts,
            Amherst
MWA   American Antiquarian Society, Worcester
MWC   Goddard Library, Clark University, Worcester

Michigan

MiU   University Library, University of Michigan, Ann
            Arbor

Minnesota

MnU   Andersen Library, University of Minnesota, Twin
            Cities, Minneapolis

New Jersey

NjP   Princeton University Library, Princeton

New Mexico

NmRM   Horgan Library, New Mexico Military Institute,
            Roswell

New York

N   New York State Library, Albany
NGenoU   Milne Library, State University of New York at
            Geneseo, Geneseo
NN   Manuscripts and Archives Division, The New
            York Public Library, New York

NN-BGC Albert A. and Henry W. Berg Collection, The New York Public Library, New York

NNR Cohen Library, The City College of The City University of New York, New York

NNPM The Morgan Library & Museum, New York

NRRI RIT Libraries, Rochester Institute of Technology, Rochester

NRU Rush Rhees Library, University of Rochester, Rochester

Ohio

OAkU Bierce Library, University of Akron, Akron

OClJC Grasselli Library, John Carroll University, University Heights

Pennsylvania

PClvU Myrin Library, Ursinus College, Collegeville

PPi Carnegie Library of Pittsburgh, Pittsburgh

PPiU Hillman Library, University of Pittsburgh, Pittsburgh

Rhode Island

RP Providence Public Library, Providence

RPB-JH John Hay Library of Rare Books and Special Collections, Brown University, Providence

Texas

TxAuHRH Harry Ransom Humanities Research Center, University of Texas at Austin, Austin

TxHR Fondren Library, Rice University, Houston

TxU Perry-Castañeda Library, University of Texas, Austin

Vermont

VtMiM Middlebury College Library, Middlebury

Virginia

ViU University of Virginia Library, Charlottesville

Washington

WaSpW Cowles Memorial Library, Whitworth College, Spokane

Canada

CaAEU Bruce Peel Special Collections Library, University of Alberta, Edmonton, Alberta

Historical Introduction

Excursions contains nine prose narratives and natural history essays: "Natural History of Massachusetts," "A Walk to Wachusett," "The Landlord," "A Winter Walk," "A Yankee in Canada," "An Address on the Succession of Forest Trees," "Walking," "Autumnal Tints," and "Wild Apples." They are here arranged in the order of their original whole or partial publication in serials. Nine individual Headnotes, one at the beginning of the editorial apparatus for each piece, describe the biographical circumstances of the essays' composition, their early forms as platform lectures (in the last five instances), and the genesis of the texts. Moreover, the Headnotes account for the surviving fair and draft manuscripts; the printings during Thoreau's lifetime and soon after his death in annuals, magazines, and newspapers; the editorial changes made by contemporary editors; the corrections and revisions Thoreau himself made to the pieces following their original publications; and the versions chosen by his posthumous editors and publisher for the first collected edition, *Excursions* (Boston: Ticknor and Fields, 1863), and for *A Yankee in Canada, with Anti-Slavery and Reform Papers* (Boston: Ticknor and Fields, 1866), where the Canadian narrative was first published in its entirety. The Headnotes also identify the copy-text or base text chosen for the present critical edition and detail the procedures used to verify the copy-text and other relevant forms of the text and the sources for emendations of the copy-text in the present edition. This Historical Introduction is limited to the histories of the 1863 *Excursions* and the 1866 *A Yankee in Canada* and their textual successors in the Ticknor and Fields–Houghton, Mifflin and Company family of publishers through 1906.

Excursions was edited by Henry Thoreau's only surviving sibling, Sophia, probably assisted in some measure by Ralph Waldo Emerson, and possibly assisted
in mechanical matters by her friend and neighbor
Elizabeth Hoar. It is likely that James T. Fields, the
publisher, intervened editorially in matters of substance, and it is certain that the volume was styled to
accord with Ticknor and Fields house practice. The
book opened with Emerson's twenty-six-page "Biographical Sketch" of Thoreau. This was a slightly revised reprint from the *Atlantic Monthly* for August
1862 (10:239-249) of a memorial essay that was itself an
expanded version of Emerson's eulogy for Thoreau
delivered at his funeral in Concord, Massachusetts,
May 9, 1862.[1] The *Excursions* essays by Thoreau were
the same pieces and in the same order as in the present edition, with two exceptions: "A Yankee in Canada" was not included, and a piece titled "Night and
Moonlight" was printed at the end. "A Yankee in Canada," set largely from Thoreau's manuscript, was held
until 1866, when it was combined with "Anti-Slavery
and Reform Papers" in the last of Ticknor and Fields's
posthumous collections of Thoreau.[2] "Night and
Moonlight," like "Walking," "Autumnal Tints," and
"Wild Apples," had appeared in the *Atlantic Monthly*
after Thoreau's death. But it followed the three others
in the *Atlantic* by a full year and more, its publication (November 1863; 12:579-583) coinciding closely
enough with *Excursions* itself (October 10 or 14, 1863)
as to give it modest promotional value for the new
book, which was advertised as "now ready" and "just

[1] See Joel Myerson, "Emerson's 'Thoreau': A New Edition from
Manuscript," *Studies in the American Renaissance*, ed. Joel Myerson (Boston: Twayne Publishers, 1979), pp. 17-92, esp. pp. 17-21.
[2] A second, authorially revised, edition of *A Week on the Concord and Merrimack Rivers*, based on a marked copy of the 1849
first edition, was issued by the firm in 1868.

issued" in the November issue's bound-in Ticknor and Fields "List of Forthcoming Books To be Published in the Autumn of 1863."[3] William L. Howarth speculates that Sophia assembled "Night and Moonlight" at the request of Fields, who may have needed another piece for *Excursions* to fill out fourteen pages of the book's last signature. Howarth concludes that the text was not authorized by Thoreau and that Sophia constructed it from draft and lecture sheets her brother had not touched since 1860.[4]

The editorial background of the 1863 *Excursions*, the records of its production, the publicity afforded it in the Boston *Commonwealth* and elsewhere, its critical reception, and its reimpressions through 1892 will be examined subsequently in this Historical Introduction. First, however, the contents of two later collections of Thoreau's short natural history works and walking narratives intended for publication will be enumerated. Both collections were issued by Houghton, Mifflin and Company, the corporate descendant of and heir to Ticknor and Fields, and both contained the word "Excursions" in their titles.

[3] November 1863 *Atlantic* copy in wrappers, collection of Joseph J. Moldenhauer. Raymond Borst, in "Thoreau Advertisements from *The Atlantic Monthly*: 1862-1868," *Thoreau Society Bulletin* 129 (Fall 1974): 4-6, notes that the October issue also advertised *Excursions* in a similar list. An *Atlantic* ad the previous February had announced it "in preparation," giving the title as "Field Notes."

[4] Howarth, "Successor to *Walden*? Thoreau's 'Moonlight—An Intended Course of Lectures,'" *Proof: The Yearbook of American Bibliographical and Textual Studies*, ed. Joseph Katz, vol. 2 (Columbia: University of South Carolina Press, 1972), pp. 89-115, esp. pp. 106-112. Although typographically signed in eights, the book was folded and assembled in twelve-leaf gatherings throughout the life of the plates: see printing details later in this Introduction. In *Thoreau the Poet-Naturalist* (Boston: Roberts Brothers, 1873), p. 323, William Ellery Channing declared that toward the end of his life his friend was vainly attempting to "arrange his papers on Night and Moonlight," among other unfinished projects.

As the stereotype plates of *Walden* and the six post-humous Thoreau volumes published by Ticknor and Fields between 1863 and 1868 wore out, the partner-ship of Houghton and Mifflin determined to produce a new collected edition, one which would incorporate four books of Journal extracts lately selected and ar-ranged by H. G. O. Blake under the titles *Early Spring in Massachusetts* (1881), *Summer* (1884), *Winter* (1888), and *Autumn* (1892). The new edition was projected ini-tially in ten volumes, omitting a re-issue of *Letters to Various Persons* (1865); but late in the production se-quence a new edition of Thoreau's letters prepared by Franklin Benjamin Sanborn, *Familiar Letters*, was added, and the whole was called the Riverside Edition of The Writings of Henry David Thoreau. The moving force for this series, first run off the press in ten vol-umes in late 1893, was the senior house editor Horace Elisha Scudder, who had been detecting errors in the old Ticknor and Fields plates of Thoreau volumes for several years and ordering corrections to some of them. Except for *Walden* (which had been re-set in 1889), *Summer*, *Winter*, and *Autumn*, all the texts were wholly re-styled and typeset anew, a modest number of misprints in the original printings being corrected in the process. Local plate changes to the three sea-sonal Journal volumes not recomposed typographi-cally were extensive.[5]

Excursions in the Riverside Edition consisted of a short "Introductory Note" by Scudder, "A Yankee in Canada" (now separated from the essays on morality and politics of the 1866 volume),[6] "Natural History of

[5] For an editorial and textual history of the Riverside Edition, including an investigation of plate changes periodically effected between 1893 and 1914, see Joseph J. Moldenhauer, "Textual Insta-bility in the Riverside Edition of Thoreau," *Papers of the Biblio-graphical Society of America* 85 (1991): 347-419.

[6] These *"Anti-Slavery and Reform Papers"* were newly packaged

Massachusetts," "A Walk to Wachusett," "The Landlord," "A Winter Walk," "The Succession of Forest
Trees," "Walking," "Autumnal Tints," "Wild Apples,"
"Night and Moonlight," "May Days," and "Days and
Nights in Concord." The last two pieces were selections from Thoreau's Journal that had first been published in, respectively, the *Atlantic Monthly* for May
1878 (41:567-576), prepared by Blake as he was plan-
ning his volumes of seasonal extracts, and *Scribner's*
Monthly for September 1878 (16:721-728), prepared by
Ellery Channing from Journal transcripts in his possession. An index concluded the whole. The new *Ex-*
cursions volume's components, in sum, were identical with those of the 1863 collection except for the
omission of the Emerson biographical sketch (moved
to *Miscellanies*) and the addition of "A Yankee in Canada" (which occupied almost a quarter of the book's
pages) and the two sets of Journal extracts, plus the
new editorial introduction and index.

   Excursions and Poems, volume 5 of Houghton, Mifflin and Company's twenty-volume "Manuscript Edition" of The Writings of Henry David Thoreau (1906),[7]
contained the same prose narratives and natural history pieces, in the same order, as the Riverside Edition
Excursions, but it omitted the Journal extracts "May
Days" and "Days and Nights in Concord" as no longer
necessary: Thoreau's Journal was now printed "in its
complete form" as volumes 7-20 of the new edition.
The two translations in the Riverside Edition *Miscella-*
nies were reprinted in *Excursions and Poems*, and the
ten-poem selection in the Riverside *Miscellanies* was

---

with Emerson's "Biographical Sketch," two hitherto uncollected
pieces on the heroic life, and two translations and some original
poems, as *Miscellanies*.
   [7] It was also published in smaller physical format as the
"Walden Edition."

expanded to twenty-two for the Manuscript Edition *Excursions and Poems*. A new editorial introduction and index were supplied, as was "A List of the Poems and Bits of Verse Scattered Among Thoreau's Prose Writings Exclusive of the Journal." The 1906 typesetting of the *Excursions* essays incorporated corrections and other changes deriving from the preparation of Thoreau's manuscript Journal for print, an enterprise closely overseen by the Houghton, Mifflin editor Francis H. Allen. Allen had compared the latest printed texts of Thoreau's essays and books, in the Riverside Edition, with parallel draft sections of the Journal, and was thus able to detect various errors caused by typesetters' misreadings of Thoreau's hand during original publications in the 1840s, 1850s, and 1860s. Allen's changes were introduced into the electrotype plates of the Riverside Edition as well, for subsequent reimpressions of that popular and inexpensive edition.[8]

We return now to the original *Excursions* collection of 1863. On an undated leaf doubly headed "Books under Consideration Books under Consideration", laid into James T. Fields's "Memorandum and Account Book,"[9] the publisher wrote "Thoreaus Field Notes" and beneath it " ″ Maine Woods". This entry appears to date from near the end of 1862 or January 1863. The first title may have come to Fields through Emerson or from Thoreau's March 21, 1853, Journal entry, where he asks himself, "Might not my Journal be called 'Field Notes.'"[10] "Field Notes" appears to have been the publisher's tentative working title for a volume of uncollected Thoreau writings, the contents

---

[8] See Moldenhauer, "Textual Instability," pp. 368-402.

[9] James Thomas Fields, Papers and Addenda, Box 10 (2), c. 1863–1881, CSmH.

[10] *Journal 6*, p. 20.

undetermined for the time being but almost certainly including the three nature pieces he had accepted for the *Atlantic Monthly* in the months immediately preceding Thoreau's death. In advertisements in the February and March 1863 separate *Atlantic* numbers he announced *Field Notes* and *Maine Woods* among Ticknor and Fields books scheduled to appear during the present season (February) and among "New Books in Press" (March). By late February Fields must have determined from Sophia that manuscripts of the unpublished long third Maine narrative, "The Allegash and East Branch," and of the detailed "Appendix" required study, organization, and at least partial transcription. On the other hand, *Field Notes* would consist predominantly of pieces already published, which could be typeset from printed copy.

The catalyst for Fields's and Sophia's determination of which pieces would be collected in that first posthumous volume appears to have been reprints of "The Landlord" and "A Winter Walk" in the Boston *Commonwealth*, a weekly paper then edited by Thoreau's younger friend, the anti-slavery activist and one-time schoolmaster Franklin Benjamin Sanborn. In a commentary accompanying "The Landlord" on page one of the March 13 issue, Sanborn supplied a list of Thoreau's printed works "prepared by himself shortly before his death. . . . The arrangement is in order of time when written." The titles of Thoreau's two books and of forty-three individual poems, translations, and shorter prose pieces followed, with the periodicals in which they appeared. The list included "Walking," "Autumnal Tints," and "Wild Apples," which Thoreau readied for the *Atlantic* on his deathbed, though not "Life without Principle" or "The Allegash and East Branch," the manuscripts of which he also perfected in his last months but which had not been printed as of March 13, 1863.[11] This pattern of omissions (to say nothing of the absence of a tally in Thoreau's handwriting) casts doubt on Sanborn's assertion that Thoreau drew up the list. It was almost certainly compiled by Sanborn himself, and is anticipated by a nearly identical summary in a manuscript notebook that Sanborn labeled "Receipts and Expenditures of the Concord Society for Educating the Refugees of Port Royal and elsewhere, 1862-1863" and in which he also recorded *Commonwealth* expenditures and revenues. That notebook list excludes the same two Thoreau titles.[12] An entry dated July 14 precedes the list; entries following the list are similarly dated by month and day only, from August to December, and then February 14, 1863. The titles in Sanborn's March 13, 1863, *Commonwealth* inventory are followed by a promotional remark by the editor: "All these papers deserve to be reprinted, but particularly the *Winter Walk* and *Natural History of Massachusetts* in the *Dial*, the review of Carlyle, and the political papers. We trust that Messrs Ticknor and Fields will include these in their forthcoming volumes." Bronson Alcott pitched in, saying in the columns of the *Commonwealth* that he hoped Fields would soon reprint "Natural History of Massachusetts."[13]

Although Sanborn's reprintings of "The Landlord" and (in two installments, March 27 and April 3, 1863) "A Winter Walk" seem to have occurred without the foreknowledge or cooperation of Sophia Thoreau or

[11] "The Allegash" first appeared in *The Maine Woods* in 1864; "Life without Principle," the manuscript of which Thoreau sent to Fields on February 28, 1862, was printed in the October 1863 issue of the *Atlantic*. "Night and Moonlight" (published in the *Atlantic*, November 1863) is also missing from the *Commonwealth* list.

[12] Franklin Benjamin Sanborn Papers, Box 1, Folder 1, MWA.

[13] "The Transcendentalist Club and *The Dial*," April 24, 1863, a transcript of Alcott's Boston "Conversation" of March 23.

James T. Fields,[14] the latter apparently was inspired by
Sanborn's efforts to prepare his own list of Thoreau's
uncollected shorter prose works by title, magazine
name, and year of publication. This census of nineteen items (excluding repetitions) is written on the
white side of a loose, coated endpaper like those used
in Ticknor and Fields bindings, and is headed "Articles
for a New Volume by Thoreau". Fields includes "Life
Without Principle" and "Moonlight" in his list, and he
notes after the entries for "Excursion to Canada" and
"Cape Cod" in *Putnam's Monthly Magazine* "Not
Complete". (In the *Commonwealth* Sanborn had written "Not all.") Of the Maine narratives, Fields enumerates only the previously published "Ktaadn" and
"Chesuncook." Between his caption and the first
Thoreau title Fields added in pencil, underlined,
"Emersons Paper".[15]

On another sheet Fields recorded, evidently for
Emerson, the titles of seventeen short or incompletely
printed prose works, heading it "Thoreau's Writings–
Uncollected".[16] At the bottom he noted in parentheses, "Mͬ Emersons paper on Thoreau, (pubͩ in the atlantic) should be printed as Prefatory to the new Vol. if
Mͬ E will consent to it." Emerson's immediate consent
is suggested by his own annotations of the sheet. On
the verso he wrote "List of H. D. Thoreaus Uncollected

---

[14] In his "Memorandum and Account Book," at CSmH, Fields
recorded an address for Sanborn at the State House. Presumably
this notation was made after Sanborn was appointed Secretary for
the Massachusetts State Board of Charities, in the summer of 1863,
by Governor John Andrew. See Sanborn, *Transcendental Youth
and Age: Chapters in Biography and Autobiography*, ed. Kenneth
Walter Cameron (Hartford: Transcendental Books, 1980), pp. 199,
201.

[15] "Memorandum and Account Book," CSmH.

[16] MH-H, bMS Am 1280.214 (13). Fields later filed the leaf among
his notes on Thoreau read to the Concord Saturday Club in November 1877.

Writings, From the 'Commonwealth'". By means of pencil "x" marks next to selected items in Fields's list, and the addition in pencil of two new titles, he suggested that the projected volume consist of "A Walk to Wachusett," "A Winter Walk," "Paradise to be regained," "Excursion to Canada," "Cape Cod," "John Brown" ("A Plea for . . ."), "Walking," "Wild Apples," "Autumnal Tints," "Life Without Principle," "Chesuncook," and "Address at Framingham" ("Slavery in Massachusetts"). The last two selections were the ones Emerson himself had added. By implication, his *Atlantic* piece on Thoreau would serve as preface; his Journal shows that he was rethinking it toward the end of April.[17] In mid-May Sophia Thoreau informed Daniel Ricketson, Thoreau's close friend in New Bedford, that the Ticknor and Fields firm was "about to issue a volume of Henry's papers."[18] To her cousin Marianne Dunbar in Bridgewater, Massachusetts, she added that "Every moment of my time is occupied. I have been preparing some of my brother's MSS. for the press."[19] By that time the volume's main contents must have been fixed, and Sophia, though perhaps not yet working on the lecture manuscripts of "Night and Moonlight" for both the *Atlantic* and *Excursions* printings, would have been collecting and selectively

[17] *JMN*, 15:342-343. In July Annie Fields, the publisher's wife, referred to the projected Thoreau collection as "his [Emerson's] new volume." M. A. DeWolfe Howe, *Memories of a Hostess* (Boston: Atlantic Monthly Press, 1922), p. 14.

[18] Letter of May 18, 1863, in *Daniel Ricketson and His Friends*, ed. Anna and Walton Ricketson (Boston and New York: Houghton, Mifflin and Company, 1902), p. 157.

[19] Letter of May 19, 1863, Thoreau Society Archives, MaLiTIW. See Walter Harding, comp., "The Correspondence of Sophia Thoreau and Marianne Dunbar," *Thoreau Society Bulletin* 33 (October 1950): 2. Sophia was now doubly burdened by her care of her mother, whose health had been wrecked by a fall down a staircase in December.

marking printed copy for "Natural History of Massachusetts," "A Walk to Wachusett," "The Landlord," "A
Winter Walk," and "An Address on the Succession of
Forest Trees." On the other hand, "Walking," "Autumnal Tints," and "Wild Apples," all printed in the previous year's *Atlantic Monthly*, required little if any of her
editorial attention.[20]

On July 17, 1863, Ellery Channing erroneously informed B. Marston Watson of Plymouth, another of
Thoreau's friends, that "Mr Thoreau's last book is now
through the press".[21] He commented, dismissively,
"hardly any original matter." Although Sophia may
have done her part, as late as July 26 a portion of the
book was not yet ready for type-composition. On that
day Annie Fields complained in her diary that Emerson had not submitted the copy for his "Biographical
Sketch": "he is careful of words and finds many to be
considered again and again, until it is almost impossible to extort a manuscript from his hands."[22] About
this time, however, the project was coming to fruition,
for Emerson, who would undertake the business aspects in Sophia's behalf, reminded himself in his

---

[20] Other manuscripts on which she and Elizabeth Hoar worked
were those for *The Maine Woods* (published in 1864), *Cape Cod*
(1865), and "A Yankee in Canada" (1866), though it seems unlikely
that she would attend to even the first of these projects with *Excursions* making so urgent a claim on her labors. She might, however, have been copying some of Henry's unpublished poems, or
finding the originals, for Sanborn, who printed them intermit-
tently in the *Commonwealth* between June 19 and November 6.
Carl Bode, in the documentation for *Collected Poems of Henry
Thoreau*, enlarged edition (Baltimore: Johns Hopkins Press, 1965),
indicates that the whereabouts of the manuscripts Sanborn used
for several of these poems are unknown: all but one of these manuscripts have now been located.

[21] "The Selected Letters of William Ellery Channing the Younger
(Part Three)," ed. Francis B. Dedmond, *Studies in the American
Renaissance*, ed. Joel Myerson (Charlottesville: University Press
of Virginia, 1991), p. 318.

[22] Howe, p. 14.

"Pocket Diary" about "Ticknor & Fields / Contract for Thoreau's new book", and went on: "Moonlight & Life without principle to be first printed", "Send her Atl. with his pieces", and "Does Walden sell? Miss T. thinks that $35 or $40 may be due on Articles in the Atlantic, now." (*JMN*, 15:504; entries after July 22, before August 11.) He wrote to Fields on September 7 that Sophia had received a draft contract from Ticknor and Fields and desired him (Emerson) to negotiate in person for her. This he wished to do "within a few days." (*Letters*, 5:336.) Alcott also took it upon himself to protect his dead friend's interests, telling Fields during a break-fast visit in October, "Make Helen [he meant Sophia, not Helen, who had died in 1849] feel that Henry will receive as much for his books as if he had made his own bargain, for he was good at a bargain and they [Sophia and her mother, Cynthia] are a little hard–that is, they do not understand all the bearings of many subjects."[23]

Emerson's bargaining session with Fields eventu-ated in another draft contract being sent to Sophia, but she was not yet satisfied. On October 19–after the formal publication of the book, it should be noted–Emerson wrote Fields as follows:

I enclose the first form of contract as you re-quested, with the alterations suggested by Miss Thoreau.

1. The compensation for the engraving is to be struck out as agreed

2. She prefers a term of five years, as in the contract for "Walden," to the term herein proposed.

3. She is sorry to find that her allowance for copy-right [royalty] is to be reduced to 10 cents. But if you

[23] Howe, p. 74.

persist in the views expressed in your statement to
me, she will acquiesce. (*Letters*, 5:339)

The engraving alluded to is a plate based on Samuel
Worcester Rowse's crayon portrait of Thoreau, made
in the summer of 1854, when the subject was 37. At Sophia's behest, apparently, the engraving would be
used as a frontispiece to *Excursions*, and she was
averse to bearing the cost. The *Walden* contract per-
tained to the March 1862 reimpression of that book.[24]
The royalty figure Sophia finally received was 12 1/2
cents per copy of *Excursions*, as recorded in Ticknor
and Fields's Cost Books. That these considerations
were still being negotiated on October 19 suggests that
all or at least the latter parts of the Cost Book entry for
the first edition of *Excursions* (discussed below) were
made retroactively, not contemporaneously–copied
clean from an earlier working or rough record. Such a
record indeed survives, headed "September, 1863" and
materially identical to the "clean," final Cost Book
entry except for a notation of a surplusage of paper
and the use to which that excess was put. The bookkeeper marked it "Entd" when he copied it over but
did not note the transcription date.[25] The final publication agreement may have been reached during a
visit to Sophia that Fields told Hawthorne he thought
he would make during the week of November 9-14.[26]

The book's title remained undetermined almost
until its publication, but Emerson, in his September 7
letter to Fields, called the book "the 'Excursions,'" as

[24] See *Correspondence*, p. 638.

[25] Photocopy from microfilm, courtesy of Michael Winship.
The publisher's practice of keeping preliminary books was discontinued before 1866.

[26] William S. Tryon, *Parnassus Corner: A Life of James T. Fields*
(Boston: Houghton Mifflin Company, 1963), pp. 233-234.

[27] *The Journals of Bronson Alcott*, ed. Odell Shepard (Boston:
Little, Brown and Co., 1938), p. 358.

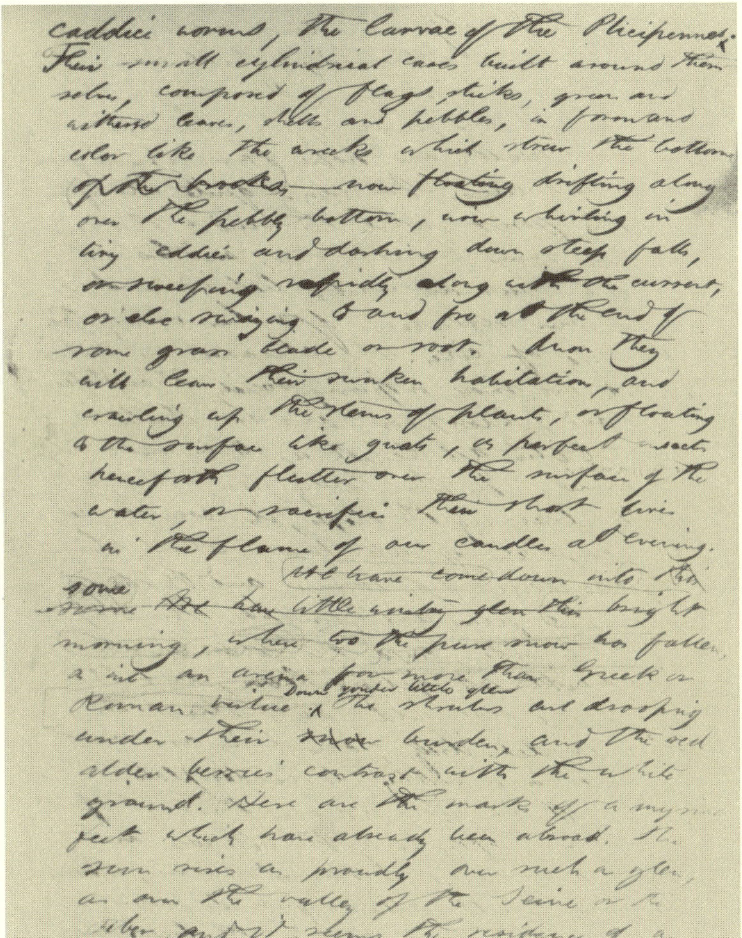
caddice worms, the larvae of the Plicipennes. Their small cylindrical cases built around themselves, composed of flags, sticks, grass and withered leaves, shells and pebbles, in form and color like the wrecks which strew the bottom ~~of the brooks~~ — now ~~floating~~ drifting along over the pebbly bottom, now whirling in tiny eddies and dashing down steep falls, or sweeping rapidly along with the current, or else swinging to and fro at the end of some grass blade or root. Anon they will leave their sunken habitation, and crawling up the stems of plants, or floating to the surface like gnats, as perfect insects henceforth flutter over the surface of the water, or sacrifice their short lives in the flame of our candles at evening. ~~We have come down into this~~ ~~Some [illegible] little winding glen this bright~~ morning, where too the pure snow has fallen, a [illegible] an arena for more than Greek or Roman virtue. Down yonder little glen the shrubs are drooping under their [illegible] burden, and the red alder berries contrast with the white ground. Here are the marks of a myriad feet which have already been abroad. The sun rises as proudly over such a glen, as over the valley of the Seine or the Tiber, and it seems the residence of a

"A Winter Walk": page from Thoreau's *Dial* manuscript

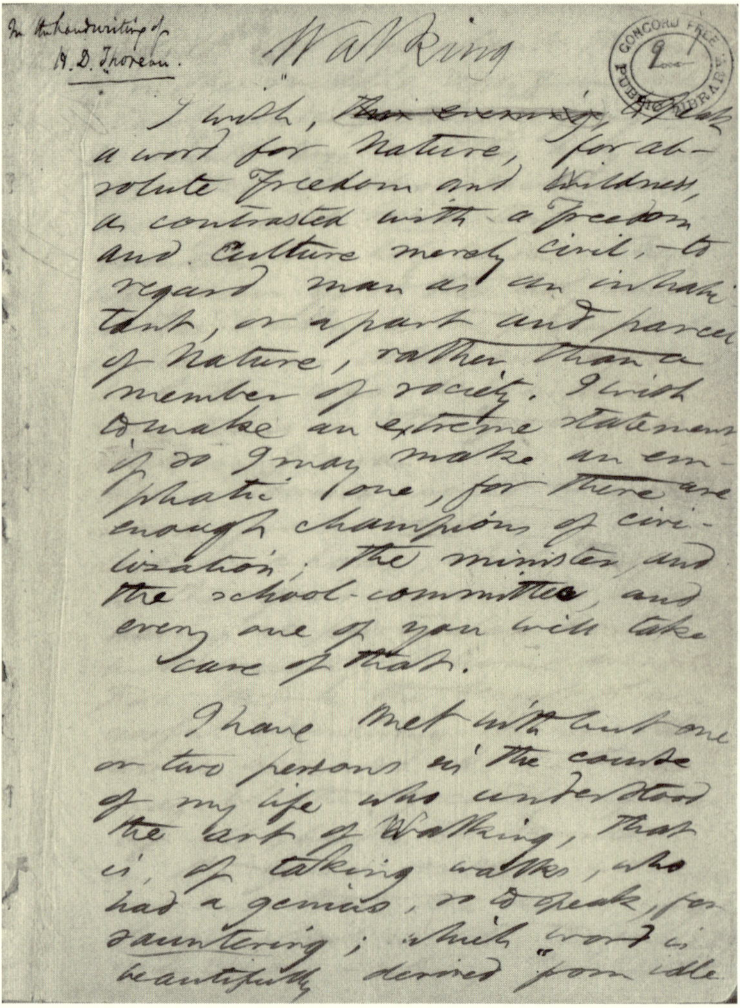

In the handwriting of H. D. Thoreau.

Walking

I wish, ~~this evening,~~ to speak a word for Nature, for absolute Freedom and Wildness, as contrasted with a Freedom and Culture merely civil,—to regard man as an inhabitant, or a part and parcel of Nature, rather than a member of society. I wish to make an extreme statement, if so I may make an emphatic one, for there are enough champions of civilization; the minister and the school-committee, and every one of you will take care of that.

I have met with but one or two persons in the course of my life who understood the art of Walking, that is, of taking walks, who had a genius, so to speak, for sauntering; which word is beautifully derived from idle

First page of Thoreau's "Walking" manuscript

H. D. Thoreau as he presented him-
self at the door of Brooklawn
Dec 25th 1854 —
Age 37.

Thoreau's traveling outfit

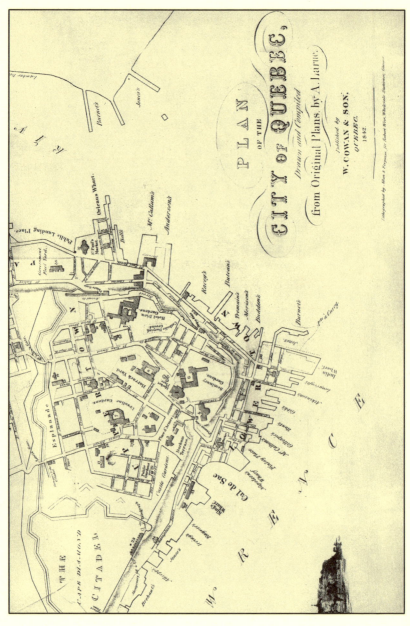

Detail from
"Plan of
the City of
Quebec"

did Alcott in a diary entry of September 11.[27] This was a favorite word of Thoreau's for his hikes and longer trips, appearing for example in the 1853 title "An Excursion to Canada"; he also used it metaphorically, as in the famous *Walden* paragraph,

> I went to the woods because I wished to live deliberately, to front only the essential facts of life ... I wanted to live deep and suck out all the marrow of life, to live so sturdily and Spartan-like as to put to rout all that was not life ... to drive life into a corner ... and, if it proved to be mean, why then to get the whole and genuine meanness of it, and publish its meanness to the world; or if it were sublime, to know it by experience, and be able to give a true account of it in my next excursion. (*Walden*, pp. 90-91)

Still, *Excursions* was not named by Thoreau, who had not even designated the contents of a collection before he died. Evidently Sophia had for a time felt reservations; she wrote to Ricketson on December 15 that she was "quite reconciled to the title."[28] Presumably in an unused draft section of Channing's nine-part memoir of his friend for the *Commonwealth* of December 25, 1863–February 19, 1864 ("Henry D. Thoreau" and "Reminiscences of Henry D. Thoreau," later to become *Thoreau the Poet-Naturalist*, 1873), or perhaps in afterthoughts thereto, he carped that the title had been selected "without *his* [Thoreau's] sensitiveness".[29] Reviewing *Excursions* in the *Commonwealth* in October, Sanborn attributed the "modest" title to "the editor," Emerson by implication. Curiously, Fields seems to have favored an expanded title, *Excursions in Field and Forest*, which he used in catalogues

[28] *Daniel Ricketson and His Friends*, p. 159.
[29] In Channing, *Thoreau the Poet-Naturalist*, revised edition, ed. F. B. Sanborn (Boston: Goodspeed, 1902), pp. xi-xiii, 272.

bound into the firm's Thoreau books and other titles.[30] A literary parlor game, one of several such diversions popular late in the nineteenth century, listed *Excursions in Field and Forest* as well as *The Maine Woods* and *Summer* under Thoreau's portrait, on its Henry D. Thoreau author card.[31] Throughout the life of the 1863 plates, however, the simple title *Excursions* was used on the titlepage, on the spine legend, and, until the Houghton, Mifflin "bevel-edge" printings of 1881-1892 (which reverted to *Excursions in Field and Forest*), on a list of Thoreau's writings available from the publisher, usually bound in the front before the titlepage.

Sanborn announced in the *Commonwealth* for August 28 that the new book was in press, but he was uninformed about the exact contents, for he declared that it would include the essay scheduled for the October *Atlantic* (that is, "Life without Principle"), as well as "Thomas Carlyle and His Works," "Resistance to Civil Government," and some other political pieces. (He also observed that Ticknor and Fields was considering a volume of Thoreau's letters and poems.)

A pre-publication announcement of *Excursions in Field and Forest* appeared in the *New-York Daily Tribune* for September 10, a notice reprinted on September 19 by the *National Anti-Slavery Standard*. On September 12, the *Springfield* (Mass.) *Republican* carried a similar preview by "Warrington" (William S. Robinson, a schoolmate of Thoreau's). The *Utica* (N.Y.) *Morning Herald* announced the forthcoming *Excursions* on September 23. Ticknor and Fields advertised

---

[30] See for example specimens of *The Maine Woods* (1864), ads dated June 1864; *Excursions* (fourth printing, 1866), ads dated September 1865; and Longfellow's *Tales of a Wayside Inn* (1863), ads dated November 1863, all in the collection of Joseph J. Moldenhauer. Advertisements in the *Atlantic Monthly* sometimes used the one title, sometimes the other. See also note 33 below.

[31] Photocopy, collection of Joseph J. Moldenhauer.

"Excursions in Field and Forest" in the October *Atlantic Monthly* as forthcoming, and listed it among "Books in Press" in *American Literary Gazette and Publishers' Circular*, a bi-weekly trade publication, on September 15, but not again until November 2, where, under "The Latest Books From the Press of Ticknor & Fields," it was characterized as "A Delightful Country Book . . . Embellished with a Fine Portrait of the Author." In the same issue, the *American Literary Gazette* reported *Excursions* in its "List of Books Recently Published in the United States," and on November 16 gave it an enthusiastic, if brief, review. This notice ended with the endorsement that "Every page of this delightful book contains a new thought, or an old one in a new garb." The November *Atlantic* advertised it as "just issued."

In the Cost Books of Ticknor and Fields, the entries for the first edition run as follows:[32]

1863	Thoreau's Excursions		1 vol	16mo			
				Houghton Stereo			
	273	pp	S. P.	777	212.121		
	$26^6/_8$	"	L. P.	943	25.225		
	$14^6/_8$	"	Bourg	1196	17.641		
	$^4/_8$	"	Min	1767	.884		
	315				255.871	82	209 81
					Correcting 7½ hrs	33	2 48
	1 p S P (½ title cancelled)				777	82	64
					Setting Greek ¾ h	33	25
					Altns in Plates 1 "		40
					7 Boxes	75	5 25	218 83

1558	First Edition		Houghton		1500		
Sep. 18	$23^5/_{20}$ Rms 22 × 37½ .60		(R.K & Co)	10.80		251 10	
			42 Tokens	90		37 80	
			Binding	13		195	
			Copyright on 1350	12½		168 75	652 65

Cost on 1350 (Inc Plates) 64½ Sells $1.25
Published Oct 10th 1863

---

[32] MH-H, bMS Am 2030.2 (17), p. 46; compare Walter Harding,

These entries need some explanation. The four lines after "Houghton Stereo" record the number of pages in each of four type fonts. "S. P." is Small Pica, "L. P." is Long Primer, "Bourg" is Bourgeois, and "Min" is Minion. The number following the typeface abbreviation is the number of ems per page in that font, and the last column records the product of that figure and the number of pages (read commas for decimal points except for the last figure, which should be read as 884). The total number of pages typeset is 315; 255,871 is the total ems; 82 (cents) is the labor cost per thousand ems; and "209 81" ($209.81) the total cost of typesetting other than Greek letters. (The casting of stereotype plates, figured separately for later Ticknor and Fields first editions of Thoreau, is included in the typesetting expense for *Excursions*.) The formes of type required 7½ hours of correcting after proofs were read (compare 92 hours each for *The Maine Woods* and *Cape Cod*, both typeset in large part from manuscript). A replacement half-title page was set in Small Pica at the same rate per thousand ems (82 cents) as the previously set 315 pages; the total (64 cents) reflects not the actual number of ems in the half-title but the number in a full page (777).[33] Special typesetting of Greek char-

---

comp., "The Early Printing Records of Thoreau's Books," *American Transcendental Quarterly* 11 (Summer 1971): 47-48. Michael Winship has kindly perfected the entries against his microfilms of the original business records and offered assistance in the interpretation of details.

[33] The Houghton Riverside Press account book also records this expense of replacing the half title, and the job entry heading reads "Excursions of a Northern Naturalist," with the last four words struck through and a period entered after "Excursions". Typesetting and plating occurred between July 6 and September 8, while the press runs took place on September 26 and October 3. See Michael Winship, " 'Printers of the Mind' Revisited–The Case of the Riverside Press," in *Books and Bibliography: Essays in Commemoration of Don McKenzie*, ed. John Thomson (Wellington: Victoria University Press, 2002), pp. 74-76.

acters cost twenty-five cents (¾ of an hour at $.33 per hour). Forty cents' worth of alteration time (one hour) was required after the plates were cast. The "Boxes," costing $.75 each, were specially made wooden containers for storing the heavy stereotype plates.

The next part of the entry itemizes the costs of paper and printing for a first edition of 1500 copies. On September 18, 1863, Ticknor and Fields ordered (or paid for) 23⁵⁄₂₀ reams of paper measuring 22 by 37½ inches and weighing sixty pounds per ream from one of its suppliers, Rice and Kendall, at $10.80 per ream, for a total paper cost of $251.10. The printing was done by the H. O. Houghton company of Cambridge, the same firm that performed the typesetting and stereo casting. A token is a unit of presswork representing 500 impressions from the plates or formes on the press bed; at $.90 per unit, the labor for 42 tokens cost $37.80. The paper size and the entry mathematics indicate that the plates were set up on the power press for half-sheet imposition; see *Cape Cod*, pp. 317-318, for an explanation of the process. Each signature or gathering consists of twelve leaves, twenty-four pages, except for the last. The press run produced good printed sheets for 1558 copies, of which 58 sets were left unbound (see the line above the "Sep. 18" dateline). The rough Cost Book reveals that only 22¹⁴⁄₂₀ reams were actually used in the press run. The discrepancy (in the final, fair Cost Book record) between 1500 copies and the 1350 on which the bookkeeper calculated unit cost and copyright (royalty) is accounted for by copies kept by the house or given gratis to friends, family members, and reviewers.

Case-binding was farmed out to Lemon, Fields & Co. of Boston, a firm of which James T. Fields's younger brother George was a member. At $.13 a copy, the 1500 sets of gatherings cost $195 to cut, fold, and bind. The expense of preparing the engraved plate of

Rowse's 1854 portrait of Thoreau for a frontispiece, of printing 1500 copies, and of tipping tissue guards into the books is not represented in the Cost Book record; see the foregoing summary of Sophia Thoreau's contract negotiations with Fields. The firm paid Sophia a royalty of twelve and a half cents per copy on the 1350 first edition copies intended for sale, for a total of $168.75. Paper, presswork, binding, and royalty added up to $652.65, which, when added to the previous subtotal, came to $871.48 as the company's total outlay for the edition, or 64½ cents per copy on 1350 copies for the trade. Ticknor and Fields priced the book at $1.25, and recorded a publication date of October 10. The *Boston Daily Advertiser*, however, announced publication on October 14.[34] A copy was deposited for U.S. copyright on the latter day.

The book's pagination is ⟨1⟩-319, 2 blank leaves; portrait frontispiece inserted. It collates ⟨1-13^{12}, 14^{6}⟩ and is signed ⟨1-19^{8}, 20^{10}⟩. *Excursions* was bound in three patterns of textured cloth, TR, BD, and Z, with deep blue-green the dominant color, although some copies in TR cloth are blue.[35]

The first reviews of *Excursions* were printed in the *Boston Post* and the Boston *Saturday Evening Gazette* for October 17, 1863. The former asserted that Thoreau's "brain was awfully out of joint, so his translations of nature are only distorted glimpses of what she is." The latter also took note of the author's "mental

[34] Emerson, *Letters*, 5:339 n.

[35] *Bibliography of American Literature*, compiled by Jacob Blanck, vol. 8, edited and completed by Michael Winship (New Haven: Yale University Press, 1990), item 20111. *BAL* reports, from the rough Cost Book, that printing took place October 2, and from other publisher's records that binding occurred October 10-16. See also note 33 above and Raymond R. Borst, *Henry David Thoreau: A Descriptive Bibliography* (Pittsburgh: University of Pittsburgh Press, 1982), item A 3.1 a.

peculiarities." Two days later a favorable notice appeared in the *Cincinnati Enquirer*, and another of the same temper was printed in the *Daily Eastern Argus* (Portland, Maine) for October 20. Also on the 20th the *New-York Commercial Advertiser* gave an enthusiastic notice. The *Cincinnati Gazette* made favorable comments on October 22, and Sanborn's review in the *Commonwealth* for October 23 was predictably long and laudatory, respecting both the book and Thoreau's character. On October 24 reviews appeared in the *Norfolk County Journal* (Roxbury, Mass.) and in the *Boston Traveller Supplement*, which echoed Emerson's biographical sketch. Emerson's memorial essay was praised in the October 28 *North American and United States Gazette* (Philadelphia). Also on the 28th, the *Baltimore American* remarked on Thoreau's "eccentricities," but welcomed this "new set of essays," "having been greatly entertained by 'Walden'." The reviewer in the *Providence Journal*, October 29, admired the author's books but disliked his character, and on October 30 the *Congregationalist* unsurprisingly regretted Thoreau's "pantheistic or naturalistic" religious tendencies. The same day a favorable notice appeared in the *New York Evening Express*. "Warrington" (William S. Robinson), who had given a pre-publication mention to *Excursions* in the *Springfield Republican*, called Thoreau an "original genius" in an October 31 review in that paper; and the *New-York Daily Tribune* of the same date spoke admiringly of Emerson's memoir and Thoreau's "remarkable . . . personal character" before reprinting long extracts from the book. Also praising the Emerson sketch was the very brief notice in the October 31 *Cincinnati Daily Commercial.*

Other reviews followed in November and December: the *Pittsburgh Gazette* (November 1); the *Worcester* (Mass.) *Palladium* (November 5, perhaps by

Thoreau's devoted friend H. G. O. Blake); the *New-York Observer* and the *Taunton* (Mass.) *Union Gazette and Democrat* (November 5), both also commendatory; the *Boston Transcript* (November 6), which thought Emerson's sketch "hardly flatters" a man whose "philosophy of life was wrong from its one-sidedness"; *Albion* (November 7), which admired Thoreau's "powerful and independent" mind, "vivacious" fancy, and "earnest and profound" sympathy with nature; the *Philadelphia Evening Bulletin* (November 7), which like so many others remarked on Thoreau's personal idiosyncrasies; the Boston *Daily Advertiser* (November 11) and New York *Evening Post* (November 12), both appreciative; *Country Gentleman* (November 12); the *Portsmouth* (N.H.) *Journal of Literature & Politics* (November 14), under the heading "Thoreau–An Eccentric"; the *Chicago Tribune* (November 15), a favorable notice; the *American Literary Gazette and Publishers' Circular* review discussed heretofore (November 16); an appreciative reading of the essays in the *Boston Transcript Supplement* (November 21); the *New England Farmer* (November 21); the *New-York Times*, November 23, whose reviewer thought the *Excursions* essays were "probably the last relics the world will receive" of Thoreau's interesting pen; the *Essex Statesman* (Salem, Mass.) of November 28, another appreciative review; the *Monthly Religious Magazine* for December, where Edmund H. Sears took a more liberal view of Thoreau than did the author of the *Congregationalist* notice; the *Continental Monthly* (December), which viewed *Excursions* as peculiarly American; the *Christian Advocate and Journal* (December 3), which despite its appreciation of Thoreau's "keenness of eye" found him "stone blind" to supernatural verities; the *Independent*, which on December 3 (like a reviewer of *Walden* in 1854) compared Thoreau to Diogenes the Cynic, with his "sharp small philosophy of life"; the *Newark* (N.J.) *Advertiser* and the *Alta California* of San Francisco (both December 4, and both favorable); *Harper's Weekly* (December 12), an appreciation penned by George William Curtis, Thoreau's editor for "An Excursion to Canada" and *Cape Cod* in *Putnam's Monthly Magazine* in the 1850s; and the *Kennebec Journal* of Augusta, Maine (December 25), which excerpted generously from the essays.

A few final notices appeared early in 1864, all in monthlies: the *American Presbyterian and Theological Review* for January; the *Boston Review* for January, which admired the essays while noting they were "not written from a Christian point of view"; *Godey's Lady's Book and Magazine* and *Arthur's Home Magazine* (both January and both admiring); and finally *Peterson's Magazine*, which, while generally friendly to the essays, thought "Autumnal Tints" should have shown "more imagination."[36]

The Cost Books show that seven reimpressions of the *Excursions* plates were made by Ticknor and Fields and its successors through 1880, the number of copies totaling 1,940. These printings occurred in 1864, late 1865, 1866 (advertised as illustrated with portrait and issued thus, but a copy in the collection of Joseph J. Moldenhauer lacks both the frontispiece and any indication that one was removed), 1875, 1877, 1879, and 1880. The price per copy gradually rose to $2.00 during this interval. Under the imprint of Houghton, Mifflin and Company as many as fourteen more printings can

[36] All the cited reviews of *Excursions* except those in the *Norfolk County Journal*, the *Cincinnati Daily Commercial*, the *Taunton Union Gazette*, *Country Gentleman*, and the *New England Farmer* are identified, summarized, and selectively quoted in Gary Scharnhorst, comp., *Henry David Thoreau: An Annotated Bibliography of Comment and Criticism Before 1900* (New York and London: Garland Publishing, Inc., 1992).

be inferred from copies with either or both a printed date or a designation of "[ordinal number] Edition."[37] Of these the *National Union Catalog, Pre-1956 Imprints* records an impression dated 1881 [?], impressions called "Fourteenth Edition," "Fifteenth Edition," "Seventeenth Edition," and "Eighteenth Edition," and impressions dated 1888, 1890, 1891, and 1892; and the collection of Joseph J. Moldenhauer contains a "Sixteenth Edition," approximately 1884-1885. The entry for the 1892 reimpression, in Houghton, Mifflin and Company's "Sheet Stock Book" covering that year, calls it the "22nd Edition." Optical collation on the Hinman machine of copies of the first edition (TxAuHRH) and the 1890 reimpression (TxAuHRH) discloses no changes in the texts of the eight essays edited in the present volume except those changes accidentally produced by damage to the stereotype plates. Such damage, concentrated along the margins and gutters, is manifested in the whole or partial loss of punctuation marks and letters.

An early reprint from *Excursions* took the form of a selection of Thoreau's prose, with Emerson's "Biographical Sketch" attached, in Houghton, Mifflin and Company's "Riverside Literature Series" (number 27), in wrappers for school use. The contents by Thoreau were "The Succession of Forest Trees," "Wild Apples," and the "Sounds" chapter from *Walden*; the compilation was published in 1887. (As early as 1890, these contents were combined with John Burroughs's "Birds and Bees" and some outdoor essays by Charles Dudley Warner in a clothbound "Riverside Literature Series" volume.[38]) A similar compilation was issued in

[37] According to the publisher's terminology, the first reimpression, 1864, would have been the second "edition," and the reimpression of 1880 the "eighth edition."

[38] An 1888 combination of the Thoreau contents with "Birds

1910 as number 100 in a monthly pamphlet series called *The School World*, issued by D. H. Knowlton & Co., Farmington, Maine. The selections were "The Succession of Forest Trees" and a short extract from the "Spring" chapter of *Walden*, with a brief, unsigned biographical essay (indebted to Emerson's) at the beginning.[39] The first British collection of short works by Thoreau, *Essays and Other Writings of Henry Thoreau*, n.d. [1891], edited by Will H. Dircks in the Walter Scott press (London and Newcastle-on-Tyne) series of Thoreau titles, contained "Walking," "A Winter Walk," "The Landlord," and "Night and Moonlight" from the 1863 Ticknor and Fields *Excursions*, plus several essays from the *Yankee* volume and letters and poems from *Letters to Various Persons*.

Early in 1865, Bronson Alcott wrote to Daniel Ricketson that "Miss Sophia" was reading proof sheets of *Cape Cod* and *Letters to Various Persons* (published in March and July of that year, respectively), and copying some of Henry's manuscripts. "You will be pleased to learn," he added, "that there remains matter for a book or two of *Politics*, one or more of *Morals*, and several more of *Field and Table Talk* . . ."[40] By "Field and Table Talk" he was presumably referring to selections from the manuscript Journal. "Politics" and "Morals" characterize the essays that would be gathered as "Anti-Slavery and Reform Papers" in the 1866 *Yankee* volume.

---

and Bees" and Hawthorne's "Little Daffydowndilly" sold poorly. Record of Book Sales, MH-H, bMS Am 2030.2 (17), HMCo Papers; information courtesy of Eric Lupfer.

[39] Not in Raymond R. Borst, *Henry David Thoreau: A Descriptive Bibliography* (Pittsburgh: University of Pittsburgh Press, 1982); copy in collection of Joseph J. Moldenhauer.

[40] *The Letters of A. Bronson Alcott*, ed. Richard L. Herrnstadt (Ames: Iowa State University Press, 1969), pp. 362-363.

The posthumous volumes of Thoreau that Fields
had published by early summer 1865 had not been un-
profitable, and he was apparently interested in adding
to his Thoreau list. Annie Fields recorded that she and
her husband went to call on Sophia on July 7, 1865.[41]
They talked about who might edit the Journal, which
Annie understood to occupy thirty-two volumes, and
about other prospective publications. Shortly afterward, on July 28, Alcott recorded in his diary that Sophia had told him "Fields wishes to print Henry's political papers, and that she has them nearly prepared
for the press. . . . The Letters are just out, and I have a
copy sent me by the publishers."[42] Those explicitly political papers, all previously published separately and
all included on Sanborn's and Fields's lists of Thoreau's writings in the spring of 1863, were "Civil Disobedience" (a somewhat revised form of "Resistance to
Civil Government"), "Herald of Freedom," "Wendell
Phillips Before the Concord Lyceum," "Slavery in Massachusetts" (the "Address in Framingham"), "A Plea
for Captain John Brown," and "The Last Days of John
Brown." To these Sophia added "Life without Principle," the Carlyle essay, "Paradise (to Be) Regained" (a
review of J. A. Etzler's utopian forecast for universal
happiness by means of mechanical improvements),
and–mistakenly–a short *Dial* essay titled "Prayers"
which had been written by Emerson though it contained a poem of her brother's. Because of its insistent
concern with government and with the striking differences between the conditions of mankind under colonial and democratic rule, "A Yankee in Canada" was
tolerably compatible with the other contents; moreover, like *Cape Cod* and *The Maine Woods*, it had been

---

[41] Howe, p. 68.
[42] *The Journals of Bronson Alcott*, p. 374.

only partially printed in magazine form, and it had not yet been collected.

Apparently the first mention of the *Yankee* volume in Fields's "Memorandum and Account Book" at CSmH is a page bearing the date 1865, where "Thoreaus Yankee in Canada &c / MSs. in Safe" follows a notation on "H H Brownells' Poems".[43] An entry on a loose sheet headed "Books to be pub^d in 1866. not yet begun." reads "Thoreaus Yankee in Canada Summer". Another list is headed "Books in Preparation /1866."; it includes "A Yankee in Canada: with Anti-Slavery & Reform Papers. By HDT. / (300 pages like 'Cape Cod'". A newspaper clipping with a Ticknor and Fields ad for titles in press, headed "Attractive Promise of New Books" and listing "A Yankee in Canada, by Henry D. Thoreau," is attached to another page headed "Books in Preparation. 1866". Yet another leaf in the Memorandum Book is captioned, "Books in Press and in Preparation. February. 1866." It lists "Thoreaus Yankee in Canada".

With the book in preparation but evidently not yet in press, Fields consulted Ellery Channing about it. Channing wrote Fields on June 22, 1866,

> I find this book of Mr Thoreau's will make about 250 pages. If you wish to enlarge the book to 300 or more, I have two months of one of his journals copied, which might be given as a specimen . . . I have written to Miss Thoreau, to see what she has to say about this. . . . I advise you not to make it appear as if this book was merely a voyage to Canada. It is not so at all. The reform papers are very remarkable. . . .[44]

[43] Henry Howard Brownell, *War-Lyrics and Other Poems* (Boston: Ticknor and Fields, 1866).

[44] "The Selected Letters of William Ellery Channing the Younger

The *Bibliography of American Literature*, item 20117, attributes the editorship of the *Yankee* volume to Sophia and Channing jointly. Samuel Arthur Jones, in a bibliographical supplement to Blake's selection, *Thoreau's Thoughts* (Boston: Houghton, Mifflin and Company, 1890), p. 136, assigns it to Channing alone, possibly because Channing had been Thoreau's companion on the trip to Canada. But in his *Bibliography of Henry David Thoreau* (New York: Printed for the Rowfant Club of Cleveland, 1894), pp. 46-47, Jones revised his opinion and declared that Channing and Sophia shared the editorial responsibility. Francis H. Allen's 1908 *Bibliography of Henry David Thoreau* (Boston: Houghton Mifflin Company), pp. 22-24, does not identify the editor or editors; and in *Thoreau's Editors: History and Reminiscence* (Thoreau Society Booklet Number Seven, 1950), p. 10, Allen declares that he has "no information as to who made up the [*Yankee*] volume." No documentary evidences of Channing's involvement in the project are known other than this letter of June 22, 1866, and a journal notation on March 1, 1867, when Channing was taking stock of his personal deficiencies: "for my part I am not only so incurious but I am so heavy and dull, that I never so much as discovered that I should have arranged H[enry]'s papers in his last book, in the series of their age, till it was all printed and then should have never done so [i.e., discovered it] but for a critic's strictures."[45] (The allusion is to Sanborn's harsh criticism of the ordering of the "Anti-Slavery and Reform Papers" in his otherwise ardent *Commonwealth* review of the volume,

---

(Part Four), ed. Francis B. Dedmond, *Studies in the American Renaissance*, ed. Joel Myerson (Charlottesville: University Press of Virginia, 1992), p. 3; year supplied by editor.

[45] Channing Diaries, MCo-SC; typed transcript by Frederick T. McGill, Jr., MH-H, bMS Am 800.6.

September 29, 1866.) Sophia gave him a copy, but its inscription, "W. E. Channing With the kind regards of S. E. Thoreau.", does not suggest that he assisted her substantially; compare his copy of *The Maine Woods*, which she inscribed to him "from his grateful friend."[46] As Channing himself acknowledged on January 4, 1868, thanking Sophia for a copy of the revised, second edition of *A Week*, his contact with her and her mother had declined sharply in recent years, which would have been especially the case after he moved from Main Street (opposite the Thoreau house) to Middle Street in late 1865. In a letter to Ricketson on May 26, 1866, Sophia had complained that Channing "*never* comes to see us."[47] Despite Channing's eagerness to supplement the contents of the volume with Journal selections, Fields proceeded with his original design.

The first advertisement by Ticknor and Fields for "The Yankee in Canada, &c.", among numerous "New Works in the Press," appeared in *American Literary Gazette and Publishers' Circular* on May 1, 1866. It was repeated on May 15, June 1, and June 15. In the August 1 and 15 issues the firm advertised "The Yankee in Canada" ("Good Reading for Summer") as "Nearly Ready." On September 15, the title was listed as forthcoming in September among "Attractive New Works, To be published this Autumn." The *American Literary Gazette* announced the book in its "List of Books Recently Published in the United States" on October 1, and reviewed it, with disapprobation of the author's "cynical individualism," on the same day. It was not advertised again by Ticknor and Fields until the November 1 issue.

[46] Both inscribed books are at NN-BGC.
[47] "The Selected Letters of William Ellery Channing the Younger (Part Four)," p. 6.

This is the firm's 1866 Cost Book record for the first edition:[48]

1866		Yankee in Canada						
		Stereotyped W. B. Co						
July 25	275 pp	L. Pr.	1000	275000				
	7 "	Bourg	1274	8918				
	4	Min	1890	7560	291478 ems	.70	204 03	
		Correcting	38 Hrs			.50	19 00	
		Stereotyping 291.478				.45	131 16	
			6 Boxes			1.25	7 50	361 69
Aug 15	1546	20⁴/₂₀ Rms	22 × 37½	.60	/GW&Co/	13.20	1500 266 64	
		⁸/₂₀ "	" " "	"	"	addl	5 28	
31		Binding				.17	255	
					Copyright	12½	187 50	752 42
		Costs 74¼			Sells 1.50			1114 11

The analysis, earlier in this introduction, of the first edition Cost Book record for *Excursions* will explain the method of the *Yankee* entry and will clarify most of the abbreviations. "W. B. Co" stands for Welch, Bigelow and Company of Cambridge; the paper provisioner "GW&Co" was Grant, Warren & Company. The amount of correction required results from the use of manuscript copy for the last two and a quarter chapters of "A Yankee in Canada"; the remainder of the book was set from printed copy. Welch, Bigelow's press run produced 1546 sets of sheets. The arithmetic of the "Binding" and "Copyright" lines indicates that 1500 copies were bound (by Sanborn, Parker & [George] Fields of Boston) and that Sophia was paid royalty on the entire bound edition. Forty-six sets of sheets remained, for the time being, unbound. The sub-total "752 42" in the rightmost column is thirty-eight dollars higher than the sum of the four figures in the column to the left which the sub-total presumably

[48] MH-H, bMS Am 2030.2 (17), p. 306. Contributions as before by Michael Winship. Compare Harding, "Early Printing Records," p. 57.

represents. This discrepancy can be explained by the absence of a presswork entry between the paper lines and the binding line. While making the Cost Book record, the bookkeeper apparently failed to copy from whatever rough record he had kept a line indicating the number of tokens, rate per token, and presswork expense. One dollar was the rate indicated in other 1866 Cost Book entries; we may therefore conjecture that the missing line read "38 tokens   1   38".

The book's pagination is ⟨i-iv⟩, ⟨1⟩-286, plus a blank leaf. Its collation is ⟨-⟩², 1-12¹², also signed ⟨-⟩², ⟨A⟩-R⁸. The bindings were in several cloth patterns, C, TR, HC, and Z, some green and others purple, with three variations of blind-stamping within the edition.[49]

A Yankee in Canada, with Anti-Slavery and Reform Papers was printed on September 3 and bound between September 6 and 12.[50] The Harvard College Library received a copy on September 17. U.S. copyright was not secured by a deposit copy until January 25, 1867, by which time a 500-copy reimpression of the plates had already been made and bound. The first review, short but favorable, appeared in the *New-York Daily Tribune* for September 15, which admired the "travel sketches" but not the "reform papers." The *Boston Transcript* (September 20) found the collection "thoroughly characteristic of the man" and advised unfamiliar readers to address it first among Thoreau's books. The *Kennebec Journal* on September 21 commended Ticknor and Fields for their "good service" in packaging Thoreau's "fugitive papers" so attractively. The *Portland Transcript* (September 22)

---

[49] *Bibliography of American Literature*, vol. 8, item 20117; see also Raymond R. Borst, *Henry David Thoreau: A Descriptive Bibliography* (Pittsburgh: University of Pittsburgh Press, 1982), item A.7.1.a.

[50] *Bibliography of American Literature*, vol. 8, item 20117.

compared Thoreau favorably as a travel writer to his world-roaming contemporary, Bayard Taylor, while the *Hartford Press* of September 22 also lauded the travel writing. So did the *Christian Register* (September 22), although its reviewer disparaged the political essays, through many of which "runs . . . a vein of impracticable and half-insane theorizing." A writer for the *Worcester Daily Spy*, perhaps an acquaintance of Thoreau's, praised the man and the book on September 22. The *Utica Morning Herald* gave a perfunctory notice on the same date. An ambivalent review in the *Albany Evening Journal*, September 22, reversed the *Portland Transcript*'s judgment of the relative merits of Thoreau and Taylor as travel writers, and regretted the "false . . . logic" and dangerous influence of the political pieces, which should not have been reprinted. Among the many notices on September 22 was one in the *Norfolk County Journal*. The *New York Herald* (September 23) admired Thoreau's stout principles while regretting some "crude opinions" and "eccentricities" in the book. Similar reservations were expressed the following day in the *Boston Post*, which thought the Carlyle essay the best piece. A reasoned reproach to Thoreau's censoriousness toward "the faults of our political and social institutions" was offered in the *Philadelphia Inquirer*, September 24, which declared that slavery was "eradicated by the instrumentalities which he regarded with the most unmitigated contempt." The anti-slavery papers were applauded, however, in the same day's *Boston Traveller*. The *Philadelphia Evening Bulletin*, September 25, praised the Canadian narrative. On September 26 reviews appeared in the *Worcester Palladium* (more reserved than its response to *Excursions*), the *New-York Commercial Advertiser*, which excerpted the text at length, and the *New York Times*, a negative reading of both the travel narrative and the political papers. The *Hartford Courant* of September 27 admired the essayist's "delightfully original and graceful" style. The *Boston Recorder* regretted Thoreau's heterodoxy on September 28. On the 29th Sanborn provided a full column of observations in the *Commonwealth*, decrying the book's editorial arrangement and contributing some anecdotes illustrative of Thoreau's just moral sense and cutting humor. "Warrington" (William S. Robinson) in the *Springfield Republican* that same day expressed his opinion that the Canada narrative was superior to the "extravagant" anti-slavery pieces, and the *Portland Transcript* excerpted a long passage from the first chapter of "A Yankee in Canada." Other reviews appeared on the 29th in the *Chicago Tribune* and *Massachusetts Ploughman* (Boston).

Subsequent notices were printed in the *Universalist Quarterly* for October; the *American Literary Gazette and Publishers' Circular* for October 1 (see p. 357 above); the *Cincinnati Daily Commercial* for October 2 (quoted without citation from the *Chicago Tribune*); the New York *Evening Post*, New York *Observer*, and *North American and United States Gazette* (Philadelphia) for October 4; the *Round Table* for October 6 (an especially hostile reaction); the *Springfield Republican* (again) and the *Green Mountain Freeman* (Montpelier, Vt.) for October 10; the New York *Evening Post* (again) and *The Independent* for October 11; the *Providence Journal* for October 12; the *Taunton Union Gazette and Democrat* for October 18, enthusiastic like all other reviews of Thoreau's posthumous books in that paper; *Alta California* for October 20; Greeley's *New-York Daily Tribune*, October 25 (one of the longest and most admiring responses); Henry C. Watson's *American Art Journal* (New York), October 25, which thought Thoreau "a healthy, vigorous writer" but found "little

in the way of novelty" in the Canadian narrative and
felt no obligation to review the political papers; the
Monthly Religious Magazine (by Rufus E. Ellis), *Hours
at Home*, and the *Eclectic Magazine*, all for November;
the *New England Farmer* for November 3; the *Christian Advocate* (November 8); the *Baltimore American*
(November 9); the London *Examiner* (brief mention,
November 17, and review, December 1); the *Ladies Repository* (December), a brief but positive notice; the
San Francisco *Evening Bulletin* (November 24); the
New Englander for January 1867, whose reviewer used
the editorial "we" to note that "We do not rank ourselves among [Thoreau's] admirers"; the *Athenæum*
for February 16, which printed a triple review of the
Yankee volume, Whittier's *Prose Works*, and E. P.
Whipple's *Character and Characteristic Men*, all marketed in Europe by Trübner & Co. (what little the reviewer had to say about the Thoreau volume was a
censure of Thoreau's treatment of "his most important topic," his unqualified support of John Brown);
and finally the *Radical* for April 1867, a notice written
by Sidney H. Morse.[51]

In addition to the reimpression recorded the same
year as the original printing, Ticknor and Fields and
its corporate successors printed four reimpressions
through 1876. The five reprintings totalled 1,008 copies, according to the Cost Books. Another printing
dated 1878 is listed in the *National Union Catalog, Pre-*

---

[51] The *Green Mountain Freeman* review and that in the *New England Farmer* are reprinted in *Thoreau Society Bulletin* 203
(Spring 1993): 5-6. The remainder, except those in the *Worcester
Daily Spy*, the *Norfolk County Journal*, the *Chicago Tribune*, the
Massachusetts Ploughman, the *Cincinnati Daily Commercial*, the
Taunton Union Gazette, the *American Art Journal*, the *Ladies
Repository*, and the second New York *Evening Post* notice, are
summarized and selectively quoted in Scharnhorst, *Annotated
Bibliography*.

1956 Imprints; the editor has seen a titlepage. Under the imprint of Houghton, Mifflin and Company the book was reprinted at least another nine times more, judging from copies listed in the *NUC*, or examined by the editor, which have either or both a titlepage date of issue and an "Edition" designation. These are the re-impressions of 1881, 1884, 1885 ("Twelfth Edition"), 1887 ("Thirteenth Edition"), 1888, 1891, and 1892. Collation on the Hinman machine of "A Yankee in Canada" in both the 1891 (CtNbT) and the 1892 (ICRC) reimpressions against the 1866 first printing (TxAuHRH) discloses no textual changes other than changes inadvertently caused by batter at the margins, gutters, and corners of the plates.

Textual Introduction

THE PRESENT EDITION of *Excursions* in the Princeton University Press series, *The Writings of Henry D. Thoreau*, is the first to be based on collation and study of all surviving authorial manuscripts related to its nine component essays as well as of the printed forms, set from copy prepared by Thoreau, that were issued during Thoreau's lifetime and shortly after his death. This edition reflects, too, the editor's analysis of such external data as correspondence by Thoreau, his friends and family, and his contemporary editors; the sources of Thoreau's quotations and paraphrases in the essays; editorial practices of the publications in which the essays were initially printed; and information about the Ticknor and Fields volumes in which the essays were first collected. The bulk of this data is cited and analyzed in the Headnotes for the individual essays, the first element in the editorial apparatus for each. Publication histories of the Ticknor and Fields collected editions, *Excursions* (1863) and *A Yankee in Canada, with Anti-Slavery and Reform Papers* (1866), have been supplied in the Historical Introduction immediately preceding. This Textual Introduction, on the other hand, will explain the editorial principles and procedures governing both the choice of copy-text for the various essays and the emendation of those copy-texts. Next, the Textual Introduction will outline the editorial apparatus documenting the exact forms of the copy-texts, the individual emendations, and the variants in other versions of the texts, variants not adopted as emendations because the editor judged them to be either nonauthorial, or authorial but superseded by authorial revision, or–in a few instances–authorial but intended for a different composition than the essay at hand, as when Thoreau attempted to incorporate parts of "A Walk to Wachusett" (1843) into *A Week on the Concord and Merrimack Rivers* (1849). Finally, the Textual Introduction details the physical means taken to prepare the Princeton Edition of *Excursions* and the safeguards against new corruption of the text in the course of production.

THEORY OF COPY-TEXT

Like all other volumes in *The Writings of Henry D. Thoreau*, and like all volumes in the other projects that originated under the auspices of the Modern Language Association's Center for Editions of American Authors and that are now submitting their results to the scrutiny of the MLA's Committee on Scholarly Editions (C.S.E.), *Excursions* is an unmodernized, purified, eclectic or critical text. The editorial theory and procedures by which this volume has been prepared conform essentially to those employed in the Centenary Edition of Hawthorne and the Northwestern-Newberry Edition of Melville. For detailed expositions, the interested reader should consult essays by W. W. Greg, Fredson Bowers, and G. Thomas Tanselle and the guidelines issued by the C.S.E.[1] What follows in these pages is a capsule discussion concentrating on the aspects of theory and practice most pertinent to the editing of the *Excursions* essays.

---

[1] W. W. Greg, "The Rationale of Copy-Text," *Studies in Bibliography* 3 (1950): 19-36; Fredson Bowers, "Current Theories of Copy-Text, with an Illustration from Dryden," *Modern Philology* 48 (1950): 12-20; Bowers, "Some Principles for Scholarly Editions of Nineteenth-Century Authors," *Studies in Bibliography* 17 (1964): 223-228; G. Thomas Tanselle, "Greg's Theory of Copy-Text and the Editing of American Literature," *Studies in Bibliography* 28 (1975): 167-229; Committee on Scholarly Editions, "Guidelines for Editors of Scholarly Editions" http://www.mla.org/resources/documents/rep_scholarly/cse_guidelines.

An eclectic or critical text is neither an exact reprint of any particular printed document nor a literatim transcription or facsimile reproduction of a manuscript document. It is an analytically constructed text whose editor selects that one of the various documentary forms of the finished text over which the author exercised the greatest degree of control, and then emends it to reproduce as nearly as possible the author's intention. The form showing the most authorial control might be, to list the most likely cases for a mid-nineteenth century American work, a manuscript from which the first printing of the text was typeset, or a set of author-corrected proofs for the first printing if the setting-copy manuscript is lost, or an authorially corrected copy of the first printing if both the setting copy and corrected proofs are lost, or an example of the first printing if all the foregoing are lost. The form of the text chosen as the base for emendation is the copy-text. Emendation of the copy-text derives for the most part from other forms of the text, including the author's working manuscripts and printed versions over which the author demonstrably or probably exercised an influence. Forms of the text showing the author's influence are relevant documents. Those materials antedating and leading to the copy-text, usually working manuscripts, are called pre-copy-texts; those postdating and issuing from the copy-text, usually revised reprints, are called post-copy-texts. It is crucial that all relevant documents (witnesses to the text) be identified and studied, for the editor selects the copy-text from among them and uses the others as guides to emendation.

The editor must be familiar with the author's style both in working papers and fair copy, with external data bearing on the composition and first publication of the text from manuscript, and, in the case of printed copy-texts, with the style norms and preferences of the editors and printers to whom the setting-copy manuscript was entrusted. Some emendations, therefore, will not derive specifically from a pre- or post-copy-text document, but rather from independent editorial judgment.

A primary assumption in modern textual theory is that the surviving finished form closest in time to the author's composition is the most reliable in its "accidentals"–the details of punctuation, spelling, word-division, capitalization, and paragraphing. The accidentals of later printed forms, even those produced during the author's lifetime, are less authoritative. This is so because prior to the age of electronic data storage a later printing was routinely typeset anew from an earlier printing, whether or not the reprint contained revisions attributable to the author. As the text was reset, further house stylings were imposed upon the accidentals, and new compositor's mistakes were introduced. Therefore, in the textual editor's choice of copy-text, the author's manuscript intended for typesetting enjoys the highest priority, followed by four other forms in this usual sequence: an amanuensis fair copy intended for typesetting, authorially corrected proofsheets for the first publication, authorially corrected post-publication copy of the first printing, and unmarked first printed copy.

Although the copy-text carries maximum general authority among relevant forms of the text with respect to accidentals, its "substantives"–the words themselves–are not binding on the editor where they differ from the substantives of a later relevant printing. Later substantives are adopted as emendations if the editor can demonstrate that they certainly or probably issued from the author's hand. Otherwise, they are rejected as likely bowdlerizations, sophistications, errors, or casual modifications by copy-editors or compositors. Those readings deemed nonauthorial are recorded in the apparatus as rejected substantives, with discussion, if needed, in textual notes.

The two steps described above, choosing a copy-text from among the relevant witnesses and emending the copy-text from the other relevant forms or from the editor's independent judgment, are the heart of the editorial process. Accordingly, the editor is obliged to identify for the reader the chosen copy-text, to explain on what grounds this copy-text was selected and verified, and to document all changes made to it for the edition at hand. This report of changes is of paramount importance, for it allows the reader to follow the editorial labor back to the original substantives and accidentals of the copy-text, and to judge the appropriateness of any particular emendation.

The edited texts in the present volume illustrate a wide variety of copy-texts. "A Walk to Wachusett," "The Landlord," and "Wild Apples" are based on first printings. The setting copy of "Natural History of Massachusetts" is also lost, but Thoreau corrected misprints and other typographer's errors in his personal copy of the *Dial*. Subsequently, he used the same copy of the *Dial* for memoranda about passages in his Journal related to the essay's contents. Some of these memoranda were entered years later; they do not represent a revision of the essay. The *Dial* as printed is therefore chosen as copy-text for this piece, and certain emendations are taken from Thoreau's marked copy. "An Address on the Succession of Forest Trees" has as copy-text the chronologically *second* printing, because editorial analysis indicates that the second, in *Transactions of the Middlesex Agricultural Society for the Year 1860*, was set independently from the same Thoreau manuscript as the first, with authorial revisions postdating the first printing. That initial print-ing, in the *New-York Weekly Tribune*, used tiny and poor newspaper type, tiny margins, crowded col-umns, and cheap paper, and thus did not lend itself to use by the printer of the second publication or by Thoreau, who wanted to correct numerous first-print-ing errors and to add material absent from the first publication.

The setting copy for the first printing of "Walking" survives intact (twelve pages of ninety-nine being in the handwriting of Thoreau's sister Sophia, who as-sisted him as a copyist during his final illness); this manuscript serves as copy-text for the essay. The set-ting-copy manuscripts of "A Winter Walk," "A Yankee in Canada," and "Autumnal Tints" survive in part, and for the sections of text corresponding to the surviving authorial and scribal leaves these leaves serve as copy-text, while the first printing provides copy-text for the remainder. "Autumnal Tints" is perhaps the simplest of these instances of composite copy-text: the setting copy for the *Atlantic Monthly* first printing survives in very fragmentary condition, and ten of the thirty ex-tant manuscript pages are scribal copies by Sophia. Copy-text for this essay therefore alternates between manuscript and the posthumous *Atlantic* printing. The setting-copy manuscript for chapters one and two of "A Yankee in Canada" as serialized in *Putnam's Monthly Magazine* survives intact and functions as copy-text for those chapters. The bulk of chapter three appeared in *Putnam's* before the serialization was sus-pended, but the corresponding manuscript pages are now lost (though they were probably returned to Thoreau in 1853). Here, the first printing in *Putnam's* is copy-text; a copy of the same *Putnam's* pages marked with his corrections and revisions was used after Thoreau's death as the source of the corresponding text in *A Yankee in Canada, with Anti-Slavery and Re-form Papers* (1866). The final quarter of chapter three, and all of chapters four and five, were first printed in the *Yankee* volume, doubtless from an authorial man-uscript, but that manuscript and the marked *Putnam's* printing of most of chapter three no longer survive, probably having been discarded in the printshop. The *Yankee* printing necessarily provides copy-text for the last two and a quarter chapters.

The most curious copy-text problem occurs in "A Winter Walk," where two-thirds of Thoreau's setting-copy pages for the first printing in the *Dial* survive. On these twenty-nine pages, however, Ralph Waldo Emerson, then editor of the quarterly, independently made various editorial deletions and revisions before sending the manuscript to the printer. Thoreau him-self had (typically) submitted a manuscript that was not, strictly speaking, a fair copy, but rather one that contained numerous revisions and corrections within and between the lines. For the determination of copy-text readings on the surviving "Winter Walk" manu-script pages the editor needed to differentiate Emer-son's editorial changes from Thoreau's compositional ones, and the distinctions were often subtle. The man-uscript, never returned to Thoreau, was retained by Emerson. Once again Thoreau turned to his personal copy of the *Dial* to correct misprints, and, more im-portantly, to attempt a reconstruction from memory of passages altered by Emerson. The author-corrected *Dial* copy serves as copy-text for the portions of the essay where the manuscript has not survived.

The Headnote for each of the nine *Excursions* essays contains full documentation and analysis of the avail-able textual materials for the essay; and the arguments for copy-text choice are there elaborated in detail.

Each copy-text chosen for *Excursions* has been emended to eliminate demonstrably nonauthorial features and to recover as nearly as possible Thoreau's intentions regarding the work's substantives and those accidentals which have substantive effect. The documents supporting most of the emendations are (1) relevant post-copy-text printings, (2) pre-copy-text manuscripts–drafts, lecture versions, and related materials in Thoreau's manuscript Journal and extract notebooks, and (3) Thoreau's printed sources for quotations and paraphrases in the several essays. Certain other emendations are based on the editor's study of the house styles and preferences of Thoreau's lifetime and immediately posthumous publishers. Yet other emendations have no explicit basis in documents, but are grounded in the editor's recognition of implausible copy-text readings and his knowledge of Thoreau's handwriting, which facilitates conjecture as to what word or character in a lost setting-copy manuscript was misconstrued during type composition. No effort has been made in this edition to modernize the texts or to impose an artificial consistency upon the style of an author whose practice in many matters of spelling, punctuation, and capitalization was decidedly variable. The editor has emended only when certain or strongly confident that copy-text readings represent errors or impositions by the copy-text compositors and editors, or inadvertent copying errors by Thoreau (or his amanuensis) as he prepared his manuscripts for publication.

1. Instances of *emendation from printed post-copy-text* may be found in all nine essays. Whether the copy-text is an authorial manuscript, a first printing,

or an author-annotated copy of the first printing, the features of a printed post-copy-text adopted as emendations will be either corrections of positive errors in the copy-text or revisions the editor attributes to Thoreau while he prepared the text for a revised reprint. In "A Yankee in Canada," for example, the manuscript copy-text for the first two chapters is emended from the first printing in *Putnam's Monthly Magazine* and also from the revised reprint in the 1866 *Yankee* volume. Copy-text for the bulk of chapter three is *Putnam's*, with emendations being taken from the *Yankee* volume. No emendations from post-copy-text occur in the conclusion of chapter three and the last two chapters because there is no relevant post-copy-text, Thoreau's involvement in the form of the text having ceased with his death in 1862.

Substantives comprise the most important emendations from post-copy-text. However, not every substantive variant in a post-copy-text is adopted as an emendation; each is judged on its own merits, and only those which manifestly or plausibly result from authorial revision are admitted into the text. In "Walking," for example, the editor rejects the *Atlantic Monthly*'s "though many may" and "he is to" as emendations of the manuscript copy-text's "though Christians may" and "he is, is to" at 216.31 and 220.35 on the grounds that these variants result from the post-copy-text editor's preference and a compositor's carelessness, respectively. In "Succession of Forest Trees" the omission in post-copy-text *Abstract of Returns of the Agricultural Societies of Massachusetts for 1860* of the *Transactions* copy-text's three opening paragraphs and three concluding paragraphs is likewise judged to be a nonauthorial change, dictated by the *Abstract* editor's space constraints or, more likely, his opinion that the omitted material was not germane.

All rejected post-copy-text variants are recorded as such in the apparatus.

Where accidentals have substantive effect–most obviously in the spellings of proper nouns–decisions to emend or not emend to variant post-copy-text forms are made according to the same norms as decisions involving variant post-copy-text substantives. Adopted post-copy-text accidentals of this sort are reported as Emendations; rejected ones as Rejected Substantives. Apart from emendations of accidentals supported by an analysis of post-copy-text house style and of Thoreau's manuscript habits (see subsection 6, below), only a few accidentals are emended to post-copy-text forms. Emendations of accidentals occur only when the rejected copy-text forms seriously obscure Thoreau's meaning or when they can confidently be identified as nonauthorial. Textual Notes provide explanation in such instances.

The texts of the nine *Excursions* component pieces as they appeared in the Riverside Edition (1894) and Manuscript Edition (1906) of *The Writings of Henry David Thoreau*–see Historical Introduction, pp. 333-335–have been collated against the first collected versions in *Excursions* (Boston: Ticknor and Fields, 1863) and *A Yankee in Canada, with Anti-Slavery and Reform Papers* (Boston: Ticknor and Fields, 1866). Predictably, these later-generation revised reprints normalize accidentals and introduce errors and sophistications as well as making corrections. In the present edition, emendations which coincidentally may first have been effected in the Riverside or Manuscript Edition are not assigned to either in the lists of Emendations. Neither are erroneous or sophisticated readings in the Riverside and Manuscript Editions reported in Rejected Substantives. The present editor has studied all the relevant material that was available to the Riverside and Manuscript Edition editors, as well as much material that they did not study.

2. *Emendation on the basis of pre-copy-text manuscript* is generally limited to substantives, accidentals with substantive effect, and the replacement of copy-text accidentals that seriously obscure Thoreau's meaning. The editor has borne in mind that Thoreau doubtless made changes in both substantives and accidentals when developing setting copy from his working drafts. The criterion for emending a printed copy-text to a manuscript reading is, therefore, that the latter is clear and plausible while the former is obscure or less plausible, or even absurd. Because so much manuscript material survives for eight of the nine *Excursions* pieces, the editor developed means for systematic comparison of the copy-text with these foul papers. Where copy-text is a printed form, a photocopy or a transcript of that printing was marked with labelled boxes to show the corresponding (and sometimes overlapping) draft pages that survive. For essays with manuscript copy-texts, a transcript of the setting-copy manuscript was similarly keyed to draft pages. In the collation of copy-text and draft manuscripts facilitated by these place markers, a record of variant substantives was kept, usually in the margins of the photocopy or transcript. A somewhat different technique was used to guide the editor to parallels between the copy-texts and Thoreau's Journal: staff members at the Textual Center began with electronic transcripts of the copy-texts, then bold-faced the phrases, sentences, and paragraphs which had Journal antecedents, each bold-faced section being followed by a parenthetical notation of the Journal entry date and the location in the most authoritative printed version, either a Princeton Edition *Journal* volume or, beyond *Journal 5* (after March 8, 1853), the 1906 Manuscript

Edition *Journal of Henry David Thoreau*. Photocopies of the manuscript Journal equivalents to *Excursions* essay passages were also provided by the Textual Center. Again, significant variations between the copy-text and its Journal antecedents were noted by the editor. Together with the reports on sight collations of relevant printed forms, these records of manuscript variants were essential resources for editorial decisions to emend or not emend the copy-texts.

3. *Emendation on the basis of printed source readings* poses special risks of error as well as special opportunities to recover the author's intention. Thoreau incorporated material from his extensive reading in science, travel, folklore, history, anthropology, and literature into all nine pieces collected in this volume, particularly "Wild Apples" and the latter chapters of "A Yankee in Canada." For the volume as a whole, the bibliography of Thoreau's printed sources runs to about 150 titles of books, plays, poems, magazine articles, and newspaper pieces quoted, paraphrased, or alluded to in the *Excursions* texts. Typically Thoreau does not assist his reader by providing an adequate citation of his source, and sometimes he fails to supply even a partial identification. Because the language of the derived passages was just as susceptible to corruption as Thoreau's original language while the *Excursions* texts were typeset and reset, the editor has attempted in each instance to find Thoreau's source in the edition he used, so that it could be compared with the copy-text and any surviving manuscript versions.

When Thoreau consulted a source text in two or more different editions, or when he encountered the same information in two or more different sources (as often happens in "A Yankee in Canada"), all of the relevant printings were consulted. When the edition of a source work that Thoreau read could not be identified, the editor consulted all the potential printings. The sources of all but ten quotations or references–at 28.11, 38.20-21, 58.1-6, 75.34, 98.31-32, 111.9-12, 122.26-29, 146.36-147.5, 150.2 (and 158.14), and 248.15-18–remained un-identified by the time the press put *Excursions* into production. Textual Notes for several of these offer hy-potheses about the exact sources. Those persons who contributed to the determination of printed sources are identified in Acknowledgments.

As in earlier volumes of *The Writings of Henry D. Thoreau*, the editor has refrained from systematically adjusting the substantives of Thoreau's quotations to known source readings.[2] To impose exactitude upon the quotations, as a matter of editorial principle, would be to misrepresent Thoreau's practice as a reader and writer. Many of his extracts from known specific editions survive among the *Excursions* draft manuscripts, and often the draft (or Journal or com-monplace book) version anticipates the discrepancy between the printed source passage and the copy-text treatment of that passage. Occasionally a quotation appears in two different draft stages, its substantives varying from the source increasingly between the ear-lier and the later draft and tending in the direction of copy-text substantives. See, for example, Textual Note 113.18 for "A Yankee in Canada." Even when the source, the draft manuscripts, and the copy-text agree in sub-stantives, the draft accidentals usually vary from the source, and the copy-text accidentals differ even more. It should be remembered that when Thoreau copied out his final, setting-copy manuscripts he had opportunity to modify the accidentals and substan-tives of quoted material beyond the working draft

---

[2] See the discussion in the "Textual Introduction" to *Cape Cod*, p. 346.

stage. Doubtless he often did so. Moreover, for some quoted material no draft manuscript version survives, leaving wholly in question whether discrepancies between source and printed copy-text readings originated with Thoreau's lost setting copy, with an amanuensis, with a contemporary editor, or with a typesetter.

These circumstances call for caution. Textual Notes specify each substantive variation and every important accidental variation between source readings and copy-text readings. These notes report any extant readings among Thoreau's manuscripts. In deciding whether or not to emend quotations and paraphrases in the copy-text the editor has tried to negotiate between two objectives–recognizing the author's habit of modifying his sources, and purifying the text of errors arguably caused by editors and compositors. To these ends, certain guidelines have been applied. (a) Variations that adjust a quotation to the specific demands of Thoreau's context are, of course, allowed to stand. (b) Other substantive variations from the source *that do not cause a significant change of meaning* are also allowed to stand unemended, even when a surviving draft version follows the source. This provision leaves room for the possibility of minor authorial changes in wording between draft and lost setting copy. Any disposition of these modest discrepancies between source and copy-text risks error. To forbear emending in such instances is to risk erring on the side of a cautious respect for the copy-text. But (c) in the absence of specific contextual signals for an authorial change in the meaning or application of the quotation, substantive variations between the source and copy-text *that garble or distort the sense of the original* are emended to the original source substantives. Whether or not manuscript versions of these quotations survive, the editor assumes that Thoreau wished to respect the basic sense of the original unless he distinctly signalled otherwise. Most of the emendations in this category involve the restoration of dropped words essential to the sense, the restoration of the source language where the copy-text reading reflects a compositor's difficulty with Thoreau's penmanship, and the proper placement of quotation marks to distinguish where the source author ends and Thoreau (or a different source author) takes up. The Textual Notes provide numerous instances of the application of these policies concerning substantive variation between source and copy-text, with all relevant evidence adduced; see, for example, Textual Notes 35.12, 113.32, 199.21, and 282.5-6.

Source accidentals being even more susceptible than source substantives to alteration by Thoreau in the drafts and setting copy, the editor emends the copy-text to source forms only when the variation has distinct substantive effect, as in spellings of proper nouns, or when the copy-text reading obscures or distorts the sense of the original. When Thoreau miscopies a proper noun or misspells or mispoints a term from a foreign language source, the editor emends, as he would if the error occurred in Thoreau's own prose. But where Thoreau's source contains the same error as the copy-text, the copy-text reading stands unemended. Again, Textual Notes explain all emendations of source accidentals and all problematical decisions to forgo emendation. See, for example, Textual Notes 73.23-74.24, 79.7, 165.25, and 257.34.

To summarize, these policies for the treatment of quotations and paraphrases seek to eliminate errors probably introduced by typesetters and house editors, but also to avoid making Thoreau seem more scrupulous than he was in the use of secondary sources.

4. *Positive spelling errors* are corrected, whether they are authorial, nonauthorial, or of undetermined origin. The editor has checked unusual spellings against five dictionaries of which Thoreau owned copies, and has respected the copy-text spellings if they are listed in at least one of the five. The lexicons consulted are Nathan Bailey, *An Universal Etymological English Dictionary*, 17th ed. (London: T. Osborne et al., 1759); Samuel Johnson and John Walker, *Johnson's English Dictionary ... with Walker's Pronouncing Dictionary ...*, Boston Stereotype Edition (Boston: Charles Ewer and T. Harrington Carter, 1828); John Walker, *A Critical Pronouncing Dictionary ... of the English Language* (New York: Collins and Hannay, 1823); Noah Webster, *An American Dictionary of the English Language*, 15th ed. (New York: N. and J. White, 1836); and John Oswald, *An Etymological Dictionary of the English Language* (Philadelphia: E. C. Biddle, 1844).[3]

5. *Typographical blunders* in printed copy-texts, such as missing end-of-line hyphens in non-compound words, or characters missing due to poor plate-casting, are corrected and listed among Emendations.

6. Some features of printed copy-texts may reflect *house styling* by the editors and compositors to whom Thoreau's manuscripts were entrusted. We may fairly assume that many accidentals in printed copy-texts are nonauthorial, but because of Thoreau's own inconsistency in capitalization, word-division, punctua-

---

[3] The surviving records of Thoreau's personal library do not give the exact editions of the Bailey, Johnson-Walker, and Webster dictionaries he owned; the editions named are thought by the editor to duplicate or approximate those on Thoreau's shelves. See Walter Harding, *Thoreau's Library* (Charlottesville: University of Virginia Press, 1957), expanded and refined in Harding, "A New Checklist of the Books in Henry David Thoreau's Library," *Studies in the American Renaissance*, ed. Joel Myerson (Charlottesville: University Press of Virginia, 1983), pp. 151-186.

tion, and tolerated spellings, we can rarely be sure which copy-text features are impositions. To regularize copy-text accidentals to the statistically dominant forms in Thoreau's manuscripts–a task difficult in practice as well as questionable in theory, since the manuscripts often disclose no steady preference–would be to misrepresent Thoreau's normal, that is, inconsistent, prose texture, and to alter what may actually be authorial readings in the copy-text.

James T. Fields, the owner and editor of *The Atlantic Monthly* and the co-owner and editorial policy-maker for Ticknor and Fields, regularly replaced "further" in Thoreau's manuscripts with "farther." While the form "farther" is not unknown among Thoreau's manuscripts, his preference for "further" is pronounced. Despite the temptation to emend all instances of printed copy-text "farther" to "further," the editor is mindful that Thoreau could have written "farther" in an uncharacteristic instance. Surviving draft manuscripts for the particular instance at hand have served as the guide and grounds for emendation. Where a printed copy-text (or an amanuensis page by Sophia) reads "farther" and a draft version of the same sentence has "further" the editor confidently emends to the draft reading. Where corresponding manuscript versions are lost, instances of "farther" in printed copy-text are allowed to stand. Textual Notes report on all appearances of "farther" in copy-texts, whether emended or not.

DOCUMENTATION

Several kinds of documentation are provided for each of the nine works by Thoreau comprising *Excursions*: Headnote, Textual Notes, Emendations, Alterations (where the copy-text is a manuscript), Corrections and Revisions in Thoreau's Copy of the *Dial* (in an instance where Thoreau annotated the *Dial* printing of an essay, attempting to reconstruct the language of a manuscript no longer available to him), Rejected Substantives, and End-of-Line Hyphenation. These reports are grouped in the Editorial Appendix by essay, in the order given above, except for the lists of End-of-Line Hyphenation (see description below), which are given for the volume as a whole at the end.

Line references in the apparatus are by literal tally; that is, blank lines are disregarded, but every line of type, whether normal, reduced, or display type, is included in the count. On pages of solid normal type the line-guide may conveniently be used to locate features cited by page and line in the back matter.

1. The *Headnote* is an essay examining the biographical background of the piece, the genesis and development of the text, and the circumstances of its first publication and revised or unrevised reprints up to either *Excursions* (1863) or *A Yankee in Canada* (1866). In addition to this historical information, the Headnote enumerates and analyzes the extant manuscript versions (setting copy where it survives, Journal entries, lecture reading copies, and foul papers), and gives the rationale for the choice of copy-text. The means used for verifying the copy-text readings and for determining differences in post-copy-texts are reported. These consist of machine collations of specimens of printed copy-texts and multiple sight-collations of the copy-text against the other forms; the exact specimens used in machine collation are identified.

2. *Textual Notes* report features of the copy-text, pre-copy-text manuscripts, relevant post-copy-texts, Thoreau's other works and correspondence, and his printed sources, which are pertinent to editorial decisions to emend or not emend. Here and in the Historical and Textual Introductions and Headnotes,

contextual end-punctuation for quotations appears outside the close-quotation marks when ambiguity about punctuation in the quoted document would result from using standard style. Before the first Textual Note, abbreviations used to signify different versions of the text are identified. The format of each Textual Note is as follows: page and line number in the Princeton Edition; the feature (i.e., the word or phrase appearing on that page and line) which the Textual Note discusses; a colon; and the discussion, in continuous prose form. The following example is drawn from the Textual Notes for "Natural History of Massachusetts":

> 23.33   still and frosty: "and" is lacking in D as printed, but Thoreau added an ampersand in CD, which Ex expanded to "and". See Textual Notes 57.30, 80.19-20, 185.34, and 223.10.

3. *Emendations* of the copy-texts are listed in tabular form, using the following format: Princeton Edition page and line number; the feature as emended; a close square bracket; the source or sources of the Emendation, given by means of an abbreviation; a semicolon; the feature as it appears in the copy-text (unemended). An asterisk preceding the page and line number indicates that the Emendation is discussed in a Textual Note. A virgule (/) indicates the end of a line. Before the first Emendation the abbreviations used in the table are defined. The example below is taken from the Emendations for "Natural History of Massachusetts":

> *21.33   May]   CD   Ex;   April

Together with the lists of Alterations and End-of-Line Hyphenation, the list of Emendations allows the reader to reconstruct the exact readings and most of the physical details of the copy-text.

4. Where the copy-text is a manuscript, the entries in *Alterations* report changes that Thoreau made on the manuscript page while preparing his finished copy. Sometimes a copy-text page is in the handwriting of Sophia Thoreau, who served as her brother's amanuensis during his final illness. In those instances, alterations Sophia herself made are differentiated from alterations Thoreau made while reviewing Sophia's copy. Markings by editors and typesetters on manuscripts that served as setting copy for the first publication are also reported and differentiated from changes made by Thoreau or Sophia. In "A Winter Walk," the editorial revisions made by Emerson on Thoreau's setting-copy manuscript for the *Dial* are sometimes so complex that they cannot adequately be recorded in tabular form. In such instances the Alterations entry refers the reader to an explanatory Textual Note. The other pieces which use a complete or partial final authorial manuscript as copy-text, and for which a list of Alterations is provided, are "A Yankee in Canada," "Walking," and "Autumnal Tints." Before the first Alterations entry, the abbreviations used in the table are defined. Where two writing media are present in the manuscript they are distinguished in the entries. Again the Princeton Edition page and line number occupies the left-hand column, followed by the feature on that page and line, a close bracket, and an account of the alteration. A virgule (/) indicates the end of a line. The editor's descriptive terms for each Alteration are printed in italics, as illustrated in this example from "A Winter Walk," where Thoreau's primary writing medium was ink:

57.3   the new day]   new *interlined in pencil with caret;* day *followed by interlined pencilled* time *cancelled in pencil*

5. *"Autograph Corrections and Revisions in Thoreau's Copy of the* Dial*"* is a type of apparatus unique to "A Winter Walk." The format of that list, slightly different from Alterations, is described before the first entry.

6. The *Rejected Substantives* list gives, from relevant post-copy-texts, all variant substantive readings and all accidental variants with substantive effect that have *not* been adopted as Emendations because the editor has judged them to be nonauthorial. In addition, some problematical rejected variant readings in pre-copy-text are recorded. At the head of the list, abbreviations for the post- and pre-copy-texts are defined. The Princeton Edition page and line number occupies the left-hand column, followed by the feature on that page and line, a close bracket, the variant reading, and the source of the variant. The following example comes from the first chapter of "A Yankee in Canada," where copy-text is Thoreau's setting-copy manuscript for *Putnam's Monthly*. An asterisk preceding the page and line number indicates that the rejected variant is discussed in a Textual Note. A virgule (/) indicates the end of a line.

*85.18-20   Donolly ... Donolly]   Donothy ... Donothy
                P; Donouy ... Donouy Y

7. *End-of-Line Hyphenation* lists are provided at the close of the volume for all nine texts in sequence, with the list formats being there explained. Every instance of end-of-line hyphenation of a hyphenated or possibly hyphenated compound word in the copy-texts (List A) required an editorial decision as to how the compound term should be typeset for this edition, e.g., "moth-like" or "mothlike" in "Natural History of Massachusetts" (20.8). Such editorial judgments were based, wherever possible, on Thoreau's treatment of

the term in the surviving draft version or versions of that specific instance. Where drafts did not survive, or where drafts did not use the term, or where drafts gave the term as two words without hyphen ("moth like"), the judgment was based on other appearances of the term in the drafts and in the copy-text itself. When the compound is part of a quotation from a secondary source and no manuscript transcript by Thoreau survives, the treatment in the exact source edition Thoreau read guided the editor. Each compound term in List A is given in the form to which the editor resolved it. By coincidence, some few compound terms, such as "blackberries" (226.32-33) and "purple-veined" (227.19-20) in "Autumnal Tints," are hyphenated at the end of the line in *both* the copy-text and the present edition; these are also reported in the forms to which the editor resolved them, notwithstanding the new typesetting.

List B records those compound terms hyphenated at the end of the line in the Princeton Edition–the present volume–that appeared with hyphens in the copy-text. Terms divided with a hyphen at the line end in the present edition and not reported in List B were single words in the copy-text. (Again, since the present typesetting occasionally duplicates copy-text end-of-line hyphenations, certain entries in and omissions from List B reflect editorial decisions: "semicircle" at 137.27-28, for instance, is hyphenated at the end of the line in both the copy-text and this edition, but since the editor resolves it as a single word it is excluded from List B, while "farm-book" at 146.4-5, hyphenated at the end of the line in both, is included in List B because the editor resolves it as a hyphenated form.) The information provided in List A will enable the reader to reconstruct copy-text forms that would otherwise be disguised, while the information in List B will permit accurate transcription of the text for the purposes of quotation and reprinting.

Certain editions of works by Thoreau and Emerson, as well as a few reference works, are cited so often in Introductions, Headnotes, and Textual Notes that the editor has abbreviated the titles. In a section of apparatus called Short Titles, these brief titles are expanded into full bibliographical citations. Another list, Library Symbols, is a directory for identifying the institutional repositories of manuscripts and specific copies of printed works that the editor designates by codes in the Historical and Textual Introductions, Headnotes, Textual Notes, and tables.

DESIGN CHANGES

Since the present edition of *Excursions* is not intended as a facsimile of the copy-texts, various details of copy-text handwriting, typography, and design are not here duplicated. Unindented paragraphs at the openings of *Putnam's Monthly Magazine* installments ("A Yankee in Canada") are normalized. Notifications of continuation at the beginnings and ends of the same installments are omitted. The original pagination of the copy-texts, printer's signature markings, and smudges are of course disregarded. Broken but legible printed characters are treated as though they were whole. All centered titles in the copy-texts have been moved to the left margin in keeping with Princeton Edition design, and chapter numbers have been lowered to the title line. Display type is used for the beginning of "St. Anne," which in *Putnam's* fell in the middle of the second installment and was not given the same typographical treatment as the first two chapter openings. At a few points, spaced one-em dashes in compound dates, e.g., "1542 — 43" (158.29), are changed to unspaced one-en hyphens. Wide-spaced contractions in printed copy-texts, such as "You 'll" and "there 's" in "A Yankee in Canada" (150.12, 162.22) are closed up. No changes in the above categories are regarded as emendations or are reported in the tabular apparatus.

PRINCETON EDITION COPY PREPARATION

For all nine *Excursions* pieces, staff members at the Thoreau Edition Textual Center, under the direction of the Editor-in-Chief, provided files, both electronic and paper, for editorial use: photocopies of all printed versions of the pieces through the 1863 and 1866 Ticknor and Fields collected editions; photocopies of all pertinent manuscripts (including setting copies); reports of sight and machine collation; notes from the study of archival materials by editors and Textual Center staff members; drafts of historical essays by Center staff and former editors; photocopies of pages from known or conjectured Thoreau sources; photocopies of relevant manuscript letters by Thoreau, his family, his friends, and his editors; electronic files–in WordPerfect–intended to correspond to the copy-texts; type-facsimile transcripts of all setting-copy manuscripts and of many draft manuscripts (the setting-copy transcripts had been "perfected," usually at least twice, against the original manuscripts, and made to conform exactly); and printouts of the electronic text files modified to show where Thoreau's Journal anticipated the essay texts.[4]

---

[4] For "A Yankee in Canada," the Textual Center provided a microfilm, not photocopies, of the copy-text for chapters one and two and of the pre-copy-text manuscripts at the Henry E. Huntington Library. A perfected transcript of chapters one and two was also supplied, but not an electronic file. (The text of those chapters was later recorded in electronic form, using WordPerfect, from the transcript and the microfilm.) Subsequent aspects of the editorial work on and Textual Center review of "A Yankee in

The editor read clean printouts from the electronic files against perfected transcripts of setting-copy manuscripts and also against photocopies of those same manuscripts, achieving a file that was a verbatim type-equivalent of the copy-text. For essays or parts of essays based on printed copy-texts, the editor read the Textual Center electronic files in printout against actual print specimens of the copy-texts wherever possible, and against photocopies in the case of unique or very rare publications. Again, the Center text file was brought into exact correspondence with the printed copy-text.

Working with these true equivalents of the copy-texts, the editor introduced emendations and resolved end-of-line hyphenations resulting from his study of pre- and post-copy-text material, of Thoreau's sources of quotations and paraphrases, and of the before-mentioned lexical guides. Emendations and end-of-line hyphenation resolutions were recorded in the margins of a perfected copy-text file printout, for subsequent listing in apparatus sections. An electronic copy of the copy-text file was modified to incorporate emendations and end-of-line hyphen resolutions. This constituted the edited text file. The list of Alterations in manuscript copy-texts was developed from perfected transcripts and photocopies used in tandem; occasionally an ambiguity in the record called for a review of the original manuscript. The Rejected Substantives list for each essay was based on the reports of sight collations of copy-texts and post-copy-texts, conflated into a master list. To this were

---

Canada" are the same as for the other eight *Excursions* pieces, except that the edited text of chapters four and five, where the 1866 printing is copy-text, was submitted to the Center in the form of marked photocopy pages of the print, and was entered into electronic form at the Center.

added some important rejected substantives from pre-copy-text drafts. The four tabular forms of apparatus (Emendations, Alterations, Rejected Substantives, End-of-Line Hyphenation) were prepared as WordPerfect electronic files, as were the Headnotes, Textual Notes, a special list of Thoreau's notations in his copy of the *Dial*, Textual Introduction, Historical Introduction, and Acknowledgments. Electronic files of these edited texts, apparatus, and other back matter were sent to the Textual Center.

At the Textual Center, the edited text files were coded for computer-driven typesetting, and then read exactingly against the copy-texts and apparatus. Questions about the text arising from these readings were resolved in consultation with the editor before the text files were sent to Princeton University Press to be put into page proof. The index to the text was prepared from page proof, and page and line numbers in the apparatus files were brought into agreement with the page proof. List B of End-of-Line Hyphenation was also created now. Inconsistencies and anomalies of form and content in the apparatus had earlier been resolved in consultations between the editor and the Textual Center. Finally, the Textual Center staff prepared the Short Titles and Library Symbols lists, and the front matter, consulting with the editor when appropriate. All this editorial matter was sent in coded electronic form to Princeton University Press.

In accordance with guidelines established by the Modern Language Association's Committee on Scholarly Editions, this volume has been inspected by an independent textual expert, Professor Joel Myerson.

Natural History of Massachusetts

Headnote

MARGARET Fuller informed Ralph Waldo Emerson in mid-March 1842 that because of ill health and exhaustion she could no longer serve as editor of the *Dial*, the Transcendentalists' quarterly journal. The forthcoming April issue was the last she would edit. Almost by default, and with little appetite for the task, Emerson took over editorial management of the magazine.[1] Promptly assuming his new responsibilities with diligence, if not high enthusiasm, Emerson set about soliciting contributions for the July number. On his previous visit to Boston, as he told Fuller on April 10,[2] he had obtained from the Secretary of State four volumes of botanical and zoological catalogues which the Legislature had commissioned at the urging of the Boston Society of Natural History, an organization to which Emerson belonged. Having read a bit in those "'Scientific Surveys' of Massachusetts by Messrs Harris[,] Dewey[,] Storer[,] Gould [and] Emmons", he had that day "set Henry Thoreau on the good track of giving an account of them in the Dial, explaining to him the felicity of the subject for him as it admits of the narrative of all his woodcraft boatcraft & fishcraft."[3]

The surveys were D. Humphreys Storer and William B. O. Peabody, *Reports on the Fishes, Reptiles and*

[1] *The Letters of Margaret Fuller*, ed. Robert N. Hudspeth, vol. 3 (Ithaca: Cornell University Press, 1984), pp. 53-54; Emerson, *Letters*, 3:33-34, 35-36, 38-39. Although Emerson had nominally been co-editor from the outset, Fuller accepted or rejected submissions for the first eight numbers of the *Dial* and oversaw its production.

[2] Emerson, *Letters*, 3:47.

[3] Emerson, *Letters*, 3:47. Emerson's Boston visit took place on Saturday, March 26. Emerson, *Letters*, 3:38.

Birds of Massachusetts (Boston: Dutton and Went-
worth, 1839); Chester Dewey and Ebenezer Emmons,
*Reports on the Herbaceous Plants and on the Quadru-
peds of Massachusetts* (Cambridge: Folsom, Wells, and
Thurston, 1840); Augustus A. Gould, *Report on the Invertebrata of Massachusetts* ... (Cambridge: Folsom,
Wells and Thurston, 1841); and Thaddeus William Harris, *A Report on the Insects of Massachusetts, Injurious
to Vegetation* (Cambridge: Folsom, Wells and Thurston, 1841). Emerson declined to carry home Edward
Hitchcock's ponderous *Final Report on the Geology of
Massachusetts* (Northampton: J. H. Butler, 1841), although Thoreau would use a copy while writing *Cape
Cod*. Besides regarding Thoreau as a protégé, Emerson
was sharing his home with the younger man, who had
moved in fifty-four weeks before. In return for room
and board, Thoreau worked in the garden (*inter alia*,
teaching Emerson to graft apple trees) and performed
"what [other] labor he chooses to do"; by April 10, 1842,
Emerson could also jocosely describe Thoreau to
Fuller as "private secretary to the President of the Dial,
[whose] works & fame may go out into all lands, and,
as happens to great Premiers, quite extinguish the tit-
ular Master."[4]

Heavily dependent on Thoreau's now-fragmentary
early Journal notebooks, the finished essay, Thoreau's
first public venture into natural-history prose, incor-
porates almost seventy passages from forty-six entries, the earliest dated November 28, 1837, and the latest April 3, 1842 (*Journal 1*, pp. 15-16 and pp. 400-402).
Apart from these, only a few scattered pages of notes
and draft survive to suggest the process by which
Thoreau composed "Natural History of Massachusetts." He listed topics for the essay on the back of one

[4] Emerson, *Letters*, 2:393-394, 395, 402; Thoreau, *Journal 1*,
p. 304; Emerson, *Letters*, 3:47.

draft leaf of his translation of *Prometheus Bound* at CSmH (HM 926): "Pilgrims cup. / May flower. / meadow mice. / Not to be trusted as an accurate catalogue. / The Cape Cod limit / The shrill roll-call of the harvest fly / The loon / American Bittern / 8 kinds of toortoises / 12. kinds of snakes / 9 frogs and toads / 9 Salamanders / and 1 lizzard / 286 birds".[5] The versos of two other leaves of the same translation draft, and available space on the recto of one, bear early versions of passages in "Natural History of Massachusetts": 9.23-24 ("The first flock ... seen beating"), 9.29-34 ("The fish-hawk . . . time to time"), and 19.25-34 ("roots of the . . . equipped for"; in part duplicating a Journal entry for April 9, 1839, in a notebook of transcriptions [see *Journal 1*, pp. 71, 596-597]). Another group of three manuscript leaves, at MHvFM, includes an early version of Thoreau's opening commentary on books of natural history and a draft of the text from 11.24 to 13.5 ("With the autumn . . . it throws"). At NNPM (MA 608) is a fragment containing seven lines of verse (three cancelled) torn from the bottom of one of those pages, 12.16-19 ("Thou dusky spirit . . . summer's day,"). A version of "Upon the lofty elm tree sprays" (11.20-23) appears on a draft of Thoreau's letter of September 8, 1841, to Lucy Jackson Brown, at MaLiTIW.

By May 9, a month after his first letter about the project, Emerson was able to report to Fuller that Thoreau "announces fifty or sixty pages of MS in a state approaching completion & I shall be summoned soon for a reading." The new editor listed the essay for the July number in his "Dialling" notebook and sent

---

[5] The *Prometheus Bound* translation was published in the *Dial* for January 1843. In Thoreau's list the several items are deployed from top to bottom of the page, usually separated by rules, and some items were lined through, perhaps to indicate that Thoreau had dealt with them.

the manuscript to the printer about June 22.[6] The setting-copy manuscript does not survive.

Emerson prefaced the piece with a "Preliminary
Note" (transcribed in full in Textual Note 3.7), in which
he called Thoreau "a near neighbor and friend of ours,
. . . a native and an inhabitant of . . . Concord," an in-
comparable handler of "the oar and fishing line," a
man "dear also to the Muses," and a potential literary
successor to Izaak Walton and Gilbert White of Selborne. His friend, wrote Emerson, had readily undertaken "to give us such comments as he had made on
[the State reports on flora and fauna], and, better still,
notes of his own conversation with nature in the
woods and waters of this town." The finished essay
contained little by way of a reviewer's appraisal, and a
great deal of Thoreau's personal "conversation with
nature" in Concord township.

Such contemporary notices as Thoreau's contribution to the July *Dial* received, in the Boston *Morning
Post*, *New-York Daily Tribune*, and *Knickerbocker*
magazine, praised it. Concord's new citizen Nathaniel
Hawthorne relished Thoreau's piece to the point of
recommending the author to the editor of a Boston
magazine as a potential contributor. Bronson Alcott
thought the essay "worthy of Isaac Walton himself"
when a copy of the *Dial* reached him in England. Margaret Fuller, however, seems to have found fault with
"Natural History of Massachusetts," for on July 19,
1842, Emerson wrote, "I am sorry that you, & the world
after you, do not like my brave Henry any better. I do
not like his piece very well, but I admire this perennial
threatening attitude. . . ."[7]

---

[6] Emerson, *Letters*, 3:54; *JMN*, 8:484; Emerson, *Letters*, 3:65, 66-
67.
[7] Joel Myerson, "Thoreau and the *Dial*: A Survey of the Contemporary Press," *Thoreau Journal Quarterly* 5 (January 1973): 5; *The*

The relative freedom of the *Dial* first printing from typographical errors and printers' misreadings of Thoreau's handwriting suggests that he himself corrected proof copy, a plausible inference because of his presence in Emerson's household. The same personal circumstance makes it unlikely that Emerson would have taken such editorial liberties with his young friend's text as he did with "A Winter Walk" fifteen months later, when Thoreau lived on Staten Island (see "A Winter Walk" Headnote). After "Natural History of Massachusetts" was published, and apparently on more than one occasion, Thoreau marked his personal copy of the printed essay with a variety of pencilled notations. Three of these, on *Dial* pp. 36 and 37, correct mistakes that were missed in the pre-publication proofreading: the word "may" was added before "study", an ampersand was inserted between "still" and "frosty", and a misplaced comma was relocated in the word-string "summer and winter forever, is" (see Textual Notes 23.25, 23.33, and 24.31-32). Four more, on *Dial* pp. 29 and 35, are revisions based on the author's reconsideration or his desire to clarify, rather than corrections of features caused by a defective printing or an imperfect printer's manuscript: the phrase "from this vicinity" was added after "disap-

---

Centenary Edition of the Works of Nathaniel Hawthorne, vol. 15, *The Letters, 1813-1843*, ed. Thomas Woodson, L. Neal Smith, and Norman Holmes Pearson (Columbus: The Ohio State University Press, 1984), pp. 656-657; *The Letters of A. Bronson Alcott*, ed. Richard L. Herrnstadt (Ames: Iowa State University Press, 1969), p. 88; Emerson, *Letters*, 3:75. If Fuller gave her criticism in a letter, it does not survive. Raymond L. Borst, in *The Thoreau Log: A Documentary Life of Henry David Thoreau* (New York: G. K. Hall & Co., 1992), p. 79, asserts that Fuller's implied objections were to "The Service," the tone and theme of which perhaps merit the characterization "threatening attitude"; but Fuller had rejected that piece when Thoreau submitted it to the *Dial* fully a year and a half before (*Correspondence*, pp. 41-42).

peared" and, in the following clause, "here" was added after "seen"; "May" was substituted for "April" and "lichens" for "moss" (see Textual Notes 15.22, 15.23, 21.33, and 22.19). Six of the remaining seven notations, one of which Thoreau could not have written before February 1860, point to natural history works Thoreau read and cross-refer to his Journal notebooks of the 1840s. These six notations, unlike those in the corrected *Dial* "A Winter Walk" (see "A Winter Walk" Headnote), do not appear to be shorthand instructions for a prospective revised reprinting of "Natural History of Massachusetts." With the seventh notation, "V. S. [vide slip or scrap or sheet] about birds. & other Autumn Things", at *Dial* p. 26, Thoreau might have wanted to instruct a subsequent editor to add a passage, but the editors of *Excursions* (1863) made no change to the *Dial* as printed at this juncture. The supplementary document in question might by 1862-1863 have become separated from the printing or lost; it is not identifiable with confidence at the present time. See Textual Notes 10.26, 11.25, 15.15, 16.32, 18.9, 18.23, and 25.21, where these corrected *Dial* notations are transcribed and discussed.

In the absence of any setting-copy manuscript or proof sheets, copy-text for "Natural History of Massachusetts" is the first printing in the July 1842 issue of the *Dial* (3:19-40; NjP). Thoreau's corrections and clarifications in his own set of the *Dial* at ICarbS are accepted as emendations from post-copy-text. His cross-references to Journal passages and to his reading, in that same ICarbS *Dial*, perhaps signal his intention to modify the essay in part or whole for inclusion in *A Week on the Concord and Merrimack Rivers*, as he was doing in 1845-1847 with a number of his early compositions. Strengthening this last possibility is the fact that four cross-references are to a notebook he called his "Long Book," a volume in which he had transcribed, from earlier notebooks, passages intended for *A Week* (see *Journal 2*, pp. 1-152). The cross-references were disregarded by the editors of *Excursions* (1863) when they used the author-corrected *Dial* as the basis for their text; and the cross-references are not treated as incipient grounds for emendation in the present edition. *Excursions* does, however, supply emendations of one typo and two misspellings that Thoreau failed to catch in his *Dial* copy.

In the preparation of "Natural History of Massachusetts" text for the present edition, copies of the *Dial* printing at ICarbS and TxAuHRH were compared on the Hinman Collator. No typesetting differences were discovered. (Optical collation of the posthumous second printing in *Excursions* [1863] is discussed in the Historical Introduction.) For the determination of textual variations between the first two printings, the *Dial* was sight-collated with *Excursions* five times, using copies of both at NjP and MaLiTIW. Six substantive variants in *Excursions*, not adopted as Emendations, are listed as Rejected Substantives in the apparatus.

Textual Notes

FOR the format of the Textual Notes, see the Textual Introduction, pp. 381-382. Copy-text is the July 1842 *Dial* essay as printed (D). CD stands for Thoreau's copy of the *Dial* at ICarbS, with his autograph corrections and annotations. Ex represents *Excursions* (1863). The abbreviation "MS" followed by a repository symbol in parentheses identifies a manuscript reading. See the Headnote for a discussion of surviving manuscripts.

3.7 State.: Followed in D and CD by Emerson's "PRELIMINARY NOTE.":

—WE were thinking how we might best celebrate the good deed which the State of Massachusetts has done, in procuring the Scientific Survey of the Commonwealth, whose result is recorded in these volumes, when we found a near neighbor and friend of ours, dear also to the Muses, a native and an inhabitant of the town of Concord, who readily undertook to give us such comments as he had made on these books, and, better still, notes of his own conversation with nature in the woods and waters of this town. With all thankfulness we begged our friend to lay down the oar and fishing line, which none can handle better, and assume the pen, that Isaak Walton and White of Selborne might not want a successor, nor the fair meadows, to which we also have owed a home and the happiness of many years, their poet.

EDITOR OF THE DIAL.
Concord, Mass.

9.25 gingle: Thus in the copy-text. Despite the inconsistency with "jingled" at 24.20, the spelling "gingle" is accepted by three of Thoreau's dictionaries and may be authorial.

10.14 with the other: Thoreau's source, Thomas Nuttall, *A Manual of the Ornithology of the United States and of Canada* (Cambridge: Hilliard and Brown; Boston: Hilliard and Gray, 1832-1834), 1:82, reads "in the other". This wording variation is well within the range of changes Thoreau might make while copying from his sources. The same is true at 26.25, where Thoreau's quotation from Augustus Gould's *Report on the Invertebrata* (see Headnote), p. 316, changes Gould's "intermingling" to "mingling".

10.26   anywhere described.:   Thoreau later added in pencil in CD (leaf trimmed, lost letters editorially supplied): "Belon & Aldrovandi seem to have known this & Thomson v. 'Dom Ha of Birds L. U." He refers to the following descriptions of the bittern's booming call: Pierre Belon, *L'Histoire de la nature des oyseaux* (Paris: B. Cauellat, 1555), 4:192-193; Ulisse Aldrovandi, *Ornithologiae hoc est de avibus historiae* . . . (Bononiae: Apud Io: Baptistam Bellambamgam, 1603), 3:403; James Thomson, *The Seasons* ("Spring"), lines 21-23; [James Rennie], *The Domestic Habits of Birds* (London: C. Knight, 1833), 3:98-99. The meaning of "L. U.", a doubtful reading, is undetermined. Thoreau's acquaintance with Belon's *Histoire* dates from February 1860, when he withdrew it from the Harvard College library. Ex adds nothing to D at this point.

11.25   spring.:   Followed in CD by a caret and, in the margin, "V. S. about birds & other Autumn Things". Thoreau's abbreviation "V. S." means "vide [see] scrap" or "sheet" or "slip". The material he refers to cannot be confidently identified, but a passage answering the general description appears on one side of a leaf laid into an album of natural history observations by John and Henry Thoreau, with some entries by Sophia, also used by Henry as a literary draft book. This album is housed at NN-BGC ("[Nature and Bird Notes]"). The relevant leaf has at least two levels of composition. Thoreau wrote the original text in ink on one side of the leaf, perhaps for the first or second draft (1845, 1847) of *A Week*, and then revised and amplified it in pencil to read as follows:

> Among the earliest indications of the advancing year The clear whistle of the oriole is occasionally heard among the elms late in the summer–as if he sung out of a perennial near lying spring. harmonizing with the aftermath [?] spring under our feet. This bird resumes its strain as if it were still the love [?] season, and he had paused but a moment to secure his prey.
> The faint flitting note of the goldfinch which indicates the turning point of the year is heard in the gardens a month earlier than this, as if this little pensioner, the harbinger of the Fall, were prompting nature to make haste–

> This lisping peeping note late in the summer or early in autumn–so incessant and universal that it is hardly distinguished more than the crickets–is one of nature's ground-tones [*possibly* grand-tones]. It is associated with the rustling of the leaves–shuddering at the first cool blast–and the swift lapse of time.
>
> The birds are the true heralds of the seasons, and they no doubt appreciate a thousand delicate changes in the atmosphere which is their peculiar element–of which men are unconscious.

Ex adds nothing to D at this point.

15.15   spring.:   Followed in CD in the margin by "V muskrat in long book", probably referring to related text written after March 11, 1845 (*Journal 2*, pp. 126-127; see Headnote). Ex adds nothing to D at this point.

15.22   disappeared from this vicinity; the: "from this vicinity" is interlined in CD with a caret following "disappeared;". Ex fails to incorporate this addition, perhaps because it makes no sense as positioned after the semicolon. Thoreau evidently misplaced the caret, intending "from this vicinity" to modify "have disappeared" rather than "seen" in the next clause about the otter.

15.23   seen here at: Thoreau added "here" with a caret in CD, a revision adopted in Ex.

16.32   distance: Followed in CD by "V skating after fox–in long book", referring to a passage that originally appeared in a Journal entry written after January 7, 1844 (*Journal 1*, pp. 494-495), which Thoreau later revised and transcribed in his "Long Book," *Journal 2*, p. 89. Ex adds nothing to D at this point.

17.15-16   "Can these things ... a summer's cloud?":   Thoreau takes a characteristic liberty with his source, *Macbeth*, 3.4.158-159, in *The Dramatic Works of William Shakespeare*, ed. George Steevens (Hartford, CT: Andrus & Judd, 1833), 1:320. The original has "such things".

18.8-9   I see the civil sun ... faster flow.:   In the complete text of his poem, "The Thaw," in his Journal for January 11, 1839 (*Journal 1*, pp. 65-66), Thoreau used the past tense for the verbs of these lines, "saw" and "flowed". Here the present tense is contextually appropriate.

18.9   flow.:   Followed in CD by "V. verses in long book p 197", referring to poetry at 116.10-18 in *Journal 2* (written after August 1, 1844). There, Thoreau transcribes the second stanza of "The Thaw" from *Journal 1*, p. 66, and replaces the third stanza with a new one. Neither of the elegiac third stanzas is appropriate in theme or mood for inclusion in "Natural History of Massachusetts." Ex adds nothing to D at this point.

18.23   treasury.:   Followed in CD by "v. verses in long book p 197", referring to poetry at 116.20-25 in *Journal 2* (written after August 1, 1844). Perhaps he intended to add these lines at the beginning of the poem on the freshet, 18.24-19.18, in agreement with manuscript versions of the same poem in *Journal 1*, pp. 111-113, and MS (TxAuHRH).

18.36   Nahshawtuck: Thus in D and CD; Thoreau's usual spelling of the aboriginal name for this Concord site (Lee's Hill) is "Nawshawtuct," as in an earlier manuscript version of the poem (see the February 24, 1840, entry in *Journal 1*, p. 112). The copy-text spelling has the authority of Lemuel Shattuck, *A History of the Town of Concord . . .* (Concord: Russell, Odiorne, and Company, 1835), p. 3. A single instance found via the indexes of Emerson's writings, in *JMN*, 11:278, is spelled "Nashawtuck". The entry dates from autumn 1850.

19.37   cucullo: A variant spelling of the Spanish "cucuyo" or "cucujo" (see *OED*), a West Indian firefly which emits bright phosphorescent light from spots on its body.

21.33   May: Thoreau changed "April" in D to "May" in CD, probably after his May 1854 field researches into the habits of the snapping turtle. On May 17 he concluded, "This then is the season for hunting them—now that the water is warmer before the pads are common" (*Journal 8*, p. 129). Ex adopts this revision.

22.19   take: "takes" in D, CD, and Ex. When Thoreau changed "moss" to "lichens" in CD (see Emendation 22.19), he failed to alter "takes" to agree with the plural subject. Ex retains "takes" but alters "lichens" to "lichen".

22.21   wreaths: "wreathes" in D, uncorrected in CD; "wreaths" in Ex.

23.2-3   *their* discontent: With the emphasized pronoun Thoreau calls attention to his deliberate alteration of the opening line of Shakespeare's *Richard III*: "Now is the winter of our discontent".

23.25   but may study: Thoreau added "may" with a caret in CD, a revision adopted in Ex.

23.33   still and frosty: "and" is lacking in D as printed, but Thoreau added an ampersand in CD, which Ex expanded to "and". See Textual Notes 57.30, 80.19-20, 185.34, and 223.10.

24.31-32 winter forever, is: D has a comma following "winter" but none after "forever". In CD Thoreau cancelled the printed comma and added a pencilled comma after "forever", a correction or revision adopted in Ex.

25.21 rapid?: Followed in CD by "V. Tahitian planting nails in journal", referring to an undated passage, after July 30, 1848, in *Journal 3*, p. 8. Ex adds nothing to D at this point.

25.34 crystallization: The original version of this sentence, in a Journal entry for December 19, 1837 (*Journal 1*, p. 21), reads "crystallizations".

28.10-11 when,–"Water . . . hill,"–may: The original version, in a Journal entry for October 11, 1840 (*Journal 1*, p. 187), dispenses with all punctuation save the open and close quotation marks.

Table of Emendations

FOR the format of this table, see the Textual Introduction, p. 382. Sources for the emendations are Thoreau's corrected copy of the *Dial* (CD), the 1863 edition of *Excursions* (Ex), or the editor's own authority, designated "PE" for the Princeton Edition, when the emendation is not anticipated in CD or Ex. In two cases, CD is identified as the source of readings that differ from the copy-text (*Dial*) and/or Ex readings.

* 3.7	State.] PE; State. *followed by* Preliminary Note. *by editor of the Dial*
7.32	skilful] Ex; skiful
*15.22	disappeared from this vicinity; the] PE; disappeared; from this vicinity the CD; disappeared; the
*15.23	seen here at] CD Ex; seen at
21.17	lizard] Ex; lizzard
*21.33	May] CD Ex; April
22.19	lichens] CD; moss *(see Textual Note 22.19)*
*22.19	take] PE; takes
*22.21	wreaths] Ex; wreathes
*23.25	but may study] CD Ex; but study

*23.33   still and frosty]   Ex;   still & frosty   CD;
                  still frosty

*24.31-32   winter forever, is]   CD   Ex;   winter, forever
                  is

Rejected Substantives

FOR the format of this table, see the Textual Introduction, p. 384. The table reports variant substantives in the 1863 edition of *Excursions* (Ex). Thoreau's
memoranda in the margins of his corrected copy of
the *Dial*–other than the corrections and revisions
adopted as Emendations–are reported in Textual
Notes.

3.1   Massachusetts.]   MASSACHUSETTS.* /
                  [1842.]   Ex

3.2-7   *Reports . . . State.]   printed as asterisked*
                  footnote   Ex

12.31   murmuring]   murmurings   Ex

13.34   here was]   was here   Ex

21.21   seem]   seems   Ex

22.19   lichens]   lichen   Ex *(see Textual Note 22.19)*

A Walk to Wachusett

Headnote

WRITING from Concord to Margaret Fuller on July 19, 1842, R. W. Emerson mentioned that "This morning your brother Richard . . . set out with H. T. on the road to Wachusett."[1] Richard Fuller was a nineteen-year-old Harvard College undergraduate, on his summer vacation; Thoreau, twenty-four, was in his second year of residence in Emerson's household, tending the garden, doing indoor chores, and writing.

By Thoreau's own account in "A Walk to Wachusett," the hike took three days; the companions camped on the mountain the second night, having spent the first at an inn in Sterling. On the fourth morning, July 22, they parted at Harvard village, where they had passed the night. Fuller walked home to Groton while Thoreau "took his separate and solitary way to the peaceful meadows of Concord" (46.6-7). If Thoreau kept field notes during the excursion, they do not survive. The Journal notebook he was using at the time, MS Volume 7, is now broken up and incomplete, but entries for August 8, August 9, between August 9 and 23, and August 23 (*Journal 1*, pp. 435-437) describe aspects of the trip; and images from an entry of July 18 (*Journal 1*, p. 433) are incorporated into the narrative.

The first extant draft of "A Walk to Wachusett" is in an album at NN-BGC ("[Nature and Bird Notes]") which also contains observations of nature, mostly of birds, by Thoreau and his brother John, as well as

[1] Emerson, *Letters*, 3:75. Richard left a contemporary record of the trip, interspersed among wordy philosophical reflections. The opening of the manuscript account survives and has been transcribed in the *Thoreau Society Bulletin* 121 (Fall 1972): 1-4.

entries by his sister Sophia. The draft consists of twenty-five pages of clean copy with only a few insertions and deletions. At several places Thoreau pencilled page numbers, all between "107" and "124," that can be related to MS Volume 7 of his Journal. Pages "107" to "118" and "121" to "150" are missing from that now-fragmentary book, but dated passages on surviving numbered pages indicate that the pages Thoreau refers to were written during the last three weeks of August; they may have contained a first draft of the narrative.[2] Thoreau's next draft of the essay, perhaps setting copy, probably dates from during or after the last week in August. That document is not extant.

Nathaniel Hawthorne, newly domiciled in the Old Manse with his bride, Sophia, first met Thoreau before August 5, 1842. He was favorably impressed by Thoreau's character and by the literary strength of "Natural History of Massachusetts" in the July *Dial*.[3] In October he would recommend Thoreau, "a fine scholar . . . but withal a wild, irregular, Indian-like sort of fellow," to the editor of *Sargent's New Monthly Magazine* as a potential contributor of poetry and natural history prose.[4] It may have been Hawthorne who suggested

[2] At the place where Thoreau wrote "120" in the nature album draft, the first printing of the essay in the *Boston Miscellany* presents a passage found in an earlier state on page "120" of the Journal volume (cf. 32.28-35 and *Journal 1*, pp. 436-437). None of the other Journal pages cued by Thoreau survives, but in the *Boston Miscellany* version, material has been added at each place where he added pencilled numbers to the nature album draft.

[3] *The Centenary Edition of the Works of Nathaniel Hawthorne*, vol. 8, *The American Notebooks*, ed. Claude M. Simpson (Columbus: Ohio State University Press, 1972), p. 355.

[4] Hawthorne to Epes Sargent, October 21, 1842, in *The Centenary Edition*, vol. 15, *The Letters, 1813-1843*, ed. Thomas Woodson, L. Neal Smith, and Norman Holmes Pearson (Columbus: Ohio State University Press, 1984), pp. 656-657. Sargent had printed two of Hawthorne's sketches early in the year.

The Boston Miscellany of Literature and Fashion as an outlet for "A Walk to Wachusett": this monthly was edited by Nathan Hale Jr., with the assistance of his brother Edward Everett Hale. They were the sons of Nathan Hale, editor of the Boston *Daily Advertiser*. Published by Bradbury, Soden and Company, the *Boston Miscellany*, which offered good pay to its contributors, had in November 1841 released its first number, dated January 1842.[5] Young Hale had printed one of Hawthorne's sketches in the May issue of the *Boston Miscellany*, after giving a favorable review in February to the expanded second edition of *Twice-Told Tales*. Ellery Channing was also a contributor, with a sketch in the July number.[6] Emerson may also have played a part in the submission of the new essay. The older man took the liveliest interest in the literary career of "my brave Henry," as he had called him in the July 19 letter to Margaret Fuller quoted above.

"A Walk to Wachusett" appeared in six double-column pages of the January 1843 issue, with almost a score of misprints affecting the sense, errors that may be referred as much to Thoreau's penmanship as to a compositor's ignorance or carelessness. Whatever their causes, these errors bear witness that Thoreau was not given proofsheets to correct. The printer read "dark" for "dank", "when" for "where", "severely" for "serenely", "Schina's" for "Schiraz'", "breaking" for "brawling", and "nesthatch" for "nuthatch". With the very next number, of February 1843, the *Boston Miscellany* failed. Thoreau was never paid for his contribution, despite his attempts to collect from Bradbury in

[5] Frank Luther Mott, *A History of American Magazines 1741-1850* (Cambridge: Harvard University Press, 1939), pp. 510, 718-720.

[6] See Hawthorne, *Letters, 1813-1843*, pp. 598, 619 and *American Notebooks*, pp. 357, 643.

person and efforts by his *Dial* associate Elizabeth Peabody and by Emerson to collect for him from what the
latter labeled the "faithless booksellers."[7]

Some time after mid-summer 1844, Thoreau prepared a redaction of "A Walk to Wachusett," probably
for the second draft of *A Week on the Concord and
Merrimack Rivers*. Six leaves at MH-H, catalogued
bMS Am 278.5, folder 10, contain continuous text starting just after the long opening poem in the *Boston Miscellany* version but lacking a conclusion.[8] Another,
single leaf in the same MH-H folder bears a new form
of the essay's opening–the prose content of the first
two paragraphs, also omitting the poetry found in
both the nature album draft at NN-BGC and the *Boston Miscellany* printing of "A Walk to Wachusett." Although this leaf is of a different paper type than the six
leaves stored adjacent to it, it is regarded by Linck C.
Johnson as belonging to the same 1847 draft of *A*

[7] See Peabody's letter to Thoreau of February 26, 1843, Thoreau's letters to Emerson of June 8 and August 7, Emerson's to
Thoreau of June 10 and July 20, and Thoreau's to his mother, July
7 (*Correspondence*, pp. 93, 112, 118, 121, 126, 134).

[8] One phrase in this draft of *A Week* gives it a *terminus a quo*:
where the nature album draft of "A Walk to Wachusett" and both
the *Boston Miscellany* and *Excursions* read "But Monadnock, rearing" (42.9; without comma in the nature album draft), the MH-H
version has "But Monadnock on whose rocky brow we have since
pitched our tent rearing". Thoreau first climbed Mount Monadnoc in the summer of 1844: see Walter Harding, *The Days of Henry
Thoreau* (New York: Alfred A. Knopf, 1970), p. 171.

[9] *Thoreau's Complex Weave: The Writing of* A Week on the Concord and Merrimack Rivers (Charlottesville: University Press of
Virginia, 1986), pp. 26-27. Howarth, in *LMHDT*, item D5k, anticipates Johnson's conclusion. Lauriat Lane Jr., in "Thoreau at Work:
Four Versions of 'A Walk to Wachusett,' " *Bulletin of the New York
Public Library* 69 (1965): 3-16, misconstrues the MH-H pages as the
first draft and the nature album draft as the second. For manuscripts of the poem "The Mountains in the Horizon" other than
that in the nature album draft, see Textual Note 29.6. The poem
had been rejected by Margaret Fuller, then editor of the *Dial*, on
October 18, 1841: see *Correspondence*, pp. 56-57.

Week.[9] Apparently related to the surviving six-leaf draft of *A Week* is a single leaf housed at RPB-JH. On this leaf Thoreau repeats five words from the end of the last MH-H page, and goes on to the end of the Wachusett narrative. For all these efforts to adjust his *Boston Miscellany* essay to *A Week*, Thoreau finally included only a short summary of the excursion.[10]

The text of the essay in *Excursions* (1863) varies considerably in substantives and accidentals, though not in theme or execution, from that in the *Boston Miscellany*. Collation with earlier authorial versions (including passages in the Journal for July and August 1842, the first draft in the nature album at NN-BGC, the manuscript redaction at MH-H, the single leaf at RPB-JH, and *A Week*) demonstrates that more than half of the 1863 variants can be assigned to Thoreau. Sophia Thoreau and those who helped her to edit *Excursions* must have used a copy of the *Boston Miscellany* text corrected and revised by Henry.[11] His copy of the *Boston Miscellany* is not extant; since the periodical had ceased publication almost two decades before Thoreau's editors undertook *Excursions*, copies were doubtless hard to come by, and his own marked copy may have gone to Ticknor and Fields and been discarded after serving the printers.

Comparison of the *Excursions* (1863) text with the

[10] *A Week*, pp. 163-166. In this Headnote and the Textual Notes page numbers are from the Princeton Edition, but the readings are those of the 1849 first edition unless otherwise specified.

[11] Thoreau's practice of reworking his texts even after publication is displayed in his copy of the *Dial* (ICarbS), in a marked copy of the *Union Magazine* "Ktaadn" text (1848), in several extant copies of the 1849 *Week* (including the one, now lost, from which the much-revised 1868 second edition was set), and in his copy of *Walden* (VtMiM). See the Headnotes for "A Winter Walk" and "A Yankee in Canada" in this volume for evidence that posthumous reprints from magazine first printings were based on pages marked by him.

nature album first draft and the MH-H redaction reveals that when the versions vary, *Excursions* (1863)
agrees with the MH-H text almost twice as often as
with the nature album draft. Whether Thoreau revised
the essay in his copy of the *Boston Miscellany* before or
after undertaking the redaction cannot be determined, if indeed his changes to the magazine text took
place at one sitting. The redaction pages themselves
display extensive internal revision, made over at least
two working sessions.[12]

Copy-text for the present edition of "A Walk to Wachusett" is the NjP copy of the first printing in the *Boston Miscellany* 3 (January 1843): 31-36. Most of the substantive variants in *Excursions* (1863) are adopted as
demonstrably authorial. In addition to the readings of
Boston Miscellany and *Excursions* (1863) against the
several manuscript witnesses to "A Walk to Wachusett," textual variations were ascertained by three
sight collations of *Boston Miscellany* and *Excursions*
(1863). The integrity of the first printing was ascertained by optical collation on the Lindstrand Com-
parator of *Boston Miscellany* copies at NjP and N.

---

[12] Although Thoreau climbed Wachusett again on October 19
and 20, 1854, he made no changes to the essay as a result; see 1906,
7:64-65.

Textual Notes

FOR the format of the Textual Notes, see the Textual Introduction, pp. 381-382. Copy-text is the printing in the January 1843 *Boston Miscellany* (BM). Ex stands for *Excursions* (1863). The abbreviation "MS" followed by a parenthesized owner's name or a repository symbol and in some cases an accession number identifies a manuscript reading. Except in Textual Notes 35.12 and 35.14, "MS (NN-BGC)" refers to the nature album kept by Henry and John. See the Headnote for a discussion of surviving manuscripts.

29.4   JULY 19:   The copy-text reads "July, 19", changed to "*July* 19" in Ex. On his own authority, the present editor accepts the removal of the comma, but not the italics, which are probably house styling.

29.6   in our horizon: Thus in Ex; lacking in MS (NN-BGC), BM, MS (MH-H), and *A Week*, p. 163. Three manuscript versions of the poem at 29.16 to 31.17 are called "The Mountains in the Horizon": MS (CSmH, HM 926 and HM 13201) and MS (MH-H, bMS Am 1280.214.1, folder 2).

29.14-15   Thus ... cliffs.–:   Ex provides this reading, absent in the copy-text. *A Week*, p. 163, reads "Standing on the Concord Cliffs we thus spoke our mind to them.–"

31.4   windows of: Thus in the copy-text; also in a Journal entry for May 2, 1841 (*Journal 1*, p. 307), MS (NN-BGC), and *A Week*, p. 165. The Ex reading, "windows on", is probably a compositor's error.

31.9   know'st: Thus in Ex; also in a Journal entry for May 2, 1841 (*Journal 1*, p. 307), MS (NN-BGC), and *A Week*, p. 165. The copy-text reads "knowst".

31.12   canst: Thus in MS (NN-BGC) and *A Week*, p. 165, emended from the 1868 second edition. The copy-text, Ex, a Journal entry for May 2, 1841 (*Journal 1*, p. 307), and the 1849 first edition of *A Week* read "can'st".

31.20   bound: Thus in Ex; the copy-text, like MS (NN-BGC), reads "bounds", while MS (MH-H) and *A Week*, p. 165, read "bounded". Similar changes in tense or narrative reference from present to past occur at 32.14, 33.22, 34.19-21, 34.27, 37.24-25, and 37.35-36.

32.4 dank: Thus in Ex, as in a Journal entry for August 8, 1842, (*Journal 1*, p. 435), and MS (NN-BGC). The copy-text prints "dark", probably an editorial sophistication if not a compositor's misreading of the manuscript.

32.9 lowing of kine: The copy-text reading, "herd of days", is changed in Ex to "lowing kine". Presumably Thoreau's alteration of the phrase on the lost BM copy used by the Ex editors and typesetters was unclear, resulting in the loss of the preposition. The sentence logic requires that the sound of the mower's rifle (whetstone) be heard mingled with the *sound* of the cattle, not with the cattle themselves. Later in the narrative (38.31-32), Thoreau uses this phrase again, the copy-text reading there matched by MS (MH-H).

32.14 then: Ex thus replaces "now" in the copy-text. See Textual Note 31.20.

32.17 lurk the gales which: Thus in Ex; "fresh gales are born to" in the copy-text. MS (MH-H) is similar to Ex: "in whose recesses the gales lurked which refreshed".

33.3 we, wayfarers, begin: Ex adds "wayfarers" and the associated commas to "we begin", evidently an authorial change. In the previous phrase, Ex adds a comma after "us", probably without authority. MS (NN-BGC) and the copy-text lack punctuation at that spot.

33.28 Wachusett, the object: Thus in Ex; name lacking in the copy-text. MS (MH-H) reads "the mountain the object".

33.29 lowering: Thus in Ex; the copy-text's "coming" is a compositor's error. MS (NN-BGC) reads "lowring"; see also Textual Note 42.20.

34.5 on New: The copy-text has "on the New". Ex returns to the authorial reading without the article, as in MS (NN-BGC) and MS (MH-H).

34.19-21 we had that . . . had gone . . . had heard: Thus in Ex, as also in MS (MH-H), where "that morning" is added in pencil. The copy-text, like the early draft MS (NN-BGC), reads "we have this . . . have gone . . . have heard". See Textual Note 31.20.

35.1 side is, by far, the: The copy-text's "side, is by far, the" reflects either careless comma placement in the lost setting copy or a typesetter's error. Ex deletes the second comma. In MS (NN-BGC), the phrase lacks punctuation: "side is far the".

35.5   these were: The copy-text reading, "there were", is relatively implausible in this context. Thoreau's "r" and "s" are often difficult to distinguish, and a typesetter's error is suspected. The phrase does not occur in MS (MH-H); in MS (NN-BGC) an ink blot obscures the letter in question.

35.12   Hassan: Corrected thus in Ex from the copy-text's "Haman", a compositor's error. Both a manuscript common-place book at NN-BGC and MS (MH-H) read "Hassan", as does Thoreau's source, William Collins, *Oriental Eclogues*, "Eclogue II. / Hassan; or, the Camel-Driver," in *The Works of the English Poets, from Chaucer to Cowper* . . ., ed. Alexander Chalmers (London: Printed for J. Johnson et al., 1810), 13:196.

35.14   Schiraz':   Corrected in Ex from the copy-text's "Schina's", a compositor's error. Both the manuscript com-monplace book at NN-BGC and MS (MH-H) read "Schiraz'", as does Thoreau's source, Collins, *Oriental Eclogues*, II, in Chalmers, 13:196.

35.33-34   As . . . refreshed: Thus revised in Ex from the copy-text's "On we went, and late in the afternoon re-freshed". The MS (NN-BGC) reading, "And as we went along our way late in the afternoon we refreshed", is similar to Ex.

37.9   brawling: Thus corrected in Ex from the copy-text's "breaking", a compositor's error. MS (NN-BGC) also has "brawling".

37.15-16   action . . . as if: Thus in Ex; the copy-text reads "action seemed consistent with a lofty prudence, as well as agreeable to the palate, as if". The early MS (NN-BGC) is al-most identical to the copy-text: "action seemed consistent with a lofty prudence, as well as pleasant to our palates, as if"; MS (MH-H) reads "we fancied that the juices of this fruit had relation to the thin air of the mountain-top–and that they were a suitable diet for those who climbed these hills,–As if". The omission of the copy-text phrase about the raspberries' flavor for the Ex printing appears to be authorial.

37.24-25   but . . . had relation: Thus revised in Ex from the copy-text's "but surely the juices of this berry have rela-tion". While MS (NN-BGC) is identical to the copy-text, "we fancied that the juices of this fruit had relation" in MS (MH-H) is similar to Ex. See Textual Note 31.20.

37.29   auger: The phrase between "wood" and "then" is an evidently authorial addition in Ex, but there "auger" is misspelled "augur".

37.35-36   reached . . . felt: Thus in Ex, revised from the copy-text's "have reached . . . feel". MS (NN-BGC) reads "have reached . . . have", but the verb forms in MS (MH-H) are identical to Ex. See Textual Note 31.20.

38.1   east.:   Thus in Ex, as in MS (MH-H). The copy-text reads "east, so withdrawn and solitary it seems." The additional phrase occurs in MS (NN-BGC), though in a somewhat different context.

38.2   sight.:   Thus in Ex. The copy-text, MS (NN-BGC), and MS (MH-H) all include another phrase here: BM reads "sight, thus easily triumphing over the height of nature."; MS (NN-BGC) reads "sight, thus easily triumphing over nature."; MS (MH-H) reads "sight, thus easily triumphing over the heights of nature."

38.4   cuckoo: Thus in Ex, as in MS (MH-H); MS (NN-BGC) reads "cucccu" and the copy-text has "cuckoos".

38.14   blue berries: The copy-text's "blueberries", not corrected in Ex, appears to reflect a carelessly written phrase in the lost setting copy, or a typesetter's mistake. MS (MH-H) provides the correct reading.

38.18-20   could . . . rising nearly: Thus revised in Ex from the copy-text's "could dimly see Monadnock, rising in simple grandeur, in the north-west, nearly". MS (NN-BGC) is similar to the copy-text: "could dimly see Monadnock rising in the north in simple grandeur–".

38.21   The first: Thus in Ex, as in MS (MH-H). The copy-text reads "But the first".

38.27   like a larger island: Ex adds the adjective, anticipated by MS (MH-H).

38.29   it. A blue: Thus in the copy-text, as also in MS (MH-H). A Journal entry from between August 9 and August 23, 1842 (*Journal 1*, p. 436), reads "earth. A blue". The reading in Ex, "it, a blue", may be editorial styling to eliminate Thoreau's sentence fragment.

39.29   altis: The copy-text reading, "attis", is a compositor's error, corrected in Ex. See also MS (MH-H) and Thoreau's source, Virgil, *Eclogues*, I, 83-84, in *Opera . . . Ad Usum Serenissimi Delphini . . .* (Philadelphia: M. Carey & Son, 1817), p. 7.

39.34-40.1   went into: Revised in Ex, as also in MS (MH-H), from the copy-text's "withdrew to". MS (NN-BGC) has "drew to".

40.17 thrilling: Thus in Ex, as in MS (MH-H). The copy-text and MS (NN-BGC) read "a rich treat".

40.27 reach as: Thus in Ex, as in MS (NN-BGC). The copy-text has a comma after "reach".

41.11 nuthatch: Thus in Ex, as in MS (NN-BGC) and MS (MH-H). A typesetter is responsible for the copy-text's "nest-hatch".

42.1 summits: Thus in Ex, as in MS (NN-BGC) and MS (MH-H). The copy-text reads "summit".

42.13 on that: Thus in both MS (NN-BGC) and MS (MH-H). The copy-text reads "or that".

42.14-16 air,– . . . born to: Thus in Ex, an authorial revision from the copy-text's "air. These rival vales, gradually extending their population and commerce along their respective streams, to". MS (MH-H) is similar in substantives to Ex.

42.20 lowering: Ex thus corrects the copy-text's "causing", a compositor's error. MS (NN-BGC) reads "lowring", while MS (MH-H) has "louring". See also Textual Note 33.29.

42.24 on the land: Although "in the land" in MS (NN-BGC) might seem a superior reading, this edition, like Ex, follows the copy-text's "on the land".

42.33 bearings referred: Without punctuation in Ex, as in MS (NN-BGC). The copy-text confusingly puts a comma after "bearings".

43.4 such even is: Ex adds "even" to the copy-text reading.

43.26 use.: So punctuated in Ex, as in MS (NN-BGC). The copy-text's "use?" is evidently a compositor's error.

43.34 impetus, we: Worded thus in Ex, as in MS (MH-H). The copy-text reads "impetus, (the reader will excuse the abruptness of the descent,) we".

44.13 river: Thus in Ex; also a Journal entry in a manuscript volume transcribed in 1842 (*Journal 1*, p. 417), and *A Week*, p. 324. The copy-text reads "rivers".

44.30 Sweavens: Thus, correctly, in a Journal entry from after April 8, 1847 (*Journal 2*, p. 377), MS (NN-BGC) and MS (RPB-JH). "Swearers" in the copy-text and Ex is an error that Thoreau apparently overlooked when he marked his copy of BM. A commonplace book version (*Thoreau's Literary Notebook in the Library of Congress*, ed. Kenneth Walter Cameron [Hartford, CT: Transcendental Books, 1964], p. 117) also reads "Sweavens", an archaic word meaning "dreams," as does

Thoreau's source, Joseph Ritson, ed., *Robin Hood: A Collection of All the Ancient Poems* . . . (London: Printed for T. Egerton and J. Johnson, 1795), 1:116.

45.30-46.3   And now . . . horizon.:   Thus in Ex; in the copy-text this paragraph follows 46.4-16, ending the essay. MS (NN-BGC) is similar to the copy-text; no later manuscript version survives. The present editor follows Ex on the assumption that it is unlikely that so large a change in an essay obviously reworked by Thoreau would have been made by anyone but him.

45.30   desultory: Thus in Ex, as in MS (NN-BGC). The copy-text reads "desert", an apparent typesetter's error.

45.31   import: Thus in Ex, as in MS (NN-BGC). The copy-text reads "impart", an apparent typesetter's error.

46.1   from it,:   By omitting the pronoun the copy-text, followed in Ex, creates a confusing and ungrammatical construction. The emendation in this edition is drawn from MS (NN-BGC), the only extant manuscript witness, which reads, "There is an elevation in every hour, no part of earth is so low and withdrawn that the heavens may not be seen from it."

Table of Emendations

For the format of this table, see the Textual Introduction, p. 382. Sources for the emendations are the 1863 edition of *Excursions* (Ex) or the editor's own authority, designated "PE" for the Princeton Edition, when the emendation is not anticipated in Ex. In *37.29, Ex is identified as the source of the reading before emendation, because that reading does not appear in the copy-text (*Boston Miscellany*).

*29.4	JULY 19] PE; July, 19
29.6	mountains in our horizon, to] Ex; mountains, to *(see Textual Note 29.6)*
29.13-16	Teneriffe. Thus . . . cliffs.– /With] Ex; Teneriffe. / With *(see Textual Note 29.14-15)*
*31.9	know'st] Ex; knowst
*31.12	canst] PE; can'st

*31.20	bound] Ex; bounds
31.30	At a cool and early hour] Ex; *no* ¶ Taking advantage of the early hour,
*32.4	dank] Ex; dark
*32.9	lowing of kine] PE; herd of days
32.11	hops, which plant perhaps supplies] Ex; hops. Perhaps there is no plant which so well supplies
32.12-13	may remind the traveller] Ex; reminds the traveller so often
32.13	France, whether] Ex; France, as this, whether
*32.14	then] Ex; now
*32.17	lurk the gales which] Ex; fresh gales are born to
32.21	vast] Ex; immense
33.1	probably] Ex; perhaps
*33.3	we, wayfarers, begin] Ex; we begin
33.11	the inhabitants;] Ex; a farmer by the road-/side;
33.14	them] Ex; him
33.15	Their tongues] Ex; His tongue
33.16	where] Ex; when
33.16	they] Ex; it
33.20	highlands overlooking] Ex; highlands in the western part of Bolton, overlooking
33.20-21	Lancaster, (affording . . . west,) and] Ex; Lancaster, and affording . . . west, and
33.22	there] Ex; here
*33.28	Wachusett, the object] Ex; the object
*33.29	lowering] Ex; coming
33.32	its] Ex; the
*34.5	on New] Ex; on the New
34.16	serenely] Ex; severely
*34.19-21	we had that . . . had gone . . . had heard] Ex; we have this . . . have gone . . . have heard
34.22	of neighboring] Ex; of the neighboring
34.23	hills, and she] Ex; hills. She
34.24	sky on that side, and] Ex; sky, and
34.27	made] Ex; makes
*35.1	side is, by far, the] PE; side, is by far, the
35.3	the Nashua] Ex; that river
*35.5	these were] PE; there were

*35.12	Hassan] Ex; Haman
*35.14	Schiraz'] Ex; Schina's
*35.33-34	As . . . refreshed] Ex; On we went, and late in the afternoon refreshed
36.16-17	In the small villages which we entered,] Ex; As we entered upon its street,
36.25	But we] Ex; But though we met with no very hospitable reception here at first, we
36.26	inn, "You] Ex; inn, and were comforted, "You
36.28	you," and were contented.] Ex; you."
37.2	slumberous] Ex; slumbrous
*37.9	brawling] Ex; breaking
*37.15-16	action . . . as if] Ex; action seemed consistent with a lofty prudence, as well as agreeable to the palate, as if
*37.24-25	but . . . had relation] Ex; but surely the juices of this berry have relation
37.28	a grand sugar maple] Ex; a maple
37.28-29	wood, which bore the marks of the auger, then] Ex; wood, then
*37.29	auger] PE; augur Ex
*37.35-36	reached . . . felt] Ex; have reached it, we feel
*38.1	east.] Ex; east, so withdrawn and solitary it seems.
*38.2	sight.] Ex; sight, thus easily triumphing over the height of nature.
*38.4	cuckoo] Ex; cuckoos
*38.14	blue berries] PE; blueberries
38.18	could see] Ex; could dimly see (see Textual Note 38.18-20)
*38.18-20	could . . . rising nearly] Ex; rising in simple grandeur, in the north-west, nearly
*38.21	The first] Ex; But the first
*38.27	like a larger island] Ex; like an island
39.7	stars."] Ex; stars "
*39.29	altis] Ex; attis
*39.34-40.1	went into] Ex; withdrew to
40.7-8	moon, so bright] Ex; moon, so that we enjoyed uninterrupted light, so bright
40.8-11	read distinctly . . . night, which] Ex; read Wordsworth distinctly, and when in the

	evening we strolled on the summit, there was a fire blazing on Monadnock, which
* 40.17	thrilling] Ex; a rich treat
* 40.27	reach as] Ex; reach, as
* 41.11	nuthatch] Ex; nesthatch
* 42.1	summits] Ex; summit
* 42.13	on that] PE; or that
* 42.14-16	air,–. . . born to] Ex; air. These rival vales, gradually extending their population and commerce along their respective streams, to
* 42.20	lowering] Ex; causing
* 42.33	bearings referred] Ex; bearings, referred
* 43.4	such even is] Ex; such is
43.12	purified; and as many] Ex; purified. As many
43.13-14	folly no doubt do not] Ex; folly do not
43.17-18	We get a dim notion of the flight of birds, especially of such] Ex; It adds not a little grandeur to our conception of the flight of birds, especially of the duck tribe, and such
43.18	by having] Ex; to have
43.19-20	mountains] Ex; they
* 43.26	use.] Ex; use?
* 43.34	impetus, we] Ex; impetus, (the reader will excuse the abruptness of the descent,) we
* 44.13	river] Ex; rivers
* 44.30	Sweavens] PE; Swearers
45.30-46.16	And now . . . horizon. We rested . . . heavens.] Ex; ¶ We rested . . . heavens. ¶ And now . . . horizon. *(see Textual Note 45.30-46.3)*
* 45.30	desultory] Ex; desert
* 45.31	import] Ex; impart
* 46.1	from it,] PE; from,

Rejected Substantives

For the format of this table, see the Textual Introduction, p. 384. The table records variant substantives in the 1863 edition of *Excursions* (Ex), *A Week* (Princeton Edition), and two bodies of manuscript, abbreviated "MS" followed by the repository symbol in parentheses. The manuscript at NN-BGC is pre-copy-text; that at MH-H is post-copy-text.

29.1	Wachusett.] WACHUSETT. / [1843.] Ex
*31.4	windows of] windows on Ex
*31.20	bound] bounds MS (NN-BGC); bounded MS (MH-H) *A Week*
40.19	was, in its elements, simple] was in its elements, simple Ex
*42.24	on the land] in the land MS (NN-BGC)
43.9	summit] summits MS (NN-BGC)
45.23	and as we passed] and we passed Ex

The Landlord

Headnote

VERY little external evidence exists about the composition of "The Landlord," and no manuscript drafts survive other than a phrase in a Journal entry of August 14, 1843 (*Journal 1*, p. 459). In November and December 1841 Thoreau had borrowed from the Harvard College Library the first volume of Alexander Chalmers's collection, *The Works of the English Poets, from Chaucer to Cowper*, 21 vols. (London: J. Johnson et al., 1810). Into a commonplace book, perhaps intended in part for his uncompleted project on English poetry, Thoreau copied many pages of Chaucer's verses. (The notebook is published in facsimile as *Thoreau's Literary Notebook in the Library of Congress*, ed. Kenneth Walter Cameron [Hartford, CT: Transcendental Books, 1964]; the Chaucer extracts begin at p. 142.) Not present among his extracts from the "General Prologue" to the *Canterbury Tales* are the materials he later used in "The Landlord": the description of the host or landlord of the Tabard Inn, and the host's first declaration to the pilgrims (52.32-53.6 and 53.12-14). Possibly these passages were transcribed on the partial leaf that Thoreau excised near the end of his "General Prologue" transcriptions. The essay was probably composed rapidly during the late summer of 1843, while Thoreau was living on Staten Island and trying to write for periodicals based in New York; it was printed in the October 1843 issue of the *United States Magazine, and Democratic Review*, edited by John L. O'Sullivan.

Nathaniel Hawthorne had introduced Thoreau to O'Sullivan the preceding January in Concord, and

O'Sullivan had invited Thoreau to contribute to his magazine (*Correspondence*, p. 77). Sometime after his arrival in New York in May 1843, Thoreau sent O'Sullivan an essay-review of J. A. Etzler's utopian tract, *The Paradise Within the Reach of All Men, Without Labor, by Powers of Nature and Machinery* (London: J. Cleave, 1842). On July 28, O'Sullivan rejected the piece but suggested he might print it if it were revised (with Thoreau's concurrence) to conform to his own ideas (*Correspondence*, p. 130), which were sympathetic to reformist communities. He also asked Thoreau to submit literary matter, "some of those extracts from your Journal, reporting some of your private interviews with nature," referring in all likelihood to Thoreau's *Dial* essay, "Natural History of Massachusetts" (July 1842), and perhaps also to "A Walk to Wachusett" (*Boston Miscellany*, January 1843).

In a draft letter to O'Sullivan of August 1, Thoreau responds by asking for the return of the manuscript of his Etzler review, promising, "If I should find any notes on nature in my journal which I think will suit you I will send them." He also asks O'Sullivan if he would be interested in the translations from Greek drama he was currently working on.[1]

No later correspondence between the two men survives, but their dealings were clearly not at an end. Most probably, Thoreau had no suitable nature essay to send, O'Sullivan was not interested in his Greek translations, and Thoreau submitted "The Landlord" instead. It appeared in the October issue (pp. 427-430), with Thoreau identified as the author. The following month the *Democratic Review* published the Etzler piece, "Paradise (To Be) Regained,"[2] perhaps in its

---

[1] CSmH, HM 13193, a complete rough draft translation of *The Seven Against Thebes*, p. "24". See *Translations*, p. 169.

[2] See *Reform Papers*, pp. 19-47, 237-238, 275-277.

original form after all, though without indication of authorship; O'Sullivan's July 28 letter had declared this was his policy with articles of a political cast. On October 1 Thoreau wrote his mother that "The Landlord" had been printed, describing it as "a short piece which I wrote to sell," and later that month he responded to his sister Helen's request for a copy by saying "I did not send the Dem Rev because I had no copy, and my piece was not worth fifty cents" (*Correspondence*, pp. 142, 147). But eventually he procured one, perhaps from O'Sullivan, and inscribed it on the front wrapper "Henry D. Thoreau   Staten Island."

That personal copy of the *Democratic Review*, now at MCo-SC, has had the pages containing "The Landlord" removed, suggesting later editorial use. The essay was reprinted posthumously from the *Democratic Review* in the Boston *Commonwealth* weekly newspaper for March 13, 1863, p. 1, and in *Excursions* (1863), pp. 97-108. Collation suggests that both the *Commonwealth* and *Excursions* texts were set separately from uncorrected copies of the *Democratic Review*, but one shared textual variant, "every honest fellow" for the original "every one", indicates communication between the *Commonwealth* editor, Franklin B. Sanborn (a friend and future biographer of Thoreau's) and one or more of the following persons: Sophia Thoreau, who had primary editorial responsibility for *Excursions*; R. W. Emerson, whose biographical sketch introduced the volume and who may have participated in its editing; Ellery Channing, Thoreau's favorite walking companion and later a close friend of Sanborn's, who also may have helped to edit *Excursions*; James T. Fields, the volume's publisher: see Textual Note 52.20.

In the absence of Thoreau's setting-copy manuscript and the magazine proofs, copy-text for "The

Landlord" in this edition is the first printing in the *United States Magazine, and Democratic Review* 13 (October 1843): 427-430. The copy used was that at NGenoU. Collation on the Hinman machine of two other copies, VtMiM in wrappers and MaLiTIW (from a bound volume), disclosed no textual differences. The *Democratic Review* text was collated with that in the *Commonwealth*, the *Democratic Review* was collated with *Excursions* (1863), and *Commonwealth* was collated with *Excursions* (1863). For substantive differences revealed by these sight collations, see Rejected Substantives.

Textual Notes

FOR the format of the Textual Notes, see the Textual Introduction, pp. 381-382. Copy-text is the printing in the October 1843 *Democratic Review* (DR). Com stands for the *Boston Commonwealth*, and Ex for *Excursions* (1863).

48.30   tavern: Thus in the copy-text and Ex; "house" in Com seems the result of a typesetter's eye-skip to "house" later in the sentence.

50.4   faggots: Spelled thus in the copy-text. Thoreau's dictionaries give only "fagot," but the *OED* recognizes "faggot" equally, giving instances from throughout the nineteenth century.

52.20   every one: Thus in the copy-text; "every honest fellow" in Com and Ex, probably a sophistication originating with the Com editor or one of the persons involved in the posthumous publication of the volume. The pages containing "The Landlord" are, however, missing from Thoreau's copy of DR, and this change is conceivably an authorial alteration.

Table of Emendations

FOR the format of this table, see the Textual Introduction, p. 382. Sources for the emendations are the Boston *Commonwealth* (Com), the 1863 edition of *Excursions* (Ex), or the editor's own authority, designated "PE" for the Princeton Edition, when the emendation is not anticipated in Com or Ex.

47.1	The Landlord.] PE; THE LANDLORD. / BY HENRY D. THOREAU.
48.7	fair-weather-and-foul] Com Ex; fair-weather-and foul
49.17	essentials] Com Ex; essentiais
50.10	ascend] Ex; ascends
50.31	idiosyncrasies] Ex; idiosyncracies
51.35	sheaves] Ex; sheafs

Rejected Substantives

For the format of this table, see the Textual Introduction, p. 384. The table records variant substantives in the Boston *Commonwealth* (Com) and the 1863 edition of *Excursions* (Ex).

47.1	The Landlord.] Miscellaneous. / {*rule*} / From the Democratic Review, Oct. 1843. /THE LANDLORD. / BY HENRY D. THOREAU. Com; THE LANDLORD. /[1843.] Ex
48.9	philanthropy, nor] philanthropy, not Com
48.30	ask] asks Com
*48.30	tavern] house Com
50.30	so all] so that all Com
52.2	and he cracks] and cracks Com
52.5	catholic] Catholic Com
*52.20	every one] every honest fellow Com Ex

A Winter Walk

Headnote

THOREAU'S conception of an essay describing a winter walk in Concord seems to have originated in his Journal immediately prior to October 14, 1842 (MS Volume 7, *Journal 1*, pp. 439-441), where a version of the third paragraph and the draft of a winter poem used in the account follow fifteen excised leaves. Forty-seven leaves are excised after an interrupted January 16, 1843, entry, and an undetermined number of leaves are missing from the end of the same notebook, interrupting an April 13 entry (*Journal 1*, pp. 447-449). Another textual fragment of "A Winter Walk" is on the first remaining pages of MS Volume 8, where an excision of seventy-one leaves precedes it and another of seventeen leaves follows (*Journal 1*, pp. 453-454). Still more fragments appear in entries for April [18] and 19 (followed by five missing leaves), April 27 (followed by a missing leaf), and May 19, followed by an excision of 126 leaves after a June 19 entry (*Journal 1*, pp. 454-458). Although Thoreau had several other compositions in progress during that busy winter and spring, it is safe to assume that some of these many missing Journal pages contained draft versions of passages for "A Winter Walk." Before putting the essay into final form Thoreau went back to the Journal entry of December 15, 1838, for a poem; and to October 24, 1838; February 7, 19, and 26, 1841; December 14, 15, 25, 26, and 31, 1841; and January 1, 1842, for sentences and phrases to incorporate into the text.[1] Long extracts of verse by

[1] All of these entries are in *Journal 1*. For December 15, 1838, see pp. 59-60; for October 24, 1838, see pp. 57-58; for February 1841 entries, see pp. 254-275; for December 1841 entries, see pp. 343-354; and for January 1, 1842, see pp. 354-355.

Gawin Douglas that Thoreau made at the end of 1841 in a commonplace book (*Thoreau's Literary Notebook in the Library of Congress*, ed. Kenneth Walter Cameron [Hartford, CT: Transcendental Books, 1964], pp. 95-96), he later recopied for "A Winter Walk" (73.23-74.24, 76.23-26, 77.3-19). He interrupted his work on the "Winter Walk" project in order to translate Æschylus's *Prometheus Bound* for the January 1843 *Dial* (then under Emerson's editorship) and to prepare his lecture on "The Life and Character of Sir Walter Raleigh" for the February 8 meeting of the Concord Lyceum.[2] Other tasks Thoreau had in hand in the autumn of 1842, the winter of 1842-1843, and the ensuing spring were his preparation of setting copy for "A Walk to Wachusett," which appeared in the January 1843 *Boston Miscellany*, his Anacreon translations and "Dark Ages" essay for the April 1843 *Dial*, and a study of the English poets.[3]

On May 6, before completing "A Winter Walk," Thoreau undertook a major, and ultimately frustrating, life-change when he left home for Staten Island, New York, in order to serve as tutor to Haven and Willie Emerson, the older sons of R. W. Emerson's brother William. Not yet twenty-six years old, he hoped to use his proximity to the New York magazines, publishing-houses, and cosmopolitan friends of Emerson to advance his literary career, but little came of the sojourn save a couple of pieces in the *Democratic Review*[4] and his friendship with Horace Greeley.

[2] For *Prometheus Bound* see *Translations*, pp. 3-53, 159-165; for "Sir Walter Raleigh" see *Early Essays and Miscellanies*, pp. 178-218, 391-393.

[3] "The Laws of Menu," printed in the January *Dial*, seems to have been completed at least six months earlier: see *Early Essays and Miscellanies*, pp. 380-382.

[4] "The Landlord," pp. 47-54, and "Paradise (To Be) Regained," *Reform Papers*, pp. 19-47.

First he suffered a severe and persistent cold and bronchitis, probably contracted during the sea-voyage from Boston to New York, and an uncharacteristic spell of somnolence. He disliked the city's meanness and materialistic pretentiousness; he missed his mother and sisters and Lidian Jackson Emerson, and he expressed his homesickness through invidious comparisons of his current whereabouts with Concord in his affectionate letters to family and friends. He took some solace in the botany of Staten Island (tropical relative to that of eastern Massachusetts) and in the wildness of the seashore. His self-exile lasted only until December 1843, when he gratefully returned to Concord, never again to dwell elsewhere.

Emerson wrote to Thoreau on May 21 while he was putting together the July number of the *Dial*, asking for "something good" by June 10 at the latest.[5] The essay was dispatched on June 8, barely short of Emerson's deadline, with a demeaning characterization: "I have very hastily written out something for the Dial, and send it only because you are expecting something,–though something better. It seems idle and Howittish,[6] but it may be of more worth in Concord, where it belongs" (*Correspondence*, p. 112). Emerson received the parcel on June 15, while writing to Thoreau a letter, begun five days before, rich in Concord news and expressions of his own pleasure about "Our Dial," with its contributions for the upcoming issue by

[5] *Correspondence*, p. 102; Thoreau's May 23 reply hints that Emerson had made the same request before Thoreau's departure for Staten Island. In that reply Thoreau sent "some verses from my journal" and promised to provide soon "an account of a winter's walk in Concord" if he could finish it "in the midst of a Staten Island summer" (*Correspondence*, p. 107).

[6] In the manner of William Howitt, *The Book of the Seasons* (Philadelphia: Carey & Lea, 1831); see *Early Essays and Miscellanies*, pp. 26-36, 343.

Ellery Channing, Samuel G. Ward, B. P. Hunt, and Charles Lane. He may have felt relief at having already made up the remaining sheets for the July issue, which he would carry to Boston the next day. There is a hint of reservation as he tells Thoreau he will keep "A Winter Walk" for the October number, "subject however to your order if you find a better disposition for it" (*Correspondence*, p. 118). To this last suggestion Thoreau replied in brief near the end of his July 8 letter to Waldo and Lidian: "As for the 'Winter's Walk' I should [?] be glad to have it printed in the D. if you think it good enough, and will criticise it–otherwise send it to me and I will dispose of it" (*Correspondence*, p. 125). Emerson concluded his next, newsy letter (July 20, 1843) with a noncommittal remark about the piece: "I will soon send you word respecting The Winter Walk" (*Correspondence*, p. 127).

Indeed, on reading the essay Emerson felt a strong aversion to it, which he recorded in his journal notebook "U":

H. D. T. sends me a paper with the old fault of un- limited contradiction. The trick of his rhetoric is soon learned. It consists in substituting for the obvi- ous word & thought its diametrical antagonist. He praises wild mountains & winter forests for their do- mestic air; snow & ice for their warmth; villagers & wood choppers for their urbanity[;] and the wilder- ness for resembling Rome & Paris. With the con- stant inclination to dispraise cities & civilization, he yet can find no way to honour woods & woodmen except by paralleling them with towns & townsmen. W[illiam] E[llery] C[hanning] declares the piece is excellent: but it makes me nervous & wretched to read it, with all its merits.[7]

[7] *JMN*, 9:9-10; undated entry.

On the eve of the printer's deadline for the October *Dial* Emerson again wrote to Thoreau about the fate of his submission, providing, in somewhat measured terms, the criticism that Thoreau had solicited in July and that Emerson had expressed so bluntly in the privacy of his journal:

> I mean to send the Winter's Walk to the printer to-morrow for the Dial. I had some hesitation about it, notwithstanding its faithful observation and its fine sketches of the pickerel-fisher and of the wood-chopper, on account of *mannerism*, an old charge of mine,–as if, by attention, one could get the trick of the rhetoric; for example, to call a cold place sultry, a solitude public, a wilderness *domestic* (a favorite word), and in the woods to insult over cities, whilst the woods, again, are dignified by comparing them to cities, armies, etc. By pretty free omissions, however, I have removed my principal objections. I ought to say that Ellery Channing admired the piece loudly and long, and only stipulated for the omission of Douglas and one copy of verses on the Smoke. (*Correspondence*, pp. 137-138, September 8, 1843; corrected from *Atlantic Monthly* 69 [1892]: 593)

He concludes the paragraph by informing Thoreau of some of the number's other contents, bemoaning the paucity of verse contributions, and asking whether Thoreau might have ready some translations from the Greek.

Emerson did not exaggerate when he spoke of his "pretty free omissions." As reported in Textual Notes and Alterations, he made numerous revisions of diction (chiefly to reduce the paradoxes he found so irritating, but also to omit or tone down some boldly heterodox religious sentiments), and he deleted Thoreau's quotations, at the end, from the description of winter in Gawin Douglas's Scots dialect translation of the *Æneid*. The identity of the "copy of verses on the Smoke" is not so easily determined, the leaf of Thoreau's setting copy on which one deleted original poem was probably written having been lost. See Textual Note 63.12-64.8 for the evidence allowing the lines of verse to be identified and restored. Thoreau replied with as much grace as he could muster before actually seeing the results of Emerson's revision, "I doubt if you have made more corrections in my manuscript than I should have done ere this, though they may be better, but I am glad that you have taken any pains with it" (*Correspondence*, p. 139). In the same September 14 letter he told Emerson he had no new translations on hand for the *Dial*, and reported his almost total failure to sell his work to New York periodicals, naming the *New Mirror*, *Brother Jonathan*, the *New World*, and the *Knickerbocker* as magazines incapable of or uninterested in paying for what little he wrote. Only John L. O'Sullivan of the *Democratic Review* had accepted a submission of his, and that after misgivings, an initial rejection, and a long delay.

As edited by Emerson with the advice of Ellery Channing, "A Winter Walk" was printed in the *Dial* 4: 211-226. Thoreau had not been shown proof-sheets of his essay, and Emerson's proofreading was evidently slipshod. Having examined a copy, Thoreau wrote to Emerson on October 17, praising the issue as a sort of "circular letter [of Concord news] itself" and noting in particular the wit of Channing's prose contribution and the solid style of Charles Lane's. He admired Emerson's "Letter" to contributors and liked the poetry. Of "A Winter Walk" he wrote, ambiguously, "I see that I was very blind to send you my manuscript in such a state, but I have good second sight (?) at least. I could still shake it in the wind to some advantage, if it would hold together." But no obscurity marks the next sentence: "There are some sad mistakes in the printing" (*Correspondence*, p. 145). The metaphors of blindness and second sight are particularly germane in view of Thoreau's immediately preceding comments concerning the editorial judgment he was exercising on his English verse project: "I feel as if I were ready to be appointed a committee on poetry, I have got my eyes so whetted and proved of late, like the knife-sharpener I saw at the Fair certified to have been in constant use in a gentleman's family for more than two years. . . . I ride along the ranks of the English poets casting terrible glances, and some I blot out, and some I spare." It is also apposite that later in the letter he spends almost a page savaging the rhyme and diction of Emerson's "Ode to Beauty," also printed in the latest *Dial*.

Horace Greeley, in the first of his many acts as Thoreau's literary promoter, reprinted an excerpt under the title "Winter Scenery" in his *New-York Daily Tribune* for October 27, p. 4. The *Dial* essay also received praise from a reviewer in the *Knickerbocker* for November.[8]

The "Winter Walk" manuscript, much of which survives, was not returned to Thoreau but remained among Emerson's papers,[9] a fact that overshadowed the essay's later fortunes. In his personal copy of the *Dial*, now at ICarbS, Thoreau corrected numerous misprints and tried to reconstruct passages that Emer-

---

[8] Joel Myerson, "Thoreau and the *Dial*: A Survey of the Contemporary Press," *Thoreau Journal Quarterly* 5 (January 1973): 5.

[9] On a leaf now at VtMiM, perhaps given to an autograph seeker, Emerson wrote and signed an attestation as to the authorship. The penultimate leaf (NNPM, MA 1719) came into the hands of F. B. Sanborn, who published a selective transcription in *The Personality of Thoreau* (Boston: Charles E. Goodspeed, 1901), pp. 31-33.

son had revised or deleted. All these notations are recorded in Autograph Corrections and Revisions in
Thoreau's Copy of the *Dial*. When his sister Sophia
assembled copy for the posthumous collection *Excursions* (1863), she apparently consulted that marked
copy of the *Dial*: the corrections Thoreau entered
there–though not the cross-references and his efforts
to remember what Emerson had cut–were reflected
in the 1863 typesetting. Setting copy for the *Excursions* printing was probably another group of *Dial*
pages marked by Sophia to duplicate her brother's
corrections. Half a year before the publication of *Excursions* Frank Sanborn reprinted "A Winter Walk" in
his weekly newspaper, the Boston *Commonwealth*
(March 27, p. 1, and April 3, 1863, p. 1), using the uncorrected *Dial* as his source.

The choice of copy-texts for "A Winter Walk" and
the treatment of those copy-texts once chosen are seriously complicated by the textual history of the piece
and the characteristics of the surviving and incomplete manuscript. Of all the works in this edition of *Excursions*, "A Winter Walk" involves the most complex
editorial apparatus and the greatest number of difficult decisions. That Emerson revised Thoreau's manuscript for the *Dial* is not in question; but apart from
the single instance where he clearly identified to
Thoreau material he had deleted ("Douglas": see
73.23-74.24 and 74.38, and 77.3-19), those editorial alterations must be distinguished by the textual scholar
from changes Thoreau himself made while composing
his setting copy, before sending it to Emerson on June
8. As documented in the list of Alterations, the surviving twenty-nine pages are extensively revised in both
ink and pencil.

Some of the changes cannot but be authorial: omitted words basic to the sense are added between lines

with carets, in a hand consistent with that of the on-line text; and false starts, involving groups of letters and entire words, are cancelled in the on-line text within paragraphs. Many other alterations, however, involve interlined words and phrases not basic to the original sense of the on-line text, but intelligible rather as parts of a pattern of cancellation and revision. Here, because of the restricted space for new copy, the handwriting necessarily differs somewhat from that of the on-line Thoreau text. It also differs somewhat from Emerson's free handwriting in his 1843 letters to Thoreau. Vexingly, moreover, the two writers' penmanships are in most respects quite similar, and on the "Winter Walk" manuscript both men use ink and pencil for their revisions.

In close paleographic study of the original manuscript pages, three Princeton Edition editors (Joseph J. Moldenhauer, Robert Sattelmeyer, and Elizabeth Hall Witherell) have attempted to distinguish Emerson's individual alterations from Thoreau's by reference to several important features. First, Thoreau's handwriting differs consistently from Emerson's in the shaping of lower-case g, terminal n, and initial s. Examining added words–words written in the margins and between the lines–the editors have attended particularly to these letters. A second difference is the two men's characteristic modes of cancellation: for omissions of up to two lines, Thoreau prefers to isolate the passage between parentheses, signifying doubt, and then to cancel it with a wavy horizontal line–a technique Emerson seems not to employ. For longer cancellations, both writers use single or multiple vertical lines, though Emerson's are typically accompanied by large square pencilled brackets and pencilled X marks in the margin. Third, Thoreau's ink alterations are effected in ink of the same hue as the on-line text of the manuscript; Emerson uses ink of another, and usually darker, hue. When interlined words in ink show a pencil substratum, the revision is typical of Thoreau's technique: he seems to have done a provisional editing of his final manuscript with pencil before tracing over his changes with a pen. The general character of Emerson's criticisms of "A Winter Walk" in his journal and correspondence serves as yet another guide to distinguishing his cancellations and insertions from Thoreau's. Excisions of unorthodox religious sentiments, though these excisions sometimes damage the style or logic of the passage as originally written, are accompanied by Emerson's large marginal X and square brackets in pencil.

Where the setting copy for the *Dial* survives, the stratum of the document that is Thoreau's own serves as copy-text for this edition, with Emerson's revisions and the compositor's marks stripped away. Where the setting copy is lost, copy-text is Thoreau's corrected *Dial*, with occasional pencilled notes, such as marginal question marks, that do not constitute clear directions for revision being deleted by editorial emendation and recorded in the apparatus.[10] Some emendations of the manuscript copy-text sections are drawn from the earliest post-copy-text, the printed *Dial*, which is usually identical at these points with the subsequent *Commonwealth* and *Excursions* typesettings. Others are drawn from the corrected *Dial*.

At two or three points in the corrected *Dial* where Thoreau left minor revisions incomplete, *Excursions* clarifies them, as the editor of the present edition would do even if *Excursions* had not. Emendations to

---

[10] An identical text in these sections where setting copy is missing would have resulted from the choice as copy-text of the *Dial* as printed, with Thoreau's corrections to his copy being adopted as editorial emendations.

the corrected *Dial* copy-text sections that are not anticipated in *Excursions* typically involve following Thoreau's shorthand instructions to insert sentences from the Journal in order to reverse Emerson's cuts. Thoreau also signals the inclusion of a poem from the one remaining pre-copy-text draft, a manuscript fragment at ICarbS: see 63.13-64.8 and its Textual Note.

The *Dial* manuscript consisted of forty-three numbered pages, probably written on only twenty-two leaves of an inexpensive stationery. The surviving fifteen leaves of setting copy are white wove type 11 (*LMHDT*, p. 377), a relatively porous paper which, when inscribed closely in ink on both sides as all the leaves are but the last, compounded the *Dial* typesetter's difficulties in reading Thoreau's hand. Missing are the leaves bearing pages "1"-"4", "9"-"16", and "19"-"20". The remaining twenty-nine pages of text, written on the rectos and versos of fourteen leaves and the recto of the fifteenth, are currently housed in five institutional repositories. Pages "5"-"6" and "7"-"8" are at MH-H, catalogued bMS Am 1280 T3911 P.800; pages "25"-"26", also at MH-H, are catalogued bMS Am 1280.214.1, folder 5. Nine leaves are at DeU; these comprise pages "17"-"18", "21"-"22", "23"-"24", "29"-"30", "31"-"32", "33"-"34", "35"-"36", "37"-"38", and "39"-"40". A leaf at VtMiM is paginated "27"-"28". A leaf at NNPM comprises pages "41"-"42" and is catalogued MA 1719. Finally, the last leaf ("43"), blank on the verso save for Emerson's docketing notation when the essay reached him in June 1843, is at MCR-S, catalogued "178 New England Women's Club, Vol. I, Oversize." In this edition of "A Winter Walk" the pages at MH-H provide text for 56.23-59.2 ("has lain ... be called in") and 66.32-67.35 ("to its ... oceans know."). Those at DeU supply the text for 62.1-63.7 ("caddis worms, ... the trees, and"), 64.27-66.32 ("baked his pot

. . . direct the traveller"), and 69.13-76.2 ("Before night
. . . to the view,"). The leaf at VtMiM comprises the text
for 68.1-69.12 ("domestic . . . forest path."). The text on
the NNPM leaf begins at 76.3 ("Shines out intensely
keen;") and runs through 77.14 ("elrische skreik."),
plus Thoreau's footnote 3. The MCR-S leaf contains
the last four lines of the Gawin Douglas extract (77.15-
18) and material in Emerson's hand, chiefly his own
copy of twenty of the Douglas lines struck from the
essay, the spelling modernized in a tentative effort to
make the material accessible to *Dial* readers before he
decided to exclude it altogether.

Textual variations among the various printed forms
of "A Winter Walk" were determined by the following
sight collations: *Dial* (as printed) against *Commonwealth*, twice; *Commonwealth* against 1863 *Excursions*
(twice); *Dial* (as printed) against 1863 *Excursions*
(three times). Thoreau's autograph revisions on his
copy of the *Dial* were ascertained by three independent readings of the original at ICarbS.

Textual Notes

FOR the format of the Textual Notes, see the Textual Introduction, pp. 381-382. Copy-text is a composite of Thoreau's setting copy for the *Dial*, twenty-nine of an original forty-three manuscript pages (here identified as DMS; located in various libraries as detailed in the Headnote), and, where the setting copy is lost, Thoreau's marked text of the essay in his personal copy of the October 1843 *Dial* (CD). The copy-text is identified as DMS or CD before the first of each group of notes about material from that copy-text; contents of MS pages are correlated with the text of the present volume in the Headnote and the table of Alterations. D stands for the *Dial* as printed, Ex for *Excursions* (1863), Com for the Boston *Commonwealth*, and PE represents the Princeton Edition, the present volume.

CD is the copy-text for 55.1-56.23 A Winter Walk . . . where it

55.1   A Winter Walk.:   "A WINTER WALK. / [1843]" in CD and Ex, adding to D the year of first publication. It would be misleading, however, to retain this date in PE, which adopts revisions from CD and the manuscript Journal that Thoreau probably made after 1843. See the Headnote. The title on the lost first page of DMS might have been "A Winter's Walk." Thoreau first referred to the essay as "an account of a winter's walk in Concord" in his May 23, 1843, letter to Ralph Waldo Emerson; Emerson wrote Thoreau on June 15 acknowledging receipt of "the Winter's Walk" manuscript; Thoreau referred to the essay as "the Winter's Walk" in a letter to the Emersons on July 8; on July 20, however, Emerson promised to send word soon "respecting The Winter Walk"; and, finally, Emerson wrote Thoreau on September 8, "I mean to send the Winter's Walk to the printer to-morrow . . ." (*Correspondence*, pp. 107, 118, 125, 127, 137). On the verso of the last page of manuscript, Emerson wrote "The Winter's Walk / H.D.T. June 1843". Their use of "Winter's" may be only casual, or it might imply an unauthorized change to "Winter" in

DMS by Emerson or in D by a compositor. Thoreau's use of adjectival winter/winter's elsewhere in the essay is inconsistent (55.22, 59.26, 61.11, 64.10, 64.34, 69.15, 73.6, 75.18, 75.27). In a pencilled note in his Journal he does refer to the essay as "winter walk", but the note was probably written after D was published (see Textual Note 75.4). Lacking more conclusive evidence that "Winter" in D and CD is an editor's or compositor's corruption of "Winter's" in lost DMS, PE retains the CD copy-text form.

55.22   At length we awake: "at length awake" in CD, originally "We sleep and at length awake" in D. Thoreau cancelled "We sleep and", but did not provide the sentence with a new pronoun. PE "we" follows the personal pronoun used elsewhere in this paragraph and repeats cancelled "We".

56.17   night is crowded: "night crowded" in CD. Because Thoreau did not supply a new verb when he cancelled "is", his intention is unclear.

56.19-21   along . . . clear: Thoreau added a question mark in the margin next to these two printed lines in CD, but his intention is unclear.

DMS is the copy-text for 56.23-59.2 has lain . . . be called in

56.24   stubble; while far: "For" in D is a compositor's misreading of blotted "Far" in DMS. In CD, Thoreau altered D "For" to "While Far" by adding "While" and a caret in the margin and by cancelling "o" and substituting "a" in the margin. "While" changes Thoreau's original sentence to a dependent clause. PE follows Ex, joining main and subordinate clauses by emending the incongruous accidentals of Thoreau's incomplete CD revision. PE emends other incomplete revisions of accidentals in CD; see Emendations 57.22-23, 58.1, 58.13-14, and 60.8.

57.12   'T has been . . . new wind: Thus in DMS; "It has gone down the glen with the light wind" in D. The absence of an alteration by Emerson in DMS suggests that he made the change in the proofs for D.

57.30   and even: DMS has an ampersand, which Thoreau expected his publisher to change routinely to "and" except where it occurred in commercial titles and "&c". D followed this practice here. See also Emendation 60.11-12, where the ampersand occurs in an interpolation from the Journal, and see Textual Notes 23.33, 80.19-20, 185.34, and 223.10.

57.34-35   it is . . . that it: Followed by a faint dash in mar-

gin in CD. Thoreau's intention is unclear. He may be query-
ing the change of DMS "becomes as much a source of delight
as anything" to "becomes a source of delight" in D (57.35-36).
The lack of an alteration by Emerson in DMS suggests that he
or a compositor made this change in proofs for D.

58.1   it, as they: In DMS Thoreau's "it, as those" is altered, apparently by Thoreau himself, to "it. Those", the
reading printed in D. In CD, however, he seems to have decided to reverse the change in part, and to institute yet another, adding "As" between "it." and "Those", and interlining
"ey" above the latter word. His apparent intention, "it, as
they", is adopted in this edition; Ex reads "it. As they".

58.1-6   as they ... pernicious to the health.":   Thus in
DMS. This information derives ultimately from David Crantz
(Cranz), *The History of Greenland: Containing a Description
of the Country and Its Inhabitants* (London: Printed for the
Brethren's Society, 1767), or from the Moravian missionary
Hans Egede's *A Description of Greenland*, the original Danish
version of which (1757) was probably Crantz's original.
Crantz, 1:43, writes, "the sea reeks like an oven, especially in
the bays. This is called the frost-smoke. . . . the frost-smoke is
more apt to raise blisters than the dry cold . . . it freezes to
little ice-particles, which are driven on with the wind, and
create such a cutting cold on the land, that one can scarce go
out of the house without having hands and feet seized on by
the frost." Egede, in the second English edition (London:
Printed for T. and J. Allman, 1818), p. 56, has, "in the winter
season [the inhabitants] are likewise plagued with the vapour
called frost smoke, which, when the cold is excessive, rises
out of the sea as the smoke out of a chimney, and is as thick
as the thickest mist, especially in the bays, where there is any
opening in the ice. It is very remarkable, that this frost, damp,
or smoke, if you come near it, will singe the very skin of your
face and hands." Thoreau is not known to have read Crantz
until late 1860, when he took notes on it in the Journal (ad-
dendum to July 7 entry [1906, 13:395]), a commonplace book,
and one of the Indian Notebooks. There is no explicit record
of his having read Egede. It appears that Thoreau derived his
slightly different version of the frost-smoke account from an
intermediate source, but the present editor has searched in
vain for one in Thoreau's extensive recorded readings in
high-latitude travel and in other possible sources such as the
notes to James Montgomery's epic, *Greenland*.

CD is the copy-text for 59.2-62.1 for shelter . . . cottages of the

59.11-61.3   There is . . . about him.:   CD contains manuscript revisions which Ex follows only in part. D prints three
paragraphs: first, "At length . . . taller grass?", with the sentence "They are glad . . . as in summer." following immediately upon "banked up with snow."; second, "There is a
slumbering . . . into that by-place."; and third, "This subterranean fire . . . and the lark." Thoreau drew a marginal line in
pencil along the paragraph "At length . . . taller grass?" and
marked it "2", for transposition with the following pair of paragraphs, "There is . . . that by-place." and "This subterranean
fire . . . and the lark.", which he similarly marked with a marginal line and numbered "1". He also added three notations,
signalling the addition of copy from his Journal. After
"banked up with snow." he wrote "v no 3 p 102"–that is, "see
Journal MS Volume 3, page 102." After "taller grass?" he wrote
"v no. 3 p 90" and "V no 6 p 15". The Journal entries so keyed
are entries Thoreau revised both in preparation for the 1843
publication of "A Winter Walk" and subsequently, perhaps
intending to restore, in CD (and in any future publication
based on CD), readings Emerson changed from DMS, which
was not available to him. The revised Journal entries contain
"domestic," heroic, and vernal imagery of the sort Emerson
objected to in DMS. Ex follows CD in transposing paragraphs, but does not add matter from the Journal, probably
because the Ex editors could not interpret Thoreau's cross-
reference notations. Here and in comparable instances elsewhere in "A Winter Walk" PE adopts revised Journal readings
only where DMS for the parallel passages is lost, and only
where Thoreau's notations in CD and the cited Journal passages are unequivocal.

The first notation (in the order of paragraphs in D as
printed), "v no 3 p 102", refers to a Journal entry for December 28, 1840, *Journal 1*, pp. 210-211, with post-D revisions. In
the Journal margin at "Our voices . . . household echoes."
(60.10-13) Thoreau noted in pencil "v p 214"–a reference to
the CD page where he wished to have the sentence inserted.
Following "household echoes." he wrote "They are glad &c",
signalling a return to the CD text beginning with those three
words.

Thoreau's first notation after the CD reading "They are
glad . . . taller grass?" refers to a revised entry of December 16,

1840, in Journal MS Volume 3, p. 90, *Journal 1*, p. 205. PE adopts the revised Journal text at this point: "Nothing is so beautiful . . . his blanket about him." (60.32-61.3). The second Journal passage ("no 6 p 15") signalled after "taller grass?", however, parallels a passage Thoreau had used elsewhere in DMS ("Again we have wandered . . . wind in July.", 67.32-68.8) and which Emerson had revised for the D printing. At 67.32-68.8 PE follows Thoreau's text in surviving DMS; here, at 61.3, PE omits the parallel Journal text from MS Volume 6, p. 15 (November 15, 1841; *Journal 1*, pp. 343-344), which Thoreau signals to appear after "about him." As revised, the Journal entry reads:

> In the woods there is an inexpressible happiness– Their mirth is but just repressed.

> In winter, when there is but one green leaf for many rods, what warm content is in them– They are not rude but tender even in the severest cold. Their nakedness is their defence. All their sounds and sights are elixer to my spirit. They possess a divine health   God is not more well. Every sound is inspiriting–and frawght with the same mysterious assurance from the creaking of the boughs in January to the soft sugh of the wind in July.

Besides marking paragraphs for transposition and keying revised manuscript Journal passages, Thoreau made minor pencilled alterations in this section of CD; he marked "At length we have reached" to read "At length having reached" (60.7), changed the period after "town" to a comma (60.8), corrected a compositor's error, "lanes", to "lawns" (60.31), and changed "our back" to "our backs" (59.30). In the two passages interpolated from the manuscript Journal, PE effects necessary emendations of the sorts outlined in the Textual Introduction, pp. 374-375. All Emendations are individually recorded as such.

59.36   traveller: Thoreau invariably spelled this word, as well as "travelled" and "travelling," with two "l"s. The single-l spelling is not D house style (see, for example, the printed D reading in the next paragraph, at 60.18) and probably resulted from a typesetter's lapse or personal preference.

DMS is the copy-text for 62.1-63.7 caddis worms, . . . the trees, and

62.1   caddis: "caddice" in DMS, a spelling followed in D, Com, and Ex, and not revised in CD. None of Thoreau's dictionaries authorize "caddice"; Johnson, Walker, and Webster have only "caddis" and Bailey has neither spelling. Although the *OED* records the alternative spelling "caddice," no cited instance antedates 1847. The insect's habit of building cases in the aquatic larval state is described by James Rennie in *Insect Architecture* (London: Charles Knight et al., 1830), a book Thoreau owned. Rennie's exposition, pp. 185-189, consistently uses the spelling "caddis." So do William Kirby and William Spence, in *An Introduction to Entomology*, seventh ed., in one vol. (London: Longman, Brown, Green, Longmans, and Roberts, 1858), pp. 264-265. Thoreau's library reportedly included a one-volume London edition of 1856, but no such printing is recorded in *The National Union Catalog, Pre-1956 Imprints* (London: Mansell, 1968-1981). Presumably his copy was struck from the same plates as the 1858 printing. Two other books Thoreau read and owned, both by Thaddeus William Harris, use the spelling "cadis": *A Report on the Insects of Massachusetts, Injurious to Vegetation* (Cambridge: Folsom, Wells, and Thurston, 1841)–one of the state surveys that were the occasion for "Natural History of Massachusetts"–p. 12, and a slightly revised edition of the same under the title *A Treatise on Some of the Insects of New England Which Are Injurious to Vegetation* (Boston: White & Potter, 1852), p. 11.

62.11-12 or floating ... henceforth flutter: Thus in the copy-text. The D compositor garbled this passage badly: "or floating on the surface like gnats, or perfect insects, henceforth flutter". Attempting to reconstruct his meaning in the absence of DMS, Thoreau revised CD to read "or to the surface like gnats, as perfect insects henceforth, flutter", the reading followed by Ex. The original manuscript version is clearly superior.

62.15-18 We have come ... shrubs: Altered by Thoreau in the process of drafting DMS, this passage was marked for further revision, apparently by Emerson, before being largely cancelled. Thoreau wrote, and cancelled, "We have" before repeating the same words in the blank space above and continuing the sentence, "come down into this little wintry glen" through "Roman virtue." Cancelling "this" before "little", he wrote "some", cancelled it, and repeated it above. A pencilled bracket in the margin marking the sentiment about classical virtue is assuredly by Emerson, who probably also supplied the pencilled circlings of "We have come", the "to" of "into", "some", and "this bright morning, where too". Finally, the whole sentence is cancelled with ink and pencilled lines. It is conceivable that Emerson's bracket at "Roman virtue" is intended to tell the compositor to set the following matter flush left rather than indenting for a paragraph. Thoreau's next sentence began with the words "The shrubs". A new beginning is interlined, with a caret, in ink in Emerson's hand: "Down yonder little glen", with a possible incomplete pencilled cancellation of Thoreau's "The" being explainable as an inadvertent extension of the pencilled line cancelling the end of the previous sentence. D follows these cancellations and begins the passage with the words "Down yonder little glen the shrubs", without a paragraph indentation. In CD, Thoreau entered a question mark, at the line beginning "Down yonder . . . ".

62.35-36 which shame ... Rome,: The technique by which this phrase (omitted in D) is cancelled in DMS–with pencilled square brackets and cancellation lines–is typical of Emerson's alterations in this manuscript. The omitted matter is, moreover, the sort of phrase about which Emerson complained to Thoreau, and in his journal, when he edited the essay for D. The editor judges it to be a nonauthorial change. See Alteration 62.35-36.

62.36 pines: "spruces" in D; a misreading or unauthorized change by the compositor or a substitution by Emerson in proofs.

63.4 As ... reflected: In CD "118" is written in pencil in the margin beside this text, but the handwriting is not clearly Thoreau's and its purpose remains uncertain. In Ex this text appears on p. 119, facing p. 118. Thus it may be an Ex proofreader's notation, possibly William Ellery Channing's or Sophia Thoreau's. CD remained in Sophia's possession until her death in 1876, at which time she left it to F. B. Sanborn. If Sanborn or a subsequent owner of CD made this notation, he probably did so after the editing of texts relevant to PE.

63.6-7 the icicles ... trees, and: This line in DMS, the last on the autograph page, is marked with Emerson's marginal "X" and with an open square bracket before "and". The changes, if any, that Emerson made affected only the portion of text immediately following, for which the autograph leaf is missing.

CD is the copy-text for 63.7-64.27 the nut-hatch . . . where he

63.12-64.8 strong meats. / The apples ... glow.: After "strong meats." in CD, Thoreau wrote "v. verses", apparently signifying that he wished to include some poetry. The DMS page paginated "18" ends with "trees, and" at 63.7; page "21" commences at "baked his pot" at 64.27; the intervening leaf, "19"-"20", is lost, and the text as printed in D contains only a little more copy–223 words of prose–than Thoreau wrote on *single* pages of the surviving manuscript. DMS pages "17" and "18" average 204 words of prose, in twenty-nine lines each. What D prints in the DMS textual gap corresponding to "19"-"20" would have occupied about thirty-two autograph lines. The contents of slightly under one page of original DMS autograph are thus unaccounted for in the D printing. From Emerson's letter to Thoreau of September 8, 1843, it is clear that some of Thoreau's poetry, as well as his quotations from Gawin Douglas, was eliminated from the D version ("omission of ... one copy of verses on the Smoke" [*Correspondence*, p. 138]). Demonstrably, Emerson excised Thoreau's seventeen-line winter poem beginning "Pray to what earth" (76.5-21), which, together with some prose passages, comes between two extended Douglas extracts in the surviving DMS. Thoreau's note in CD suggests that additional "verses" were dropped here at 63.13. The winter poem added in PE at this point as the most likely realization of Thoreau's purpose is from MS (ICarbS), a fragmentary leaf paginated "177" and of a different paper type than DMS. On the reverse is a draft of prose material at 62.23-36, "[subsis]tent valor ... Florence and Rome." An earlier and longer version of the same poem (eighty-four lines in twenty stanzas) and a draft of the immediately preceding "Winter Walk" prose paragraph (63.4-12) appear as continuous text in a Journal entry for October 13 [?]-14, 1842 (*Journal 1*, pp. 440-442). PE follows Thoreau's pencilled alterations and apparent revised ordering of stanzas in the MS (ICarbS) fragment; Thoreau altered "We" (63.18) in pencil from "I" to agree in person and number with "we" in the preceding prose paragraph (63.5, 10). The eight-stanza poem on the ICarbS fragment occupies sixteen lines in double columns, with extra space after each four-line stanza. From top to bottom in the left column are the stanzas beginning "The Rabit leaps", "The ferret weeps", "The apples thaw", and "To their retreat". The right column has the stanzas beginning "The willows droop", "The catkins green", "The snow dust falls", and "The traveller dreams". Pencilled

lines to the left of each column group the first two and last
two pairs of stanzas into units. Outside the lowermost grouping line in the left column is a short, somewhat irregular pencilled mark which might be a "1"; a more distinct "1" is placed
against the lower grouping line in the right column. These
marks suggest that Thoreau intended the original stanzas 3
and 4 to be transposed with original stanzas 1 and 2, and intended the original stanzas 7 and 8 to be transposed with
original stanzas 5 and 6. This order is adopted in PE. Arguably, on the lost leaf of DMS the poem, again inscribed in
double columns, would have taken up nineteen lines, beginning about line 7 of p. "19" and ending at the bottom of that
page or near the top of p. "20". It must be noted that neither
"Pray to what earth" nor the poem supplied here deals with
smoke; Emerson's report to Thoreau about omissions was
both incomplete and inaccurate. The ICarbS fragment or another manuscript of the poem and the last few unpublished
pages of DMS (if not more of DMS) came through the hands
of F. B. Sanborn when Sanborn and Henry S. Salt edited
Thoreau, *Poems of Nature* (London: John Lane [-] The Bodley
Head; Boston: Houghton, Mifflin & Co., 1895). There, the
poem is titled "A Winter Scene" (pp. 90-92) and is footnoted,
"These stanzas formed part of the original manuscript of the
essay on 'A Winter Walk,' but were excluded by Emerson." In
terms of their original (ICarbS) manuscript order, Thoreau's
four-line units are arranged thus: 1-2-3-4-7-8-5-6. Sanborn
deploys them as four stanzas of eight lines each, and reverses
Thoreau's revision "we" to "I" after "To their retreat". For evidence of Sanborn's access to DMS, see his *The Personality of
Thoreau* (Boston: Charles E. Goodspeed, 1901), pp. 31-33, and
Textual Note 77.18. In *The First and Last Journeys of Thoreau*
(Boston: The Bibliophile Society, 1905), 1:141, 144-146, Sanborn
prints an eighty-two-line form of the eighty-four-line Journal
text (rearranging the material), in eleven stanzas, under the
title "A Winter and Spring Scene." This Sanborn says was
"used in part" in the manuscripts of "A Winter Walk," but
was omitted from D by the "scrupulous" editor, Emerson.
Houghton, Mifflin's Manuscript Edition (1906) of Thoreau's
Writings, vol. 5, *Excursions and Poems*, reprints from *Poems
of Nature* at pp. 410-411 "A Winter Scene" and Sanborn's footnote. Finally, in *The Life of Henry David Thoreau* (Boston:
Houghton Mifflin Company, 1917), pp. 261-264, Sanborn
prints as "verses excluded by Emerson from the 'Winter

Walk,'" and again under the title "A Winter and Spring Scene," the eighty-two-line poem of *The First and Last Journeys*, now in ten stanzas, with small changes in the accidentals and formatting, and one new corruption: "fair" for "air". See also Carl Bode, ed., *Collected Poems of Henry Thoreau*, enlarged edition (Baltimore: The Johns Hopkins Press, 1965), pp. 239-242, 263-265, and 337-338; Bode was evidently unfamiliar with the ICarbS manuscript.

64.25   phœbes: "phæbes" in D, uncorrected in CD; Ex follows D and Com emends D to "phebes". "phæbes" is probably a compositor's error; it is not authorized by Thoreau's usual practice, dictionaries, or ornithological handbooks.

DMS is the copy-text for 64.27-77.18 baked his pot ... rebound:"–

65.19-22   What ... sun.:   Although "ourselves" at the end of this passage in DMS is cancelled by Thoreau, and although the substitution of "his" for "its" is also apparently authorial, the cancellation of both sentences in their entirety is evidently Emerson's work. His "X" appears in the margin, and the passage was set off with square brackets before being lined through with several vertical strokes.

66.2   human ... life.:   The interlined pencilled "rural homestead" above this cancelled phrase, accompanied by a marginal pencilled "X", seems to be by Emerson. While the words afford none of the distinctive points of Emerson's or Thoreau's handwriting, the substitution makes the sentence redundant in order to excise the word "domestic", which Emerson found overused and paradoxical in Thoreau's essay. Other changes deemed to be Emerson's are also accompanied by the marginal "X".

66.10   wreaths: "wreathes" in DMS, but Thoreau clearly intends the noun rather than the verb form. See Textual Note 22.21 for another instance of this error.

67.4-8   whatever ... But now: The passage is heavily revised, apparently by Thoreau, and contains a major pencilled cancellation, probably by Thoreau since it is consistent with an ink revision in Thoreau's hand. See Alterations 67.4-5 through 67.7. The cancellation of "We should wither and dry up if it were not for lakes and rivers, and by the distant thought of them we are made limber and supple- / jointed. Our bodies derive their juices thence, as much as the herbage on their brinks." seems to have occurred after Thoreau signalled the transposition of "In summer . . . surface." to follow "again in the spring.", and changed "their surface" to "its surface" for the sake of consistent reference. Given the transposition, "their brinks" (the brinks of lakes and rivers) does not accord with "conceals it" (the woodland lake) in the following sentence. The cancellation of "We should . . . their brinks." is of a piece with the cancelling of the circle Thoreau drew around "In summer . . . surface.": the result is that the sentence containing "conceals it" again follows immediately after "its surface."

67.12 beech: The copy-text reads "beach", a spelling not accepted for the tree in Thoreau's dictionaries, and first corrected to "beech" in Ex. While conceivably he intended a play on words in this context, it is more likely that Thoreau misspelled the tree name.

67.20-21 midst . . . scene: The interlined "interior of a larger house" again appears to be by Emerson, and is accompanied by a pencilled "X" in the margin. The alteration eliminates "domestic" at the cost of weakening, by repetition, Thoreau's "a larger culinary preparation" two sentences below. In the interlined phrase, the "g" of "larger" and the "s" of "house" vary from Thoreau's letter formations and resemble those of Emerson.

67.29-30 seem not . . . scenery and: Thoreau originally wrote "seem not once unworthy of the scenery and"; he cancelled "once unworthy of" and interlined "separate", apparently intending to revise to "seem not separate from the scenery". This revision proved abortive, however, for Thoreau cancelled the interlineation in pencil and entered, below the line, "unworthy of" in pencil and ink. At some point he heavily cancelled "and" (it may originally have been "but" altered to "and" by overwriting), but then restored "and" by repeating it above the cancelled word.

67.35-68.1 It is . . . thrilling as: The marginal pencilled "X" and the ink and pencilled revision to "To me it has a strange sound of home," are evidently by Emerson, showing characteristics of his hand, although the clarifications of "thrilling as" are Thoreau's. The D compositors read the latter portion as "strange sound of home, thrilling"–neglecting to follow Thoreau's "and", which Emerson had left intact.

68.5 God . . . well.: The sentence is cancelled in pencil, with pencilled parentheses around it that are somewhat squared off, like those at "a protestant warmth," at 58.15.

No marginal "X" or marginal bracket permits the confident identification of this change as Emerson's, but the editor judges it to be his because the sentiment omitted so much resembles that of other passages Emerson cancelled.

69.10   faggot: Spelled thus in the copy-text. Thoreau's dictionaries give only "fagot," but the *OED* recognizes "faggot" equally, giving instances from throughout the nineteenth century.

69.20-22   The river ... towns, and ... The fields: Thoreau originally wrote, "We see the fields and forests from a new side and wilder side, for the river flows in the rear of the towns, and the fields". He cancelled the first occurrence of "side", probably in the initial course of composition. Later he marked the two clauses for transposition with circlings in pencil and ink, the numerals "2" and "1" in ink over pencil in the margin, and a marginal pencilled instruction, "tr". The first word of the original sentence, "We", is heavily cancelled in ink over pencil, and "we" interlined in ink over pencil; "for" is cancelled in pencil; and "the" before "river" is changed to "The" in ink over pencil. Either before or after the transposition other changes were made, probably by Thoreau: the cancellation of "fields and forests" in pencil and the interlining in ink over pencil of "nature", which was then cancelled and replaced with "all things" in ink.

69.23-24   a   sort ...   front upon: Pencilled brackets around "sort of unpretension and" suggest that the pencilled cancellation of this phrase and other changes in the sentence are Emerson's. After "frankness," he interlined in pencil with a caret, "& freedom from pretension which they do not wear" and cancelled, in pencil, "as they do not front". The interlined words show some of the tendencies of Emerson's handwriting, though the features are not definitive.

70.4   plane: The copy-text reads "plain", an apparently deliberate spelling in the context of Thoreau's original witticism, "descending into the plain, or by one gentle inclined plain, to the sea." The cancellation of the first four words (see Alteration 70.3) made "inclined plain" less pointedly a pun, but the original spelling was respected in D. In CD, however, Thoreau cancelled the last two letters of "plain", entering "ne" in the margin. The original of this sentence, in a Journal entry for April 19, 1843 (*Journal 1*, p. 455), has "gently inclined plane".

72.15   towns. Go: "towns." was originally followed by the following sentences, later cancelled in at least two stages: "He is, as it were, earth-born, (γηγενης) like the Titans, a brother of the sun and moon. His breath is a kind of zephyr, his step like a quadruped, and his mood the season. His clumsy motions have a sort of grace about them, for he moves not as somewhat finding a place, but for which a place is already found, as if through vallies, as the brook flows at the bottom of the meadow. His uncouth words are of the very substance of the air, and perchance fall naturally on the ear, like the rustling of leaves or the crackling of fire. The heavens seem more above him than ourselves, for he never stood from under them, and from his mole-like, lack-lustre eyes, he looks at the stars with an answering ray[.] All nice moral distinctions are trivial and out of place in his presence, yet go". In a sequence that cannot be exactly determined, Thoreau introduced pencilled parentheses before "He" and after "season." and around "perchance", a pencilled open parenthesis before "His clumsy", and an ink over pencil close parenthesis after "yet". He cancelled "He . . . like" with wavy ink lines, cancelled "stars" and interlined "sun" (in ink), cancelled "yet" in ink, cancelled the entire passage ("He" through "yet") with a series of vertical ink lines, and reformed "go" to "Go".

72.25   gathered: The word "again" interlined with a caret after "gathered" shows Emerson's "g".

72.27-30   The nearest . . . feathers.:   See Textual Note 73.15.

73.15   art.:   In CD Thoreau here noted "V no 6 p 34"; on the front fly-leaf of Journal MS Volume 6 Thoreau wrote in pencil "V p 34 falling snow". Thoreau thus identifies, in a Journal entry for December 30, 1841 (*Journal 1*, p. 352), a version of a passage on the appearance of driving snow cancelled in DMS, perhaps by Emerson (see Alteration 72.27-30). Although the DMS cancellation might be authorial, Thoreau evidently wished to restore the passage as he reviewed the D printing; DMS was not available to him. Instead of following the DMS cancellation at 72.27-30 and interpolating the Journal version here at 73.15, PE restores the text and original placement of the copy-text version. Ex, which in following D had omitted 72.27-30, ignores as well the CD marginal notation.

73.23-74.24   Douglas' . . . strive."– *and* 74.38 [5]briars . . . [8]tamed: (This Textual Note also discusses features of 76.22-77.19, "But to return . . . [3]went.") The cancellation, by means of a single pencilled line in DMS, where all the glosses follow the first eighteen lines of the poem without separation, resembles none of the earlier authorial cancellations but duplicates Emerson's in the final pages. At the end of the cancelled passage is a pencilled square bracket. Writing to Thoreau on September 8, 1843, Emerson declared that Ellery Channing had stipulated for "the omission of Douglas" from the essay (*Correspondence*, p. 138). Thoreau's source for these lines by Gawin Douglas and for the lexical glosses is *Chronicle of Scottish Poetry* (Edinburgh: Printed for J. Sibbald, 1802). He borrowed all four volumes of James Sibbald's historical collection from the Harvard College Library in December 1841 and meticulously copied several pages of Douglas into a commonplace book. This notebook is published in facsimile as *Thoreau's Literary Notebook* (see Headnote); for the lines from "A Description of Wynter" later used in "A Winter Walk," see pp. 95-96. In Sibbald's edition those same lines appear at 1:430-431. As he copied, Thoreau underlined several Scots terms and provided marginal definitions from the glossary in volume four. The notebook verses and glosses, perhaps originally intended for Thoreau's English poetry project, were recopied to DMS. With infrequent exceptions, the DMS transcript replicates the shared Sibbald-notebook readings, and those discrepancies are chiefly accidentals not affecting the sense: the source has colons after "sike", "hout", and "law", a comma before "syne", and a period after "glyde"; and it gives the spellings "perellus", "tak", and "regioun". In these instances the DMS pointings and spellings do not interfere with the sense of the text; they are left unemended in the present edition. Four other miscopyings in DMS are, however, deemed to have substantive effect and are here emended: at 73.31 a comma is supplied after "Woddis" and a period deleted after "blout"; at 74.6 "Quhirlit" is changed to "Quhislit"; and at 76.23 "Repartirrit" is changed to "Repatirrit". In each case the emended reading restores the printed source and the earlier transcript. See the Textual Introduction, pp. 375-378, for emendation policy respecting Thoreau's quotations and paraphrases from printed sources.

75.4 sound of the flail: Thoreau may have thought to add a Journal passage to CD at this point; he pencilled a note in the left margin and above the first paragraph of his Journal entry for November 13, 1837 (see *Journal 1*, p. 11): "V threshing flail in winter walk. It is a sure evidence of the health & innocence of the beholder if the senses are alive to the beauty of nature". However, there is no "vide" note in CD calling for the addition of Journal matter.

75.18 winter: The mark following this word in DMS may be an apostrophe, indicating unfinished "winter's", but may be a stray mark instead. Thoreau's use of adjectival "winter/ winter's" is inconsistent elsewhere in the essay (see Textual Note 55.1).

75.19-20 But even ... man.: Not marked for deletion, but absent from the D printing. Emerson likely cancelled it in proof for its iconoclasm.

76.4 pole.": The pencilled "H.D.T." following this line should almost surely be assigned to Emerson.

76.5-27 Pray ... we lend: Not marked for cancellation, but absent from the D printing. The original poem may be the "copy of verses on the Smoke" for whose omission Emerson told Thoreau Ellery Channing had "stipulated" (*Correspondence*, p. 138); see also Textual Note 63.12-64.8. For the omission of lines by Douglas (from his translation of the *Æneid*), see Textual Note 73.23-74.24. Emerson's deletion of a transitional prose passage by Thoreau, "From our comfortable pillows ... gate of a city." (76.27-77.2) was not reported to the author.

76.27-77.19 our warm ... ³went.: Cancelled with a single vertical line, and absent from the D printing. For textual problems in the lines from Gawin Douglas, see Textual Note 73.23-74.24.

77.18 rebound:"–: Followed by a semi-modernized transcript, in Emerson's hand, of the Douglas text at 76.23-26 and 77.3-18 plus the three pertinent glosses (76.36 and 77.19). The words "Emerson's autograph" appear in the handwriting of F. B. Sanborn in the left margin of this final page; and the verso, otherwise blank, bears the pencilled legend "The Winter's Walk / H. D. T.   June 1843" in Emerson's hand.

Table of Emendations

FOR the format of this table, see the Textual Introduction, p. 382. Sources for the emendations are the *Dial* as printed (D), Thoreau's corrected *Dial* text

(CD), the *Commonwealth* printing (Com), the 1863 edition of *Excursions* (Ex), or the editor's own authority, designated "PE" for the Princeton Edition, when the emendation is not anticipated in one of the earlier versions. Because copy-text alternates between the surviving pages of Thoreau's fair copy (DMS) and CD where setting-copy pages are lost, the copy-text is identified by abbreviation following the original reading in each emendation entry.

CD is the copy-text for 55.1-56.23 A Winter Walk . . . where it

*55.1	A Winter Walk.] PE; A WINTER WALK. / [1843] CD
*55.22	At length we awake] PE; at length awake CD
*56.17	night is crowded] D Com Ex; night crowded CD
*56.19-21	along . . . clear] D Com Ex; *preceded by question mark in margin* CD

DMS is the copy-text for 56.23-59.2 has lain . . . be called in

*56.24	stubble; while far] Ex; stubble. Far DMS
57.22-23	cock. Though the] Ex; cock. Though The CD; cock. The DMS
57.26-27	bottom, they] PE; bottom. They DMS
57.28	horizon, as] D CD Com Ex; horizon,, as DMS *(see Alteration 57.27-28)*
57.29-30	ragged. The] D CD Com Ex; ragged, the DMS *(see Alterations 57.29 and 57.30 The)*
*57.30	and even] D CD Com Ex; & even DMS
*58.1	it, as they] PE; it. Those DMS *(see Alteration 58.1)*
58.12	steps] D CD Com Ex; *possibly* step DMS *(see Alteration 58.12)*
58.13-14	Meanwhile we] Ex; Meanwhi We CD *(alteration runs off margin)*; We DMS
59.8	leafless] Com Ex; leafeless CD

CD is the copy-text for 59.2-62.1 for shelter . . . cottages of the

*59.11-61.3   There is . . . about him.]   PE
*59.36   traveller]   Com   Ex; traveler   CD
 60.8   town, we]   Ex;   town, We   CD
 60.10-13   snow. Our . . . echoes. They]   PE;   snow. v
                 no 3 p 102   They   CD *(see Textual Note 59.11-
                 61.3)*
 60.11-12   chamber and]   PE;   chamber &   MS
                 Journal *(see Textual Note 59.11-61.3)*
 60.32   taller grass?]   PE;   taller grass?–v no. 3 p
                 90   V no 6 p 15   CD *(see Textual Note 59.11-
                 61.3)*

*DMS is the copy-text for 62.1-63.7 caddis worms, . . . the trees,
and*

*62.1   caddis]   PE;   caddice   DMS
 63.1   side,]   D   CD   Com   Ex;   side,,   DMS
                 (see Alteration 63.1)

CD is the copy-text for 63.7-64.27 the nut-hatch . . . where he

 63.13-64.8   The apples . . . glow.]   PE;   v. verses   CD
                 (see Textual Note 63.12-64.8)
 63.20   apple's]   PE;   apples   MS; *lacking*   CD
 63.24   wood.]   PE;   wood   MS; *lacking*   CD
 63.29   Rabbit]   PE;   Rabit   MS; *lacking*   CD
*64.25   phœbes]   PE;   phæbes   CD

*DMS is the copy-text for 64.27-77.18 baked his pot . . .
rebound:"–*

 65.10-11   wood-chopper and of]   D   CD   Com   Ex;
                 wood-chopper and and of   DMS
 65.22   sun.]   PE;   sun   DMS
 65.26   a long]   D   CD   Com   Ex;   along   DMS
 65.27   profanity]   D   CD   Com   Ex;   prophanity
                 DMS *(however, see Textual Note 94.11)*
*66.10   wreaths]   PE;   wreathes   DMS
 66.12   important]   D   CD   Com   Ex;   *last letters
                 off edge of page*   DMS
 66.18   brink of this]   D   CD   Com   Ex;   brink
                 this   DMS
 66.24   pines]   D   CD   Com   Ex;   *possibly* pine
                 DMS
 67.5   herein,]   D   CD   Com   Ex;   herein   DMS
                 (see Alteration 67.4-5)

*67.12	beech] Ex; beach DMS
68.6	assurance] D CD Com Ex; assuranance DMS
69.22	side.] D CD Com Ex; side, DMS
*70.4	plane] CD Ex; plain DMS
70.27	swamp's] D CD Com Ex; swamps DMS
71.18	winter, or] D CD Com Ex; winter,, or DMS
71.21	surface.] D CD Com Ex; surface DMS
71.27	swollen] D CD Com Ex; swolen DMS
72.6	sprightliness] D CD Com Ex; sprightiness DMS
*73.15	art.] PE; art. V no 6 p 34 CD
73.26	Bedowin[1]] PE; Bedowin *with* 1 *added above* e DMS
73.26	donkis[2]] PE; donkis *with* 2 *added above* n DMS
73.26	sike;[3]] PE; sike; *with* 3 *added above* s DMS
73.31	Woddis, forestis] PE; Woddis forestis DMS *(see Textual Note 73.23-74.24)*
73.31	blout] PE; blout. DMS *(see Textual Note 73.23-74.24)*
73.34	derne[4]] PE; derne *with* 4 *added above* r DMS
73.34	doun] PE; *possibly* down DMS
74.1	ronnys[5]] PE; ronnys *with* 5 *added above first* n DMS
74.3	hidlis[6] and hirnys[7]] PE; hidlis and hirnys *with* 6 *added above first* i *in* hidlis *and* 7 *added above* n *in* hirnys DMS
74.6	Quhislit] PE; Quhirlit DMS *(see Textual Note 73.23-74.24)*
74.11	dantit[8]] PE; dantit *with* 8 *added above* a DMS
74.28	warm-blooded] D CD Com Ex; warm-bloodded DMS
74.30	traveller.] D CD Com Ex; traveller, DMS
74.30	traveller. It does] D CD Com Ex; traveller, does DMS

*75.18	winter] D CD Com Ex; winter' DMS
76.1	ethereal] D CD Ex; etherial DMS
76.23	Repatirrit[1]] PE; Repartirrit *with* 1 *added above* R DMS *(see Textual Note 73.23-74.24)*
76.23	bekit,[2]] PE; bekit, *with* 2 *added above* b DMS
76.34	us. Or] PE; us., Or DMS
77.3	bownit[3]] PE; bownit *with* 3 *added above* w DMS
77.16	Attour] PE; *possibly* Altour DMS
77.18	the horisont] PE; The horisont DMS

Table of Alterations

For the format of this table, see the Textual Introduction, p. 383. For the differentiation of Thoreau's compositional alterations on the setting copy from Emerson's editorial markings and revisions, see the Headnote. Surviving and lost setting-copy manuscript pages are correlated with the Princeton Edition text using page and line numbers and keywords. Another table gives the autograph changes in Thoreau's copy of the *Dial*.

Four MS pages missing, 55.1-56.23 A Winter Walk . . . where it

Two MS leaves, pages "5"-"6", "7"-"8", at MH-H, 56.23-59.2 has lain . . . be called in

57.3	the new day] new *interlined in pencil with caret;* day *followed by interlined pencilled* time *cancelled in pencil*
57.27-28	bell-like and from a greater distance in the horizon, as] and . . . horizon, *interlined in ink over pencil, with caret positioned between* bell-like *and comma (see Emendation 57.28)*
57.29	ragged] *followed by comma and* for then nature is never silent nor rarified, but now the farthest and faintest sounds take possession of the vacuum, and *set off by pencilled parentheses and cancelled in pencil*

57.30   The] *altered in pencil from* the

57.30   sonorous] *preceded by* tense *and set off by ink over pencilled parentheses and cancelled in ink*

57.30   wood, and even] *comma changed in ink from period;* & *added and* Even *changed to* even *in ink over pencil (see Emendation 57.30 and Textual Note 57.30)*

57.32-33   There . . . possible] *followed by* ¶ There is the least possible *cancelled in ink*

57.38   polished] *preceded by* pure *and set off by parentheses and cancelled in ink over pencil*

*58.1   it, as they] it, as those *altered to* it. Those *in ink over pencil (see Emendation *58.1)*

58.9   The sun] *preceded by* We step hastily *cancelled in ink*

58.9   woods] *interlined in ink with ink caret*

58.12   steps] *interlined in ink with ink caret*

58.12   that] *interlined in ink with ink caret*

58.15   a protestant warmth,] *set off in pencilled square brackets and cancelled in pencil, with pencilled* ? *and* X *in margin, apparently by Emerson*

58.15-16   enjoying] *preceded by* and *cancelled in ink over pencil;* ing *added to* enjoy *in ink over pencil*

58.30-32   In the coldest . . . a foothold.] *preceded in margin by pencilled* X *(apparently Emerson's)*

59.1   things] *interlined in ink over pencil above* God's creatures *cancelled in ink over pencil*

Eight MS pages missing, 59.2-62.1 for shelter . . . cottages of the

One MS leaf, pages "17"-"18", at DeU, 62.1-63.7 caddis worms, . . . the trees, and

62.2   Plicipennes.] *period altered in ink from semicolon*

62.2   Their] *altered in ink from* their

62.5   the bottom] *originally* the bottoms *with last letter cancelled in pencil*

62.5   the bottom] *followed by* of the brooks, *set off by pencilled parentheses and cancelled in ink*

62.6	drifting] *preceded by* floating *cancelled in ink*
*62.15-18	We have come . . . shrubs] *heavily revised and cancelled in pencil and ink by Thoreau and Emerson*
62.18	burden] *preceded by* snow *cancelled in ink*
62.23-24	pure . . . never] *marked with pencilled bracket in margin, apparently by Emerson*
62.24	witnessed;] *possibly altered in ink from* witnessed,
62.33	more] *preceded by* a *cancelled in pencil*
62.33	companions] *interlined in ink over pencil above* intercourse *cancelled in ink over pencil*
*62.35-36	which shame. . . Rome,] *set off in pencilled square brackets and cancelled, probably by Emerson*
63.1	side,] *followed by* and the alder and the birch with its yellow leaves *set off in pencilled parentheses and cancelled in ink*
63.2	oats] *followed by* stand *cancelled in ink over pencil*
*63.6-7	the icicles . . . trees, and] *marked with pencilled* X *in margin, probably by Emerson;* and *preceded by pencilled bracket*

Two MS pages missing, 63.7-64.27 the nut-hatch . . . where he

Two MS leaves, pages "21"-"22", "23"-"24", at DeU, 64.27-66.32 baked his pot . . . direct the traveller

64.33	only;] *altered in pencil from* only,
65.3	See] *preceded by pencilled* James James *(compositor's stint mark)*
65.7	round it] *followed by comma in ink over pencil, finally cancelled in ink*
65.10	wood-chopper] *altered in ink and erasure from* world-chopper
65.11	world] *followed by comma cancelled in ink and* if we would but read it. *set off by pencilled parentheses and cancelled in ink over pencil; period added after* world *in ink over pencil*
65.13	a log] a *interlined in ink over pencil above* this *cancelled in ink over pencil*
65.14	tattle] tl *reformed; original word perhaps* tales

65.15 High-streets, and Broad-ways] *altered in ink from* high-streets, and broad-ways

*65.19-22 What . . . sun.] *set off in pencilled square brackets and cancelled in pencil, with pencilled* X *in margin, apparently by Emerson*

65.20 his] *interlined in pencil and ink above* its *cancelled in pencil and ink*

65.22 sun] *followed by* ourselves. *set off in pencilled parentheses and cancelled in ink*

65.28 cheerfully] *followed by* ech *cancelled in ink*

65.29 the axe] the *reformed in ink from another word, possibly* an

65.32 Now] *indented; preceded by ink paragraph sign in margin*

*66.2 human . . . life.] *cancelled in pencil and* rural homestead *interlined in pencil, marked with pencilled* X *in margin, probably by Emerson*

66.4 the vapor from] *cancelled in ink; cancellation then reversed by erasure (scraping) of cancel line*

66.4 spring] *followed by* by the vapor rising *cancelled in ink*

66.12 important] *preceded by* domestic *cancelled in ink*

66.14 ensign,] *comma possibly added; followed by* is *cancelled in ink*

66.18 And now] *interlined in ink above* Again *cancelled in ink*

66.18 again] *interlined in ink with caret*

66.18 the brink] *interlined in ink with caret*

66.28 In summer it is] *added in ink over pencil before* ¶ In summer it is *cancelled in ink over pencil*

One MS leaf, pages "25"-"26", at MH-H, 66.32-68.1 to its . . . strange

67.4-5 whatever . . . herein] *interlined in ink above* all *cancelled in ink; the* filfth of the wood, and *cancelled in pencil; the* accumulated impurities of the winter, have been rinsed herein, *cancelled in ink*

67.6   in the spring.]   *followed by* We should wither
                and dry up if it were not for lakes and rivers,
                and by the distant thought of them we are
                made limber and supple-jointed. Our bodies
                derive their juices thence, as much as the
                herbage on their brinks. *preceded by ink over
                pencilled caret and pencilled paragraph sign
                and cancelled in pencil (see Textual Note
                67.4-8)*

67.6-7   In summer . . . surface.]   *circled in ink over
                pencil and led to ink over pencilled caret after*
                spring. *with pencilled* tr *in margin. Circling
                later cancelled in pencil (see Textual Note
                67.4-8)*

67.7   its]   *interlined in ink over pencil above* their
                cancelled in pencil (see Textual Note 67.4-8)

67.7   surface. But]   *altered in ink over pencil from*
                surface, but

67.13   rocking still,]   *comma added in pencil*

*67.20-21   midst . . . scene]   *cancelled in ink, with*
                interior of a larger house *interlined in ink
                above, apparently by Emerson, with pencilled*
                X *in margin*

*67.29-30   seem not . . . scenery and]   *originally* seem
                not once unworthy of the scenery and *then*
                once unworthy of *cancelled in ink;* separate
                interlined in ink and cancelled in pencil;
                unworthy of *repeated in ink over pencil;*
                and *cancelled in ink and interlined in ink
                above*

67.33   its]   *added in ink after* their *cancelled in ink*

67.35   oceans]   *altered from* ocean's *by ink
                cancellation*

67.35-68.1   It is a strange]   *cancelled in pencil*

One MS leaf, pages "27"-"28", at VtMiM, 68.1-69.12 domestic
. . . forest path.

68.1   domestic . . . voice]   *marked with a marginal*
                X *in pencil;* domestic *cancelled in ink;* To me
                it has a strange *interlined in ink with ink caret
                before* sound *and* of home *interlined in ink
                with ink caret after* sound *and pencilled
                comma added after* home *(all changes*

apparently by Emerson; see Textual Note
67.35-68.1)

68.1   thrilling] *altered in ink from another word,
                possibly* thringing *apparently by Thoreau;
                then cancelled in ink and* thrilling *interlined
                in ink above*

68.1   as] *first letter reformed*

*68.5   God . . . well.] *set off in pencilled parentheses
                and cancelled in pencil, possibly by Emerson*

68.8   soft sough] *preceded by* creaking of the
                cancelled in ink

68.17   Summer] *altered in ink from* summer

68.23   Summer's] *altered in ink from* summer's

68.29   Bringing] *altered in pencil from* Brining

68.29-69.12   Bringing . . . forest path.] *in left margin:*
                Autograph pages of Henry D. Thoreau. Attest
                R. W. Emerson. *(wavy line)*

*Six MS leaves, pages "29"-"30", "31"-"32", "33"-"34", "35"-"36",
"37"-"38", "39"-"40", at DeU, 69.13-76.2 Before night . . . to the
view,*

69.13   Before night] *interlined in ink over pencil
                above* Ere evening *cancelled in ink over pencil*

69.20-22   The river . . . fields] *Textual Note 69.20-22
                gives details of alterations*

69.22   The fields] *altered in pencil from* the fields

*69.23-24   a sort . . . front upon] *altered, evidently by
                Emerson*

69.25   earth.] *followed by* You see the natural side
                of the village, and *cancelled in ink over
                pencil*

69.25   Our eyes are] *altered in ink over pencil from*
                your eye is

69.28   we] *interlined in ink over pencil above* you
                cancelled in ink over pencil

70.2   its] *cancelled ink mark interlined above*

70.3   conducts him] *followed by* like a skilful
                leach, *set off with pencilled parentheses and
                cancelled in ink*

70.3   steps] *followed by* descending into the plain
                *set off with pencilled parentheses and
                cancelled in ink*

71.17   that] *third and fourth letters reformed*

71.18	winter,] *followed by* and wholly cease to flow, *set off with pencilled parentheses and cancelled in ink*
71.18	else] *followed by* be *cancelled in ink*
71.20	their] *altered in ink from* the
71.21	surface] *followed by* of the streams *cancelled in ink*
71.30	round,] *comma added in ink over pencil*
72.15	towns.] *Textual Note 72.15 gives details of alterations*
72.15	Go] *altered from* go *in ink over pencil*
*72.25	gathered] *followed by pencilled caret and interlined pencilled again in Emerson's hand*
72.27-30	The nearest . . . feathers.] *set off with ink over pencilled parentheses and cancelled in ink (see Textual Note 73.15)*
72.32	Quadrupeds] *first letter altered in ink from lower case; preceded by* The *set off by pencilled parentheses and cancelled in ink*
73.7	incessant] *preceded by pencilled lines, with pencilled* 225 *in margin (compositor's mark; Dial p. 225 begins here)*
73.15	her] *interlined in ink over pencil above* nature *cancelled in pencil*
73.15	art.] *followed by pencilled lines, probably compositor's mark*
73.16	The surly] *preceded by pencilled* Set *and line (compositor's marks)*
73.23-74.24	Douglas' . . . strive."–] *cancelled with vertical pencilled line, probably by Emerson (see Textual Note 73.23-74.24)*
73.24	for] *added in ink in margin before* of *cancelled in ink over pencil*
74.15	be] *preceded by* by *cancelled in ink*
74.27	rather] *preceded by* would *set off in ink parentheses and cancelled in ink*
74.27	him as] him *preceded by* t *cancelled in ink*
74.27	a merry] *preceded by* an old ma *cancelled in ink*
74.29	Summer] *altered in ink from* summer
74.30	traveller] *followed by* for it is not trivial, and *set off by pencilled parentheses and cancelled in pencil*

74.30   It] *interlined in pencil, probably by Emerson*
               to complete Thoreau's revision (see previous
               Alteration)

74.30   us] *altered in pencil to* him *with alteration*
               reversed by erasure

74.31   but has] *interlined in pencil with pencilled*
               caret covering preceding period; followed by It
               is *cancelled in pencil*

74.36   the house] *preceded by vertical pencilled*
               line, probably compositor's mark (new
               printed line begins here)

74.37   are] *interlined in ink above* must be
               cancelled in ink

74.38   [5]briars . . . [8]tamed] *cancelled with vertical*
               pencilled line, probably by Emerson (see
               Textual Note 73.23-74.24)

75.4   the flail] *altered in ink from* threshing *by*
               reformation of third letter, cancellation of
               eshing *and interlining of* flail *(see Textual*
               Note 75.4)

75.13-14   The good] *interlined in pencil above* How
               can we accept that *cancelled in pencil*

75.14   revelation] *followed by* as sufficient, which
               cancelled in pencil

75.15   snow.] *altered in pencil from* snow?

One MS leaf, pages "41"-"42", at NNPM, 76.3-77.14 Shines out
intensely keen; . . . elrische skreik. and 77.19 [3]went.

*76.4   pole."] *followed by* H. D. T. *in pencil*
               beneath the line, probably by Emerson

76.16   the flower] the *interlined in ink above* some
               cancelled in ink

76.22   Douglas.] *period altered in ink from comma*

76.27-77.18   our warm . . . rebound:"-] *cancelled with*
               vertical ink lines, probably Emerson's

76.32   and traverse] and *interlined in ink over*
               pencil above We *cancelled in ink over pencil*

76.32-33   and traverse . . . glaciers] *originally placed*
               after about us. *but marked for transposition*
               in ink over pencil with caret and circling in
               ink over pencil

76.34   Or] *altered in ink over pencil from* or

76.34   we] *added in margin in ink over pencil*

One MS leaf, page "43", at MCR-S, 77.15-18 The wyld . . . rebound:"–

*77.18	rebound:"–] *followed below by partly modernized text in Emerson's hand of 76.23-26 and 77.3-18 and three glosses as footnotes (76.36 and 77.19); on verso in Emerson's hand in pencil:* The Winter's Walk / H. D. T. June 1843

Autograph Corrections and Revisions in Thoreau's Copy of the *Dial*

ALL of the following corrections and revisions were made in pencil. They are listed in the order of their appearance in the printed *Dial* "Winter Walk" text, not their order in the text of the Princeton Edition, the present volume (PE). Their location by page and line in the *Dial* is given in the leftmost column; the PE page and line numbers of the equivalent PE text appear in the next column. A virgule indicates the end of a line. Keywords for the alteration listing, before the close bracket and record of the autograph change, come from the *Dial* text as printed and often do not match exactly the PE version. It should be remembered that the *Dial* printing was the only text available to Thoreau–he did not have access to the original setting-copy manuscript–and that the *Dial* printing differed frequently from the setting copy; Thoreau often only approximated the restoration of his original readings when he entered his corrections and revisions. "No DMS" and "DMS" indicate by block of text the loss or survival of setting-copy manuscript pages; where the manuscript survives, the editor has compared the altered readings in Thoreau's *Dial* with the original readings.

Dial   PE

No DMS for 55.1-56.23 A Winter Walk . . . where it

211.1	55.1	A Winter Walk.] *followed by* [1843] *beneath (perhaps not Thoreau's)*
211.11	55.13	door, has] *comma cancelled*
211.12	55.14	work.–The] *period and* T *cancelled and* t *written in margin*
211.17	55.19-20	flakes, descending] *comma cancelled*
211.19	55.22	We sleep and at length awake] *first 3 words cancelled (see Textual Note 55.22)*
212.9	56.17	night is crowded] *is cancelled (see Textual Note 56.17)*
212.12-13	56.19-21	along . . . clear] *question mark written in margin*

DMS for 56.23-59.2 has lain . . . be called in

212.16-17	56.24	stubble. For] *caret and* While *written in margin after* stubble. *(see Emendation 56.24 and Textual Note 56.24)*
212.17	56.24	For] o *cancelled and* a *written in margin (see Emendation 56.24 and Textual Note 56.24)*
213.7	57.22	cock. The] *caret after* cock. *and* Though *written in margin*
213.19	57.34-35	it is . . . that it] *faint horizontal line written in margin (see Textual Note 57.34-35)*
213.23	58.1	it. Those] As *interlined after* it. *and* ey *interlined above* Those *(see Textual Note 58.1)*
213.36	58.13	mountains.] *followed by caret and* Meanwhi *written in (trimmed) margin (see Emendation 58.13-14)*

No DMS for 59.2-62.1 for shelter . . . cottages of the

214.26	60.7	we have] X *written in margin and* we *cancelled and* ing *interlined above cancelled* e *of* have

Dial	PE	
214.26-215.5	60.7-32	At length . . . taller grass?] *marked with vertical line and 2 (for transposition) in margin (see Textual Note 59.11-61.3)*
214.27	60.8	town. We] *period changed to comma*
214.29	60.10	banked up with snow.] *followed by caret and interlined v no 3 p 102 (see Textual Note 59.11-61.3)*
215.5	60.31	lanes] ne *cancelled and* wn *written in gutter*
215.5	60.32	taller grass?] *followed by short horizontal line and* v no. 3 p 90 V no 6 p 15 *in margin (see Textual Note 59.11-61.3)*
215.6-36	59.11-60.6	There is a . . . and the lark.] *marked with vertical line and 1 (for transposition) in margin (see Textual Note 59.11-61.3)*
215.25	59.30	back] *followed by caret and* s *added in margin*
216.3	61.14	distinction] *followed by caret and* s *added in margin*
216.14	61.25	The grey-squirrel] T *cancelled and* T—*added to cancel paragraph break*

DMS for 62.1-63.7 caddis worms, . . . the trees, and

216.25	62.2	caves] v *cancelled and* s *written in margin*
216.33-34	62.11	floating on] *cancelled and* to *written in margin (see Textual Note 62.11-12)*
216.34	62.12	or perfect] or *cancelled and* as *written in margin (see Textual Note 62.11-12)*
216.34	62.12	insects,] *comma cancelled (see Textual Note 62.11-12)*
216.34-35	62.12	hence- / forth flutter] *comma added after* hence- / forth *and* /, *written in margin (see Textual Note 62.11-12)*

Dial	PE	
216.36	65.15-18	Down yonder . . . drooping under] *question mark written in margin (see Textual Note 62.15-18)*
217.10	62.32	the statesmen] the *cancelled*
217.17	63.4	As the day] 118 *written in margin (see Textual Note 63.4)*

No DMS for 63.7-64.27 the nut-hatch . . . where he

217.24	63.11	expands] *partially cancelled and* hales *interlined*
217.25	63.12	meats.] *followed by* v. verses *in blank part of line (see Textual Note 63.12-64.8)*
217.36	64.19	foaming] *second and third letters cancelled and* u *written in margin*

DMS for 64.27-77.18 baked his pot . . . rebound:"–

219.23	66.23-24	on the pines] o *cancelled and* i *written in margin*
220.1	67.9	except when] n *cancelled and* re *interlined*
222.25	70.4	plain] in *cancelled and* ne *written in margin (see Textual Note 70.4)*
222.28	70.7	dominion] *cancelled and* domain *written in margin*
223.2	70.24	on the swamp] o *cancelled and* i *written in margin*
225.1	73.7	top] *followed by caret and* s *written in margin*
225.6	73.12	deeper on] o *cancelled and* i *written in margin*
225.9	73.15	art.] *followed by* V no 6 p 34 *in blank part of line*
225.26	74.32	merry] *curved line leads from* m *to* che *written in margin*
225.40	75.12	cured] ured *cancelled and* ruel *written in margin*
226.10	75.24	adequately of] of *cancelled and* to *written in margin*
226.24	76.4	H. D. T.] *followed by deletion symbol (perhaps not Thoreau's)*

Rejected Substantives

For the format of this table, see the Textual Introduction, p. 384. The table records variant substantives in Thoreau's corrected copy of the *Dial* (CD) where the setting-copy manuscript (DMS) survives, and also in *Dial* as printed (D), the *Commonwealth* reprint (Com), and the 1863 edition of *Excursions* (Ex).

CD is the copy-text for 55.1-56.23 A Winter Walk . . . where it

*55.1	A Winter Walk.] A WINTER WALK. / [1843] CD Ex; Miscellaneous. / {*rule*} / A WINTER WALK. / BY HENRY D. THOREAU. Com
*55.22	At length we awake] We sleep and at length awake D Com Ex

DMS is the copy-text for 56.23-59.2 has lain . . . be called in

56.24	far] For D Com *(see Textual Note 56.24)*
*57.12	'T has been . . . new wind] It has gone down the glen with the light wind D CD Com Ex
57.22	Though] *lacking* D Com
58.1	as they who] Those who D Com *(see Textual Note 58.1)*
58.13-14	Meanwhile we step] We step D Com

CD is the copy-text for 59.2-62.1 for shelter . . . cottages of the

59.11-60.27	There is . . . by-place. ¶This . . . lark. ¶At length . . . taller grass?] At length . . . taller grass? ¶There is . . . by-place. ¶This . . . lark. D Com *(see Textual Note 59.11-61.3)*
59.23	swamps] swamp Com
59.30	backs] back D Com
60.2-3	in winter] in the winter Com
60.7	At length having] At length we have D Com
60.10-13	Our voices . . . echoes.] *lacking* D Com Ex *(see Textual Note 59.11-61.3)*
60.31	lawns] lanes D Com

60.32-61.3	Nothing is so . . . blanket about him.] *lacking* D Com Ex *(see Textual Note 59.11-61.3)*
61.14	distinctions] distinction D Com
61.32	Still, in the midst] *preceded by* Miscellaneous. /{*rule*} / A WINTER WALK. / PART II. /BY HENRY D. THOREAU Com

DMS is the copy-text for 62.1-63.7 caddis worms, . . . the trees, and

62.2	cases] caves D Com
62.11	or floating to] or floating on D Com; or to CD Ex *(see Textual Note 62.11-12)*
62.12	as perfect] or perfect D Com *(see Textual Note 62.11-12)*
* 62.15-18	We have come . . . shrubs] Down yonder little glen the shrubs D CD Com Ex
62.30	of richer] of a richer D CD Com Ex
62.31-32	than statesmen] than the statesmen D Com
62.35-36	hues, which . . . Rome, where] hues, where D CD Com Ex *(see Textual Note 62.35-36)*
* 62.36	pines] spruces D CD Com Ex

CD is the copy-text for 63.7-64.27 the nut-hatch . . . where he

63.11	exhales] expands D Com
63.13-64.8	The apples . . . glow.] *lacking* D Com Ex *(see Textual Note 63.12-64.8)*
64.14	Hecatompolis] Hectatompolis Com
64.19	fuming] foaming D Com

DMS is the copy-text for 64.27-77.18 baked his pot . . . rebound:"–

65.4	chopper's] choppers's Com
* 65.19-22	What . . . sun.] *lacking* D CD Com Ex
* 66.2	human . . . life] rural homestead D CD Com Ex
66.23	waves] wave Com
66.23-24	in the pines] on the pines D
67.9	except where] except when D Com
67.13	would soon start] would start Ex
* 67.20-21	midst . . . scene] interior of a larger house D CD Com Ex

68.1	domestic sound] sound of home D CD Com Ex
68.1	and thrilling] and *lacking* D CD Com Ex
*68.5	God . . . well.] *lacking* D CD Com Ex
68.9-69.12	When Winter . . . forest path.] *lacking* Com
68.20	the last] that last Ex
69.5	I crack me with] I gambol with D CD Ex
69.21	towns] town Com
69.23	a sort of unpretension and frankness] a frankness and freedom from pretension D CD Com Ex *(see Textual Note 69.23-24)*
69.23-24	as they do not front upon] which they do not wear on D CD Com Ex *(see Textual Note 69.23-24)*
*70.4	plane] plain D Com
70.7	domain] dominion D Com
70.11-12	in the long] in long Com
70.14	shoes] marshoes Com
70.24	in the swamp] on the swamp D Com
70.25	warblers now following] warblers following Ex
70.35	birds'] bird's D CD Com
72.25	gathered, and] gathered again, and D CD Com Ex *(see Textual Note 72.25)*
72.27-30	The nearest . . . feathers.] *lacking* D CD Com Ex *(see Textual Note 73.15)*
73.7	tops] top D Com
73.12	in the bosom] on the bosom D Com
73.23-74.24	Douglas' . . . strive."–] *lacking* D CD Com Ex *(see Textual Note 73.23-74.24)*
74.32	cheery] merry D Com *(see Autograph Corrections and Revisions in Thoreau's Copy of the* Dial *225.26 74.32)*
74.38	[5]briars . . . [8]tamed] *lacking* D CD Com Ex *(see Textual Note 73.23-74.24)*
75.5-6	a skilful physician] a physician Com
75.11	fates grow] fate grows D CD Com Ex
75.12	cruel] cured D Com
*75.19-20	But even . . . man.] *lacking* D CD Com Ex

75.23-24	scripture speaks] scriptures speak D CD Com Ex
75.24	adequately to] adequately of D Com
75.33	glistering] glittering D CD Com Ex
75.33-34	equanimity] unanimity Com
*76.4	pole."] pole."/H.D.T. D
76.5-77.19	Pray . . . ³went.] *lacking* D CD Com Ex *(see Textual Notes 76.5-27 and 76.27-77.19)*

A Yankee in Canada

Headnote

THE opportunity for Thoreau to visit "Canada East" or Quebec in late September and early October 1850 came in the form of a special, cut-rate, round-trip, combination railroad and steamboat fare between Boston and Quebec City. This excursion was one of a series arranged by the owner of a moving panorama depiction of the St. Lawrence and Saguenay rivers, then midway through a sensational Boston engagement. William Burr's "Moving Mirror of the Lakes, the Niagara, St. Lawrence and Saguenay Rivers," often advertised as "Burr's Seven Mile Mirror," was painted in 1848-1849 under Burr's supervision and unrolled to the accompaniment of a narration and music. It enjoyed a highly successful fifteen-week run in New York; next, it moved to Boston for an engagement lasting, with two interruptions, from February 4, 1850, to July 4, 1851. It opened in Amory Hall but soon moved to the larger Melodeon, and it was seen in Boston by up to a million people. The spectators possibly included Thoreau, who refers to it obliquely in "A Yankee in Canada" (154.18-20) and records having attended two other river panoramas in 1848-1849.[1]

Burr apparently was the American innovator of the cheap rail excursion, by which he encouraged groups from distant parts of Massachusetts, and from elsewhere in New England, to visit Boston for a day and

[1] For a full study of Burr's panorama, its relation to the American moving panorama craze of the late 1840s and early 1850s, and its influence on "A Yankee in Canada" and Nathaniel Hawthorne's *The House of the Seven Gables*, see Joseph J. Moldenhauer, "Thoreau, Hawthorne, and the 'Seven-Mile Panorama'," *ESQ: A Journal of the American Renaissance* 14 (4th Quarter 1998): 226-273.

attend the panorama. The first involved 700 travelers from Lynn, on May 22, 1850. Burr's agent for negotiating with the numerous regional railroad companies and arranging these group tours was Josiah Perham, who became the panorama's proprietor at the end of October 1850. Capitalizing on his experience with mass travel and the notoriety of his enormous painting, Burr promoted three early-autumn excursions from Boston to Montreal, with optional continuation to Quebec. The itinerary followed a rail link to Burlington, Vermont, completed the previous winter, the steamer route down Lake Champlain and the Richelieu River to St. Johns, Canada, and a stretch of Canadian rail from St. Johns to Laprairie on the St. Lawrence, opposite Montreal. Burr's round-trip fare to Montreal was only $5.00, with an overnight steamer trip to Quebec and return available for $2.00 more. The first of these tours, leaving Boston on September 25 with a flexible return schedule within ten days, attracted 1,346 subscribers, among them Thoreau and his walking companion and close friend, the poet Ellery Channing.[2]

The terms of the ticket allowed subscribers to use the regularly scheduled trains on the tracks of the Fitchburg Railroad, the Cheshire Railroad, and the Rutland and Burlington Railroad between Boston and Burlington, not only returning but also departing. This is the alternative Thoreau and Channing chose, leaving from Concord rather than incurring the added expense and inconvenience of going to Boston and boarding the special, nineteen-car excursion train that carried Mr. Burr and most of his tourists.[3] After an

[2] The second tour left Boston on October 9, and the third on October 15.

[3] Thoreau's aversion to his fellow-Yankee tourists on those parts of the trip where their propinquity was unavoidable, as

unscheduled overnight layover in Burlington, and another delay of nearly three hours in St. Johns, the companions arrived in Montreal early in the afternoon of
September 26, visiting the city only until dusk, when
the steamer *John Munn* cast off moorings for Quebec.
On the 27th they explored the Upper Town of Quebec
and its fortifications, touring the Citadel twice, and
walked on the Plains of Abraham. In mid-afternoon
they set out on foot across the Dorchester Bridge on
their way downriver.[4]

With some difficulty, because there were no inns
and the travelers could not understand the Quebecois
pronunciation of French, Thoreau and Channing
found lodging for the night with the family of Jean
Baptiste Binet in Beauport village, eight miles from the
city. On September 28 they viewed the nearby cataract
of Montmorenci from above and below and resumed
their muddy walk toward Ste. Anne. After a stop in
Chateau Richer, they secured a bed for the night with
another *habitan* family. On Sunday, September 29,
they visited the parish church of Ste. Anne de Beaupré
(since replaced by a huge basilica) and observed with
Protestant skepticism the display of crutches and
other tokens of miraculous healings attributed to the
holy mother of the Virgin Mary. A forest hike brought
them to their principal destination, the great falls of
the River Ste. Anne du Nord. Exploring the cascade
until early afternoon, they retraced their steps up the
St. Lawrence, detouring briefly to the falls of the

---

between St. Johns and Montreal, is evident in the narrative. For
his contemptuous remarks on excursion trains see also *Walden*,
p. 37.

[4] Generally, details of Thoreau's trip that do not appear in the
printed text are drawn from the lecture drafts at CSmH, HM 949
and HM 953 (b): see "Lecture Versions, Drafts, and Setting Copy,"
below.

Rivière du Sault à la Puce. Disappointed in their hope of crossing the St. Lawrence north channel to the Isle d'Orleans by rowboat, they spent the night near the boundary of l'Ange Gardien and Chateau Richer with a farm family and its hired men. On September 30 they had a surly reception from a mill owner on the Chi-pré (Petit-Pré) stream, examined the church in Beauport, and re-entered Quebec's Upper Town. Here they hired a buggy and driver to take them to another cele-brated waterfall, that of the Chaudière River, just up-stream of Quebec on the right (south) bank of the St. Lawrence. This required a ferry trip to Point Levi, the toll being added to the driver's charge. They observed the fall and its remarkable rainbow until evening, missing the last ferry. In Point Levi they engaged a room in a pension, whose hostess, at Thoreau's re-quest, stitched a cloth lining into his cheap summer straw hat: he had caught the head cold of which he would complain in the opening paragraph of his narrative.

This indisposition may have determined the travel-ers to shorten their maximum Canadian sojourn by one day. On Tuesday, October 1, they crossed by ferry to Quebec and immediately secured berths on the steamer *Lord Sydenham* for passage to Montreal that night. Once more they walked around the Upper Town, visiting the museum, studying the fortifica-tions, and enjoying the magnificent view down the St. Lawrence from the summit of Cape Diamond. In a spare hour or so before the steamer's departure time, Thoreau returned to a restaurant where he had no-ticed a large map of Canada and copied various of its features. The boat left at 5 p.m., reaching Montreal at 7 the next morning, October 2. What first attracted Thoreau and Channing there was Mount Royal, for which the city was named, a hill they climbed as Car-

tier had done in 1535. After taking in the prospect from
the summit, they descended to the city and perambu-
lated as far as the Lachine canal locks and railroad
depot, at the southwest end of the island which Montreal occupies. Late in the afternoon they crossed to
Laprairie, took the railway to St. Johns, and boarded
the steamboat for Burlington there. Reaching Burlington in the early morning of October 3, they spent the
remainder of that Thursday in railroad cars and arrived home in the evening.

Judging from dated entries in his Journal, Thoreau
began his account of the Canadian excursion on October 17. The opening forty-three words of the Journal
account survive, but the following eighty-four pages,
on forty-two leaves, were excised for use in the lecture
draft.[5] Toward the end of the month he made the first
of five visits to the Harvard College Library in order to
study old maps and to read accounts of the early exploration and settlement of the northeastern coasts of
America–an intense exercise of scholarship that resulted in his filling a large commonplace book with
notes (the "Canadian Notebook": see item B in "Reading Notes and Extracts" below) and that found issue in
both *Cape Cod* and "A Yankee in Canada." Thoreau's
lecture topic for the 1849-1850 season had been his first
(October 1849) Cape Cod excursion, but he had taken
another trip to the Cape in June 1850 and incorporated
his experience into the lecture, which he read twice
in January 1851. The drafting of the "Excursion to
Canada" lecture apparently did not begin until August
22, 1851,[6] in preparation for the 1851-1852 season. He

[5] *Journal 3*, p. 124. Scattered passages pertaining to the narrative
appear later in this notebook, e.g., at *Journal 3*, pp. 124-125 and 136.
See inventory of manuscripts later in this Headnote.

[6] On that date he composed a lecture opening in his Journal:
see *Journal 4*, pp. 7-8.

delivered the new lecture in a single session for the
Lincoln, Massachusetts, Lyceum on the evening of December 30, 1851. For his Concord Lyceum presentation he spread the account over two parts, reading the
first on January 7, 1852, and the second on March 17.[7]

Twelve days before the second Concord lecture,
Thoreau approached his friend and literary advocate,
Horace Greeley, publisher of the *New-York Tribune*,
about finding a print outlet for the narrative. It appears from Greeley's response on March 18 to Thoreau's March 5 letter that Thoreau had already sent a
legible copy:

> As to your longer account of a canadian tour, I don't
> know. It looks unmanageable. Can't you cut it into
> three or four, and omit all that relates to time? The
> cities are described to death; but I know you are at
> home with Nature, and that she rarely and slowly
> changes. Break this up if you can, and I will try to
> have it swallowed [by one of the magazines] and di-
> gested. (*Correspondence*, p. 277)

Greeley's advice to omit temporal references probably
reflects his sense that Canadian group tours were no
longer novel. His political editor for the *Tribune*,
Charles A. Dana (also an associate of George William
Curtis's on the staff of *Putnam's Monthly Magazine*,
where "An Excursion to Canada" was eventually accepted) had the previous summer gone to Montreal,
Quebec, and even the Saguenay, from New York via
Hudson steamer to Troy and rail through Saratoga to

---

[7] Bradley P. Dean and Ronald Wesley Hoag, "Thoreau's Lectures Before *Walden*," *Studies in the American Renaissance*, ed.
Joel Myerson (Charlottesville: University Press of Virginia, 1995),
pp. 201-203, 205-206. Dean and Hoag speculate that the Lincoln
and first Concord readings covered only the beginning of the excursion, and that Thoreau was still writing the latter part, which
he presented in the second Concord lecture.

Whitehall on the shore of Lake Champlain. William Rischmuller, George Batchelor, and George Stanley were the tour organizers, and Dana's account was printed in the *Tribune* as a series of five travel letters between August 29 and September 26, 1851.[8]

John Sartain, the New York engraver and publisher of *The Union Magazine*, was approached by Greeley on Thoreau's behalf and accepted two extracts from the *Walden* manuscript, "The Iron Horse" and "A Poet Buying a Farm." Greeley reported his success to Thoreau on March 25, 1852, and repeated his earlier advice: "If you break up your 'Excursion to Canada' into three or four articles, I have no doubt I could get it published on similar terms" (*Correspondence*, p. 278). It was at this point, evidently, that Greeley returned the manuscript for revision and division, because on April 20 he urged Thoreau to make haste:

> But your Quebec notes don't reach me yet, and I fear the 'good time' is passing. They ought to have appeared in the June Nos. of the Monthlies, but now cannot before July. If you choose to send them to me all in a bunch, I will try to get them printed in that way. (*Correspondence*, p. 281, corrected from a photocopy of the manuscript)

The parcel of manuscript–201 pages in five chapter groups, according to a non-authorial note on the first page (CSmH, HM 953 [a])–apparently reached Greeley soon afterward and was immediately offered to the *Whig Review*, which rejected it, as did another magazine (Greeley to Thoreau, May 26 and June 25, 1852; *Correspondence*, pp. 281-282). By now Thoreau was so hard up that he asked his friend for a loan of seventy-

[8] The series was titled "A Week's Vacation," though the excursion actually lasted fifteen days: see the classified ads for the tour in the *Tribune* for August 1-23.

five dollars, a request Greeley gladly granted on July 8. The newspaperman retained the "Excursion to Canada" manuscript.

Thoreau's *Cape Cod* project, meanwhile, was nearing maturity on his desk. He had learned of the formation of a new magazine, *Putnam's Monthly*, and had corresponded with George William Curtis, its literary editor and an acquaintance from the Walden years, about serial publication of the Cape Cod narrative. Curtis expressed interest, and on November 16 Thoreau sent a hundred-page manuscript comprising the first three chapters. Greeley was ignorant of these developments, for about the same time he gave "An Excursion to Canada" directly to George Palmer Putnam for publication in the magazine. Thoreau was surprised and disturbed by what Greeley obviously assumed would be welcome news; Greeley, pained in turn, defended his actions and urged Thoreau to accept G. P. Putnam's offer of three dollars per double-column, sixty-five-line printed page for the Canada piece, to be published anonymously like all the magazine's contents. Once more Greeley cited the narrative's lack of timeliness: "Your 'Canada' is not so fresh and acceptable as if it had just been written on the strength of a last summer's trip, and I hope you will have it printed in Putnam's Monthly."[9]

When the maiden number of *Putnam's* was issued, shortly before New Year's 1853, Thoreau was dismayed to see that Curtis had editorially removed from the first chapter of "An Excursion to Canada," "Concord to Montreal," a sardonic comment critical of Catholicism: "I am not sure but this Catholic religion would

[9] Greeley to Thoreau, November 23, 1852; *Correspondence*, pp. 289-290. The letter implies that Curtis had mentioned to Thoreau a rate of pay higher than $3.00. See *Cape Cod*, pp. 258-260.

be an admirable one if the priest were quite omitted. I think that I might go to church myself sometimes, some Monday, if I lived in a city where there was such a one to go to" (88.33-89.2).[10] The expurgation so angered Thoreau that he wrote to Curtis threatening to withdraw the remainder of the manuscript or perhaps even demanding its return. On December 29 he reported these developments to Greeley and repaid $20 of Greeley's loan. The journalist replied on January 2:

> I am sorry you and Curtis cannot agree so as to have your whole MS. printed. It will be worth nothing elsewhere after having partly appeared in Putnam. I think it is a mistake to conceal the authorship of the several articles, making them all (so to speak) *Editorial*; but *if* that is done, don't you see that the elimination of very flagrant heresies (like your defiant Pantheism) becomes a necessity?– If you had withdrawn your MS. on account of the abominable misprints in the first number, your ground would have been far more tenable.[11]

The second (February 1853) number of *Putnam's*, containing all but the last few paragraphs of Thoreau's second section, "Quebec and Montmorenci," appeared at the end of January or the beginning of the next month. It ended with a parenthetical "To be continued."–though the first installment had not. The third or March issue completed "Quebec and Montmorenci" and gave the first three-quarters of section three, "St. Anne." This installment also ended without the promise of another, and it was in fact the last. On

[10] There is no evidence to suggest that Thoreau read proof for this installment or either of the others.

[11] ALS, Horace Greeley Papers, NN. The $20 check may have been G. P. Putnam's payment (at $4 per printed page) for the first installment, which ran to a little over five pages.

or just before March 8, in a letter he misdated February 9 but which bears a March 8 Concord postmark, Thoreau sent his friend Greeley

> ... Putnam's check for 59 dollars, which together with the 20 ″ sent last December–make, nearly enough, principal & interest for the $75 which you lent me last July– ... I am sorry that my manuscript should be so mangled, insignificant as it is, but I do not know how I could have helped it fairly, since I was born to be a pantheist–if that be the name of me, and I do the deeds of one. (*Correspondence*, p. 294)

If the $59 check was his payment for the February and March installments ($20 having apparently been paid for the January contribution), Thoreau's rate of remuneration for all the copy published in *Putnam's* was about $4.25 per printed page, a figure close to the $4.00 *Putnam's* pay rate he told another editor he received later that year.[12] Acknowledging receipt of the check on March 16, Greeley asked Thoreau to "Consider me your friend who *wished* to serve you, however unsuccessfully." He closed his letter urging Thoreau not to alienate Curtis or Putnam (*Correspondence*, pp. 301-302).

In a long moralizing letter of February 27 to his Worcester disciple H. G. O. Blake, Thoreau referred demeaningly to the series in *Putnam's*, which Blake had been reading:

> I do not wonder that you do not like my Canada story. It concerns me but little, and probably is not worth the time it took to tell it. Yet I had absolutely

---

[12] *Correspondence*, p. 308. If $59 was his payment for the whole, the rate per page would have been a little over $3.00.

no design whatever in my mind, but simply to report what I saw. I have inserted all of myself that was
implicated or made the excursion. It has come to an
end at any rate, they will print no more, but return
me my mss. when it is but little more than half done
. . . because the editor Curtis requires the liberty to
omit the heresies without consulting me–a privilege
California is not rich enough to bid for. (*Correspondence*, p. 299)

Thoreau's dealings with *Putnam's Monthly Magazine* about his Canadian essay were still not concluded. He wrote to Curtis in a mood of exasperation
on March 11, complaining that only part of his "Excursion to Canada" manuscript had been returned to him
by G. P. Putnam, and that was a portion of what had
been printed. Putnam had told him that the remainder
apparently was lost at the printshop. He entreated the
editor to undertake a diligent search (*Correspondence*,
p. 301). As discussed in the manuscript inventory
under CSmH, HM 953 (a), the missing setting copy of
chapters 3-5 seems to have come to light and into
Thoreau's hands.

No textual significance attaches to the reprint of the
third installment in a collection, *Pictures and Readings
from American Authors, Being the Choice Volume of
Putnam's Magazine* (New York: Leavitt and Allen,
1855).[13] The ending of chapter 2 and the bulk of chapter 3 are taken directly from the March 1853 issue's
stereotype plates, complete to the page numbers, 321
through 329. It is unlikely that Thoreau was aware of
this publication.

[13] *Bibliography of American Literature*, compiled by Jacob
Blanck, vol. 8, edited and completed by Michael Winship (New
Haven: Yale University Press, 1990), item 20107; copy at Madonna
University, Livonia, MI.

Thoreau's correspondence and Journal contain no later references to the Canada project, but he obviously continued working on it with a view to its future complete publication. His ongoing work on *Cape Cod*–another *Putnam's* serialization, suspended in August 1855 after three installments–played into the historical emphasis of the latter half of the Canadian narrative. The record of his book borrowings from the Harvard College Library indicates a steady pattern of reading about early North American exploration, missionary activity, natural history, and ethnography, the most obvious fruits of which appear in the manuscript volumes of Thoreau's "Extracts relating to the Indians" (NNPM, MA 596-606). As late as May 1860 Thoreau was studying material from Harvard that would find its way into "A Yankee in Canada."[14]

During the last months of Thoreau's life, his sister Sophia may have helped him to complete "A Yankee in Canada," among other unfinished projects, for eventual publication. After his death, it was also Sophia who did the lion's share of editorial work to bring those projects into print. A detailed account of the preparation and publication of *A Yankee in Canada, with Anti-Slavery and Reform Papers* (1866) may be found in the Historical Introduction to the present volume.

The surviving and conjectured manuscripts pertinent to "A Yankee in Canada" are recorded below in approximate chronological order within each category. Any field notes that Thoreau made during his Canadian excursion, September 25–October 3, 1850, have been lost.

[14] Philip Gosse, *The Canadian Naturalist*; see Kenneth Walter Cameron, "Books Thoreau Borrowed from Harvard College Library," in *Emerson the Essayist*, 2 vols. (Raleigh, NC: Thistle Press, 1945), 2:191-208, esp. 196-198.

THE MANUSCRIPT JOURNAL

Drafts of matter used in his lecture on the trip and in the published narrative survive in Thoreau's MS Volume III (April-May 1850–September 19, 1850); see *Journal 3*, p. 115; and MS Volume IV (after September 19, 1850–December 2, 1850); see *Journal 3*, pp. 122, 123, 124-125, 134, 136, 144-145. Excised material originally in this notebook and now lost fell on pp. "7"-"90" (forty-two leaves), definitely on the Canada trip; on pp. "99"-"101" (two leaves), possibly on Canada; on pp. "127"-"128" (one leaf), possibly on Canada; and on portions of eight other pages, one definitely on Canada. The excised pages were used up as Thoreau drafted his lecture. Additional Journal drafts include those in MS Volume V (December 4, 1850–July 7, 1851) and possibly on excised pages; see *Journal 3*, pp. 222, 242; and MS Volume VI (July 8–August 20, 1851); see *Journal 3*, pp. 327, 328, 333, 335, 373, 374, 375. A manuscript leaf bearing pertinent material is missing: see p. 327. Other material survives in MS Volume VII (August 21–October 7, 1851); see *Journal 4*, pp. 3, 7-8, 11, 17, 49, 72, 115-116; and MS Volume VIII (October 7, 1851–January 11, 1852); see *Journal 4*, pp. 164, 175. Moreover, at p. 164 four-fifths of a leaf, notebook pp. "53"-"54", have been excised, probably for use in the Canada lecture draft. MS Volume IX (January 12–March 28, 1852) contains pertinent material; see *Journal 4*, pp. 261, 320, 335, 337, 379-380. Again, half a leaf (notebook pp. "209"-"210") is missing at p. 379. Finally, there is a relevant Journal passage in MS Volume X (March 29–April 27, 1852), written before Thoreau gave the third of his lectures on the Canadian excursion, on March 17, 1852, and apparently after he had sent a manuscript of the narrative to Horace Greeley for the first time (March 5, 1852; see *Correspondence*, p. 277) for sale to one of the magazines with whose editors and publishers Greeley had influence; see *Journal 4*, p. 429.

READING NOTES AND EXTRACTS

A. A quotation from Middleton and Rowley's *The Fair Quarrel*, taken from a collection of poetry "specimens" edited by Charles Lamb, appears in Thoreau's poetry commonplace book at DLC; it was used in the "Concord to Montreal" chapter. See the facsimile edition by Kenneth Walter Cameron, *Thoreau's Literary Notebook in the Library of Congress* (Hartford, CT: Transcendental Books, 1964), p. 340. Thoreau's transcript of the lines seems to date from between 1845 and 1848.

B. The so-called "Canadian Notebook," NNPM, MA 595, a double-ender, contains reading extracts and notes relevant to Canada, from the records of the earliest explorations in the sixteenth century to contemporaneous books by British travelers and colonial officials, on pages "2" through "37", plus loose sheets [20], "21", "30" and, in the inverted *Cape Cod* section of the notebook, on p. "23". On the first page of the Canada "end" of the notebook is a reading list by Thoreau of "Books on Canada at Cam. [Harvard College Library, Cambridge]," including items dated 1851 and 1852. At p. "9", between reading notes, are several sentences of original narrative and description that would be used in Thoreau's account. The notebook's earliest entries date from November 18, 1850 (as Thoreau was working with materials destined for use in both "A Yankee in Canada" and *Cape Cod*); see discussion earlier in this Headnote and *Cape Cod*, pp. 256-257, 299.

C. Five pages of notes made at Harvard on the maps in Champlain's *Voyages*, 1613 and 1632 editions, Lescarbot's *Histoire de la Nouvelle France*, and DeLaet's *Novus Orbis*, apparently in late 1850 and early 1851, were formerly in the collection of Raymond R. Borst. These are more germane to *Cape Cod* than to "A Yankee in Canada."

D. The third of Thoreau's books of extracts relating to the Indians, NNPM, MA 598, contains material used in the narrative at fols. 3 (from Warburton), 8-9 (from Cartier), and 18 (from Champlain). These notes were made about 1851. Two later "Indian Notebooks," NNPM, MA 599 and MA 604, contain relevant details from other sources–Charlevoix, Lahontan, and Morton.

E. In May 1860 Thoreau borrowed Philip Gosse, *The Canadian Naturalist*, from the Harvard College Library, and took notes from it. One partial leaf survives at ViU, Barrett Collection number 6345-g. The extracts on this manuscript were not used in "A Yankee in Canada," though another passage from Gosse was.

LECTURE VERSIONS, DRAFTS, AND SETTING COPY

A. The earliest draft of Thoreau's "Excursion to Canada" lecture of the winter of 1851-1852 survives complete at CSmH, HM 949. Written in ink and pencil, its 194 pages (on 101 leaves, paginated by Thoreau "1"-"101" on the rectos) are heavily revised. All the leaves but one are on white wove type 18 stationery marked "Goodwin Hartford," with an anchor inside a circle (*LMHDT*, p. 377), and the manuscript is now bound.

B. A subsequent, revised, incomplete reading version and essay draft, also at CSmH, HM 950, consists of sixty-eight pages, on fifty-seven leaves numbered by Thoreau on the rectos, of the same white wove type 18 paper. The text, in ink, with ink and pencil revisions leading to the *Putnam's* publication, corresponds to the first third, approximately, of the finished essay, from the beginning to 105.28 in the present edition, "when we can get that at home." The manuscript is now bound. See the description of CSmH, HM 953 (b) for the original relationship of HM 950 to that body of manuscript.

C. A composite of setting copy for publication and essay-lecture draft at CSmH, HM 953, consists of 214 pages on 169 leaves, all but five of them on white wove type 18 paper. The text is in ink and pencil, and the manuscript is now bound.

HM 953 (a). The first seventy-four leaves of HM 953, numbered lightly in pencil by Thoreau on the rectos, are the setting copy of "An Excursion to Canada," chapters 1 and 2, for *Putnam's Monthly Magazine*, to 110.26 in the present edition. The versos are blank. Written in ink with a few pencilled additions and revisions, the setting copy bears the doubly underlined title "An Excursion to Canada" in the left margin of page "35", the beginning of chapter 2, in another hand, probably that of a *Putnam's* editor or typesetter. There are various signs of printshop use, notably stint marks and the names of compositors ("Brooks", "Burnham", "Dillon", "Murray", "Murry", "Forbes", "Roulston", "Welling", "Burton"). Cancelled at the bottom of p. "74" is the opening of the first paragraph of chapter 3 (110.28-111.5). When the serial publication of "An Excursion to Canada" was interrupted after the third (March 1853) installment, Thoreau complained to Curtis that "Mr Putnam sends me only the first 70 or 80 (out of 200) pages of the 'Canada,' all which having been printed is of course of no use to me." (These must be the first seventy-four pages of HM 953, sent to Thoreau with a check for $59 by George Palmer Putnam before March 8, 1853: see above.) "He states," Thoreau continued, "that 'the remainder of the mss. *seems* to have been lost at the printers'.' You will not be surprised if I wish to know if it *actually is* lost, and if reasonable pains have been taken to recover it" (*Correspondence*, p. 301). Thoreau goes on to press it upon Curtis as a moral duty to attempt recovering the manuscript, since it was "you to whom I entrusted it."

The present editor infers that the 127 mislaid setting-copy pages were in fact found, pursuant to Thoreau's urging, and were returned to the author. With revisions and additions, these pages served as the Ticknor and Fields setting copy for the heretofore unpublished last quarter of chapter 3, and all of chapters 4 and 5, in the 1866 first complete publication of *A Yankee in Canada*. The setting-copy pages for the portion first published in 1866 are lost, probably having been discarded in the printshop. Collation shows that for the opening three-fifths of the narrative, that is, chapters 1 and 2 plus the first three-quarters of chapter 3, the printers for Ticknor and Fields used a copy of the *Putnam's* printing, marked by Thoreau with corrections, restorations, and revisions. It is no longer extant. (Thoreau's personal copy of the March 1853 issue, which contained the third installment, survives and is housed at ICarbS; pages 321-330 have been excised.) Among lesser revisions on the *Putnam's* pages that he left for the printer, Thoreau restored the material on Catholicism that Curtis had expurgated. See Rejected Substantives for *Putnam's* readings deemed non-authorial in chapters 1 and 2; and see Emendations for changes deemed Thoreau's in chapters 1, 2, and the *Putnam's* part of 3 that first occurred in *A Yankee in Canada* (1866).

The whereabouts of the setting copy for the part of chapter 3 originally published in *Putnam's* are unknown. The first page would at one time have been paginated "75" by Thoreau for use at the magazine printshop. Possibly Thoreau kept the chapter 3 manuscript intact when it was returned to him, even though it had been partially printed, and this whole chapter (together with the manuscript of chapters 4 and 5, and the marked *Putnam's* pages for the first two and three-quarter chapters) was provided to Fields by Sophia for the 1866 printing. In that event, the manuscript for the opening of chapter 3 would have met the same fate as the remainder of the setting copy for matter first printed in *A Yankee in Canada, with Anti-Slavery and Reform Papers*.

HM 953 (b). The remaining ninety-five leaves (142 pages) of HM 953 are apparently contemporary with HM 950 (the partial lecture reading copy–see item B) and begin textually exactly where HM 950 breaks off, at 105.28. Like HM 950, HM 953 (b) is written in ink and pencil with extensive revisions. This manuscript, though now incomplete, seems to have served Thoreau as a back-up copy in 1852 for the setting-copy text of chapters 3, 4, 5, and the ending of chapter 2, just as HM 950 would have functioned as back-up copy for the first sixty-two (setting-copy) pages of HM 953 when those pages were at *Putnam's*. It is paginated on the rectos in dark pencil by Thoreau "75"-"169", the numbering manifestly having been made after *Putnam's* returned the seventy-four-page setting copy of chapters 1 and 2, and perhaps well after the (conjectured) return of setting-copy chapters 3, 4, and 5. Previous pencilled pagination beginning with "58" (continuing from HM 950's p. "57") was erased before this numbering commencing with "75" was entered. Pages "75"-"83" of HM 953 (b) in fact are draft for the HM 953 (a), setting copy, pages "63"-"74". A likely occasion for Thoreau's renumbering of the leaves was his work on chapter 10 of *Cape Cod*, "Provincetown," between September 1855 and 1861 (see *Cape Cod*, pp. 283-284).

Although Thoreau's page numbering in HM 953 (b) is continuous, the text is not; there are lacunae of syntax and sense after pp. "104", "123", "129", "130", "147", "157", and "165", suggesting that prior to receiving the pagination in dark pencil the manuscript contained other leaves, now lost or scattered.[15] The text through p. "155" generally tracks the printed text (to 157.35) while the remainder is either not used in "A Yankee in Canada," or used out of textual sequence. Page "166" contains matter relevant to *Cape Cod*, and ends with the authorial notation, in pencil, "Missing pages transferred to Cape Cod". Page "167" has material used in *Cape Cod*; page "168" contains both "Yankee" and *Cape Cod* material. Pages "165" and "169" contain "Yankee" text printed at pages 158.19-24 and 150.30-151.7, respectively, the manuscript text in each instance beginning in the middle of a sentence. On page "169" the draft breaks off in mid-sentence, and the entire conclusion of the narrative as printed is missing. Apart from the early lecture draft (HM 949), reading notes in the Canadian Notebook, an Indian Notebook 3 phrase, and a few Journal sentences and phrases, no manuscript equivalent survives for the last five pages of the essay, from 158.24 ("We were soon abreast of Cap Rouge . . .") onward. However, some of the *intermediate* textual lacunae in HM 953 (b) are or might be filled by manuscript leaves now in other collections, most of which were disseminated with sets of the Manuscript Edition of 1906. See the following twelve entries.

D. Two draft pages on two leaves of white wove type 18 paper[16] are at MH-H, catalogued bMS Am 278.5, folder 12. The text, in ink and pencil, corresponds to

[15] The conjecture about the re-pagination of the manuscript that is now HM 953 (b) after parts of it had been removed is supported by authorial page numbers on surviving scattered leaves in other collections.

[16] The scattered manuscripts accounted for in "D" through "O" are all on the same type paper.

130.4-36 ("did, and he pronounced it . . . *petite étoffe.*")
plus a chapter title variant of "IV. The Walls of Quebec.", 135.29. It may not originally have been from the
same continuous draft stage as the surviving paginated HM 953 (b), since it overlaps textually with
pages in the latter, and the text is revised beyond the
equivalent in HM 953 (b). Indeed, most of these revisions are not incorporated in the 1866 printed text: see
Textual Note 130.5-36. Adjacent to these MH-H leaves
in folder 12 is a pencilled list of terms and topics that
Thoreau made while taking notes from his printed
(chiefly historical) sources, plus a few topics reflecting
his own experience ("woodbine", "what journey
cost"). Many items in the list are lined through, as if to
indicate the topics had been covered in the course of
composition.

E. Three draft pages, in ink and pencil, on three
leaves paginated by Thoreau "133", "134", and "137",
are at NN-BGC. The first two pages correspond to
133.24-134.22 ("them in the Indian way . . . selling
strong"), while the last includes a single sentence corresponding to 135.17-19 ("of the English was . . . enterprise of traders."). This same sentence was also used
in *Cape Cod*, p. 185. Yet other material on page "137"
was used in *Cape Cod*, pp. 180, 185, 187-188. The text on
pages "133"-"134" overlaps with that on pages "156"
and "157" in HM 953 (b). Three pencilled revisions are
not incorporated in the 1866 printed text: see Textual
Note 133.24-134.22.

F. One draft page, in the collection of Paul Brown, is
mounted in Manuscript Edition set number 284. The
mounting conceals any numbering it may bear. The
text is written in ink and pencil and corresponds to
137.10-25 ("we saw that the Canadians . . . which this
tremendous"). There is no equivalent text in HM 953
(b) and the leaf is thus perhaps originally from the

same draft stage. The text is continuous with that on the leaf next described.

G. One draft page at NmRM is mounted in Manuscript Edition set number 491. No pagination can be seen because of the mounting frame. The text is written in ink and pencil and corresponds to 137.25-138.3 ("fall produced . . . like the beak of"). Since there is no equivalent text in HM 953 (b), the NmRM leaf possibly belonged once to that draft stage. See item F.

H. One draft page at MiU comes from Manuscript Edition set number 370. The text, written in ink and pencil, corresponds to 138.34-139.12 ("unengaged berths . . . for musketry"). In the absence of equivalent text in HM 953 (b), this leaf may have originally belonged to the same draft stage.

I. One draft page at ViU, Barrett Collection number 6345, bears the pencilled pagination "152" in Thoreau's hand, perhaps reflecting the same pagination sequence as "133"-"134" in item E. It is written in ink and pencil, and the text corresponds to 139.16-140.6 ("visitor then in the city . . . St. Louis Street"). There is no equivalent text in HM 953 (b), and the leaf was thus perhaps originally from the same draft stage. However, the text overlaps with another NN-BGC manuscript (item J).

J. Two draft pages at NN-BGC are written on two leaves in ink and pencil. No pagination is visible. The text corresponds to 140.2-141.8 ("The Government Garden . . . at the gates."). There is no equivalent text in HM 953 (b), and the leaves thus possibly belonged originally to the same draft stage. See item I: this NN-BGC manuscript and the ViU manuscript cannot *both* be from the draft stage of HM 953 (b), since they overlap textually with one another.

K. One draft page at PPi ends textually where HM 953 (b) p. "131" begins, and thus appears to have been originally in the same draft stage. The text is written in ink and pencil, and corresponds to 141.31-142.10 ("him that it . . . but I"), with some intervening sentences absent, and it includes the sentence "However, I think . . . Sappers and Miners" (142.14-16), not present on p. "131" of HM 953 (b). The PPi manuscript text overlaps with and antedates that of the IdU manuscript (item L).

L. A draft leaf (two pages) at IdU is mounted in Manuscript Edition set 496. The recto is paginated "156" in pencil by Thoreau. See the remarks on pagination in items E and I. The text, written in ink and pencil, corresponds to 142.3-31 ("At the ramparts . . . England's"). Besides post-dating and overlapping with item K, the IdU manuscript also overlaps textually with HM 953 (b) p. "131".

M. A draft leaf (two pages), in the collection of Suzanne Y. H. Kurtz, is mounted in Manuscript Edition set 220. It is paginated "175" in pencil by Thoreau; see pagination remarks in items I and L. The text, in ink and pencil, corresponds to 151.7-24 ("with the cries . . . had grown in Canada"). Page "169" of HM 953 (b) breaks off at "streets resounded", where the Kurtz manuscript begins; the Kurtz leaf was apparently once part of the same draft stage as HM 953 (b). It also overlaps with and post-dates a ViU manuscript (item N).

N. A draft page at ViU, Barrett Collection number 6345-g, is written in ink and pencil, the text corresponding to 151.14-23 and 158.12-19 ("travelling once . . . Boston.'" and "I had already . . . stood on it, and"). There is no equivalent text in HM 953 (b); the leaf at one time was adjacent to HM 953 (b) p. "165", which begins in mid-sentence where the ViU manuscript leaves off. No pagination is evident. See item M.

O. One draft page in the collection of James Dawson is mounted in Manuscript Edition set 288. It is written in ink and pencil and paginated "178" by Thoreau. The text corresponds to 152.24-33 ("associations ... the clear air,") and has no equivalent in HM 953 (b). The manuscript might thus have once belonged to the same draft stage. See remarks on pagination in items I, L, and M.

From this inventory of scattered draft leaves (D through O), two conclusions are inevitable: first, that substantial parts of the narrative went through draft revision (subsequent to the first lecture stage, HM 949) requiring the re-inscription of the same material on two or more sheets of stationery; and second, that in the first years of the twentieth century, after Thoreau's manuscripts had been sold to a dealer by E. Harlow Russell, H. G. O. Blake's heir, a large handful of "Yankee in Canada" leaves–leaves not then physically within the body of HM 953 (b) that Thoreau had continuously repaginated "75"-"169"–were appropriated for commercial purposes including, but not necessarily limited to, the enhancement of sets of the 1906 Manuscript Edition. In the Manuscript Edition sets that have been recovered, seven out of twelve surviving "Yankee" leaves that were thus appropriated were from chapter 4, textually in close proximity to one another. Two were from chapter 3 and three from chapter 5, near the beginning.

The copy-text for "A Yankee in Canada" in this edition is necessarily a composite, since for different segments of the text different documents constitute the most authoritative surviving form.[17] The setting copy of chapters 1 and 2 for the *Putnam's* printing, CSmH, HM 953 (a), best represents Thoreau's intentions for

[17] See the general discussion of copy-text and emendation from earlier and later relevant forms in the Textual Introduction to this volume, pp. 365-375.

those chapters (79.1-110.26). A typescript prepared
from microfilm of the manuscript was perfected twice
against the original. For the first three-quarters of
chapter 3, the part printed in the March *Putnam's* installment, that version of the text closest in descent or
transmission to Thoreau's lost setting copy is the
Putnam's printing itself, 1:322-329, and this serves as
copy-text in the present edition (110.27-130.5 "in its
way."). A typescript based on the NjP copy was used.
The earliest finished forms of the conclusion of chapter 3 and all of chapters 4 and 5 are in the 1866 first
printing of *A Yankee in Canada, with Anti-Slavery and
Reform Papers*, beginning at line 27 on p. 57 and ending on p. 93, set from a lost authorial manuscript (130.5
"This man's farm"–163.15). For the small section of
chapter 3, a typescript based on a first edition (Walter
Harding copy, now at MaLiTIW) was prepared. For
chapters 4 and 5, an enlarged clear photocopy was
used, with emendations and other directions written
in the photocopy margins for entry into computer
files; this text was read for substantives and accidentals against the editor's copy of the first edition. No
later printing than the 1866 *Yankee* offers fresh authority for any part of the narrative. The editor draws
emendations for all parts of the work from draft manuscripts–principally HM 949 and HM 953 (b)–when the
draft readings clarify otherwise obscure authorial intentions. This is especially important where the text
is based on *Putnam's* or the 1866 *Yankee*, in both of
which typesetters' errors and house styling sometimes
manifestly distort Thoreau's meaning or violate his
habitual practices. Wherever copy-text is a print form,
the editor has taken pains to read the text closely
against the surviving manuscript witnesses. "A Yankee
in Canada" is freighted, like chapters 2, 3, and 10 of
Cape Cod, with quotations and paraphrases from nu-

merous printed sources, often unidentified by Thoreau. As a check against compositors' errors and even of inadvertent copying mistakes by Thoreau that distort his sources, the editor has identified these sources in the exact editions Thoreau employed, and has collated the derived "Yankee" passages with the originals. Occasional emendations have resulted from this comparison: see, for example, Textual Notes 79.5, 79.7, and 114.2.

Emendations to the manuscript and *Putnam's* copy-texts are usually drawn from later authoritative versions. Where *Putnam's* corrects an error in the setting copy of chapters 1 and 2–for example, by supplying an inadvertently omitted letter in a word–the emendation in the present edition is assigned to *Putnam's*. Some emendations to the manuscript copy-text of chapters 1 and 2, where *Putnam's* agrees with the manuscript, are changes in 1866 *Yankee* deemed by the editor to be Thoreau's own revisions and corrections of his earlier text, presumably marked by him in the margins of a copy of the magazine printing or supplied on slips of paper attached to the marked copy. A few emendations to chapters 1 and 2 are made on the editor's own authority. These, designated "PE" in the Emendations list, are typically discussed in Textual Notes. For the first three-quarters of chapter 3, where *Putnam's* is copy-text, most of the emendations are drawn from *Yankee* (1866). For the remainder of chapter 3, and all of chapters 4 and 5, where the copy-text is the 1866 *Yankee* printing, all emendations are assigned to the present editor. These typically are drawn from draft manuscripts and are discussed in Textual Notes.

No type variations other than batter damage in the portions of text printed in *Putnam's* were disclosed by optical collation on the Hinman machine of two pairs of copies, TxU and TxAuHRH, and NjP and the Walter

Harding copy. The integrity of the original printing of the complete text in *Yankee* (1866), including chapters 4, 5, and the portion of 3 first published there, was determined by Hinman machine collation of two TxAuHRH copies, and of the Walter Harding copy with copies at MnU and N: see *Reform Papers*, p. 260. Three machine collations of the 1866 text of the narrative against later printings from the 1866 stereotype plates are recorded in *Reform Papers*, p. 260; two more were performed using a TxAuHRH copy of the first, 1866, printing and (1) an 1891 printing at CtNbT and (2) the ICRC copy of the 1892 printing, the last on record from these plates. Apart from titlepage information changes (publisher's name; date of publication) and broken characters resulting from plate batter, no differences were detected in these comparisons. Variant substantives and significant accidentals were identified through the following sight collations: setting copy of chapters 1 and 2 versus *Putnam's* equivalent, three times; setting copy versus the 1866 *Yankee* equivalent, three times; and *Putnam's* versus the equivalent parts of 1866 *Yankee*, six times.

Textual Notes

FOR the format of the Textual Notes, see the Textual Introduction, pp. 381-382. Copy-text for chapters 1 and 2 is Thoreau's setting-copy manuscript for *Putnam's Monthly Magazine*, HM 953 (a) at CSmH. For chapter 3, up to 130.5, "in its way.", copy-text is the printing in the March 1853 *Putnam's* (P). For the remainder of chapter 3, and for all of chapters 4 and 5, copy-text is *A Yankee in Canada, with Anti-Slavery and Reform Papers*, 1866 (Y). The first textual note after the copy-text changes identifies the new copy-text. The abbreviation "MS" followed by a parenthesized owner's name or a repository symbol and in some cases an accession number identifies a manuscript reading. For the identification of draft manuscripts cited in textual notes, see the Headnote.

79.1 A Yankee in Canada.: Thoreau's title in the manuscript copy-text and in the P printing based on the copy-text is "An Excursion To [altered from "to"] Canada." The editor regards as authorial the change of title in the 1866 book publication of the narrative, the first complete printing, Y. Of the substantive additions and revisions in those portions which were first published in P, the great majority appear to originate with Thoreau, increasing the likelihood that the change of title is also his. No evidence has been found among the records of the publisher or among the surviving papers of Sophia Thoreau and Ellery Channing to suggest that the change was an editorial imposition. A study of the seventeen instances of the term "Yankee" in the text, and of the two dozen references to the intellectual and moral constitution of New Englanders (usually in explicit contrast to the British or the French Canadians), reveals that Thoreau usually identifies with the categories "Yankee," New Englander, and citizen of Massachusetts. To be sure, there are exceptions: the size of the "Yankee" excursion party to Canada–some 1,500 travelers–and the tendency of those travelers to do their sightseeing en masse offend Thoreau's individualistic instincts; moreover, he believes his countrymen carry far too much luggage. The image of the umbrella as an American's weapon (literal or symbolic), capable of defeating the British soldiery with its firearms, is introduced by "some of our party" and is overheard by Thoreau (85.21); Thoreau later adopts the title "knights of the umbrella and the bundle" for himself and Channing (105.12; 140.26), and he depicts himself with his umbrella as a substantial and moral superior to the "spectral" British sentinel with his musket (143.30-31). For these reasons the editor judges the title "A Yankee in Canada" to reflect Thoreau's own intention for the revised and complete piece, published after his death, despite the relative anomaly in his books and essays of a main title that calls attention to the author's own person.

79.2-12   "*New England* . . . Montreal.:   The first epigraph, from Josselyn, occurs in the copy-text, but the second, from Morton, was added in Y. In the copy-text the Josselyn material follows the chapter number and chapter title, though P puts it in its logical position just after the main title, where it remains in Y.

79.5   Rarities: Thoreau copies correctly from John Josselyn's *New-England's Rarities Discovered* (London: Printed for G. Widdowes, 1672), when taking notes from the Harvard copy in his third Indian Notebook, MS (NNPM, MA 598). The term is also correctly spelled in the 1868 second edition of *A Week on the Concord and Merrimack Rivers* (see *A Week*, p. 29), in an authorial addition to the original *Week* text. The copy-text and two earlier drafts, MS (CSmH, HM 949) and MS (CSmH, HM 950), read "Rareties", however, a form followed by P and Y.

79.7   1637:   "1632" in Y, the first appearance of this epigraph, perhaps due to a misreading of Thoreau's hand. In the tenth Indian Notebook, MS (NNPM, MA 604), Thoreau correctly copies the publication date while taking notes from Morton, *New English Canaan* (Amsterdam: by Jacob Frederick Stam, 1637). At 79.10, Thoreau changes Morton's "that first" (p. 97) to "who first". The spelling "Monsier" occurs in the source.

79.30   exciting, suggesting: Thus in P; in the copy-text the comma, if present, merges with the "l" of "least" on the next manuscript line.

80.10   Keene: The copy-text and draft spelling, "Keen", has no authority among Thoreau's maps and reference works.

P repeats the misspelling here and at 80.32 and 81.3. In all three instances Y emends to "Keene".

80.13-20 I have also . . . street.: Thoreau's source, Salma Hale, "Annals of the Town of Keene" in *Collections of the New-Hampshire Historical Society* (Concord, N.H.: Jacob B. Moore), 2 (1827): 73-74, 77, records that the main street was widened from four rods by vote at a proprietors' meeting on September 30, 1736, but it does not include the quotation or give the new width.

80.19-20 far and: The copy-text has an ampersand, which P routinely changed to "and", as Thoreau expected his publishers to do except when the ampersand occurred in "&c" and in real or imaginary commercial titles like "Somebody & Co." (*Maine Woods*, p. 13). The same expansion of the ampersand occurs twenty-nine more times in the setting-copy manuscript, as detailed in Emendations. See Textual Notes 23.33, 57.30, 185.34, and 223.10.

81.33-82.3 Mt Holly . . . Mᵗ Holly: P normalizes to "Mount Holly". Although John Hayward, *The New England Gazetteer* (Concord, N.H.: Israel S. Boyd and William White; Boston: John Hayward, 1839), gives "Mount Holly," another of Thoreau's reference works for traveling, Wellington Williams, *Appletons' Railroad and Steamship Companion* (New York: D. Appleton & Company, 1848), gives on its map no. 9 the abbreviation with the "t" superscribed and a period beneath, and "Mount Holly" on pp. 90, 91. A later edition, titled *Appleton's Northern and Eastern Traveller's Guide* (New York: D. Appleton & Company, 1850), gives in its text both "Mt. Holly Gap" (p. 90) and "Mount Holly" (p. 91), and on its maps no. 9 and 28 "Mt. Holly" with the "t" superscribed and a period beneath.

83.18-20 The oldest . . . 1535.: Cartier does not mention Lake Champlain, as the text may imply, but only the Richelieu River or "Rivière des Iroquois," which drains the lake into the St. Lawrence. Thoreau's source is "Les Trois Voyages de Jacques Quartier au Canada, en 1534, 1535 et 1540," in *Voyages de Découverte au Canada* (Quebec: Chez William Cowan et Fils [for la Société Littéraire et Historique de Québec], 1843), p. 56.

84.10 Richelieu: Thus in P, emended from the copy-text's "Richlieu". The latter was Thoreau's habitual spelling of the name, whether in reference to the river or to other

Canadian places bearing Cardinal Richelieu's name. Among the numerous instances in the draft manuscripts for this narrative, Thoreau includes the "e" in the first syllable only once, at 111.15. In studying the maps and books that Thoreau consulted, the editor has encountered the form "Richlieu" (River, Rapids) only in John MacGregor, *British America* (Edinburgh: William Blackwood; London: T. Cadell, 1832), 2:496, 499, 500, and 502; the same work also gives "Richelieu" at 2:433. See also Emendation 94.19.

84.21   Johns: Thoreau inconsistently supplies or omits the apostrophe when writing this name in the copy-text and its antecedent manuscripts. The inconsistency is shared by his source books and maps.

85.18-20   Donolly . . . Donolly: Thus in the copy-text and preceding drafts. The P compositor misread the name as "Donothy", and Y sophisticated this error to the French-sounding "Donouy". Possibly this last development resulted from Thoreau's writing "ll" over "th" in his copy of the P text, a correction misunderstood as a large "u" by the compositor and editors of Y.

86.23   Sault Norman: Thus, correctly, in the copy-text and in MS (CSmH, HM 949). P corrupts to "Sault Vorruan" and Y restores the manuscript reading. Of the numerous contemporary maps examined by the editor, only one gives this name to a rapid between Isle St. Paul and St. Helen's Island. This is the detail map of "Island of Montreal" on Edward Staveley's "A Map of Canada Compiled from the Latest Authorities" (Montreal: Printed for Armour & Ramsay, 1848). The guide-book purchased by Thoreau, probably at the publisher's own bookstore in Montreal, was *The Canadian Guide Book, with a Map of the Province* (Montreal: Armour & Ramsay, 1849). The Staveley map was also advertised for separate sale, either at 8s 9d on a roller, or at 6s 3d in pocket form. It was the folding pocket version that accompanied *The Canadian Guide Book*, glued onto the back fixed endpaper of the one intact copy the editor has seen, at CSmH.

87.4-5   five hundred and forty: Thoreau's reading notes in the Canadian Notebook, MS (NNPM, MA 595), twice record the figure 580 miles for the distance of Montreal from the Gulf of St. Lawrence: first from Joseph Bouchette, *A Topographical Description of the Province of Lower Canada* (London: W. Faden, 1815), p. 45, and second from John Ramsay McCulloch, *M'Culloch's Universal Gazetteer. A Diction-*

ary, Geographical, Statistical, and Historical, of the Various Countries, Places, and Principal Natural Objects in the World (New-York: Harper & Brothers, 1846), 2:art. "Laurence, or Lawrence (St.)". In both MS (CSmH, HM 949) and MS (CSmH, HM 950), Thoreau wrote "580" in ink and "540?" in pencil, with an accompanying pencilled query, "Bouchette?", in the former instance. The MS (CSmH, HM 949) section corresponding to 156.9-13 also includes "580" revised in pencil to "540".

87.24   prophane: Thus in the copy-text, but emended to "profane" in P. See Textual Note 94.11.

90.2   Edinburgh: Thoreau's habitual misspelling in the copy-text, "Edinburg", is thus emended in P. See also Emendation 100.21.

90.16   not to smile: In MS (CSmH, HM 949) this passage continues in a more sharply iconoclastic tone: "–so demure & hypocritical I thought that nothing would be so good for them as a smart switching– They waited demurely on the side-walk for a truck to drive in at the gate of the Seminary of St Sulpice. The truck was laden with raisins, by the way, were they for some jolly fat friar to nibble? or to flavor his porridge?"

90.33-34   regarding: Thus in P; the copy-text reads "re-guarding". Thoreau intends an aural pun on "guarding," but not a visual one. In MS (CSmH, HM 950) he first wrote "reguarding" and corrected by overwriting the "ua" with an "a". In drafts of the "St. Anne" chapter, he usually miswrote the place-name "Ange Gardien" as "Ange Guardien," and its translation "Guardian Angel" as "Gardian Angel."

91.11   any more: Although the copy-text hyphenates after "any" at the end of the line, both the previous draft, MS (CSmH, HM 950), and P read "any more".

92.10-14   Two fifths ... and others.:   Thoreau's source, *The Canadian Guide Book*, p. 24, reads "tenth" and "tenths" where the copy-text reads "fifth" and "fifths"; but the source figures only add up to five tenths in all. Thoreau corrects the fraction, but otherwise follows the source.

93.23   Longueil: While the spelling of this place-name is properly "Longueuil," from the fief and title of nobility given an early Canadian soldier and seigneur, Charles Le Moyne, Sieur de Longueuil (1626-1685), variations ("Longueil," "Longueil") were frequent in the guidebooks, sources, and maps Thoreau consulted. The form Thoreau uses in the copy-text and drafts, "Longueil," occurs on Staveley's map in *The Canadian Guide Book*; and on map no. 10 and in the text, p. 185, of *Appletons' Railroad and Steamboat Companion* (see Textual Note 81.33-82.3).

94.2   names.:   Thoreau ends this rhetorical question with a period not only in the copy-text but twice in the drafts. P emends to a question mark.

94.6   it; all: "it; All" in the copy-text; in the previous draft, MS (CSmH, HM 950), Thoreau ended the sentence with a period after "it" and began a new one with "All" but then reconsidered and wrote a dash over the period.

94.11   profaned: Although Thoreau has spelled the verb and adjective with a "ph" in the second syllable twice earlier in the copy-text (87.24; 89.5), here he revises in pencil to "profaned". Webster prefers the spellings with "f" but lists "prophane" as an alternate form. In all three places P gives "profane" or "profaned". See Emendation 65.27, where the present editor, on his own authority, emends Thoreau's manuscript "prophanity" (not accepted in his dictionaries) to "profanity", adopting a change first made in the initial (*Dial*) printing of "A Winter Walk."

95.8   Chaudiere: Thoreau omits the grave accent over the first "e" in the copy-text, but the omission is consistent with the practice of many of his sources, including the Staveley map in *The Canadian Guide Book* and map no. 28 in *Appletons' Railroad and Steamboat Companion*. See also p. 186 in the latter. P, followed by Y, emends to "Chaudière".

95.31-37   *Hierosme . . . heads.":   The footnote, added for Y, reflects Thoreau's reading in early 1857 of this volume of the Jesuit Relations, *Relation de ce qvi c'est passé de plus remarqvable és missions des peres de la compagnie de IESVS, en la Novvelle France, es annees 1647. & 1648* (Paris: Sebastien Cramoisy, 1649), p. 101. As usual when translating from French, Thoreau follows the word order of the original.

96.6-12   about 45000 . . . and others.:   P changes Thoreau's columnar list to connected phrases in a single sentence, spells out the numerals as words, and replaces some of the ditto marks with the words they represent in the copy-text, ignoring some others.

98.7   Poniatowski: Thoreau alludes to Prince Jozef Anton Poniatowski (1763-1813), a Polish general and a marshal in the army of France. The copy-text spelling, "Poniatowsky", followed in P and Y, has no authority.

98.29-31 those lines . . . journey: Thus in the copy-text. Although Thoreau accurately quotes from Claudian's minor poem *De sene Veronensi qui Suburbium nunquam egressus est* in his Journal for May 10, 1841 (*Journal 1*, p. 310), and uses the same two lines with a loose translation of his own in *Walden* (p. 322), there is nothing in the poem about gates or the difficulty of getting through them. A search of Claudian by means of an index-concordance of his works (for *porta* and *iter*) yielded nothing pertinent. Abraham Cowley's translation or "Imitation," "Claudian's Old Man of Verona," with which Thoreau might well have been familiar, also offers no solution to the problem of this allusion. Nor does the translation by Francis Fawkes in Alexander Chalmers, ed., *The Works of the English Poets, from Chaucer to Cowper* . . . (London: Printed for J. Johnson et al., 1810), 16:253. Thoreau says he tried to read the entire collection: see *Walden*, p. 259.

101.3 Tryggvesson: The copy-text reads "Trygvesson", corrupted to "Trygresson" in P and then to "Trygesson" in Y. Thoreau's source is Snorro Sturleson (Snorri Sturluson), *The Heimskringla; or, Chronicle of the Kings of Norway*, translated by Samuel Laing (London: Longman, Brown, Green, and Longmans, 1844), 1:399. Laing consistently gives the correct patronymic form, "Tryggvesson," from "Tryggve." Taking notes from Laing in a commonplace book, MS (NN-BGC), Thoreau follows the source spelling, as he does in another notebook, the "Fact Book," published in facsimile as *Thoreau's Fact Book in the Harry Elkins Widener Collection in the Harvard College Library*, vol. 1, ed. Kenneth Walter Cameron (Hartford, CT: Transcendental Books, 1966); "Tryggvesson" is on p. 64. The original of this sentence appears with the same spelling in Thoreau's Journal for November 6, 1851 (*Journal 4*, p. 164). The first surviving draft of "An Excursion to Canada," MS (CSmH, HM 949), also has "Tryggvesson", but the following draft, MS (CSmH, HM 950), shifts to the incorrect copy-text form of the name.

105.34-106.2 the Canadians . . . cold: Thoreau's source is Hugh Gray, *Letters from Canada, written during a residence there in the years 1806, 1807, and 1808* (London: Longman, Hurst, Rees, and Orme, 1809), p. 263. Copying from Gray in the Canadian Notebook, MS (NNPM, MA 595), Thoreau follows the source with "currying-comb" and "increased quantity of fur".

106.26   farther: Although two draft versions of the sentence have Thoreau's almost invariable "further", the reading "farther" in the copy-text here is unquestionable.

107.11-12   *Anglais*:   Thus in two draft versions of the passage and in P, which emends from the copy-text's slip of the pen, "*Anglois*".

107.20   *ce nuit*:   Thus in the copy-text and two preceding drafts; emended to the correct feminine "*cette nuit*" in P. Thoreau is accurately representing his poor conversational French.

107.26   *Y a-t-il*:   The copy-text reads "*Y-a-t'il*"; P removes the illogical hyphen after the first word of the construction; and Y completes the correction by replacing the illogical apostrophe between "*a-t*" and "*il*" with the requisite hyphen.

108.17   Patterson: Thoreau's sources vary between this copy-text spelling and "Paterson," the latter appearing in Joseph Bouchette, *The British Dominions in North America* (London: Longman, Rees, Orme, Brown, and Green, 1831), 1:279, 280, and Alfred Hawkins, *The Quebec Guide . . . with a plan of the City* (Quebec: W. Cowan and Son, 1844), p. 155.

110.5   It is: P thus emends from the copy-text's "They are", resulting from an incomplete revision. In the first draft, Thoreau paired "these falls" with "described them" and "They are"; in the next draft he repeated the original wording but then altered "these falls . . . described them" to "this fall . . . described it", leaving "They are" as the opening of the next sentence. The error carries over into the copy-text.

110.27   III. St. Anne.:   In the absence of setting-copy manuscript, copy-text from this point until 130.5, "masterpiece in its way.", is the first printing, P, 1 (March 1853): 322-339. See Headnote.

111.9   the map: Thoreau could be referring to a map he owned, "Map of the Eastern and Middle States &c. and also the British Provinces," in *Appletons' Railroad and Steamboat Companion* (see Textual Note 81.33-82.3), or to any of a number of other maps of the 1830s through early 1850s. Neither of the hand-traced or -copied maps of Canada in the Henry David Thoreau Papers, MCo-SC, shows the legend "Canada East": see Robert F. Stowell, *A Thoreau Gazetteer*, ed. William L. Howarth (Princeton: Princeton University Press, 1970), map 15, map 16, pp. 28, 30. Nor do the maps (also owned by Thoreau) accompanying Israel D. Andrews's *Report . . . on the Trade and Commerce of the British North American*

Colonies, Executive Documents, no. 136, House of Representatives, 1 session, 32 Congress (Washington: R. Armstrong, 1853). One of these maps is by Thomas C. Keefer; a second by Henry F. Perley; and a third drawn under the direction of the editor, *American Rail Road Journal*.

111.22-23 Cape Tourmente: Thus in the copy-text. Thoreau's notebooks and drafts show various treatments of the name: Cap Tourmente, Cape Tourmente, Cap Tourment, and Cape Tourment. These variations also appear among Thoreau's maps, guide-books, and other sources.

111.28-29 Bouchette's ... Canadas: The information given comes from Joseph Bouchette's *The British Dominions*, 1:177-178, rather than from the same author's earlier *A Topographical Description*. Thoreau took notes from both sources in the Canadian Notebook, MS (NNPM, MA 595).

111.29 Beaupré: Not accented in the copy-text, but thus twice in Thoreau's Canadian Notebook extracts, MS (NNPM, MA 595), and in Y.

112.6-7 Ange ... Angel: In his drafts, for this and later references to this place, Thoreau repeatedly misspelled the French adjective as "Guardien" and the English equivalent as "Gardian".

113.11-12 sometimes one-half ... sixty: This fact is put more clearly in the source, Bouchette's *The British Dominions*, 1:364: "It is not uncommon to meet with lands in the seigniories, whose dimensions are half an arpent in front by thirty in depth, forming a rectangular farm, whose breadth is to its length in the relative proportion of 1 to 60." In the Canadian Notebook, MS (NNPM, MA 595), Thoreau abbreviated the sentence to "Sometimes 1/2 arpent by 30 or 1 to 60".

113.18 land: Thus in the copy-text, as in the most recent surviving draft, MS (CSmH, HM 953 [b]). In an earlier draft, MS (CSmH, HM 949), and in the Canadian Notebook, MS (NNPM, MA 595), however, Thoreau writes "lands", reflecting the source, Bouchette, *The British Dominions*, 1:379.

113.31 their parishes: In the Canadian Notebook, MS (NNPM, MA 595), Thoreau translates from the source, Pierre-François-Xavier de Charlevoix, *Histoire et Description Générale de la Nouvelle France, avec le Journal Historique d'un Voyage fait ... dans l'Amérique Septentrionnale* (Paris: Chez Rollin Fils, 1744), 2:160, using the first person plural of the royal decree order as Charlevoix does: "that they should reduce our habitations to the form of our parishes, as much as

possible." The original, "nos Habitations", means "our settlements." A draft of the present passage gives the copy-text
reading, "their parishes", however. It is unclear whether
Thoreau's alteration of "habitations" to "parishes" is deliberate or inadvertent.

114.2   Hontan: A misreading by the compositor caused
the copy-text's "Houtan", corrected in Y. The source is Louis
Armand de Lom d'Arce, baron de Lahontan, *Voyages du
baron de La Hontan dans l'Amérique Septentrionale*, 2d ed., 2
vols. (Amsterdam: Chez F. l'Honore, 1705), which Thoreau
borrowed from the Harvard College Library. In the 1703 first
edition, differently paginated and titled *Nouveaux Voyages
. . .*, the quoted phrases fall at 1:272.

115.7   for summer: These words are followed in the
drafts, MS (CSmH, HM 949) and MS (CSmH, HM 953 [b]), by
"and a thick tight one for winter".

115.11   woollen: Here and at 120.2 and 138.21 the drafts
show Thoreau's habitual spelling, "woolen". However, one
draft instance has "woollen" with one "l" cancelled.

115.11   gray: The drafts for this sentence give Thoreau's
usual, but not invariable, spelling, "grey". For an authorial
"gray", see 86.35. At 100.1 the setting copy reads "grey" while
the preceding draft, MS (CSmH, HM 950), has "gray".

115.27   standing on: Thus in the drafts, MS (CSmH, HM
949) and MS (CSmH, HM 953 [b]). The less plausible copy-
text reading, "standing in", results from a copying error on
the part of Thoreau or, more likely, the P compositor. It is
retained in Y.

115.33   *Inri*:   Thoreau evidently did not know the meaning of the initials INRI placarded at the tops of crucifixes
(IESUS NASARENUS REX IUDAEORUM), for his drafts read
"*iniri*", and Y restores this misspelling in response, doubtless, to an authorial revision on a copy of the P printing.

115.34   symbolical: This word, from Y, appears to be an
authorial addition to the copy-text.

116.2-5   a weathercock . . . St. Peter: Thus in the copy-
text. In the draft, MS (CSmH, HM 949), Thoreau gives freer
vent to his iconoclastic impulses: "as we were walking along
the road we heard a creaking sound for it was a gusty day and
looking up saw a rusty weather-cock on the top of a cross by
the roadside–in a nich of which as usual there was a picture
of the Virgin Mary–and on the weathercock itself was the
word–which by its creaking it seemed to pronounce Ιησυς–

Iησυς– We went on our way admiring the miracle–though we could not help thinking that Iησυς needed greasing."

116.29 *"repose,"*: Y emends to *"Repose,"* but Thoreau clearly intends the word as an alternative to *"git"*, a third-person singular indicative verb between *"Ici"* and the name of the person who lies or reposes here (*ici* or *ci*).

116.33-34 appeared. . . . he answered: Y restores the sentence division that Thoreau intended, as is evident from the draft, MS (CSmH, HM 953 [b]). A misreading by the P compositor produced the construction "appeared to our *Parlez-vous Anglais? Even he answered . . ."*

117.20 immigrant: A draft version of the sentence, MS (CSmH, HM 953 [b]), reads "emigrant", consistent with the source title, Sir Francis B. Head, *The Emigrant* (London: John Murray, 1846); see p. 39. Yet the context allows for "immigrant", which may have been the reading in Thoreau's lost printer's copy for this chapter.

117.27 and even beans: Thus in the copy-text, though Thoreau cancels "even" in a draft version, MS (CSmH, HM 953 [b]).

117.33 *snells*: Thoreau accurately represents what he heard, both in the copy-text and in a surviving draft. The French and French-Canadian term "senelle" or "cenelle" (see Textual Note 159.19), meaning hawthorn-fruit (haw), is pronounced with the first "e" elided. Moreover, in his reading about Canadian geography, Thoreau would have encountered the place-name "Anse [cove, small bay] aux Snelles" on the lower St. Lawrence at the mouth of the Mitis River: see, for example, Bouchette, *The British Dominions*, 1:319. The editor has found the word spelled "snelle" at Domaine des Fleurs, a botanical garden near Kamouraska, Que., July 1995, in reference to the fruit of a hawthorn, apparently *Crataegus brainerdi*.

118.13 *à la*: Accented thus in the draft, MS (CSmH, HM 949), and in Y; the copy-text gives *"a"* without the accent. Thoreau also writes "Sault à la Puce" in the draft of a later reference to this river, at 126.25.

118.30-31 *Ste. Anne ... Ste. Anne*: In the drafts, MS (CSmH, HM 949) and MS (CSmH, HM 953 [b]), here and later, Thoreau uses the French abbreviation for Saint or Holy (feminine), "Ste.", sometimes with the "e" superscribed, when using the name in French language contexts. The copy-text anglicizes to *"St. Anne"*, possibly with a view to consistency

with the place-name in an English context ("between Chateau Richer and St. Anne") in the first half of the sentence.
See 120.34, 121.23.

118.35   we had grand: Thus in the copy-text; in the draft,
MS (CSmH, HM 953 [b]), Thoreau writes "we had had grand".
It is not clear whether the change is a revision by Thoreau or
a copying or typesetting error.

119.32   eleven miles: Thoreau quotes from McCulloch,
M'Culloch's Universal Gazetteer, 2:art. "Laurence, or Lawrence (St.)." There, the breadth of the St. Lawrence below the
Isle of Orleans is properly given as "11 m." Thoreau added the
footnote at 119.31-37 to the text for Y, where, probably due to
a compositor's misreading, the distance was given as "a
mile". He knew from personal observation that the river widened substantially a few miles below Quebec; in the drafts he
twice writes that the breadth at St. Anne is eleven miles, and
once he writes "a dozen".

119.33   Point Pelee: Thus in McCulloch and in the Canadian Notebook, MS (NNPM, MA 595), where Thoreau transcribes from the source. "Point Peter" in Y results from a
compositor's difficulty with Thoreau's handwriting on the
accompanying slip of paper or the marginal notation on
the pages from P which constituted printer's copy for this
portion of chapter 3. The proper form of the name, given by
at least two others of Thoreau's sources, is "Pelée" (see
Bouchette, *A Topographical Description*, p. 51, and Head, *The
Emigrant*, p. 241).

120.2   woollen: See Textual Note 115.11.

120.9-10   He shouted . . . breed).:   Thus in Y, an authorial
revision to the copy-text's "He said *Brock!*" Although at the
time–and while writing the drafts on which the P setting copy
was based–Thoreau seemed to mean that he asked his host
the dog's name, he realized afterward that the reply, "Brock"
(or rather "Braque", pronounced like "Brock" in English),
was a breed name, and adjusted the text accordingly.

120.10   We . . . called: Thus in Y, an authorial revision
from the copy-text's "At Binet's they called the cat".

120.14-15   *vent*," if . . . wind. They: Thus in Y, which restores the sentence division of the drafts. In the copy-text a
period replaces the comma after "*vent*", "if" is changed to
"If", a comma replaces the period after "wind", and "They" is
changed to "they". A compositor's or editor's sophistication
is suspected.

120.26 *plus beau*: In Y Thoreau corrects his French from "*plus bel*". Assuming that the controlling noun is the masculine *saut*, rather than the feminine *chute d'eau* or *cascade* (which would require *belle* and *grande*), *beau* is the proper form of the adjective. *Bel* would be proper as the masculine adjective if the following word were a noun beginning with a vowel or a silent "h."

120.35 book: Singular in the draft and Y, though "books" in the copy-text. Thoreau draws the quotation from *The Canadian Guide Book*, pp. 77-78.

121.15-18 In early . . . there.: This sentence, which occurs in both drafts, MS (CSmH, HM 949) and MS (CSmH, HM 953 [b]), seems an essential connective for the immediately preceding and following material. It is omitted in the copy-text, and is not restored in Y.

121.33 observed: The copy-text reads "observes", inconsistently with the rest of the sentence and contrary to "observed" and "said" in two drafts of the statement about Charlevoix.

122.30 tumbled: Y thus corrects the copy-text, which reads "tumbles". The draft also uses the past tense.

124.8 *a black streak*: If the italics in the copy-text are in fact authorial, Thoreau's purpose in thus emphasizing the phrase is unclear. In two draft versions, "a black streak" is not underlined.

124.34 a field: The copy-text reading, "the field", appears not to be authorial. Two draft versions of the sentence, in MS (CSmH, HM 949) and MS (CSmH, HM 953 [b]), support the emendation to the indefinite article.

125.10-12 They have . . . for us.: Compare *Cape Cod*, p. 185, and see Textual Note 135.9-19.

125.12 *prairie*: The emphasis shown by underlining in the draft is thus restored by Y. The copy-text prints "prairie" in roman.

125.32 *St. Fereole*: So spelled (twice) in the drafts and in Y, which emends the copy-text's "*St. Fercole*", a compositor's misreading. The spelling and accentuation of this place-name, a village north of St. Anne, vary a good bit among the contemporary maps studied by the editor, and among Thoreau's sources: "Fereol" ("Map of the Provinces of Lower & Upper Canada, Nova Scotia, [etc.] . . . [by] Joseph Bouchette, Jun. Engraved by J. & C. Walker London [1831]," in three large sections, and "Map of the Provinces of Canada,

New Brunswick, Nova Scotia, Newfoundland, and Prince Edward Island ... compiled ... by Joseph Bouchette 1846 Engraved by Sherman & Smith, New York"); "Féréol" (Hawkins, *The Quebec Guide*); "Fèrèol" (MacGregor, *British America*). In the Canadian Notebook, MS (NNPM, MA 595), quoting from Bouchette's *A Topographical Description*, p. 552, Thoreau respects the Surveyor-General's "Féréole". In MS (CSmH, HM 949), he notes that the inhabitants usually gave to a mountain the name of its nearby village, and he specifically gives the example of the mountain called St. Fereole.

125.33 *Belange*: The copy-text reads "*Bélangé*", an error not remedied by a change in Y, "*Bélange*". In the draft, MS (CSmH, HM 949), Thoreau writes, "pointing toward Cap Tourmen[te] I inquired its name of a habitant whom we met, he hazzarded the name Belange–or fair Angel, or perhaps he referred to some other *mt*–". The original version of that sentence, in the Journal for November 11, 1851 (*Journal 4*, p. 175), likewise has the phrase "Belange–or fair angel".

125.34 *St. Hyacinthe*: Thus in the copy-text; Thoreau spells the name without the terminal "e" in the draft of this passage. Once again, the practice of Thoreau's sources and contemporary maps varies. *The Canadian Guide Book* has "St. Hyacinthe" (pp. 119, 121), though its map by Staveley and map 10 of *Appletons' Railroad and Steamboat Companion* have "St. Hyacinth"; Bouchette's maps of 1831 and 1846, Bouchette's *A Topographical Description*, p. 213, and MacGregor, *British America*, 2:417, read "St. Hyacinthe". The spelling with the "e" appears in a reference by Emerson during his April 1852 Montreal trip, in *JMN*, 13:22.

125.35 *St. Johns*: The draft of this sentence gives an "s" at the end of the name, as is Thoreau's practice in all his manuscript references to this fort and town on the Richelieu River (see Textual Note 84.21). In the copy-text and Y it is given as "*St. John*".

126.3 *Longueil*: See Textual Note 93.23.

126.3 *Bartholomy*: Thus in the drafts, MS (CSmH, HM 949) and MS (CSmH, HM 953 [b]), as in the copy-text. The earliest surviving version of this sentence is in the Journal for July 22, 1851. There Thoreau writes, "the names of the mountains & the streams & the villages reel with the intoxication of poetry–Longoeil Chambly–Barthillon? Montilly?" (*Journal 3*, p. 328). The editor has not been able to discover either "Barthillon" or "Bartholomy" in Thoreau's sources or on maps of

Quebec. A hamlet on the north bank of the St. Lawrence near Berthierville, opposite the mouth of the Richelieu River, is named St. Barthélemy. Whether Thoreau misheard or mis-remembered this name, or whether "Bartholomy" was a name of only local currency, like "Belange," cannot be confidently conjectured.

126.10   Bay were: The copy-text's comma after "Bay", preserved in Y, obscures the syntax of Thoreau's sentence. In both early and late drafts, MS (CSmH, HM 949) and MS (CSmH, HM 953 [b]), "the woods . . . France and Germany" is an independent clause, without internal punctuation.

127.4-22   Most . . . world.:   This material, lacking in the copy-text but represented in an early draft, MS (CSmH, HM 949), was first printed in Y. "Catskill" and "Katterskil", the latter used in the draft, were both accepted spellings for the celebrated falls near a resort called the "Mountain House," west of present-day Catskill, New York, about 95 miles by river from New York City. "Bashpish" or "Bash Bish" or "Barshaspiss" Falls are in the Taconic range of extreme southwestern Massachusetts, near the village of South Egremont. See *A Week*, p. 245, for another reference by Thoreau.

127.7-8   "two . . . falls":   Thus in Y and the draft, MS (CSmH, HM 949), and thus worded in the Canadian Notebook, MS (NNPM, MA 595), where Thoreau copies from Bouchette, *A Topographical Description*, p. 553. The original reads "two or three very romantic falls".

127.13   they: Underlined in the draft, MS (CSmH, HM 949).

127.16   drunk: Thus in the draft, MS (CSmH, HM 949), though "drank" in Y. At 108.2 Thoreau's setting copy reads "drunk" as a past participle, while both P and Y give "drank".

129.18   *snells*:   See Textual Note 117.33.

130.5   This man's: The P serialization having concluded with the previous sentence, copy-text for the remainder of chapter 3 (and for all of chapters 4 and 5) is Y.

130.5-36   This man's . . . *étoffe*.:   This material is represented on two heavily revised draft leaves at MH-H. The leaves show a compositional stage, chiefly in pencil, *beyond* the text as it appears in Y. Whether Thoreau decided not to update the statistics on Montmorenci County, or whether the revisions failed to be incorporated in Y for some other reason, cannot be determined. At 130.8, before "In 1827," a chapter division is introduced: "No. 4. The Character of the

Canadians, & the Fortifications of Quebec."; 130.8, "In 1827" cancelled; 130.8, "to which" cancelled and "not including" interlined; 130.9, "which" interlined after "Orleans"; 130.9, "since" cancelled and "recently" interlined; 130.9, "was" cancelled and "is" interlined; 130.10-11, "being the . . . in extent" cancelled; 130.14-17, "I quote . . . recent growth" cancelled and "I am obliged partly to guess at the number for want of any recent statistics" interlined, referring to the ink sentence, "Lying as it were under the walls of Quebec, its population was then only 3.782.", revised in pencil to read "population is only some 4 or 5000"; 130.17, "were" cancelled and "are" interlined; 130.17-18, "this county . . . date, five" cancelled and "it only a dozen" interlined; 130.18-19, "and no others . . . presbyteries" cancelled; 130.19, "or 3" interlined before "schools"; 130.19, "two corn-" cancelled and "a few grist" interlined; 130.20, "four" cancelled and "&" interlined; 130.20-21, "perhaps not many years since" interlined before "no medical man"; 130.21-25, "five shopkeepers . . . tons!" cancelled and "I saw nothing which we should call a tavern– hardly even a grocery or mechanic's shop & as for [its?] tonnage there are only a few pirogues & sail boats" interlined; 130.26, "This" cancelled (in ink); 130.28, "banks" altered to "bank" (in ink; see Textual Note 130.28); 130.28-33, "This describes . . . account for." cancelled; 130.33, "were" cancelled and "are" interlined.

130.11   Lower Canada: In at least three instances Thoreau modified "Lower Canada" in MS (CSmH, HM 953 [b]) to "Canada East". In the revised draft version of this sentence, MS (MH-H), the mention of Lower Canada is simply deleted.

130.19-20   two corn-mills: Thus in the copy-text. Taking notes in the Canadian Notebook, MS (NNPM, MA 595), from Bouchette, *The British Dominions*, 1:350, Thoreau wrote "3 corn mills".

130.22   *sign*:   The copy-text prints "sign" in roman, but in MS (MH-H) and MS (CSmH, HM 949), Thoreau's underlining conveys his intention to pun. See 119.14-19.

130.24-25   river craft: Thus in the source (Bouchette, *The British Dominions*, 1:351), the Canadian Notebook, MS (NNPM, MA 595), and the drafts, MS (MH-H) and MS (CSmH, HM 949). The copy-text reading, "river crafts", seems nonauthorial.

130.28   bank: Thoreau's revision in MS (MH-H) is superior to the earlier reading, "banks", reflected in the copy-text, since Montmorenci County is confined to the north bank of the St. Lawrence.

131.2 soccage: Consistently so spelled in Thoreau's sources, in his Canadian Notebook extracts, MS (NNPM, MA 595), and in his drafts. The immediate source here is Bouchette, *The British Dominions*, 1:182, 300-301, though several of Thoreau's other sources explain the soccage tenure. Here and at 131.30 and 132.33 the copy-text reads "socage".

131.13 fines. According: Thus in the copy-text. In the draft, MS (CSmH, HM 953 [b]), Thoreau has "fines.–according". It is not clear whether he intends the dependent clause to stand as a sentence fragment.

131.23-24 all the grain: Thoreau's source, Bouchette, *A Topographical Description*, p. 13 (see also Bouchette, *The British Dominions*, 1:378), reads "all grain"; but Thoreau introduced the article in the Canadian Notebook, MS (NNPM, MA 595), and retained it in the draft, MS (CSmH, HM 953 [b]).

132.2-5 In 1846 . . . Parliament: Thoreau here draws on Eliot Warburton (i.e., George Drought Warburton, Eliot's brother), *Hochelaga; or, England in the New World* (New York: Wiley & Putnam, 1846), 1:300, from which he had copied in the Canadian Notebook, MS (NNPM, MA 595): "one out of six in the whole population having the power of voting". But Warburton's remarks about the qualifications for suffrage and the proportion of inhabitants qualified to vote for the Legislative Assembly (the lower house of Parliament) refer collectively to both Canada East and Canada West, rather than, as Thoreau implies, to Canada East specifically.

132.10-11 In some . . . incredibly filthy.: The draft, MS (CSmH, HM 949), reads "this was the most filthy of any peo[ple I have seen]". Earlier in the same manuscript, Thoreau was more specific about the habits that offended him, the open disposal of human waste by the road-side: "Privies were scarcely to be seen if they existed at all, but there was frequently a disgusting deposit which had been long accumulating on the opposite side of the way directly in front of a house, which the foot-traveller came near falling into. It evinced such filthiness in the inhabitants as I had never dreamed of; Yet strange to say from the openness of it it was very little offensive to the nostrils."

132.29-33 Parliament . . . &c.: The matter in quotation marks, from Bouchette, *The British Dominions*, 1:382-383n, is inexact.

132.35   peasants.:   At this point in the draft, MS (CSmH, HM 953 [b]), Thoreau writes, "Yes–peasants–for though any inhabitant of the northern U S would feel insulted if you should call him a peasant–that is the proper title of a French Canadian."

133.1   immigrants: The draft, MS (CSmH, HM 953 [b]), has "emigrants"; but see Textual Note 117.20.

133.7   Denonville: Thoreau accurately copied this name from Charlevoix, *Histoire*, 2:324-325, in the Canadian Notebook, MS (NNPM, MA 595). In the fourth Indian Notebook, MS (NNPM, MA 599), taking extracts from Charlevoix and Lahontan, he again spells the name correctly. The copy-text reads "Denouville".

133.10-11   to think . . . error: Charlevoix reads "de reconnoître qu'on se trompoit", which Thoreau translates more idiomatically in the Canadian Notebook, MS (NNPM, MA 595), "to think themselves mistaken".

133.24-134.22   them . . . selling strong: Two leaves of almost fair copy, with limited pencilled revisions, survive for this section in MS (NN-BGC), in addition to rougher worksheets in MS (CSmH, HM 953 [b]). As with the MS (MH-H) leaves corresponding to 130.5-36, some revisions on MS (NN-BGC) go beyond the Y state of the text: 133.27, "fashions.'" followed by interlined "This is in some measure true today &"; 133.27, "Thus" cancelled and "while" changed to "While"; 134.13, "on me" followed by interlined "also"; 134.20, "live in earnest and" cancelled and "work & get their living" interlined.

134.8   1630:   Thus in the copy-text, as on MS (NN-BGC); an earlier draft version in MS (CSmH, HM 953 [b]) and Thoreau's notes based on Charlevoix in the Canadian Notebook, MS (NNPM, MA 595), give the erroneous date "1632". Quebec was yielded to an English fleet in July 1629, and was ceded back to the French in 1632.

134.31   foothold: In the surviving draft, MS (CSmH, HM 953 [b]), where this sentence appears as a marginal addition in pencil, Thoreau underlines "foothold", perhaps to stress a play on words in light of the image of the French holding on by the fur of wild animals.

135.9-19   Yet . . . traders.:   This passage comes close to duplicating *Cape Cod*, pp. 184-185. A leaf in MS (NN-BGC) begins "of the English was that of sailors who land but for a day, and their enterprise the enterprise of traders." It continues with matter appearing in *Cape Cod*, pp. 185, 187-188, and 180. For the overlap of Thoreau's efforts on his Cape Cod and Canada projects, see the Historical Introduction and Textual Introduction to *Cape Cod* (pp. 256-257, 258-259, 299-300), and the Headnote.

135.28 a poor man.: At this point in the draft, MS (CSmH, HM 953 [b]), Thoreau introduces several pages of extracts on the manners of the French Canadians prefaced by the following statement: "As I have presented a rather unfavorable view of him, perhaps from having gone so little way behind the scenes in my rapid excursion, I will refer the Reader to 'A Political & Historical Account of Lower Canada, by a Canadian,' which exhibits him in a more pleasing light." Thoreau drew this material from Bouchette, *The British Dominions*, 1:403-416.

136.1 *Chi-pré*: Thus in the copy-text and in the draft, MS (CSmH, HM 949); the actual name of the stream is (la Rivière du) Petit Pré. The first syllable of *petit* is radically shortened in Quebecois pronunciation.

136.9-10 in Canada.: At this point in an early draft, MS (CSmH, HM 949), Thoreau writes, "just beyond [Montmorenci Falls] met Col. Whiting and Mr. Scherb upon an omnibus." The first was William Whiting of Concord, and the second E. V. Scherb, an emigré poet and literary scholar from Basel, a friend of Julia Ward Howe and Henry Wadsworth Longfellow.

136.22 Chaudière: Thus accented in the copy-text, a possible imposition by an editor or compositor. In the surviving drafts, all apparently antedating 1853, Thoreau consistently writes this name without the accent. Various of his maps and source-books do the same, e.g., the Staveley map accompanying *The Canadian Guide Book*, map no. 28 of *Appletons' Railroad and Steamboat Companion* and pp. 186, 189; Gray, *Letters from Canada*, p. 94; the large Bouchette maps of 1831 and 1846; and the H. V. Nelson map, "North America. British Provinces of New Brunswick, Nova Scotia, & Part of Canada ...," London [184–]. See Textual Note 95.8.

137.14-22 Chaudière ... Chaudière: Thoreau omits the grave accents in each instance in the surviving draft, MS (Paul Brown). See Textual Note 136.22.

138.20 checkered: Possibly a nonauthorial spelling. A draft version, MS (CSmH, HM 949), reads "checquered".

138.21 woollen: See Textual Note 115.11. The draft, MS (CSmH, HM 949), has "woolen".

138.24-25 in the streets.: In MS (CSmH, HM 949) Thoreau follows this sentence with some personal details. The loss of later drafts makes it impossible to determine when this material was eliminated from the narrative: "By this time I had got cold in my head from wearing a palmleaf hat without lining in that wintry climate– So in the morning I asked our hostess–Pouvez vous coudre pour moi du drap epais dedans mon chapeau? She did it very neatly, and I have kept it in ever since in remembrance of her & Canada."

139.28 Governor's Garden: This name is inconsistent with "Government Garden" at 140.2, but the surviving manuscripts have the same two readings in the two sentences.

142.8 were faithfully: In a draft leaf, MS (PPi), Thoreau cancels "were" and interlines "are". A later draft, MS (IdU), reads "are", but the copy-text reading is more likely to be a reflection of the author's reversal to the original tense in the lost setting copy than the result of a compositor's error or sophistication.

142.13 further: Although the copy-text has "farther", MS (IdU) spells this word "further", Thoreau's preferred form, in a pencilled addition to the ink text.

142.23 get: MS (IdU) reads "got"; the copy-text's present tense may result from a compositor's error.

143.21 Bucaniers: Thus in the copy-text and MS (CSmH, HM 953 [b]), the latter altered from "Buccaniers". The earliest surviving manuscript version of the sentence is in the Journal for August 18, 1851, where the word is spelled "Buccaniers" (*Journal 3*, p. 374); in MS (CSmH, HM 949) Thoreau has "buccanniers". See *Maine Woods*, p. 134, for Thoreau's remarks on the derivation of the term (there spelled "buccaneer"). His French lexicon, (Abel) *Boyer's French Dictionary* (Boston: T. Bedlington, and Bradford & Peaslee, 1827), gives "Boucanier," and Webster gives both "Bucaneer" and "Bucanier."

144.20-23 yet Wolfe ... fortifications.: See *Cape Cod*, p. 210, for another expression of this same event and sentiment. "Hinderance" is the spelling approved in Thoreau's dictionaries.

145.11 in case of: In the Canadian Notebook, MS (NNPM, MA 595), Thoreau accurately copied "in cases of" from his source, Benjamin Silliman, *Remarks Made on a*

Short Tour Between Hartford and Quebec, 2d ed. (New-Haven: S. Converse, 1824), p. 297, but by a late draft stage, MS (CSmH, HM 953 [b]), he had changed the quoted phrase to the copy-text form.

146.3 if desired: Thoreau continues the mock advertisement in the draft, MS (CSmH, HM 953 [b]), as follows: "Payment made easy & possession given immediately, as the subscriber is going to invest his capitol in other business. Address, postpaid, V. R. Strand." This material is isolated with horizontal ink lines and is marked vertically with a single pencilled line, a "use mark" of the sort that normally indicates that a passage had been recopied.

146.22 verdigrease: Thus in the copy-text as in the draft, MS (CSmH, HM 953 [b]). While three of Thoreau's dictionaries (Johnson, Walker, and Webster) give only the modern spelling, "verdigris," Bailey has "verdegrease," and the *OED* notes instances of "verdigrease."

148.21 *white*: Underlined in the draft, MS (CSmH, HM 953 [b]). Thoreau's emphasis there is part of a pattern of pencilled revision to an ink sentence that originally began "What makes our government slaveholding as it is, more tolerable, is the fact . . ." The copy-text prints "white" in roman.

148.32 and its tools: Thus in the copy-text, in MS (CSmH, HM 949) (with "its" added after first writing), and in MS (CSmH, HM 953 [b]); both drafts use the ampersand for "and". In the original version of the passage, a Journal entry for August 21, 1851 (see *Journal 4*, p. 3, line 30, and Later Revision 3.30, p. 763), the entire sentence is a pencilled addition, reading "It goes out onto the plains of abraham & exhibits itself & toots [–] whistles so that you can not mistake it". The image of conspicuous whistling is carried over to both MS (CSmH, HM 949) and MS (CSmH, HM 953 [b]), but is cancelled in both those drafts, where "its tools" are clearly the two foregoing words. The crossing stroke of the fourth letter of "toots" in the Journal manuscript is conceivably a stray mark. Evidently on the basis of the Journal manuscript, 1906, 5:84, substitutes "and toots" for "and its tools".

149.24 restaurants: The copy-text, like MS (CSmH, HM 953 [b]), reads "restaurateurs". But an earlier draft, MS (CSmH, HM 949), has "restaurants" in this sentence. Perhaps seeing "Restaurateur" after the proprietor's name on the sign or window of an eating-establishment, Thoreau became confused as to the application of the latter term. When away from Concord, Thoreau was accustomed to taking his meals at a private house or an inn, or carrying them with him, or preparing them over a campfire. See also Textual Note 158.15.

150.2   a large map of Canada: This map has not been and probably cannot be positively identified. The largest pre-1851 chart including upper and lower Canada that the editor has examined is Joseph Bouchette's of 1846, which due to its relative recency is a more likely candidate than the same cartographer's large three-part map of 1831 (for full identifications see Textual Note 125.32). For another hypothesis, involving "[V. H.] Nelson's New Map of British Provinces of North America" (1840), see Stowell, *A Thoreau Gazetteer*, p. 29. The present editor has examined several Nelson maps of the 1840s, plus maps of the same decade and 1850-1852 by J. Sleath, Ensign & Thayer, S. Augustus Mitchell, and Johnson, without being convinced that any of them is more likely to meet Thoreau's description than those by Bouchette.

150.30   further: Two surviving draft versions, both in MS (CSmH, HM 953 [b]), give this, Thoreau's preferred spelling. The copy-text, which in earlier instances replaced P's "further" with "farther", apparently did the same with the lost manuscript that served as setting copy for this chapter. See Rejected Substantives 106.26, 111.20-21, and 125.17.

151.8   "*Qui . . . tôt!*":   Thus in the copy-text, and, save for "*&*" after "*donc!*", in two surviving drafts, MS (CSmH, HM 949) and MS (Suzanne Y. H. Kurtz). In *Journal 3*, p. 134, Thoreau records a conversation on November 8, 1850, with his French-Canadian woodchopper friend Alex Therien, who gave "March-donc" as his countrymen's expression for "giddyap." The Journal entry, the drafts, and the copy-text all misspell the French imperative (second person singular) *Marche* by dropping the terminal letter. One of Thoreau's sources, Warburton's *Hochelaga*, represents the drivers' cries as "*Marchez! marchez!*" and "*marchez donc*" (1:23, 75). "Qué! vaches! qué!" and "Quien! p'tits! quien!" are given as farmers' calls to cattle in Sylvia Clapin, *Dictionnaire Canadien-Français*, 1894 (rpt. Québec: Les Presses de l'Université Laval, 1974).

152.3   *Que bec!*:   In a version of this story that Thoreau took from Claude Bacqueville de La Potherie, *Histoire de l'Amérique Septentrionale* (Paris, 1722), via Alfred Hawkins, *Hawkins's Picture of Quebec* (Quebec: Printed by Neilson &

Cowan for the Proprietor, 1834), p. 114, and copied into the Canadian Notebook, MS (NNPM, MA 595), the wording was "*Quel bec!*" But in the early lecture draft, MS (CSmH, HM 949), Thoreau uses the form that the copy-text was to follow. *The Canadian Guide Book*, pp. 50-51, also assigns "*Que bec!*" to Cartier's Norman pilot. Thoreau also encountered the story in Peter (Pehr) Kalm, *Travels into North America*, transl. John Reinhold Forster (London: for the Editor, 1770-1771), 3:111, where the words uttered are represented as "*Que bec*", annotated "Meaning *Quel bec.*"

152.11 Edinburgh: "Edingburg" in the Canadian Note-book, MS (NNPM, MA 595), where Thoreau takes extracts from Hugh Gray, and "Edinburg" in MS (CSmH, HM 949). See Textual Note 90.2.

152.26-34 I still ... direction.: This passage, one phrase of which appears in the Canadian Notebook, MS (NNPM, MA 595), and all of which is represented in two drafts, MS (CSmH, HM 949) and MS (James Dawson), has parallels in Hawkins's *Picture of Quebec*, pp. 6-7, and the same author's *The Quebec Guide*, pp. 50-53.

153.1 portal of: Thus in the copy-text. Thoreau's source, *The Canadian Guide Book*, p. 52, reads "portal to", as does the surviving draft, MS (CSmH, HM 949).

153.3-6 It is but ... Africa.: The source, Bouchette's *The British Dominions*, 1:281-282, reads "country for ten leagues to the northward", "capital of British North America", and "as little or less known", but the differences in the copy-text's paraphrases are anticipated in the Canadian Notebook, MS (NNPM, MA 595).

153.9-10 her history: Thoreau underlines "her" in a sur-viving draft version, MS (CSmH, HM 949).

153.19 "Hochelaga" ... "Saguenay,": On the Ortelius map "Americae sive novi orbis nova descriptio", following p. 2 of the source, the first place-name is misspelled "Hoch-gelaga" and the second is rendered "Saguenai". On the world map, "Typus orbis terrarum" following p. 1, the first does not appear and the second is spelled "Saguenay".

154.5-6 Schoolcraft ... Mississippi.: Thus in the copy-text. The source is Henry R. Schoolcraft, *Information Re-specting ... the Indian Tribes of the United States* (Philadel-phia: Lippincott, Grambo & Company, 1851-1857), 1:133; 3:32. Taking extracts from volume one in the Canadian Notebook,

MS (NNPM, MA 595), Thoreau writes, "& [Schoolcraft] also says p 133, 'It appears, from the archaeological collections of *Ternaux Campans*, that the mouth of the Mississippi was discovered by the Spanish from Cuba, under M. Narvaez, in the month of Novembermber, 1527, during an expedition made with boats to trace the Floridian coasts of the Gulf westwardly.'" At a later date Thoreau cancelled this entry with a notation, "Ap[pears] to have been misled by Gallatin". The occasion of this comment may well have been Thoreau's encountering in Schoolcraft, 3:32, the following footnote to a more detailed recital of the ill-fated adventure (1528) of Pamphilio (Pamphilo) de Narvaez: "It has been stated by Mr. Gallatin, vide Am. Eth. Trans., Vol. II, p.—, that he discovered the mouth of the Mississippi; but this is not sustained by De Vaca and there is no other authority." The De Vaca referred to is Alvar Nuñez Cabeça (Cabeza) de Vaca, a member of Narvaez's party who survived, and whose *Narrative* Schoolcraft read in Buckingham Smith's English translation (Washington: privately printed, 1851). The paper by Albert Gallatin on which Schoolcraft evidently based his statement at 1:133 is a long introduction to "Hale's Indians of North-West America, and Vocabularies of North America," *Transactions of the American Ethnological Society*, 2 (New York: Bartlett & Welford, 1848). At pp. liv-lvii, Gallatin summarizes Cabeza de Vaca's narrative as printed in a collection by (Henri) Ternaux-Compans; and at p. lvii Gallatin asserts that a river mouth passed by Narvaez was the Mississippi and that the date of this discovery was October 30 or 31, 1528 O.S. The present editor acknowledges the parenthetical nature of this sentence and the next–which Thoreau probably added to the lost setting copy in the form of an attached slip–by emending with marks of parentheses before "Schoolcraft" and after "say so."

154.6 De Vaca: The copy-text reads "De Vega", apparently an error by Thoreau or the printer. No manuscript for the short sentence survives, but see preceding Textual Note on Schoolcraft and Gallatin. Thoreau almost certainly refers to Schoolcraft's correction of himself in *Information*, 3:32n. In Buckingham Smith's translation of Cabeza de Vaca's *Narrative*, the translator does not commit himself to specifying which geographical feature in the account, if any, corresponds to the Mississippi, though surely some of the starving Spaniards passed or crossed it while proceeding westward.

At one point Cabeza de Vaca writes that they entered a bay with many islets, where they "took fresh water from the sea, for the stream entered it impetuously" (p. 38). This could, however, have been any of a number of rivers in flood–the Alabama, for example. Narvaez, in another boat from Cabeza de Vaca, tells the latter to go his own way; and it is subsequently reported to Cabeza de Vaca by survivors who had remained with Narvaez that during a respite on the coast their commander insisted on spending the night aboard his makeshift vessel, and was blown out to sea, alone, in a storm (p. 59). Buckingham Smith conjectures (p. 131) that this occurred at the mouth of the Perdido River, just west of Pensacola Bay. His only mention of the Mississippi is in a note, pp. 128-129, intended to demonstrate that the coast between the Florida peninsula and Mexico had been explored as early as 1519 by Francisco Garay, and that Florida and the Mississippi's mouth appeared on a map "in the geography of Ptolomeus, printed at Venice in 1513." A remote possibility remains, however, that by "De Vega" Thoreau intended to designate Garcilaso de la Vega ("El Inca"), whose history of the exploits of Hernando de Soto, *La Florida del Inca* (1605), includes various statements about the enterprise of Narvaez in North America nine years prior to De Soto's. An English translation available to Thoreau was Theodore Irving, *The Conquest of Florida, by Hernando de Soto*, rev. ed. (New-York: George P. Putnam, 1851).

154.11   winter: Two surviving draft versions, MS (CSmH, HM 949) and MS (CSmH, HM 953 [b]), read "winters", and the copy-text may reflect a printer's error.

154.34   *Marsouins*:   The modernized spelling is probably Thoreau's. His source, Pierre Boucher, *Histoire veritable et naturelle . . . du pays . . . dite le Canada* (Paris: Chez Florentin Lambert, 1664), p. 74, reads "Marsoins".

154.35-36   P. H. Gosse: The copy-text gives "A." as Philip Henry Gosse's middle initial, probably because the compositor mistook Thoreau's "H" for an "A". *The Canadian Naturalist* was published by John Van Voorst, London, in 1840. A partial leaf of Thoreau's extracts from this volume, including the author's name but not the remark about the white dolphin (Beluga), survives (MS [ViU]).

155.8   "America" of 1670:   In the copy-text the close quotation mark falls after the date; but the date is not part of the title of John Ogilby's *America; Being an Accurate Description of the New World* (London: Printed by T. Johnson for the Author, 1670). Two draft versions, MS (CSmH, HM 949) and MS (CSmH, HM 953 [b]), use neither quotation marks nor underscores for the citation.

155.10   Niew: So spelled in the copy-text and in two draft versions of the sentence, MS (CSmH, HM 949) and MS (CSmH, HM 953 [b]). The Ogilby map has "Nieu", accurately followed in the Canadian Notebook, MS (NNPM, MA 595), and in a Journal entry for November 17, 1850 (*Journal 3*, p. 145). For the variable spelling of this adjective in the seventeenth-century maps Thoreau studied for an understanding of the history of the northeastern portion of North America, see *Cape Cod*, Textual Note 178.25.

155.15   Cataraqui: So spelled in Thoreau's immediate source for the various names of the river along its course, McCulloch, *M'Culloch's Universal Gazetteer*, 2:art. "Laurence, or Lawrence (St.)," and also in Bouchette, *The British Dominions*, 1:126-127, and Bouchette, *A Topographical Description*, p. 43. The copy-text and two draft versions of the sentence, MS (CSmH, HM 949) and MS (CSmH, HM 953 [b]), read "Cateraqui". No precedent has been found for Thoreau's spelling of the name.

155.16   St. Mary's: "St. Mary" in McCulloch, *M'Culloch's Universal Gazetteer*, while Bouchette, *The British Dominions*, 1:127, calls the same stretch of river "the Narrows, or the Falls of St. Mary". Thoreau's form is anticipated in Israel D. Andrews's *Report*, p. 49 (see Textual Note 111.9).

155.36   near . . . five (?):   An early draft, MS (CSmH, HM 949), lacks the parenthetical question mark. In a later version, MS (CSmH, HM 953 [b]), however, Thoreau expresses a measure of doubt when he adds a pencilled marginal comment, "retain the 105". The figures Thoreau provides come from both Bouchette's *The British Dominions*, 1:165-167, and *A Topographical Description*, pp. 48-51. The differing estimate of the river's width between Cape Rosier and the Mingan Islands comes from "Chart of the Gulf and River St. Lawrence, including the Coast from Breton Island to Cape Cod, and the Island and Banks of Newfoundland. Compiled from the Surveys of Capt. H. W. Bayfield [and Others]. London: James Imray & Son." The present editor has managed to find (at DLC) only a copy dated 1858–the *National Union Catalogue, Pre-1956 Imprints* lists another dated 1858 at MB–but Thoreau examined an earlier one. On the first page of the Canadian Notebook, MS (NNPM, MA 595), among titles of works on Canada he intends to consult, Thoreau records having seen at [David?] Loring's two charts of the St. Lawrence, both published by Imray: a chart of the river up to Montreal, London, 1850, and one dated 1851, on a smaller scale, of the Gulf and river up to Quebec, "Capt. Byfield & other's Survey". On a late page of the same notebook he takes notes from "the Chart of the Gulf of the St Lawrence & the River up to Quebec–Surveyed by Capt. Bayfield & others & pub. by James Imray London '51". The notes include the present reference to the river's width.

156.25   *Psamma arenaria*:   The specific name is mistakenly given as "*arenarium*" in the copy-text and, without underlines, in the surviving draft, MS (CSmH, HM 953 [b]). Thoreau's principal authority for beach-grass in *Cape Cod* is Chester Dewey, *Reports on the Herbaceous Plants . . . of Massachusetts* (Cambridge: Folsom, Wells, and Thurston, 1840), pp. 238-239, *P. arenaria* under Psamma. Other taxonomic names for this plant are *Arundo arenaria* and *Calamagrostis arenaria*, the genus and species terms in each case feminine. See *Cape Cod*, pp. 87, 158-159. Thoreau's source for this sentence is Kalm, *Travels into North America*, 3:201, 210-212. Kalm gives the Linnaean name *Arundo arenaria* for beach-grass, which he calls "sand-reed."

156.34-35   more . . . million: Thus in the copy-text, as in the surviving draft, MS (CSmH, HM 953 [b]). The source is Arnold Guyot, *The Earth and Man*, 3d ed. (Boston: Gould and Lincoln, 1851), p. 208, which reads "nearly a million", wording that Thoreau paraphrased "a little less than a million" in the Canadian Notebook, MS (NNPM, MA 595).

157.3-4   almost: The compositor mistook this word in the lost setting copy for "about". Guyot, *The Earth and Man*, p. 209, reads "almost", as does Thoreau's extract from Guyot in the Canadian Notebook, MS (NNPM, MA 595), and a draft version in MS (CSmH, HM 953 [b]).

157.4   water: Guyot, *The Earth and Man*, p. 209, and Thoreau's extract in the Canadian Notebook, MS (NNPM, MA 595), read "waters", but the copy-text reading is anticipated in the draft, MS (CSmH, HM 953 [b]).

157.8-9   more . . . thousand (?):   The copy-text's wording and parenthetical question mark are anticipated in the draft, MS (CSmH, HM 953 [b]). The apparent source, *The Canadian*

Guide Book, p. 98, has "nearly a thousand". Thoreau found a lower figure, in fathoms, marked on Bayfield's "Chart of the Gulf and River St. Lawrence," which may account for his expression of uncertainty.

157.14-15   MacTaggart: Thoreau spells the name correctly, in keeping with the source title page, twice in his Canadian Notebook (MS [NNPM, MA 595]) extracts from John Mactaggart, *Three Years in Canada* (London: Henry Colburn, 1829). But the copy-text treatment, "McTaggart", occurs twice in a late draft version of the passage, MS (CSmH, HM 953 [b]), and once, changed from "MacTaggart", in the earlier MS (CSmH, HM 949).

157.17   Gray: Although Thoreau headed his Canadian Notebook extracts, MS (NNPM, MA 595), with the author's name correctly spelled–"Gray's Canada 1806-7-8" (see Textual Note 105.34-106.2)–he wrote "Grey" in both MS (CSmH, HM 949) and MS (CSmH, HM 953 [b]), and in the lost setting copy which the copy-text misspelling reflects. In the first of the copy-text sentences quoted from Gray, the source, *Letters from Canada*, p. 36, includes "Rhones" before "Rhines". Thoreau omits "Rhones" in MS (CSmH, HM 949) and MS (CSmH, HM 953 [b]), as he had done in the Canadian Notebook. The interpolation "as where he happened to be" is set off in square brackets, not parentheses, in all three manuscript versions, and the copy-text pointing, though not ambiguous, may be nonauthorial.

157.21-27   "There . . . waterfalls.":   Thoreau again quotes from Gray, *Letters from Canada*, pp. 42-43. The source reads "majestic country", "every thing", and "the grand scale"; all three copy-text changes, to "majestic scenery", "everything", and "a grand scale", are anticipated in MS (CSmH, HM 953 [b]) and all but the first in the Canadian Notebook, MS (NNPM, MA 595).

158.11-12   for Montreal: Thoreau continues the sentence, in MS (Suzanne Y. H. Kurtz), with a comma and these words: "having on board two priests, a long and a short one, a discharged soldier, and I know not how many discharged Yankees." The same construction survives in a later version, MS (CSmH, HM 953 [b]), although there "a long & a short one" is cancelled in pencil.

158.13   an hour and a half: In a late draft, MS (ViU), "& a half" is cancelled in pencil; but Thoreau probably changed his mind while preparing the lost setting copy.

158.15 restaurant: The copy-text reads "restaurateur", as the lost setting copy probably did as well; the late draft, MS (ViU), has "Restaurateur". In an early draft, MS (CSmH, HM 949), Thoreau writes, "I returned to the first restaurant in the upper town, asked liberty to look at a large map of Canada which I had seen hanging in the parlor in my search . . ." This sentence he revised to read, "remembering a large map of Canada which I had seen hanging in the parlor of the first Restaurant I had entered in the upper town . . .": the spelling "restaurant" occurs twice on this draft page. See Textual Note 149.24 for a discussion of Thoreau's uncertainty about the correct term.

158.23 or my own: In an early draft, MS (CSmH, HM 949), Thoreau ends the sentence here and continues, evidently with reference to broken bottle-necks (i.e., opened bottles), "These days were a Saturnalia for the Yankees in Quebec." However, by the next draft stage, MS (CSmH, HM 953 [b]), the copy-text wording had been established.

158.30 (I translate . . . original): Thoreau's source is "Voyage du Sieur de Roberval, au Canada. 1542.", in *Voyages de Découverte au Canada*, pp. 93-94. In the Canadian Notebook, MS (NNPM, MA 595), Thoreau took fourteen pages of notes, mainly in French, from this collection of early voyages. As the editor of the volume indicates parenthetically between the title of the Roberval section and the first chapter heading, p. 91, that narrative is itself translated into French from the English version in Hakluyt. It appears in the expanded 1598-1600 edition of *The Principal Navigations Voyages Traffiques & Discoveries of the English Nation*; in the twelve-volume reprint of that edition by James MacLehose and Sons, Glasgow (1903-1905), the Roberval narratives appear at 8:283-289, the passages about the company's diet and discipline falling on p. 286.

159.10 Cap Tourment: Thus in the copy-text; no manuscript version survives. Thoreau's source is an anonymous narrative, "Voyage depuis l'entrée du Golphe Saint Laurent jusques à Montreal," printed as a supplementary chapter to Jerome Lallemant, *Relation de ce qvi s'est passé de plvs remarqvable aux missions des peres de la compagnie de Iesvs en la Novvelle France, és années 1662. & 1663.* (Paris: Chez Sebastien Cramoisy, et Sebast. Marbre-Cramoisy, 1664), p. 135, misnumbered "145". There, the author writes "le Cap de Tourmente"; but see Textual Note 111.22-23 for the spelling variations of this place-name in both French and English. The copy-text form is probably authorial.

159.12-13 houses of the company: The source, "Voyage ... à Montreal," p. 135 (misnumbered "145"), reads "les maisons de la campagne", that is, houses of the country. Although no manuscript survives to confirm the conjecture, it is likely that Thoreau in his haste misread "campagne" as "compagnie," or confused the two terms. In the next sentence, Thoreau or the compositor omits the source's "de Beaupré" ["of Beaupré"] from the beginning of the list of seigniories.

159.14 Notre Dame: Thus in the source (see preceding Textual Note), p. 135, misnumbered "145". The copy-text reads "Notre Dames". The same vicinity, downstream of Quebec, is named correctly in another Jesuit Relation, cited at 95.31-37; see Textual Note.

159.19 *senelles*: Erroneously "*semelles*" in the copy-text, but thus spelled in the source, "Voyage ... à Montreal," p. 142, misnumbered "152". The fruits, haws, are the same as those Thoreau calls "snells" at 117.33 (see Textual Note) and 129.18.

160.29-30 McTavish ... McTavish: Thoreau's source, Silliman, *Remarks*, p. 354, gives the fur trade entrepreneur's name correctly as "McTavish" and the company name as "North Western." (The proper title is "North West Company.") In the Canadian Notebook, MS (NNPM, MA 595), Thoreau follows Silliman in these particulars, but in a surviving draft of the passage, MS (CSmH, HM 949), the forms "Mac Tavish" and "North-Western" have superseded the source. "Northwestern" in the copy-text may not be authorial.

161.8 St. Hyacinth: Thus in the draft, MS (CSmH, HM 949), and in the copy-text. See Textual Note 125.34.

161.10 St. Ann's: This is the village called "Ste. Anne de Bellevue" on modern maps, at the southwest point of Montreal Island where the Ottawa River joins Lac St. Louis, an expansion of the St. Lawrence. *The Canadian Guide Book*, pp. 102-103, which quotes Thomas Moore's "A Canadian Boat-Song," reads "St. Anne" or "St. Anne's" four times. It is also so spelled in *Appletons' Railroad and Steamboat Companion*, p. 184. Another of Thoreau's sources, McGregor, *British America*, 2:503, has "St Ann" in an allusion to Moore's poem. Bouchette, *A Topographical Description*, has "St. Anne" (pp. 133, 152, 167), but also "St. Ann" (p. 132). The copy-text spelling is anticipated in the draft, MS (CSmH, HM 949). For Thoreau's use of Moore's poem in "Ktaadn, and the Maine Woods" (1848), see *Maine Woods*, pp. 38-39, 409.

161.21-24 and where also . . . *vu le bout*: Thus in the copy-text; Thoreau quotes from and translates the narrative of Jacques Cartier's second voyage, in *Voyages de Découverte au Canada*, p. 56. Cartier here reports what Chief Donnacona and other natives in "Canada" (the region of Quebec) told him upon his return from Hochelaga to winter at the harbor of Ste. Croix (the mouth of the St. Charles River at Quebec); the geography is necessarily obscure, but the Ottawa River, rather than the St. Lawrence, seems to be meant in the original reference to a watercourse leading to great lakes and a fresh-water sea. Cartier consistently uses "Fleuve" for the St. Lawrence and "Rivière" for subordinate streams such as the Saguenay. According to his informants, the river Saguenay led toward a rich country named Saguenay, a month's journey west-northwest (from its mouth), but after eight or nine days' travel the river became too shallow for any vessels but canoes. However, the best route (to the country Saguenay, where there were many people and towns, and much gold and copper) was by means of the St. Lawrence to above Hochelaga, where a river descending from the country Saguenay entered the St. Lawrence. Beyond Saguenay that tributary river–the Ottawa?–led to two or three great lakes and a fresh-water sea: "Et avons entendu par le Seigneur *Donnacona* . . . que la Rivière devant dite, et nommée la Rivière de *Saguenay*, va jusques au dit *Saguenay*, qui est loin du commencement de plus d'une Lune de chemin vers l'Ouest Nor-Ouest; et que passé huit ou neuf journées elle n'est plus parfonde que pour bateaux; mais que le droit et bon chemin et plus sûr est par le dit Fleuve jusques au dessus de *Hochelaga* à une Rivière que descend du dit *Saguenay* et entre au dit Fleuve, (ce que avons veu) et que de là sont une lune à y aller. . . . Et nous ont dit que le tout de la terre depuis la dite première Rivière jusques au dit *Hochelaga* et *Saguenay* est une Isle, laquelle est circuite et environnée de Rivières et du dit Fleuve: et que passé le dite *Saguenay* va la dite Rivière entrant en deux ou trois grands lacs d'eau fort larges: puis que l'on trouve une mer douce, de laquelle n'est mention avoir vue le bout, ainsi qu'ils ont ouï par ceux du *Saguenay*; car ils nous ont dit n'y avoir été." The notion of a direct water connection between the Saguenay and Ottawa rivers, making all of southern Quebec province on the north bank of the St. Lawrence an island, is fanciful; but as the voyageurs discovered, the Ottawa gave easy access via Lake Nipissing to Lake Huron, and thus to the other Great Lakes. Copying part of this passage in the Canadian Notebook, MS (NNPM, MA 595), Thoreau interpolated "[either Ottoway or Saguenay, probably former]" between "Rivière" and "entrant en deux ou trois grands lacs"; but by the time he composed MS (CSmH, HM 949) he appears to have associated the route to the Great Lakes with the St. Lawrence. The normalization of "*avoir vue*" to "*avoir vu*" may not be authorial.

163.4-5   two guidebooks . . . half cents: One of the books was manifestly *The Canadian Guide Book*, the price of which included a folding map by Staveley (see Textual Note 86.23). The second may well have been Hawkins, *The Quebec Guide* (see Textual Note 108.17). Hawkins provides a plan of the city and detailed information about points of interest in the vicinity, including Montmorenci Falls, the Chaudière Falls, the Falls of Ste. Anne, Chateau Richer, the Ste. Anne Church, the Isle of Orleans, the scenery of the St. Lawrence below Quebec, and the scenery of the Saguenay. Presumably Thoreau's statement about purchases is not meant to include *Appletons' Railroad and Steamboat Companion*, which he already owned.

163.9   Mackenzie: In MS (CSmH, HM 949), the only surviving manuscript version, Thoreau wrote "Mackenzie", then cancelled the "c" and wrote "c" over the "a". The copy-text reads "McKenzie". Thoreau spelled Alexander Mackenzie's name correctly when transcribing portions of the explorer's *Voyages . . . to the Frozen Sea and Pacific Ocean* in his final Indian Notebook, MS (NNPM, MA 606).

163.14-15   perhaps . . . called: Thus in the copy-text, but "perhaps" is cancelled in the surviving draft, MS (CSmH, HM 949), where Thoreau also considered the wording, "to be called". It is obvious that Thoreau reversed these early revisions.

Table of Emendations

FOR the format of this table, see the Textual Introduction, p. 382. Sources for the emendations are the January, February, and March 1853 *Putnam's Monthly Magazine* (P), *A Yankee in Canada*, 1866 (Y), or the editor's own authority, designated "PE" for the Princeton Edition, when the emendation is not anticipated in P or Y. In *79.7, 95.34, 119.32, 119.33, and *127.16, Y is identified as the source of the reading before emendation, because the reading does not appear in the copy-text (setting-copy manuscript or P). Copy-text is Thoreau's setting-copy manuscript for 79.1-110.26, P for 110.27-130.5 "in its way.", and Y for 130.5 "This man's farm"-163.15.

*79.1	A Yankee in Canada.] Y; An Excursion To Canada.
*79.5	Rarities] PE; Rareties
79.6-11	And still . . . America."] Y; *lacking*
*79.7	1637] PE; 1632 Y
79.12	I. Concord to Montreal.] P; *precedes Josselyn epigraph; chapter number on separate line (see Textual Note 79.2-12)*
*79.30	exciting, suggesting] P; *possibly* exciting suggesting
80.7	Monadnoc] P; Monadnoc Monadnoc
*80.10	Keene] Y; Keen
*80.19-20	far and] P; far &
80.32	Keene] Y; Keen
80.34	surveyed and] P; surveyed &
80.35	here and] P; here &
81.3	Keene] Y; Keen
81.9	distance] P; distances
81.30	everywhere] P; *possibly* every where
82.19	yellow-birch.] P; yellow-birch
83.8	were in Burlington] Y; reached Burlington
83.14	waste and] P; waste &
84.2	fruits".] PE; *possibly* fruits."
*84.10	Richelieu] P; Richlieu

84.22	hundred and] P; hundred &
84.33	dress and] P; dress &
85.14	talk] Y; speak
85.19	name!" though] Y; name!" Though
86.30	Bonsecours] P; Bonsecours Bonsecours
87.5-6	here two] P; here 2 two
87.10	again and] P; again &
87.30	thought and] P; thought &
88.3	kneeled] P; kneeld
88.24	tinsel] P; tinsel tinsel
88.26-27	serious and] P; serious &
89.8	baboons] P; babboons
89.12	only its sleeping] P; only its its sleeping
*90.2	Edinburgh] P; Edinburg
90.12	bonnets and] P; bonnets &
90.32	back and] P; back &
*90.33-34	regarding] P; reguarding
90.34	and disregarding] P; & dis /regarding
*91.11	any more] P; any-/more
91.19	idiosyncrasies] P; idiosyncracies
91.36	and tyrannical] P; & tyranical
92.12	Irish, and] P; Irish, &
92.13	people, and] P; people, &
92.28	*cerises*] P; *cerises* cerises
92.31	pocket. Since] P; pocket.–Since *(see Alteration 92.31)*
92.32	sweet] P; sweet weet
93.7	foot and] P; foot &
93.20	II.] P; NO. 2.
94.1	hear and] P; hear &
*94.6	it; all] PE; it; All
94.15	low and] P; low &
94.19	Richelieu] P; Richlieu *(see Textual Note 84.10)*
94.31	tells.] P; tells
95.27	abolished.*] Y; abolished.
*95.31-37	*Hierosme . . . heads."] Y; *footnote lacking*
95.34	arrived] PE; ar /rived Y *(see Textual Note 95.31-37)*
96.1	and though] P; & though
96.12	Scotch and] P; Scotch &
96.36	hundred and] P; hundred &
*98.7	Poniatowski] PE; Poniatowsky

98.8	hat and] P; hat &
98.15	Louis and] P; Louis &
98.28	thick and] P; thick &
100.21	Edinburgh] P; Edinburg *(see Textual Note 90.2)*
*101.3	Tryggvesson] PE; Trygvesson
101.15	home and] P; home &
102.5	water-power] P; *possibly* Water-power
102.12	New and] P; New &
102.18	regular and] P; regular &
104.30	nieces] P; nieces nieces
105.22-23	asked us where] Y; inquired where
*107.11-12	*Anglais*] P; *Anglois*
107.12	*non*] PE; *initial n possibly N*
*107.26	*Y a-t-il*] Y; *Y-a-t'il*
109.24	simple and] P; simple &
109.32	ferns and] P; ferns &
*110.5	It is] P; They are
110.8	waterfall] P; waterfal
110.23	and full] P; & full
*111.29	Beaupré] Y; Beaupre
113.32	possible."] Y; possible.
*114.2	Hontan] Y; Houtan
*115.27	standing on] PE; standing in
*115.34	symbolical] Y; *lacking*
116.33	appeared. To] Y; appeared to *(see Textual Note 116.33-34)*
116.34	*Anglais?* even] Y; *Anglais?* Even *(see Textual Note 116.33-34)*
*118.13	*à la*] Y; *a la*
*118.30-31	*Ste. Anne . . . Ste. Anne*] PE; *St. Anne . . . St. Anne*
119.11	mouth.*] Y; mouth.
119.31-37	*From . . . across."] Y; *footnote lacking*
*119.32	eleven miles] PE; a mile Y
119.33	Pelee] PE; Peter Y *(see Textual Note 119.33)*
*120.9-10	He shouted . . . breed).] Y; He said *Brock!*
*120.10	We . . . called] Y; At Binet's they called the cat
*120.14-15	*vent,"* if . . . wind. They] Y; *vent."* If . . . wind, they
*120.26	*beau*] Y; *bel*

120.34   Ste. Anne]   PE;   St. Anne *(see Textual Note 118.30-31)*

*120.35   book]   Y;   books

*121.15-18   In early . . . there.]   PE;   *lacking*

121.23   Ste. Anne]   PE;   St. Anne *(see Textual Note 118.30-31)*

*121.33   observed]   PE;   observes

*122.30   tumbled]   Y;   tumbles

*124.34   a field]   PE;   the field

*125.12   *prairie*]   Y;   prairie

*125.32   *Fereole*]   Y;   *Fercole*

*125.33   *Belange*]   PE;   *Bélangé*

*125.35   *St. Johns*]   PE;   *St. John*

*126.10   Bay were]   PE;   Bay, were

*127.4-22   Most . . . world.]   Y;   *lacking*

*127.16   drunk]   PE;   drank   Y

*130.22   *sign*]   PE;   sign

130.25   craft]   PE;   crafts *(see Textual Note 130.24-25)*

*130.28   bank]   PE;   banks

*131.2   soccage]   PE;   socage

131.30   soccage]   PE;   socage

132.33   soccage]   PE;   socage

*133.7   Denonville]   PE;   Denouville

135.29   IV.]   PE;   CHAPTER IV.

139.22   cleated]   PE;   cleeted

*142.13   further]   PE;   farther

*148.21   *white*]   PE;   white

149.10   V.]   PE;   CHAPTER V.

*149.24   restaurants]   PE;   restaurateurs

*150.30   further]   PE;   farther

154.5-7   (Schoolcraft . . . say so.)]   PE;   Schoolcraft . . . say so. *(see Textual Note 154.5-6)*

*154.6   De Vaca]   PE;   De Vega

*154.35-36   P. H. Gosse]   PE;   P. A. Gosse

*155.8   "America" of 1670]   PE;   "America of 1670"

*155.15   Cataraqui]   PE;   Cateraqui

*156.25   *Psamma arenaria*]   PE;   *Psamma arenarium*

*157.3-4   almost]   PE;   about

*157.14-15   MacTaggart]   PE;   McTaggart

*157.17   Gray]   PE;   Grey

*158.15   restaurant]   PE;   restaurateur

*159.14   Notre Dame]   PE;   Notre Dames

*159.19   *senelles*] PE; *semelles*
*160.29-30   McTavish . . . McTavish]   PE;   Mac Tavish
                 . . . Mac Tavish
*163.9   Mackenzie]   PE;   McKenzie

Table of Alterations

For the format of this table, see the Textual Introduction, pp. 383. The surviving setting-copy manuscript for the *Putnam's* printing covers chapters 1 and 2 only. Unless specified to the contrary, alterations are in ink and were made by Thoreau.

79.3-18   north . . . ten miles]   *pencilled* In 5 parcels.
                 201 pages in all from Henry D. Thoreau *in left*
                 margin; not Thoreau's hand
79.3-4   so called . . . Cane]   *set off in ink parentheses*
                 cancelled in pencil
79.12   I.]   *preceded by pencilled* No *in another hand*
79.12   Concord]   *preceded by erased pencilled* III *in*
                 another hand
79.16   Fare]   *followed by cancelled dollar sign*
80.7   Monadnoc]   *pencilled* Monadnoc *interlined*
                 above
81.9   distance,]   *followed by cancelled false start,*
                 perhaps fu
81.13   ash-trees]   -trees *perhaps added later; word*
                 runs off edge of page
81.36   through]   *last letter perhaps added later*
82.1   Mountains]   M *altered from lower case*
82.8   You]   *followed by* You *cancelled in pencil*
82.23   five]   *added in margin before cancelled* 5
83.31   high]   *added later*
84.4   The number]   *preceded by pencilled* Brooks
                 (compositor) in margin; not Thoreau's hand
84.7   whirled]   *word reformed*
84.20   Vermont]   V *altered from lower case*
84.20   New]   N *possibly altered from lower case*
84.22   three . . . six]   *interlined with a pencilled*
                 caret above cancelled 306

84.28   and English]   *followed by cancelled comma*
                 and cancelled by the
85.5-6   Canadian]   *interlined with a caret*
85.6   gentlemen]   *interlined with a caret above*
                 cancelled men
85.24   Yankee]   *altered from* Yankees *by*
                 cancellation in pencil
85.29   Englishman,]   *comma added in pencil*
86.15   novel, but]   but *interlined above* though
                 cancelled in pencil
86.30   Bonsecours]   *pencilled* Bonsecours
                 interlined above
87.6   two miles]   2 *interlined above* two
87.14   home-spun]   *altered from* homespun
87.22   eighty]   *preceded by cancelled* 8
88.10   Catholics]   C *altered from lower case*
88.10   and]   d *added in pencil*
88.24   tinsel]   *pencilled* tinsel *interlined above*
88.28   enter]   *followed by cancelled* d
88.28   our]   *interlined in pencil below* those
                 cancelled in pencil
88.29   Sundays]   S *altered from lower case*
89.16   creative]   *interlined with caret before*
                 thought
89.20-23   I heard ... oil.]   *pencilled* Burnham
                 (compositor) in margin in another hand with
                 pencil line led to pencilled asterisk before I
                 heard
89.28   city]   c *altered from another letter, perhaps* s
90.6   States]   S *altered from lower case*
90.10   Sisters]   S *altered from lower case*
90.11   Shaker-shaped]   S *altered from lower case*
91.36   if]   *followed by cancelled* if
92.17-18   Montreal ... ours]   *pencilled* Dillon
                 (compositor, possibly Hilton*) in margin, with*
                 pencil line led to Montreal *(not Thoreau's*
                 hand)
92.28   cerises]   *pencilled* cerises *interlined above*
92.31   pocket.]   *period added; followed by dash and*
                 cancelled for it looked li familiar.
92.32   sweet]   *interlined above* Sweet *with* S
                 cancelled
92.33   us]   *followed by cancelled false start*
93.2   charettes]   *followed by cancelled* &c &c

93.2	and similar] and *interlined in pencil above* or *cancelled in pencil*
93.2	vehicles] *interlined above cancelled* carriages
93.3	more.] *followed by* vehicles *set off in parentheses and cancelled, with following period also cancelled*
93.20	Quebec and Montmorenci.] *in pencil; preceded by pencilled* NO. 2. *(see Emendation 93.20)*
93.20	Quebec and Montmorenci.] *doubly underlined* An Excursion to Canada *in left margin; not Thoreau's hand*
*94.11	profaned] f *interlined above cancelled* ph *apparently in Thoreau's hand*
94.19	still] *interlined with a caret*
94.31	This is . . . tells.] *interlined with a caret (see Emendation 94.31)*
94.31	it] *interlined above cancelled* this
95.18	one fifth] one *followed by* one *cancelled in pencil*
96.2	seventeen] *preceded by cancelled* from 1 /
96.4-5	I may . . . state that] *interlined; following* in *altered from* In
96.16	Stairs] S *altered from lower case*
96.17	narrow] *interlined above cancelled* massive
96.29	for security] for *altered from* fore *by cancellation*
96.30	them!] *period changed in pencil to exclamation point*
97.10-13	At a . . . answered] *pencilled* Murray *(compositor) in left margin with pencil line led to paragraph opening; not Thoreau's hand*
97.19-22	coppers . . . Barracks] Murry *(compositor)* and 2 *in left margin; not Thoreau's hand*
97.22	Jesuits'] *preceded by partial square bracket (stint mark or type line break); not Thoreau's hand*
97.24	Major] j *altered from* y
98.15-16	a holy] a *reformed*
98.27	or even] *preceded by cancelled* ore
98.35	road] d *reformed*
99.7	psychological] s *reformed*

99.10	having] av *reformed*
99.15-17	This is . . . since.] *added in left margin with caret after* French. *and connecting line*
99.18	manoeuvred] v *reformed*
99.27	destitute] *preceded by cancelled* desp
99.33	naturally] y *reformed*
99.36	or that] or *reformed*
99.36	drill] *preceded by cancelled* edu
100.2-3	marching . . . rest,] *interlined with a caret after* devil,
100.3-4	to pay . . . gait.] *followed by pencilled* Forbes (compositor) *and horizontal pencil line across page; not Thoreau's hand*
100.8	thistles] *first letter reformed*
100.9	Diamond] a *reformed*
100.30	red-coated] *first* d *reformed*
100.31	him,] *comma added in pencil*
100.32	he did] h *reformed*
101.2	bad] b *reformed*
101.20	marry] y *reformed*
101.21-22	whom . . . patronizing] *interlined above cancelled* with whom he was talking
101.29-30	to do . . . thousand] *pencilled question mark in left margin*
101.30	twenty] *interlined above cancelled* two
101.30	thousand] h *reformed*
102.5	water-power,] w *reformed (see Emendation 102.5)*
102.5	water-power,] *followed by cancelled* like
102.12	New] N *altered from lower case*
102.14	little] i *reformed*
102.23	sledges] l *reformed*
102.24	dog] *interlined in pencil with pencilled caret after* middle-sized
103.6	Meadows] M *altered from lower case*
103.32	certificate] *first* t *reformed*
103.35	dressed] *first letter reformed*
104.1	dine] e *reformed*
104.2	going] *first letter reformed*
104.8	to preserve] t *reformed*
104.11	gentleman] a *altered from* e
104.12	gloss] g *reformed*
104.14-16	frequent . . . consult] *pencilled* Roulston

(compositor) in left margin; not Thoreau's
hand

104.21   hitch] *first letter reformed*

104.30   nieces] ie *altered from* ei *and* nieces
interlined above

104.31   liked] l *reformed in pencil*

104.32   aboard] *second* a *reformed*

104.36   reflection] l *reformed*

105.8   literally] e *reformed*

105.11   bundle] u *reformed*

105.19   in particular] *interlined with a caret after*
nowhere

105.20   were] *preceded by cancelled* wh

105.28   where] h *reformed*

106.27   referred] *altered from* referrred *by*
cancellation

106.27-28   perhaps] *followed by cancelled* as much

106.28   transparency of] of *reformed*

106.29   whitewash] *written over erased* atmosphe

106.30-31   We were . . . one road.] *pencilled* Welling
(compositor) in left margin, with pencil line
led to paragraph beginning; not Thoreau's
hand

106.34   the road] t *reformed*

106.36   began] g *reformed*

107.4   knocked] *first letter reformed*

*107.11-12 Anglais] *interlined above cancelled*
underlined Francais *(see Emendation *107.11-*
12)

107.34   English] E *altered from lower case*

108.6   assured] *interlined above cancelled*
answered

108.11   communicate] *second* c *reformed*

108.25   low] *followed by cancelled* d

108.26   home-made] o *reformed*

108.26   ones] s *reformed*

109.2-3   French Canadians.] *added after cancelled*
Canadian French.

109.4-5   After . . . mile, and] *pencilled* Burton
(compositor) in left margin, with pencil line
led to paragraph beginning; not Thoreau's
hand

109.6   among] g *reformed*

109.22	perpendicularly] ic *reformed*
109.27	looked] l *reformed*
110.2	thus] *word reformed*
110.14	side] *altered from* sides *by cancellation*
110.14	chasm,] *comma added in pencil*
110.14	slate] e *reformed*
110.16	In] I *reformed*
110.26	use.] *followed by beginning of chapter 3, cancelled in ink and pencil:* By the middle of the forenoon, though it was a rainy day, we were once more on our way down the north bank of the St. Lawrence in a north-easterly direction, toward the falls of St. Anne, which are about thirty miles from Quebec. The settled and more level and fertile portion of Canada East may be described rudely, as a triangle with its apex slanting toward the north-east; about one hundred miles wide at its base, and from two to three or even four hundred miles long if you reckon its narrow north-

Rejected Substantives

For the format of this table, see the Textual Introduction, p. 384. The table records variant substantives in *Putnam's* (P) where copy-text is Thoreau's setting-copy manuscript, and also in *A Yankee in Canada* (Y) and various pre-copy-text manuscripts, designated by "MS" followed by the owner's name or the repository symbol in parentheses. Variants from several manuscripts at CSmH are reported; to avoid confusion, accession numbers for these manuscripts follow the repository symbol. See the Headnote for an inventory of manuscripts. Copy-text is Thoreau's setting-copy manuscript for 79.1-110.26, P for 110.27-130.5 "in its way.", and Y for 130.5 "This man's farm"-163.15.

79.12	I.] CHAPTER I. Y
79.16	25th 1850, for] 25th, ——, for P
79.24	woods for an] woods of an P Y
79.29	was not a] was a P Y
80.36	Capitol] capital P
81.23	Bellows' Falls] Bellows Falls MS (CSmH: HM 949) MS (CSmH: HM 950) Y
81.33	Mt Holly] Mount Holly P Y *(see Textual Note 81.33-82.3)*
82.2-3	Mt Holly] Mount Holly P Y *(see Textual Note 81.33-82.3)*
82.23	eaves] eves P
82.34	name Lucerne] name of Lucerne Y
83.18	these waters] the Richlieu river & Lake Champlain MS (CSmH: HM 949) *(see Textual Note 83.18-20)*
83.18-19	have met with] have yet seen P Y
83.27	withdraw] withdrew P
83.31	was snow] was more P
83.34	Hiroquois] Iroquois P Y
84.7	toward] towards P Y
84.11	were flat] are flat P Y
*84.21	Johns] John's P Y
85.14	no great] as great P
*85.18-20	Donolly . . . Donolly] Donothy . . . Donothy P; Donouy . . . Donouy Y
85.20	do. It] do, it P
86.5	Johns] John's P Y
86.11	toward] towards P Y
86.20	Helens] Helen's P Y
86.23	Norman] Vorruan P *(see Textual Note 86.23)*
86.23	further] farther P Y
87.17	ashore . . . soon] ashore, with a single companion. I soon P
87.21	two hundred fifty-five] two hundred and fifty-five P Y
88.6	farmers' sons] farmer's sons P Y
88.24	stalactites] stalactics P Y
88.28-29	thousand of our churches] thousand churches MS (CSmH: HM 949); thousand of those churches MS (CSmH: HM 950)

88.29	only on Sundays] only Sundays P Y
88.33-89.2	I am not sure . . . to go to.] * * * * P *(see Headnote)*
89.9	and poetry] and to poetry P Y
89.10	beside] besides P Y
89.18	symbols] symbol Y
89.20-21	candles here were] candles were P Y
89.25	here, as elsewhere] here or elsewhere P Y
89.35	felt] feel P
90.2	made] make P Y
91.26	quire] choir Y
93.9	slopes] slope P Y
93.11	come] came P
93.20	II.] CHAPTER II. Y
94.16-17	the most interesting] the more interesting P Y
95.7	Cap Rouge] Cape Rouge P Y
*95.8	Chaudiere] Chaudière P Y
95.16	rock] rocks P Y
96.9	" 8000 " " " British"] about eight thousand British P Y
96.10	7000 " natives] seven thousand natives P Y
96.11	1500 " " " England] one thousand five hundred natives of England P Y
98.15	Gates] Gate P Y
98.31	greater part] greatest part MS (CSmH: HM 950)
99.4-5	deadest] deadliest P
100.2	as the devil] as an eel P
100.14	semblance] resemblance P
*101.3	Tryggvesson] Trygresson P; Trygesson Y
102.16	horses] houses P
102.27	youth] youths P
104.5	do. Why, a man] do, and a man P Y
104.13	soon made] home-made P
104.21	hitch] pitch P
104.29	perchance] perhaps P Y
105.3	studies] study P Y
105.28-30	There was . . . story.] *lacking* P Y
106.3	is true] be true P Y

106.4	was approaching] were approaching P Y
106.15	afterward] afterwards Y
*106.26	farther] further MS (CSmH: HM 949) MS (CSmH: HM 953 [b])
106.31	road. The houses] road, the houses P
107.14	Canadian] Canadians P Y
*107.20	*ce nuit*] *cette nuit* P Y
107.30	lodging] lodgings P Y
108.2	drunk] drank P Y
108.29	crowded] loaded P Y
109.1	Genevieve] Geneviève P Y
109.23	164] one hundred and sixty-four Y
109.35	immigrant] emigrant P Y
110.7	squares] square P Y
110.27	III.] CHAPTER III. Y
111.20-21	further and further] farther and farther Y
112.1-2	property of the Seminary] property of the ecclesiastics of the seminary MS (CSmH: HM 949) MS (CSmH: HM 953 [b])
*113.18	land] lands MS (NNPM: MA 595) MS (CSmH: HM 949)
113.20	seigneurs'] seigneur's Y
114.12-13	part of the road] part of it Y
*115.7	for summer] for summer and a thick tight one for winter MS (CSmH: HM 949) MS (CSmH: HM 953 [b])
*115.33	*Inri*] *iniri* MS (CSmH: HM 949) MS (CSmH: HM 953 [b]); *Iniri* Y
116.11	kneeled] kneeled and crossed themselves MS (CSmH: HM 953 [b])
117.9	*appris à parler*] appris parler MS (CSmH: HM 949) MS (CSmH: HM 953 [b])
*117.20	immigrant] emigrant MS (CSmH: HM 953 [b])
*117.27	and even beans] and beans MS (CSmH: HM 953 [b])
*118.35	we had grand] we had had grand MS (CSmH: HM 953 [b])
120.16	as usual] as was usual MS (CSmH: HM 949) MS (CSmH: HM 953 [b])
120.24	said that they] said they MS (CSmH: HM 953 [b])
120.31	called a *potage*] called *potage* Y

121.27   meet since]   meet with since   MS (CSmH: HM 949)   MS (CSmH: HM 953 [b])

123.12   by giant steps]   by natural giant steps   MS (CSmH: HM 949)   MS (CSmH: HM 953 [b])

123.29   terminating at the bottom]   terminating at bottom   MS (CSmH: HM 949)   MS (CSmH: HM 953 [b])

125.17   further]   farther   Y

*125.33   *Belange]   *Bélangé*   P;   *Bélange*   Y

125.36   see it]   see the inside of it   MS (CSmH: HM 953 [b])

126.22   *quatres lieue]   *quatres de lieue*   MS (CSmH: HM 949)   MS (CSmH: HM 953 [b])

126.27   pronounced them]   pronounced these   MS (CSmH: HM 949)   MS (CSmH: HM 953 [b])

128.7-8   sharp-featured French]   sharp-featured voluble French   MS (CSmH: HM 949)   MS (CSmH: HM 953 [b])

129.20   said that they]   said they   Y

*130.5-36   This man's . . . *étoffe*.]   *Textual Note 130.5-36 gives pencilled variants in MS (MH-H)*

*130.19-20   two corn-mills]   3 corn mills   MS (NNPM: MA 595)

130.21   or notary]   nor notary   MS (MH-H)

130.22   though]   but   MS (MH-H)

132.31   burdens]   burthens   MS (CSmH: HM 953 [b])

*133.1   immigrants]   emigrants   MS (CSmH: HM 953 [b])

133.6   conformed than]   conformed and assimilated than   MS (CSmH: HM 953 [b])

133.23   weed of]   weed from   MS (CSmH: HM 953 [b])

*133.24-134.22 them . . . selling strong]   *Textual Note 133.24-134.22 gives pencilled variants in MS (NN-BGC)*

*135.28   a poor man.]   *Textual Note 135.28 gives variants in MS (CSmH: HM 953 [b])*

136.5-6   compensation]   accommodation   MS (CSmH: HM 949)

140.3-4   beside the common]   beside common   MS (CSmH: HM 949)   MS (ViU)   MS (NN-BGC)

141.36	That is] That's MS (CSmH: HM 949) MS (PPi) MS (IdU)
*142.8	were faithfully] are faithfully MS (PPi) MS (IdU)
*142.23	get] got MS (IdU)
145.22	one another] each other MS (CSmH: HM 949) MS (CSmH: HM 953 [b])
151.8	*donc!" "March*] *donc! & March* MS (CSmH: HM 949) MS (Suzanne Y. H. Kurtz) *(see Textual Note 151.8)*
151.14	who were] who are MS (Suzanne Y. H. Kurtz)
153.13	The most] far the most MS (CSmH: HM 949)
*154.11	winter] winters MS (CSmH: HM 949) MS (CSmH: HM 953 [b])
155.24-25	in circumference] in circumference following the windings of the shore MS (CSmH: HM 949)
156.34	more than] a little less than MS (NNPM: MA 595) *(see Textual Note 156.34-35)*
*158.13	an hour and a half] an hour MS (ViU)

An Address on the Succession of Forest Trees

Headnote

THOREAU's address on tree succession was prepared for a specific occasion, the annual Middlesex County Cattle-Show (agricultural fair) in Concord, rather than for multiple lecture presentations. It was delivered only once, on September 20, 1860, was well received by its auditors and widely distributed in print, and was the next-to-last public reading by Thoreau of any of his work.

His interest in plant species springing up where seemingly they had not grown before can be dated as far back as July of 1850, when he wrote, "There is in our yard a little pitch pine 4 or 5 years old & not much more than a foot high with small cones on it . . . & yet I do not know of another pitch pine tree within half a mile" (*Journal 3*, p. 92). Journal entries that found their way into the address were made on December 9, 1852 (*Journal 5*, p. 407); January 10 and September 3, 1853 (*Journal 5*, pp. 439-440 and *Journal 7*, pp. 33-35); December 22, 1855 (1906, 8:56-57); May 13 and June 3, 1856 (1906, 8:333-335 and 363-364); September 24, 1857 (1906, 10:39-41); September 22, 1859 (1906, 12:339-342); and September 1, 1860 (1906, 14:69-71). The catalyst for Thoreau's study of the oak and pine alternation puzzle may be identified in a Journal passage for April 28, 1856:

> Observing the young p[itch]. pines by the road S of Loring's lot that was so heavily wooded Geo. Hubbard remarked that if they were cut down oaks would spring up–& sure enough looking across the

road to where Lorings White pines recently stood so densely–the ground was all covered with young oaks– Mem. let me look–at the site of some thick pine woods which I remember–& see what has sprung up. Eg. The p. pines on Thrush alley–& the wht pines on Cliffs–also at Baker's Chestnuts–& the chestnut lot on the Tim. Brooks farm.[1]

By May 13 he appears to have settled on the basic elements of his theory of tree succession, namely that seeds of hardwoods are carried into pine groves by birds, squirrels, and the wind and are annually germinating, but not thriving, in the shade of the pines; only when the pines are cut down do the "oaks &c having got just the start they want–& now secured favorable conditions immediately spring up to trees."[2]

This long genesis is consistent with Thoreau's remark to Horace Greeley nine days after the address that its text was "part of a chapter on the Dispersion of Seeds" (*Correspondence*, p. 590). The extensive manuscripts of the "Seeds" project and several other late, unfinished natural history studies survive at NN-BGC; Bradley P. Dean has made an editorial reconstruction of the first in *Faith in a Seed* (Washington: Island Press, 1993). Only a few months prior to the 1860 Cattle-Show, the Concord Farmers Club, meeting on April 12, heard a talk on forest trees by one of its members, Charles L. Heywood. The ensuing discussion, as recorded in the minutes, touched on the question of oaks succeeding pines and vice versa.[3] Whether Thoreau attended this meeting is unrecorded, but his inter-

[1] NNPM, MA 1302:27, pp. [31-32] (1906, 8:315-316).

[2] NNPM, MA 1302:27, p. [75] (1906, 8:335).

[3] Louisa Kussin, "The Concord Farmers Club and Thoreau's 'Succession of Forest Trees,'" *Thoreau Society Bulletin* 173 (Fall 1985): 1-3.

est in the subject was of long standing and needed no special stimulus from Heywood's paper or other club members' comments thereon. Indeed, he might already have been invited by the officers of the county Agricultural Society to give the Cattle-Show address that September.

The Middlesex Agricultural Society had its origins in the Western Society of Middlesex Husbandmen (officially founded in 1803), which renamed itself in 1824 as the Society of Middlesex Husbandmen and Manufacturers.[4] The name was again changed, in 1852, to Middlesex Agricultural Society. Beginning in 1820, the organization sponsored an annual exhibition–held in Concord except for 1851, when it took place in Lowell–of agricultural products, innovations, equipment, and skills.[5] At these so-called Cattle-Shows, in all years but the first, a speaker addressed the society members and visitors. Edward Everett, Unitarian clergyman, Harvard Professor of Greek literature, and statesman who was the most distinguished New England orator of his time, gave the address in 1827; in 1851 he made briefer ceremonial remarks on "The Husbandman, Mechanic, and Manufacturer." The historian and Free-Soil politician John Gorham Palfrey was the speaker in 1846. Ralph Waldo Emerson's 1858 discourse was titled "The Man with the Hoe."[6] Typically these speakers affirmed in patriotic or religious terms the nobility of farming and its importance to the maintenance of democratic virtues and institutions. Thoreau's address would have been conspicuous for

[4] Lemuel Shattuck, *A History of the Town of Concord . . .* (Boston: Russell, Odiorne, and Company and Concord: John Stacy, 1835), p. 231.

[5] Walter Hesford, " 'Too Happy Husbandmen': Addresses Given to Middlesex Farmers from the 1820s to 1860," *The Concord Saunterer* 14 (Summer 1979): 8, 11.

[6] Hesford, " 'Too Happy Husbandmen'," 10, 11, 13.

its specificity and scientific thrust, as well as for its barbed comments about his neighbors' unfamiliarity with their own woodlots.

A full day was given to the activities of the Middlesex Cattle-Show, which

> usually began at 9 A.M. with a plowing match, followed by a "trial of working oxen." Then came the cattle-show proper, and the formal exhibition of produce and craft work. The Society processed about noon to an assembly hall, and listened to the annual address, the cultural climax of the affair. The address was often followed by a dinner, after which there were brief remarks, reports, poems, and, at 4 P.M., the presentation of cash awards. Band music accompanied the competitions and procession. Throughout the day, travelling showmen and operators served up a great variety of entertainment and, one gathers, a fair amount of liquor.[7]

On September 20, 1860, as reported by Levi Stockbridge for the *Eighth Annual Report of the Secretary of the Massachusetts Board of Agriculture*, ed. Charles Flint (Boston: William White, 1861), a bovine epidemic prevented the exhibition of cattle, and a drenching rain kept most of the spectators under shelter. After Thoreau's discourse to an appreciative audience in the Town Hall there were shorter speeches by President Cornelius Conway Felton of Harvard College (Thoreau's Greek teacher a quarter-century before) and Charles Hudson of Lexington. Toward the end of the day the festivities were marred by an "intoxicated Irishman," who "stabbed two men severely, and, as was feared at the time, fatally."[8]

[7] Hesford, " 'Too Happy Husbandmen'," 7.
[8] Printed in facsimile in Walter Hesford, "The 1860 Concord Cattle-Show: An Official Account," *Thoreau Society Bulletin* 132

Thoreau sent his manuscript of the address to Horace Greeley on September 29, inviting Greeley to print it whole in the *New-York Tribune*, and observing that the text "*is due to [for inclusion in] the Societys* 'Report' a month or 6 weeks hence" (*Correspondence*, p. 590). By the Society's "Report" Thoreau meant the *Transactions of the Middlesex Agricultural Society for the Year 1860*, to be printed for the Society in Concord by Benjamin Tolman before the year's end. Thoreau asked Greeley to return the manuscript immediately if he chose not to publish it entire in his newspaper, implying that the author had in mind submitting the *Tribune* text to *Transactions* if it were available by the deadline.

Under the captions "*Interesting To Farmers*" and "The Succession of Forest Trees. An Address Before the Middlesex (Mass.) Agricultural Society" and Thoreau's name in the by-line, Greeley printed the piece in full in his *New-York Weekly Tribune*, Saturday, October 6, 1860, pp. 6-7, reprinting it (apparently from the same typesetting though with altered column breaks) in the Tuesday, October 9, 1860, *New-York Semi-Weekly Tribune*, p. 7. He sent Thoreau a number of copies containing the address, and, it appears, the original manuscript (see discussion of the *Transactions* text below). Bradley P. Dean has discovered a subsequent exchange of letters concerning forest re-propagation, printed in the *Weekly Tribune* for February 2, 1861, pp. 6-7. In the first letter, dated December 13, 1860, Greeley questions Thoreau's premise, asserting that in conflagrations of northern pine-forests

(Summer 1975): 6-7; see also Bradley P. Dean and Ronald Wesley Hoag, "Thoreau's Lectures After *Walden*: An Annotated Calendar," *Studies in the American Renaissance*, ed. Joel Myerson (Charlottesville: University Press of Virginia, 1996), pp. 339-342. In "Autumnal Tints," pp. 245-246, Thoreau alludes to rowdiness requiring law enforcement on the village's festive days.

and on lands where hardwood trees are cleared and burned, the earth itself is charred so deeply that any dormant seeds must be killed; yet young birches appear on the burnt forest floor and fireweed sprouts densely in the agricultural clearings. Thoreau replied on December 30, acknowledging receipt of the copies Greeley had sent him, challenging Greeley's assumption that the birches and fireweed had generated spontaneously, and questioning not only the accuracy of Greeley's description of the Maine and New Brunswick forests as uniformly composed of pine, but also the time interval for re-vegetation in Greeley's second example.[9] By the same mail as his letter, Thoreau sent Greeley "a copy [of his address] slightly amended", i.e., a copy of the *Transactions* printing.[10]

Writing from Cincinnati on November 26, Moncure D. Conway, a young Unitarian minister, espouser of liberal causes, former Concord resident and acquaintance of the Transcendentalists, asked Thoreau to let him reprint the "Agricultural Address" in the *Dial*, which Conway had begun anew as a monthly the previous January (*Correspondence*, p. 601). Any reply Thoreau may have made is lost; but since the new series *Dial* ceased publication with the December 1860 issue, the prospect of reprinting "The Succession of Forest Trees" in Cincinnati was rendered moot.

However, a partial reprint–from *Transactions*, not the *Tribune*–did appear in *Abstract of Returns of the Agricultural Societies of Massachusetts for 1860*, ed.

[9] Dean, "Henry D. Thoreau and Horace Greeley Exchange Letters on the 'Spontaneous Generation of Plants,'" *New England Quarterly* 66 (December 1993): 630-638; also Dean and Hoag, "Thoreau's Lectures After *Walden*," pp. 343-345.

[10] Dean, *New England Quarterly* 66 (December 1993): 633; Dean and Hoag, p. 343. Thoreau presented another copy to the Boston Society of Natural History the next day, December 31: see Raymond Borst, *The Thoreau Log: A Documentary Life of Henry David Thoreau* (New York: G. K. Hall, 1992), p. 581.

Charles L. Flint (Boston: William White, State Printer, 1861), pp. 11-23, bound with *Eighth Annual Report of the Secretary of the Massachusetts Board of Agriculture* ... (Boston: William White, State Printer, 1861). This text drops from its source the first three paragraphs and the opening phrase of the third, and also the last three paragraphs, besides making several smaller unauthorized changes (see Rejected Substantives). The satirical and philosophical matter omitted by the *Abstract* editor must have struck him as superfluous. Another reprint, this one from the curtailed *Abstract* version, appeared in consecutive issues of *The Country Gentleman and Cultivator*, an agricultural weekly, on May 16, May 23, May 30, and June 6, 1861.

The text on certain pages of the 338-page "Dispersion of Seeds" manuscript at NN-BGC[11] predates the Cattle-Show address and its publication in the *New-York Tribune*. These portions agree in wording with the *Tribune*, wording altered by Thoreau for the later *Transactions* printing. In the weeks following his oration Thoreau continued working on the larger project and perhaps widened its scope. On two pages of the manuscript he waxed short clippings from the *Tribune* to leaves of stationery and adjusted his handwritten text to the excerpts both spatially and contextually: the manuscript matter on these pages was written subsequently to the attachment of the print matter. Thoreau also fastened other *Tribune* clippings to the margins of pages bearing already written (earlier) draft, or actually over that draft. On yet another page Thoreau writes, following a single-sentence paragraph, "Apparently there were only pines &c &c as far as 2 ¶s on p. 15 printed report". This citation, manifestly entered after *Transactions* was issued in late 1860, is to

[11] *LMHDT*, F30. Robert D. Richardson Jr. and Dean in *Faith in a Seed* give two different page-counts: 354 (p. 3) and 304 (p. 223).

the consecutive paragraphs on printed page 15 that begin "Apparently, there were only pines" and "In this neighborhood," paragraphs Thoreau told himself he wanted to insert into the "Dispersion" text at this point.

The insertion of *Tribune* clippings and the cross-reference to the *Transactions* printing signify neither Thoreau's preference of one printed version over another nor the sequence of the two kinds of citation in the "Dispersion" manuscript. It is only clear that the attachment of clippings cannot antedate October 6 and that the reference to *Transactions* cannot antedate the printing of that volume in (probably) late December 1860. Thoreau did not hesitate to cut up one of the several copies of the *Tribune* typesetting he had received from Greeley. Of *Transactions* he had obtained the copy he sent Greeley, the copy he presented to the Boston Society of Natural History, and a copy he kept for his own use–but not necessarily any besides. No clippings from *Transactions* appear among the "Dispersion" papers.

In the absence of Thoreau's manuscript for the address, the text of the present edition of "The Succession of Forest Trees" must be based on one of the first two typesettings. Analysis of the relationship between the *Tribune* and *Transactions* printings dictates the choice of copy-text for the address. Normally it can be demonstrated that a later nineteenth-century printing was set from an earlier one, and this holds true for various reprints of Thoreau's work before and immediately after his death, even when the manuscript survived its use in the printshop (see, for example, the discussion of the first two chapters of "A Yankee in Canada" in the Headnote for that essay). Thoreau's handwriting was difficult to read, and typesetters preferred to work from printed copy when it was available. The *Transactions* version of "The Succession of Forest Trees" contains many substantive alterations from the *Tribune* version, which was derived from the manuscript Thoreau sent Greeley on September 29. By their nature these alterations must have issued from Thoreau's hand (moreover, various pages of the "Dispersion" manuscript display substantive readings different from the *Tribune* but identical to *Transactions*). See the list of Rejected Substantives for authorial *Transactions* readings that superseded those in the *Tribune*.

Three possible scenarios present themselves for the transmission of text among the address manuscript (now lost), the *Tribune*, and *Transactions*. All three alternative explanations assume that the accidentals of the manuscript would have been brought into agreement with the different house styles of the two publications when the address was printed. The least probable hypothesis is that Thoreau prepared a second setting copy for the *Transactions* editor or printer some weeks after he dispatched the first to Greeley. On this hypothetical second setting copy, after September 29, Thoreau would have incorporated the revisions that differentiate the *Transactions* version from that in the *Tribune*. While this hypothesis accounts for the superiority of the later printing over the earlier, it assumes a duplication of time and effort by Thoreau at the final-copy stage that does not occur in other Thoreau projects with which the editor is familiar. The Journal for the six weeks beginning September 30 is rich in Thoreau's field observations of natural phenomena, giving no indication that he was housebound while laboriously constructing a near-duplicate of the address.[12] Had he created two setting copies, more-

[12] See 1906, 14:97-241.

over, there would probably be far less similarity in accidentals and substantives between the two print versions.

The next most plausible scenario is that Thoreau marked up for *Transactions* one of the copies of the *Tribune* printing that Greeley gave him, correcting typographer's misreadings and entering substantive revisions. In support of this possibility one can point to the like labor-saving procedures Thoreau demonstrably or probably adopted with the second edition (1868) of *A Week on the Concord and Merrimack Rivers*, with the portions of *Cape Cod* (1865) and *A Yankee in Canada* (1866) that had been printed in *Putnam's Monthly Magazine* during the 1850s, and with the magazine texts of "Ktaadn" (1848) and "Chesuncook" (1858) for their inclusion in *The Maine Woods* (1864). Specific magazine printings survive that Thoreau marked with a view to subsequent, revised publication, the *Dial* essays being conspicuous examples. However, the *Tribune* typeface was so minute and the columns so closely set, with vertical rules in lieu of margins, that Thoreau could hardly have entered corrections and revisions on the newsprint itself: he would have had to paste one-column wide sections of the printing onto writing paper, penning his alterations on the newly created broad margins and drawing lines between these changes and the relevant parts of the printed text. Another counter-indication for this hypothesis is that none of the *Tribune* typesetters' misreadings of one word as another, e.g. "thin ferns" as "their ferns", "found" as "bound", "pack" as "pick", and "about" as "abort", are repeated in the *Transactions* text. Thoreau was not a fastidious proofreader, and one would expect some of these errors to have contaminated the second printing had it been set from the *Tribune*.

The third hypothesis best accounts for the similarities and differences between the *Tribune* and *Transactions* versions, and is most consistent with the biographical context and the timetables under which Thoreau had to work. It is that Greeley, publisher of the *Tribune*, instructed his typesetters to preserve his friend Thoreau's manuscript and returned it to the author with copies of the newspaper printing by mid-October. The manuscript may have borne a few editor's or compositor's marks, including one that affects the text of *Transactions*. For Thoreau's spelling "height" in a quotation about tree-farming, the *Tribune* substituted "hight," one of Noah Webster's "reformed" spellings: see Textual Note 173.23. (Alternatively, "hight" may have been the *Transactions* editor's preference as well as the *Tribune*'s.) With his manuscript again in hand, Thoreau made on it the numerous alterations that are listed in Rejected Substantives as non-erroneous differences in the *Tribune* printing. Then he delivered the manuscript to the *Transactions* printer or editor. The chief arguments against this scenario are that (1) Thoreau in the September 29 letter did not ask Greeley to preserve the manuscript if the address were printed in the *Tribune*, (2) Greeley's return of the manuscript to Thoreau cannot be proven from surviving records, and (3) an accidental ("hight") present in the *Tribune* but uncharacteristic of Thoreau recurs in *Transactions*. But the third of these objections is not definitive proof that *Transactions* was set from a marked *Tribune* print; as suggested above, that spelling could have been preferred by the editors of both publications.

The editor selects the third of these possibilities as most consistent with the known facts, textual and otherwise, and uses *Transactions of the Middlesex Agricultural Society for the Year 1860*, pp. 12-24, as copy-text in the present edition. The specific copy employed was that at MHi, though others were also used in collations and proofreading: MBAt, MH, MBH, MU. As recorded in the list of Emendations, three superior accidental readings are drawn from the *Tribune*; four others are adopted from the 1863 *Excursions* text of the address, which itself derives from *Transactions*.[13] It is not known whether Thoreau read proof copy of the *Transactions* typesetting and no proofs survive.

The following collations have been performed: *Weekly Tribune* against *Semi-Weekly Tribune*, once; *Transactions* against *Weekly Tribune*, once; *Transactions* against *Abstract*, three times; *Transactions* against 1863 *Excursions*, four times; *Abstract* against *Weekly Tribune*, once; *Abstract* against *Excursions* (1863), once; *Excursions* (1863) against *Weekly Tribune*, once; and, on the Hinman machine, revealing no textual differences, the MHi copy of *Transactions* against the MBH copy.

[13] This copy-text approach has seemed to the editor to produce the same result, with far greater efficiency, than the adoption of a "radiating text" approach, where each individual difference, accidental or substantive, between two printings from the same manuscript must be recorded in the apparatus and adjudicated on its own merits. See Fredson Bowers, "Multiple Authority: New Problems and Concepts of Copy-Text," *The Library*, 5th ser., 27 (1972): 81-115, and G. Thomas Tanselle, "Editorial Apparatus for Radiating Texts," *The Library*, 5th ser., 29 (1974): 330-337.

Textual Notes

For the format of the Textual Notes, see the Textual Introduction, pp. 381-382. Copy-text is the printing in *Transactions of the Middlesex Agricultural Society for the Year 1860*. NYT-W stands for the chronologically prior printing in the October 6, 1860, *New-York Weekly Tribune*, Abstr. for *Abstract of Returns of the Agricultural Societies of Massachusetts for 1860*, and Ex for *Excursions* (1863). For the relationships among these texts, see the Headnote. The abbreviation "MS" followed by a repository symbol in parentheses identifies a manuscript reading.

172.26   woods evidently: In the copy-text a comma follows "woods", apparently reflecting an incomplete revision by Thoreau in the printer's copy for *Transactions*. That copy originally read "woods, as I have said, evidently"–the text as printed in NYT-W. A version of the sentence among Thoreau's "Dispersion of Seeds" papers, MS (NN-BGC), has "hard woods as I have said evidently".

173.18   among: The source, Alexander Milne as quoted in John Claudius Loudon, *Arboretum et Fruticetum Britannicum; or The Trees and Shrubs of Britain . . .*, 2d ed. (London: the author, 1844), 3:1803, reads "amongst". Thoreau follows this form in a version of the passage among the "Dispersion of Seeds" papers, MS (NN-BGC), but it is entirely possible that the lost setting-copy manuscript for "Succession of Forest Trees" read "among".

173.21   inclosures: The source, Milne as quoted in Loudon, 3:1803, reads "enclosures", a spelling followed by Thoreau in his "Dispersion of Seeds" papers, MS (NN-BGC). The copy-text spelling "inclosures" may, however, accurately reflect Thoreau's lost setting copy. It appears also in NYT-W, Abstr., and Ex.

173.23   height: Thus in the source, Milne as quoted in Loudon, 3:1803; in a version of the passage among Thoreau's "Dispersion of Seeds" papers, MS (NN-BGC); in Abstr.; and in Ex, which emends to Thoreau's characteristic spelling of the word. The copy-text, like NYT-W, imposes Webster's "reformed" spelling. See *Cape Cod*, Textual Note 15.24, for comment on an emendation from "hight" in a *Putnam's Monthly Magazine* copy-text of 1855.

173.23   five or six feet,:   The source, Milne as quoted in Loudon, 3:1803, reads "5 ft. or 6 ft.," followed by "which they will do in as many years,". Thoreau copies Milne in the "Dispersion of Seeds" papers, MS (NN-BGC), and then cancels his transcript of the following eight words.

173.35   but pine: The source, Milne as quoted in Loudon, 3:1803, reads "but pines". Thoreau's extract in the "Dispersion of Seeds" papers, MS (NN-BGC), also has "but pines", though the copy-text's form may accurately reflect the lost setting copy.

175.3   chestnutting: Thus in Ex; the copy-text, NYT-W, and Abstr. all read "chestnuting". In a Journal passage for January 10, 1853, that serves as the original version of this sentence Thoreau writes "a chestnutting" (*Journal 5*, p. 439). A subsequent version, among Thoreau's "Dispersion of Seeds" papers, MS (NN-BGC), reads "chestnutting".

177.1   stealing Nature's "thunder":   "thunder" is not set off with quotation marks or otherwise emphasized in a version of this sentence among the "Dispersion of Seeds" papers, MS (NN-BGC).

178.28-29   nuciferous: The source, Alexander Wilson, *Wilson's American Ornithology, with Notes by Jardine . . .*, by T. M. Brewer (New York: H. S. Samuels, 1852), p. 5, reads "ruciferous", an error corrected by Thoreau.

179.2   few years: Thus in the copy-text. The source, Wilson/Brewer, p. 5, reads "few years'".

179.19   beech mast: The copy-text has "beach mast", a misspelling of the tree name anticipated in NYT-W and followed in Abstr. Ex reads "beechmast"; the source, Loudon, 3:1968, has "beech . . . mast". In a draft of the present sentence among the "Dispersion of Seeds" papers, MS (NN-BGC), Thoreau writes "beech mast". None of Thoreau's four dictionaries accepts the copy-text spelling for the common name of *Fagus grandifolia* (American beech) or *Fagus sylvatica* (European beech). In his setting-copy manuscript of "Chesuncook" Thoreau spells the name "beech": see *Maine Woods*, p. 96.

Table of Emendations

FOR the format of this table, see the Textual Introduction, p. 382. Sources for the emendations are the *New-York Weekly Tribune* (NYT-W), the 1863 edition of *Excursions* (Ex), or the editor's own authority, designated "PE" for the Princeton Edition.

167.8	wind, water]	NYT-W; wind water
169.1	persuade]	NYT-W; pursuade
*172.26	woods evidently]	Ex; woods, evidently
*173.23	height]	Ex; hight
*175.3	chestnutting]	Ex; chestnuting
175.27	sufficient]	NYT-W; suf / ficient
179.19	beech]	Ex; beach *(see Textual Note 179.19)*
182.20	talismans]	PE; talismen

Rejected Substantives

FOR the format of this table, see the Textual Introduction, p. 384. The table records variant substantives in the *New-York Weekly Tribune* (NYT-W), the *Abstract of Returns of the Agricultural Societies of Massachusetts* (Abstr.), and the 1863 edition of *Excursions* (Ex).

165.1-2   An Address ... Trees.] *INTERESTING TO FARMERS.* / THE SUCCESSION OF FOREST TREES. / AN ADDRESS BEFORE THE MIDDLESEX (MASS.) AGRICULTURAL SOCIETY. / By Henry D. Thoreau.   NYT-W; SUCCESSION OF FOREST TREES. / From an Address before the Middlesex Agricultural Society. / By Henry D. Thoreau.   Abstr.; / THE SUCCESSION OF FOREST TREES.* / [1860.] / *An Address read to the Middlesex Agricultural Society, in Concord, September, 1860. *(footnote)*   Ex

165.3	Ladies and Gentlemen] *lacking* NYT-W Abstr. Ex
165.4-166.22	Every man . . . referred to,] *lacking* Abstr.
165.4	Cattle-show] Cattle-shows NYT-W
166.25	commonly] *lacking* NYT-W
166.31	hereabouts] *lacking* NYT-W
166.31	single forest tree] single tree NYT-W
168.34	the centre of] the of NYT-W
168.35	earthy] earthly NYT-W
169.3-4	swallow these, as the birds do when] swallow these like the birds when NYT-W
169.4-5	it being the shortest] as the shortest NYT-W
169.23	then an oak] then the oak NYT-W
169.29	have lain] have been lying NYT-W
169.30	not lain] not been lying NYT-W
169.34	about] abort NYT-W
169.35	unmixed] exclusive NYT-W
170.9	the oldest seedlings] the plants NYT-W
170.13	The shade] Apparently, the shade NYT-W
170.14	of the same species] *lacking* NYT-W
170.22-23	and moreover, if the wood was old, the sprouts will be feeble or entirely fail] *lacking* NYT-W
170.25	for this] for the same NYT-W
171.12-13	it, covered] it and covered NYT-W
172.4-5	another] an / other *(missing type)* NYT-W
172.11	tree in it] tree on it NYT-W
172.14	thin ferns] their ferns NYT-W
172.21	this case] his case NYT-W
172.26	seven or eight years] some years NYT-W
*172.26	woods evidently] woods, as I have said, evidently NYT-W
172.29	diseased] *lacking* NYT-W
172.30	prostrated, though] prostrated, as if by the wind, though NYT-W
173.19	soil might be] soil be NYT-W
173.19	found] bound NYT-W
174.7	appear] appeared Abstr.
174.8	and that they] and they Abstr.
174.22	which twigs have] which have NYT-W
175.35	of these before] of those before NYT-W

176.3   for these are]   and these are   NYT-W
176.14   chestnuts]   chestnut   Ex
176.23   the store the same]   the store at the same
             Abstr.
176.27   pack]   pick   NYT-W
177.24   almost constant]   most constant   NYT-W
178.2   gets]   get   Abstr.
178.10   sit to crack]   sit and crack   NYT-W
178.26   Bartram]   Bertram   NYT-W
179.23   sprouted or decayed.]   sprouted.   NYT-W
180.31   date 1703]   date of 1703   Abstr.
180.36-181.1 and I consider]   and consider   NYT-W
181.2   seeds]   seed   NYT-W
181.11   botrys]   botry-   NYT-W
181.12   Solanum]   Solanium   NYT-W
181.34-183.8 Though I do not . . . rather than light.]
             lacking   Abstr.
182.12   there were]   there was   Ex
182.19   never was]   was never   NYT-W
182.27-28   points the]   points to the   Ex
183.5   farmers']   farmers   NYT-W

Walking

Headnote

THE origins of this essay lie concentrated in Thoreau's Journal entries of November 1850 and January-February 1851, although scattered phrases and sentences used in it occur as early as the 1842-1844 Journal and as late as that of February 1852.[1] The first public expression of this material was a lecture, "Walking or the Wild," before the Concord Lyceum, meeting in the Unitarian Church on April 23, 1851, near the end of the Lyceum's lecture season. Thoreau read the same lecture in Worcester on the last day of May, in the parlor of his friend H. G. O. Blake's school on Warren Street. The text was so long–163 pages–as to require extensive omissions to fit the limits of a lecture (see the excerpt from Thoreau's February 6, 1857, letter to Blake quoted below). By May 23, 1852, Thoreau had separated the two major parts of the piece, titling the first lecture "Walking" and the second "The Wild." He read them both on the same day, a Sunday morning and evening, at Leyden Hall, Plymouth, Massachusetts.[2]

"The Wild," a version of the second 1852 lecture somewhat revised and reduced by the relocation of material to his new lectures on "Moonlight" and

[1] For November 1850 and January-February 1851, see *Journal 3*, pp. 125-156 and 170-201; for the 1842-1844 Journal, see *Journal 1*, pp. 354-497, and *Journal 2*, pp. 1-120; for February 1852, see *Journal 4*, pp. 313-368.

[2] Bradley P. Dean and Ronald Wesley Hoag, "Thoreau's Lectures Before *Walden*: An Annotated Calendar," *Studies in the American Renaissance*, ed. Joel Myerson (Charlottesville: University Press of Virginia, 1995), pp. 198-201, 208-211. Parts of the original manuscript for the April-May 1851 lectures, including the last page, survive at MH-H, catalogued bMS Am 278.5, folder 21B.

"What Shall It Profit" (later titled "Life Misspent" and finally published as "Life without Principle"), was delivered on November 21, 1854, at the Spring Garden Institute of Philadelphia, a mechanics' institute. During the same platform oratory season Thoreau read "Moonlight" in Plymouth and "What Shall It Profit" in Providence, New Bedford, Nantucket, Worcester, and Concord. While visiting the Quaker reformer Marcus Spring's nascent Eagleswood community at Perth Amboy, New Jersey, in order to survey the grounds and to give three lectures, he read "Walking" on the estate, in an auditorium called Unionists' Hall, on November 2, 1856. Bronson Alcott was in attendance, as also, evidently, were the writer Caroline Kirkland, Theodore Weld, his wife Angelina Grimké, and her sister, Sarah Grimké, the last four being members of the community and the last three active Abolitionists. It is not entirely clear whether Thoreau's text was part one of the divided project dating from 1852 or something approximating the original combined version of 1851. He next lectured before the Amherst, New Hampshire, Lyceum on an unusually cold December 18, 1856. Although the topic was advertised in that day's newspaper as "Getting a Living" (another title for "What Shall It Profit") and although Thoreau wrote in his Journal concerning this event, "Lectured in basement (vestry) of the orthodox church, and I trust helped to undermine it" (1906, 9:188), he told Blake in a letter of December 31 that he had read in Amherst the old lecture "which I call 'Walking, or the Wild'" (*Correspondence*, p. 461).[3]

[3] Dean and Hoag, "Thoreau's Lectures After *Walden*: An Annotated Calendar," *Studies in the American Renaissance*, ed. Joel Myerson (Charlottesville: University Press of Virginia, 1996), pp. 249-283, esp. 255-260, 276-277, 279-283. Dean and Hoag identify the Eagleswood lecture as "Walking, or the Wild" without explanation, but Alcott referred to it as "Walking" in both his journal

The Fitchburg, Massachusetts, Athenaeum sponsored Thoreau's lecture of February 3, 1857, in City Hall. Apparently the text was the second part of the large divided manuscript, for a writer (perhaps Blake) reported eight days later in the *Worcester Daily Spy* that he had heard "The Wild" in Fitchburg, and that the same lecture would be given on February 13 at Brinley Hall in Worcester. Conscious of having delivered the original "Walking or the Wild" lecture to a Worcester parlor audience more than five years earlier, Thoreau wrote to Blake on February 6:

> I will come to you on Friday Feb. 13th with that lecture. You may call it "The Wild"–or "Walking" or both–whichever you choose. I told [Theo] Brown that it had not been much altered since I read it in Worcester, but now I think of it, much of it must have been new to you [in Fitchburg?], because, having since divided it into two, I am able to read what before I omitted. Nevertheless, I should like to have it understood by those whom it concerns, that I am invited to read in public . . . what I have already read, in part, to a private audience.[4]

One of Thoreau's four presentations of the 1860-1861 lecture season (his last season on the platform) may have been "Walking" or "The Wild." An association of Spiritualists in Lowell, Massachusetts, negotiated with him to give two Sabbath lectures for the price of one, at Welles Hall on September 9, 1860. Dean and Hoag

---

and a letter. Thoreau probably didn't go back to–or restore–the original lecture of 1851, "Walking or the Wild." The present editor thinks it more likely that he gave the same "Walking" lecture as he read in Plymouth the morning of May 23, 1852. This is also Dean and Hoag's understanding of his Amherst Lyceum topic: see pp. 282-283.

[4] Dean and Hoag, "Thoreau's Lectures After *Walden*," pp. 287-289; *Correspondence*, p. 465.

speculate that the morning text might have been "Walking"; they conjecture more confidently that the afternoon lecture was "Life Misspent."[5]

During his final illness Thoreau made a concerted effort to prepare his unpublished lectures for print. This enterprise required the help of amanuenses. In late 1861 or January 1862 James T. Fields (possibly with the encouragement of Bronson Alcott, F. B. Sanborn, Emerson, or other friends of the dying Thoreau) solicited various shorter pieces for publication in the *Atlantic Monthly*, which Fields now edited as well as owned. Thoreau replied in a letter he dictated to his sister Sophia on February 11, 1862, pleading "extreme illness" for the delay. He tentatively agreed to the publication of "the papers you refer to" and asked what the editor would pay for them. They had been used, he wrote, "as lectures of the usual length,–taking about an hour to read." He asked how many pages of his text the *Atlantic* would print at once, since he felt they could not "be divided without injury." He also firmly cautioned that "no sentiment or sentence" in the papers should "be altered or omitted without my consent." Clearly he had in mind the editorial meddling that had marred his contributions to *Putnam's Monthly Magazine*–"An Excursion to Canada" and *Cape Cod*–and to the *Atlantic* itself four years earlier under the editorship of James Russell Lowell–"Chesuncook." He specifies that he will retain copyright of the papers after they are printed in the magazine, and seeks to guard against piracy by asking "Is your monthly copyrighted?" Thoreau names none of the "papers" by title, but his subsequent correspondence with Fields–or more precisely, with the Ticknor and Fields firm–indicates which pieces had been re-

[5] Dean and Hoag, "Thoreau's Lectures After *Walden*," pp. 336-338.

quested. He sent manuscripts of "Autumnal Tints" on February 20, "The Higher Law" ("Life without Principle") on February 28, "Walking" on March 11, and "Wild Apples" on April 2, scarcely a month before his death. With the exception of one dated February 18, Thoreau's eight letters to Fields were all written in Sophia's hand and signed by her for her brother.[6]

Fields's response about payment for the essays must have satisfied Thoreau, who on February 18 accepted "the offer contained in your last". The rate of payment was probably about $6.00 per double-column printed page, since on March 4 Thoreau acknowledged receiving Ticknor and Fields's "check for one hundred dollars on account of manuscript sent to you." By then he had sent "Autumnal Tints" and "The Higher Law." It is unlikely that the latter had been typeset (Fields was unhappy with the title, and the essay was eventually published as "Life without Principle" in eleven pages and a fraction); the former occupied sixteen and one-half printed pages. Had the hundred-dollar check been intended as payment in full for both essays, the figure would have been only $3.64 per printed page, an unusually low rate for the time.

On March 11, together with corrected proofs of "Autumnal Tints," Thoreau forwarded the ninety-nine-page manuscript of "Walking" in two bundles tied with string. He had already proposed a division of the seventy-four-page "Autumnal Tints" into two installments, and now he suggested dividing "Walking" a little less than halfway through, at the end of page "44",

---

[6] *Correspondence*, pp. 635-640, 645, plus Thoreau to Messrs Ticknor & Fields, February 18, 1862, MS at CU-SB, tipped in PS 3049 .A1 1849, c. 2. For "An Excursion to Canada," see Headnote for "A Yankee in Canada"; for *Cape Cod*, see *Cape Cod*, "Historical Introduction," pp. 263-277; for "Chesuncook," see *Maine Woods*, "Textual Introduction," pp. 361-362, and Textual Note 122.14-16.

the last page of the first bundle. This ninety-nine-page manuscript, from which the *Atlantic* text of "Walking" was set, survives intact. It serves as copy-text for the present edition, and will receive detailed description below.

Who read the proofs of "Walking" is not known. Thoreau died on May 6, 1862, and the essay was the lead article of the June *Atlantic* issue. If "Walking" proofsheets were prepared soon after Fields received the manuscript in mid-March, they might have reached Concord for correction during the last month of Thoreau's life. The author's diminished energies and eyesight in those final weeks enhance the likelihood that Sophia, if anyone in Concord, was the proofreader. The proofs do not survive.

In the April number, Fields had advertised that Thoreau would "publish in the 'Atlantic' during the present year his new Essays. One on 'Walking' will be printed in the June issue." The advertising copy in June read, "During the latter weeks of his life, Mr. Thoreau corrected the proof-sheets of several articles for this Magazine, the first of which series, 'Walking' appears in this Number. His papers on 'Autumnal Tints', 'Wild Apples' will be printed during the year, in their proper seasons."[7]

"Walking," the first of Thoreau's posthumously published writings, runs to a bit over seventeen *Atlantic* pages (9:657-674). The editor and typesetters routinely normalized Thoreau's punctuation, capitalization, and eccentric spellings; they normalized the ampersand to "and"; they supplied necessary letters in words incompletely written in the manuscript, and necessary end-punctuation where the manuscript

[7] Raymond Borst, "Thoreau Advertisements from *The Atlantic Monthly*: 1862-1868," *Thoreau Society Bulletin* 129 (Fall 1974): 3-4.

lacked it; and they deleted inadvertently repeated words and authorial notes as to text sequence (*Atlantic* anticipates the present edition in some of these changes; see Emendations). Besides making a number of inconsequential alterations in Thoreau's wording and word-order (see Rejected Substantives), Fields was responsible for a cluster of changes near the end that justify Thoreau's apprehensions about the integrity of his text and recall the bowdlerizations in "Chesuncook" and "An Excursion to Canada." All of them affect heterodox references to Christianity, references which Fields presumably felt would irritate the *Atlantic* readership. At 216.13 he deleted "both of heaven and earth" after "laws". At 216.27 he deleted "Christ" from a list of spiritual seekers ("Christ, Dante, Bunyan, and others . . ."). Thoreau began the next sentence with "Even Mahomet, though Christians may scream at his name . . ."; Fields revised "Christians" to "many" (216.31), essentially emasculating the author's criticism of Christian hypocrisy. And finally, at 220.31-33, Thoreau's setting-copy manuscript lauds the resolute walker's philosophy by saying the wisdom suggested "by it [is] not in Plato nor the New Testament. It is a newer testament–the Gospel according to this moment." As edited by Fields, the passage runs, "by it that is a newer testament,–the gospel according to this moment." Such changes add to the argument that Thoreau did not read *Atlantic* proof of "Walking," and that if Sophia did, in the time of worry and grief surrounding his death, she could not have rigorously compared the print with the manuscript.

Fields retained the final manuscript of "Walking" and presented it, bound, to MCo-SC when that library was founded in 1873. It is housed there still, in the Thoreau Collection; as of 2001, its binding complicated somewhat the interpretation of a pencilled note or two in the gutters. Evidently at least some of the leaves were sewn together, possibly into the two bundles to which the covering letter refers, prior to the formal binding for Fields. Here and there this amateur stitchery is visible. On the verso of page "99" appears the title, in pencil, in Thoreau's handwriting. On the recto of a final, unpaginated leaf Thoreau wrote in pencil "p 44 Divide". Of the manuscript's ninety-nine numbered pages (on eighty-six leaves), twelve are wholly or primarily in Sophia Thoreau's neat handwriting: p. "13", 188.34-189.17 ("No doubt temperament . . . out of doors.'"), p. "15", 189.32-190.12 ("natural remedy . . . air. Of"), p. "19", 191.11-18 ("A people who . . . standing in the"), p. "20", 191.18-22 ("middle of . . . surveyor."), p. "23", 192.10-31 ("and there consequently . . . to travel but"), p. "24", 192.31-193.18 ("not from choice . . . I fear for no good."), p. "25", 193.19-194.6 ("No other man . . . But travellers none."), p. "26", 194.7-33 ("Cenotaphs . . . the thawing."), p. "27", 194.34-37 ("If with fancy . . . Marlboro Road."), p. "36", 198.9-31 ("'And now the sun . . . is made for"), p. "85", 216.30-217.6 ("Even Mahomet . . . ear so soon?'"), and p. "88", 217.28-218.6 ("The walker . . . anniversary."). Most of these amanuensis pages have cancellations, transpositions, insertions, and other revisions by Thoreau, as detailed in the list of Alterations. Four paper types are represented in the setting copy. The bulk of the leaves (arguably survivals from Thoreau's most recent lecture version) are on white wove types 12 and 18, while all the text in Sophia's hand is written on white laid type 5 paper stock and on three leaves of an anomalous white laid (*LMHDT*, pp. 377-378). The manuscript also bears stint notations by the typographers who set "Walking" for the *Atlantic Monthly*, and a brief note by Fields on page one, authenticating the manuscript (see Alterations).

Much pre-copy-text material survives, scattered in single leaves and larger groupings among numerous institutional and private collections. The Manuscript Edition of *The Writings of Henry David Thoreau* (Boston: Houghton Mifflin and Company, 1906) was the initial means for dispersing most or all of the single draft leaves. Leaves in Thoreau's handwriting that overlap textually with copy-text pages inscribed by Sophia are presently located at MH-H (bMS Am 278.5, folder 21B); the Brandywine Conservancy, Inc., Chadds Ford, PA; ViU (Barrett Collection number 6345-e); collection of Richard F. Mullen; MH-H (bMS Am 278.5, folder 21B); collection of David Fuller; CaAEU; and collection of Paul R. Bernier. These eight leaves, in order, parallel in part or whole the following seven copy-text sections in Sophia's hand: pages "13", "19" and "20", "23", "24", "36", "85", and "88" (see the preceding paragraph for page and line equivalents in the present edition). Preceding even these materials in the composition of "Walking" are eighty-seven passages from twenty-eight dated entries in Thoreau's Journal. Earlier yet, Thoreau copied into a commonplace book several Zoroastrian and Chaldean oracles from a collection called *The Phenix*, including one used in "Walking": see Textual Note 216.1-4.

In the present edition the text is based on Thoreau's setting-copy manuscript for the *Atlantic Monthly*. The text on pages in Sophia's handwriting, whether or not revised by Henry, has been read against pre-copy-text to guard against copying errors on her part. The editor draws numerous necessary emendations of accidentals from the *Atlantic*, using the copy at NGenoU. The first collected printing of "Walking," in *Excursions* (1863), is based on the *Atlantic* text but introduces seven new substantive readings, none carrying authority (see Rejected Substantives). Collations performed by members of the Thoreau Edition staff include one of the setting-copy manuscript (photocopy) against the *Atlantic*, one of a transcript of the setting-copy manuscript against the *Atlantic*, one of the transcript against *Excursions* (1863), and four of *Excursions* (1863) against the *Atlantic*. The transcript was repeatedly read against the photocopy of manuscript and was perfected against the original manuscript at MCo-SC.

Textual Notes

FOR the format of the Textual Notes, see the Textual Introduction, pp. 381-382. Copy-text is Thoreau's setting-copy manuscript at MCo-SC. AM represents the first printing in the June 1862 *Atlantic Monthly*, and Ex stands for *Excursions* (1863). The abbreviation "MS" followed by a repository symbol or owner's name in parentheses identifies a manuscript reading.

185.1 Walking: For the publication of the essay in AM Thoreau conflated lectures he had presented between April 1851 and September 1860 under the titles "Walking, or the Wild," "Walking," and "The Wild." See Headnote.

185.2 WISH to: The copy-text page, from a lecture manuscript, originally read, "I wish, this evening, to speak". When Thoreau altered the copy-text for magazine use, he cancelled the phrase "this evening" with its terminal comma, but failed to cancel the comma following "wish". For other emendations of features resulting from incomplete revision, see 186.14, 188.5, 189.13, 189.32, 190.8, 191.23, 197.3, 197.21, 198.30, 206.11, 206.15, 206.32, 211.11, 212.31, 215.27, 216.14, and 217.28.

185.15-16 in the middle ages,: This phrase, with its following comma, is Thoreau's addition to his source, Johnson, s.v. "saunter." In the copy-text he initially set off "in the middle ages," from the rest of the quotation with square brackets, but later he cancelled the brackets.

185.22 Some, however: Although these words are not indented as a new paragraph, the previous sentence ends in mid-line.

185.34 forth and: In the copy-text Thoreau uses an ampersand for "and" here and at thirty-three other places, as detailed in Emendations. The typesetters for AM routinely changed each of these to "and", as Thoreau expected them to do. At 211.20, while revising a page to serve as setting copy, Thoreau first pencilled an ampersand between two words, and later wrote "and" in ink over it. See also Textual Notes 23.33, 57.30, 80.19-20, 223.10. See the discussion in *Maine Woods*, Textual Introduction, pp. 394-395, of Thoreau's use of the ampersand in his manuscripts and the print practices of contemporary editors and publishers.

186.10   are prepared to: Thus in the copy-text. AM, followed by Ex, prints "are ready to", perhaps an editorial change to avoid repeating "are prepared to" in the previous sentence. On the other hand, a lecture-draft leaf, MS (MH-H), wholly in pencil, shows "prepared" cancelled and "ready" interlined at this point. Possibly the copy-text wording was altered in proof by Sophia.

186.14   a walk.:   Following these words on the copy-text page are references in Thoreau's hand to pages in earlier lecture forms of the essay, his back-up copy. The page references evidently served to guide him in the preparation of subsequent pages of copy for AM. See Alteration 186.14 for the content of these notes.

186.18   Equestrians: Thoreau entered a dieresis above the third letter, perhaps inadvertently adopting a convention for writing Latin *eqüus*. None of Thoreau's English dictionaries uses a diacritical in this word.

188.8   o'clock: Here and at 188.9 the copy-text reads "o clock", though Thoreau provides the apostrophe at 188.7 and, for all three instances, in a draft leaf, MS (MH-H).

188.30   bed.–:   Thus in the copy-text. The draft page, MS (MH-H), reads "bed!"

189.6   taking exercise: Thus in the copy-text, p. "13", in Sophia's hand. Thoreau puts quotation marks around "taking exercise" on a draft page, MS (MH-H).

189.32   natural: This word, added by Thoreau in pencil, is the last writing on copy-text page "14", two-thirds of the way down the page. He apparently intended it to serve as a catch word for the following, transcribed, page. Written in Sophia's hand (her copy of a superseded draft page), page "15" begins in mid-sentence with the word "Natural". She later corrected the capital initial to a minuscule, but the repetition of the word was allowed to stand. Similar occurrences of uncancelled catch words signalling transitions between pages from different compositional or transcription stages of the copy-text are emended at 206.15, 215.27, 216.14, and 217.28. Most of the other repetitions emended in this edition are on pages where Thoreau cancelled several lines of material between blocks of text he wished to retain, and added, just before the cancellation, the word or words that began the next uncancelled passage. See, for example, 212.31.

190.1 selfrespect: Thus in the copy-text, p. "15", in Sophia's hand. The only previous version of the sentence, in the
Journal for November 11, 1851 (*Journal 4*, p. 175), lacks this
compound term, which Thoreau might have treated differently–with a hyphen or as two words. It appears hyphenated
in drafts F and G of *Walden* (CSmH, HM 924) and in the first
edition (see *Walden*, pp. 213, 321).

190.11 Platans: AM changes this copy-text spelling to
"Platanes", but Thoreau follows the spelling in his source,
John Evelyn, *Sylva, or a Discourse of Forest-Trees ... [together
with] Terra ... Pomona ... [and] Kalendarium Hortense*, 3d
ed. (London: Printed for John Martyn, 1679), p. 117. The information in the remainder of the sentence is taken from the
same page of *Sylva*.

191.12-13 consumed, their: The needed comma is missing in the copy-text, page "19", written by Sophia. It is present, however, in a lecture draft page in Thoreau's hand, MS
(ViU).

191.23 ten, fifteen, twenty,: The copy-text originally read
"10–15–20–" before Thoreau cancelled "10" and "15" and
wrote above, for the printer, "ten, &c".

192.22 vile: Not underlined in the copy-text, page "23",
in Sophia's hand, but underlined in Thoreau's lecture draft
page, collection of Richard F. Mullen.

192.24 way-worn: Spelled "way-worne" both in the
copy-text, p. "23" (Sophia's hand), and in the Richard F. Mullen collection draft.

192.34 nature: Thus with minuscule initial in the copy-
text, p. "24", in Sophia's hand, though capitalized on Thoreau's lecture draft of this passage, MS (MH-H). AM capitalizes it.

193.7-8 Marlboro: The name occurs thus six times on
copy-text pages "24"-"27", all transcriptions by Sophia. Thoreau's treatment in the surviving lecture draft pages in his
hand, MS (MH-H), varies between "Marlboro" and "Marlboro'". AM consistently spells it "Marlborough".

193.32 Old: The copy-text page, in Sophia's hand, is ambiguous as to the initial, but it is plainly a capital in Thoreau's
draft version, MS (MH-H). The same is the case at 194.37. In
both instances AM capitalizes.

193.36 Christians: Sophia gives this term a minuscule
initial in her transcription (p. "25"), though Thoreau capitalizes it in a surviving earlier manuscript version of the line, a

Journal entry written after July 29, 1850 (*Journal 3*, p. 104). He also capitalizes "Christian" at 212.34, from a copy-text page in his own handwriting. At 216.31, from another of Sophia's amanuensis pages, "Christians" is capitalized.

194.5   guide boards of stone: Thus in the copy-text, p. "25", in Sophia's hand. The only surviving manuscript version of the line in Thoreau's hand, a Journal entry written after July 29, 1850 (*Journal 3*, p. 104), underlines "boards", playing on the contradiction between "board" and "stone". Although Thoreau made pencilled corrections to a draft copy of the poem, MS (MH-H), also a transcription of Sophia's, he did not there add underlining to "boards".

194.13   wondering–:   Thus in the only known version in Thoreau's hand, a Journal entry written after July 29, 1850 (*Journal 3*, p. 104). The copy-text lacks punctuation; AM supplies a period.

194.23-26   Grave all that is known / Which . . . read / In his extreme need. / I know: Punctuated thus in both the Journal draft of these lines, written after July 29, 1850 (*Journal 3*, p. 105) and a draft copy of the poem, MS (MH-H), in Sophia's hand with Thoreau's pencilled revisions. When Sophia recopied this matter to p. "26" of the copy-text, she altered the punctuation, thus garbling the sense of the lines: "[where a traveller might] Grave all that is known. / Which another might read, / In his extreme need, / I know [some lines a man could remember]." On his own authority, the present editor emends to the earlier pointing. The AM printing makes similar, but not identical, adjustments in the punctuation of the copy-text.

198.9   sun . . . stretched: The copy-text page on which this quotation from the conclusion of Milton's "Lycidas" appears, p. "36", is in Sophia's hand except for revisions by Thoreau, including a sentence added by him at the foot. On a draft leaf, MS (David Fuller), Thoreau capitalizes "Sun" and puts an apostrophe over the second e of "stretched", possibly intending "stretch'd". In one edition Thoreau is known to have used, *The Poetical Works of John Milton . . .*, ed. Henry John Todd (London: Printed for J. Johnson [et al.] by Bye and Law, 1801), 5:50, the readings are "sun" and "stretch'd". Another, *The Works of the English Poets, from Chaucer to Cowper . . .*, ed. Alexander Chalmers (London: Printed for J. Johnson et al., 1810), 7:474, has "Sun" and "stretch'd".

198.29   goes further–further than: The copy-text page

("36") is in Sophia's hand. At this point, copying from a lost draft page, she wrote "[Guyot] goes farther than I am quite ready to follow him," wording Thoreau modified by adding a dash after "farther", interlining "further" (his characteristic spelling of the term), and cancelling "quite". In the following sentence she wrote "He says further on", though Thoreau cancelled "further on" in association with other revisions (see Alterations 198.29 to 198.30 "'As" for all changes in this section of text). Thoreau's preference here is clearly for "further" over "farther".

199.13-16 "From what ... globe.": Thoreau adds the word "naturally" in his translation from the French of François André Michaux, *Voyage à l'Ouest des Monts Alléghanys* ... (Paris: Dentu, 1808), p. 68. Michaux gives the pioneer's question in both English and French: "*From what part of the world are you coming?* (De quelle partie du monde êtes-vous venu?)" Ignoring the English of the source, Thoreau provides a more idiomatic translation, "From what part of the world have you come?"

199.21 that "in: In the copy-text, Thoreau fails to enter the open-quotation mark for this quotation from Francis B. Head, *The Emigrant*, 3d ed. (London: John Murray, 1846), p. 1. At 199.31, Thoreau follows Head's "the rivers larger" (*The Emigrant*, p. 2), a reading sophisticated to "the rivers longer" in AM.

200.26 ethereal: Emended from the copy-text's "etherial". None of Thoreau's four dictionaries accepts the spelling of the manuscript.

201.2 star: Thus in the copy-text, though the source, Bishop George Berkeley's "Verses on the Prospect of Planting Arts and Learning in America," line 21, reads "course". The line is proverbial, but Thoreau may have known it in *A Collection of Poems ... by Several Hands* (London: Printed for J. Dodsley, 1775), 6:311-312.

203.5 Cumming: The copy-text's "Cummings" is in error. Thoreau cites Roualeyn Gordon-Cumming, *Five Years of a Hunter's Life in the Far Interior of South Africa* (New York: Harper & Brothers, 1850), 1:218.

203.13 trapper's: The copy-text omits the apostrophe, but it is present on a draft leaf at OAkU.

203.19 exchanges: By curious coincidence, this word is hyphenated after "ex" at the end of the line in a surviving draft version, MS (OAkU), in the manuscript copy-text, in

AM, and in Ex. No word-play by Thoreau requiring the maintenance of the hyphen is perceptible in this context.

206.34   in some respects: In the copy-text this phrase is
interlined with a caret above "and more". The syllable "re"
fell just before the ascender of the letter d of "and"; Thoreau
wrote a hyphen after "re" and finished the word, "spects", to
the right of the ascender. It is unlikely that he intended the
reading "re-spects".

210.28   friends: The copy-text reads "frinds". Curiously,
a draft of the passage, formerly in the collection of Anne
Wanzer, has "frends".

211.2   Buffalo: Spelled thus, though with a minuscule initial, on a draft leaf, MS (MdU-BC). The copy-text has "Buffa-
loe", a spelling not authorized by Thoreau's dictionaries.

211.10   unwieldly: Spelled thus in the copy-text, changed
to "unwieldy" by an AM compositor or editor, and restored
as "unwieldly" in Ex. The copy-text spelling is anticipated in
the only other surviving version of this sentence, part of a
Journal entry for November 21, 1850 (*Journal 3*, p. 147). Of
Thoreau's dictionaries, Johnson and Webster give only "unwieldy"; Bailey lacks the term in either spelling; and Walker,
which records "unwieldily" and "unwieldiness", lists the adjective as "unwieldly". This last may be a mistake, however,
for the phonetic data immediately after the term shows
the pronunciation to be "unwieldy". The *OED* records
"unwieldly" as an alternative to "unwieldy," giving several
instances.

211.14-18   *who!* ... Who!:   Thus in the copy-text, Thoreau's preferred representation of the teamster's "stop" command to his draft animals. See *Walden*, p. 324, and Walter
Harding, ed., *The Variorum Walden and the Variorum Civil
Disobedience* (New York: Washington Square Press, 1968),
p. 318, note 24. AM substitutes the spelling "Whoa" in both
instances.

212.4   Confucius: Two earlier versions give the name in
this, correct, spelling: a Journal entry for May 6, 1851 (*Journal
3*, p. 217), and a lecture-draft leaf (photocopy courtesy of
Larry E. Rutter Books and Autographs). In the copy-text
Thoreau writes "Confufucius" here, though "Confucius" at
206.6.

213.26   men.:   The elongated mark after "men" in the
copy-text may be intended as a short dash, though the punctuation of a draft leaf, MS (ICarbS), is distinctly a period.

213.36   Niepce: Thus in the copy-text. AM prints "Ni-épce", but Thoreau is faithful to his source, Robert Hunt, *The Poetry of Science* (Boston: Gould, Kendall, and Lincoln, 1850), pp. 126, 128. In the next sentence, Thoreau changes Hunt's "during daylight" (p. 133) to "during the day-light".

215.7   Great Fields: It is difficult to tell whether in the copy-text the initial of the first word is a capital or a minuscule; but it is clearly a capital in two draft leaves: MS (CtY-BR) and MS (William A. Strutz).

216.1-4   ΄ως τι . . . Chaldean Oracles.:   Thus in the copy-text. Thoreau's source is Thomas Taylor's collection of "The Chaldæan Oracles of Zoroaster," in *The Phenix: A Collection of Old and Rare Fragments* (New York: William Gowan, 1835), p. 168. This particular oracle (number 167), attributed by Taylor to "the Theurgists," reads in the source, "You will not understand it as when understanding some particular thing." When Thoreau copied this saying into his commonplace book (ca. 1840–1848), he translated it back into Greek and wrote, "You will not understand that as understanding a particular thing" (*Thoreau's Literary Notebook in the Library of Congress*, ed. Kenneth Walter Cameron [Hartford, CT: Transcendental Books, 1964], p. 40). For "Walking," he changed the English verbs from "understand" and "understanding" to "perceive" and "perceiving".

216.13   both of heaven and earth: AM deletes this phrase, evidently in deference to the religious sensibilities of its readers. For like reason, "Christ" is removed from Thoreau's list of deep thinkers at 216.27, and Thoreau's phrase at 216.31, "though Christians may scream", is bowdlerized to "though many may scream".

216.35   a railroad: Thus in the copy-text, a page ("85") transcribed by Sophia. A draft leaf, MS (CaAEU), reads "the railroad".

217.4   storms: The copy-text page ("85") is a transcription by Sophia. Thoreau's draft leaf, MS (CaAEU), has a semicolon after the word, accurately following the source, James Macpherson, "Ca-Lodin," in *The Genuine Remains of Ossian . . . with a Preliminary Dissertation. By Patrick MacGregor* (London: Smith, Elder & Co., 1841), p. 121.

217.28   the familiar: The copy-text page ("88") is a transcription by Sophia. Thoreau's draft leaf, MS (Paul R. Bernier), reads "these familiar".

219.9-10   cohabitancy: None of Thoreau's dictionaries

includes this noun form, which may be a coinage of his; they list only "cohabitation".

219.32   payed: AM's editorial change of this copy-text term to "paid" nullifies Thoreau's pun on the nautical sense of "pay": "to daub or besmear [with tar, pitch, or grease] . . . to preserve [the object so treated] from injury by water or weather" (Webster).

221.36   gilded: In the copy-text Thoreau miswrites this word as "guilded", but at 222.4 he correctly spells "gilding".

Table of Emendations

FOR the format of this table, see the Textual Introduction, p. 382. Sources for the emendations are the first printing in the *Atlantic Monthly* (AM) or the editor's own authority, designated "PE" for the Princeton Edition, when the emendation is not anticipated in AM or *Excursions* (1863).

*185.2	WISH to] AM; wish, to
185.14	"from] AM; "fom
*185.34	forth and] AM; forth &
186.5	Half] AM; Haf
186.5	is] AM; *second letter illegible*
*186.14	a walk.] AM; a walk. V p 5 . . . also 9 *(see Alteration 186.14)*
*186.18	Equestrians] AM; Eqüestrians
186.24	State and] AM; State &
188.4	shops and] AM; shops &
*188.8	o'clock] AM; o clock
188.9	o'clock] AM; o clock
188.11	one's] AM; ones
188.13-14	sympathy.] AM; sympathy
188.15	four and] AM; four &
188.15	five] AM; 5 five
189.13	you] AM; You
*189.32	natural] AM; natural natural
189.34	day,] AM; *possibly* day– *(see Alteration 189.34)*
190.6	fields and] AM; fields &

190.8	mall?] AM; mall.? *(see Alteration 190.8)*
190.10	themselves] AM; them / selves
190.27	happen.–] PE; happen–
*191.12-13	consumed, their] AM; consumed their
*191.23	ten, fifteen, twenty,] AM; ten, &c–20– *(see Alteration 191.23)*
191.27	brook, and] AM; brook, &
191.27	meadow and] AM; meadow &
191.29	civilization] AM; *extra stroke between* l *and* i
191.33	trade and] AM; trade &
191.34-35	them all–I] PE; them all– –I
192.9	year's] AM; years
192.11	man.] AM; man
192.14-15	a trivial] AM; A trivial
192.19	to and from] AM; to & from
*192.22	*vile*] PE; vile
192.23	liable to.] AM; liable to,
*192.24	way-worn] PE; way-worne
193.9	me. I] AM; me I
*193.32	Old] AM; *possibly* old
*193.36	Christians] AM; christians
*194.13	wondering–] PE; wondering
194.23	known] PE; known. *(see Textual Note 194.23-26)*
194.24	read] PE; read, *(see Textual Note 194.23-26)*
194.25	need.] AM; need, *(see Textual Note 194.23-26)*
194.37	Old] AM; *possibly* old
195.2	narrow and] AM; narrow &
195.4	road;] PE; road.;
195.15	heedlessness and] AM; heedlessness &
196.3	sometimes] AM; *possibly* sometime
196.34	we] AM; *possibly* We
197.3	before it] AM; before, it *(see Alteration 197.3)*
197.13-14	some, crossing] AM; some crossing
197.21	town] AM; town town *(see Alteration 197.20-21)*
198.1	enveloped] AM; envelopped
198.15	fertile and] AM; fertile &
198.15-16	productions, and] AM; productions, &
198.18	that "the] AM; that " "the

198.22	size."] AM; size"
198.29	goes further] PE; goes farther *(see Textual Note 198.29)*
198.30	he] AM; He *(see Alterations 198.29 him, and 198.29-30)*
198.36-199.1	preceding] AM; preceeding
199.19	fruit.] AM; fruit
*199.21	that "in] AM; that in
199.30	vivider–the] PE; vivider– –the
199.32	broader.–"] PE; broader:–"
199.34	world and] AM; world &
200.14-15	philosophy and] AM; philosophy &
*200.26	ethereal] AM; etherial
200.31	breadth and] AM; breadth &
201.11	studying] AM; study / ing
201.20	and Rolandseck and] AM; & Rolandseck &
201.35	Dubuque and] AM; Dubuque &
202.12	plow and] PE; plow &
202.13	forest and] AM; forest &
202.15	Romulus and] AM; Romulus &
202.25-26	strength and] AM; strength &
203.3	to which] AM; To which
*203.5	Cumming] PE; Cummings
203.9	Nature] AM; *possibly* nature
*203.13	trapper's] AM; trappers
203.16-17	wardrobes and] AM; wardrobes &
203.31	say–] PE; say– –
204.20	there–the] PE; there– –the
204.21-22	lamb-kill, azalea] AM; lamb-kill azalea
204.22	and rhodora] AM; & rhodora
204.25	plots and] AM; plots &
204.29	cellar.] AM; *possibly* cellar–
205.17	moisture and] AM; moisture &
206.10	or resort to] AM; or, resort to
206.11	A hundred] AM; A hundred A hundred
206.14	hardened] AM; hardenened
206.14	hardened and] AM; hardenened &
206.15	Ah! already] AM; Ah! already Ah! already
206.18-19	tar and] AM; tar &
206.32	the farmer] AM; The farmer
206.34	respects] AM; re-spects *(see Textual Note 206.34)*
207.21	begrimed] AM; begrimmed

207.22	Indian's] AM; *possibly* Indians'
208.23	Nature] AM; *possibly* nature
208.34	annually] AM; anmually
210.21	In short] AM; [In short *(bracket possibly typesetter's: see Alteration 210.21)*
210.26	beasts] AM; ea *blotted*
*210.28	friends] AM; frinds
210.30	awful] AM; aweful
211.1	swollen] AM; swolen
*211.2	Buffalo] PE; Buffaloe
211.5	cattle and] AM; cattle &
211.8	Any] AM; Any Any *(second* Any *blotted; first* Any *possibly intended to cancel paragraph break)*
211.11	even] AM; even even
*212.4	Confucius] AM; Confufucius
212.5	they] AM; they they
212.31	At present] AM; At At present *(see Alteration 212.31)*
*213.26	men.] AM; *possibly* men–
214.9	original] AM; *possibly* originals
214.19	meadow and] AM; meadow &
214.20	immediate] AM; immeadiate *with* a *smeared*
*215.7	Great Fields] AM; *possibly* great Fields
215.27	The highest] AM; The highest The highest *(see Alteration 215.27)*
216.14	"That is] AM; That is "That is
217.28	The walker in] AM; The Walker The walker in *(see Alteration 217.28)*
217.30	owners'] AM; owners
217.30-31	as it were] AM; As it were
217.35	these bounds] AM; These bounds
218.2	they fade] AM; They fade
218.5	trace, and] AM; trace, &
218.23	path] AM; parth
219.7	is only] AM; is [only
219.12-13	few and fewer] AM; few & fewer
219.14-15	few and fewer] AM; few & fewer
219.24	itself. Our] AM; itself. *(wavy pencil line)* Our *(see Alteration 219.24)*
220.20	ones.–] PE; ones–
221.10	awful] AM; aweful

*221.36	gilded] AM; guilded
222.12	till] AM; Till

Table of Alterations

For the format of this table, see the Textual Introduction, p. 383. A dozen of the manuscript's ninety-nine pages are in the handwriting of Sophia E. Thoreau, most with revisions and additions by her brother. These pages are identified, and the alterations they bear are assigned, as applicable, to Sophia (ST) or Henry (HDT). Thoreau often set off with parentheses phrases he was considering deleting; hence, in entries that record deletions, the deleted phrases may include parentheses that would otherwise be inappropriate marks of punctuation. Unless specified to the contrary, alterations are in ink.

185.1	Walking] the handwriting of *underlined* H. D. Thoreau. *added in the hand of James T. Fields*
185.2	I WISH] *followed by* this evening, *set off with pencilled parentheses and cancelled in ink over pencil (see Textual Note 185.2)*
185.2-5	absolute . . . inhabitant] Hennessy *(typesetter) faintly pencilled in left margin*
185.3	Freedom] F *altered from lower case in ink over pencil*
185.3	Wildness] W *altered from lower case in ink over pencil*
185.3	Freedom] F *altered from lower case in ink over pencil*
185.4	Culture] C *altered from lower case in ink over pencil*
185.9	school-committee] *last letter reformed or written over other letter(s)*
185.12	Walking] W *altered from lower case*
*185.15-16	in the middle ages,] *set off by square brackets cancelled in ink over pencil*

185.22   mean. Some]   *linked by pencilled line to*
                cancel paragraph break
185.24   sense, will]   *comma added in pencil*
185.27   sits]   sit *reformed*
185.28   Saunterer,]   S *altered from lower case;*
                comma added in pencil
185.29   sense, is]   *comma added in pencil*
185.30   river,]   *comma added in pencil*
185.31   sea. But]   *linked by pencilled line to cancel*
                paragraph break
*186.14   a walk.]   *followed by erased pencilled*
                notations: V p 5 of Duplicate of [4 or 5 illegible
                words] 8 also 9
186.15   To come]   *preceded by* If you are prepared to
                leave father and mother, and brother & sister,
                & wife and child and friends, and never see
                them again. If you have payed your debts, and
                made your will, and settled all your affairs,
                and are a free man, then you are ready for a
                walk *cancelled in pencil (see 186.9-14)*
186.19   Walkers]   W *altered from lower case in ink*
                over pencil
186.23   Errant. He]   *linked by pencilled line to cancel*
                paragraph break
186.25   We have felt that]   *preceded at top of page by*
                cancelled seeming to them to be in league
                with the Devil, going about seeking whom he
                may devour, and plotting all the treasons. He
                is not a good citizen, for he has no fixed
                abode, but merely squats somewhere, though
                it may be fast by the Tree of Knowledge.
                Hence, if I were sure that you would
                understand my words in a sufficiently liberal
                sense, I might say that those twain who act a
                principal part in the history of the world,
                (who *cancelled)* appearing to stand close
                together though there is a considerable
                interval between them, were well enough
                named the Devil and Tom *Walker.*
186.25   hereabouts]   *interlined in ink over pencil*
                with a caret in ink over pencil
186.31   God]   G *altered from lower case*
186.34   Walkers]   W *altered from lower case*

187.5   class. No]   *linked by line to cancel paragraph break and* no break *written in margin*

187.8   outlaws]   out laws *joined with line*

187.27   upon–]   *followed by* it is a cruel truth– *cancelled in ink over pencil*

188.6   I know]   *preceded by pencilled* / / *at beginning of line*

188.6-7   sitting there]   *followed by* with Dutch sturdiness taking Holland–I do not mean Holland gin– *cancelled in ink over pencil*

188.7-9   3 o'clock . . . morning courage]   Use[d?] this in iron horse *pencilled in margin and erased; see* Walden *pp. 118-119 and* Sartain's Union Magazine *July 1852*

188.15   four]   *interlined above cancelled* 4

188.15   five]   *interlined above uncancelled* 5

188.24   a summer]   *interlined above* the *cancelled in pencil*

188.25   skirts]   k *reformed*

188.31   which]   *preceded by cancelled* –

188.34-189.17   No doubt . . . out of doors."]   *text in ST's hand*

188.34-36   No doubt . . . follow]   *underlined* Cormack *(typesetter) pencilled in left margin*

189.12   him.]   *followed by* The seeming necessity of swinging dumb-bells proves that he has lost his way. When he finds it his bells will no longer be dumb, *(followed by* bells *cancelled in pencil)* but will ring out a melodious peal. *all cancelled in pencil by HDT*

189.13   Moreover,]   *added by HDT*

189.14   ruminates]   te *clarified in pencil*

189.15   traveller]   ll *clarified in pencil*

189.25   say]   *followed by cancelled* think *or* thank

189.28   moral]   *interlined in pencil with a caret*

189.32   that the]   *followed by pencilled* natural *(catch word)*

189.32-190.12   natural remedy . . . air. Of]   *text in ST's hand*

189.32   natural]   N *of* Natural *cancelled in pencil and* n *added in pencil*

189.34   day,]   *comma written over dash or vice versa, apparently by ST*

190.2   thrills]   ll *clarified in pencil*

190.3   mere] *added in left margin, apparently by*
                 ST
190.4   white,] *comma added in pencil*
190.5   callus] o *of* callous *cancelled by HDT*
190.8   mall?] *question mark pencilled above*
                 uncancelled period
190.11   Platans"] *close quotation mark clarified in*
                 pencil
190.13   course] *preceded by text cancelled in pencil*
                 occupying recto of same leaf: in the true sense
                 of that word, both in spirit and in fact, as my
                 neighbors, and more so than many of them
                 who are longer about it. But however that
                 may be, I am satisfied that the walking of
                 which I am thinking is better than any mere
                 work of the hands that I can do. = You must
                 walk like a camel which is said to be the only
                 beast which ruminates when walking. When
                 a traveller asked Wordsworth's servant to
                 show him her *(pencilled over cancelled* his*)*
                 master's study; she *(s added in pencil)*
                 answered "Here is his Library; but his Study *(S*
                 altered from lower case) is out of doors." Shall
                 we suppose that if he spent his time well in his
                 Library, he spent it less profitably in his out-
                 of-door Study? *(S altered from lower case)*
                 (pencilled ¶) When we walk we naturally go
                 to the fields and woods; What would become
                 of us if we walked only in a garden or a mall?
                 *(*Even some *interlined in pencil with a caret*
                 and v l p *pencilled in margin)* Of
190.21   body is;] *followed by cancelled* –
190.30-31   exhausted] *followed by pencilled caret and*
                 illegible erased pencilled matter
190.33   walking] ing *added*
190.35   as good as] *followed by cancelled* Cairo or
                 Damascus, or
191.4-5   It will . . . you.] *added*
191.5   you.] *followed by cancelled* After how few
                 steps–how little exertion–the student stands
                 in pine woods, above
191.6   Now a days] *interlined above cancelled* At
                 present, in this vicinity

191.11-18   A people who . . . standing in the]   *text in ST's
                   hand; see next entry*
191.11   A people who]   *preceded on page by text in
                   ST's hand, cancelled in pencil by HDT:*
                   Though his route is across-lots, fences are not
                   necessarily an obstacle to the Walker. If the
                   divisions correspond to natural ones, which is
                   the case to a considerable extent, as mowing,
                   pasture, wood land and the different kinds of
                   tillage, they will not much offend the eye. The
                   fence that separates one of natures provinces
                   from another, we do not feel to be an
                   obstruction; but the fence which is set up
                   arbitrarily, or according to the whim of the
                   owner, or which merely parts your land from
                   another's, *(apostrophe added in pencil)* we
                   do not love to get over, and we do not repair
                   it with so good a grace when we have tumbled
                   it down. However what the farmer calls
                   mowing, pasture &c is not often such to me.
191.18-22   middle of a . . . his surveyor.]   *text in ST's
                   hand*
191.19   fen]   f *altered from* p *apparently by HDT*
191.23   I can easily walk]   *preceded by* the Solomon's
                   seal and the cow-wheat–in a place still
                   unaccountably wild to him and his pursuits,
                   & to all civilization. This so easy and so
                   common, though our literature would imply
                   that it is so rare. We in the country make no
                   report of the wildness amid which we live to
                   those in the city–nor do they remind us of the
                   seals and sharks in their harbor. We send
                   them only our huckle berries at most, not
                   free wild thoughts. *cancelled in pencil and*
                   solomon's *changed to* Solomon's *in ink;
                   possibly erased* here or hereafter? *pencilled in
                   margin*
*191.23   ten, fifteen, twenty,]   *originally* 10–15–20–
                   altered to ten, &c–20–
191.34-35   the most . . . all,–]   *interlined in ink over
                   pencil with a caret above cancelled* for that is
                   the name for them all here today
192.7-10   In one half . . . to another]   *possibly added*

192.10   another] *followed on verso by memoranda in pencil about text sequence and ink text cancelled in pencil:* and there consequently politics are not for they are but as the cigar smoke of a man. *(see 192.10-11)*
v s n p 161 *(or* p. 61*)* In the village

Some do not walk at all; others walk in the high-ways; a few walk across lots. Roads are made for horses and men of business. I do not travel in them much comparatively, because I am not in a hurry to get to any tavern, or grocery, or livery stable, or depot to which they lead. I am a good horse *(*a good horse *altered in pencil from* as good as a horse*)* to travel, but not from choice a roadster– The landscape painter uses the figures of men to mark a road– He would not make that use of my figure *(*The landscape . . . my figure *interlined in pencil with a caret)* When I have liberty I walk out into a nature such as the old prophets and poets–Menu–Moses–Homer Chaucer–walked in. You may name it America,–but it is not America. Neither Americus Vespucius, nor Columbus, nor the rest, were the discoverers of it. There is a truer account of it in the Mythology than in any History of America so called that I have seen. *(see 192.26-193.4); added in pencil and separately cancelled:* I sit on the hills overlooking my native town *(*my native town *altered in pencil from* Concord*)* & I do with America what I will. My neighbors are at the mercy of my thoughts. I think hard of them sometimes; but oftenest I do not think of them at all.

To any one whom you can call a philosopher his country and nation are not very prominent facts. There is danger that

192.10-194.37   and there consequently . . . By the Old Marlboro Road.] *text in ST's hand*

192.12   The village] Schubarth *(typesetter) pencilled in left margin*

192.14   which] *interlined by HDT in ink over pencil with a caret in ink over pencil*

192.33	He] H *altered from lower case in ink over pencil by HDT*
193.3	of it] *interlined in pencil with a caret by HDT*
193.3	Mythology] *preceded by* the *cancelled in pencil by HDT*
193.7	nearly] *interlined in ink over pencil above* well nigh *cancelled in ink over pencil by HDT*
193.7	Old] O *altered from lower case by ST*
193.8-9	methinks,] *comma added in pencil*
193.9	unless] *followed by comma cancelled in pencil*
193.9-11	I am . . . every town.] *added in ink over pencil by HDT*
194.1	What is it, what is it] *followed by* ? *cancelled in pencil*
194.4	somewhere?] *period altered to question mark in pencil by HDT*
194.38	At present,] *cancelled in pencil (cancellation erased) and* As yet, *written in pencil, cancelled, and erased above*
194.38	vicinity] neighborhood *written in pencil and erased below*
195.6	grounds.] *followed by cancelled –*
195.8	true] *interlined in ink over pencil with a caret in ink over pencil*
195.8	it.] *followed by cancelled –*
195.9	come.] *followed on verso by cancelled ¶* However, there are a few old roads that may be trodden with, profit, as if they led some where (profit, . . . some where *interlined in pencil with a pencilled caret)* now that they are well nigh discontinued. There is the Old Marlboro Road, which does not go to Marlboro' now methinks, unless that is Marlboro where it carries me. *(see 193.5-9)*
195.31	south-south-west. The] *linked by ink over pencilled line to cancel paragraph break*
196.6	me. It] *linked by ink over pencilled line to cancel paragraph break*
196.8	Wildness] W *altered from lower case*
196.8	Freedom] F *altered from lower case*
196.16	wilderness.] *followed by pencilled caret*
196.16-19	should . . . must] *interlined in ink over*

pencil above I must walk toward Oregon, *with
original* must *cancelled in ink over pencil and
preceded in margin with cancelled pencilled* I
or &

196.22   Within] *preceded by* It is true, that *set off in
pencilled parentheses and cancelled in ink
over pencil*

196.22   Within]   W *altered from lower case in ink
over pencil*

196.27   experiment.]   *followed by* We envy more the
towns which bound us on the west, than
those which bound us on the east. The former
have one permanent advantage over us.
cancelled in ink and pencil

196.30   East]   E *altered from lower case*

196.32   We go eastward]   Cormack *(typesetter)
pencilled in left margin*

196.35   adventure. The]   *linked by ink over pencilled
line to cancel paragraph break*

197.3   before]   *followed by* in the course of ages, *set
off in pencilled parentheses and cancelled in
ink over pencil (see Emendation 197.3)*

197.4   Styx]   S *and* y *reformed*

197.5   three]   *interlined above cancelled* 3

197.8   walk]   *followed by* , or fronting even to his
favorite chamber or window in a chamber
cancelled in ink and pencil

197.9   race;]   *followed by cancelled* –

197.11   some]   *interlined in ink over pencil above
cancelled* one

197.11   instances]   *second* s *added in pencil*

197.13   say some]   *interlined in ink over pencil with
an ink caret*

197.17   which affects]   which *followed by* is known)
to *set off with pencilled parentheses cancelled
in ink over pencil and an* s *added in ink over
pencil to* affect

197.18   referred]   *followed by* solely *set off with
pencilled parentheses and cancelled in ink
over pencil*

197.20   Not]   *preceded by pencilled* \\

197.20-21   our town]   *interlined in ink over pencil with
a pencilled caret above* this town *with* town
cancelled in ink over pencil

197.22   if] *cancelled false stroke (beginning of capital I?) above*

197.28   Sun] S *altered from lower case*

198.3   Hesperides] H *altered from lower case*

198.8   afar.–] *followed by cancelled period or comma*

198.9-31   "And now . . . is made for] *text in ST's hand*

198.12   new."] *followed by* There seems to be sufficient testimony to the greater habitableness if not fertility and promise of the western continent. *cancelled by HDT*

198.13-17   Where on the Globe . . . as this is?] *added by HDT over erased pencilled matter at bottom of page and marked with marginal line and* 1 *for insertion*

198.14   that] *followed by cancelled* that

198.17-31   Michaux . . . made for] *marked by HDT with marginal line and* 2 *to follow* Where on . . . as this is?

198.23   his observations] *interlined in ink over pencil by HDT above* what he says *cancelled in ink over pencil by HDT*

198.29   –further than] *dash and* further *interlined in ink over pencil with a caret in ink over pencil by HDT (see Textual Note 198.29)*

198.29   ready] *preceded by* quite *cancelled by HDT (see Textual Note 198.29)*

198.29   him,] him. *(see Textual Note 198.29)*

198.29-30   yet not when] *interlined in pencil by HDT above* He *with* yet *only partially visible in bound gutter (see Textual Note 198.29)*

198.30   says] *followed by* further on *cancelled in pencil by HDT (see Textual Note 198.29)*

198.30   "As] A *altered from lower case by ST (see Textual Note 198.29)*

199.10   times. The] *linked by line to cancel paragraph break*

199.15   meeting] *followed by underlined* reunion *cancelled in ink and pencil and enclosed in uncancelled brackets*

199.18-19   From . . . fruit.] *added in ink over pencil*

199.20   Sir Francis] *preceded in margin with pencilled paragraph sign*

199.26	old] *reformed*
199.26	world." "The] *linked by ink over pencilled line to cancel paragraph break*
199.32-34	This statement . . . productions] *added in ink and pencil*
200.2-3	Romans] s *added in ink over pencil*
200.11	Europe] *preceded by cancelled* America
201.1	To Americans] Hector *(typesetter) pencilled in left margin*
201.1	To Americans] *altered from* To an American audience *by cancellation in ink over pencil and addition of* s
201.3	As] *added before cancelled* As *to eliminate paragraph break*
201.7-8	though we . . . south] *set off by erased pencilled lines, with pencilled* retain *in margin*
201.10	their] i *reformed*
201.10	inheritance. It] *linked by line to cancel paragraph break*
202.3	kind] *interlined with a caret*
202.5-6	this was . . . itself] *underlined in ink over pencil*
202.7	of men.] *followed by pencilled* Divide here if necessary
202.8	The West] *preceded at top of page by* than of the past or present–I saw that this was a Rhine stream of a different kind, that the foundations of castles were yet to be laid, and the famous bridges were yet to be thrown over the stream,–and I felt that this was the heroic age itself–though we know it not. for the hero is commonly the simplest & obscurest of men *cancelled in ink and pencil and* for the hero . . . men *added in pencil (see 202.1-7)*
202.8	The West] *paragraph sign pencilled above*
202.8	West] W *altered from lower case*
202.9	Wild;] *followed by cancelled* –
202.10	Wildness] W *altered from lower case in ink over pencil*
202.11	Wild] W *altered from lower case in ink over pencil*

202.14-15   savages. The] *linked by ink over pencilled line to cancel paragraph break*

202.25-26   for strength and] *interlined with a caret*

202.25   strength] *altered from* strengths

202.31   soft.] *followed by cancelled* –

202.35   of. Give] *linked by ink over pencilled line to cancel paragraph break*

202.35   Wildness] W *altered from lower case*

203.1   border] b *reformed*

203.2   migrate] *followed by cancelled comma*

203.8   much] *followed by* of *cancelled in ink over pencil*

203.14   musquash] *altered from* musk- / rats *in ink over pencil*

203.14   even;] *followed by cancelled* –

203.22   and perhaps] *interlined above cancelled* Is not

203.23   woods.] *period altered from question mark*

203.29   Ben] *ink over pencilled paragraph sign inserted after* fields."

203.33   Life] *inserted before cancelled* Life *to eliminate paragraph break*

203.33   Wildness] W *altered from lower case in ink over pencil*

204.6   Hope] *underlined* Bradford *(typesetter) pencilled in left margin*

204.17-18   (*Cassandra calyculata*)] *interlined in ink over pencil with a caret in ink over pencil*

204.21-22   azalea] *interlined in ink over pencil with a caret in ink over pencil*

204.31   Nature] N *altered from lower case*

205.2   not] *interlined with a caret*

205.2-3   me. Bring] *linked by ink over pencilled line to cancel paragraph break*

205.8   if it] *preceded by cancelled* though

205.17   fertility] *interlined in ink over pencil above* muck *cancelled in ink over pencil*

205.22   existence."] *followed by* Returning from it, "The air of cities will suffocate you, and the care-worn and cadaverous countenances of citizens will haunt you like a vision of judgment." *cancelled in pencil*

205.27   When] *followed by cancelled* outward dreariness. Give me the ocean, the desert, or

the wilderness. V Burton   When *(*V Burton
interlined in pencil and When *cancelled in
pencil)*

205.30   *sanctum sanctorum*]   *underlined in pencil*

205.31   Nature]   N *altered from lower case*

206.9   To]   *interlined in ink over pencilled above* If
we would *cancelled in ink over pencil*

206.9   implies generally]   generally implies *marked
for transposition with* tr *in margin and ink
over pencilled line; preceded by* it *cancelled in
pencil*

206.10-11   So is it with man. A hundred]   *interlined
above cancelled* Man is to be preserved by a
similar method. *with erased means pencilled
above* method

206.13   there]   *altered from* where

206.13-14   methinks]   *interlined with a caret*

206.15   Ah!]   *preceded at top of page by* cannot
furnish a load of bark–where the forest has
lost its shagginess. *cancelled in ink and pencil*

206.28   down]   *interlined in ink over pencil with a
caret in ink over pencil*

206.29   It is said to be]   *interlined below* Guyot says
that it is *cancelled in ink over erased pencil*

206.31-32   I think that]   *interlined in ink over pencil
with a caret in ink over pencil*

*206.34   in some respects]   *interlined in ink over
pencil with a caret in ink over pencil*

207.14-15   I refer . . . class.]   *interlined in ink over pencil
with a caret in ink over pencil*

207.14-15   I refer . . . class.]   *followed by cancelled* The

207.16   The weapons]   The *added in left margin and
preceded by paragraph sign*

207.22   field. The]   *linked by ink over pencilled line
to cancel paragraph break*

207.28   In Literature]   *preceded on the line above by
cancelled* In Literatur *following* spade.

208.8   English literature]   *underlined* Hector
(typesetter) pencilled in left margin

208.16   animals,]   *interlined in ink over pencil with a
caret in ink over pencil*

208.20-21   learning of]   *followed at bottom of page by
erased pencilled* mankind, enjoys no
advantage over Homer. *(see 208.21)*

208.24   him;]   *semicolon added in pencil, followed*
                  by period and Who wandered by the brook
                  sides for years till he found the fit word which
                  has no synonyme–who sometimes held up
                  the thing like a savage, and spoke not;
                  cancelled in pencil

208.30   that]   *possibly added*

208.30   would]   *interlined in ink over pencil with a*
                  caret in ink over pencil

208.30   appear]   *altered from* appeared *in ink over*
                  pencil

208.31   the buds]   the *possibly added*

208.34   sympathy]   p *and* t *reformed*

209.2   Wild]   W *altered from lower case*

209.17-18   this is like . . . as old as]   *question mark*
                  pencilled in margin

209.17-18   the Western isles]   *interlined in ink over*
                  pencil above Africa *cancelled in ink over*
                  pencil, with ink caret

209.19   long;]   *followed by cancelled* –

209.25-26   produce. Perchance]   *linked by ink over*
                  pencilled line to cancel paragraph break

209.27   it is]   *followed by* now *set off with pencilled*
                  parentheses and cancelled in pencil

209.30   even,]   *comma added in ink over pencil*

210.3   prophesy]   es *reformed*

210.13   will]   *interlined in ink over pencil above* may
                  cancelled in pencil

210.21   In short]   *underlined* 669 *(AM page no.) and*
                  Hector *(typesetter) pencilled in left margin;*
                  pencilled open bracket inserted before In

210.23   voice]   *followed by cancelled comma*

210.27   understand. Give]   *linked by ink over*
                  pencilled line to cancel paragraph break

211.8   Any]   *added in left margin before blotted* Any

211.12   perceived]   *interlined in ink over pencil*
                  above saw *cancelled in ink over pencil*

211.17   Evil One]   *interlined above cancelled* Devil

211.20   time,]   *comma added, possibly over period*

211.20   and Man]   and *added over pencilled*
                  ampersand

211.25   I rejoice]   Cormack *(typesetter) pencilled in*
                  left margin

212.4   says] *added in left margin*
212.11   military officers or of] *interlined with a caret*
212.12-13 once more] *interlined in ink over pencil with a caret in ink over pencil*
212.13   nothing] *preceded by* commonly *cancelled in ink and pencil*
212.13   a name.] *followed by cancelled* As the names of the Poles and Russians are to
212.22   of course] *interlined in ink over pencil with a caret in ink over pencil*
212.23   dogs.] *followed by text cancelled in ink and pencil:* We know what are dogs' names; we know what are mens' names.

We have but few names in proportion to the number of us, and hence they are additionally insignificant. Is it that *(*that *interlined with a caret)* men cease to be original when genuine and original names cease to be given? Have we not enough character to establish a new patronymic?
˙ We are wont to think that those youths who are christened George Washington now-a-days, are not fairly dealt with by their parents; but if we look at the principle of the thing, in what respect is this a less honest and proper name than the common ones Adam–Abraham–Moses David–Thomas–Richard, or Henry, & the like, one or the other of which each one of us bears.

212.31   own. At] *followed by text cancelled in ink and pencil:* To name all mankind thus particularly, yet superficially, is as if you were to give names in the Caffre dialect to the individuals in a herd of spring-bocks or gnus. It may be a convenience to the herdsman, but the ceremony of baptism connected with this kind of naming does not deserve to be called a sacrament.
212.31   At] *added, with pencilled line at indented* At *to eliminate paragraph break*
212.31   only true] *interlined in ink over pencil above* truest *cancelled in ink over pencil*
212.34   Some] *preceded at top of page by* there was

no doubt a true baptism, whether with water
or blood, or without. *cancelled in pencil*

212.35   but] *followed by* had it to *cancelled in ink over pencil*

212.35-36   earned it,] ed it, *added in ink over pencil*

214.28   referred.] *followed by cancelled paragraph:*
Education often makes but a straight-cut
ditch of a free meandering brook. (but
reformed)

214.29   have] *followed by* have *cancelled in ink and pencil*

214.29-31   of a Society . . . Methinks] *underlined*
Bradford *(typesetter) pencilled in left margin*

214.33   Beautiful] B *altered from lower case*

214.33   Knowledge] K *altered from lower case*

215.1   ignorance;] *followed by cancelled –*

215.13   May;] *followed by cancelled –*

215.16   So,] *comma added in pencil*

215.16   frequently] *interlined with a caret*

215.17   treats] s *added in ink over pencil*

215.17   treats] *preceded by erased pencilled caret
and text, perhaps* of Agriculture

215.17   its] *interlined in ink over pencil above* their
cancelled in ink and pencil

215.27   The highest] *added in ink over pencil at
bottom of page to eliminate paragraph break
for* The highest *at top of next*

215.28   Knowledge] K *altered from lower case*

215.28   Sympathy] S *altered from lower case*

216.14   his] *interlined in ink over pencil above* and
cancelled in ink over pencil

216.14   Law-maker.] *followed by text cancelled in
ink and pencil:* The man for whom law exists–
the man of forms–the mere conservative, is a
tame man.
> "Give me a spirit that on life's rough sea
> Loves to have his sails filled with a lusty
>   wind
> E'en till his sail-yards tremble, his masts
>   crack,
> And his rapt ship run on her side so low
> That she drinks water and her keel plows air;
> There is no danger to a man that knows

> Where life and death are; *(are interlined in*
> *pencil above* is *cancelled in pencil)* there
> *(*t *of* there *altered from capital)* is not any
> law
> Exceeds his knowledge, neither is it needful
> That he should stoop to any other law;
> He goes before them and commands them
> all,
> That to himself is a law rational."

216.14   That is]   *added at bottom of page (catch*
           phrase) with s *of* is *running off margin*

216.19   It is remarkable]   *preceded at top of page by*
           of infants? We have not fathomed the
           heavens–we have not exhausted any source
           of life–any joy–any sentiment. *cancelled in*
           pencil

216.30-217.6   Even Mahomet . . . so soon?"]   *text in ST's*
               hand

217.15   Beauty]   B *altered from lower case*

217.18   part]   p *reformed*

217.18   Nature]   *followed by* , whose Elysian fields
           never reach quite up to our doors– *cancelled*
           in ink and pencil

217.22   seem to]   *interlined in ink over pencil with a*
           caret in ink over pencil

217.26   it. Nature]   *linked by ink over pencilled line*
           to cancel paragraph break

217.28   The walker]   *preceded on foregoing page as*
           catch phrase by The Walker *with* W *changed to*
           w *or vice versa*

217.28-218.6   The walker . . . anniversary.]   *text in ST's*
               hand

217.32   Concord,]   *followed by* suggests *cancelled by*
           ST

217.34   suggested.]   *followed by* For this actual
           Concord with its slight rural and commercial
           bustle, its little fame and its monument which
           pins it to earth's roof, is no more than some
           sad but transient second thought of a child at
           play. *cancelled by HDT in pencil and ink*

218.1   through]   r *interlined with a caret by ST*

218.4   beneath.]   *followed by cancelled* our eyes,
           and by forgetfulness can we remember it.

218.14   Sun]   S *altered from lower case*

219.5   But I find]   Schubarth *(typesetter) pencilled in left margin*

219.9-10   cohabitancy. If]   *linked by ink over pencilled line to cancel paragraph break*

219.19   us.]   *followed by cancelled* – –

219.24   Our winged]   *preceded by wavy pencilled line to eliminate paragraph break*

219.27   hear of.]   *followed by paragraph cancelled in pencil:* It is not necessary for them to take the ether for exhiliration, who in their sane and waking hours are ever translated by a thought, nor for them to see with their hind heads, who sometimes see out of their fore-heads, nor for them to listen to the spiritual knockings, who attend to the intimations of reason and conscience.

220.4   fertile]   *interlined in ink over pencil above cancelled* female

220.11   ancient]   *altered from* ancients

220.18   blossoms]   *interlined in ink over pencil above* and beautiful flowers *cancelled in ink over pencil*

220.22   seen them.]   *followed by cancelled paragraph:* The trees do not brag. I have seen a pine tree in the wind sowing the seeds of a future forest which perchance would cover acres of ground for centuries to come. Yet I heard no other herald of this deed than the sough of that same wind, through its boughs. The planting was completed in a single gale, and no man was notified of it.

220.24   over]   *interlined in ink over pencil above* above *cancelled in ink and pencil*

221.9   joy? When]   *linked by line to cancel paragraph break*

221.15   We had a]   *preceded by* / /

221.27   When]   *added before cancelled* When *to eliminate paragraph break*

221.36   musquash]   *altered from* muskrat

222.3   stump.–]   *followed by cancelled* –

222.12   Land]   L *altered from lower case*

Rejected Substantives

For the format of this table, see the Textual Introduction, p. 384. The table records variant substantives in the *Atlantic Monthly* (AM) and the 1863 edition of *Excursions* (Ex).

185.1	Walking] WALKING. / [1862.] Ex	
*186.10	are prepared to] are ready to AM Ex	
186.24	outside to Church] outside of Church AM Ex	
186.36	walk] walks AM Ex	
188.8	Buonaparte] Bonaparte AM Ex	
188.14	these times] this time AM Ex	
190.28-29	though I have walked almost every day for so many years] though for so many years I have walked amost every day AM Ex	
193.7-9	Marlboro . . . Marlboro . . . Marlboro] Marlborough . . . Marlborough . . . Marlborough AM Ex *(see Textual Note 193.7-8)*	
193.12	Marlboro] MARLBOROUGH AM Ex *(see Textual Note 193.7-8)*	
193.32	Marlboro] Marlborough AM Ex *(see Textual Note 193.7-8)*	
194.37	Marlboro] Marlborough AM Ex *(see Textual Note 193.7-8)*	
196.4	the thousandth] a thousandth Ex	
196.11	towards] toward Ex	
196.12	and that there are] and there are Ex	
198.29	further than] farther than AM Ex *(see Textual Note 198.29)*	
199.31	rivers larger] rivers longer AM Ex *(see Textual Note 199.21)*	
200.13	higher, the] higher, and the AM Ex	
201.26	a heroic] an heroic AM Ex	
201.29	the stream in] the river in AM Ex	
202.5	the stream; and] the river; and AM Ex	
202.18-19	It is because] It was because AM Ex	
203.8	much a] much like a AM Ex	
204.19	further] farther AM Ex	

204.23	I would like] I should like AM Ex
204.28	only, to] only to AM Ex
205.11	dismal swamp] Dismal swamp Ex
205.16	desert a pure] desert pure AM Ex
206.20-21	are sustained] have been sustained AM Ex
206.28	on to his] on his AM Ex
*211.10	unwieldly] unwieldy AM
211.14	*who!*] *Whoa!* AM Ex *(see Textual Note 211.14-18)*
211.18	Who!] "Whoa!" AM Ex *(see Textual Note 211.14-18)*
211.21	and ox] and the ox Ex
211.31	disposition, is] disposition, this is AM Ex
*213.36	Niepce] Niépce AM Ex
214.6	observed "that those] observed that "those AM Ex
215.20	beside] besides AM Ex
216.13-14	laws both of heaven and earth, by virtue] laws, by virtue AM Ex *(see Textual Note 216.13)*
216.27	farce. Christ, Dante] farce. Dante AM Ex *(see Textual Note 216.13)*
216.31	though Christians may] though many may AM Ex *(see Textual Note 216.13)*
217.20	occasional and transient] occasional and transional and transient Ex
218.12	seated] settled AM Ex
218.28	notwithstanding that I] notwithstanding I AM Ex
219.6	now that I] now while I AM Ex
*219.32	payed] paid AM Ex
220.31-32	by it not in Plato nor the New Testament. It is a newer testament] by it that is a newer testament AM Ex
220.35	he is, is to] he is to Ex
222.16	so warm] as warm AM Ex

Autumnal Tints

Headnote

THE origins of Thoreau's "Autumnal Tints" lecture and essay, and of the larger project, "The Fall of the Leaf," of which he considered "Autumnal Tints" but a part, may be traced in his Journal back to entries of the early 1850s. The fancy of making a book of exactly colored copies of ripe leaves, a volume to be called "October Hues or Autumnal Tints" (see 225.4-10), is first expressed in the Journal for November 22, 1853 (*Journal 7*, p. 172). Entries as early as September 1851 are reflected in the essay text. Comparison of the essay with antecedent Journal passages reveals that Thoreau's interest in the phenomena of leaf ripening surged in August through November 1853 (forty extracts ultimately used in the essay), subsided in 1854 and 1855, and then resumed strongly in October 1856 (ten extracts), fall 1857 (thirty extracts), and late August through early November 1858 (eighty extracts of the total of 175).[1] It appears that he composed the "Autumnal Tints" lecture in the fall and winter of 1858.

Thoreau gave the lecture its first reading in Worcester, in the parlor of his friend H. G. O. Blake, the evening of February 22, 1859.[2] He delivered it next before the Concord Lyceum on March 2, and again in Emerson's house a week later, to Bronson and Abby Alcott,

---

[1] For August through November 1853, see *Journal 6*, pp. 283-306, and *Journal 7*, pp. 3-185; for October 1856, see 1906, 9:96-136; for September through November 1857, see 1906, 10:21-217; for August 15 through November 15, 1858, see 1906, 11:105-322.

[2] Bradley P. Dean and Ronald Wesley Hoag, "Thoreau's Lectures After *Walden*: An Annotated Calendar," *Studies in the American Renaissance*, ed. Joel Myerson (Charlottesville: University Press of Virginia, 1996), p. 293.

the Emersons, Ellery Channing, and "some young people of the village." On April 26 he repeated it at the new Frazier Hall in Lynn, Massachusetts, accompanied on the trip by Channing.[3] The recorded responses to all four presentations are positive, although a Lynn reviewer complained about the lecturer's unenthusiastic delivery. Well over a year later, on December 11, 1860, Thoreau read "Autumnal Tints" again in Waterbury, Connecticut, for the Young Men's Institute. Already suffering from hoarseness and a bad cold, he spent the afternoon and night of December 10 with Blake in Worcester, proceeding to Waterbury the next morning. The weather was cold and stormy, probably hastening Thoreau's decline into the tubercular condition that caused his death. A review in the Waterbury *American* faulted the lecture as monotonous in delivery and neither practical nor particularly poetic in content.[4] It was the last lecture of Thoreau's career; he devoted his remaining intellectual energies to the completion of manuscripts for publication.

As he informed James T. Fields on February 18, 1862, while accepting Fields's offer for the publication of his late essays in the *Atlantic Monthly*, he had culled "Autumnal Tints" from "a very large imperfect" botanical study; he requested the return of the manuscript so as to restore the project's integrity.[5] This study he referred to on a manuscript leaf now at ICarbS as "[The] Fall of [the] Leaf." Another large project (related in substance to "The Succession of Forest Trees") he called "The Dispersion of Seeds." A third, from which the "Wild Apples" lecture and essay emerged, was called "Wild Fruits."

---

[3] Dean and Hoag, pp. 297, 299, 301.

[4] Dean and Hoag, pp. 348-353.

[5] Thoreau to Messrs Ticknor & Fields, February 18, 1862; MS at CU-SB, tipped in PS 3049 .A1 1849, c. 2.

It is not the purpose here to attempt reconstructing "The Fall of the Leaf." Its papers–including those sheets of "Autumnal Tints" setting copy that survive– are numerous and scattered, many of them having been dispersed by Houghton, Mifflin and Company in the 1906 Manuscript Edition. Markings in Thoreau's Journal manuscripts back to September 1851 indicate his retrospective accumulation of raw data on leaf ripening. A number of pages, loose rather than entered in notebooks like the Journal, consist of extracts on leaf maturation from Journal entries, often organized according to the late summer and autumn calendar. Apart from the Journal itself, the identifiable or probable manuscript survivals from "The Fall of the Leaf," including the "Autumnal Tints" lecture and essay, are listed below.

Thoreau sent a complete setting-copy manuscript of seventy-four pages to Ticknor and Fields on February 20, 1862, with a covering letter he dictated to his sister Sophia (*Correspondence*, pp. 636-637). Because of the essay's length, Thoreau concluded "that it will have to be divided," and asked that the division occur at the end of page "42" (see Alterations 223.1, 242.18). Of the seventy-four setting-copy pages, thirty, on nineteen leaves, survive and serve as copy-text for the corresponding sections of the essay in the present edition. The setting-copy pages are numbered in pencil at the top, possibly in Sophia's hand. Most leaves have text on both the recto and verso sides. The paper types represented include a white wove and two white laid papers.[6] The writing medium is ink, with corrections and revisions in both ink and pencil. Unless otherwise indicated in the descriptions that follow, the

---

[6] White wove type 13 and white laid types 2 and 5, as described in *LMHDT*, pp. 377-378.

text was penned by Thoreau rather than being a
scribal copy in Sophia's hand. Evidently the text on the
white wove leaves is from an earlier stage of composition–perhaps lecture manuscript–than that on white
laid, and all the pages in Sophia's handwriting are on
the type 5 laid paper. The Table of Alterations records Thoreau's revisions of manuscript pages he and
Sophia inscribed, markings in yet other autographs
(typesetters' names, for example), and Sophia's corrections and revisions on the manuscript pages she
herself had inscribed. The manuscript copy-text descriptions below include the parameters of the text in
the present edition by page and line and by opening
and closing words.

Pages "1"-"2" are at NNPM, catalogued MA 2255;
they cover 223.1-223.31 ("Autumnal ... evidence").
Pages "5"-"6", in the Thoreau Society Archives at
MaLiTIW, correspond to 225.2-23 ("October ...
notes."). Pages "8"-"9" are at NNR, and cover 226.9-
227.6 ("Close . . . frosts."). Page "12" (three-fifths of the
recto and all the verso blank) is at MH-H, catalogued
bMS Am 278.5, folder 13E; it covers 228.5-15 ("clear . . .
To walk"). Pages "20"-"21", with half of "21" in Sophia's
handwriting–232.16-23 ("Some single . . . object can")–
are at MH-H, catalogued bMS AM 278.5, folder 13B,
and correspond to 231.23-232.23 ("The Red . . . can").
Pages "25"-"26", in the same MH-H group as that immediately above, cover 233.33-235.4 ("Notwithstanding . . . over the"); they are in the handwriting of Sophia, with revisions by Henry. Page "27", written by
Sophia with revisions apparently by Henry, is in the
same MH-H group as the two preceding manuscripts.
It covers the text at 235.4-20 ("sheeny . . . horse-sheds
for."). Page "30", at MH-H, catalogued bMS Am 278.5,
folder 13E, corresponds to 236.20-26 ("or . . . reap.").
The verso is blank, and part of the recto consists of a

cancelled passage. Pages "35", "36"-"37", and "38"-"39" are all at MH-H, catalogued bMS Am 278.5, folder 13B. They correspond, respectively, to 238.22-239.7 ("At one swamp . . . river."), 239.7-240.14 ("When I . . . Whether"), and 240.14-241.18 ("we . . . forest."). All five of these pages are amanuensis copies by Sophia, with revisions in Henry's handwriting. The lower half of page "37" consists of thirteen and one-half lines of text in Henry's hand, 240.4-14 ("And painted . . . Whether"), written after Sophia had inscribed the top half. Page "43", 242.18-243.4 ("The Sugar . . . side of the"), in Sophia's hand with revisions by Henry, is also at MH-H, catalogued bMS Am 278.5, folder 13E. Pages "48"-"49", at NN-BGC, correspond to 245.10-246.23 ("What do . . . should"). Pages "52"-"53", at VtMiM, cover 247.24-248.30 ("which almost . . . infirm."). A partial sheet paginated "54" (verso blank) at PClvU corresponds to 248.31-249.1-2 ("The Scarlet . . . acquaintance"). The text on pages "55"-"56", at NjP, is that of 249.2-251.8 ("with 12 . . . whittling"). Pages "59"-"60", formerly at TxHR, cover 252.14-253.10 ("By the 26th . . . fight."). Pages "70"-"71" are at ViU, Barrett Collection number 6345-e, and correspond to 257.4-258.7 ("botanical . . . woodcocks, he"). And finally, page "74", in Sophia's hand with a revision by Henry, corresponding to 259.12-24 ("in his mind . . . vicinity."), is at MH-H, catalogued bMS Am 278.5, folder 13B. On the verso are pencilled calculations by Thoreau, relating to the proposed division of the essay in the *Atlantic* and to the placement in the text of the Scarlet Oak illustration.

The present whereabouts of pages "13"-"14"–a leaf once and perhaps still mounted in volume one of a set of the Manuscript Edition–are undetermined, but a partial (and manifestly inaccurate) transcript of its text covering 228.15-18 ("To walk . . . eye") appears in the catalogue of Sale No. 1889, March 25, 1959, by Parke-Bernet Galleries, Inc., lot 430. See Textual Note 228.17.

Manuscripts in numerous libraries and private collections are related to the "Fall of the Leaf" project, but it can only be conjectured which of them held a place in the lecture, and which are working materials for the "large imperfect" study or preliminary drafts for the lecture. They were not part of the setting copy for the *Atlantic Monthly*. Those in the following group contain phrases or sentences that end up in the "Autumnal Tints" essay: MH-H, five leaves (two in Sophia's hand with Henry's revisions) and four partial leaves; CLjC, one half leaf; MA, one leaf; MWC, one leaf; NN-BGC, one leaf; OClJC, one leaf; PPiU, one leaf; RP, one leaf; TxAuHRH, one leaf; VtMiM, one leaf; Martin Bodmer Foundation, Geneva, Switzerland, one leaf; formerly collection of Mr. and Mrs. Morton H. Baker (one leaf); collections of James Dawson (two leaves), Theodore Hassan (one leaf), R. W. Knight (one leaf), Mrs. John J. McDevitt III (one leaf), Daniel Siegel (one leaf); two leaves sold by Doris Harris Autographs, Los Angeles, CA. A leaf of manuscript once in the possession of Richard Adamiak, Rare and Scholarly Books, Chicago, IL, is available to the editor only in unverified transcript. In the editing of "Autumnal Tints" for this volume, the editor has compared the worksheets with the copy-text equivalents, exercising special care where the setting copy was lost or where the manuscript setting-copy leaf was by Sophia, as a check against possible typesetting or copying errors.

Materials related to the "Fall of the Leaf" project that have no specific textual equivalents in the finished "Autumnal Tints" essay are to be found at MH-H, CSdS, CSmH, CtNlC, CU-SC, IaU, ICarbS, IPB, NN-BGC, NRU, PPiU, ViU (three leaves), and WaSpW; and in the collections of James Dawson (one and one-half leaves), J. M. Dorsey, and Edward Scibilia.

Finally, *American Book Prices Current*, vol. 10, no. 9496, indicates that a six-page manuscript, "Part of the essay 'Autumnal Tints,'" was sold at auction as lot 1474 in the Kennard sale, April 26, 1904, by Libbie's (Boston). Quite possibly these leaves are among those listed in the foregoing inventory of extant "Autumnal Tints" manuscript materials, but the editor has not traced the provenance of any of the latter to the Kennard sale.

Those portions of the essay where setting copy is lost and the first printing in the *Atlantic* is necessarily copy-text for the present edition are taken from the bound copy at NGenoU. Verification that the *Atlantic* text of "Autumnal Tints" is uniform was achieved by Hinman machine collation of copies in the collection of the editor (issued in wrappers, then bound) and at TxU (evidently originally issued in a bound volume). No differences were detected.

In the same February 18, 1862, letter to Ticknor and Fields quoted above, the last known letter in his handwriting, Thoreau alludes to his illness and asks the publisher to "have a sharp-eyed reader" save him the labor of a thorough review of the "Autumnal Tints" proofsheets. In the same sentence, however, he asks to see the proofs himself, "chiefly that I may look after my peculiarities." The "peculiarities" are probably his unorthodox views of religion and society. For the concern about editorial alteration of his text that Thoreau expresses to Fields in this late correspondence, and for inferences about the rate of pay for his *Atlantic* essay manuscripts, see the "Walking" Headnote.

Fields promptly set his typesetters to work on Thoreau's manuscript. On March 11, a mere nineteen days after the setting copy had left Concord, Thoreau returned the proofs of "Autumnal Tints" (together with the setting copy of "Walking") to his publisher (*Correspondence*, p. 640). It seems unlikely that the proofs received rigorous scrutiny by the author or Sophia. Henry lacked the strength, and his sister was engaged in the demanding work of copying, clarifying, and arranging her brother's manuscripts. Probably, however, Henry or Sophia looked at the "peculiarities" to which Henry had referred on February 18: the *Atlantic* printing reveals no bowdlerizations of Thoreau's text. Sophia might also have scanned the proofs rapidly for sense, but could not have compared them systematically with the setting copy–if Fields returned it with the proofs–or alternatively with Thoreau's superseded and incomplete drafts. For variant substantive readings in the *Atlantic* where the setting copy survives, see Rejected Substantives. The "Autumnal Tints" proofsheets are not extant. For Thoreau's negotiations with Fields about an illustration for the essay, see Textual Note 251.34-35.

The March 11 covering letter returns to the subject of dividing "Autumnal Tints." In the *Atlantic* proofs Thoreau found the text interrupted at the point he had specified (just before the section on the Sugar Maple, 242.18), but he objected to the editorially introduced terms "In Two Parts / I." and "In Two Parts / II." (See Alterations 223.1, 242.18.) "I do not quite like to have the Autumnal Tints described as in two parts," he dictated to Sophia, "for it appears as if the author had made a permanent distinction between them, Would it not be better to say at the end of the first portion 'To be continued in the next number'?"

Fields held the essay for a seasonally appropriate issue of the *Atlantic*, October 1862, where it was the lead article, volume 10, pp. 385-402. Some time after the proof copy was returned from Concord, Fields decided to stereotype and print "Autumnal Tints" *en bloc* rather than in installments; that decision could have been made as late as August 1862, when the contents of the October issue were being laid out. When "Autumnal Tints" was collected in *Excursions* (1863), no significant substantive changes from the *Atlantic* were introduced, and there is no evidence of fresh authority.

Collations performed by members of the Thoreau Edition staff include two of the composite copy-text for the present edition against the *Atlantic Monthly*, one of the composite copy-text against *Excursions* (1863), and two of the *Atlantic* against *Excursions* (1863). For a Hinman machine collation of the *Atlantic*, see above. The manuscript copy-text portions were read in photocopy against their *Atlantic* equivalents, and both the *Atlantic* portions (where Thoreau's manuscript does not survive) and the portions of the manuscript in Sophia's handwriting were read against pre-copy-text.

Textual Notes

For the format of the Textual Notes, see the Textual Introduction, pp. 381-382. Copy-text is a composite of Thoreau's setting copy for the October 1862 *Atlantic Monthly*, thirty of an original seventy-four pages (now located in various libraries and collections as detailed in the Headnote), and, where the setting copy is lost, the *Atlantic* printing. Copy-text is specified as either manuscript or print in each note. AM stands for the *Atlantic Monthly* and Ex for *Excursions* (1863). The abbreviation "MS" followed by a repository symbol or owner's name in parentheses identifies a manuscript reading. For Journal entries later than September 3, 1854, the manuscript version was consulted. Citation is made to the 1906 edition when it reproduces the manuscript reading; when 1906 has regularized a reading, the manuscript is cited.

223.2 surprised: On the manuscript copy-text Thoreau miswrote the word as "surprized", although it is correctly spelled in two draft versions, MS (VtMiM) and MS (MH-H), and elsewhere in the text, e.g., "surprise" at 223.23. AM corrects the error.

223.6 most that: Emended from "most, that" in the manuscript copy-text, the result of an incomplete revision in the preceding draft version, MS (MH-H). A still earlier draft, MS (VtMiM), reads "most that". AM drops the illogical comma.

223.6 Thomson: Thoreau misspells the name of James Thomson as "Thompson" here in the manuscript copy-text as in two drafts, MS (VtMiM) and MS (MH-H). The correction is first made in AM.

223.10 and dun: Here and frequently later in the manuscript copy-text Thoreau used the ampersand, assuming that his publisher would expand the symbol. See Textual Notes 23.33, 57.30, 80.19-20, and 185.34, and also the Textual Introduction to *Maine Woods*, pp. 394-396. The fifty emendations of ampersands in "Autumnal Tints" are recorded individually in Emendations.

223.11   wan-declining: Thoreau evidently desired to follow his source, "Autumn," in Thomson's *The Seasons*, by including the hyphen in this phrase. He read the poem in Alexander Chalmers, ed., *The Works of the English Poets, from
Chaucer to Cowper* . . . (London: Printed for J. Johnson et al.,
1810), 12:442. Two drafts, MS (VtMiM) and MS (MH-H), include the hyphen, though the manuscript copy-text lacks it.

223.12   To: The present edition emends "to" in the manuscript copy-text to agree with this line opening in Thoreau's
source (Thomson, "Autumn," in *The Works of the English
Poets*, 12:442) and in two drafts, MS (VtMiM) and MS (MH-H).
In AM the verses are formatted differently.

226.20   rhexia: Thus with the lower-case initial in the
manuscript copy-text. At 226.4, where AM serves as copy-text
in the absence of manuscript, the plant name is capitalized.
Thoreau's practice in the setting copy is inconsistent; sometimes he uses capital initials for plants, sometimes lower
case, and sometimes he changes lower case to capitals. AM
normalizes to capital initials in almost every instance.

228.17   tasting: The copy-text for 228.16-18 "amid . . .
eye" is a transcript in a Parke-Bernet auction catalogue: see
the Headnote. The transcriber's "tasking" is obviously an
error, running counter to the imagery of wine in casks and
pipes that the connoisseur tastes with his eye. See *Journal 4*,
p. 69, for the original version of the poke passage in an entry
for September 10, 1851, including this sentence: "What need
to taste the fruit to drink the wine–to him who can thus taste
& drink with his eyes?"

231.1   impurpled: Thus in the AM copy-text, a possible
house spelling imposed on the lost manuscript. Thoreau's
Journal entry for August 29, 1858 (1906, 11:131), has "empur-
pled" in the original version of this passage.

235.4   stripe: The copy-text is a leaf of setting copy in Sophia Thoreau's handwriting. In the first version of the passage, a Journal entry for October 7, 1857 (1906, 10:71), Thoreau
writes "strip". See also *Cape Cod*, Textual Note 94.11.

243.20   further: The AM copy-text has "farther", but this
was clearly the preference of the editor and typesetters, who
had converted Thoreau's setting-copy term "further" at 239.1
to "farther" in the first printing. The original Journal version
of the passage, October 18, 1858 (1906, 11:218), reads "further",
consistently with Thoreau's usual habit. See Textual Notes
106.26, 142.13, 150.30, and 198.29, as well as *Maine Woods*,

Textual Notes 13.11, 128.11, and 161.10, and *Cape Cod*, pp. 351-353 and Textual Notes 24.8, 44.9, 50.2, 84.21, 96.3, 118.21, 119.10, 135.20, 140.24, 149.29, 161.17, 188.11, 194.5, and 204.17.

244.9 studious are: Emended from "studious is" in the AM copy-text on the basis of the original version in Thoreau's Journal entry for October 18, 1858 (1906, 11:219). The plural form in the Journal is a more satisfactory reading.

244.9 taught colors: "taught color" in the AM copy-text, but with the more plausible plural reading in the original Journal entry, October 18, 1858 (1906, 11:219), the only surviving manuscript version of the passage. The AM compositor may have been influenced by "color" in the previous sentence.

244.25 further: Thus in the original version of the sentence, in a Journal entry for October 22, 1858 (1906, 11:240). The AM copy-text reads "farther"; see Textual Note 243.20 above.

246.10 fawns: Thus in the manuscript copy-text, a spelling accepted for this sense of the word by one of Thoreau's dictionaries (Bailey's), but not by Johnson's, Walker's, or Webster's: see Textual Introduction, p. 379.

247.4-5 vine, at present covering: Thus in the AM copy-text. The only surviving manuscript version of the sentence, Thoreau's Journal entry for October 19, 1858 (1906, 11:227), reads "woodbine at present covering", which leaves open the possibility that Thoreau intended "at present" to modify the noun rather than the participle.

247.6 *never sear*: Thoreau alludes to John Milton's elegy "Lycidas," line 2, "Ye Myrtles brown, with Ivy never sere". At 256.20 the AM copy-text gives the spelling "sear" as it does here, though in the latter instance the only surviving manuscript version, a Journal entry for November 4, 1858 (1906, 11:285), has "sere". Among Thoreau's dictionaries, Webster's records "sear" as a more usual spelling of the word than "sere," while Bailey's, Walker's, and Johnson's list both without indicating a preference. See the Textual Introduction, p. 379, for the lexical norms employed in this edition.

247.16-17 Tupeloes: Spelled thus in the AM copy-text, though "tupelos" in the only surviving manuscript version of the passage, Thoreau's Journal entry for October 18, 1858 (1906, 11:220). Among Thoreau's dictionaries, only Webster's lists the tree name, and then only in the singular, "tupelo."

248.18 "enlarged ... repaired": The quotation marks

occur in the manuscript copy-text and suggest that Thoreau is alluding to a church document or local history, possibly in *Collections of the Massachusetts Historical Society* (1801-1846), John Warner Barber's *Historical Collections . . . Relating to the History and Antiquities of Every Town in Massachusetts* (1839), Timothy Dwight's *Travels in New England and New York* (1821-1822), Thomas Prince's *Chronological History of New-England in the Form of Annals* (1736, 1755), Thomas Hutchinson's *History of the Colony of Massachusetts Bay* (1764), or John Hayward, *The New England Gazetteer* (1839). Thoreau was fond of reading and quoting such materials.

248.21-23 Themselves . . . they could . . . They *planted* . . . conscious *trees*:   Thus in the manuscript copy-text. Thoreau wittily alters R. W. Emerson's "The Problem," lines 21-25, in *Poems* (Boston: James Munroe and Company, 1847), p. 18. The original lines, dealing with church architecture, read, "Wrought in a sad sincerity; / Himself from God he could not free; / He builded better than he knew;– / The conscious stone to beauty grew."

251.34-35 *The original . . . pile.:   In the manuscript copy-text Thoreau interlined, above the paragraph beginning "Or bring one home", "I picked this one from such a pile." Sending the "Autumnal Tints" manuscript to AM on February 20, 1862, Thoreau directed Fields's attention to the pages describing the Scarlet Oak leaf and remarked that in his lectures he had "always carried a very large & handsome one displayed on a white ground, which did me great service with the audience" (*Correspondence*, pp. 636-637). Although he probably knew that AM had rarely included illustrations, he urged Fields to print a line cut of a Scarlet Oak leaf, with a cut of a White Oak leaf on the facing page, at the appropriate point in the text. Thoreau said he would supply the leaves to be copied. Apparently Fields expressed a reluctant willingness to print one illustration only, for on March 1 Thoreau sent a Scarlet Oak leaf, "the smallest one in my collection," with a request for "simply . . . a faithful outline engraving of the leaf bristles & all." He asked that his pencilled note in the setting copy be "altered into a note for the bottom of the page" facing the line cut, and that it read " 'The original of the leaf on the opposite page was picked from such a pile' " (*Correspondence*, p. 639). He appears to have assumed that the footnote and the line cut would be on facing pages. This was not the case with AM, where Thoreau's footnote text, on

printed page 397, was editorially altered to read "*The original of the leaf copied on the next page was picked from such
a pile." In a letter of March 11, returning the proofs of "Autumnal Tints," Thoreau reverted to the illustration matter:
"As for the leaf, I had not thought how it should be engraved,
but left it to you. Your note suggests that perhaps it is to be
done at my expense. What is the custom? and what would be
the cost of a steel engraving? I think that an ordinary wood
engraving would be much better than nothing" (*Correspondence*, p. 640). The engraving in this edition is photographic-
ally copied from AM 10:398.

   252.23   pitch pine is: A pencilled comma after "pine" in
the manuscript copy-text may be a stray mark.

   256.7   great: Thus in the AM copy-text. The sole surviving manuscript version, a Journal entry for November 2, 1858
(MS [NNPM, MA 1302:33]), has "greate". Thoreau might have
intended "greater" in the Journal or "Autumnal Tints," or
both, to contrast with "our gardening", which is "[c]ompara-
tively . . . on a petty scale" (256.1-2).

   257.34   Emanuel: The manuscript copy-text's misspelling of Swedenborg's Christian name, "Immanuel," is anticipated in a draft, MS (Theodore Hassan), and in the original
Journal version, November 4, 1858 (1906, 11:286). AM follows
the manuscript, and Ex does not correct the error.

Table of Emendations

   For the format of this table, see the Textual Introduction, p. 382. Sources for the emendations are
the *Atlantic Monthly* (AM) where the copy-text is the
setting-copy manuscript, or the editor's own authority, designated "PE" for the Princeton Edition, either
where the copy-text is the AM printing or where a
needed emendation of manuscript copy-text is not
precisely anticipated in AM. PE emends the AM copy-
text portion in only four places, 243.20, 244.9 (twice),
and 244.25, on the basis of Journal readings superior to
those of AM. The latter evidently reflect editorial pref-

erence in three instances and an apparent copyist's or compositor's misreading in the fourth. For a special case involving Thoreau's footnote to a linecut for the AM printing, see Textual Note 251.34-35. All other emendations are to manuscript copy-text.

*223.2	surprised] AM; surprized
*223.6	most that] AM; most, that
*223.6	Thomson] AM; Thompson
*223.10	and dun] AM; & dun
*223.11	wan-declining] PE; wan declining
*223.12	To] PE; to
223.20	seen] AM; seeen
225.5	tree, shrub] AM; tree shrub
225.12	maples, hickories] PE; maples hickories
226.10	and made] AM; & made
226.16	combine] AM; Combine
226.19-20	and supplies] AM; & supplies
226.23	selvedges] PE; selevedges
226.29	hay and] AM; hay &
226.33	and neglected] AM; & neglected
226.33	neglected, withered] AM; neglected withered
226.33	and wiry] AM; & wiry
226.36	beauty] AM; beuty
227.2	and paint] AM; & paint
227.4	and rounded] AM; & rounded
227.5	and it] AM; & it
228.11	and branch] AM; & branch
228.15	and see] AM; & see
228.15	To walk] AM; To walk To walk
228.17	and diffuse] AM; & diffuse (see Textual Note 228.17)
*228.17	tasting] AM; tasking
232.8	and there] AM; & there
232.17-18	evergreens, are more] AM; evergreens are, more
234.18	yellow, scarlet] AM; yellow scarlet
234.27	and scarlet] AM; & scarlet
234.35	Yet] AM; slightly indented, perhaps for paragraph (see Alteration 234.35)

235.1	meadow] AM; medow
235.6	scarlet, orange] AM; scarlet orange
236.22	and ready] AM; & ready
239.4-5	bend, where they] PE; bend where, they
239.6	they] AM; the
239.7	When] AM; When When *(see Alteration 239.7)*
239.18	bank.] AM; bank
239.19	when] AM; whe
239.27	bay, each] AM; bay,, each *(see Alteration 239.27)*
240.5	and float] AM; & float
240.14	a-gossiping] AM; a-gossipping
240.21	them. She] PE; them She
240.22	all. Consider] AM; all, Consider
240.30	sulphur] AM; sulpher
241.11	down. The] PE; down, The
241.11	particolored] PE; parti colored
241.14	it. They] AM; it.. They
242.23	there. As] AM; there, As
242.32	other. They] AM; other, They
*243.20	further] PE; farther
*244.9	studious are] PE; studious is
*244.9	taught colors] PE; taught color
*244.25	further] PE; farther
245.11	amber, and] AM; amber, &
245.13	keepers,] AM; *comma written over dash*
245.14	and Chobdars] AM; & Chobdars
245.16	America and] AM; America &
245.20	and shrubs] AM; & shrubs
245.23	and distinctions] AM; & distinctions
245.23	joy and] AM; joy &
245.23-24	exhilaration] AM; exhiliration
245.27-28	and innocent] AM; & innocent
245.32	peace; and] PE; peace; And
246.5	hollow and] AM; hollow &
246.10	fawns, satyrs] PE; fawns satyrs
246.10	and wood-nymphs] AM; & wood-nymphs
246.18-19	and button-bushes] PE; & button-bushes
247.24	them. An] AM; them– An
247.29	and cheering] AM; & cheering
247.29-30	and superstition] AM; & superstition
247.33	shall be sure] AM; shall be be sure

248.1	and milk-can] AM; & milk-can
248.3	and houses] AM; & houses
248.6	and forlorn] AM; & forlorn
248.9-10	and call] AM; & call
248.18	"enlarged and] PE; "enlarged &
248.25-26	and century] AM; & century
249.4	and see] AM; & see
249.6-7	double, treble] AM; double treble
249.7-8	ethereal] AM; etherial
249.12	entire, simple] AM; entire simple
249.12-13	and lumpish] AM; & lumpish
249.14-15	and higher] AM; & higher
249.15	and sublimated] AM; & sublimated
249.19	and grasp] AM; & grasp
249.22	slenderness and] AM; slenderness &
249.30-31	lobes and] AM; lobes &
251.3	and study] AM; & study
251.34	*The original . . . was picked from] PE; *I picked this one from *(see Textual Note 251.34-35)*
*252.23	pitch pine is] PE; pitch pine, is
252.26	Oaks. I] AM; Oaks I
252.28	withered] AM; with- withered
252.29	trees. Most] AM; trees.. Most
252.33	perfect and] AM; perfect & and
252.34	high] AM; heigh
252.36-253.1	you and] AM; you &
253.1-2	dye. The] AM; dye–, The
257.15	walk, or] AM; walk. or
257.18-19	*Juncaceae* and] AM; *Juncaceae* &
257.23	poet and] AM; poet &
257.26	and tell] AM; & tell
*257.34	Emanuel] PE; Immanuel
257.35	and set] AM; & set
257.36	and let] AM; & let
258.7	and woodcocks] AM; & woodcocks
259.21	tint, and] PE; tint. and

Table of Alterations

For the format of this table, see the Textual Introduction, p. 383. Of the thirty surviving setting-copy pages, nine full and two half pages are in the handwriting of Sophia E. Thoreau, with revisions and additions by her brother. These pages are identified, and the alterations they bear are assigned, as applicable, to Sophia (ST) or Henry (HDT). Unless specified to the contrary, alterations are in ink. Surviving and lost setting-copy manuscript pages are correlated with the Princeton Edition text using page and line numbers and keywords.

One MS leaf, pages "1"-"2", at NNPM, 223.1-223.31 Autumnal . . . evidence

223.1   Autumnal Tints.]   *preceded by underlined pencilled* Oct *and underlined pencilled* Hector *(typesetter) diagonally in margin, and followed by pencilled* In Two Parts / 1. *in a hand other than HDT's (see Headnote)*

223.17   our poetry.]   *followed by* High-colored as, in one sense, are most political speeches, no one will pretend that there is any reflection even from the October tints in them, but they are comparatively as lifeless & colorless as the herbage in November.
    The year, with these dazzling colors on its margin lies spread open like an illustrated volume, but one would say that the volume which the preacher handles had lost all its luster. *cancelled in ink and pencil*

223.30   ones. I]   *linked by line to cancel paragraph break*

Two MS pages missing, 223.31-225.2 that . . . setting.

One MS leaf, pages "5"-"6", Thoreau Society Archives, MaLiTIW, 225.2-23 October . . . notes.

225.11   reddening]   nin *reformed*
225.15   be!]   *exclamation changed from question mark*

225.19   still. I] *linked by line to cancel paragraph*
                break
225.20   all] *interlined in ink over pencil with a caret*
                in ink over pencil
225.22-23   The following . . . my notes.] *written in ink*
                over similar, partly illegible text in pencil, and
                followed by erased pencilled some extracts
                from my notes V next page but one By the
                20th Aug.

One MS page missing, 225.24-226.9 The Purple . . . around me.

One MS leaf, pages "8"-"9", at NNR, 226.9-227.6 Close . . .
frosts.

226.9-10   Close at hand] *preceded by cancelled*
                flower
226.15   earth.] *followed by cancelled* very much.
226.15   Such] S *altered from lower case*
226.19   With its] *preceded in margin by underlined*
                diagonal pencilled word, possibly typesetter's
                name
226.21   and it is] it *interlined with a caret*
226.22   August. The] *linked by line to cancel*
                paragraph break
226.26-28   Or, it may be . . . timothy.] *interlined with a*
                caret and Or *altered from* or
227.5   slopes,] *followed by cancelled dash*
227.6   frosts.] *followed by cancelled* In the latter 3[d]
                of the month the changing of the woodbine is
                generally noticed. Dogsbane & Milkweed
                (k *reformed)* are turning yellow, some of the
                former a clear light yellow, some leaves of the
                rhodora yellowish, & in low grounds & about
                pools are observed the yellow patches of
                cyperus strigosus & phymatodes in flower.
                Looking southwest at the river meadows from
                a hill-top in

Two MS pages missing, 227.7-228.4 In . . . still

One MS leaf, page "12", at MH-H, 228.5-15 clear . . . To walk

228.9-10   an ornament . . . What] *preceded by*
                pencilled question mark in margin
228.11   branch,] *followed by cancelled* as

228.11-12   glowing . . . decay, like]   *interlined with a*
                 caret
228.12   Poke!]   P *altered from lower case*
228.12   Poke! I]   *linked by line to cancel paragraph*
                 break

Seven MS pages missing, 228.16-231.22 amid . . . hunting-
grounds.; 228.15-18 To walk . . . eye printed in Parke-Bernet
catalogue offering pages "13"-"14"

One MS leaf, pages "20"-"21", at MH-H, 231.23-232.23 The Red
. . . can

231.23   THE RED MAPLE]   *added in pencil*
231.24   Red Maples]   R *and* M *altered from lower*
                 case
231.26   single]   *originally underlined; underline*
                 cancelled
231.27   brilliant. I]   *linked by line to cancel*
                 paragraph break
231.34   it]   *interlined above cancelled* that tree
231.34-232.1   down. I]   *linked by line to cancel paragraph*
                 break
232.1-2   my town]   my *pencilled over* our
232.8   there. Sometimes]   *linked by line to cancel*
                 paragraph break and no break *written above*
232.16-23   Some single . . . object can]   *text in ST's hand*
                 on half-sheet waxed or pasted over bottom of
                 page "21"
232.17-18   evergreens]   n *interlined with a caret,*
                 possibly by HDT

Three MS pages missing, 232.23-233.32 there . . . scarlet.

Two MS leaves, pages "25"-"26", "27", at MH-H, 233.33-235.20
Notwithstanding . . . horse-sheds for.

233.33-235.20   Notwithstanding . . . horse-sheds for.]   *text*
                 in ST's hand
233.33   Notwithstanding]   *preceded by marginal,*
                 diagonal, underlined pencilled Haney [?]
                 (typesetter)
233.33   Red Maple]   R *and* M *altered from lower case*
                 by ST
233.34   Sugar Maple]   S *and* M *altered from lower*
                 case by ST

234.3	still] *followed by* perfectly *cancelled with heavy stroke*
234.8	palm. A] *linked by pencil line to cancel paragraph break*
234.9-10	of all . . . things] *interlined in pencil by HDT above* phenomenon of the year, *cancelled in pencil*
234.14	Maples] M *altered from lower case*
234.15	Pines] P *altered from lower case*
234.20	Maples] M *altered from lower case*
234.24	veins] *preceded by* ven *cancelled by ST*
234.29	wind. It] *linked by line to cancel paragraph break and* no break *written above by HDT*
234.32	a simple] a *added*
234.33	and hues] *interlined by ST with a caret above cancelled* *and*
234.34	tree top] *interlined by ST with a caret or* X
234.35	Yet] Y *altered from lower case by ST*
234.36	off.] *followed by HDT's heavy paragraph sign over horizontal line*
235.3	Maple] M *altered from lower case by ST*
235.4	hill, a] *comma added before cancelled dash*
235.5	deep, of] *comma added before cancelled dash*
235.8	hill] *last two letters reformed*
235.12	color. One] *period added before cancelled dash*
235.17	blaze] z *written by HDT over another letter, possibly* s
235.18	then. Perhaps] *period added before cancelled dash*

Two MS pages missing, 235.21-236.20 The Elm . . . granary

One MS leaf, page "30", at MH-H, 236.20-26 or . . . reap.

236.24	thought, blasted] *comma added before cancelled dash*
236.25	cob-meal] *hyphen interlined above* cobmeal
236.26	reap.] *followed by cancelled* Is there then indeed (deed *underlined; then* indeed *set off in parentheses and cancelled)* no thought under this ample husk of convention and manners? There is the book husk, & *(last four*

words set off in parentheses and cancelled) the sermon husk, and the lecture husk, and the conversation husk–all which, unless some seed go with them, are good only to make into *(*into *interlined with a caret)* mats & tread under our feet.

Four MS pages missing, 236.27-238.22 Fallen . . . them.

Three MS leaves, pages "35", "36"-"37", "38"-"39", at MH-H, 238.22-241.18 At one swamp . . . forest.

238.22-240.4	At one swamp . . . launching.] *text in ST's hand*
238.24	rail,] *comma added in pencil*
238.27	the sixteenth] *added in pencil with a caret by HDT*
238.27	covered] *followed by* with them *cancelled in pencil, apparently by HDT*
238.28	Willow,] *comma added in pencil*
238.29	moored,] *comma added in pencil*
238.34	Assabet,] *comma added in pencil*
238.35	surface,] *comma added in pencil*
238.36	tack,] *comma added in pencil*
238.36	shore,] *comma added in pencil*
239.1	up,] *comma added in pencil*
239.2	width,] *comma added in pencil*
239.3	Alders,] *comma added in pencil*
239.3	Maples,] *comma added in pencil*
239.4	with] *interlined in pencil with a caret by HDT above* the *cancelled in pencil*
239.5	where] *followed by pencilled comma (see Emendation 239.4-5)*
239.5	wind,] *comma added in pencil*
239.6	crescent,] *comma added in pencil*
239.7	river.] *followed by pencilled* When *in HDT's hand*
239.7	When I turn] *preceded by* concealing the water for a rod in width, under and amid the Alders (A *altered in pencil by HDT from lower case)* and Button-bushes (B *altered in pencil by HDT from lower case)* amid Maples, still perfectly light and dry with fiber unrelaxed.

	And *all cancelled in pencil by HDT; illegible words interlined in pencil above* and Maples *and* unrelaxed. And
239.7	When] W *altered in pencil by HDT from lower case*
239.9	dry] *interlined by HDT above cancelled* crisp
239.9	substances] *interlined in pencil by HDT above cancelled* boats
239.10	which] *interlined with a caret by ST*
239.14	sound. Higher] *linked by line to cancel paragraph break*
239.16	eddy] *altered in pencil by HDT from* eddie
239.18	bank] *interlined in pencil with a caret by HDT*
239.19-25	Perchance . . . great fleet] *added by ST on a slip waxed over other text and* Perchance *preceded by pencilled open square bracket by HDT*
239.19	Perchance,] *comma added in pencil*
239.19	day,] *comma added in pencil*
239.20	reflections,] *comma added in pencil*
239.21	stream,] *comma added in pencil*
239.25	want of purpose,] *comma added in pencil*
239.27	bay,] *followed by* which is not stirred by a breath *cancelled in pencil, apparently by HDT*
239.28	sun's] *preceded by* rains *cancelled by HDT*
239.28	sun's] *apostrophe added in pencil*
239.36-240.1	together. ¶How] *linked by pencilled line to cancel paragraph break; line then cancelled in pencil by HDT*
240.2	yet,] *comma added in pencil*
240.4-14	And painted . . . Whether] *added by HDT*
240.4-5	Wood-duck] W *altered from lower case*
240.9	leaves] *preceded by cancelled* fields
240.14	Nature] N *altered from lower case*
240.14-241.18	we drink . . . forest.] *text in ST's hand*
240.15	as yet,] a *added in pencil before cancelled* A *and comma added in ink*
240.16	these] *altered by HDT from* their
240.16	leaves,] *followed by* leaves *cancelled by HDT*
240.16	coppers,] *comma added*
240.21	husbandman] b *reformed*

240.22	Consider] C *altered from lower case*
240.25	with] *interlined with a caret by ST*
240.25	interest–] *followed by* for *cancelled by HDT*
240.26	it.] *period added; flourish on* t *cancelled by HDT*
240.28	Nature] *altered by HDT from* natures
240.32	or] *interlined with a caret by HDT above cancelled* on
241.2	yellow] *interlined in pencil by HDT above* flavidness *cancelled in pencil*
241.2	the grains] *interlined in pencil by HDT above* corn *cancelled in pencil*
241.4	Maple, the] *altered by HDT from* Maple. The
241.5	Sumac] S *reformed*
241.5	blazing] blaz- / ing *altered by HDT from* bla- / zing
241.5	mulberry] m *interlined in pencil by HDT above* M *cancelled in pencil*
241.6	Ash] A *overwritten by HDT*

Three MS pages missing, 241.19-242.17 It . . . Cemetery.

One MS leaf, page "43", at MH-H, 242.18-243.4 The Sugar . . . side of the

242.18	THE SUGAR MAPLE] *added in pencil by HDT; preceded in margin by underlined pencilled* nov *(November) and underlined pencilled* n *and pencilled* Aut. Tints In Two Parts / II. *and pencilled* Hennessy *(typesetter), all in handwritings other than HDT's*
242.19-243.4	But think . . . east side of the] *text in ST's hand*
242.21-243.4	smallest Sugar . . . east side of the] *on earlier-written leaf waxed or pasted onto page numbered "43", apparently later-written,* The Sugar Maple . . . Autumn. The *(see 242.18-21)*
242.21	smallest] *preceded by* The *cancelled in pencil by HDT*
242.22	in our streets] *interlined with a caret by ST*
242.27	Red] R *altered from lower case by ST*
242.27	White] W *reformed*
242.27	White Maples] *followed by cancelled comma*

242.27-28	are bare . . . Sugar Maples] *interlined with a caret by ST*
243.2	golden] *originally underlined; underline cancelled*
243.3	Yet] Y *reformed*

Four MS pages missing, 243.4-245.10 Common . . . ultra-marine?

One MS leaf, pages "48"-"49", at NN-BGC, 245.10-246.23 What do . . . should

245.10-15	What do we . . . wherever else.] *interlined above* I do not see . . . America *following cancelled* one of our most brilliant American flowers after the colors *(s cancelled)* of the cloak worn by a particular set of functionaries in a distant country–whom *(altered from* whose*)* we never see & hope we never shall see here? *(question mark cancelled)*
245.11	amethyst,] *followed by cancelled dash*
245.14	honor,] *followed by cancelled dash*
245.14	Nabobs,] *followed by cancelled dash*
245.15	I] *reformed in pencil*
245.15	why,] *followed by cancelled dash*
245.20	as well as flowers] *interlined with a caret*
245.23	color,] *followed by cancelled dash*
245.24	excite. Already] *linked by line to cancel paragraph break*
245.25	street,] *followed by cancelled dash*
245.26	variety,] *followed by cancelled dash*
245.27	holiday,] *followed by cancelled dash*
245.29	marshals,] *followed by cancelled dash*
245.30	licensed,] *followed by cancelled dash*
245.30-31	rum-sellers,] *followed by cancelled dash*
245.32	peace;] *semicolon written over dash (see Emendation 245.32)*
245.33	Maple] M *altered from lower case*
245.34	powder,] *followed by cancelled dash*
245.36	waving.] *interlined above cancelled* run up
246.4	Fair] F *altered from lower case*
246.4	October,] *followed by cancelled dash*
246.6	Red Maple] R *and* M *altered from lower case*
246.6	a-blaze,] *interlined above cancelled* aglow

246.8-23   Gypsies . . . should] *on blank verso of a business letter, waxed over an earlier-written version of 246.8-9* Gypsies *beneath and* 246.19-23 rows . . . should *in ink with pencilled revisions*

246.9   capable] p *reformed in pencil*

246.10   fawns] *followed by* & *cancelled in pencil*

246.11   earth?] *followed by cancelled dash*

246.11   Or] O *altered from lower case*

246.12   choppers,] *followed by cancelled dash*

246.12   lots,] *followed by cancelled dash*

246.13   of?] *followed by cancelled dash*

246.20   perhaps] *interlined in ink over pencil with a caret in ink over pencil*

246.22   Nature's–] *followed by cancelled comma*

Two MS pages missing, 246.23-247.23-24 hang . . . picture

One MS leaf, pages "52"-"53", at VtMiM, 247.24-248.30 which almost . . . infirm.

247.24   which almost . . . behind them.] *interlined above and below cancelled* Our picture is already painted with each sunset behind it.

247.27   C——.] *interlined below cancelled* Concord

247.28-30   A village . . . embowered] *preceded by underlined pencilled* Gough [?] *(typesetter) in left margin and pencil line led to paragraph break*

247.30   superstition] st *reformed*

247.33   suicides,] *possibly followed by cancelled dash (MS margin obscured by paper mounting)*

248.1   wash-tub,] *comma added in pencil*

248.1   milk-can,] *comma added in pencil*

248.1   and grave-stone] *first two letters of* and *reformed*

248.3   Arabs] *followed by cancelled* bet

248.9   perchance] *interlined with a caret*

248.11   Maples] M *altered from lower case*

248.15   What] *preceded by paragraph sign*

248.17   re-painting,] *followed by cancelled dash*

248.18   repaired"] *close quotation mark added in pencil (see Textual Note 248.18)*

248.27   unction] *ascender of* t *enlarged to cover a*
                preceding letter, perhaps a

One MS leaf, page "54", at PClvU, 248.31-249.1-2 The Scarlet
. . . acquaintance

248.31   THE SCARLET OAK] *added in pencil*
248.32-249.2   remarkable . . . acquaintance] *preceded in*
                left margin by underlined pencilled Aut. Tints
                (not in HDT's hand)
248.33-34   Scarlet Oak leaves surpass] *originally*
                scarlet oaks surpass *then* ks *overwritten as* k
                and leaves *added and* S *and* O *altered from*
                lower case
248.34   Oaks] O *altered from lower case*

One MS leaf, pages "55"-"56", at NjP, 249.2-251.7-8 with 12 . . .
whittling

249.2-3   which I have seen,] *interlined with a caret*
249.5   sky,] *followed by cancelled dash*
249.6   midrib] *followed by dash cancelled in*
                pencil
249.6   double] *followed by* or *cancelled in pencil*
                and ink
249.11   are] *altered from* as
249.11   like] *added in margin*
249.12   more] *preceded by cancelled* are
249.20   light,] *comma added in pencil, followed by*
                dash cancelled in pencil
249.20   points,] *comma added in pencil, followed by*
                dash cancelled in pencil
249.22   with it] *preceded by open parenthesis*
                cancelled in pencil
249.27   with] *interlined in pencil with a caret, above*
                by *cancelled in pencil*
249.33   in] *preceded by cancelled* of
251.1-2   they remind . . . tin.] *followed by* I picked
                this one from such a pile. *interlined in pencil*
                (see Emendation 251.34)
251.5-6   character–] *followed by pencilled semicolon*
                cancelled in ink
251.6   Stone] S *altered from lower case*

Two MS pages missing, 251.8-252.13 stone . . . there?

One MS leaf, pages "59"-"60", formerly at TxHR, 252.14-253.10
By the 26th . . . fight.

252.14	26th] *followed by* Or from the 22nd to November *(last five letters of* November *added in pencil with a caret)* 2nd at least, this year (1859)– *(first two numerals interlined in pencil with a caret)* I first thought that the 22nd was the day (q.v), *(parenthetical notation cancelled)* then the 24th (q v) *all set off in parentheses and cancelled*
252.14	of October] *interlined with a caret*
252.14	Scarlet] S *altered from lower case*
252.15	usually] *interlined in pencil above cancelled* generally
252.17	blaze. This] *linked by line to cancel paragraph break*
252.17	our] *followed by cancelled* Concord
252.17	our] *underlining possibly later revision related to cancellation of* Concord
252.18	Dogwood] D *altered from lower case*
252.20	glory.] *followed by cancelled* Of the [word] the pitch pine [words] is still commonly bright
252.24	But it requires] *preceded by pencilled paragraph sign*
252.26	Scarlet Oaks] S *and* O *altered from lower case*
252.26-29	I do not . . . large trees.] *interlined in pencil and ink with a caret*
252.31	brilliant] *preceded by cancelled* memorable and
252.32	yet lit.] *followed by zero crossed with diagonal line*
252.33	perfect and] and *interlined below cancelled ampersand (see Emendation 252.33)*
252.33	forty] *interlined in pencil with a caret above* 40 *cancelled in pencil*
252.34	which] *added*
252.35	the 26th,] *interlined in pencil and ink with a caret*
252.36-253.1	between . . . sun as if . . . dye] *originally* as if . . . dye–between . . . sun *then marked for transposition*

253.1 dye.] *followed by* and it has been so, apparently, for 2 or 3 days. *cancelled in pencil and ink, with pencilled* two *and* three *interlined with carets and cancelled in pencil (see Emendation 253.1-2)*

253.2 The whole tree] *interlined with a caret above cancelled* It

253.4 ten] *interlined in pencil with a caret above* 10 *cancelled in pencil*

253.9 Scarlet ones] S *and* O *altered in pencil from lower case and* O *then rubbed out*

253.10 fight.] *followed by cancelled* Perhaps their leaves, so finely cut, are longer preserved, partly because they present less surface to the elements. For a long time, as I remember, some of them "hold out to burn–"
    It is remarkable that this species, though it is quite abundant here,

Nine MS pages missing, 253.11-257.4 The sap . . . my

One MS leaf, pages "70"-"71", at ViU, 257.4-258.7 botanical . . . woodcocks, he

257.7 Hudson's] n's *reformed*

257.7 Bay–] *dash preceded by cancelled comma and* y *reformed*

257.15-16 or at most . . . shadows.] *interlined with a caret*

257.17 eye,] *followed by cancelled open parenthesis*

257.17 locality] *followed by cancelled close parenthesis*

257.18 as] *last letter reformed*

257.18-19 *Juncaceae*] J *altered from lower case*

257.19 *Gramineae*] G *altered from lower case*

257.25 Select Man] S *and* M *altered from lower case*

257.28 best,] *followed by cancelled dash*

257.28 (aye . . . likes)] *parentheses added in pencil*

257.31 meeting-houses] *second* e *reformed*

257.34 woodlot.] *followed by cancelled dash*

257.34 Caesar–or] or *interlined above cancelled* and

257.34-35 Swedenborg–or] or *interlined above cancelled* and

257.35 him] *altered from* them

257.35-36	Or suppose . . . together and] *interlined with a caret*
257.36	let] l *altered from capital*
258.5	elbow] *altered in pencil from* elbows

Two MS pages missing, 258.7-259.12 must . . . clearly

One MS leaf, page "74", at MH-H, 259.12-24 in his mind . . . vicinity.

259.12-24	in his mind . . . vicinity.] *text in ST's hand*
259.23	nearly] *interlined by HDT above cancelled* about

Rejected Substantives

For the format of this table, see the Textual Introduction, p. 384. The table records variant substantives in the *Atlantic Monthly* (AM), the 1863 edition of *Excursions* (Ex), and pre-copy-text manuscripts, either "MS Journal" followed by the entry date in parentheses or, for lecture and other draft papers, "MS" followed by the repository symbol or owner's name in parentheses.

223.1	Tints.] TINTS. / [1862.] Ex
223.13	And the line] and in the line AM Ex
223.20-21	rather ripe] rather the ripe AM Ex
224.9	physiologist says] physiologists say MS (RP)
224.24	which we eat] *which we eat* MS (RP)
224.30	valued] regarded MS (RP)
224.34	month of painted] month for painted Ex
226.23	selvedges] selvages AM Ex *(see Emendation 226.23)*
227.3-5	It grows either . . . diameter on the gentle slopes] It grows on the gentle slopes, either in a continuous patch, or in scattered and rounded tufts a foot in diameter AM Ex
227.7	In most . . . calyx is] With most plants the

	corolla or calyx are MS (formerly Mr. and Mrs. Morton H. Baker)
227.8-9	in many] With many MS (formerly Mr. and Mrs. Morton H. Baker)
227.9	in others] With others MS (formerly Mr. and Mrs. Morton H. Baker)
227.10	in others still] with others still MS (formerly Mr. and Mrs. Morton H. Baker)
230.18	walked over those] walked those MS (NN-BGC)
230.27	your appreciation] my appreciation MS (NN-BGC)
231.15	but in scattered] but scattered MS (NN-BGC)
231.20	passed] *possibly* paused MS Journal (September 6, 1858)
231.26	*beginning*] beginning AM Ex
232.1-2	my town] our town AM Ex
233.33	Notwithstanding that the] Notwithstanding the AM Ex
234.21	flakes, as] flakes, like AM Ex
234.28	or like snow] or snow MS (MWC)
235.1	towards] toward AM Ex
*235.4	stripe] strip MS Journal (October 7, 1857)
235.9	frame of] frame to MS Journal (October 7, 1857)
236.8	the scene of] *lacking* MS (OClJC)
236.15	burden] burdens MS (OClJC)
237.25	earth] ground MS (MH-H)
237.25	like] just like MS (MH-H) MS Journal (October 14, 1856)
237.32	would] should MS Journal (October 14, 1857)
237.34	and they] and that they MS (MH-H)
238.24	into the water] into water MS (MH-H) MS Journal (October 19, 1853)
239.1	further] farther AM Ex *(see Textual Note 243.20)*
240.11	dropped] drooped MS Journal (October 18, 1856)
241.20	beautifully] beautiful MS Journal (October 20, 1853)
242.20	if one] as one AM Ex

242.21	fallen] falling Ex
242.23	any trees] any other trees AM Ex
245.30	gamblers nor] gamblers or AM Ex
245.31	nor requiring] not requiring Ex
247.24	which almost daily is] which is daily AM Ex
248.14	dahlia stems!] dahlia-stems? AM Ex
250	[*leaf engraving*]] *lacking* Ex *(see Textual Note 251.34-35)*
*251.34-35	*The original . . . pile.] *lacking* Ex
251.34	leaf on the opposite page] leaf copied on the next page AM *(see Textual Note 251.34-35)*
254.5	myriad of fine] myriad fine MS Journal (October 31, 1858)
254.33	Methuselah] Methusaleh MS Journal (November 1, 1858)
*256.7	great] greate[r?] MS Journal (November 2, 1858)
256.28	concealed from us] concealed to us MS Journal (November 4, 1858)
257.8	months I go] months or years I go MS (Theodore Hassan)
257.20	in their midst] in the midst of them AM Ex

Wild Apples

Headnote

THOREAU'S earliest surviving references to the lecture and essay topic were made in his Journal, at Walden Pond, during the summer of 1845, and a flurry of passages on the wild apple appeared in November and December 1850.[1] By 1859 Thoreau seems to have regarded "Wild Apples" as part or outgrowth of a large project of his later years, "Wild Fruits." Most of the working papers of that project, including some early and late draft leaves for the lecture and essay, are housed at NN-BGC.[2]

He delivered the "Wild Apples" lecture twice in rapid succession. The initial reading occurred in Concord, at the Brick School House, on Wednesday, February 8, 1860. It was the ninth of fifteen lectures in the Concord Lyceum's program for that season, and it was well received; one auditor afterward declared it had been the best of the entire series.[3] Six days later he

[1] See *Journal 2*, p. 165, and *Journal 3*, pp. 125-170. The report of a one-page manuscript of 1850 headed "Places to Walk to" and containing a reference to wild apples has not been confirmed. That manuscript was presumably sold at a Parke-Bernet auction on February 17, 1957 or 1959, but the firm's New York sale catalogues archived at NN do not include a sale on the first date (a Sunday) or the second (a Tuesday), and the catalogues for book and manuscript auctions in January and February of both years fail to list the reputed document.

[2] Large portions of this 681-page manuscript ("[Notes on Fruits]")–catalogued in *LMHDT* as F29h, F29b, F29e, and F29j–are published as *Wild Fruits*, ed. Bradley P. Dean (New York: W. W. Norton & Company, 2000); for the "Wild Apples" draft leaves, see pp. 74-92, 244-248; see also *Huckleberries*, ed. Leo Stoller (Iowa City: The Windhover Press of the University of Iowa and the New York Public Library, 1970), reprinted in *The Natural History Essays*, ed. Robert Sattelmeyer (Salt Lake City: Peregrine Smith Books, 1980), pp. 211-262.

[3] Bradley P. Dean and Ronald Wesley Hoag, "Thoreau's

read it again in nearby Bedford.[4] For most of the lecture material Thoreau drew on his Journal, using entries as late as January 1860; subsequently he incorporated passages about the wild crab-apple from the notes he made on his trip to Minnesota during May and June of 1861.[5]

"Wild Apples" was the last of four lectures he prepared during his final illness for publication as essays in the *Atlantic Monthly*. For a discussion of the others, including "Life without Principle," see the Headnotes to "Walking" and "Autumnal Tints." The first Headnote examines Thoreau's correspondence with James T. Fields about these essays in the early months of 1862 and estimates the rate at which Thoreau was paid for them. In the preparation of *Atlantic* setting copy for "Wild Apples," as with "Walking" and "Autumnal Tints," Thoreau required the assistance of amanuenses.

From the surviving foul papers, Thoreau appears to have revised the lecture version extensively. Some of these foul papers are in the handwriting of Elizabeth Hoar. A friend of Thoreau's from their school days in the Concord Academy, Hoar was a Main Street neighbor,[6] the daughter of Concord's leading citizen, Samuel Hoar. She was an intimate of Emerson's and So-

---

Lectures After *Walden*: An Annotated Calendar," *Studies in the American Renaissance*, ed. Joel Myerson (Charlottesville: University Press of Virginia, 1996), pp. 332-333.

[4] *Ibid.*, pp. 333-334.

[5] See 1906, 13:71-117, and "Thoreau's Notes on the Journey West," in *Thoreau's Minnesota Journey: Two Documents*, ed. Walter Harding (Geneseo, NY: The Thoreau Society, Inc., 1962), pp. 1-44.

[6] Elizabeth Maxfield-Miller, "Elizabeth of Concord: Selected Letters of Elizabeth Sherman Hoar (1814-1878) to the Emersons, Family, and the Emerson Circle [Part One]," *Studies in the American Renaissance*, ed. Joel Myerson (Charlottesville: University Press of Virginia, 1984), p. 231.

phia Thoreau's and the sister of Edward Hoar, Thoreau's companion on excursions in Concord, on the Allagash and East Branch Penobscot rivers of Maine, and to the White Mountains. Returning in September 1859 from her first trip to Europe, Hoar assisted Sophia Thoreau in transcribing letters of Horace Mann for a biography by his widow, Mary Peabody Mann. She undertook another European tour in April 1861, returning to Concord in mid-September. By early March 1862 Sophia had enlisted her to assist with arranging and copying Henry's unpublished manuscripts, in which capacity she served until at least July.[7]

Thoreau's final letter to Fields, dictated to Sophia on April 2, 1862, accompanied "the paper on Wild Apples." The essay would appear in the November 1862 *Atlantic*, a little less than six months after Thoreau's death on May 6. The printer's copy of "Wild Apples" is not known to have survived, and it is futile to guess how much of it was in Thoreau's own handwriting. While one may reasonably assume that the copy consisted at least in part of pages in an amanuensis hand, one cannot know how extensively or carefully such pages were corrected by Thoreau. Nor, in the absence of a full documentary record, can one know which pages other than three at MH-H were transcribed as

[7] *Ibid.*, pp. 262, 264. Thomas Blanding correctly identifies Hoar's hand on "Wild Apples" pages in "Beans, Baked and Half-Baked," *Concord Saunterer* 11, no. 3 (Fall 1976): 13. It matches the handwriting on photofacsimiles illustrating Maxfield-Miller, "Elizabeth of Concord . . . (Part Three)," *Studies in the American Renaissance*, ed. Joel Myerson (Charlottesville: University Press of Virginia, 1986), pp. 135, 152, 157, 192, and 195. Besides the *Atlantic* essays, amanuensis labor was required for the "Allegash and East Branch" and "Appendix" portions of *The Maine Woods* (1864), for chapters 6 through 10 of *Cape Cod* (1865), and for the portions of "A Yankee in Canada" (1866) that remained in manuscript after the incomplete *Putnam's Monthly Magazine* publication of 1853. For the textual history of the last of these pieces, see the "Yankee" Headnote.

final or intermediate copy by Hoar. The examples of "Walking" and "Autumnal Tints" suggest that the setting copy included pages in Thoreau's hand that had required little or no correction. Bronson Alcott might have carried the manuscript and the April 2 covering letter to Fields when he went to Boston on April 3. Thoreau retained what he called a "Duplicate" consisting of superseded lecture sheets, essay drafts, and transcripts by Hoar–a body of material now textually quite incomplete and possibly never complete, and certainly not an exact duplicate of the setting copy sent to Fields.

The extant portions of this "Duplicate" or draft are presently distributed among eleven institutional and private collections. The largest part, at MH-H, bMS Am 278.5, folder 9, comprises ten leaves, written by Thoreau in pencil on one side only, and representing a late but not final stage of composition. It corresponds to the first thirteen paragraphs of the printed essay (to 263.32) and thence, discontinuously, to 264.27-36, 270.31-272.6, 263.4-6, 269.2-3, 276.31-33, and 269.30. In addition, the MH-H material includes (1) a leaf written by Thoreau in pencil on both sides and partially cancelled, an account of Thoreau's discovery of the wild crab in Minnesota, including 271.19-272.2; (2) a leaf written by Thoreau on one side and cancelled, corresponding loosely to 263.4-6, 269.2-3, and 276.31-33; (3) an amanuensis page by Hoar, in ink on a single leaf, copied from the preceding item and cancelled in pencil with a single vertical line; (4) a double-sided leaf written in ink by Hoar and bearing on the recto very extensive pencilled revisions by Thoreau, the whole corresponding roughly to 276.8-277.21; (5) a one-sided leaf in ink by Thoreau, with his pencilled revisions, consisting of the first twelve verses copied from the book of Joel (King James Version), much of which transcript Thoreau used in the "Wild Apples" conclusion; (6) a leaf written by Thoreau in pencil on both sides and corresponding to 280.29-281.14; and (7) a leaf written by Thoreau on one side in pencil, consisting of a paragraph from the essay section on the wild apple's growth habit (276.24-30) plus a cancelled outline of the lecture or essay as a whole, with estimated page counts. This page also bears the title, "Duplicate of Wild Apples", in Thoreau's hand, in large, dark pencilled letters, as though it had once been the topmost page of a sheaf of manuscript leaves. Added to these full-size pages at MH-H are one leaf (verso blank) partially written in ink by Thoreau with sentences on cider, including 287.13-16, and ten ink or pencilled passages written on nine paper scraps of various sizes and shapes, the contents often quotations and paraphrases from Thoreau's reading.

The next largest body of "Wild Apples" draft matter, that at NN-BGC, consists of four leaves, each written on both sides in ink with extensive revision in ink and pencil, plus three single-sided scraps and one double-sided scrap, all in Thoreau's handwriting and representing an earlier draft stage than the surviving equivalent manuscript copy elsewhere. The opening twelve paragraphs of the printed essay (261.5-263.13), the end of the section on naming wild apples (284.16-285.4), and the beginning of "The Last Gleaning" (285.5-12) are (roughly) represented by the NN-BGC manuscript.

The remaining ten leaves (twenty pages) known to survive from the "Wild Apples" lecture and essay draft are now scattered among several institutional and private collections: FMU, text corresponding to 263.33-264.26; CU-S, text possibly related to 269.25-30; NRRI, text corresponding to 272.34-274.1; ViU, two leaves (Barrett Collection numbers PS 3040 1906c and 6345-e), text corresponding to 277.8-9, 277.32-278.7, 281.29-282.20,

283.16-33; VtMiM, text corresponding to 278.12-33; CoCA, text corresponding to 278.15-28 and related to 282.30-283.2 and 283.13-14; ICarbS, text corresponding to 283.12-14, 288.11-289.7, 287.7-11; and the collections of Amy Wallace and David Wallechinsky (text corresponding to 287.11-288.9) and Dr. George A. Snook (text corresponding to 288.9-289.1). The last two leaves are paginated "52", "53", "54", and "55", perhaps in Thoreau's hand. Most of those ten leaves are now or were formerly tipped into sets of the 1906 Manuscript Edition of Thoreau's *Writings*. How many more "Wild Apples" draft leaves were distributed by Houghton, Mifflin and Company in 1906 and have not yet reappeared it is impossible to determine. An ink notation on the Wallace and Wallechinsky leaf reads, "This MS. is in H. D. Thoreaus handwriting. J. T. Fields." While the publisher's authentication might suggest that the leaf had been part of the setting copy, retained by the editor and bestowed on a Thoreau fancier or collector of literary memorabilia, it resembles some of the surviving draft leaves with its cancellations, overwritings, and interlineations. The more likely explanation of Fields's memorandum is that this and a cognate leaf, which also survives, were acquired by an admirer from among Thoreau's working papers after his death and were submitted to Fields for verification of the handwriting.

Approximately half the essay, or thirteen and one-half of twenty-six printed *Atlantic* text columns, is represented in the surviving worksheets and scraps (exclusive of the Journal passages), and some of the draft pages involve duplication or overlap in that they present the same textual matter twice, at different stages of development.

Although Fields ordered the printshop to prepare proofs of "Autumnal Tints" very soon after he obtained the manuscript, it is unlikely that he sent proof copy of "Wild Apples" to Concord before Thoreau died on May 6. Proofs of "Walking" seem not to have reached Thoreau by April 2, when he dispatched the "Wild Apples" manuscript, and the publication of "Walking" in the *Atlantic* preceded that of "Wild Apples" by five months. The probability is that Sophia Thoreau, Elizabeth Hoar, or some other Concord volunteer read "Wild Apples" proofsheets, if they were read at all outside the printshop and editorial office.

The essay appeared as the lead article in the November 1862 issue of the *Atlantic Monthly* (10:513-526), just before a chapter on "Katahdin and the Penobscot" from Theodore Winthrop's serialized *Life in the Open Air*. For the 1863 version in *Excursions*, where "Wild Apples" was the penultimate essay (before "Night and Moonlight"; see Historical Introduction), the printing in the *Atlantic Monthly* served as setting copy. The book followed the substantives of the magazine copy except in two instances, and those of no great importance.

For the Princeton Edition *Excursions* also, the *Atlantic* printing (NGenoU) serves as copy-text. This magazine text has been collated with all the surviving draft or "Duplicate" pages (including scribal copies) and Journal antecedents in order to identify variants which might have resulted from a misreading of Thoreau's handwriting by either a copyist or a compositor. Five sight collations of the *Atlantic* and *Excursions* texts have been performed. In the course of the *Atlantic* press run or runs the final letter of "most" (267.12) disappeared; the word is intact in one copy issued in wrappers (collection of Joseph J. Moldenhauer) and one bound volume of *Atlantic* (NGenoU), but absent in three other bound volumes (collection of Joseph J. Moldenhauer; TxU). A copy of the essay in an individual monthly number of the magazine, issued in wrappers (collection of Joseph J. Moldenhauer), has been collated on the Hinman machine against the essay in a bound volume (TxU). This optical comparison disclosed no other differences.

Textual Notes

FOR the format of the Textual Notes, see the Textual Introduction, pp. 381-382. Copy-text is the first printing in the November 1862 *Atlantic Monthly* (AM). The abbreviation "MS" followed by a repository symbol in parentheses identifies a manuscript reading. For an inventory of surviving manuscripts, see the Headnote.

261.5-8 the order of the *Rosaceæ* ... on the globe.: Thoreau's paraphrase of his source, Hugh Miller, *The Testimony of the Rocks* ... (Boston: Gould and Lincoln, 1857), pp. 78-79, entails a syntactical ambiguity. The phrase "also the true Grasses" is in parallel with "the *Rosaceæ*" and "the *Labitæ*" rather than with "the Apple". The same ambiguity occurs in two draft versions, MS (MH-H) and MS (NN-BGC).

261.20 milk, sheep: Thus in the copy-text; the source of the quotation is Berthold Georg Niebuhr, *The History of Rome* ..., tr. J. C. Hare and C. Thirlwall (Philadelphia: Thomas Wardle, 1835), 1:64. Thoreau's version omits "kine, swine" between "milk," and "sheep", and drops "should" before "agree" as required by the structure of his sentence. These changes are anticipated in the surviving drafts, MS (MH-H) and MS (NN-BGC).

261.21 ways: Thus in two draft versions, MS (MH-H) and MS (NN-BGC), as in Thoreau's source, Niebuhr, *The History of Rome* ..., 1:64. The copy-text reads "way".

262.31 frigid zone: "torrid zone" in Thoreau's source, John Claudius Loudon, *Arboretum et Fruticetum Britannicum*, 2d ed. (London: Printed for the Author, 1844), 2:894. In the earliest surviving draft, MS (NN-BGC), Thoreau follows Loudon. In a subsequent draft, MS (MH-H), Thoreau repeats "torrid zone" but then, realizing that his source was probably in error (no part of Europe being south of the Tropic of Cancer), he cancelled "torrid" and interlined "frigid".

263.20 further: Thus in the surviving draft, MS (MH-H); the copy-text has "farther", most likely a normalization according to AM (and Ticknor and Fields) preference. See *Maine Woods*, pp. 400, 406, 435, and 450, and *Cape Cod*, pp. 351-352 and Textual Notes 24.8, 50.2, and 84.21.

263.32   wild-boar: The hyphen, absent in Thoreau's source (Loudon, *Arboretum et Fruticetum Britannicum*, 2:896) and in a draft version, MS (MH-H), may result from a liberty taken by an amanuensis or from a typesetter's interpretation of the lost setting copy.

265.18   gnarly: Thus in a Journal entry for August 9, 1851 (*Journal 3*, p. 362), as in the copy-text. See, however, Textual Note 282.16-17, where the manuscript evidence indicates "gnurly" and "gnurliest". Thoreau's dictionaries (Johnson, Webster, Walker) all offer "gnarled" for "knotted," but none of them has the term "gnarly" or "gnurly." In the *Dictionary of American Regional English*, ed. Frederic G. Cassidy (Cambridge: The Belknap Press of Harvard University Press, 1996), "gnurl" is identified as a variant of "knurl"; and "nurly," "gnurly," and "gnarly" are recorded from printed and oral sources, principally of New England origin, meaning "warty," "cross-grained," "knotty," "gnarled," "tough," and "ill-tempered."

268.12   Hurra!:   Two of Thoreau's sources on the folklore of apples, both English publications, give the Briticism "Huzza!" here: John Brand, *Observations on the Popular Antiquities of Great Britain* (London: Henry G. Bohn, 1849), 1:29; and Loudon, *Arboretum et Fruticetum Britannicum*, 2:900. The change to an American form is probably authorial; no manuscript version remains.

268.18-23   "Stand fast, root! . . . enow . . . a cow's horn: In addition to repunctuating this passage from Brand, 1:9-10, Thoreau alters the spelling from the source's "enou" and the wording from "the cow's horn". No manuscript version survives.

268.31   do: "so" in the copy-text, an apparent misreading of Thoreau's final manuscript by an amanuensis or a compositor. Herrick's wording in *Hesperides*, "Another [Christmasse-Eve Ceremonie]," followed by Brand, 1:30 (and by a previous [1813] edition of Brand), is "do". No manuscript version survives.

268.34   Phillips: Thus in the copy-text; no manuscript survives. A selection of poems by John Philips (1676-1708), including his "Cider, . . . in Two Books," appears in Alexander Chalmers, ed., *The Works of the English Poets, from Chaucer to Cowper . . .* (London: Printed for J. Johnson et al., 1810), 8:369-393. But Thoreau's source for the name spelling closest in time to the composition of "Wild Apples" was probably

Loudon, *Arboretum et Fruticetum Britannicum*, 2:901. Loudon's reference to the poet as "Phillips" and his sample of some lines from "Cider" appear just after the passage on "grippling" quoted by Thoreau at 277.26-31.

271.15-17 "if, on being cultivated ... celebrated: This part of François André Michaux's conclusion is only a paraphrase of the source, *The North American Sylva, or A Description of the Forest Trees of the United States, Canada, and Nova Scotia* . . ., translated from the French of F. Andrew Michaux (Paris: Printed by C. D'Hautel, 1819), 2:68-69. The words after "celebrated" are those of Michaux; in a draft version, MS (MH-H), as in the copy-text, Thoreau placed the open quotation mark before "if, on being cultivated".

273.4-5 "The same cause ... brought me,": Thoreau purposively modifies his source, R. W. Emerson's "The Rhodora: On Being Asked: Whence Is the Flower," *Poems* (Boston: James Munroe and Company, 1847), p. 59, "The self-same Power that brought me there brought you."

273.32 clipped: Thus in the copy-text, a possible normalization by a copyist or typesetter. In a surviving draft, MS (NRRI), Thoreau spells the word "clipt".

276.31 Columella: Thus in two draft pages, MS (MH-H), one in Thoreau's hand and the other in Elizabeth Hoar's, a copy of the first. Thoreau's source for the quotation is Lucius Junius Columella, *De Re Rustica*, Book X ("De Cultu Hortorum"), line 16, in *Rei Rusticae Auctores Latini Veteres, M. Cato [,] M. Varro [,] L. Columella [,] Palladius* . . . ([Heidelberg]: ex Hier. Commelini Typographio, 1595), p. 404. Thoreau borrowed a copy of this volume from Bronson Alcott in August 1851. A last-minute confusion on the part of Thoreau or an amanuensis may have produced the copy-text reading, "Palladius". The ascription to Palladius for another observation, at 265.5-7, is correct. The source has "iniussi", but variorum editions of Columella record "iniussa" and "iniussu" (equivalent to the copy-text reading "injussu") at this point in the poem among the codices.

276.35-277.1 best stocks: Thus in the copy-text, though "best stock" in Elizabeth Hoar's hand on a copied draft leaf, MS (MH-H), heavily revised in pencil by Thoreau. In reading a subsequent recopy he apparently corrected the singular to plural. The arcane word "inteneration" that Thoreau quotes in the next sentence comes from a passage by John Evelyn on the wilding (crab or wild apple) as the source of the best stocks for grafting; see *Sylva, Or, a Discourse on Forest-Trees . . . to which is annexed Pomona: or, an Appendix concerning Fruit-Trees in relation to Cider . . .* (London: Printed for John Martyn, 1679), p. 345.

278.30 "Seek-no-furthers,": The last element is spelled "farthers" in the copy-text. Thoreau's source for these two sentences on varieties listed by "pomological gentlemen" is one of the printings of A. J. Downing, *The Fruit and Fruit Trees of America* (first published in 1845). In the edition of 1857, revised and corrected by Charles Downing (New York: Wiley & Halsted), the list of apple varieties runs from p. 71 to p. 231. The "Seek-No-Further" is described on p. 110; "Hub-bardston Nonesuch" on pp. 82-83; "William's Favourite" on p. 111, and "Monk's Favourite" on p. 173. In a draft of the passage, MS (VtMiM), Thoreau writes "Seek-no-furthers".

279.17 one Newburgh: The copy-text reads "one Dr. Newburg". Thoreau draws on Evelyn's *Sylva . . . [and] Pomona*, p. 395, in an appendix of "Observations Concerning the Making, and Preserving of Cider: by John Newburgh Esq." When copying the sentence into his "Fact Book" Thoreau prefaces the quotation with "Newburg says": see *Thoreau's Fact Book in the Harry Elkins Widener Collection in the Harvard College Library*, ed. Kenneth Walter Cameron (Hartford, CT: Transcendental Books, 1966, 1987), 1:105. The change of Newburgh's "hath" to "has" in the copy-text is well within the range of liberties Thoreau assumed when quoting. But the assignment of a medical or theological "Dr." to the gentleman may be due to memorial contamination from "Dr. Symonds" in the previous sentence, either by Thoreau in the lost draft, or by an amanuensis, or by the AM compositor. A printed marginal note in *Sylva . . . [and] Pomona*, p. 369, refers to Newburgh as "Mr."

280.32-281.2 One Peter Whitney . . . of the tree.: Thus in the copy-text. Thoreau's source for this material is in *Memoirs of the American Academy of Arts and Sciences* (Boston), 1 (1785): 386-387. Whitney's communication to the Academy is headed "An Account of a Singular Apple-Tree . . .," with Thoreau's quotation coming from the same extended heading.

282.5-6 Deuxan . . . Queening: Emended from "Deuxan . . . Greening" in the copy-text. Thoreau's source is Francis Quarles, *Emblems, Divine and Moral* (Chiswick: Printed by C. & C. Whittingham, 1825), p. 262 (Book V, Emblem 2), where the reading is "deuzan ... queening". The Deusan, Deuzan, or Deuxan variety of apple was so named for its property of keeping for two years (Fr. *deux ans*). On a draft leaf, MS (ViU), Thoreau copies the seven lines of verse in the margin, writing "deuxan" and "queening". "Greening" is probably an error by a copyist or a compositor; it is the name of another variety of apple.

282.16-17   gnarly ... gnarliest: Thus in the copy-text, though "gnurly ... gnurliest" in both the original Journal entry of October 31, 1851 (*Journal 4*, p. 157) and a surviving draft, MS (ViU). Thoreau used both spellings of this regional term, and the copy-text may accurately reflect his last draft; see Textual Note 265.18.

283.13   fairy: Thus in the copy-text. Thoreau's spelling in a surviving draft, MS (ICarbS), and in a Journal version of November 11, 1850 (*Journal 3*, p. 137), is the archaic "faery," not recognized in his dictionaries. He uses the form "fairies" in a later Journal passage, dated October 5, 1851 (*Journal 4*, p. 121).

285.8-9   chickadee: Thus in the copy-text. Thoreau's usual spelling, "chicadee," occurs on a draft leaf, MS (NN-BGC).

Table of Emendations

FOR the format of this table, see the Textual Introduction, p. 382. The source for all seven emendations is the editor's own authority, designated "PE" for the Princeton Edition; these emendations are not anticipated in *Excursions* (1863).

*261.21	ways] PE; way
*263.20	further] PE; farther
*268.31	do] PE; so
*276.31	Columella] PE; Palladius
*278.30	"Seek-no-furthers,"] PE; "Seek-no-farthers,"
*279.17	one Newburgh] PE; one Dr. Newburg
282.6	Queening] PE; Greening *(see Textual Note 282.5-6)*

Rejected Substantives

FOR the format of this table, see the Textual Introduction, p. 384. The table records variant substantives in the 1863 edition of *Excursions* (Ex) and in pre-copy-text manuscripts, either "MS Journal" followed by the entry date in parentheses or, for lecture and other draft papers, "MS" followed by the repository symbol or owner's name in parentheses.

261.1	Apples.] APPLES. / (1862) Ex
261.10	lately] recently MS (MH-H)
261.13	entire black] entire but black MS (MH-H)
262.1-2	heroes were employed] heroes employed MS (MH-H) MS (NN-BGC)
262.35	it is thought] is thought Ex
267.1	remembered] remember Ex
267.22-23	evenings] eve- / ings Ex
268.21	bough] bow Ex
271.21	so far as] as far as MS (MH-H)
*276.35-277.1	best stocks] best stock MS (MH-H)
281.3	Nawshawtuct] Nawshawtuck Ex *(see Textual Note 18.36)*
281.8-9	Provence is] Provence are MS (MH-H) MS (MH-H)
282.18	eye] eyes MS Journal (October 31, 1851)
282.28	harvest] harvests MS Journal (October 31, 1851)
284.18	good only] only good MS (NN-BGC)
285.7	ground, and] ground but MS (NN-BGC)
287.12	sensitive] sensible MS (Amy Wallace and David Wallechinsky)
288.28-29	so extensive] as extensive MS (Dr. George A. Snook) MS (ICarbS)
288.29	my town] this town MS (Dr. George A. Snook) MS (ICarbS)
289.4	plat] plot MS Journal (November 16, 1850)

End-of-Line Hyphenation

THE compounds in list A, below, are hyphenated at the end of the line in the copy-texts. Using the criteria described in the Textual Introduction, pp. 384-385, the editor has resolved each of these ambiguous features to the form recorded in list A. List B records only those compounds hyphenated at the end of the line in the present edition that should be transcribed with the hyphen in order to duplicate the copy-text forms.

	LIST A	70.16	muskrat
		71.2	dry-shod
15.17	musk-rat	74.28	warm-blooded
18.3	north-east	75.9	fire-places
20.8	moth-like	81.2	coach-wise
20.11	light-bringer	81.18	Westmoreland
22.9	daylight	81.20	West-more-land
24.6	landscape	81.32	rail-road
26.7	flower-stalks	84.35	Englishman
33.12	*Wor*-tatic	85.1	grandfatherly
37.8	Stillwater	85.3	rail-road
38.7	gooseberries	86.15	north-east
42.5	north-west	88.7	Cattleshow
44.4	hop-fields	90.3	bookstore
48.7	sunshiny	90.11	Shaker-shaped
49.5	gingerbread	90.23	side-walk
49.9	raspberries	92.16	fair-looking
51.3	weather-cock	94.27	daybreak
53.18	statesman	97.19	bung-town
55.35	landscape	98.3	Highlanders
57.27	bell-like	100.7	broadleaved
58.27-28	moss-grown	106.29	whitewash
61.30	wood-chopper	108.33	breakfast
62.32	statesmen	109.21	mill-wright's
65.15	High-streets	112.5	grist-mill
65.21	loose-strife	114.24	whitewashed
66.10	housewife	115.6	ice-house
69.24	highway	115.12	night-caps

116.2	weathercock	218.22	sunbeams
120.20	cow-hide	219.26-27	*a-ate*
122.20	drift-wood	220.6	straightway
129.9-10	landholder	225.11	woodbine
129.32	jolly-looking	225.33	hill-side
130.19-20	corn-mills	226.15	flower-like
131.14-15	purchase-money	226.32-33	blackberries
133.24	bark-boats	227.19-20	purple-veined
136.1	*Chi-pré*	229.32	fine-eared
139.11	loopholed	230.7	afternoons
139.22	loophole	231.3	wine-colored
140.3	nose-gays	237.25	crimson-spotted
140.32	shell-fish	238.31	tomorrow
146.4-5	farm-book	240.21	husbandman
146.21	wash-leather	241.23-24	resting-place
147.33	methinks	242.12	Loose-strife
150.16	water-side	242.13	Huckleberry-bird
152.1	cloud-built	242.13-14	woodman
161.31	eating-house	243.15-16	to-day
163.4	guidebooks	244.14-15	paint-boxes
166.17	to-day	244.27	dye-house
168.3	seed-bearing	245.25	throughout
175.21	evergreens	247.10	gun-house
177.27	squirrel-hunter	251.15	half-dozen
186.24	outside	252.10	headlands
187.25	afternoon	253.16	Oak-wine
188.32	forever	253.27	evergreens
191.3-4	three- / score- years	255.32	near-sighted
		257.31	meeting-houses
192.1	highway	258.25	head-wind
192.13	highway	259.7	huckleberries
195.31	south-south- / west	261.24	apple-tree
		262.26	apple-spray
196.5	Eastward	264.9	woodpecker
196.7	landscapes	264.17-18	half-rolled
196.23	south-eastward	265.15-16	handkerchief
201.30	steamboats	265.33	godlike
204.36	front-yard	266.27	three-quarters
207.22	hard-fought	269.2	apple-trees
209.16	overshadow	271.14	sweet-meats
211.22	thenceforth	271.22	half-fabulous
215.3	newspapers	272.19-20	Easterbrooks

279.3	high-colored	130.19-20	corn-mills
279.11	hogshead	144.12-13	horse-load
281.8	plum-tree	146.4-5	farm-book
283.23	cider-mill	149.13-14	flag-staff
283.29	rain-bow	151.23-24	crook-neck
285.28-29	lurking-places	156.24-25	sea-milkwort
286.14	hedge-hog	161.27-28	stone-built
		165.16-17	weak-bodied
		168.23-24	bird-cherries
	LIST B	169.35-36	pitch-pine
		175.3-4	mid-winter
7.14-15	roll-call	175.5-6	wood-mouse
17.27-28	foot-print	175.28-29	white-pine
23.24-25	out-door	187.23-24	shop-keepers
25.29-30	needle-shaped	188.18-19	house-bred
26.26-27	ninety-seven	189.7-8	dumb-bells
29.10-11	many-peaked	189.10-11	dumb-bells
38.12-13	mountain-ash	192.26-27	high-ways
40.26-27	fellow-travellers	196.4-5	south-west
45.5-6	way-worn	205.5-6	Front-yards
54.1-2	good-morning	205.19-20	single-minded
56.12-13	barn-yard	208.5-6	hearth-stone
56.21-22	wood-sled	212.18-19	*tol-tan*
58.27-28	moss-grown	212.31-32	nick-names
64.18-19	pitch-pine	217.22-23	moss-trooper
80.33-34	Washington-city	219.26-27	*a-ate*
81.11-12	sugar-maples	221.21-22	hill-side
84.22-23	twenty-four	222.1-2	black-veined
84.26-27	log-house	227.19-20	purple-veined
92.35-36	ferry-boats	228.32-33	Poke-stems
96.2-3	twenty-four	234.20-21	crimson-tipt
98.28-29	tunnel-like	236.24-25	pig-corn
100.7-8	golden-rod	240.4-5	Wood-duck
101.20-21	would-be	241.23-24	resting-place
102.2-3	wood-saw	243.15-16	to-day
104.31-32	custom-house	243.24-25	bean-poles
106.10-11	four-pence	244.14-15	paint-boxes
112.4-5	parsonage-house	245.30-31	rum-sellers
115.34-35	knick-knacks	254.23-24	rallying-point
118.8-9	road-side	256.18-19	hill-top
119.20-21	old-fashioned	261.3-4	Apple-tree
123.13-14	close-hugging	262.33-34	apple-tree